THE GUIDE TO CHINESE COOKING

HANDA CHENG

120 RECIPES

35 TECHNIQUES

The Guide to Chinese Cooking

家常便饭

A JOURNEY THROUGH CHINA'S FAVOURITE DISHES

DK

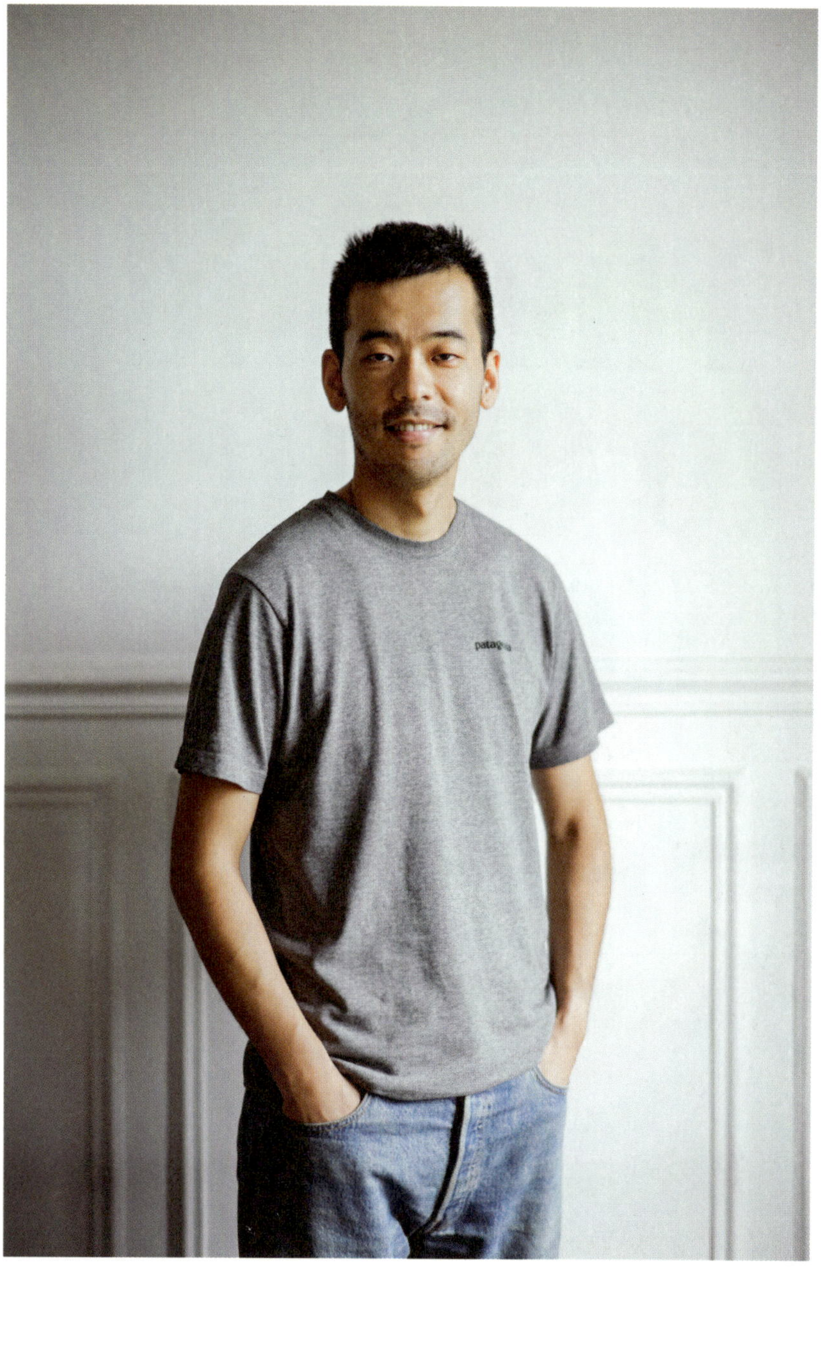

Seven Essential Things in Life: Firewood, Rice, Oil, Salt, Soy Sauce, Vinegar and Tea

中国人的开门七件事，
柴米油盐酱醋茶

When I was asked to write a book on Chinese cuisine, I was flattered but somewhat daunted by the task. Tackling this massive topic without reducing it to a stack of recipes is not a simple feat.

I spent the first eleven years of my life in Wenzhou, a city located in the south-east of the country. It was the '90s, during a time of social and economic change in China. That era of my life gave me a love for hot and savoury breakfasts, the smell of noodle stalls, and a passion for seafood. After arriving in Paris, my story mirrors thousands of other immigrant families, for whom food became the bridge that connects us to our homeland. But my culinary interest really developed during my various trips back to the country as an adult, when I felt both like an insider and an outsider.

In China, food is at the heart of all social interactions, so much so that the phrase "How are you?" can be translated to "Have you eaten?" From marriage to funerals, from catching up with friends to the most serious of business meetings, everything is settled around a large meal. The day begins with an incredible choice of breakfast foods (bao, noodles, pancakes...) at every street corner, and finishes with fried rice at a street food stall at 2 o'clock in the morning. Whether they are dealing with popular street food (incredible), imperial food (sophisticated), family food (frugal) or Buddhist food (vegetarian), Chinese people are always striving for a balance between colour (色, *sè*), aroma (香, *xiāng*) and taste/texture (味, *wèi*). Multiply this notion by the immensity of the country, with its various regions, 56 ethnic groups and a rich, 5,000-year-old history, and you might get a glimpse of the diversity of Chinese cuisines.

For a long time, in the West, Chinese cuisine was a watered-down version of Cantonese cuisine, the region from which the first Chinese immigrants left. That cheap cuisine, represented by countless caterers, all-you-can-eat buffets and other small joints, has the merit of showing a small glimpse of the "Chinese taste". But it is very far from the Chinese cuisine that I'm familiar with.

The book you are holding is, first and foremost, a collection of family recipes (家常菜, *jiā cháng ca*). In other words, dishes that best represent everyday cooking in China, in my personal (and thus subjective) opinion. Extraordinary dishes for ordinary people. It was also important to me to include thematic pages, to help the reader better understand cooking techniques, eating habits, customs... In short, everything that the word "eat" represents for a Chinese person.

Use this book as a guide, as a source of inspiration to familiarize yourself with basic ingredients and techniques. And after familiarizing yourself with the basics, feel free to adapt the recipes according to the season, the region and your personal tastes; that is also part of the Chinese cuisine philosophy. Through these recipes, I hope I might present Chinese cuisine in a new light: frugal, balanced cooking, with an emphasis on freshness and seasonality. You can then add a personal touch in your daily cooking, using condiments, spices or cooking techniques, to truly make the recipes yours.

HANDA CHENG
程汉达

Intro
简介
P. 8

Cold Dishes
冷菜
P. 52

Vegetables
蔬菜
P. 78

Tofu
豆腐
P. 116

Eggs
鸡蛋
P. 138

Soups
汤
P. 156

Meat
肉
P. 180

Fish
鱼
P. 210

Noodles
面条
P. 230

Dumplings
饺子
P. 256

Bao Zi
包子
P. 274

Rice
米饭
P. 288

Snacks
小吃
P. 314

Condiments
酱料
P. 336

Sweets
甜品
P. 350

CHAPTER
01

Intro
简介
JIĂN JIÈ

PP. 10-11: Map of Chinese Cuisines ■ **P. 12:** Map of Starchy Foods
P. 13: Map of Chilli Pepper ■ **P. 14:** Map of Alcohols ■ **P. 15:** Map of Teas ■ **PP. 16-17:** When Do We Eat?
PP. 18-19: At the Table ■ **P. 20:** Creating a Meal ■ **P. 21:** *Dos* and *Don'ts* ■ **PP. 22-23:** Street Food
PP. 24-27: Essential Ingredients ■ **PP. 28-29:** Essential Aromatic Ingredients ■ **PP. 30-31:** Spices ■ **PP. 32-35:** Dried Food
PP. 36-37: Chilli Peppers ■ **PP. 38-39:** Fermented Products ■ **PP. 40-41:** Unclassifiable Precious Ingredients
PP. 42-43: Wok and Accessories ■ **PP. 44-45:** Essential Utensils ■ **PP. 46-47:** Stir-Frying with a Wok
PP. 48-49: Steam Cooking ■ **PP. 50-51:** Making a Hong Shao

Map of Chinese Cuisines

MAP 1

23 PROVINCES, 56 ETHNIC MINORITIES, HUNDREDS OF DIALECTS, A BORDER STRETCHING FROM SIBERIA IN THE NORTH TO TROPICAL ISLANDS IN THE SOUTH; CHINESE CUISINE IS THE REFLECTION OF INCREDIBLE DIVERSITY AND A 5,000-YEAR-OLD HISTORY.

SHANDONG CUISINE

- Shandong, home of Confucius, is the cradle of Northern Chinese cuisine, including Beijing and Dongbei (north-east). It is considered to be the oldest, most complex and most technical form of cooking, and was the root of imperial cuisine during the Ming (1368–1644) and Qing (1644–1912) dynasties.

Jiao zi dumplings should be cited as one of its cornerstone dishes; they are native to the region and are still made to this day in all northern households during the Chinese New Year. That province has a marked preference for savoury dishes, spiced up with different fermented soy bean pastes such as *huang dou jiang* or *tian mian jiang*, p. 38. Finally, the use of garlic, cultivated for more than 2,000 years in Shandong, is another common feature of all northern cuisines. While it is enjoyed throughout China, few people eat raw garlic cloves!

→ **RECIPES**: Jian bing (p. 322), julienned potato salad (p. 110), fried cockles with garlic and chilli (p. 220), zha jiang noodles (p. 242)

JIANGNAN CUISINE

- Jiangnan means "south of the Yangtze River". This vast region located around the mouth of the Yangtze River includes the Jiangsu and Zhejiang provinces, part of Anhui and Shanghai, where they speak the same family of dialects (Wu). I feel particularly close to this region, as I was born and raised there until the age of 11.

In China, Jiangnan is synonymous with abundance. The countless lakes and streams around Shanghai are rich in freshwater fish and crustaceans. The mountainous areas of Zhejiang are ideal for rice crops and tea plantations. The mild and humid climate allows for plenty of fruit and vegetables all year round. Generations of poets and gourmets have fallen in love with the region and boosted the reputation of its delicate cuisine, for both its taste and its appearance.

Compared to other regions, Jiangnan cuisine is lighter and softer (清淡, *qing dan*). It doesn't overly rely on chilli or oil, to favour the "natural taste" (原味, *yuan wei*) of the products. The region's basic diet consists of rice, aquatic vegetables (water grass, lotus roots) or mountain plants (bamboo shoots), tofu, meat (pork and poultry), freshwater fish and seafood (crustaceans, algae, etc.). Soy sauce, rice vinegar and Shaoxing wine are its three basic condiments, along with aromatic ingredients, such as ginger and onion. Umami is created by many dried products (mushrooms, ham, seafood) or fermented ingredients (tofu, Chinese mustard). Note that the inhabitants of Shanghai and Suzhou are known for their sweet tooth.

→ **RECIPES**: Tofu jerky (p. 136), sweet and sour pork ribs (p. 200), stir-fried squid with celery (p. 224), four happiness kaofu (p. 64)

GUANGDONG CUISINE

- Cantonese cuisine is the epitome of superlatives; the ingredients, spices, dishes, techniques and specificities are so diverse, depending on the city of origin, that it is hard to know where to even begin.

Facing the South China Sea and boasting a subtropical climate, the Guangdong province is located in the far south of the country. Cantonese ports have had commercial links with the rest of the world since the 16th century. This cultural exposure allowed the Cantonese to appropriate ingredients and techniques from other parts of the world very early on, but also to export their cuisine along with waves of emigrants from the 19th century.

Most Chinese restaurants in the world mainly serve Cantonese dishes, from San Francisco's Chinatown, to the streets of Lima, to Parisian caterers. However, its philosophy, based on preserving the ingredients' extreme freshness, their seasonality, and their natural taste, is seldom reflected.

The Cantonese have a reputation for eating everything. It is true that exotic animals are consumed there, especially for medicinal cooking (see p. 378). But the daily diet consists mainly of rice (also in the form of flour), meat (a lot of poultry, pork and beef), fish and seafood, and green vegetables. Various offal (duck tongue, chicken leg, trotter) are very popular, but they are also found in other parts of China. As for the condiments, in addition to the classics such as rice wine and soy sauce, we should mention oyster sauce, fish sauce, douchi (p. 346), hoisin sauce, and XO sauce.

→ **RECIPES**: White radish cake (p. 332), stir-fried chow fun with beef (p. 252), crispy pork (p. 194), clay pot rice (p. 298)

SICHUAN CUISINE

▪ Sichuan, sometimes spelled Szechuan, is a huge province in South-Western China. Geologically, it is a large and very fertile basin (where Chengdu and Chongqing are located) surrounded by high mountains, far from the rich coastal provinces. This isolation has led to a unique cultural and culinary identity in Sichuan.

It is impossible to talk about Sichuan cuisine without mentioning its two key ingredients: Sichuan pepper and Sichuan peppercorn. The former, originally from America, made its way to China via Portuguese traders at the end of the 16th century, but it was not until the 1800s that it started to be cultivated locally. Its use is closely linked to the concept of "moisture" (湿, *shi*) in Chinese medicine (see p. 378). Due to its geographical location, Sichuan is a very humid area. Perspiration caused by chilli pepper is a great way to remove excess *shi* from the body. In Sichuan, chilli pepper is used in all its forms: fresh, dried, whole, powdered, pickled, fermented, raw, or cooked.

Sichuan peppercorn (see p. 27) is a local berry that creates a unique tingling sensation on the tongue and has a lemony taste. Combining it with chilli creates the famous mala taste 麻辣, literally "anaesthetic and spicy", found in dishes such as mapo tofu (p. 126).

For about thirty years, Sichuan cuisine has been very popular throughout China, and that trend is beginning to spread abroad. But it would be reductive to summarize it as "ingredients + chilli pepper". One can find much spicier food in other Chinese provinces (Hunan, Guizhou). The success of the "Sichuan taste" is due to its complexity. Examples include Sichuan dumplings (p. 268), which are both sweet and spicy, or pao cai (Sichuan "kimchi"), which adds acidity to the chilli pepper, and of course, Sichuan chilli oil (p. 36), which is a concentrate of *se* (colour), *xiang* (aroma) and *wei* (taste).

In China, the people of Sichuan are known for their peaceful pace of life, even in the megalopolis of Chengdu. It is no coincidence that the city has the largest number of tea houses (p. 376).

→ **RECIPES**: Dan dan noodles (p. 244), twice-cooked pork (p. 196), chilli fish pot (p. 218)

MAP 2

Starchy Foods
主食
ZHǓ SHÍ

······· **WHEAT IN THE NORTH; RICE IN THE SOUTH** ·······

🌾 *wheat-based foods*   🌿 *rice-based foods*   🌱 *Tibetan foods made from barley*   ▢ *intermediate regions*   750km

Why?

Rice farming requires a warm and humid climate, which is present in Southern China. In the north, wheat gradually replaced millet after it was introduced 5,000 years ago.

Associated Dishes

Dumplings, noodles and bao are the cornerstone of northern cuisine. In the south, rice comes in all forms: glutinous rice, congee, noodles, rice vermicelli, just to name a few.

A Regional Exception

North-eastern rice is very famous in China, despite being more recent than its counterparts. This variant, called japonica rice, is well suited to the local climate and is only harvested once per year, as opposed to twice in the south, which supposedly explains (in part) its quality.

MAP 3

Chilli Pepper

辣椒

LÀJIĀO

A FIERY CENTRE

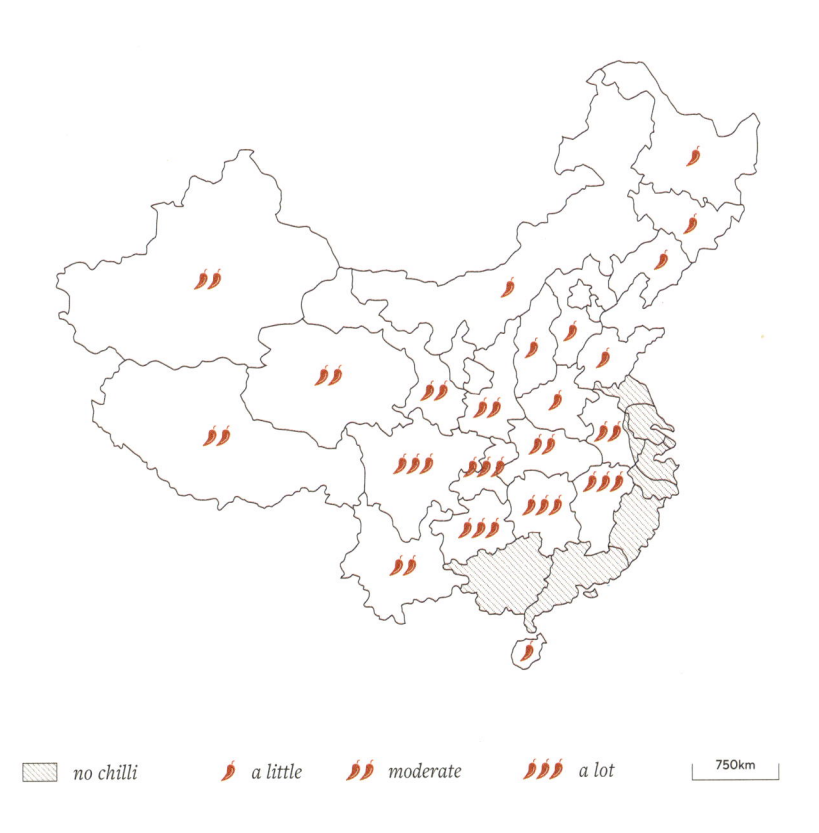

---

no chilli   *a little*   *moderate*   *a lot*   750km

A Regional Disparity

Imported by Portuguese traders at the end of the 16th century, chilli peppers are now part of the daily life of many central China regions, such as Hunan, Sichuan or Guizhou. In contrast, coastal provinces use very little chilli in their food.

The Poor Man's Spice

Coastal regions are historically richer and have easier access to fresh produce, unlike the central regions that originally used chilli peppers both to preserve food and as a seasoning, salt being rare.

The Chilli Revolution

Migrant workers, mainly from the central regions, brought their cuisine to the major coastal metropolises (Shanghai, Hangzhou, Guangzhou). Thus, chilli oil has become one of the most popular condiments in the country.

MAP
4

Alcohol

酒

JIǓ

····················· NATIONAL INEBRIATION ·····················

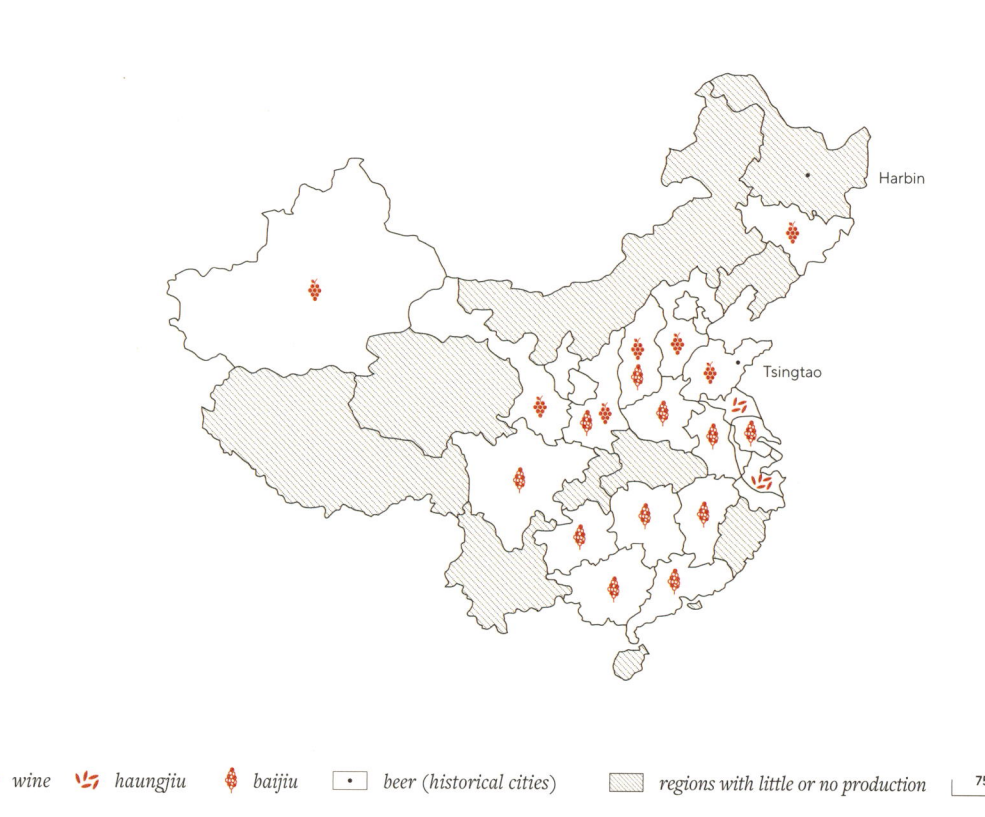

● wine   ᭣ haungjiu   ● baijiu   ▫ beer (historical cities)   ▨ regions with little or no production   750km

The National Spirit

Baijiu (35–60% alcohol) is the most widely consumed spirit in the world. Made mainly from fermented sorghum, its best bottles are a sign of prestige, and are indispensable for every great occasion.

To Drink and Cook

Huangjiu, or "yellow wine" (8–20% alcohol), is one of the oldest wines in the world, with more than 2,500 years of history. Made from rice, it is historically associated with Shaoxing City, Zhejiang. It is served at the table as well as used in the kitchen (see p. 24).

Foreign Origins

The first brewery in China was launched in Harbin by a Polish man in 1900. The Germans followed suit by launching the Tsingtao beer in 1903, in the eponymous city. Wine production really took off in the 1980s, after the country's economic reforms.

Introduction to Chinese Cuisine · · · · · Map of Alcohols

MAP

5

Teas

茶叶

CHÁ YÈ

---- **THE SOUTH'S SWEETNESS** ----

🌿 green tea   🍂 black tea   🌿 oolong tea   🍂 pu'er tea   ▨ regions with little or no production   750km

Red is Black

In China, the colour of the tea refers to the colour of the infusion, not the leaves. Thus, what is commonly called "black tea" in the West corresponds to "red tea" (红茶, *hóng chá*) in China.

Oxidation History

Oxidation is a natural chemical process that darkens tea leaves and thus changes their colour. Green tea has not oxidized and very nearly retains its original colour, while black tea is fully oxidized.

The Land of Tea

China is the only country in the world to produce all six types of tea. Besides green and black tea, there is also oolong tea (a semi-oxidized tea) and pu'er tea, a fermented tea whose taste improves over time, like good wine. White tea, and especially yellow tea, are much rarer and not visible on the map.

CULTURE 1

When Do We Eat?

IN CHINA, THE USUAL GREETING, "HOW ARE YOU?", IS REPLACED BY "HAVE YOU EATEN?" TO EAT WELL IS TO INSTANTLY FEEL BETTER. THE THREE CLASSIC MEALS ARE COMPLEMENTED BY OTHER MOMENTS THAT ARE SPECIFIC TO CHINESE CULTURE.

BREAKFAST
早餐
ZǍO CĀN

7 to 9 a.m.

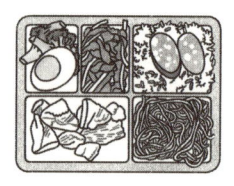

LUNCH
午餐
WǓ CĀN

11:30 a.m. to 1:30 p.m.

DINNER
晚餐
WǍN CĀN

6 to 9 p.m.

It is common in China to start the day with something hot and savoury. And there is no shortage of choices: bao zi (p. 278), you tiao (p. 326), soy drinks, noodle or wonton soups (p. 272), congee (p. 302), pancakes of all kinds (p. 226), to mention only a few major categories of dishes. Breakfast is a good representation of Chinese cuisine; the dishes are generous, varied and lively.

▪ Beyond the food, what stands out is the morning's energy and excitement. Breakfast is mostly an outdoors affair, enjoyed in thousands of small restaurants and at specialized street vendors. It is delicious and cheap, to take away or on the spot, finished in 15 minutes in a good-natured atmosphere.

▪ It is hard to choose, but my strongest childhood memory is of sticky rice with a chopped pork broth and shiitake mushrooms (p. 306), which I eat along with fresh soy milk, also salted (p. 324).

At noon, everyone, from students to office workers, tends to prefer something quick and filling. Noodle dishes (with or without soup, p. 231) are a top choice, the same with rice dishes (p. 289).

▪ Getting a delivery has become very common for young urban dwellers nowadays, but I prefer to go to canteens to have my "rice box" (饭盒, *fan he*). Similar to the Japanese bento, this lunch box may consist of three or four dishes, with a side of white rice.

▪ Dishes in this type of restaurant are usually divided into two categories: meat and fish (荤菜, *hūn cài*) on one side, and vegetables and tofu (素菜, *sù cài*) on the other. The menu changes regularly, depending on the seasons and what's available.

Dinner is eaten early in China, usually right after the end of the work day. For as long as I can remember, my grandmother has always had dinner as early as 6 p.m., or even earlier. It is often the only time of the day when the family meets to share a "real" meal, meaning several communal dishes on the table.

▪ For a household of four, for example, it is usually "three dishes and one soup" (三菜一汤, *sān cai yī tāng*), with a meat dish, a vegetable dish and a last dish which can be tofu or fish. Soup (p. 157) is an important part of the meal, as it moistens the palate and stimulates the appetite. I developed a habit as a child that I kept up to this day; when I have a bit of leftover rice in my bowl, I like to finish by mixing it with soup. It gives me a sense of warm comfort.

▪ There aren't really any desserts at the end of the meal. Instead, fresh seasonal fruit is sometimes served, such as clementines or a slice of watermelon.

GOOD TO KNOW
小提示

In China, one usually starts the day with a glass of hot water, in order to protect the stomach.

YUM CHA
早茶
ZǍO CHÁ

7 to 11 a.m.

"Morning tea" is a concept that exists in many parts of Southern China, but nowadays, it is mostly associated with the Guangdong and Hong Kong provinces. You go to this type of restaurant to have your tea (oolong, pu'er, chrysanthemum, among the most popular) and eat a few dim sum (p. 352).

- Dim sum is a set of small dishes, usually served in steamer baskets. In the most traditional restaurants, the waiter still brings the dishes on trolleys.

- Restaurants serving yum cha are now open all day, and are popular with tourists and locals alike. But the morning atmosphere remains special: in Guangzhou, I remember being among many elderly people who came after their morning gym (a very common practice in China). It's a little like going to a pub with friends, without alcohol but with a lot of good food!

XIAO CHI
小吃
XIĀO CHĪ

Throughout the Day

Xiao chi, which literally means "small snack", is synonymous with street food in a country that worships this type of food.

- Although xiao chi is not a substitute for a formal meal and is often eaten on the go, it comes in limitless variations. It can be grilled dumplings, noodle soup, ice cream or meat skewers (p. 316). The only requirement is that it is easy to eat.

- I tend to associate xiao chi with places and atmospheres, rather than specific dishes. There are "xiao chi streets" (小吃街, *xiao chī jiē*) in every Chinese city, some of which have become major tourist attractions, such as Chenghuang Miao in Shanghai or Jinli Street in Chengdu.

- After sunset, the famous night markets become an essential trip for all gourmets, where you can stop at every stall without ever seeing the same dish twice.

XIAO YE
宵夜
XIĀO YÈ

9 p.m. Until the End of the Night

It's dinner time, but Chinese style. From 9 p.m. until late, night restaurants (which are different from the night market stalls) take over to feed the night owls, especially in summer, when the heat is stifling in large parts of the country.

- Xiao ye (literally "eat at night") can be a substitute for dinner or enjoyed as an extra meal, a solitary pleasure if you have the munchies, or an accompaniment to drinking parties with friends. Imagine a dozen outdoor tables, loud voices, and free-flowing beers. Stir-fried wok dishes are the stars of xiao ye, perhaps tied with grilled dishes.

- Every Chinese person is bound to associate a dish with these moments. Personally, I will never forget the smell of good stir-fried rice (p. 296) bought at 2 a.m. on my street in Shanghai during my university exchange year, or a large rice vermicelli soup, with pork intestines simmered in a highly fragrant broth (猪脏粉), a Wenzhou speciality.

CULTURE 2

At the Table

A CHINESE MEAL IS MEANT TO BE A COMMUNAL AFFAIR; ASIDE FROM THE RICE BOWLS, ALL DISHES ARE PLACED IN THE CENTRE OF THE TABLE. IT CHANGES EVERYTHING, FROM THE INGREDIENTS' PREPARATION, TO HOW THE DISHES ARE SET UP, TO GOOD MANNERS.

THE PROGRESSION OF THE MEAL

The "starter/main course/dessert" model does not really exist in China. A daily meal is very simple: a few dishes to share, all served at the same time, accompanied by white rice. In a more formal meal, such as a large wedding banquet, a dozen dishes find their way to the table, usually in the following order.

01 — TEA AND DRINKS (茶, 饮料)

Apart from the almost systematic presence of tea, other drinks are usually placed on the table even before the guests arrive. As for alcohol, wine, *baijiu* and beers are offered. Non-alcoholic beverages such as soda, coconut milk or herbal teas in cans (*wang lao ji*) are also available.

02 — COLD DISHES (冷盘)

An assortment of small cold dishes marks the start of the meal, such as white radish pickles (p. 68), shredded chicken with sesame oil (p. 74) or steamed aubergines (p. 56). They are intended to stimulate the appetite, meaning that acidic, spicy and salty flavours are particularly welcome at this stage. There's a reason they are also called "dishes that accompany alcohol"!

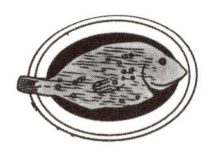

03 — MAIN DISHES (热菜)

At minimum, there are as many dishes as there are guests at a formal meal, although there can often be more. Dishes quickly cover the table. The rule is that expensive ingredients arrive first (bird's nest, sea cucumber...), meat dishes before vegetable dishes, wok dishes before braised or simmered dishes, solids before liquids (like soups).

04 — RICE & NOODLES (主食)

Starchy foods are served after hot dishes, often in the form of stir-fried noodles or rice.

05 — SWEET DISHES (甜菜)

Even though they are served at the end of the meal, sweet (and hot) dishes are not considered desserts. They can be presented as a soup, a sweet bao or a Chinese pastry.

06 — FRUITS (水果)

The meal always ends with a large plate of fresh fruits (watermelon, clementine, mango, dragon fruit, etc.) that is elegantly presented (carved fruits, colour combinations).

ROUND TABLE AND TABLEWARE

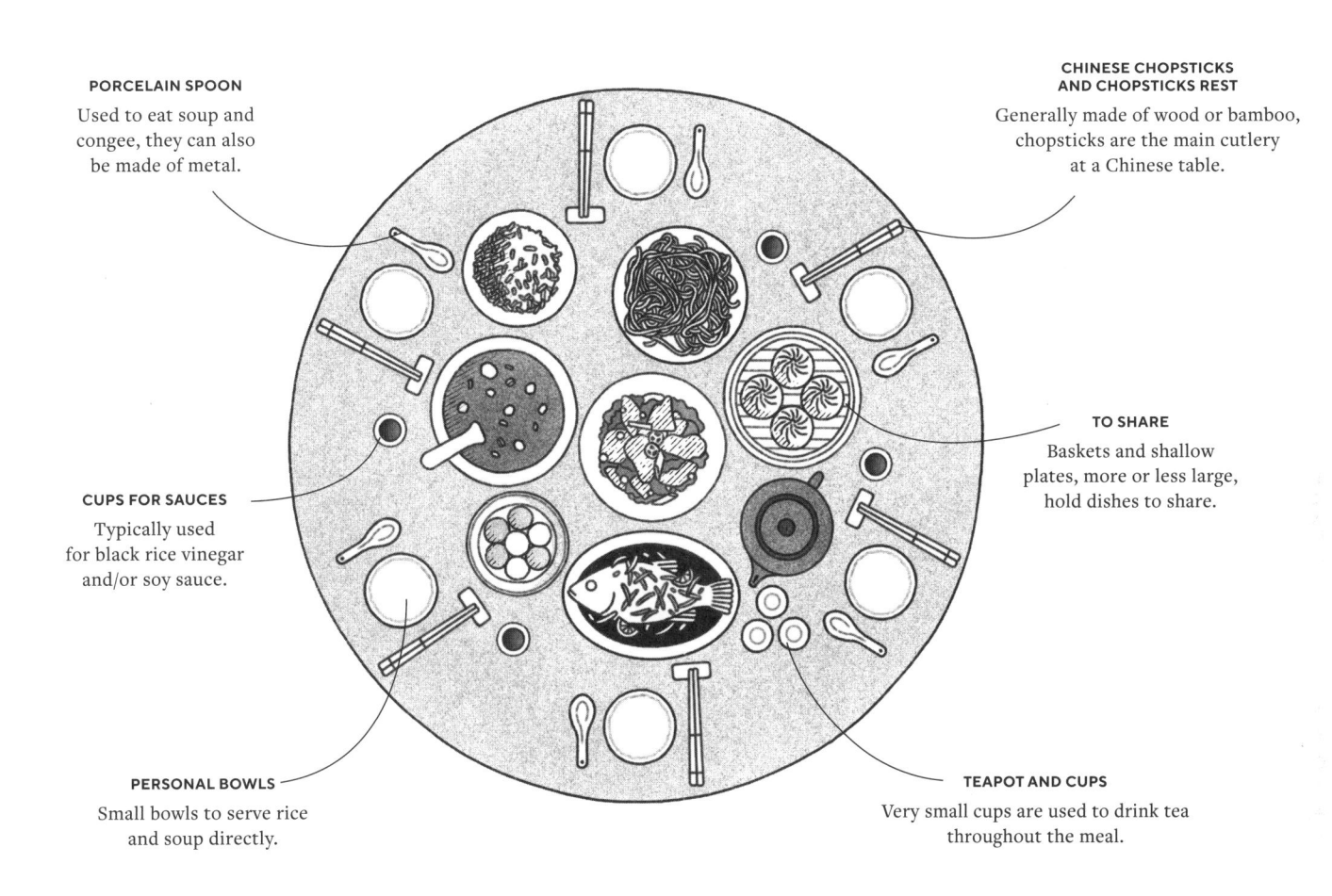

PORCELAIN SPOON
Used to eat soup and congee, they can also be made of metal.

CHINESE CHOPSTICKS AND CHOPSTICKS REST
Generally made of wood or bamboo, chopsticks are the main cutlery at a Chinese table.

TO SHARE
Baskets and shallow plates, more or less large, hold dishes to share.

CUPS FOR SAUCES
Typically used for black rice vinegar and/or soy sauce.

PERSONAL BOWLS
Small bowls to serve rice and soup directly.

TEAPOT AND CUPS
Very small cups are used to drink tea throughout the meal.

THE ROUND TABLE

Even if it is no longer in every household today, the round table remains deeply associated with meals in China, be it for philosophical or practical reasons. For a New Year's meal, a state banquet or in private lounges of restaurants, the presence of a round table is often inseparable from great moments.

The circle (圆, *yuán*) has special significance in Chinese culture. It is the symbol of perfection, balance and unity. Among other things, it evokes the representation of yin and yang (balance), the full moon during the mid-autumn festival (reunion) or the "moon gates" in classical Chinese gardens (harmony).

This table shape is also very convenient for sharing dishes:

- When they are placed in the centre, everyone has access to them. If the table is too big, the famous glass turntable takes over.

- There are no angles, and thus no loss of space.

- It avoids the problem of some people being seated at the end of the table. Everyone can see each other, which makes meals often lively.

CULTURE
3

Creating a Meal

A CHINESE MEAL IS ABOVE ALL SHAREABLE. INSTEAD OF A SINGLE DISH PREPARED FOR SEVERAL PEOPLE, SEVERAL DISHES ARE ARRANGED IN THE MIDDLE OF THE TABLE, SERVED WITH WHITE RICE. HERE ARE SOME MENU IDEAS TO START PREPARING YOUR FIRST CHINESE MEAL.

01
QUICK AND EASY
简单
JIǍN DĀN

Dishes with few ingredients that can be made in less than 20 minutes.

Menu 1
- Spinach with sesame sauce
- Hand-torn cabbage
- 5-spice tofu
- Coca-Cola-flavoured chicken wings
- White rice

Menu 2
- Sweet and sour pork ribs
- Steamed aubergine (eggplant) with soy sauce and sesame oil
- Fried cockles with garlic and chilli
- Seaweed soup with dried shrimp
- White rice

02
VEGETARIAN
素食
SÙ SHÍ

Chinese cuisine is more veggie-friendly than you would think. While meat is present in many vegetable, tofu or soup recipes, it is easily exchangeable.

Menu 1
- Smashed cucumber salad
- Fried corn with pepper and salt
- Mapo tofu (shiitake version)
- Stir-fried tomatoes and eggs
- White rice

Menu 2
- Three treasures of the Earth
- Tofu skin salad with red radishes
- Yu xiang aubergine (eggplant)
- Hot and sour soup (without meat)
- White rice

03
CHINESE DINNERS
家常
JIĀ CHÁNG

My favourite dishes, some of which require a little more effort, but I promise you will not be disappointed.

Menu 1
- Dongpo pork
- Sichuan fried green beans
- Silken tofu with century egg
- Chicken meatball and vermicelli soup
- White rice

Menu 2
- Steamed pork with dried mustard leaves
- Stir-fried celery with cashew nuts
- Dai-style fried egg salad
- Steamed scallops with rice vermicelli
- White rice

QUANTITY: The number of dishes corresponds to the number of guests; for example, 4 dishes per 4 people. You can add one or two additional dishes, depending on the occasion and the amount of time you have.

ORGANIZATION: Manage your preparation time by alternating cold and braised dishes that can be prepared in advance, while wok stir-fried dishes should be cooked at the last minute.

BALANCE: A spicy dish is handled better with other softer dishes, a soup makes the meal more digestible, a fatty dish is counterbalanced by fresh vegetables.

DOS

应该

YĪNG GĀI

HOLD YOUR BOWL OF RICE

This is the first thing children are taught. Always hold your bowl with one hand, so that it stays stable when eating rice (the other hand is busy handling chopsticks). It is also natural for most Chinese people to bring the bowl of rice closer to their mouth rather than the other way around (and incidentally, avoid making a mess).

USE SERVING CUTLERY

Although the dishes are shared, for hygiene purposes, serving chopsticks and spoons (公筷, *gōng kuai*) have become a common utensil for every dish, to avoid touching the food with your own chopsticks. If there aren't any, do not hesitate to request some; you will not offend anyone.

GIVE PRIORITY TO THE ELDERLY

Filial piety is one of the most important virtues of Chinese culture, which was influenced by Confucianism. At the table, respect for your elders translates into a well-established order; one does not begin to eat until the elders are served.

DON'TS

不应该

BÙ YĪNG GĀI

PLAY WITH YOUR CHOPSTICKS

Planting your chopsticks in your rice bowl, licking your chopsticks, pointing with your chopsticks, making noise with your chopsticks... All these small gestures can be construed as quite rude at the table.

DIG AROUND IN THE DISH

The absence of cutlery does not give you permission to dig around in the dish or, even worse, pick up a morsel and then put it back. The best practice is to visualize the morsel you want, usually in the part of the dish that is closest to you, pick it up with your chopsticks, then add it to your bowl.

OVERUSE THE TURNTABLE

A glass or wooden turntable (or "lazy Susan", its curious English nickname) is often found on large round tables, to allow all the guests to access the dishes. It is very convenient and quite fun for first-time users. You obviously cannot spin the tray while someone is in the process of helping themselves. Furthermore, you should avoid spinning it too often, or you might be perceived as a picky eater who is only interested in a few dishes.

CULTURE 4

Street Food

MAINSTREAM FOOD IS ENJOYED IN THE STREET ABOVE ALL, IN ICONIC AND UNPRETENTIOUS PLACES WHERE YOU CAN EAT ON THE GO, OR SIT DOWN FOR A GREAT DINNER WITH FRIENDS THAT CAN LAST ALL NIGHT.

MIAN GUAN
面馆
MIÀN GUǍN

These stalls that can be found all over China, whose name can be translated as "noodle house", serve, as their name suggests, fresh noodles. They offer quick service, cheap food, and above all, a lot of comfort. With or without broth, with a good dose of chilli pepper or vinegar, simmered pork or an avalanche of seafood, a bowl of wheat or rice noodles is always packed with local flavours.

While the decor has somewhat modernized compared to my memories of the '90s (the kitchen used to be at the entrance, with the steaming water pot, and plastic chairs and tables used to be at the front), the pleasure of slurping remains intact!

DAI PAI DONG
大排档
DÀ PÁI DÀNG

I first discovered the *dai pai dong* through Hong Kong movies from the '90s. These open-air restaurants appeared in Hong Kong after World War II, while the city was going through an intense period of growth. This word is synonymous with night-time meals with friends, enjoying stir-fried dishes with a lot of *wok hei*, that famous smoky taste you obtain when using a wok at very high temperatures, and drinking beer.

They came close to disappearing after the city refused to renew their licences (*dai pai dong* literally means "big licence stand") in the '80s. However, the *dai pai dong* have made a comeback in recent years, born out of the desire of protecting these culinary icons of Hong Kong.

GOOD TO KNOW
小提示

Eating out is a very commonplace activity in China, as there are options for all budgets.

BAO ZI STALLS
包子店
BĀO ZǏ DIÀN

GRILLING STAND
烧烤摊
SHĀO KĂO TĀN

Of all breakfast-serving stalls, these are probably the most recognizable. It is impossible to miss the huge steaming baskets that pile up at the entrance. Ask the boss for your favourite bao, and she will know exactly where it is in the pile.

There are generally few or no seats. You line up, order your baos and possibly some hot soy milk, then you go home to eat, or you enjoy your meal on the go.

Chinese people don't have ovens at home, and barbecues aren't part of the culture, so grilled dishes are eaten outside. Most people have discovered the pleasure of fire-cooked dishes via stands that sell skewers, always following the same ritual: take an aluminium tray, place the skewers in it (lamb, cauliflower, tofu, squid... anything is possible), give everything to the chef and patiently wait your turn. When the cooking is done, they add a brush stroke of sauce and a pinch of ground spices (cumin, chilli pepper). I promise it's worth the wait...

PRODUCTS 1

Essential Ingredients

MOST OF THE RECIPES IN THIS BOOK ARE CENTRED AROUND A FEW ESSENTIALS
THAT YOU WILL FIND IN THE MAJORITY OF CHINESE HOUSEHOLDS.
IF YOU AREN'T SURE WHERE TO START, YOU'RE IN THE RIGHT PLACE.

01 SOY SAUCE

Basic soy sauce is a fermented product made up of four ingredients: water, soy, wheat and salt. It is the "mother sauce" of Chinese cuisine, the one that adds a salty and umami taste to countless dishes. It is used as a seasoning, a sauce and a marinade base. You can find it everywhere.

A distinction is made between light soy sauce (生抽, *shēng chōu*) and dark soy sauce (老抽, *Lao chōu*). The former is the "default" soy sauce, also known as salted soy sauce, while the latter is characterized by its thicker texture, its less salty flavour and its darker hue. It is mainly incorporated in braised or simmered dishes, to add a caramel colour. It is interesting to note that in some countries you can find commercially sweetened soy sauce, which does not exist in China (p. 348).

Once the bottle is opened, there is no need to keep the soy sauce cool. I keep it on a shelf or in a cupboard, away from the light, with the cap tightly fastened. It normally does not expire, but it can become slightly less tasty after six months to one year, which isn't too much of a problem.

- **Alternative Ingredients**: To replace light soy sauce, you can use Japanese soy sauce (*koikuchi shoyu*), which is slightly sweeter and thicker, or tamari sauce if you are gluten intolerant. There are also variants of soy sauce that have reduced salt content but don't impact the dish's flavour too much. There is no substitute ingredient for dark soy sauce.

02 SHAOXING WINE

Shaoxing wine is a type of yellow wine (黄酒, *huáng jǐ*), a traditional Chinese alcohol that is made with fermented cereals (wheat, millet, rice). Its name refers to the city of Shaoxing in Eastern China, where it has been manufactured for more than 2,000 years.

Amber in colour, with an alcohol content ranging from 12 to 18%, it is a wine that can be enjoyed hot or cold at the table, as well as a cooking wine. It has quite a unique taste, which can be surprising when you try it for the first time; it is slightly sweet, deep and spicy, with a caramelized note.

It is very often used for blanching or marinating meat or fish, removing strong odours (去腥, *qù xīng*), but also to add flavour and depth to a dish.

- **Alternative Ingredients**: There is no real alternative, but sherry or other Chinese or Japanese rice wines (with a transparent colour) can work as substitutes.

03 RICE VINEGAR

Out of the five basic tastes, sourness is probably the second most important in Chinese cuisine, right after saltiness. It counterbalances greasiness (解腻, *jiě ni*). A fried dish becomes more digestible, and a rich broth seems lighter. In China, you can find rice vinegar everywhere.

Chinese vinegars are mostly cereal-based, usually rice but sometimes wheat, sorghum or millet, depending on the region. Rice vinegars are extremely varied, each including different ageing times and fermentation techniques. For the sake of simplicity, I will only mention black rice vinegar, and more particularly the variant that originates from Zhenjiang City, which is by far the most used and the easiest to find. As I grew up with it, I use that vinegar by default in all the recipes of this book, unless otherwise stated.

Zhenjiang vinegar is one of the so-called flavoured vinegars (香醋, *xiāng cù*); in addition to its strong aroma and black colour, it is mildly acidic, with a fruity note and a lingering taste. It is used both as a seasoning for stir-fried or braised dishes (the famous sweet and sour taste) and as a dumpling sauce. I remember my grandfather adding generous helpings of it in his noodle soup.

- **Alternative Ingredients**: Sherry vinegar is probably the closest thing to Zhenjiang vinegar in terms of taste (but its smell is quite distinct).

02

SHAOXING WINE

绍兴酒 | SHÀO XĪNG JIǓ

- **Purchasing Tip:** Shaoxing wine (sometimes spelled "Shao Hsing") is found in most Chinese supermarkets and is always sold as a large bottle.

- **Recommended Brand:** Pagoda Brand (塔牌)

01

SOY SAUCE

酱油 | JIÀNG YÓU

- **Purchasing Tip:** Soy sauce made with natural fermentation must not contain any additives or colouring agents (look out for the words "naturally brewed" on the label).

- **Recommended Brand:** Shinho (欣和)

03

RICE VINEGAR

香醋 | XIĀNG CÙ

- **Purchasing Tip:** Black rice vinegar can be found in any Chinese supermarket. Look out for the word "Zhenjiang" or "ChinKiang" on the bottle, or "Yongchun", named after a city in the Fujian province, which tastes similar.

- **Recommended Brand:** Heng Shun (恒顺)

05
OYSTER SAUCE
蚝油 | HÁO YÓU

- <u>Purchasing Tip</u>: The market is largely dominated by one brand of oyster sauce: Lee Kum Kee.
- <u>Recommended Brand</u>: Lee Kum Kee (李锦记, LKK for those in the know)

07
ROCK SUGAR
冰糖 | BĪNG TÁNG

- <u>Purchasing Tip</u>: You can find this in any Chinese supermarket, in the dried products or spices aisle.

06
SICHUAN PEPPERCORN
花椒 | HUĀ JIĀO

- <u>Purchasing Tip</u>: If possible, buy whole berries rather than ground (the brighter and more intense the red colour is, the better). A precise indication of the production area is another sure sign of quality, instead of a simple "made in China" or "made in Sichuan".

04
COOKING OIL
油 | YÓU

- <u>Purchasing Tip</u>: In addition to your usual rapeseed (canola) and/or sunflower oil, you can also use peanut oil or grapeseed oil.

> "Contrary to what you might expect, you only need a few ingredients to start cooking Chinese."

04) COOKING OIL

The mention of oil in Chinese cuisine is instantly associated with the wok, whether for stir-fried, braised or fried dishes.

I tend to use sunflower or rapeseed (canola) oil at home, but any vegetable oil that meets the following two criteria is suitable.

The oil must first have a high smoke point (200°C/400°F at minimum) to adapt to the wok's temperature, which can rise very quickly. These are usually refined oils, as opposed to virgin oils.

It must also have a neutral taste, to prevent it from clashing with the seasoning, unless desired, as in Sichuan cuisine, which uses roasted rapeseed (canola) oil (*cai zi you*).

05) OYSTER SAUCE

As the name suggests, oyster sauce is made from oyster extract. Legend has it that the founder of the Lee Kum Kee brand created it in 1888 by chance when he left a pot of oysters on the fire for too long. When he came back, the broth had reduced and turned into a sauce so good that he decided to market it.

Oyster sauce looks like molasses. It has a salty, slightly sweet taste, is a veritable umami bomb that replaces glutamate, and unlike other seafood sauces (such as fish sauce), which have a quite pronounced smell, it does not smell like raw oysters!

I use it mainly in stir-fried dishes, and often combined with soy sauce. Originally Cantonese, oyster sauce is mainly used in the south and east of the country. But thanks to the Cantonese influence on Chinese cuisine around the world (p. 10), it is very likely that you have already tasted it without even knowing it.

- **Alternative Ingredients:** Vegetarian "oyster" sauces are available, and are usually made from shiitake mushroom extract.

06) SICHUAN PEPPERCORN

Sichuan peppercorn (called "flower pepper" in Chinese) is inseparable from Sichuan cuisine. When combined with chilli pepper, it creates one of the most iconic flavours of Chinese cooking: *mala* (麻辣), literally "spicy anaesthetic".

It is a berry that has had its seed removed to keep only the husk, hence its oddly shaped head that looks like Pac-Man's mouth! Its taste, or rather the sensation it causes, is quite unique. It starts with a slight lemony note, rather pleasant; but very quickly there is a tingling on the tongue, before a sensation of anaesthesia takes over and diffuses throughout the palate.

While it is historically associated with Sichuan and south-west Chinese cuisine, this type of peppercorn is now an ingredient that is found in the majority of the country. It can be used whole (to infuse in oil in order to flavour a broth) or ground (as a seasoning, on its own or mixed with other spices).

There are two types of Sichuan peppercorn on the market. The red peppercorn, prized especially for its beautiful colour, is the most common. The green peppercorn has a fresher, lemony taste, and its anaesthetic effect is a little more pronounced.

- **Alternative ingredients:** Sansho or Timur berries are close neighbours. They create a lighter tingling sensation.

07) ROCK SUGAR

These cane sugar crystals, mainly used in soups (*tong sui*) or in *hong shao* dishes (see p. 50) to make caramel, are supposed to add a shine to the dish. Rock sugar isn't as sweet as powdered white sugar.

There are two versions: white crystals, shaped like small cubes of about 1cm (½in) and of identical size, and yellow crystals, much larger and unevenly shaped. The latter are made from less refined cane sugar and create a slightly more complex taste. However, their large size means they must be broken down to obtain the correct amount for the dish.

PRODUCTS 2

Essential Aromatic Ingredients

GARLIC, GINGER AND SPRING ONION ARE THE HOLY TRINITY OF CHINESE CUISINE, AND ARE PRESENT IN MOST RECIPES IN THIS BOOK, WHETHER INDIVIDUALLY OR TOGETHER.

01 GARLIC

Garlic (蒜, *suàn*) is known for its antibacterial properties. It is used fried, fermented or pickled.

- A whole garlic bulb, just cut in half horizontally, can be added directly to simmering dishes when the broth will be strained. A garlic clove can be infused in hot oil or fermented in vinegar (such as in the northern speciality Laba garlic). Once sliced, it can be made into fried garlic, and chopped garlic is the most common form for stir-fried dishes.

- In Northern China, it is not uncommon to see the locals bite directly into a clove of garlic to go along with their noodles!

- Use a knife to peel a garlic clove. Place the clove on a stable chopping (cutting) board, and gently hit it with the flat of the knife (blade facing outwards as a safety measure). The skin should come off by itself.

02 GINGER

Ginger (姜, *jiāng*) is mainly used in Chinese cuisine to remove strong odours (腥味) coming from meat or fish.

- Without peeling the skin, it is sliced and placed in water to blanch meat and neutralize its smell. It can be chopped and browned in hot oil for added flavour. It can also be grated and subtly integrated into meat stuffing (dumplings, bao).

- Or it can be used raw, usually finely julienned, to be added directly to a dish for presentation (steamed fish) or to a sauce (black rice vinegar for the classic combination).

- According to traditional Chinese medicine, it is a remedy for small, everyday ailments. Infused in hot water, it is said to relieve colds, headaches, sore throats or hangovers.

- To peel the ginger, simply scrape the skin with a teaspoon. For inaccessible corners, you can cut off a part of it and start over with the spoon. Only peel the quantity you need, to keep the rhizome fresh.

03 SPRING ONION (SCALLION)

Spring onions (葱, *cōng*, pronouncd "tsong") are the default herb in China. They belong to the onion family; their slightly spicy taste increases in strength when heated up.

- The green part, which is the most tender, is used at the end of the cooking process, or for toppings, chopped or shaped like sticks. It is possible to make spring onion "hair", by cutting it vertically and immersing it in iced water to bend it.

- The white part, which is more resistant to heat, is used in fried dishes. Much like ginger, spring onions are used to blanch meat, often tied in a knot to recover them more easily from the broth.

- The spring onions you buy from many Western greengrocers are bigger and sweeter than their Chinese counterparts or those you find in Chinese supermarkets, but they are perfectly suited to the recipes in this book. They should not be confused with Chinese spring onions (韭菜 *jiucai*), which are closer to chives, and whose taste is completely different.

- Spring onions should be chopped in order to maintain their freshness, then transferred to an airtight container and covered with kitchen paper (moisture is the enemy of spring onions). For long-term storage, there is no need to add kitchen paper, but make sure to dry the spring onions before putting them in the freezer.

| | CLOVE | CRUSHED | CHOPPED | MINCED |

01
GARLIC
蒜 | SUÀN

| | SLICED | FINELY JULIENNED | MINCED | GRATED |

02
GINGER
姜 | JIĀNG

| | KNOT | STICK-SHAPED | "HAIR" | CHOPPED |

03
SPRING ONION (SCALLION)
葱 | CŌNG

PRODUCTS 3

Spices

THERE IS A VERY WIDE VARIETY OF SPICES IN CHINA DEPENDING ON THE REGION, OFTEN LINKED TO CHINESE MEDICINE. BUT ON A DAILY BASIS, A HOUSEHOLD'S USE OF SPICES IS QUITE FRUGAL.

---

01 STAR ANISE

In my opinion, star anise is one of the most important spices there is.

It originates from China and is indispensable for a large number of braised or simmered dishes (*hong shao*, see p. 50), or for chilli oil. Its strong and characteristic fragrance makes it difficult to replace. It is generally used whole (except in the case of the 5-spice mix) and in small quantities. Incidentally, its Chinese name translates to "8 horns". I'll let you count them!

02 WHITE PEPPER

White pepper is the default pepper used in Chinese cuisine.

It is made from the same berry as black pepper (*Piper nigrum*), but is stripped of its outer casing. It has a more "direct", pungent taste. It is mainly used in its ground form in marinades, soups or stir-fried dishes, and usually added at the end of the cooking process, to preserve its flavour as much as possible.

03 CHINESE BROWN CARDAMOM

Brown cardamom can be identified by its smoky and peppery taste.

At first glance, it looks more like a very dark nutmeg, compared to its much smaller green counterpart. It is used whole in simmered dishes, broken slightly (with the flat of a knife, for example) to release its flavour.

04 CUMIN

Cumin is mainly associated with lamb skewers, which are very popular in China.

It came to China in the 7th century by the Silk Road, notably via the city of Chang'an (now Xi'an), which was the imperial capital at the time. To this day, cumin is still associated with this north-west region of China. This is one of my favourite spices. It is mainly used as a seasoning at the end of the cooking process on grilled skewers.

05 5-SPICE

A blend of the five basic spices of Chinese cuisine: Sichuan peppercorn, star anise, Chinese cinnamon, cloves and fennel seeds.

This combination is not set in stone, and seasoning sold under this name may vary. In Chinese supermarkets you will often find a more complex version called "13-spice" (十三香, *shí sān xiāng*). The 5-spice seasoning is bought in powder form, meaning it is reserved for meat marinades or simmered dishes.

06 CHINESE CINNAMON

Chinese cinnamon (*Cinnamomum cassia*) is different from Ceylon cinnamon (*Cinnamomum verum*), which is considered to be nobler.

Unless explicitly mentioned, the cinnamon you will usually find is the *Cinnamomum cassia* variant. In Chinese cuisine, it is mainly used in simmered and savoury dishes. One stick (or even half) is usually enough, thanks to its powerful flavour.

01
STAR ANISE
八角 | BĀ JIĂO

02
WHITE PEPPER
白胡椒 | BÁI HÚ JIĀO

03
CHINESE BROWN CARDAMOM
草果 | CĂO GŬO

04
CUMIN
孜然 | ZĪ RÁN

05
5-SPICE
五香粉 | WǓ XIĀNG FĚN

06
CHINESE CINNAMON
桂皮 | GUÌ PÍ

PRODUCTS 4

Dried Food

DRIED FOOD IS A PILLAR OF CHINESE CUISINE, WHETHER OF ANIMAL OR VEGETABLE ORIGIN. DRYING TECHNIQUES WERE DEVELOPED OUT OF NECESSITY TO PROLONG THE LIFE OF FRESH PRODUCTS, BUT THEY ALSO AMPLIFY THEIR FLAVOUR, INCLUDING THE FAMOUS UMAMI TASTE.

01 SHRIMP

Sun-dried shrimp are packed with umami, complemented by a sweet undertone.

It is the basic ingredient (*xia mi*) of XO sauce, arguably the most luxurious condiment in Cantonese cuisine. It is mainly used in braised and simmered dishes, to give them time to release all their flavours. *Xia pi* (literally "shrimp skins") is what we call dried micro-shrimp. Given their size, they are mostly used for presentation or for quick soups, to which they will add a salty and iodized taste. You will find them in the frozen section of Chinese supermarkets.

02 ALGAE (SEAWEED)

My family comes from a coastal region, so I maintained our habit of eating seaweed, which is naturally iodized, rich in nutrients and packed with umami.

Hai dai (*Saccharina japonica*, better known by their Japanese name, konbu) are loved for their crunchy texture in stir-fried dishes. They naturally enhance the flavours in broths and are very popular in Japanese cuisine. As for *zi cai* (literally "purple vegetables"), they are red algae (of the *Porphyra* genus) often sold dried, then toasted, and packaged like a big cake. You probably know them under the name *nori*. In Chinese cuisine, they are usually added to soups, or used as the main ingredient in popular snacks, including my favourite, *hai tai* (海苔), a very thin seaweed with spices and grilled sesame, a kind of iodized crisp!

03 BLACK FUNGUS

Also known as "wood ear fungus", these small mushrooms are prized for their crisp texture.

They are used in quick-cooking recipes, such as stir-fried dishes, or in salads. Once rehydrated (30 minutes is enough), the black fungus swells enormously (its volume is multiplied by five), so you should only use a small handful at a time.

04 MANDARIN PEELS

Only peels dried under certain conditions and aged for at least three years (their name can be translated to "aged peel") are entitled to use this name. Their price increases with their ageing time.

Well-liked in Cantonese cuisine (the one from Xinhui, in Guangdong, is very famous), *chen pi* strengthens the spleen and relieves wet coughs, according to traditional Chinese medicine. When cooking, the peels are rehydrated, then cut into thin strips or chopped. They add a complex citrus flavour, a sweet undertone and a touch of bitterness (the white part can be scratched off to soften it). The original acidity decreases with the age of the peel. I mainly use it in meat marinades (p. 202).

05 SHIITAKE

This is the most widely used mushroom in China, and almost exclusively in its dried form. Its intense flavour, which fresh shiitake does not have, is the basis of its Chinese name, which can be translated to "flavourful mushroom".

It is the key ingredient in stir-fried dishes or in many soups. Before cooking, it is rehydrated in cold water for at least 2 hours, until the hardest part (usually the stem) becomes soft. Those in a hurry can speed up the process by using warm water (30°C/86°F) and sugar (1 teaspoon per litre/4⅓ cups of water). I do not recommend hot or boiling water, which allows you to go faster but will remove a lot of flavour.

01
SHRIMP

虾米 | XIĀ MǏ, 虾皮 | XIĀ PÍ

02
ALGAE

海苔 | HǍI TÁI, 海带 | HǍI DÀI, 紫菜 | ZǏ CÀI

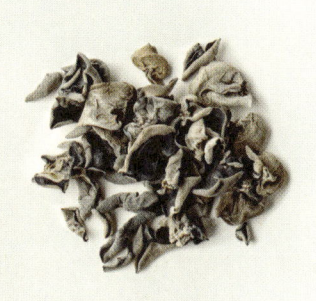

03
BLACK FUNGUS

木耳 | MÙ ĚR

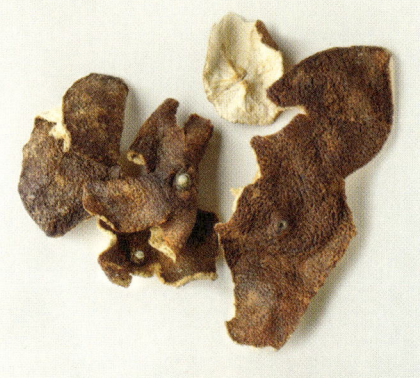

04
MANDARIN PEELS

陈皮 | CHÉN PÍ

05
SHIITAKE

香菇 | XIĀNG GŪ

06
LOTUS AND BAMBOO LEAVES
荷叶 | HÉ YÈ, 粽叶 | ZÒNG YÈ

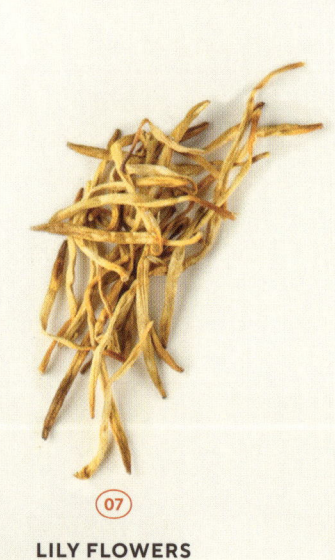

07
LILY FLOWERS
金针菜 | JĪN ZHĒN CÀI

08
GOJI BERRIES
枸杞 | GǑU QĪ

09
HUAMEI
话梅 | HUÀ MÉI

10
JUJUBES
红枣 | HÓNG ZĂO

> "Some markets in China are entirely dedicated to dried products. A true journey for the eyes and nose."

(06) LOTUS AND BAMBOO LEAVES

Dried leaves are widely used in China for cooking *en papillote*.

Unlike aluminium foil, they are naturally airtight, while allowing steam to pass through, and they flavour the food. The lotus leaf, used in *lo mai gai* (p. 308), and the bamboo leaf, used for the famous *zong zi* (p. 375), are among the best known.

(07) LILY FLOWERS

The daylily (*Hemerocallis citrina*) is one of the most common edible flowers in Chinese cuisine.

Measuring 5–6cm (roughly 2in) in length, the buds are picked before flowering and then dried. The colour changes from yellow-green to light brown, which explains their Chinese name, "golden needle". These "flowers" keep a slightly crunchy texture even after rehydration, with a subtle scent of sweet tea that I love. You can use them in a salad (they must be blanched beforehand), in a fried dish or in a meat broth (pork ribs in our region): they counterbalance the fat and add complexity to the soup.

(08) GOJI BERRIES

Considered to be a superfood in the West (sometimes with a little exaggeration), goji berries have been consumed for millennia in China.

They are one of the most popular ingredients of traditional Chinese medicine, as they are credited with many virtues; for example, they combat ageing and improve eyesight. Their bright red, pulpy flesh and slightly sweet flavour make them an ingredient that is as aesthetic as it is tasty. In China, they are used for infusions with chrysanthemum flowers, simmered in regenerative soups with other medicinal ingredients, or incorporated into congee. It is not necessary to rehydrate them if you want to add them to a salad, among other examples. The best berries come from Ningxia, in Northern China. Those of lesser quality are dried out and are a dull dark red, less sweet and more bitter.

(09) HUAMEI

These lacto-fermented plums, mixed with sugar then dried, are a popular snack in China. When cooking, they go particularly well with sweet and sour dishes (p. 200).

(10) JUJUBES

Called "red dates" in Chinese, fresh jujubes are sweet, crunchy and slightly acidic, with a taste reminiscent of apples. In their dried form, they have a higher sugar content and are eaten as snacks or added to simmered dishes.

PRODUCTS
5

Chilli Peppers

ONCE LIMITED TO A FEW CENTRAL REGIONS, THE TASTE OF CHILLI PEPPER NOW EXTENDS TO THE WHOLE COUNTRY. THE MAIN CHILLI PEPPERS USED IN CHINA AREN'T AS STRONG AS THEIR THAI OR INDIAN COUNTERPARTS. CHINESE CUISINE AIMS FOR A BALANCE BETWEEN COLOUR, FLAVOUR AND WARMTH.

RECOGNIZING AND CHOOSING CHILLI PEPPERS

The Chinese names of chilli peppers are generally very evocative and quite confusing for non-natives.

- For example, there is the "sky-facing chilli pepper" (*chao tian jiao*, 30,000 on the Scoville scale), because its tip faces the sky as it grows.

- The bird's eye chilli is called the "small rice pepper" (*xiao mi La*, 50,000 on the Scoville scale).

- One of the most iconic is *er jing tiao*, moderately spicy (15,000 on the Scoville scale) and very flavourful. Long in shape and dark red, it is widely used in Sichuan cuisine. To my knowledge, the best way to find them is to ask good Sichuan restaurants directly, as they import them from China, often in powdered form.

- Varieties of chilli peppers are rarely indicated in Chinese supermarkets, but as a general rule, note that large chilli peppers aren't as strong as the small ones. You can identify a good-quality chilli pepper by its uniform red and shiny colour, and by its texture, which is still supple and not brittle.

01 DRIED CHILLI PEPPERS

Dried chilli peppers are easy to store and are often preferred over fresh peppers, especially outside production areas.

They are typically used in stir-fried dishes, at the beginning of the cooking process, when they are fried in a bit of oil to release their flavour, along with garlic or ginger (see the frying techniques on p. 46).

02 CHILLI OIL

The term "chilli oil" refers to different aromatic oils found in China that are made using chilli.

In Sichuan, it is called "red oil". The basic version is obtained by infusing sesame seeds and three varieties of chilli pepper powder in very hot oil: *er jing tiao* for the flavour, *xiao mi la* for the intensity, and *deng long jiao* for the bright red colour. The less purist among us add spices to it to create an even more flavourful and complex oil (see p. 342). In the Shanxi province, the chilli oil is called *you po la zi*, literally "oil sprinkled on chilli pepper". Hot oil is poured directly onto chilli powder (without burning it), then a touch of vinegar is added to the mix.

03 FERMENTED CHILLI PEPPER

Fermented chilli pepper can be eaten as is, but it is most often used as a condiment to add a mixture of acidic, spicy and salty flavours to a dish.

It is not uncommon to come across a jar filled with lacto-fermented vegetables in a Sichuan kitchen. This is called *pao cai* (literally "pickled vegetables"), and chilli is inevitably one of them.

Unlike basic lacto-fermentation (which uses water and salt), spices (Sichuan peppercorn, bay leaves, star anise) and alcohol (*baijiu*) are usually added to the brine.

04 CHILLI POWDER

The powder is used as a seasoning, but it is above all an essential ingredient in various chilli oils in China.

It is made with whole dried chilli peppers, which are first lightly roasted, traditionally in a wok for the home-made version, and then crushed. The Korean version of chilli powder (*gochugaru*), used to make kimchi, is the most easily found and is a good alternative, although less flavourful and less spicy than *er jing tiao*, to name an example.

03
FERMENTED CHILLI PEPPERS
泡椒 | PÀO JIĀO

01
DRIED CHILLI PEPPERS
干辣椒 | GĀN LÀ JIĀO

02
CHILLI OIL
红油 | HÓNG YÓU

04
CHILLI POWDER
辣椒面 | LÀ JIĀO MIÀN

Fermented Products

PRODUCTS 6

WHETHER IT IS USED FOR SAUCES, CONDIMENTS, VEGETABLES OR TOFU, FERMENTATION IS THE FOUNDATION OF THE "CHINESE TASTE".

01 CHILLI BEAN PASTE

Doubanjiang has the appearance of a thick, oily paste. It is derived from the four fermented ingredients: broad (fava) beans, chilli peppers (*er jing tiao*), salt and wheat flour.

Considered to be the soul of Sichuan cuisine, *doubanjiang* is present in most classic dishes of the region (mapo tofu p. 126, twice-cooked pork p. 196, yu xiang aubergine p. 104). *Doubanjiang* is not consumed raw. It must be fried in a bit of oil over a low heat to release its "red oil", and especially its flavour, before adding the other ingredients. To get an authentic *doubanjiang*, look for the words "Pixian Dou Ban Jiang" in Chinese supermarkets.

02 SWEET BEAN PASTE

Tian mian jiang is a thick brown paste, prepared mainly with fermented wheat flour (in addition to water and salt).

Despite its name, *tian mian jiang* is not particularly sweet; it only contains natural sugar from starch fermentation. It is often compared to hoisin sauce, with which even Chinese people tend to confuse it. *Tian mian jiang* is associated with Peking duck, as the sauce is added to the pancake, or *zha jiang mian*, the capital's iconic noodles (p. 242).

03 FERMENTED BLACK BEANS

These black soy beans with a wrinkled exterior are among the oldest fermented products of Chinese gastronomy (more than 2,000 years of history).

Douchi is widely used in Sichuan cuisine (in stir-fried dishes) and Cantonese cuisine (in steamed dishes). It must be rinsed thoroughly before use (to remove salt from the surface), then roughly chopped with a knife.

04 FERMENTED TOFU

Fu ru is a fermented tofu sold in small cubes of 2–3cm (roughly 1in) in glass jars.

There are two main versions: red (made with red *koji*) and yellow. There are many variations depending on which spices were used (most notably chilli peppers). It is compared to cheese due to its soft texture (reminiscent of feta), its strongly salty taste and its powerful flavour. It is a classic accompaniment for congee, and a condiment used in some meat marinades.

05 FERMENTED STICKY RICE

Sometimes translated as "sweet rice wine", it is a low-alcohol (1–2%) concoction made by fermenting sticky rice.

It can be home-made by adding natural sourdough (*jiuqu*) to pre-cooked sticky rice. Make a hole in the middle of the rice, and a whitish and sweet alcohol will appear in it after a few days of fermentation at 30–35°C (86–95°F). it is possible to drink and/or eat *jiu niang* directly as a snack, or to use it in recipes.

06 CHINESE MUSTARDS

The different varieties of Chinese mustard (*Brassica juncea*) are widely used to make many fermented products, using all parts of the plant.

- *Suan cai* (酸菜, *suān cài*) is made by lacto-fermenting a variety of brown mustard (芥菜, *jiè cài*), and can be considered the equivalent of sauerkraut or kimchi. With a green-yellow colour, *suan cai* is both acidic and salty, and slightly crunchy. It is mainly used in soups and fish dishes (see p. 216), or in omelettes.

- *Zha cai* (榨菜, *zhà cài*) is salted, pressed, then fermented from the mustard bulb, which explains its crunchiness. Very popular throughout China, it is usually used as a filling in noodles, soups or congee. You can also find spicy variants.

- Dried mustard leaves (梅菜, *méi cài*) are popular in Zhejiang, Shanghai and Jiangsu cuisine. Making it is complex: mustard leaves are dried, fermented, and then undergo several steaming and drying processes to concentrate the flavours. A quality *mei cai* is slightly salty, relatively flexible even in its dried form, and very flavourful. It is used once rehydrated and mainly added to steamed dishes (see p. 192).

- *Ya cai* (芽菜, *yá cài*) is a fermented Sichuan speciality made from mustard stems. Its salty and strong umami taste is ideal for stir-fried dishes. It is also a classic ingredient in dan dan noodles (p. 244).

02
SWEET BEAN PASTE
甜面酱 | TIÁN MIÀN JIÀNG

03
FERMENTED BLACK BEANS
豆豉 | DÒU CHǏ

04
FERMENTED TOFU
腐乳 | FǓ RǓ

01
CHILLI BEAN PASTE
豆瓣酱 | DÒU BÀN JIÀNG

05
FERMENTED STICKY RICE
酒酿 | JIǓ NIÀNG

梅菜 | MÉI CÀI

酸菜 | SUĀN CÀI

榨菜 | ZHÀ CÀI

06
CHINESE MUSTARDS
芽菜 | YÁ CÀI

PRODUCTS 7

Other Precious Ingredients

THESE ARE SOME OF THE OTHER KEY INGREDIENTS I USE REGULARLY,
FROM FLAVOURED OILS FOR DRESSING, TO LARD FOR COOKING,
TO THE ROASTED SESAME PASTE USED IN A LARGE NUMBER OF SAUCES.

01 SESAME OIL

Unlike the type of sesame oil that is generally found in the West, the Chinese version (and also Korean or Japanese) is made from toasted sesame seeds, which give it a dark colour and, most importantly, an intense flavour that is close to hazelnuts. It is also called *xiang you* in Chinese, meaning simply "scented oil". It is usually used in small quantities (1 teaspoon is enough for most recipes), added at the very end of the cooking process, heat turned off, or at the table. Its smoke point is quite low, so do not use it as a cooking oil.

02 LARD

Once widely used, pork fat has somewhat been neglected in favour of vegetable oils, which are cheaper and generally easier to transport and store. But it remains popular in Southern China, especially in fried rice recipes; the mixture of soy sauce and lard creates a much-appreciated flavour.

03 SESAME PASTE

Unlike tahini, this paste is made with toasted sesame seeds. It has a darker colour, a more intense fragrance and a significantly different taste. Before using it, remember to mix the oil layer with the paste layer. You can dilute it with water or any other liquid seasoning to create a creamier consistency. You will find this paste in many recipes in this book (noodles, cold dishes), combined with sesame oil. If you ever need an alternative, peanut butter is the best choice.

04 SICHUAN PEPPERCORN OIL

This flavoured oil is obtained by infusing Sichuan peppercorn berries in a neutral oil (usually rapeseed/canola). Oil infused with green Sichuan peppercorn berries is a little stronger. It is widely used in cold dishes to give them a lemony and anaesthetic undertone. Do not overuse it, as a small amount is more than enough.

①
SESAME OIL
芝麻油, 香油 | ZHĪ MA YÓU, XIĀNG YÓU

④
SICHUAN PEPPERCORN OIL
花椒油 | HUĀ JIĀO YÓU

②
LARD
猪油 | ZHŪ YÓU

③
SESAME PASTE
芝麻酱 | ZHĪ MA JIÀNG

UTENSILS 1

Wok and Accessories

ONE OF THE MOST VERSATILE UTENSILS I KNOW, THE WOK IS THE ICON OF CHINESE CUISINE AND IS FOUND IN EVERY HOUSEHOLD.

01 WOK

While it is technically possible to prepare the dishes in this book using a large pan, the wok is by far the best choice. It heats up quickly, goes along perfectly with the "throwing-jumping" technique (p. 46) with its flared shape, and requires less oil thanks to its smaller base. On top of everything else, it is cheap, almost indestructible and naturally non-stick if well maintained!

It is used practically for everything in China: stir-fried dishes, of course, but also for deep-frying (less risk of splashing thanks to its rounded shape). It can also be used to blanch vegetables or cook noodles (it heats up faster than a kettle), and to steam cook or to braise vegetables. However, woks are not suitable for long cooking due to their low heat retention (which is also an asset, because the food is less likely to overcook once the heat is off). You could write an entire guide on how to choose a wok, but I recommend one with the following features:

- **Carbon Steel Composition:** This metal is light, heats up quickly and adapts to all types of heat (including induction). It is also the classic material (熟铁, *shú tiě*) used in Chinese households.

- **Flat Bottom:** Flat-bottom woks are compatible with a flat cooking surface (electric hob/stovetop), unlike traditional round-bottom woks that only work with a stove fitted with a particular type of ring.

- **Between 32 and 34cm (12–13in) in Diameter:** This is the ideal size for everyday use, and a good compromise between manoeuvrability, storage space and the amount of ingredients needed for a dish. Remember not to overload your wok, in order to be able to properly fry your ingredients and prevent the temperature from dropping too much.

- **Maximum Weight of 1.6kg (3½lb):** Beyond this weight, the wok becomes too heavy to handle with one hand.

BEFORE FIRST USE: A new wok is usually covered with a thin layer of oil (to guard against rust between the factory and the time of purchase), which should be removed. Simply wash your utensil with a sponge and warm soapy water, then dry it.

SEASONING AND MAINTENANCE: Just like any steel pan, a wok requires seasoning before its very first use, then regular maintenance to improve its performance, give it its beautiful black patina and, most importantly, gradually build its non-stick surface.

The simplest technique for seasoning is to pour a large amount of oil into the wok (one third of the volume of your wok, using vegetable oil with a high smoke point), and place over a medium heat until smoke is visible. Then turn off the heat and tilt and rotate the wok so that the oil completely coats the inside walls (be careful, the oil is very hot!) Wait for the oil to cool down, then transfer it to a jar (you can reuse it).

Using kitchen paper, spread the thin layer of oil remaining in the bottom of the wok over the entire surface. Ta-da! Your wok is ready for use. You can test it with stir-fried vegetables or an omelette, especially to check its non-stick properties. Tip: avoid acidic ingredients (such as tomatoes and lemon) the first few times.

AFTER EACH USE: Wash the wok immediately after each use with warm water, using a bamboo brush or sponge (with a scouring pad). Avoid soap as much as possible, which could damage the patina. Dry with a cloth or directly on your stovetop over a low heat, to avoid rust. It is advisable to coat your wok with a thin layer of oil the first few times you use it, or if you do not use it very often.

02 SPATULA AND LADLE

The Chinese ladle has a slightly different shape from Western ladles: it is less rounded (and therefore not a half-sphere), as it is not only used in liquid preparations, but also for some solid foods (egg fried rice, p. 296).

03 LID

A wok lid is useful for steaming and/or preparing braised dishes. It can be flat, or spherical if used with a steamer rack.

04 BAMBOO BRUSH

This traditional brush made of bamboo bristles, which are both stiff and soft, is very handy for removing residues from the wok. Bamboo is much more heat resistant than plastic, so you can use it even when the wok is still hot.

01
WOK WITH A FLAT BOTTOM
平底锅 | PÍNG DĪ GUŌ

Some woks also have an "ear", meaning a small helper handle opposite the long handle, so you can carry it more easily with two hands.

01
WOK WITH A ROUND BOTTOM
圆底锅 | YUÁN DĪ GUŌ

Aside from major brands, one of the best options for buying a carbon steel wok is to head to specialist stores, which supply Chinese restaurants (but also sell to individuals).

02
SPATULA AND LADLE
锅铲 | GUŌ CHĂN, 汤勺 | TĀNG SHÁO

The Chinese spatula is shaped like a small spade and is used to fry, stir or flip food or transfer seasonings to the wok.

03
LID
锅盖 | GUŌ GÀI

Flat lids are traditionally made of wood, while the rounded versions are made of aluminium.

04
BAMBOO BRUSH
锅刷 | GUŌ SHUĀ

The brush is less likely to be found in households, but it is used almost universally in restaurant kitchens.

UTENSILS 2

Essential Utensils

ADD A KNIFE, A CHOPPING BOARD AND A FEW OTHER ACCESSORIES TO YOUR KITCHEN, AND YOU WILL BE EQUIPPED TO MAKE ALL THE RECIPES IN THIS BOOK.

---

(01) SPIDER

This large, slightly rounded colander is very convenient for lifting out food after frying or cooking in water, two very common cooking methods in Chinese cuisine.

(02) STEAMER RACK

When an ingredient is too big to fit into a regular steamer basket (a whole fish, for exmple), the wok can be used. Simply heat your water, place this aluminium rack in the wok, add a plate and cover with the lid.

(03) CHINESE CLEAVER

Unlike the wide variety of knives found in Japan, you will find only one knife for everything in China. It may look like a meat cleaver, but it is a light knife, easy to handle and very versatile. It can be used for cutting, slicing, mincing, chopping and even for a few other less-frequent uses, thanks to its large size. For example, it can be used to crush garlic or cucumber (for the famous smashed cucumber recipe, p. 58) or to transfer aromatic ingredients to a bowl (without using a pastry cutter). It is especially important, as most foods in Chinese cuisine are chopped before cooking. (Remember that there is no knife or fork at the table!)

(04) CHOPSTICKS

Chopsticks are not only indispensable at the table, but also very useful in the kitchen. They can be used to beat eggs, remove pickles from the bottom of a large jar, mix the ingredients in a wok, provided they are made of wood, or test the approximate temperature of the oil: dip the end of a chopstick in hot oil – if small bubbles gradually rise to the surface, the oil is about 160°C (320°F). If small bubbles appear immediately and spread in all directions, the oil is above 180°C (350°F).

(05) DUMPLING ROLLING PIN

Thinner (its diameter is similar to that of a pound coin) and shorter than the Western rolling pin, this small wooden stick is mainly used to make dumpling or bao pastes.

(06) STEAMER BASKET

Traditional bamboo baskets absorb condensation during cooking. They impart a light and pleasant fragrance to the food and can be used directly as serving dishes.

(07) CLAY POT

The use of *sha guo* in China (literally "sand pots") has been documented over a period of at least 2,000 years. Unlike the wok, it is a utensil that heats slowly and retains heat. It is ideal for soups and stews, but also for one of the iconic rice-based Cantonese dishes (see p. 298). The *sha guo*, a beautiful object in itself, is relatively fragile. When using it, always start over a low heat to avoid too sudden a temperature change, which could crack it. It is also advisable to soak it in cold water to "rehydrate" its porous surface after its first use.

(08) RICE COOKER

The pressure cooker was invented in Japan in the 1940s. It is one of the top household appliances found in Chinese homes. The traditional models are extremely simple: wash the rice, add water according to the graduated marks inside the appliance, close, press the only button, and the rice, perfectly prepared, is ready in 30 minutes.

01
SPIDER
笊篱 | ZHÀO LÍ

This utensil is often used to scoop out noodles after cooking.

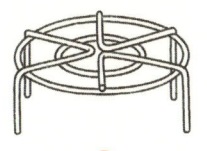

02
STEAMER RACK
蒸架 | ZHĒNG JIÀ

Combine with a rounded lid to create more space and better steam circulation.

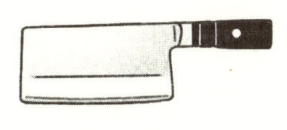

03
CHINESE CLEAVER
菜刀 | CÀI DĀO

Having good knife skills (刀工, *dāo gōng*) is essential for any self-respecting cook.

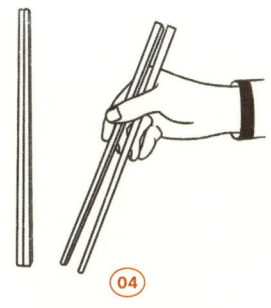

04
CHOPSTICKS
筷子 | KUÀI ZI

Chinese chopsticks are made of bamboo or wood, and are longer and thicker than their Korean or Japanese counterparts.

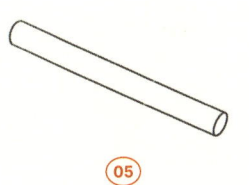

05
DUMPLING ROLLING PIN
擀面杖 | GĂN MIÀN ZHÀNG

Its dimensions are specifically made for one-handed use, while the other hand handles the dough (see technique, p. 260).

06
STEAMER BASKET
蒸笼 | ZHĒNG LÓNG

A 20cm (8in) basket is perfect to go along with a pan of the same diameter, while a 24cm (9in) basket can be placed in the hollow of a 34cm (13in) wok.

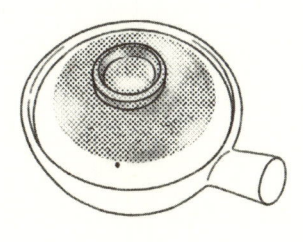

07
CLAY POT
砂锅 | SHĀ GUŌ

Usually, dishes cooked in a *sha guo* are served directly in the pot and are thus kept warm.

08
RICE COOKER
电饭煲 | DIÀN FÀN BĀO

Nowadays, rice cookers are also used to make soups, congee or steamed dishes.

TECHNIQUE 1

Stir-Frying with a Wok

STIR-FRYING WITH A WOK (CHAO) IS A HIGH-TEMPERATURE
COOKING METHOD THAT PRESERVES THE COLOUR, TEXTURE AND NUTRIENTS
OF THE INGREDIENTS BY CONSTANTLY MIXING TO DISTRIBUTE HEAT.
IT IS THE BEST EXAMPLE OF TYPICAL DAILY COOKING.

FINDING THE RIGHT MOVEMENT

*It usually takes 3 or 4 tosses per cycle to mix all the ingredients.
This takes less than 2 seconds. It is only by practising, with rice or lentils
in a cold wok, that you will find your rhythm.*

01
Slightly tilt the wok while holding the handle. Push forward with a continuous motion.

02
Straighten the handle, while trying to bring the wok towards you. After a quick motion, the wok's flared shape should allow the food to be sent upwards.

03
Continue to bring the wok towards you to catch the ingredients, then tilt the wok again to repeat step 1.

MAKE SURE TO PREPARE BEFOREHAND

Preparation is essential when making a stir-fried dish with a wok. The utensil heats up very quickly, and cooking usually only lasts a few minutes. You won't have time to grate your ginger or try to pour out the last drops of an oyster sauce bottle while the heat is on.

This restriction means that you should read the recipe beforehand and have a general understanding of the different steps, so as not to be caught unprepared.

Dried products, if any, must be rehydrated beforehand, all the ingredients (including herbs) must be chopped, the meat or vegetables must be pre-cooked if necessary, and the various seasonings and spices must be prepared in the required quantity.

Ideally, you should group similar ingredients together in small bowls, then add them at the same stage. For example: aromatic ingredients (garlic, ginger, spring onions/scallions, chilli peppers), then sauces and condiments (soy sauce, oyster sauce, white pepper, etc.), and finally your cornflour (cornstarch) and water mixture.

GOOD TO KNOW
小提示

The term "stir-fry" has been popularized in English, but the exact motion for a stir-fry dish would be "stir-toss": the ingredients are quickly stirred with the spatula, then followed by two or three vertical tosses.

HOW TO STIR-FRY WITH A WOK

炒

CHǍO

Use the following steps as a general guide to making a stir-fried dish.
You can of course adapt it, depending on the recipe.

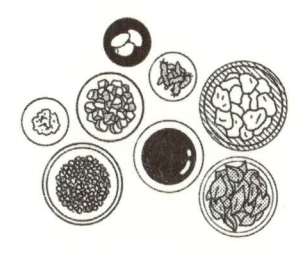

01
Before you start cooking, make sure everything is ready. Chop the aromatic ingredients, mix the condiments and pre-cook the meats and vegetables if necessary.

02
Lightly oil the wok's surface with kitchen paper before turning on the heat, which helps to prevent sticking, and will indicate if your wok is warm enough thanks to the smoke.

03
Heat the wok over a high heat until you see smoke begin to rise. You should be able to feel the heat with your hand held just above the surface.

04
Add the amount of oil indicated in the recipe and slightly tilt the wok to spread it over the entire surface of the bottom.

05
Immediately add the aromatic ingredients (garlic, ginger, Sichuan peppercorn etc.). Fry for about 10 seconds to smell their fragrance, without burning them.

06
Over a high heat, add the other ingredients (proteins, vegetables), which will lower the wok's temperature. Stir with the spatula and constantly toss.

07
Add the seasoning (soy sauce, oyster sauce, sugar, pepper etc.) and continue to stir-fry to mix well until cooked.

08
For a sauce dish, add the cornflour (cornstarch) and water mixture to create a thicker sauce. Finish with a few chopped fresh herbs (spring onion/scallion, coriander/cilantro etc.).

RECIPES TO PRACTISE

食谱

SHÍ PǓ

Hand-Torn Cabbage
(p. 86)

Egg Fried Rice
(p. 296)

Sichuan Fried
Green Beans
(p. 102)

TECHNIQUE 2

Steam Cooking

STEAM COOKING IS A UBIQUITOUS COOKING METHOD IN CHINESE CUISINE, ESPECIALLY IN THE EAST AND SOUTH OF THE COUNTRY.

TRADITIONAL UTENSILS

Hot steam, considered to be softer than other heat sources, is preferred for cooking delicate ingredients such as fish, eggs, bao, vegetables and, of course, the famous Cantonese dim sum.

01
POT + STEAMER BASKET

I mostly use a pot and a bamboo steaming basket measuring 20 or 24cm (8 or 9in) in diameter. The bamboo basket (p. 44) captures condensation, which prevents water droplets from falling onto the food while it cooks. You can stack several baskets and use them as a serving dish.

02
WOK + STEAMER BASKET

The wok lives up to its status as an all-purpose utensil. Simply place the baskets directly in the wok. Ideally, your basket's size should be slightly smaller than the wok's diameter to let it rest on the rim without touching the bottom, hence without touching the water. For example, a 24cm (9in) basket fits perfectly within a 32cm (12in) diameter wok.

03
WOK + RACK + PLATE + LID

When a dish is too large to fit in a basket (for example, a whole fish), a rack becomes necessary (see p. 44). Place the plate containing the dish directly on top, then cover. Use a domed lid rather than a flat one, to leave enough space above the dish.

GOOD TO KNOW
小提示

Steaming is also a great way to heat up food without drying it out, unlike a microwave.

HOW TO STEAM COOK

蒸

ZHĒNG

Use the following steps as a general guide to making a steamed dish.
You can of course adapt it, depending on the recipe.

01
For dry dishes (bao, dumplings): place your food in bamboo baskets and cover. To prevent the contents from sticking and to let the steam circulate, line the bottom of the basket/s with perforated baking paper (look up "otoshibuta" to make it yourself), a muslin cloth (cheesecloth) or even cabbage leaves.

02
For all other dishes: place a rimmed plate in the basket. The plate should not be too large, to let the steam rise.

03
Bring water to the boil in a pot. Place your baskets on the pot. Count the cooking time from when the steam starts to come out of the baskets.

04
Keep on medium to high heat for most recipes. Opt for a low to medium heat for bao.

05
If the water runs out while cooking, top up with boiling water. Ideally, you should add enough water from the beginning (leaving some room to avoid contact with the food).

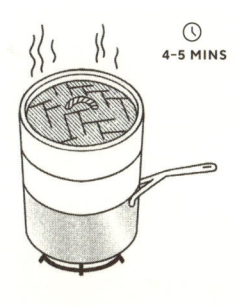

06
Once cooking is finished, turn off the heat and let the food stand for 4–5 minutes before opening the basket, to avoid steam burns.

4–5 MINS

RECIPES TO PRACTISE

食谱

SHÍ PǓ

Steamed Eggs (p. 142)

Steamed Pork with Dried Mustard Leaves (p. 192)

Steamed Sea Bream (p. 214)

TECHNIQUE 3

Making a Hong Shao

POPULAR THROUGHOUT CHINA, BUT ESPECIALLY IN THE EAST OF THE COUNTRY (SHANGHAI, HUNAN, ZHEJIANG, JIANGSU), *HONG SHAO* IS A GOOD EMBODIMENT OF FAMILY COOKING: INEXPENSIVE INGREDIENTS, LIGHT SEASONING, AND SLOW COOKING THAT REQUIRES LITTLE EFFORT.

PREPARING THE CARAMEL

Hong shao is a cooking technique that consists of braising meat, fish, tofu or certain vegetables in a soy sauce and sugar-based liquid. Hong shao dishes are characterized by their sweet and savoury taste, their bright shine and their melting texture. Hong *means red and* shao *means any type of cooking with fire.*

The "red" colour is usually obtained with a combination of rock sugar (p. 27) and light and dark soy sauce. Beloved by connoisseurs but requiring an additional step, a possible option is to caramelize the sugar, which will turn the colour closer to "jujube red" than dark red (see sweet and sour pork ribs, p. 200).

01
In a pan over a low heat, add sugar (ideally rock sugar, p. 27) and water. Follow a ratio of 1 measure of water per 2 measures of rock sugar.

02
Stir in one direction to dissolve the sugar until you obtain a syrupy texture. First thing to watch out for: as the water evaporates, the large bubbles you see at the beginning will turn into small bubbles.

03
Monitor the colour: the sugar changes from white to yellow, then to an amber colour, over the course of about 5 minutes. The colour will change rapidly from this point, which means it can quickly burn.

04
Immediately pour in boiling water, following a 1:1 ratio (never use cold water, which can cause the caramel to splutter and possibly splash you). Mix and set aside for any *hong shao* recipe.

HOW TO MAKE A HONG SHAO

红烧

HÓNG SHĀO

Most *hong shao* recipes can be divided into five steps.
Let's use pork as an example, the most iconic of ingredients.

01
Pre-Cooking the Main Ingredient

Cut the pork belly into cubes of 4–6cm (1–2in) and add to cold water with a little ginger. Bring to the boil, skimming the foam as you go. Drain and set aside.

02
Creating an Aromatic Base

Over a medium heat, add a little oil to a wok and lightly brown the meat, which will release fat. Stir-fry any herbs (at least ginger) to bring out the aromas.

03
Adding the Liquid Seasoning

As a minimum, add your caramel (or dark soy sauce + sugar), light soy sauce, Shaoxing wine and water. The spices that are usually added at this point are optional.

04
Controlling the Heat while Cooking

Transfer to a pot or *sha guo* (p. 44). Add liquid seasoning (at least caramel and soy sauce), optional spices (star anise, bay leaves, etc.) and water. Bring to the boil, then switch to a low heat and cook for at least 1 hour, covered.

05
Monitoring the Reduction

Check the food: the meat must be tender without falling apart. Turn up the heat to reduce the liquid until an amber-red coating layer is formed. Be careful, the sauce contains sugar, and therefore burns quickly.

GOOD TO KNOW
小提示

For tofu or vegetables (such as aubergines/eggplants), the main steps do not change: tofu is first blanched (as in mapo tofu, p. 126) and aubergines are fried (as in yu xiang aubergines, p. 104). But the cooking time is considerably reduced.

Once seasonings and water are added, simmer in the wok over a medium heat and uncovered for a maximum of 10 minutes. Then, reduce with a mixture of water + cornflour (cornstarch) to thicken the sauce.

RECIPES TO PRACTISE
食谱
SHÍ PǓ

Dongpo Pork (p. 186)

Lu Rou Fan (p. 300)

Coca-Cola-Flavoured Chicken Wings (p. 204)

CHAPTER 02

Cold Dishes

冷菜

LĚNG CÀI

PP. 56-57: Steamed aubergine salad ■ **PP. 58-59**: Smashed cucumber salad
PP. 60-61: Seaweed salad with cucumber ■ **PP. 64-65**: Four happiness kaofu ■ **PP. 66-67**: Spinach with sesame sauce
PP. 68-69: White radish pickles ■ **PP. 70-71**: Bamboo shoots with chilli oil ■ **PP. 72-73**: Mouth-watering chicken
PP. 74-75: Shredded chicken with sesame oil ■ **PP. 76-77**: 5-spice braised beef top rump

From All Angles

Keep Your Cool

COLD DISHES AREN'T A SIMPLE EQUIVALENT TO STARTERS (APPETIZERS) IN CHINESE CUISINE. THERE IS A WIDE VARIETY OF THEM, AND THEY HAVE PRONOUNCED FLAVOURS. ENJOYED AS A PREAMBLE DURING A FAMILY MEAL, THEY EASILY ADAPT TO EVERYDAY CRAVINGS.

MUCH MORE THAN A STARTER

Part starter and part snack, the purpose of a cold dish is to "stimulate the appetite" (开胃, kāi wèi) before hot dishes get brought out.

Jellyfish salad with a dressing, poached chicken legs to dip in soy sauce, hong shao-style duck tongue, sweet and acidic white radish pickle, thin marinated slices of beef with 5-spice. My first memories of cold dishes are of small plates presented at the beginning of meals during big banquets in Wenzhou, where I spent my childhood.

For everyday cooking, when all dishes are served at the same time, you must take care to accommodate them depending on the occasion. A fresh smashed cucumber salad (see p. 58), enjoyed with vinegar, is very popular in summer, while shredded chicken with sesame oil (p. 74) goes perfectly with a beer, in the tradition of dishes meant to "tone down the alcohol" (下酒菜, xià jiu cài).

"TONING DOWN THE ALCOHOL"

Traditionally, cold dishes accompany alcohol served at the beginning of a meal and stimulate the taste buds.

Refreshing and appetizing, cold dishes are based on strong flavours: acidic, spicy or salty. These dishes are low in fat and contain little or no sauce, to remain light.

As for the cooking, vegetables should remain crisp, ideally cooked gently (with steam or water) to preserve their colour. Seafood is barely blanched to avoid damaging its delicate flesh. Meat is poached or simmered to give it time to become as flavourful as possible.

PREPARING IN ADVANCE

Unlike most dishes that need to be cooked at the last moment, cold dishes are made well in advance.

Vegetables are usually prepared earlier so as not exude water, and you only need to mix in your sauce and aromatic ingredients when serving. As for meat, the dish will taste even better after a few more hours of marinating in a broth or sauce.

GOOD TO KNOW
小提示

This chapter's recipes are designed to be part of a Chinese meal, meaning that they are intended to be shared with other dishes. You are free to use them as an appetizer, a side or a main course.

SOME COLD DISHES TYPICAL OF WENZHOU,
MY HOMETOWN, SERVED DURING A BIG FAMILY MEAL.

PICKLED PEANUTS
卤煮花生 | LǓ ZHǓ HUĀ SHĒNG

JELLYFISH SALAD
凉拌海蜇 | LIÁNG BÀN HĂI ZHÉ

FISH CAKE
温州鱼饼 | WĒN ZHŌU YÚ BǏNG

SALTWATER EDAMAME
水煮毛豆 | SHUǏ ZHǓ MÁO DÒU

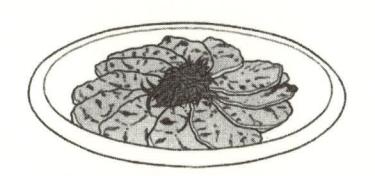

MARINATED BEEF TOP RUMP WITH SPICES
卤牛肉 | LǓ NIÚ RÒU

POACHED CHICKEN AND SPRING ONION OIL
白切鸡 | BÁI QIĒ JĪ

WHITE RADISH PICKLES
酸甜腌白萝卜 | SUĀN TIÁN YĀN BÁI LUÓ BO

BRAISED DUCK TONGUES
鸭舌 | YĀ SHÉ

BLANCHED COCKLES
花蛤 | HUĀ GÉ

Steamed Aubergine Salad

LIÁNG   BÀN   QIÉ   ZI

凉拌茄子

PREPARING 15 MINUTES

COOKING 5 MINUTES

CHINESE AUBERGINES ARE DISTINGUISHED BY THEIR SLENDER SHAPE, VERY THIN SKIN AND DELICATE FLESH. THEY CAN BE STIR-FRIED IN A WOK OR, LIKE HERE, STEAMED WITHOUT USING FAT. THIS RECIPE, SIMPLE AND QUICK, IS VERY FLAVOURFUL.

Serves 4 people

INGREDIENTS

For the aubergines

2 Chinese aubergines (eggplant), about 300g (10oz)
2 tbsp white vinegar

For the sauce

2 garlic cloves, chopped
1 tsp chopped ginger
2 tsp finely chopped spring onion (scallion), plus extra to serve
1 tsp white sesame seeds
2 tbsp neutral oil
1 tbsp light soy sauce
1 tbsp black rice vinegar
1 tbsp sesame oil
½ tsp sugar
½ tsp white pepper

FOR THE AUBERGINES

- Cut the aubergines into roughly 8cm (3in) sections, then cut them in 2 lengthways. Soak them for 5 minutes in cold water with the white vinegar, to avoid oxidation and preserve their purple colour as much as possible during cooking.

- Drain the aubergines and place them in a steamer basket, skin side up. In a pot, bring some water to the boil. Place the basket on the pot and cook for about 5 minutes over a high heat. The flesh should be tender, easy to pierce with a fork, but not completely softened. Allow to cool and slice into thin strips.

FOR THE SAUCE

- In a bowl, combine the garlic, ginger, spring onion and sesame seeds.

- Heat the neutral oil in a pan until it starts to smoke lightly. Pour it into the bowl to release the flavours of the aromatic ingredients.

- Add the soy sauce, vinegar, sesame oil, sugar and pepper. Mix, then pour the sauce over the aubergines.

- Sprinkle with a little spring onion and serve with rice.

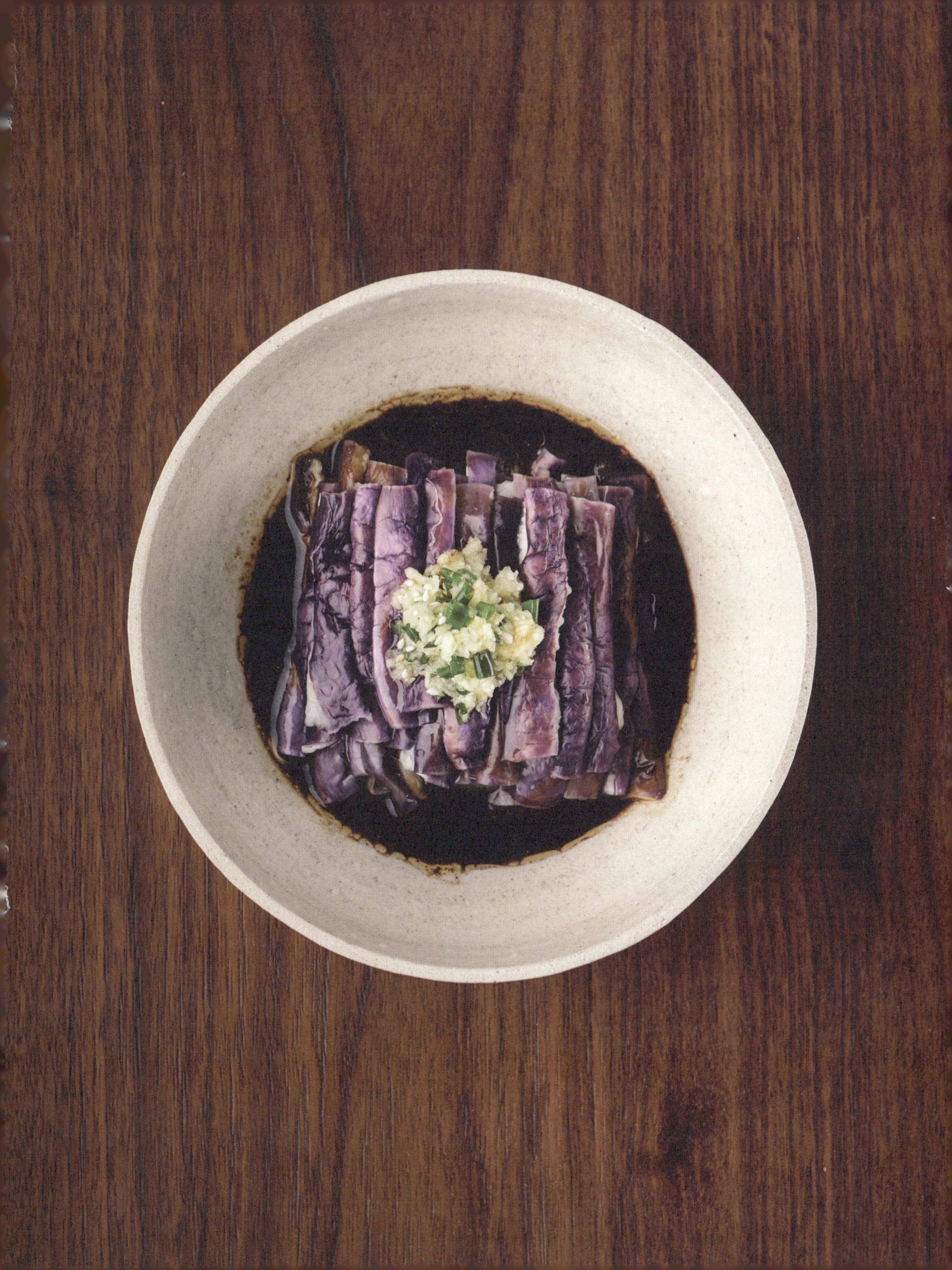

Smashed Cucumber Salad

PĀI　HUÁNG　GUĀ

拍黄瓜

PREPARING 5 MINUTES

RESTING 15 MINUTES

THIS ESSENTIAL SUMMER DISH IS ENJOYED ALL OVER CHINA. IT IS CRUNCHY, JUICY, FRESH AND EASY TO PREPARE. ITS NAME IS A NOD TO ITS PREPARATION. THE CUCUMBER IS SPLIT BY SMASHING IT WITH A KNIFE. THIS CREATES PIECES WITH IRREGULAR SHAPES, WHICH ALLOWS THEM TO BETTER RETAIN THE SAUCE. PERFECTION IN IMPERFECTION.

Serves 4 people

INGREDIENTS

For the cucumber

1 cucumber, about 400g (14oz)
2 tsp salt

For the sauce

2 garlic cloves, chopped
1 tbsp light soy sauce
1 tbsp black rice vinegar
1 tsp sesame oil
½ tsp sugar
1 tsp chilli oil, to serve (*optional*)

FOR THE CUCUMBER

- Wash the cucumber without peeling the skin.

- Smash the cucumber: on a chopping (cutting) board, give the cucumber a few controlled blows with the flat side of a Chinese knife, then cut the lightly smashed cucumber into pieces.

- In a salad bowl, mix the cucumber pieces and salt and leave to disgorge (see p. 183) for 15 minutes. Drain and set aside.

FOR THE SAUCE

- Mix all the sauce ingredients in a bowl and pour over the cucumber. Arrange on a plate and add a little chilli oil if desired (see p. 36).

- You can eat this salad straight away, but it will taste even better after 30 minutes of marinating in a cool place.

GOOD TO KNOW
小提示

In China, the most common variety of cucumber has very thin skin, is longer in shape, has a crunchy flesh and very few seeds; it is ideal for this recipe. You might sometimes find it in Chinese supermarkets. You can also make this dish with red radishes.

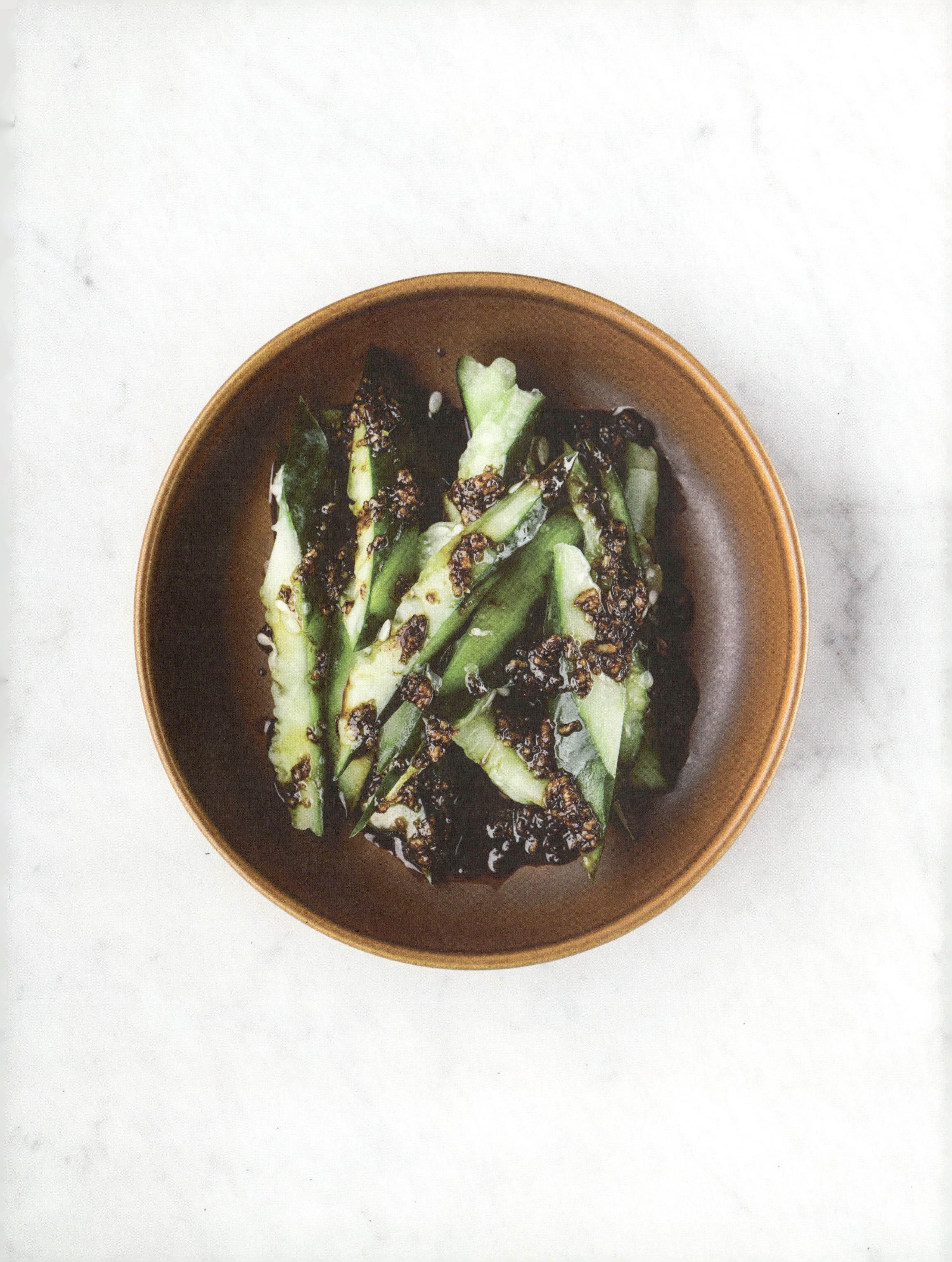

Seaweed Salad with Cucumber

HĂI   DÀI   LIÁNG   BÀN

海带凉拌

PREPARING 70 MINUTES

COOKING 5 MINUTES

HAI DAI (SEE P. 32) IS A POPULAR SEAWEED IN CHINA'S COASTAL REGIONS. IN MY REGION, IT IS MOSTLY ENJOYED AS A COLD DISH FOR ITS NATURALLY SALTY AND UMAMI TASTE, BUT ALSO FOR ITS CRUNCHY TEXTURE.

🍴 Serves 4 people

INGREDIENTS

For the salad

20g (¾oz) *hai dai* seaweed
½ cucumber, about 200g (7oz)
1 tsp white vinegar
Fresh herbs

For the sauce

2 garlic cloves, chopped
1 tbsp light soy sauce
1 tbsp black rice vinegar
1 tsp sesame oil
½ tsp sugar

RECIPE STEPS

- Rehydrate the seaweed in cold water for 1 hour until soft. It will gain a lot in volume.

- Meanwhile, julienne the cucumber. If necessary, remove the seeds, which contain a lot of water.

- Prepare the sauce by mixing all the ingredients together.

- Roll up the seaweed and julienne it. Bring a pot of water to the boil and add the white vinegar and then the seaweed (vinegar speeds up the cooking process). Blanch the seaweed for 2 minutes before immersing it in cold water, to stop cooking and preserve its crunchiness. Drain.

- Mix together the cucumber, seaweed and sauce and finish with a few fresh herbs of your choice.

GOOD TO KNOW
小提示

You can find bags of hai dai *in the form of fine julienne strips in Chinese supermarkets.*

Cold Dishes   The Guide to Chinese Cooking

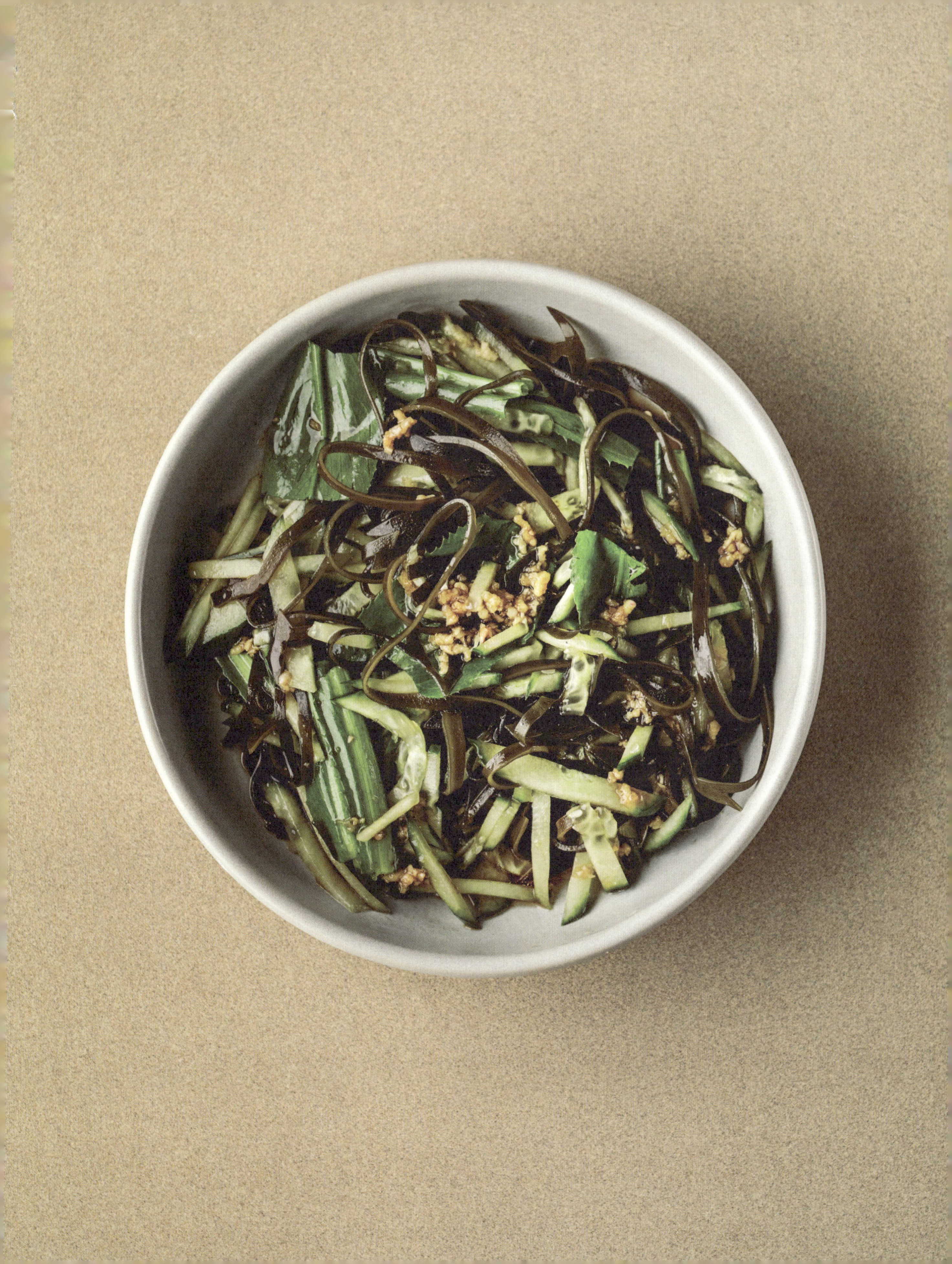

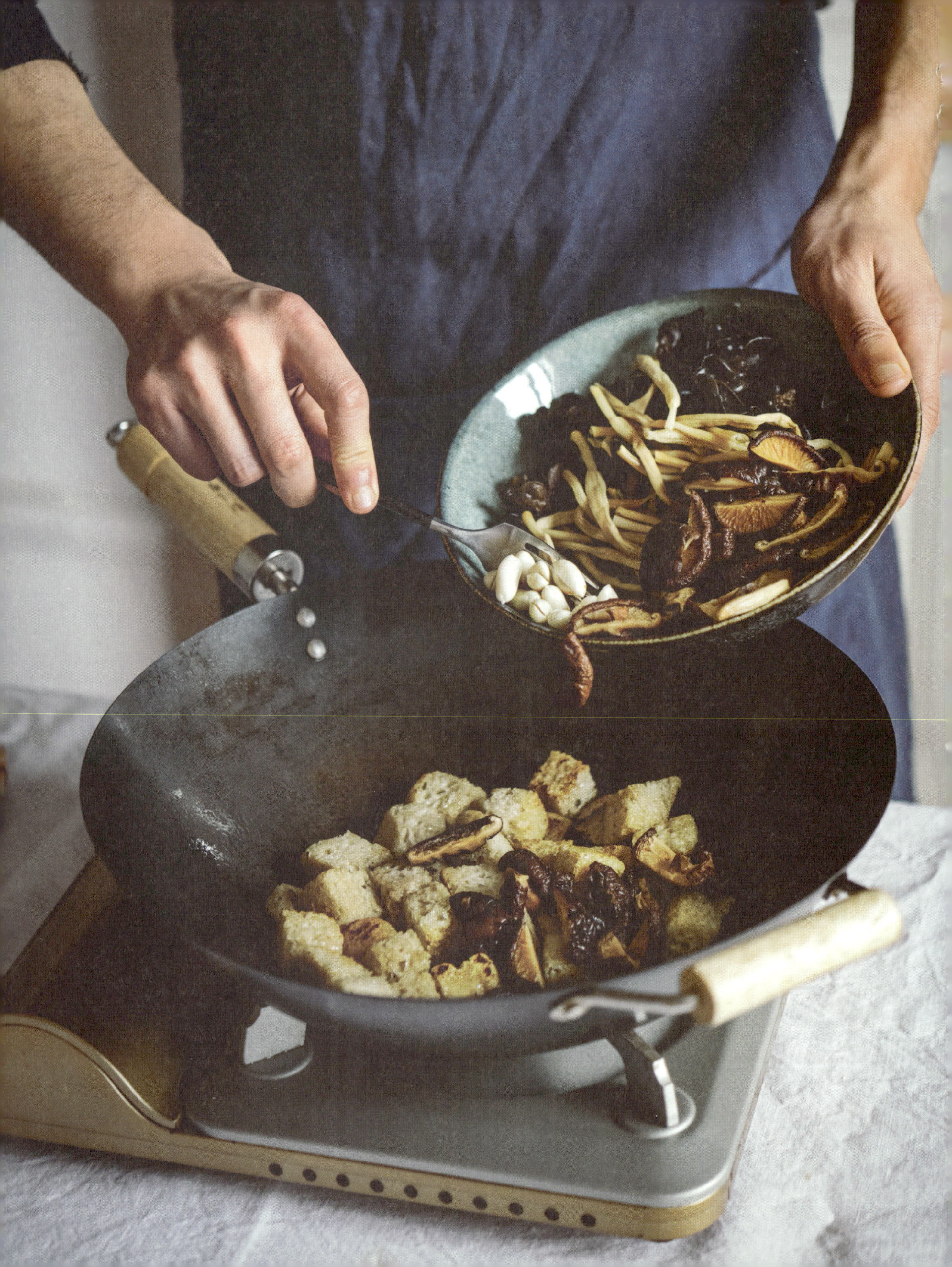

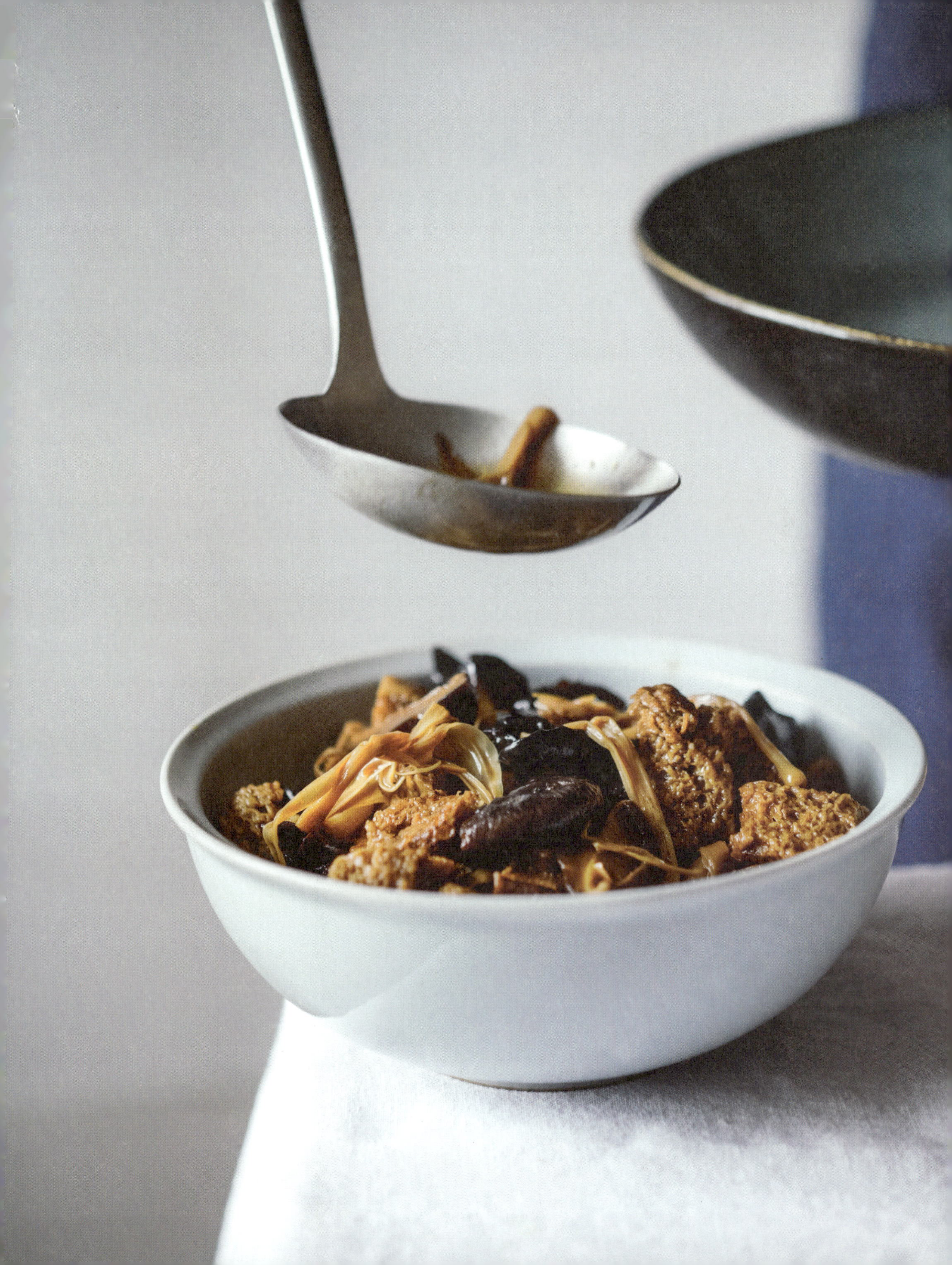

Four Happiness Kaofu

sì xǐ kǎo fū
四喜烤麸

PREPARING 35 MINUTES

COOKING 35 MINUTES

KAOFU IS STEAMED WHEAT GLUTEN, OFTEN FOUND IN ITS DRIED FORM. IT IS WIDELY USED IN CHINA IN BUDDHIST AND VEGETARIAN CUISINE. IN SHANGHAI, THIS FESTIVELY NAMED DISH IS A CLASSIC. IT IS OFTEN SERVED AS A COLD STARTER IN BANQUETS (THAT'S HOW I DISCOVERED IT). THE *HONG SHAO* COOKING METHOD IS HIGHLIGHTED HERE (SEE P. 50), WHICH IS THE MOST TYPICAL IN THE REGION.

Serves 4 people

INGREDIENTS

For the four happiness

30g (1oz) dried shiitake mushrooms
20g (¾oz) dried lily flowers (*see p. 35*)
5g (⅛oz) black fungus
80g (3oz) dehydrated kaofu
3 tbsp cooking oil
50g (1¾oz) unshelled peanuts
400ml (1¾ cups) water

For the seasonings

2 tbsp light soy sauce
1 tbsp dark soy sauce
2 tbsp Shaoxing wine
2 tbsp sugar
1 star anise
1 cinnamon stick
1 tbsp sesame oil

RECIPE STEPS

- Place the shiitake, lily flowers and black fungus in individual bowls and rehydrate with warm water. Cut the shiitake in 3 and the lily flowers in 2. Rehydrate the kaofu for 30 minutes in cold water, then rinse it 2 or 3 times, until the water is clear. Drain on kitchen paper.

- Place a wok over a medium heat, pour in the oil and add the kaofu. Fry for about 5 minutes, until the outside becomes crispy and slightly golden. Add the shiitake, black fungus, lily flowers and peanuts. Mix, then pour in the measured water (you can incorporate the shiitake soaking water to add flavour, if you like) and all the seasonings except the sesame oil. Bring to the boil, then cover. Simmer for about 30 minutes, stirring occasionally to prevent the ingredients from sticking.

- Add the sesame oil at the end of the cooking time. This dish is usually served cold, but you can also enjoy it hot.

GOOD TO KNOW
小提示

Kaofu is very popular in simmered dishes, because it acts as a sponge that absorbs all the sauce, and therefore concentrates the flavours.

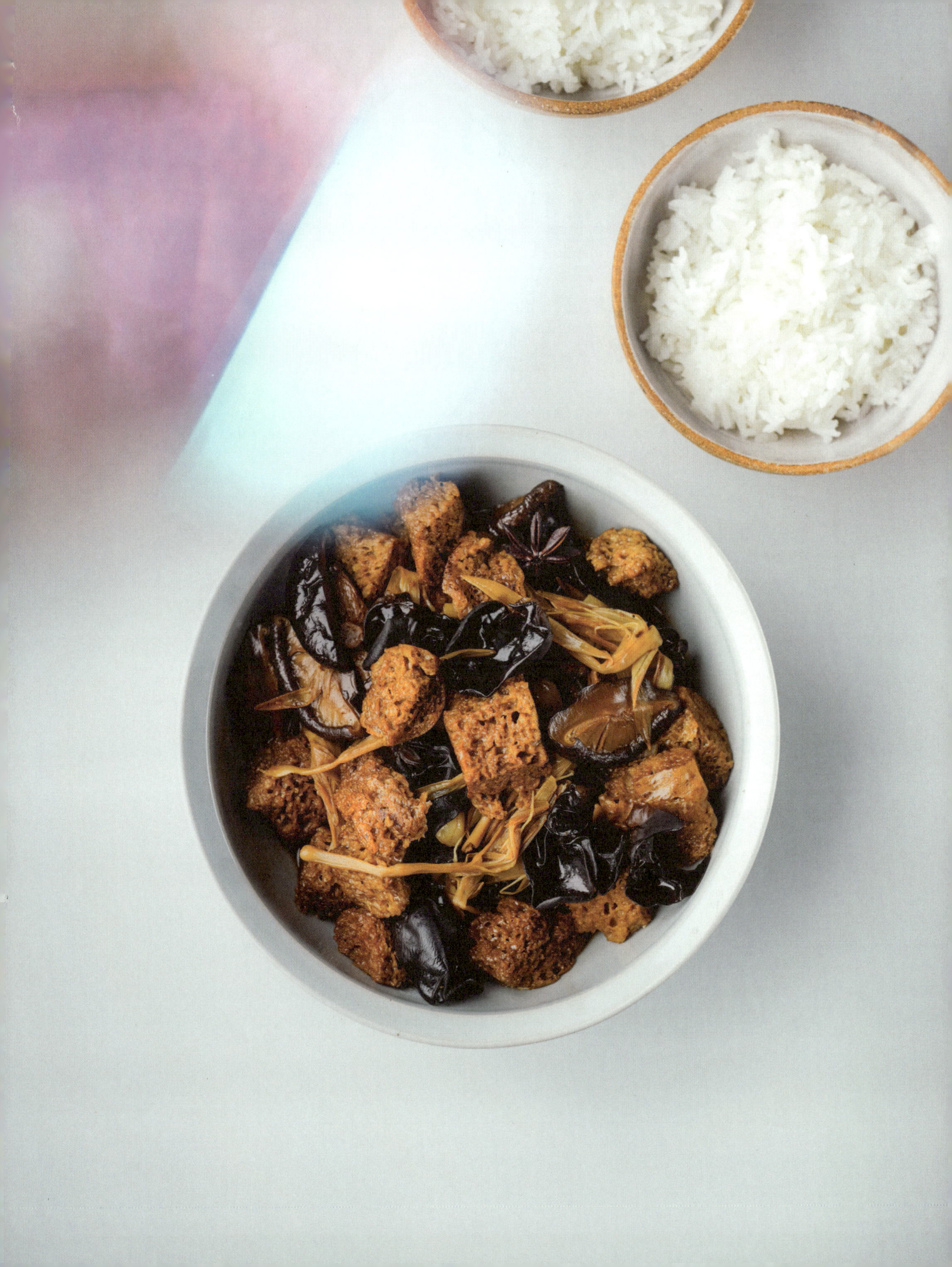

Spinach with Sesame Sauce

MÁ JIÀNG BŌ CÀI

麻酱菠菜

PREPARING 5 MINUTES

COOKING 1 MINUTE

DURING MY UNIVERSITY EXCHANGE IN SHANGHAI, I HAD A SOUTH KOREAN FLATMATE WHO ALWAYS KEPT A BOTTLE OF SESAME OIL IN THE FRIDGE, WHICH SHE POURED ON ALL HER DISHES. THE SPINACH AND SESAME COMBO WAS ONE OF HER FAVOURITES. I THEN DISCOVERED THE CHINESE VERSION OF THIS DISH, TASTIER THANKS TO THE ADDITION OF SESAME PASTE.

Serves 2 people

INGREDIENTS

For the spinach

1 tbsp salt
300g (10oz) spinach

For the sauce

1 tbsp Chinese sesame paste (*see p. 40*)
3 tbsp warm water
1 tsp soy sauce
1 tsp sesame oil
Pinch of salt

To serve

Toasted white sesame seeds

RECIPE STEPS

- For the sauce, place the sesame paste in a bowl, pour in the warm water and mix to obtain a slightly thick texture. Add the remaining ingredients and mix again.

- In a pot, bring some water to the boil with the tablespoon of salt. Immerse the spinach and blanch for about 20 seconds. Transfer the spinach immediately into cold water to stop it cooking, then drain well.

- Roughly chop the spinach and arrange in a shallow dish, then pour over the sauce. Finish with a pinch of toasted sesame seeds.

GOOD TO KNOW
小提示

The spinach should be fully drained to avoid diluting the sauce. The most effective technique (but not the most pleasant) is to wring it by hand.

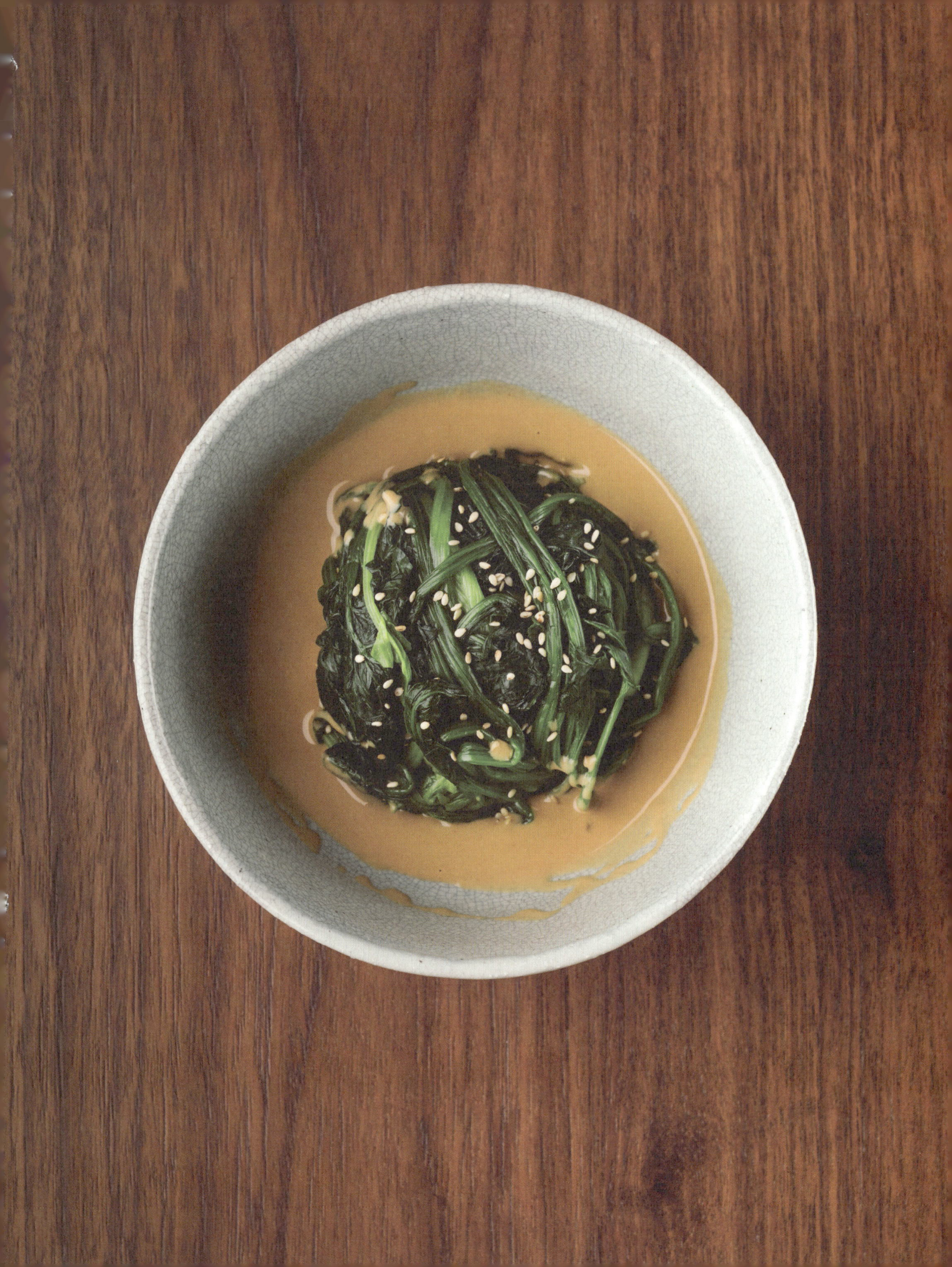

White Radish Pickles

SUĀN TIÁN YĀN BÁI LUÓ BO

酸甜腌白萝卜

PREPARING 45 MINUTES

COOKING 5 MINUTES

THESE WHITE RADISH PICKLES (ALSO CALLED DAIKON) REMIND ME OF MY GRANDMOTHER COMING BACK FROM THE MARKET IN WENZHOU. SLIGHTLY SWEET, ACIDIC, CRUNCHY, AND ESPECIALLY VERY FRESH, THIS SIDE DISH IS ESSENTIAL AT HOME. THIS IS ITS BASIC RECIPE, BUT DO NOT HESITATE TO EXPERIMENT WITH THE HERBS: FRESH CHILLI PEPPER, SICHUAN PEPPERCORN, CITRUS PEEL…

Makes 1 jar of about 1 litre (4⅓ cups)

INGREDIENTS

1 white radish (*daikon*), about 600g (1lb 5oz)
30g (1oz/2½ tbsp) salt
200ml (scant 1 cup) water
200ml (scant 1 cup) white rice vinegar
Zest of ½ lemon
40g (1½oz/3¼ tbsp) sugar

RECIPE STEPS

- Wash the radish (you can choose to keep the skin or not). Cut it into roughly 5cm (2in) sections, then into sticks. This is the ideal shape to keep it crunchy.

- Transfer the radish sticks to a bowl, add half the salt, mix and leave to disgorge for 30 minutes (see p. 83). This step will allow the radish to better absorb the marinade and reduce its pungent side.

- Rinse the radish with water, drain and transfer it to a clean jar.

- In a pot, bring the water, vinegar, lemon zest, remaining salt and the sugar to a simmer so that the granules dissolve completely. Let cool and pour over the radishes.

- Keep chilled. It can be consumed after marinating for 4 hours, but it is best to wait 2 days for the flavours to strengthen. You can keep these pickles for 1 month, chilled, in their liquid.

GOOD TO KNOW
小提示

You can replace the white radish with small, easy-to-find red radishes, and white rice vinegar with more acidic black rice vinegar; your pickles will be darker.

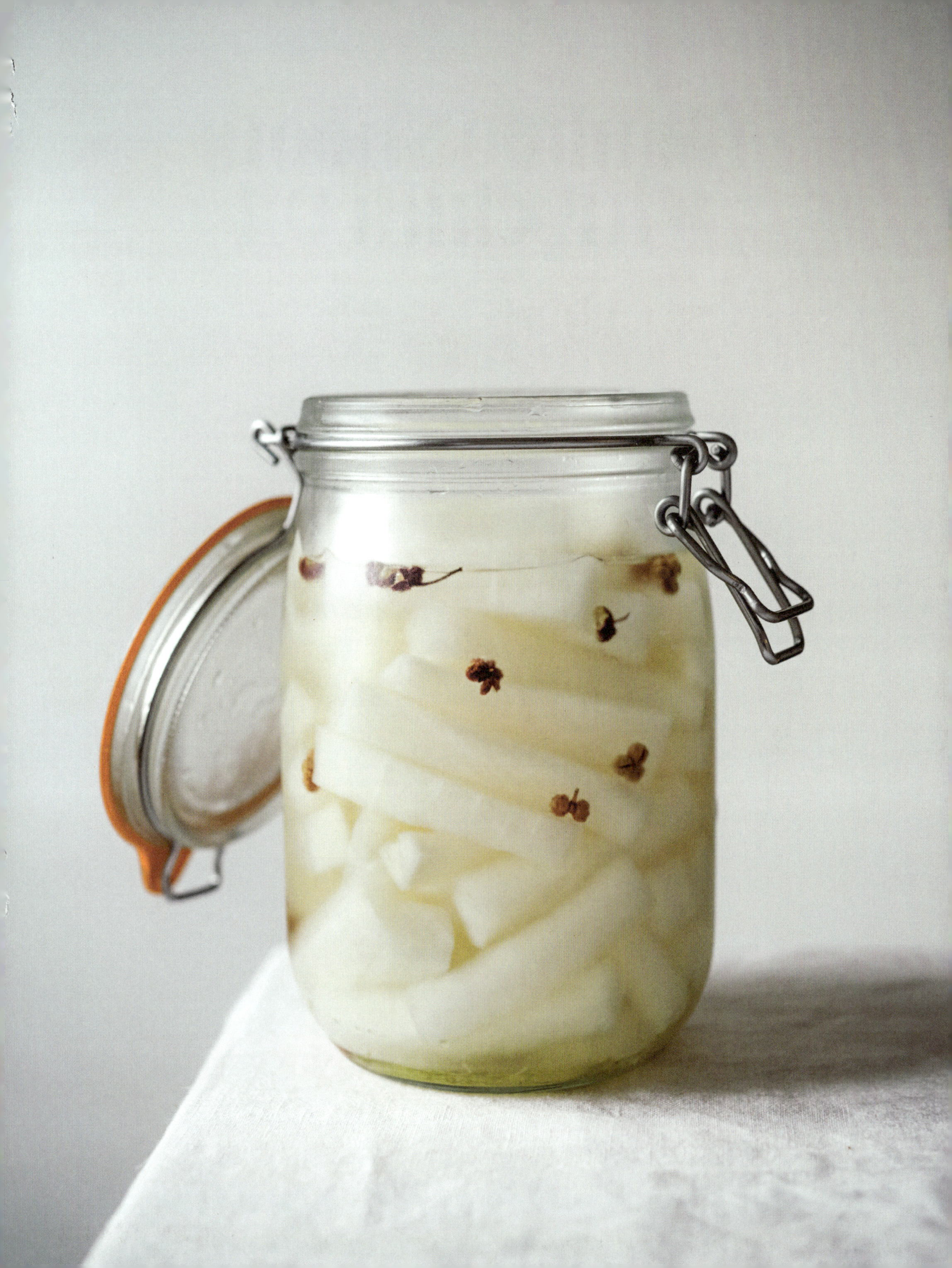

Bamboo Shoots with Chilli Oil

LÀ YÓU XIĀNG SŬN
辣油香笋

PREPARING 12 HOURS *COOKING 10 MINUTES*

THESE MARINATED BAMBOO SHOOTS ARE AN EXCELLENT CONDIMENT FOR ALL NOODLE DISHES, OR SIMPLY TO ACCOMPANY WHITE RICE. I ALMOST ALWAYS HAVE A JAR OF IT SOMEWHERE IN THE FRIDGE. DESPITE ITS NAME AND APPEARANCE, THIS RECIPE IS TAIWANESE AND THUS ISN'T TOO SPICY.

Makes 1 jar (400ml/1¾ cups)

INGREDIENTS

300g (10oz) bamboo shoots
2 tsp sesame oil
2 tsp chilli oil *(see p. 36)*
3 tbsp vegetable oil
2 tsp mirin
2 tsp white rice vinegar
2 tsp soy sauce
1 tsp salt
5 tsp sugar

RECIPE STEPS

- If using fresh bamboo shoots, remove the leaves and cut the heart into strips. If you have opted for canned or vacuum-packed shoots, cut them into thin strips.

- Blanch the bamboo strips in boiling simmering water for 3 minutes. Do not hesitate to taste to adjust the time; the shoots should be tender while maintaining a little bit of chewiness. Drain on kitchen paper.

- Mix all the other ingredients in a clean jar. Put it in the microwave for 10 seconds to thoroughly dissolve the sugar and salt. (Once you've mastered the recipe, you can vary the ratio of chilli oil or sugar to taste.)

- Add the bamboo shoots, mix well, then marinate for at least 12 hours in the fridge before eating. To avoid using too much oil, the amounts stated here will not fill the entire jar. The bamboo shoots at the bottom of the jar will be the most flavourful, so start with those!

GOOD TO KNOW
小提示

Canned or vacuum-packed bamboo shoots are sold pre-cooked but, depending on the brand you find, briny water can have a very unpleasant smell. If this is the case, rinsing the bamboo shoots with water and blanching them (with the windows open) neutralizes the smell, and the marinade will do the rest.

This recipe also works very well with artichoke hearts, which have a similar texture.

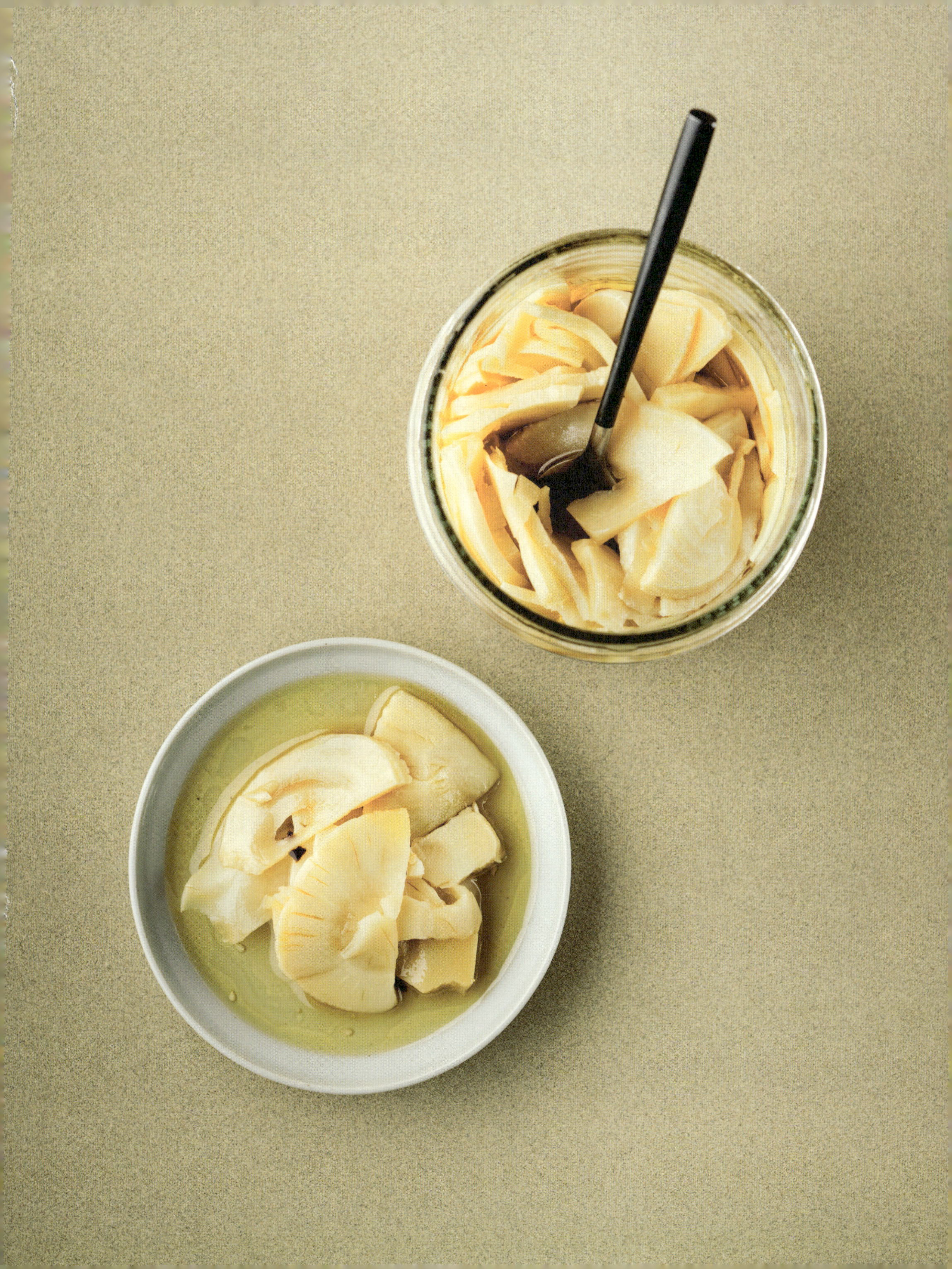

Mouth-Watering Chicken

KǑU SHUǏ JĪ

口水鸡

PREPARING 10 MINUTES

COOKING 20 MINUTES

THIS IS ONE OF MY FAVOURITE SICHUAN DISHES, AND IT'S MOSTLY DUE TO THE DELICIOUS SAUCE. CHICKEN IS USUALLY SERVED WITH BONES AND SKIN (DELICIOUS, IF YOU FOLLOW THE RECIPE), BUT IF YOU DECIDE TO DO WITHOUT, I WILL NOT HOLD IT AGAINST YOU. THE RESULT WILL ALWAYS BE MOUTH-WATERING!

Serves 2 people

INGREDIENTS

For the chicken

1 litre (4⅓ cups) water
30g (1oz/2½ tbsp) salt (= 3% of the water's volume)
3 strips of ginger
½ tsp ground turmeric
1 tsp Sichuan peppercorn
1 brown cardamom pod (optional)
1 tbsp Shaoxing wine
1 boneless chicken thigh, about 300g (10oz)

For the sauce

2 tbsp chilli oil
1 tbsp soy sauce
1 tbsp chicken broth
½ tbsp sugar
½ tbsp sesame oil
2 tsp black rice vinegar
1 tsp chopped garlic
1 tsp grated ginger
Sichuan peppercorn

To serve

Toasted white sesame seeds
Coriander (cilantro)

FOR THE CHICKEN

- Bring the water to the boil in a pot, add the salt, spices, wine and chicken. Switch to a low heat and cover. Cook for 10 minutes, then turn off the heat and leave for another 10 minutes. The meat should be tender and cooked just enough.

- Remove the chicken and immerse it in iced water for a few minutes, to make the flesh and the skin firm. Drain it and cut it into 2cm (¾in) pieces, keeping the skin. Place in a shallow dish.

FOR THE SAUCE

- Mix all ingredients in a bowl. Pour this sauce over the chicken, then finish by sprinkling with some toasted white sesame seeds and fresh coriander.

GOOD TO KNOW
小提示

In China, this dish is usually prepared with the whole chicken and served with the bones.

Cold Dishes | The Guide to Chinese Cooking

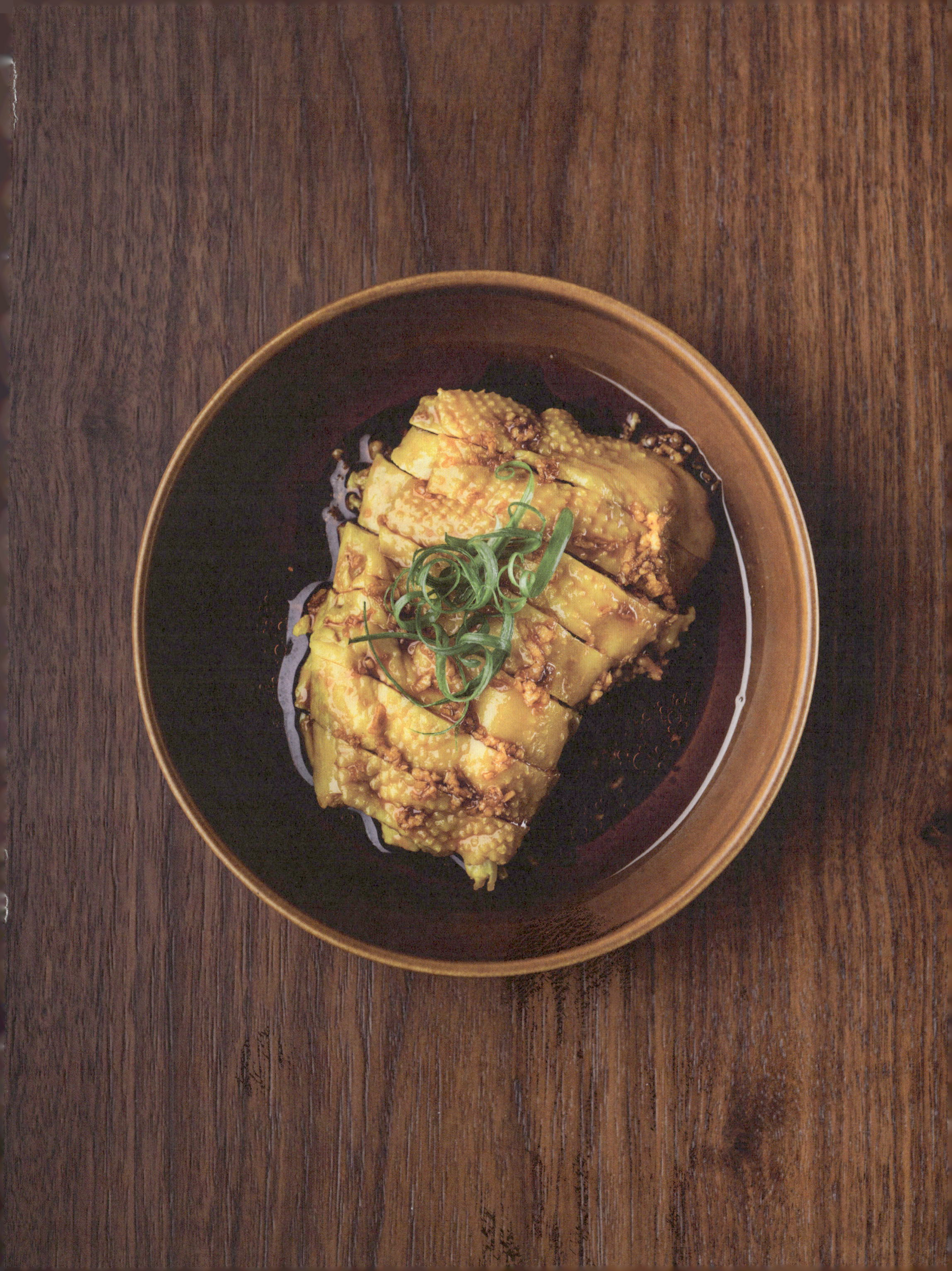

Shredded Chicken with Sesame Oil

SHǑU SĪ JĪ

手撕鸡

PREPARING 15 MINUTES • COOKING 20 MINUTES

EVERY TIME I RETURN TO CHINA, TO THE CITY OF WENZHOU, MY AUNT PICKS UP THIS DISH FROM A LADY IN THE MARKET. SHE'S PRETTY SURE IT WILL MAKE ME HAPPY; IT'S FRESH, TASTY, FLAVOURFUL, AND HASN'T CHANGED IN 20 YEARS.

🍴 Serves 2 people

INGREDIENTS

For the chicken

1 litre (4⅓ cups) water
30g (1oz/2½ tbsp) salt (= 3% of the water's volume)
3 ginger strips
1 star anise
½ tsp ground turmeric
1 brown cardamom pod (*optional*)
1 tbsp Shaoxing wine
1 boneless chicken leg, about 300g (10oz)

For the sauce

1 tsp chopped spring onion (scallion) white
1 tsp chopped red onion
1 tsp chopped coriander (cilantro)
1 tsp toasted crushed peanuts
1 tbsp sesame oil
2 tsp melted pork fat (*optional*)

FOR THE CHICKEN

- Bring the water to the boil in a pot, add the salt, spices, wine and chicken. Switch to a low heat and cover. Cook for 10 minutes, then turn off the heat and leave for another 10 minutes. The meat should be tender and cooked just enough.

- Take out the chicken, let it cool a little, then shred it into strips.

FOR THE SAUCE

- Mix the spring onion, red onion, coriander and peanuts with the sesame oil and melted pork fat, which can be melted in the microwave for ease (*see also p. 344*).

TO SERVE

- Mix the sauce with the shredded chicken. Enjoy with white rice.

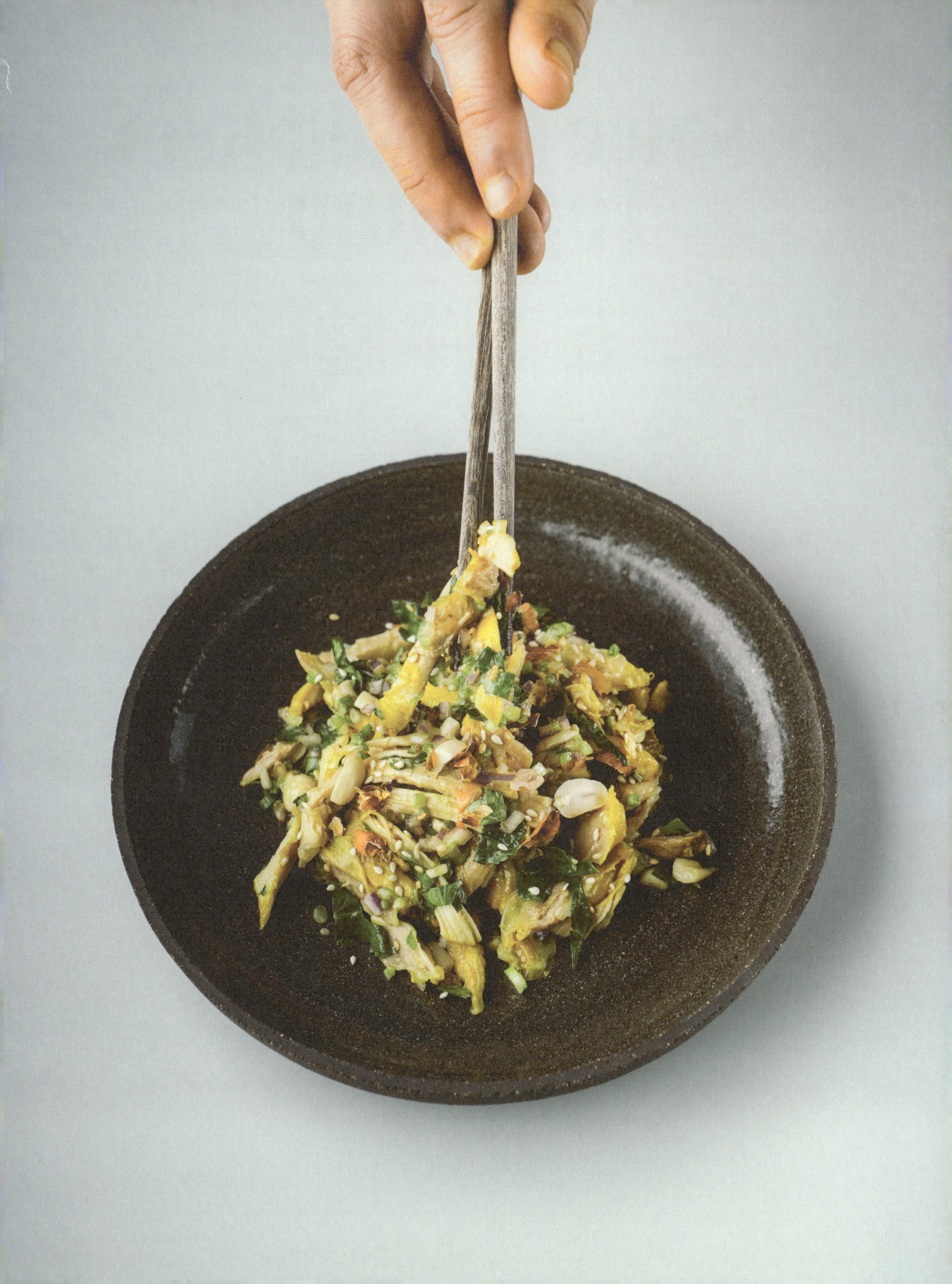

5-Spice Braised Beef Top Rump

WǓ　XIĀNG　NIÚ　JIÀN

五香牛腱

PREPARING 1 DAY

COOKING 1 HOUR

"卤" (LU) IS AN ANCESTRAL CHINESE COOKING METHOD THAT INVOLVES BRAISING INGREDIENTS IN A SOY-BASED LIQUID, THEN TURNING OFF THE HEAT AND LEAVING THEM TO MARINATE. THIS RECIPE IS A GOOD EXAMPLE OF THAT TECHNIQUE. IT REQUIRES A BIT OF PATIENCE BUT ISN'T DIFFICULT TO MASTER.

Serves 4 people

INGREDIENTS

For the beef

1kg (2¼lb) top rump
1 tbsp coarse salt
2 litres (8½ cups) water

For the seasoning

1 tbsp oil
3 shallots, peeled
3 ginger strips
1 tbsp fermented sweet soy bean paste (*tian mian jiang*, see p. 38)
400ml (1¾ cups) Shaoxing wine
600ml (2½ cups) light soy sauce
2 tbsp dark soy sauce

For the spices

2 star anise
2 cloves
5 bay leaves
½ tbsp Sichuan peppercorn
1 cinnamon stick
½ tbsp fennel seeds

FOR THE BEEF

- The day before, cut the top rump into large pieces and remove any white membrane. Massage the meat with the coarse salt and let it rest overnight.

- The next day, heat a pot over a medium heat. Add the tablespoon of oil and fry the shallots and ginger for about 1 minute to release their flavour. Add the other seasonings and pour in the water. Tie up the spices in a piece of muslin (cheesecloth), then add this to the pot and bring to the boil.

- At the same time, blanch the top rump pieces in a pan filled with cold water. Bring to the boil, removing any foam that appears as you go. Drain and transfer the meat to the pot with the broth. Taste and add salt if necessary. Bring to the boil, then simmer for 45 minutes over a low heat.

FOR THE MARINADE

- Remove the pot from the heat and let the meat marinate in the broth for at least 4 hours, but preferably 12 hours, to soak up as much flavour as possible (keep it in a cool place).

TO SERVE

- Cut the meat into thin slices of 2–3mm (⅛in). You can enjoy this as a side dish, dipping the slices in a sauce, or add to a salad or a bowl of noodles.

GOOD TO KNOW
小提示

In China, it is common to add other spices, such as fennel seeds, brown cardamom (see p. 30) or dried mandarin peels (chen pi, see p. 32). The fragrant broth (called master stock), can be reused, in the honeyed tofu jerky recipe, for example (see p. 136). In which case, make sure to freeze the stock and then bring it fully to the boil before each new use, to avoid any risk of food poisoning.

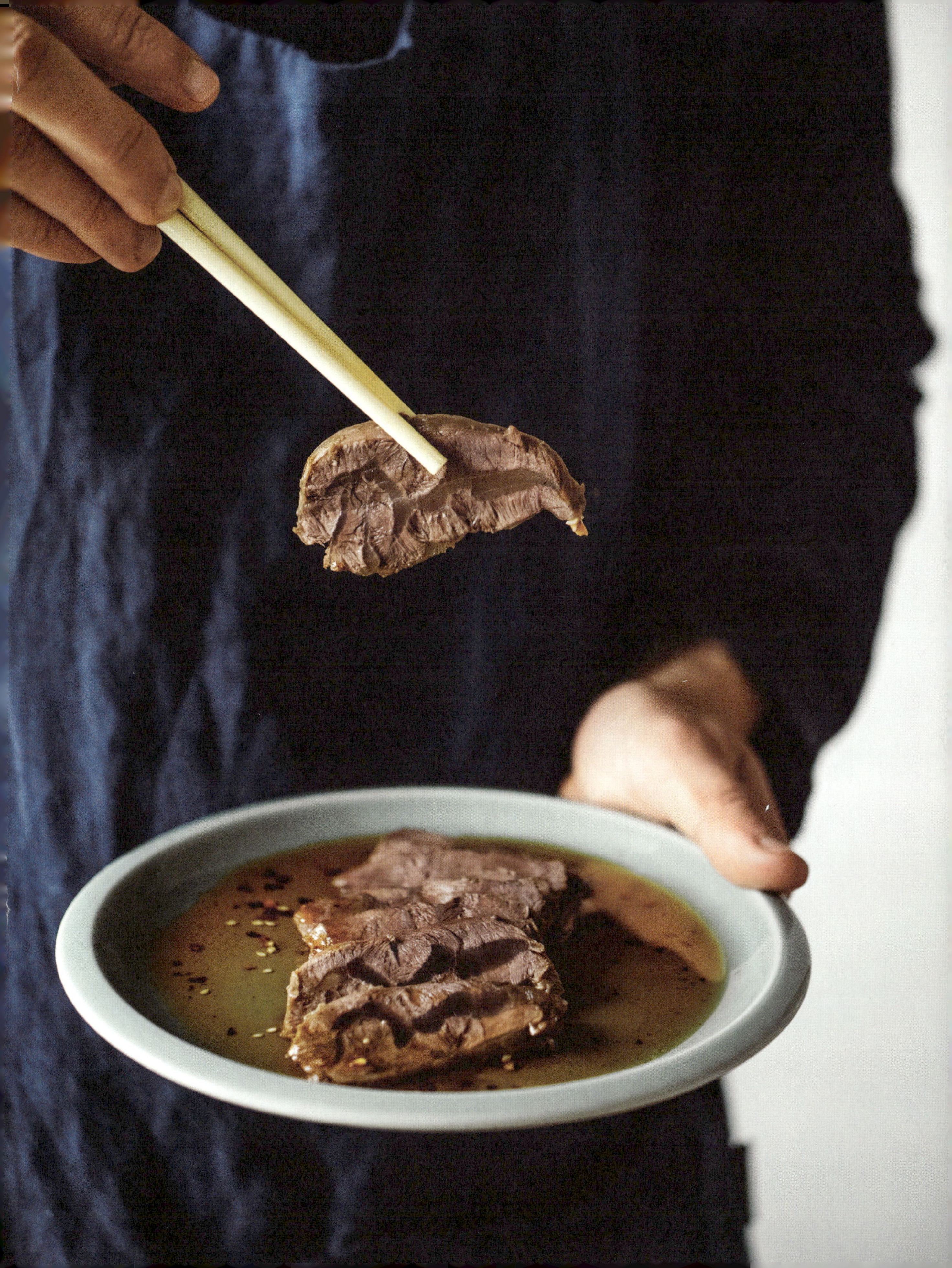

CHAPTER
03

Vegetables
蔬菜
SHŪ CÀI

PP. 84-85: Stir-fried Chinese spring onions with soy bean sprouts ■ **PP. 86-87**: Hand-torn cabbage
PP. 88-89: Wok cauliflower ■ **PP. 92-93**: Romaine lettuce with oyster sauce ■ **PP. 94-95**: Stir-fried garlic scapes and pork
PP. 96-97: Stir-fried celery with cashew nuts ■ **PP. 98-99**: Roasted asparagus in butter-soy sauce
PP. 100-101: Fried mangetout with lap cheong ■ **PP. 102-103**: Sichuan fried green beans
PP. 104-105: Yu xiang aubergine ■ **PP. 106-107**: Three treasures of the Earth ■ **PP. 108-109**: Steamed white radish balls
PP. 110-111: Julienned potato salad ■ **PP. 114-115**: Fried corn with pepper and salt

From All Angles

Vegetable–Based Cooking

FOR CENTURIES, CHINESE CUISINE CONSISTED MAINLY OF VEGETABLES AND PLANTS (RICE, WHEAT, SOY AND LOTS OF VEGETABLES), ACCOMPANIED BY FISH, WHITE MEAT AND, MORE RARELY, RED MEAT. THE SINOGRAM 菜 (PRONOUNCED "TSAI"), WHICH DESIGNATES VEGETABLES, IS ALSO A TRANSLATION OF THE WORD "DISH".

LEAFY GREEN VEGETABLES

These are usually stir-fried in a wok. This cooking method (see p. 46) helps to preserve their colour, their nutrients, and especially their texture.

They occupy a special place in the vegetable world. They are found as garnishes in noodle soups, next to rice in a lunch box (盒饭, *hé fàn*), or as stuffing in a *bao zi*.

You will find a big vegetable section in any Chinese supermarket: pak choi (also known as bok choy), Chinese cabbage, gai lan (also known as Chinese broccoli), water spinach, choy sum... All these vegetables with more or less exotic names are considered basic, everyday ingredients, especially in the south of the country.

MEAT IN PLANTS

Don't be surprised to find recipes with meat in a chapter dedicated to vegetables; this is very common in China.

As the popular saying goes, you should "cook vegetables with animal fat and cook meat with vegetable fat" (素菜荤油,荤菜素油).

Vegetarianism as it is understood in the West does not necessarily make sense in a country where, until the '70s and '80s, meat was scarce for ordinary people. In China, vegetarianism is most often associated with Buddhist cuisine; it is founded on the principle of compassion and therefore prohibits animal exploitation. This temple food, both simple and creative (*kaofu*, p. 64; tofu skin, p. 118), has existed and evolved since the introduction of Buddhism in the country 2,000 years ago.

LOST IN TRANSLATION

The same vegetable often has several names in China, a legacy of linguistic disparities in this huge country.

For example, tomato is called both *fān qié* (番茄, "eggplant from abroad") or *xī hóng shì* (西红柿, "Western persimmon"). This makes translating little-known varieties in the West sometimes complicated. To help you, I use the most common Chinese name in the recipes, as well as the alternatives you can use.

MEMORY
回忆

I experienced my first culinary shock at age 11, when I discovered steamed cauliflowers in my middle school's cafeteria, in Paris. They were soft, bland, waterlogged... so different from the cauliflowers I had always known (see p. 88).

A FEW POPULAR VEGETABLES IN CHINESE CUISINE

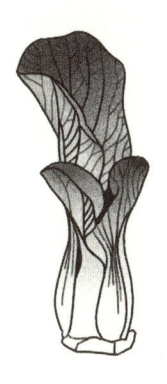

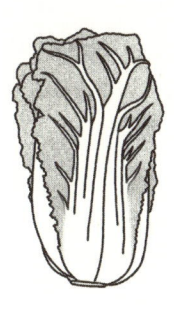

CHINESE CABBAGE
大白菜 | DÀ BÁI CÀI

CHINESE CELERY
芹菜 | QÍN CÀI

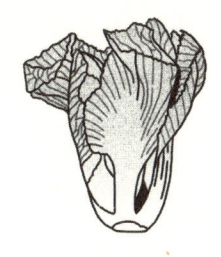

CHINESE MUSTARD
芥菜 | JIÈ CÀI

PAK CHOI (BOK CHOY)
小白菜 | XIĂO BÁI CÀI

WATER SPINACH
空心菜 | KŌNG XĪN CÀI

CHINESE BROCCOLI
芥蓝 | JIÈ LÁN

WHITE RADISH
白萝卜 | BÁI LUÓ BO

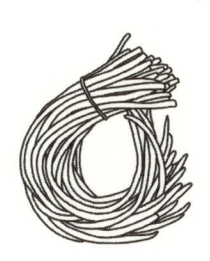

LOTUS ROOT
莲藕 | LIÁN ŎU

ASPARAGUS BEAN
长豇豆 | CHÁNG JIĀNG DÒU

TARO
芋头 | YÙ TÓU

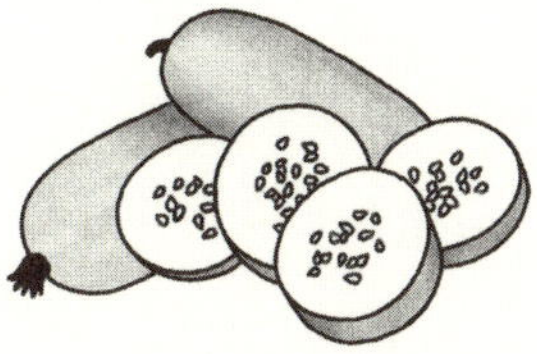

WAX GOURD
冬瓜 | DŌNG GUĀ

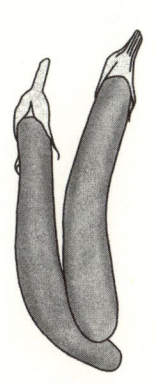

CHINESE AUBERGINE (EGGPLANT)
茄子 | QIÉ ZI

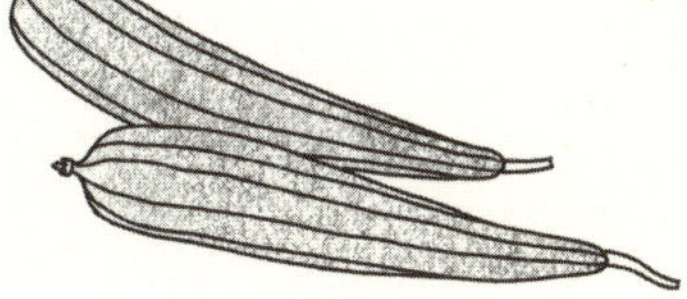

SPONGE GOURD
丝瓜 | SĪ GUĀ

BAMBOO SHOOT
春笋 | CHŪN SŬN

TECHNIQUE 4

Preparing Vegetables

BEFORE COOKING, ESPECIALLY WITH A WOK, VEGETABLES OFTEN NEED TO BE PREPARED BEFOREHAND, WHETHER TO PRESERVE THEIR TEXTURE, MAKE THEM TASTIER OR LIMIT THEIR OIL ABSORPTION. HERE ARE SOME BASIC TECHNIQUES THAT YOU WILL OFTEN COME ACROSS IN THIS BOOK.

CHOPPING
刀工
DĀO GŌNG

Chopping vegetables should highlight the ingredient's texture and, of course, be adapted to the cooking technique. Here are the three most common ways to chop in Chinese cuisine.

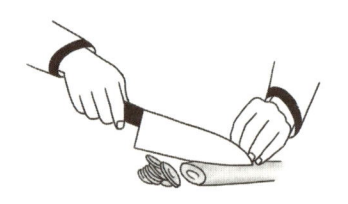

SLICES
片 / PIÀN

Vegetables are cut horizontally, vertically and often diagonally, into thin slices for stir-fried dishes, or thicker slices for longer cooking times. This is the most basic form of chopping.

JULIENNE
丝 / SĪ

Crunchy vegetables such as radishes, potatoes or carrots are first cut into slices, then finely julienned (the Chinese word for this literally means "silk thread") to be served as a salad or stir-fried quickly in a wok. Here's a tip: before starting, instead of stacking the slices to go faster, it is better to spread them out, like a deck of cards, which allows easier and more regular cutting.

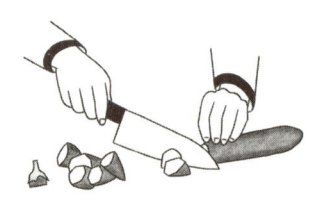

"ROLLED"
滚刀切 / GǓN DĀO QIĒ

This style is used for long-shaped vegetables (aubergines/eggplants, courgettes/zucchini, carrots) to obtain uniform pieces with two slanted sides, which gives a larger surface area and therefore faster cooking. Start by cutting the vegetable diagonally at a 45° angle, then turn at a 90° angle between each cut, until you reach the other end (think of it a bit like a pencil sharpener!).

LEARN MORE
了解更多

See how to cut aromatic ingredients on pp. 28–29.

DISGORGING

杀水

SHĀ SHUǏ

Mixing vegetables with salt allows the water to be extracted by osmosis. This allows seasonings to better penetrate the vegetables, such as cucumbers, and make them tastier. It also helps to reduce the bitterness of a plant, such as radishes, or make the flesh more firm and absorb less oil, for aubergines (eggplants), for example.

01
In a large bowl, pour salt over the cut vegetables, about 1 tsp for 500g (1lb 2oz) of vegetables. Mix to distribute well.

02
Let stand for between 15 minutes (cucumber) and 30 minutes (aubergine/eggplant) depending on the type and size of the vegetable, until droplets are visible on the surface and liquid pools at the bottom of the container.

03
Drain the vegetables on kitchen paper or squeeze gently by hand to remove as much liquid as possible. Since this process already salts your chosen vegetables, you may need to adjust the amount of salt in the rest of the recipe.

BLANCHING

焯水

CHĀO SHUǏ

Many vegetables (broccoli, celery, mangetout/snow peas...) must be pre-cooked in water (焯水, chāo shuǐ) before being stir-fried in a wok. If you don't, they may be raw on the inside and overcooked on the outside. Leafy green vegetables, on the other hand, are often eaten just blanched with a little seasoning.

01
Bring a large volume of water to the boil in a pot with some salt – 10g (¼oz) salt per 1 litre (4⅓ cups) of water. Salt will impart some flavour, but most importantly, it will preserve the colour of green vegetables by slowing down the loss of chlorophyll.

02
Add your vegetables and blanch them for between 30 seconds and 1 minute for leafy vegetables (pak choi/bok choy, spinach), or a maximum of 3 minutes for crunchier, pre-cut vegetables (cauliflower florets, julienned potatoes).

03
Transfer your blanched vegetables to cold water to stop the cooking process and then drain (really) well. This last step is very important if you plan to move on to wok cooking in hot oil, to avoid splashing.

Stir-Fried Chinese Spring Onions with Soy Bean Sprouts

JIŬ   CÀI   CHǍO   DÒU   YÁ

韭菜炒豆芽

PREPARING 5 MINUTES

COOKING 5 MINUTES

WHAT ARE COMMONLY KNOWN AS SOY BEAN SPROUTS ARE ACTUALLY YOUNG MUNG BEAN SPROUTS. THEIR CRUNCHY TEXTURE GOES WELL WITH A HIGHLY AROMATIC PLANT LIKE CHINESE SPRING ONIONS.

Serves 2 people

INGREDIENTS

For the spring onions

200g (7oz) Chinese spring onions (chives)
200g (7oz) mung bean sprouts
2 tbsp neutral oil
5–6 dried chilli peppers

For the sauce

½ tbsp soy sauce
1 tsp oyster sauce
1 tsp rice vinegar
1 tsp sugar
½ tsp salt

RECIPE STEPS

- Wash and drain the Chinese spring onions. Trim them to about the same length as the mung bean sprouts.

- Heat the oil gently in a wok over a medium heat. Once hot, add the dried chilli peppers and toast them for a few seconds to release their flavour (be careful not to let them burn).

- Switch to a high heat and add the spring onions. Stir-fry quickly for 1–2 minutes, until they soften a little. Add the bean sprouts and stir-fry for another 2 minutes. They will release some water and soften, but they should remain slightly crunchy.

- Mix all the ingredients for the sauce in a bowl, then pour this down the side of the wok and continue cooking for about 20 seconds. Serve.

GOOD TO KNOW
小提示

Eggs are often added to this recipe. They are cooked like an omelette, then stir-fried with the vegetables.

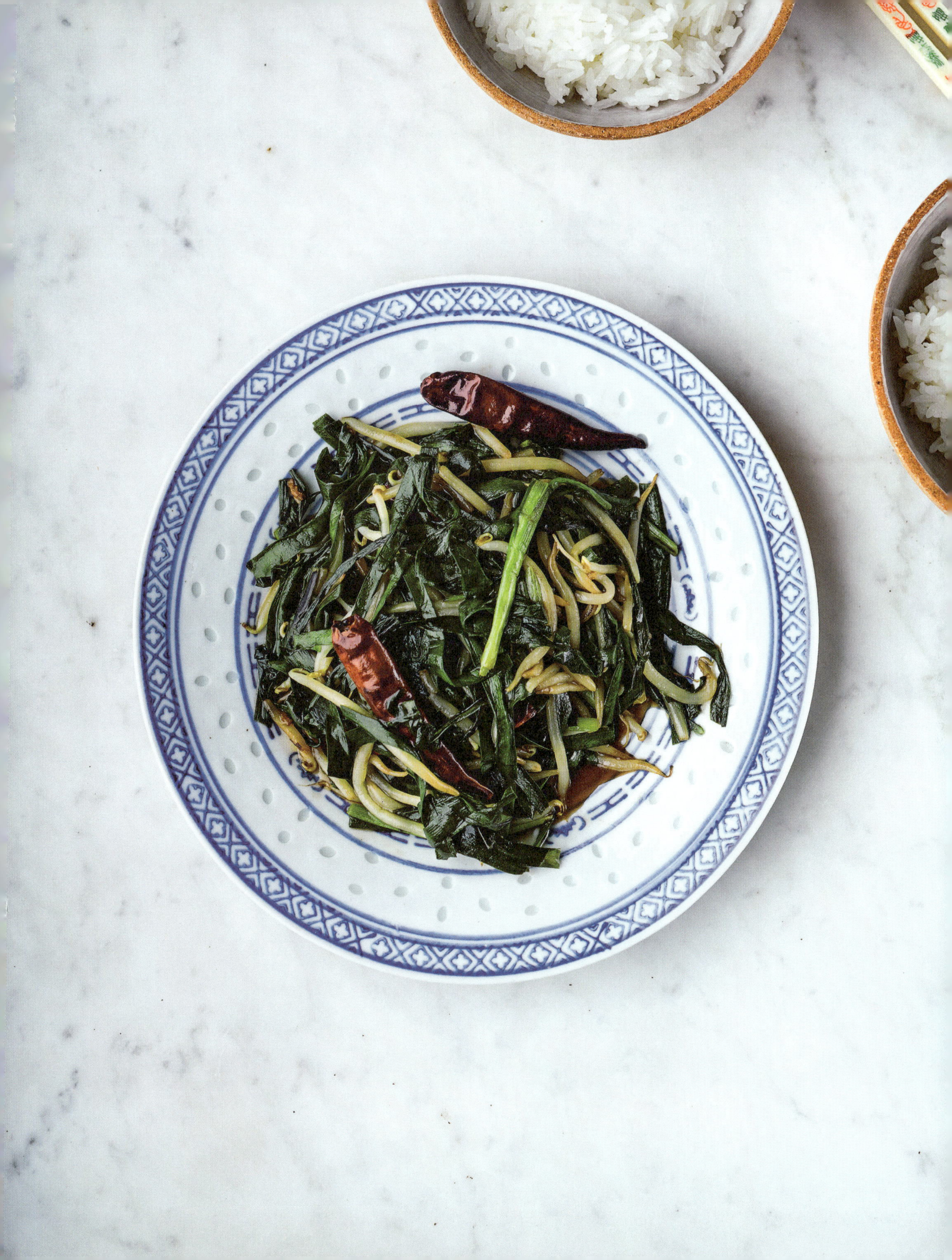

Hand-Torn Cabbage

SHŎU SĪ BĀO CÀI

手撕包菜

PREPARING 10 MINUTES

COOKING 5 MINUTES

THIS CABBAGE RECIPE IS THE MOST POPULAR (AND THE SIMPLEST) IN CHINA. THE CABBAGE LEAVES ARE TORN BY HAND, RATHER THAN CHOPPED WITH A KNIFE. THE RESULTING IRREGULAR SHAPES CREATE A LARGER CONTACT SURFACE WITH THE SAUCE AND MAKE FOR A TASTIER DISH.

Serves 2–3 people

INGREDIENTS

½ pointed cabbage
2 tbsp oil
3 garlic cloves, chopped
1 tsp chopped spring onion (scallion) white
A few dried chilli peppers (*optional*)
½ tbsp black rice vinegar
½ tsp salt
½ tsp sugar
1 tsp light soy sauce

RECIPE STEPS

- Cut the cabbage in two lengthways and remove the hard core with a knife. Tear the leaves by hand into irregular pieces of 4–8cm (1½–3in).

- Heat the wok over a high heat. As soon as it starts to smoke, add the oil, then the garlic, spring onion and dried chilli peppers (if using). Stir with a spatula for about 10 seconds, to release the flavours.

- Add the cabbage and stir-fry for 2 minutes until the leaves are slightly softened.

- Season with the black rice vinegar, salt and sugar and continue cooking for another 1 minute to mix well. The leaves should be cooked but stay a little crunchy.

- Pour the soy sauce down the sides of the wok, stir for 10 seconds and serve.

GOOD TO KNOW
小提示

If possible, use varieties of cabbage that have tender leaves, because cooking should be fast. I prefer pointed cabbage or Choudou cabbage (a type of white cabbage), which have a slightly sweet taste.

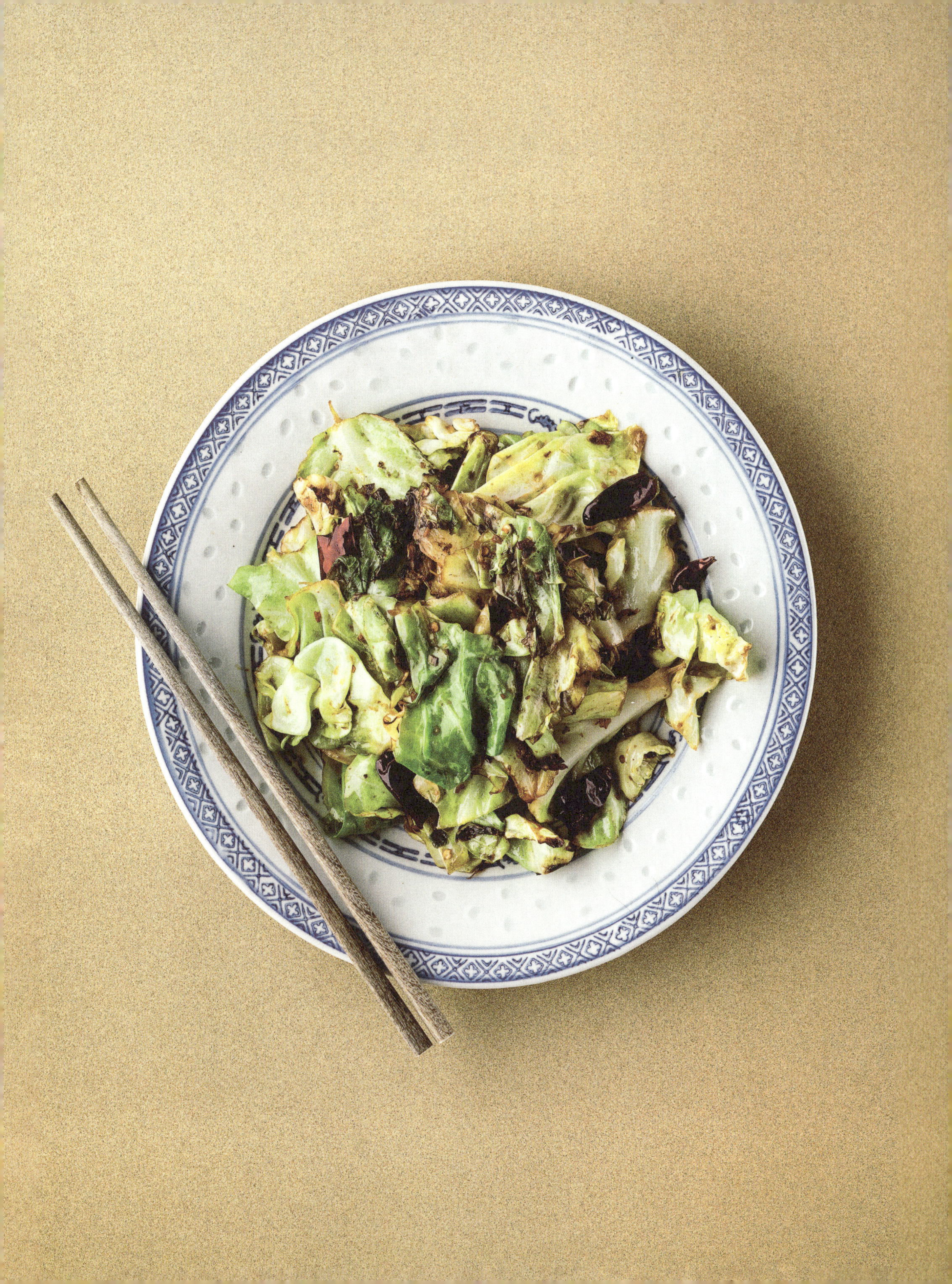

Wok Cauliflower

GĀN GUŌ HUĀ CÀI
干锅花菜

PREPARING 15 MINUTES

COOKING 10 MINUTES

A FAMILY DISH THAT MADE ME FALL IN LOVE WITH CAULIFLOWER FROM A YOUNG AGE. WOK COOKING ALLOWS A GOOD BALANCE BETWEEN TASTE (FULL OF FLAVOURS), TEXTURE (SLIGHTLY CRUNCHY) AND UMAMI (MEAT FAT).

Serves 4 people

INGREDIENTS

400g (14oz) cauliflower, broken into small florets
1½ tbsp salt
2 tbsp neutral oil
100g (3½oz) rindless pork belly, finely sliced
3 garlic cloves, chopped
1 tbsp chopped red onion
A few dried chilli peppers (*optional*)
1 tbsp light soy sauce
1 tsp dark soy sauce
½ tsp sugar
Spring onion (scallion), cut into short lengths, to serve

RECIPE STEPS

- Blanch the cauliflower florets in boiling water with 1 tablespoon of the salt for 2 minutes. The florets are ready when they become slightly crunchy but can still be easily pierced with a fork. Drain and set aside.

- Heat the wok over a medium heat. Once it becomes very hot, add the oil, then the pork belly slices, and fry the pork for 3 minutes until slightly browned.

- Stir in the remaining ½ teaspoon of salt, the chopped garlic and red onion, and the chilli peppers if using. Stir-fry for a few seconds to release the flavours.

- Switch to a high heat and add the blanched cauliflower pieces. Stir-fry them for about 1 minute to mix everything together. Season with the soy sauces and sugar and continue cooking for a few seconds, so that each cauliflower floret takes on some colour.

- Transfer to a bowl and sprinkle with the spring onion pieces to serve.

GOOD TO KNOW
小提示

If possible, use Chinese cauliflower (which you will find in the vegetable section of Chinese supermarkets), which has longer stems and fewer dense florets, similar to tenderstem broccoli/broccolini. Its texture is more suitable for wok cooking.

You can replace the pork belly with bacon (if so, do not salt), or any other type of slightly fatty meat. For a vegetarian version, use rehydrated dried shiitake, which will provide some extra umami flavour.

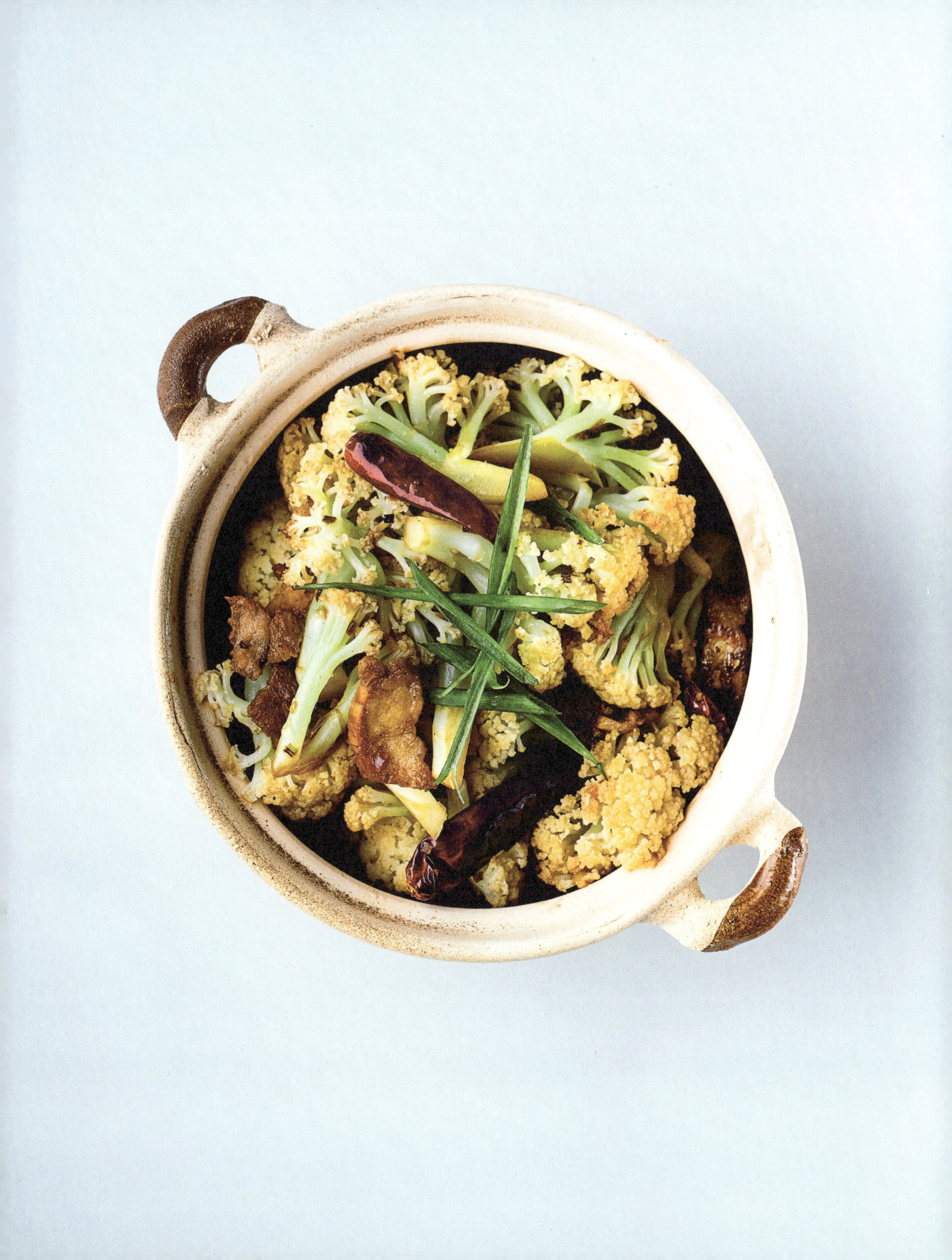

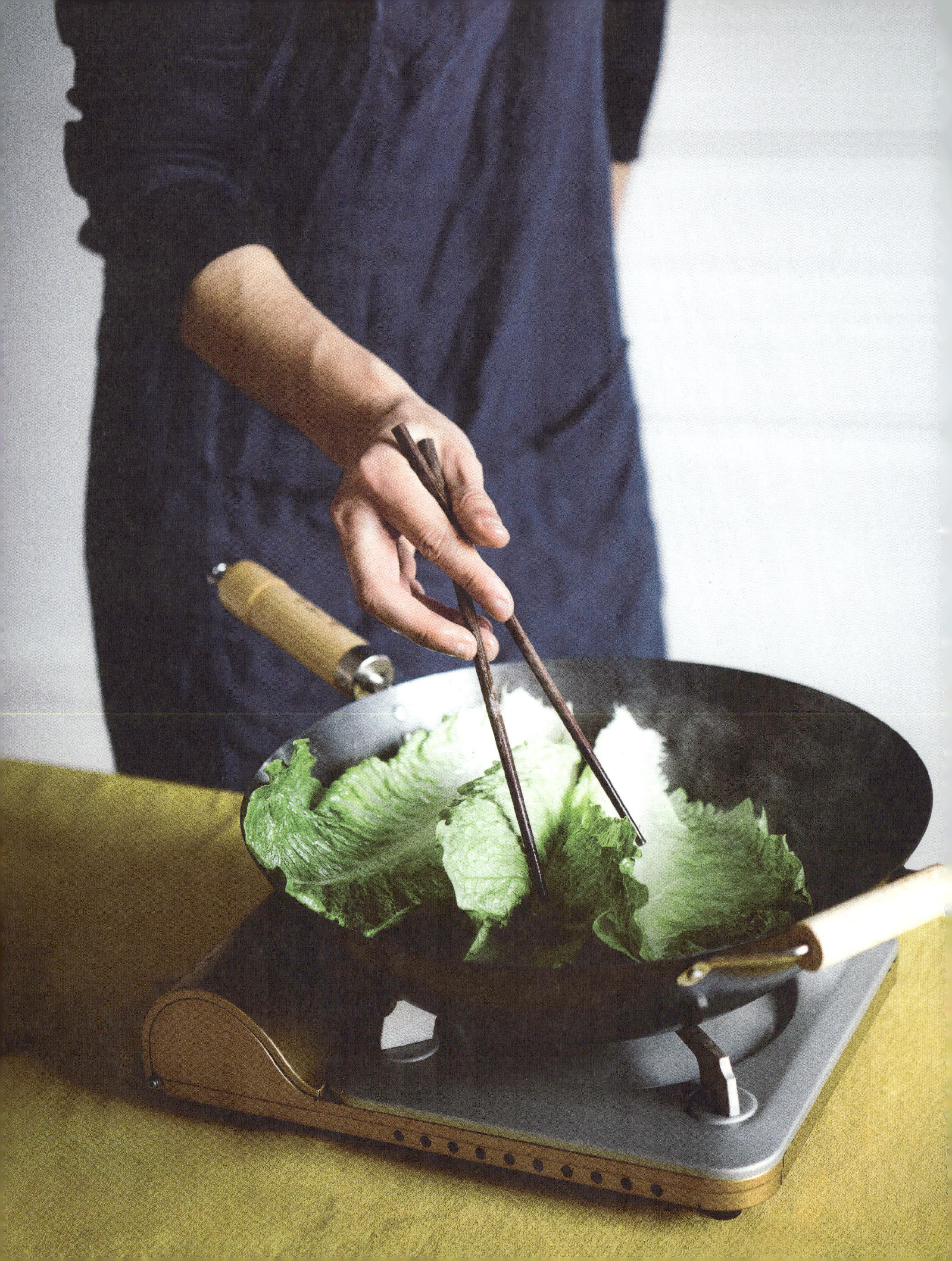

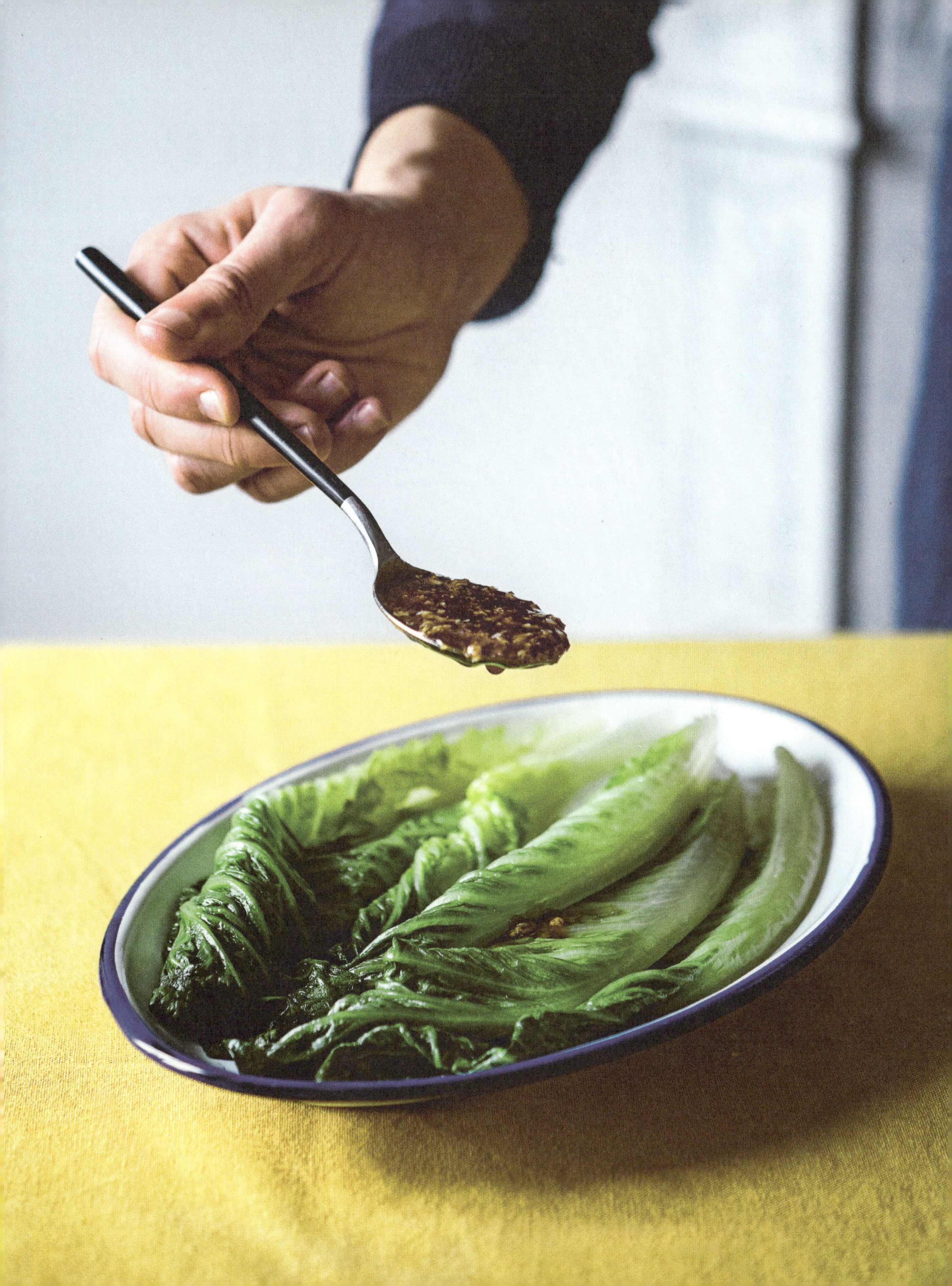

Romaine Lettuce with Oyster Sauce

SUÀN   RÓNG   SHĒNG   CÀI

蒜蓉生菜

PREPARING 5 MINUTES

COOKING 5 MINUTES

IN CHINA, IT IS RARE TO EAT VEGETABLES IN A SALAD. PEOPLE PREFER TO COOK THEM QUICKLY TO AVOID EATING THEM RAW WHILE MAINTAINING THEIR NUTRIENTS AND CRUNCHINESS AS MUCH AS POSSIBLE. THIS CANTONESE-FLAVOURED DISH IS A NOVEL WAY TO COOK LETTUCE.

Serves 2 people

INGREDIENTS

For the lettuce

1 tbsp cornflour (cornstarch)
1 tbsp water
1 Romaine lettuce, about 400g (14oz)
½ tbsp neutral oil
2 garlic cloves, chopped
Salt

For the sauce

2 tsp oyster sauce
1 tsp light soy sauce
½ tsp sugar
⅓ tsp dark soy sauce
100ml (6½ tbsp) water

RECIPE STEPS

- Mix all the sauce ingredients in a bowl and set aside.

- Mix the cornflour with the tablespoon of water and set aside.

- Separate the lettuce leaves and wash them to remove impurities.

- Bring plenty of water to the boil in your wok. Add a pinch of salt, then add the lettuce leaves. Blanch for 40 seconds – they should start to soften a little. Drain well and arrange on a plate.

- Heat the empty wok over a medium heat. As soon as it starts smoking, add the oil, then the chopped garlic, and fry for about 15 seconds. Pour in the sauce, let it reduce a little, then add the cornflour mixture, stir quickly and cook until you have a relatively thick sauce.

- Pour this sauce over the lettuce leaves and serve.

GOOD TO KNOW
小提示

This recipe also works very well with broccoli. Break into small florets and blanch for a little longer than the lettuce (about 2 minutes).

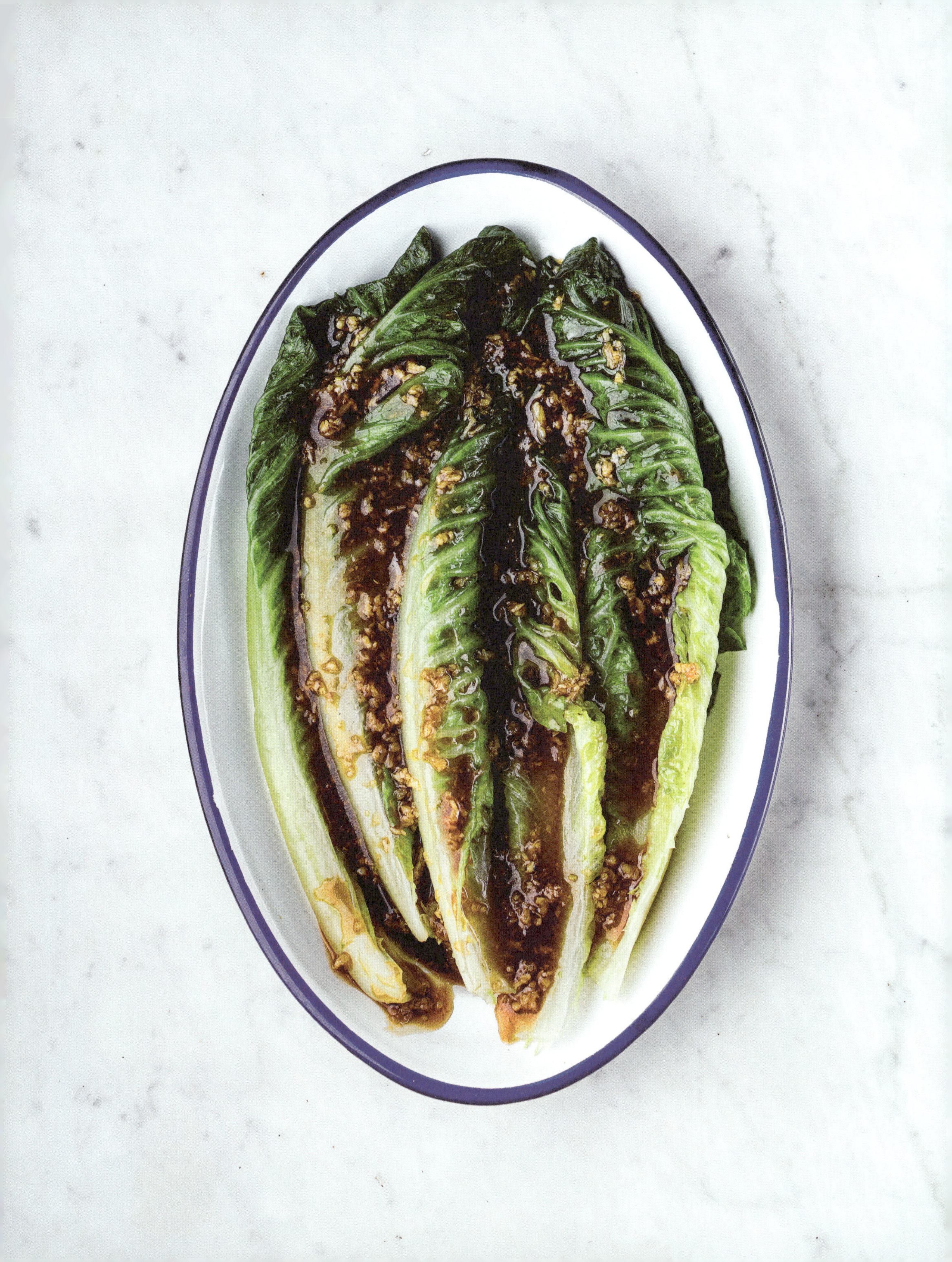

Stir-Fried Garlic Scapes and Pork

SUÀN MIÁO RÒU SĪ

蒜苗肉丝

PREPARING 5 MINUTES

COOKING 5 MINUTES

GARLIC SCAPES ARE DELICIOUS, CRUNCHY, SLIGHTLY SWEET AND VERY TENDER. THEY ARE USUALLY SOLD IN CLUSTERS OF EIGHT STEMS IN CHINESE SUPERMARKETS. THEY ARE OFTEN COOKED WITH PORK, AS IN THIS RECIPE, BUT THEY ALSO GO WELL WITH CHICKEN OR BEEF.

Serves 2 people

INGREDIENTS

For the scapes

12 garlic scapes, about 300g (10oz), cut into 5cm (2in) sticks
1 tsp light soy sauce
1 tsp oyster sauce
½ tsp sugar
1 tbsp neutral oil
1 tsp chopped ginger
Salt

For the pork

100g (3½oz) pork tenderloin
2 tsp light soy sauce
½ tsp salt
½ tsp black pepper
1 tsp Shaoxing wine
1 egg white
1 tbsp cornflour (cornstarch)
1 tbsp neutral oil

FOR THE GARLIC SCAPES

- Bring a pot of water to the boil with 2 teaspoons of salt and blanch the garlic scapes for 40 seconds, then immerse in cold water to stop cooking. They must remain crisp.

FOR THE PORK

- Cut the pork fillet into the same size pieces as the garlic scapes. Transfer to a bowl and add the soy sauce, salt, pepper and Shaoxing wine. Massage the meat well until no liquid remains at the bottom of the bowl (for about 30 seconds). Pour in the egg white and start massaging again so that the meat absorbs it completely. Add the cornflour in two stages, mixing well each time. Leave to marinate for 10 minutes.

- Heat a wok over a medium heat. As soon as it starts smoking, add the tablespoon of oil, then the marinated pork. Stir-fry quickly for about 1 minute until the meat is just cooked through. Remove the pork from the wok and set aside.

TO FINISH

- Mix the light soy sauce, oyster sauce and sugar in a bowl.

- Heat the remaining tablespoon of oil in the wok, then add the ginger and fry for 10 seconds to release the flavour. Stir in the garlic scapes and continue cooking for about 30 seconds, then add the pork and the soy sauce mixture. Stir-fry for 30 seconds, adding a little salt if necessary. Turn off the heat and serve.

GOOD TO KNOW
小提示

The technique used here to marinate the meat makes it possible to obtain a "velvety" mouthfeel (see p. 184). To make the vegetarian version, pork can be replaced by 5-spice tofu strips (see p. 130).

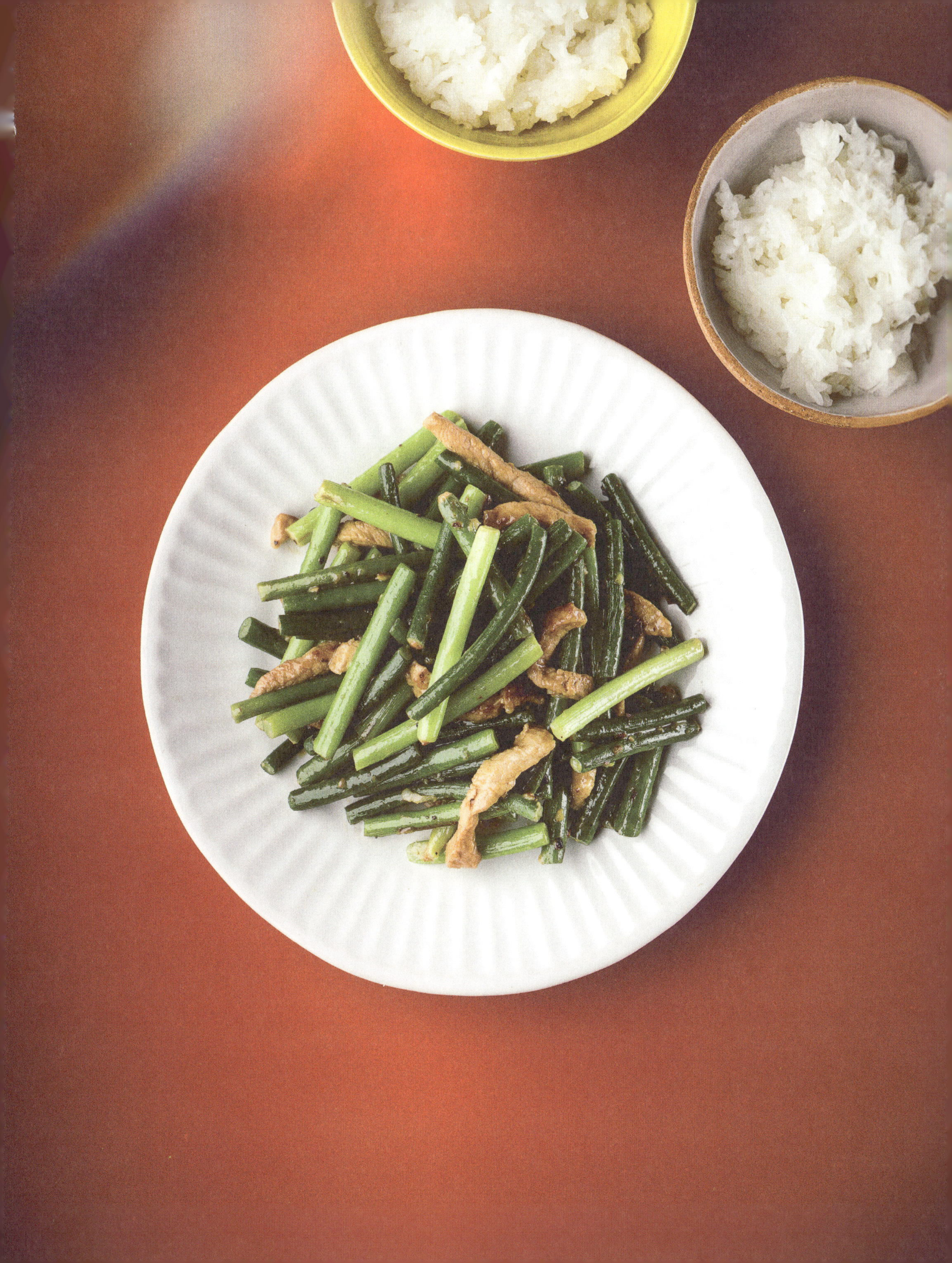

Stir-Fried Celery with Cashew Nuts

XĪ　QÍN　CHǎO　YĀO　GUǑ

西芹炒腰果

PREPARING 5 MINUTES

COOKING 15 MINUTES

A TYPICAL JIANGNAN DISH OF STIR-FRIED VEGETABLES: SWEET FLAVOURS, MINIMAL SEASONING AND HARMONY OF COLOURS, NOT TO MENTION THE MOST IMPORTANT ASPECT: DIFFERENT TYPES OF CRUNCHY TEXTURES BETWEEN CELERY, PEPPERS AND CASHEW NUTS.

Serves 2 people

INGREDIENTS

2 tsp cournflour (cornstarch)
2 tbsp unsalted broth or water
2 tbsp neutral oil
50g (1¾oz) cashew nuts
2 tsp salt
3 celery sticks, about 300g (10oz), cut on the diagonal into 1cm (½in) wide pieces
2 garlic cloves, chopped
1 tbsp chopped spring onion (scallion) white
¼ red bell pepper, about 50g (1¾oz), finely julienned
½ tsp sugar

RECIPE STEPS

- In a small bowl, mix the cornflour and broth (preferably chicken or pork) or water and set aside.

- Heat 1 tablespoon of the oil in a wok over a medium heat and add the cashews. Brown for 2–3 minutes, then transfer them to a bowl; they will become crunchy as they cool down.

- Leave the oil in the wok and pour in 1 litre (4⅓ cups) water with 1 teaspoon of the salt. Bring to the boil over a high heat, then blanch the celery pieces for 30 seconds (they should remain crisp). Drain the celery and empty the water from the wok.

- Heat the dry wok over a medium heat. When it starts smoking, add the remaining tablespoon of oil, followed by the garlic and spring onion. Quickly fry them for a few seconds, then add the celery and red pepper. Stir-fry everything for 30 seconds, then add the remaining teaspoon of salt and the sugar.

- Pour in the cornflour and water mixture, which will thicken the sauce. Finally, add the cashew nuts and mix well to serve.

GOOD TO KNOW
小提示

In China, this dish is always cooked with lily bulbs (百合, bai hé), composed of white petals that are slightly crunchy and floury. Although uncommon, the fresh version is beginning to appear in some Chinese supermarkets. Much like celery, just blanch them for a few seconds before moving on to the stir-frying.

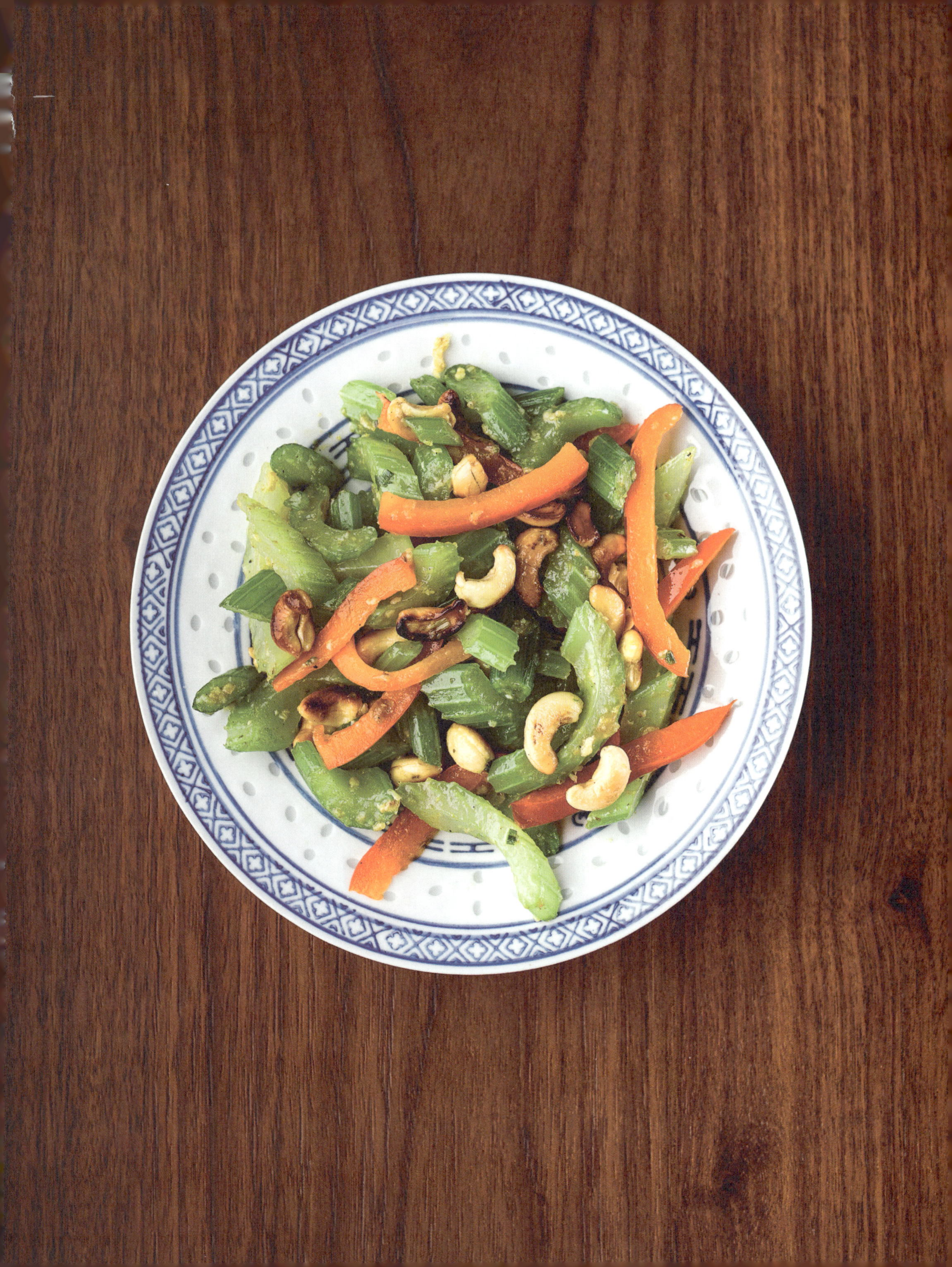

Roasted Asparagus in Butter–Soy Sauce

HUÁNG YÓU JIÀNG YÓU LÚ SǓN

黄油酱油芦笋

PREPARING 5 MINUTES

COOKING 12 MINUTES

THIS IS ONE OF THE MOST "TRIED AND TESTED" RECIPES IN THIS BOOK. THE MIXTURE OF BUTTER, SOY SAUCE AND BLACK VINEGAR IS DELICIOUS. WHILE BUTTER CERTAINLY ISN'T A CLASSIC INGREDIENT IN CHINESE CUISINE, MOST HOUSEHOLDS ARE WELL ACQUAINTED WITH IT, MOST NOTABLY THANKS TO THE GROWING POPULARITY OF WESTERN PASTRIES.

Serves 4 people

INGREDIENTS

12 green asparagus stalks
8 garlic cloves, chopped
1 tbsp light soy sauce
10g (¼oz/2 tsp) butter
1 tbsp black rice vinegar
½ tsp sugar

RECIPE STEPS

- Preheat the oven to 200°C (180°C fan/400°F/Gas 6). Meanwhile, wash the asparagus and cut off the hard part of the base, then place the spears in an oven-proof dish and sprinkle them with the garlic. Bake for 12 minutes (as oven temperatures can vary, it is a good idea to monitor) until the spears are lightly roasted.

- Meanwhile, prepare the sauce by mixing together the light soy sauce, butter, black rice vinegar and sugar. Microwave for about 20 seconds to melt the butter, then stir and pour over the asparagus.

GOOD TO KNOW
小提示

You can replace the black rice vinegar with balsamic vinegar, but if doing so, do not add sugar.

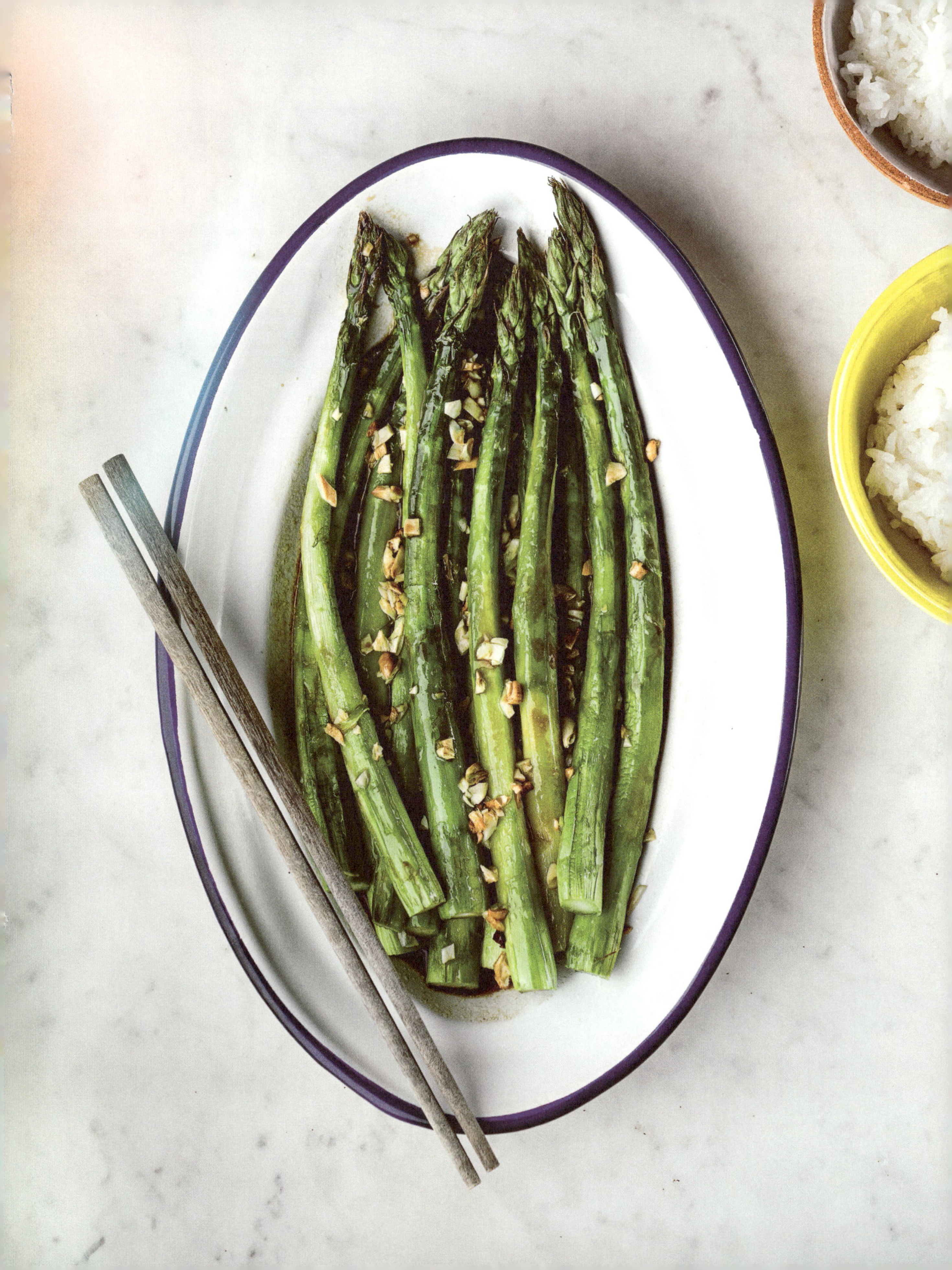

Fried Mangetout with Lap Cheong

XIĀNG CHÁNG CHǍO HÉ LÁN DÒU

香肠炒荷兰豆

PREPARING 10 MINUTES

COOKING 5 MINUTES

A VERY SIMPLE WOK RECIPE WITH TWO INGREDIENTS I REALLY LIKE: CRISP MANGETOUT AND VERY FLAVOURFUL CANTONESE SAUSAGES (LAP CHEONG). THANKS TO THEIR SLIGHTLY SWEET TASTE, THEY BLEND WELL TOGETHER AND DON'T REQUIRE MUCH SEASONING.

Serves 4 people

INGREDIENTS

1 tsp cornflour (cornstarch)
1 tbsp water
300g (10oz) mangetout (snow peas), washed and stems removed
2 tbsp neutral oil
80g (3oz) lap cheong, thinly sliced
1 tsp chopped garlic
1 tsp chopped ginger
½ tsp sugar
½ tbsp oyster sauce
Salt

RECIPE STEPS

- Mix the cornflour and water in a bowl and set aside.

- Heat 1 litre (4⅓ cups) of water in a pot (or wok) and bring to the boil. Switch to a medium heat and add 1 tablespoon of salt and the mangetout. Blanch for 1 minute; the mangetout should be cooked but remain slightly crunchy. Drain and set aside.

- Place a wok over a high heat. When it's hot, add the oil, then the lap cheong, and stir-fry quickly for 30 seconds. Add the garlic and ginger and stir to release the aromas. Then add the mangetout, sugar and ½ teaspoon of salt. Continue to stir-fry for a few seconds, then add the oyster sauce. Pour in the cornflour mixture and stir-fry until everything is mixed together. Arrange on a plate and serve with rice.

GOOD TO KNOW
小提示

Lap cheong are found in most Chinese supermarkets in the chilled section. These slightly sweet sausages are made with pork, salt, soy sauce and rose liqueur (Mei Kuei Lu).

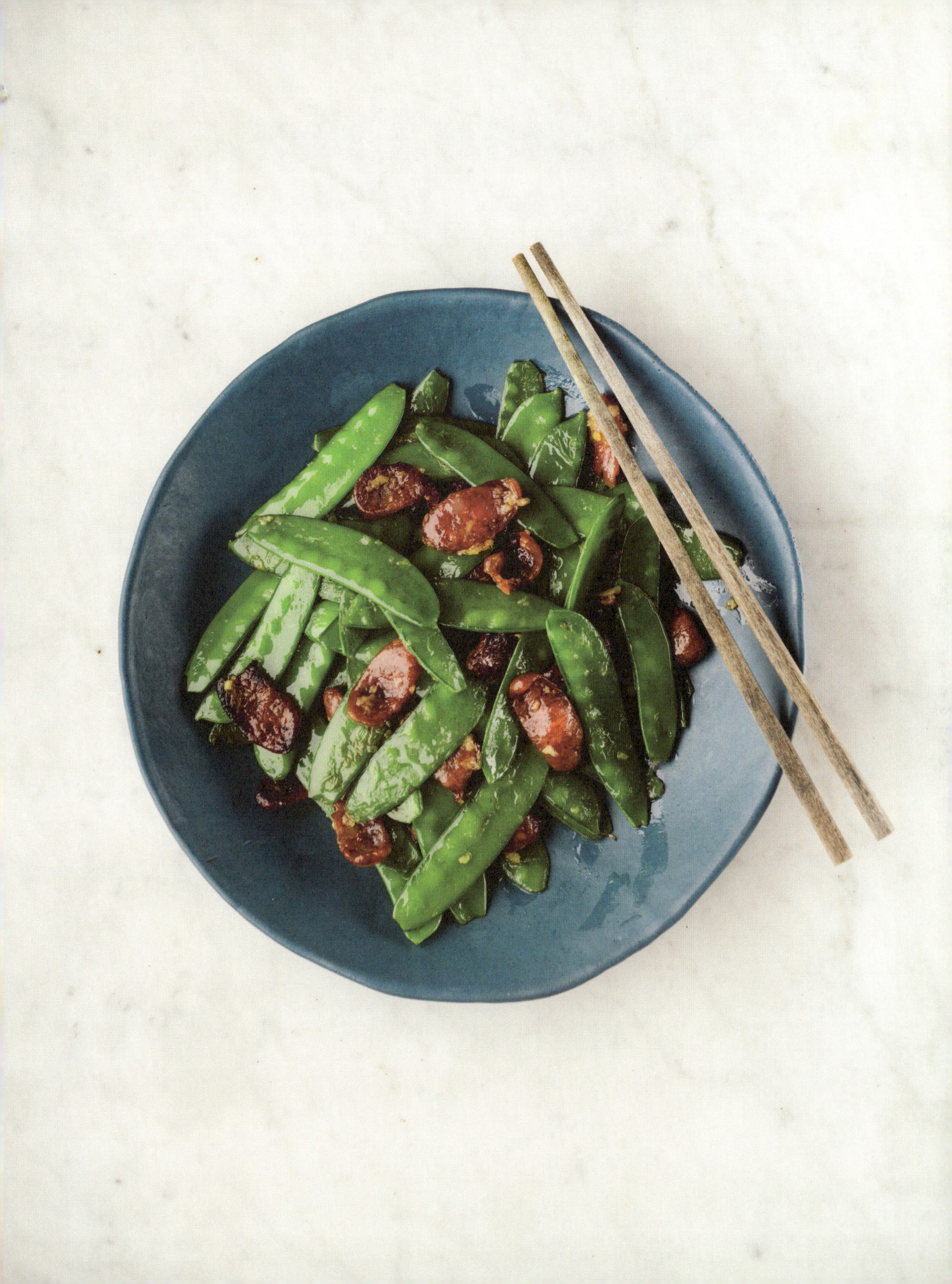

Sichuan Fried Green Beans

GĀN　BIĂN　SÌ　JÌ　DÒU

干煸四季豆

PREPARING 15 MINUTES

COOKING 10 MINUTES

THIS DISH IS A MUST EVERY TIME I GO TO A SICHUAN RESTAURANT. THESE GREEN BEANS ARE COMPLETELY ADDICTIVE!

🍴 Serves 4 people

INGREDIENTS

400g (14oz) green beans
500ml (2 cups) neutral oil
2 tsp Sichuan peppercorn
1 tsp chopped ginger
3 garlic cloves, minced
A few dried chilli peppers
100g (3½oz) pork belly, chopped
½ tbsp Shaoxing wine
½ tbsp light soy sauce
½ tsp dark soy sauce
½ tsp sugar
Salt

FOR THE GREEN BEANS

- Remove the stems from the green beans, then wash, drain well and pat dry with a towel or kitchen paper.

- Heat a wok over a medium heat and pour in the oil. When the temperature reaches 180°C (350°F), add half of the green beans and cook for about 1 minute, until lightly roasted (try to maintain a temperature of about 160°C/325°F – you will see small "wrinkles" appear on the surface of the beans). Using a spider or slotted spoon, transfer the green beans to a plate covered with some kitchen paper. Repeat with the remaining green beans.

FOR THE AROMATIC INGREDIENTS

- Remove the oil from the wok (you can filter and reuse it), leaving roughly 1 tablespoon in the wok. Fry the Sichuan peppercorn, ginger, garlic and dried chilli peppers for 20 seconds over a medium heat to release the flavours.

TO FINISH

- Add the chopped pork belly and stir-fry until lightly coloured, for about 3 minutes. Add the green beans back in and pour in the Shaoxing wine, soy sauces and sugar. Stir to mix everything together. Adjust the seasoning with a little salt, if necessary.

GOOD TO KNOW
小提示

I use Chinese dried chilli peppers called xiao mi la, which are quite hot. You can choose another variety, but the idea is to have some heat in your mouth.

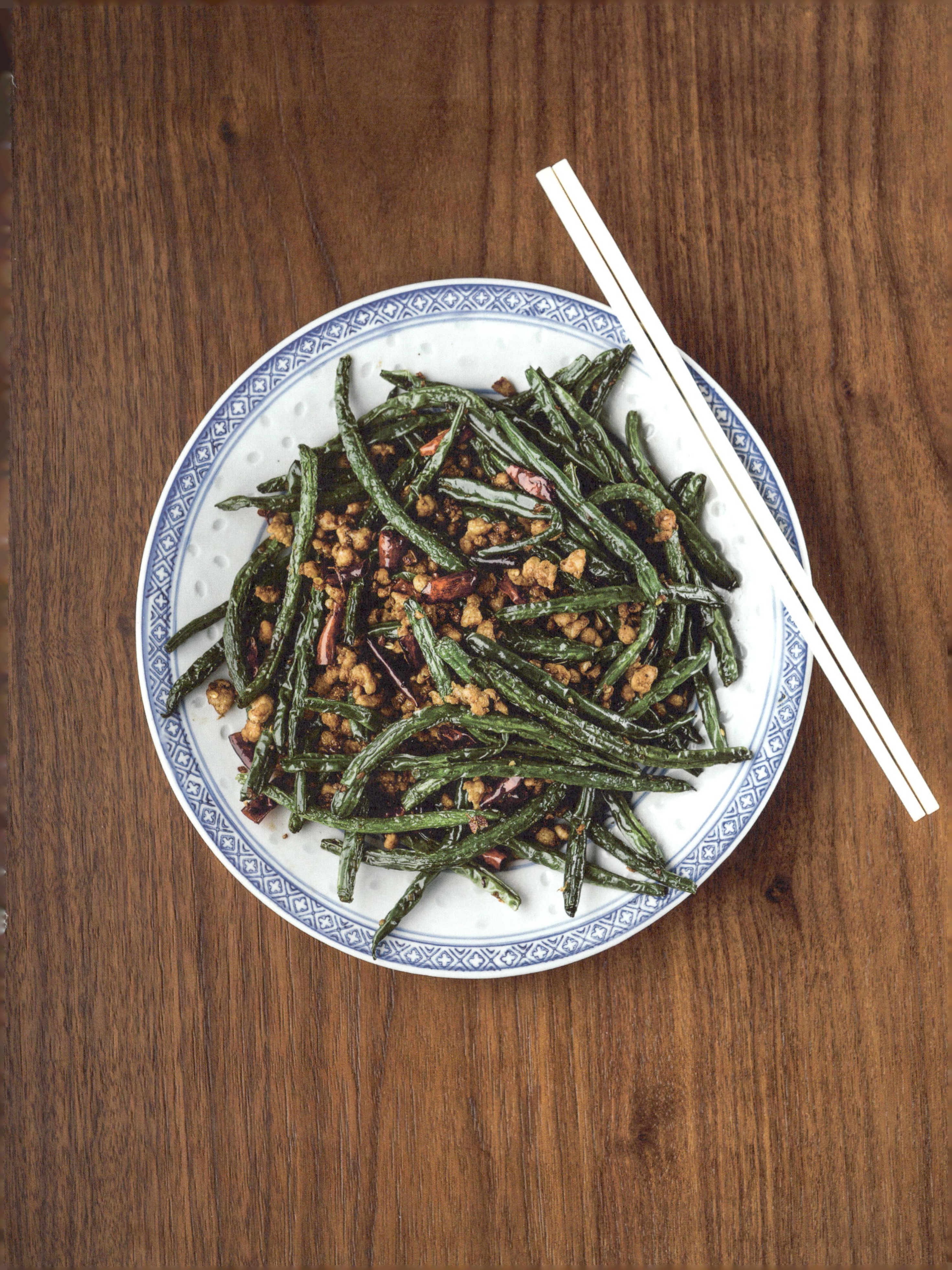

Yu Xiang Aubergine

YÚ XIĀNG QIÉ ZI

鱼香茄子

PREPARING 45 MINUTES

COOKING 10 MINUTES

I AM PARTICULARLY FOND OF AUBERGINES, WHETHER THEY ARE COOKED PROVENCE-STYLE, ITALIAN-STYLE OR LEBANESE-STYLE. SICHUAN PEOPLE HAVE DEVELOPED THE ART OF PREPARING THIS VEGETABLE: TENDER FLESH, AN EXPLOSION OF FLAVOURS OSCILLATING BETWEEN SALTY, SWEET AND ACIDIC, AND LIFTED BY THE HEAT OF THE CHILLI PEPPER. FOR THOSE WHO DO NOT LIKE AUBERGINES, THIS MAY BE A REVELATION.

Serves 4 people

INGREDIENTS

For the aubergines

2 Chinese aubergines (eggplant), about 500g (1lb 2oz)
1 tbsp salt
500ml (2 cups) oil
½ tbsp chilli bean paste (*doubanjiang*, see p. 38)
1 tsp finely chopped ginger
1 tsp finely chopped garlic
1 tsp chopped spring onion (scallion) white
1 tsp cornflour (cornstarch)
1 tbsp water
1 tsp black rice vinegar
2 tbsp chopped spring onion (scallion) green

For the sauce

150ml (scant ⅔ cup) hot water or broth
1 tbsp sugar
½ tbsp soy sauce

FOR THE AUBERGINES

- Cut the aubergines into 6cm (2½in) pieces, then cut them in half lengthways. Transfer them to a bowl, add the salt, then mix and leave to disgorge (see p. 83) for 30 minutes. Rinse and dry with kitchen paper. Meanwhile, mix the sauce ingredients together and set aside.

- Heat the oil in a wok over a medium heat. When the temperature reaches 200°C (400°F), fry the aubergines (in 3 batches, to avoid overcrowding the wok) for about 2 minutes, until lightly browned. Transfer to a plate covered with some kitchen paper.

FOR THE AROMATICS

- Remove the oil from the wok (you can filter and reuse it), leaving about 2 tablespoons. Heat over a medium heat, then add the chilli bean paste and cook for about 15 seconds (the oil will turn red and fragrant). Add the ginger, garlic and spring onion white and continue stir-frying for about 15 seconds to release the flavours.

TO FINISH

- Gently pour the sauce into the wok and add the aubergines. Simmer for 1 minute.

- Mix the cornflour with the water and add to the wok in two stages, to thicken the sauce. Finish by adding the black rice vinegar and a little of the spring onion green. Serve hot, sprinkled with the remaining spring onion green.

GOOD TO KNOW
小提示

For extra crunchiness, you can add a thin layer of cornflour to the aubergines before frying.

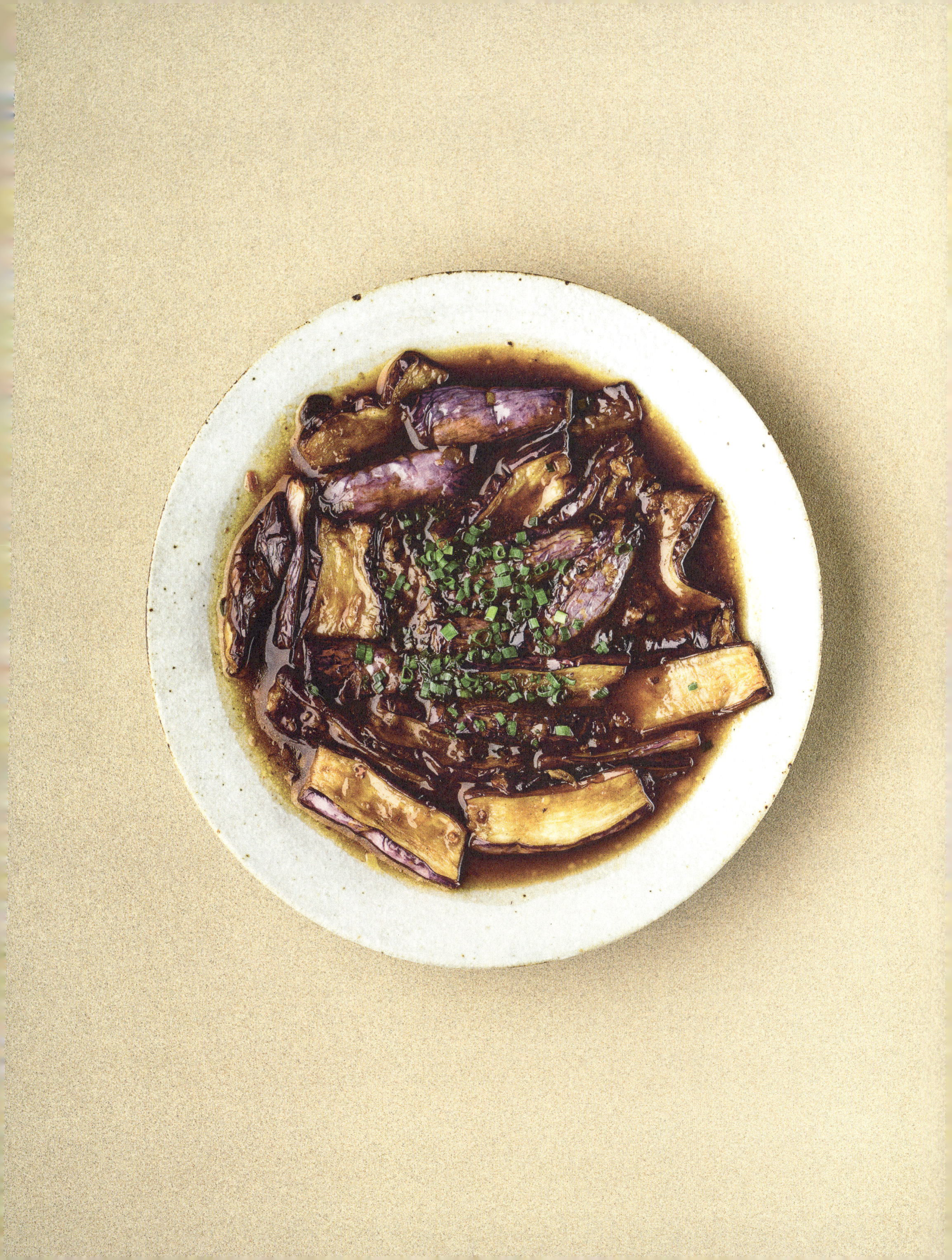

Three Treasures of the Earth

DÌ　　SĀN　　XIĀN

地三鲜

PREPARING 25 MINUTES

COOKING 15 MINUTES

DONGBEI CUISINE (NORTH-EASTERN CHINA) MAY SEEM MORE RUSTIC COMPARED TO THE DIFFERENT GASTRONOMIES OF THE SOUTH, YET IT IS RICH IN TASTE. THE THREE "TREASURES" HERE REFER TO THE THREE INGREDIENTS COMMONLY FOUND IN THIS REGION: PEPPER, POTATO AND AUBERGINE.

Serves 2 people

INGREDIENTS

For the treasures

300g (10oz) Chinese aubergines (eggplant)
2 potatoes, about 200g (7oz), preferably Agria or Bintje
1 tsp salt
2 tbsp cornflour (cornstarch)
500ml (2 cups) neutral oil
2 garlic cloves, chopped
1 tsp chopped spring onion (scallion) white
½ green pepper, cut into 1–2cm (½–¾in) strips

For the sauce

40ml (2½ tbsp) water
1 tbsp light soy sauce
1 tsp dark soy sauce
1 tbsp Shaoxing wine
½ tbsp sugar
1 tsp cornflour (cornstarch)

RECIPE STEPS

- Cut the aubergines in a "rolled" shape (see p. 82), then do the same with the potatoes, but make slightly smaller pieces, as they will take longer to cook.

- Place the aubergine pieces in a bowl, add the teaspoon of salt and mix. Leave to disgorge (see p. 83) for 15 minutes, then drain the pieces but do not wash them, as the droplets on the surface will help retain the cornflour. Add the cornflour in three batches, to prevent it from forming clumps.

- Pour the oil into a wok or a small pot. When the temperature reaches 180°C (350°F), add the aubergines and fry for 1 minute (in two batches if necessary) until the flesh is lightly browned. Remove using a spider or slotted spoon and transfer to a plate covered with kitchen paper.

- Lower the temperature of the oil to 150°C (300°F) and repeat with the potatoes, letting them fry for 5 minutes. The outsides should be golden brown and the insides should be tender when pierced with a fork.

FOR THE STIR-FRYING

- Mix all the sauce ingredients together in a bowl and set aside.

- Heat a wok over a medium heat. When it's hot, pour in 1 tablespoon of your frying oil and add the chopped garlic and spring onion. Fry them for a few seconds to release their flavours.

- Add the green pepper strips and stir-fry for 1 minute to soften them up a little. Pour in the sauce and mix until slightly thickened, then stir in the potatoes and aubergines and serve.

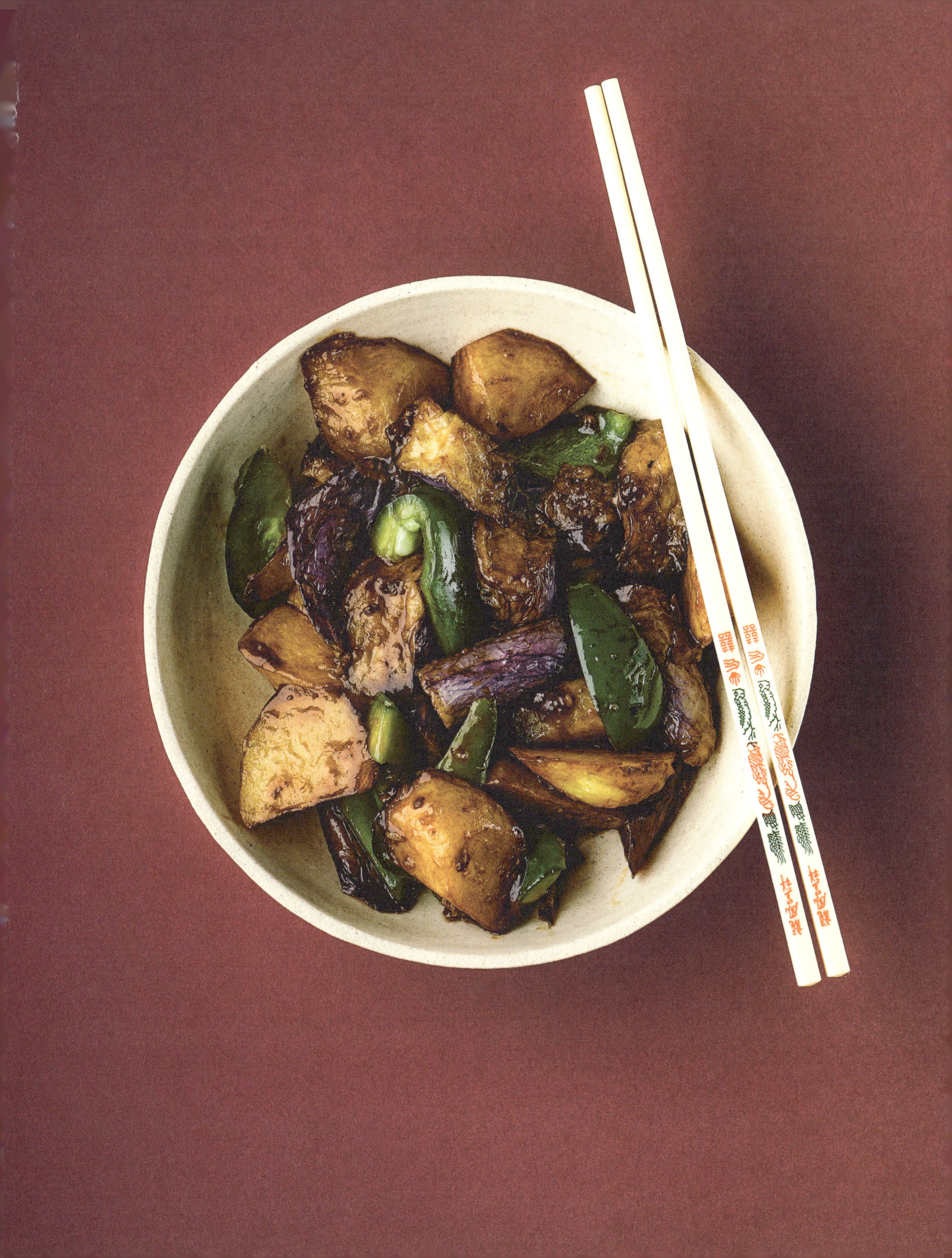

Steamed White Radish Balls

QĪNG ZHĒNG LUÓ BŬ WÁN

清蒸萝卜丸

PREPARING 75 MINUTES · COOKING 15 MINUTES

FULLY VEGETARIAN BALLS ARE RATHER RARE IN CHINESE CUISINE. THE STAR OF THIS RECIPE IS THE WHITE RADISH, WHICH HAS A VERY INTERESTING TASTE AND TEXTURE, LIFTED HERE BY THE SEASONING AND A SLIGHTLY ACIDIC SAUCE.

Serves 2 people

INGREDIENTS

For the balls

6 dried shiitake mushrooms
1 tbsp neutral oil
1 carrot, about 100g (3½oz), peeled and cut into small cubes
1 tbsp light soy sauce
1 tsp dark soy sauce
1 tsp fermented black soy bean sauce (*douchi*; see p. 346)
1 tsp white pepper
½ white radish, about 400g (14oz)
1 tbsp salt
2 tbsp finely chopped spring onion (scallion)
1 egg
2 tbsp plain (all-purpose) flour
Herbs of your choice, to serve

For the sauce

1 tbsp soy sauce
1 tbsp white rice vinegar
1 tbsp ketchup
1 tbsp cornflour (cornstarch)
100ml (6½ tbsp) water

FOR THE BALLS

- Rehydrate the dried shiitake in warm water (30°C/86°F) for 1 hour, then chop them into small cubes.

- Heat the oil in a frying pan. Fry the diced carrot and mushrooms for about 2 minutes. Add the soy sauces, black soy bean sauce and white pepper. Mix well, then turn off the heat. Transfer to a large bowl.

- Peel the radish and grate it with a mandoline into fine julienne roughly 5cm (2in) long. Transfer to a large bowl, add the tablespoon of salt and leave to disgorge (see p. 83) for 15 minutes. Wring out as much water as possible from the radish and add it to the carrot and mushroom mixture, then add the spring onion. Stir in the egg, then the flour. The texture should be sticky; if it is too liquid, add a little more flour.

- Shape the mixture into 12 balls with your hands and place them on a plate suitable for your steamer basket. Steam over a high heat for 6 minutes.

FOR THE SAUCE

- Mix all the sauce ingredients together in a pan and cook over a low heat until you have a sauce thick enough to lightly coat the balls.

TO SERVE

- Drizzle the radish balls with the sauce and sprinkle them with your choice of chopped herbs.

GOOD TO KNOW
小提示

As you can see in the photo opposite, I also added some puffed mung bean vermicelli (fried for 5 seconds in oil) to my version of this dish, which adds a little crunchiness to contrast with the tenderness of the radish balls.

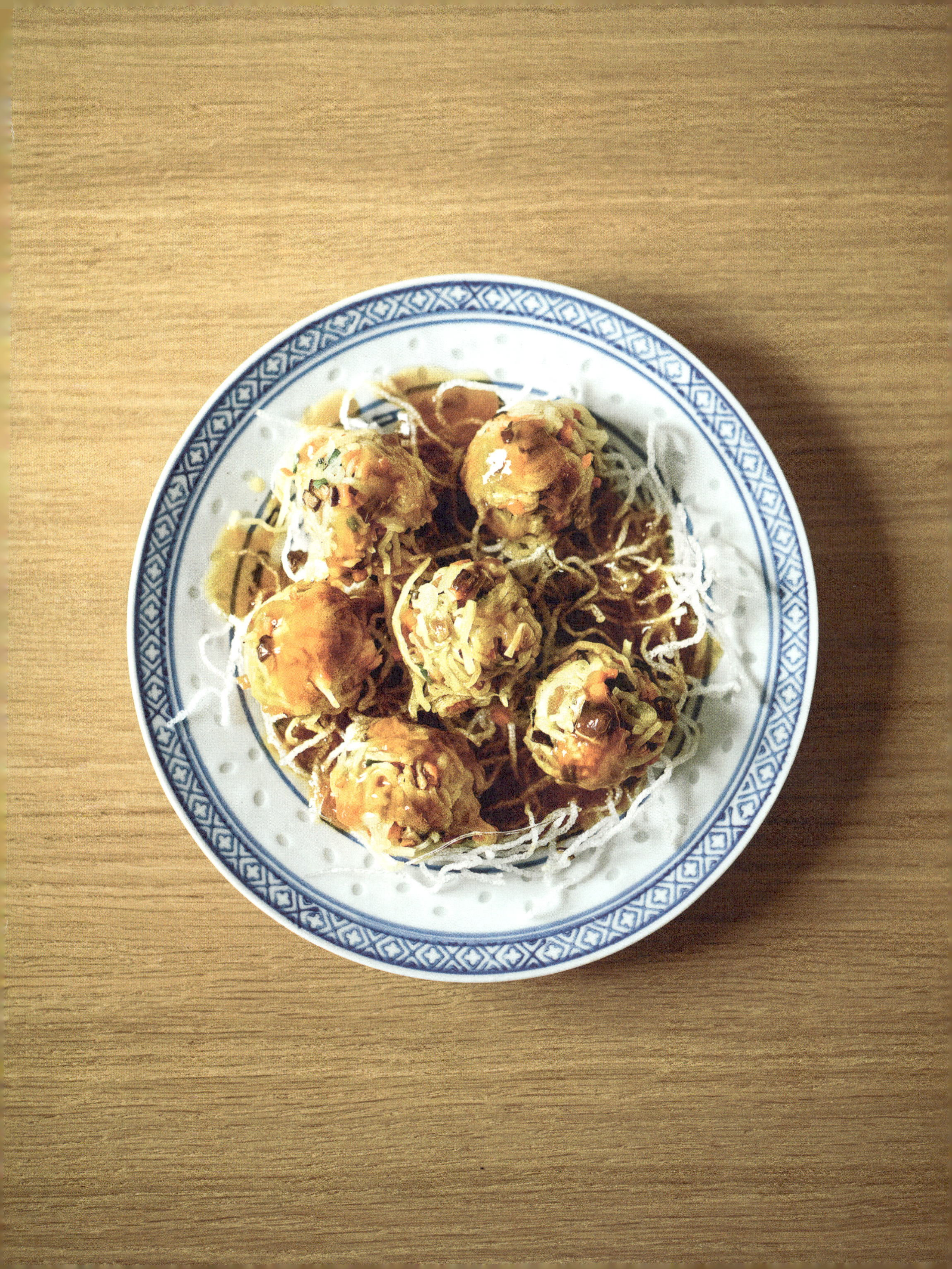

Julienned Potato Salad

TŬ DÒU SĪ

土豆丝

PREPARING 20 MINUTES

COOKING 5 MINUTES

WHEN WAS THE LAST TIME YOU REDISCOVERED THE TASTE OF AN INGREDIENT YOU'D ALWAYS KNOWN? I HOPE THESE FINE, CRUNCHY, TANGY AND SPICY POTATOES WILL DO THAT FOR YOU. THIS WOK-FRIED DISH, WHICH CAN BE FOUND IN ALL RESTAURANTS IN DONGBEI, IN NORTH-EASTERN CHINA, WILL AMAZE YOU.

Serves 2–3 people

INGREDIENTS

2 potatoes, about 300g (10oz)
2 tbsp white vinegar
2 tbsp vegetable oil
½ tsp Sichuan peppercorn
6 dried chilli peppers, halved lengthways and deseeded
1 tsp chopped spring onion (scallion) white
1 tsp black rice vinegar
½ tsp sugar
½ tsp salt
1 tsp chopped spring onion (scallion) green

RECIPE STEPS

- Peel the potatoes and very finely julienne them (see p. 82), using a mandoline or knife. Soak them in water with the white vinegar for 10 minutes. This step both removes excess starch and prevents oxidation.

- Bring a pot of water to the boil and blanch the potatoes over a high heat for 20 seconds; they should become slightly translucent. Rinse immediately with cold water and drain.

- Heat a wok over a medium heat. Once it's hot, pour in the oil, then the Sichuan peppercorn and the dried chilli peppers. Fry for 10 seconds to release their flavours. Add the spring onion white and the potatoes and stir-fry them for 30 seconds over a high heat. Pour in the black rice vinegar, sugar, salt and chopped spring onion green. Stir for a few more seconds to mix everything together. This dish can be enjoyed both hot and cold.

GOOD TO KNOW
小提示

For this recipe, choose a variety of potato with firm flesh: Charlotte, Roseval or Ratte. Don't pick ones that are too small, as it makes it difficult to properly julienne them!

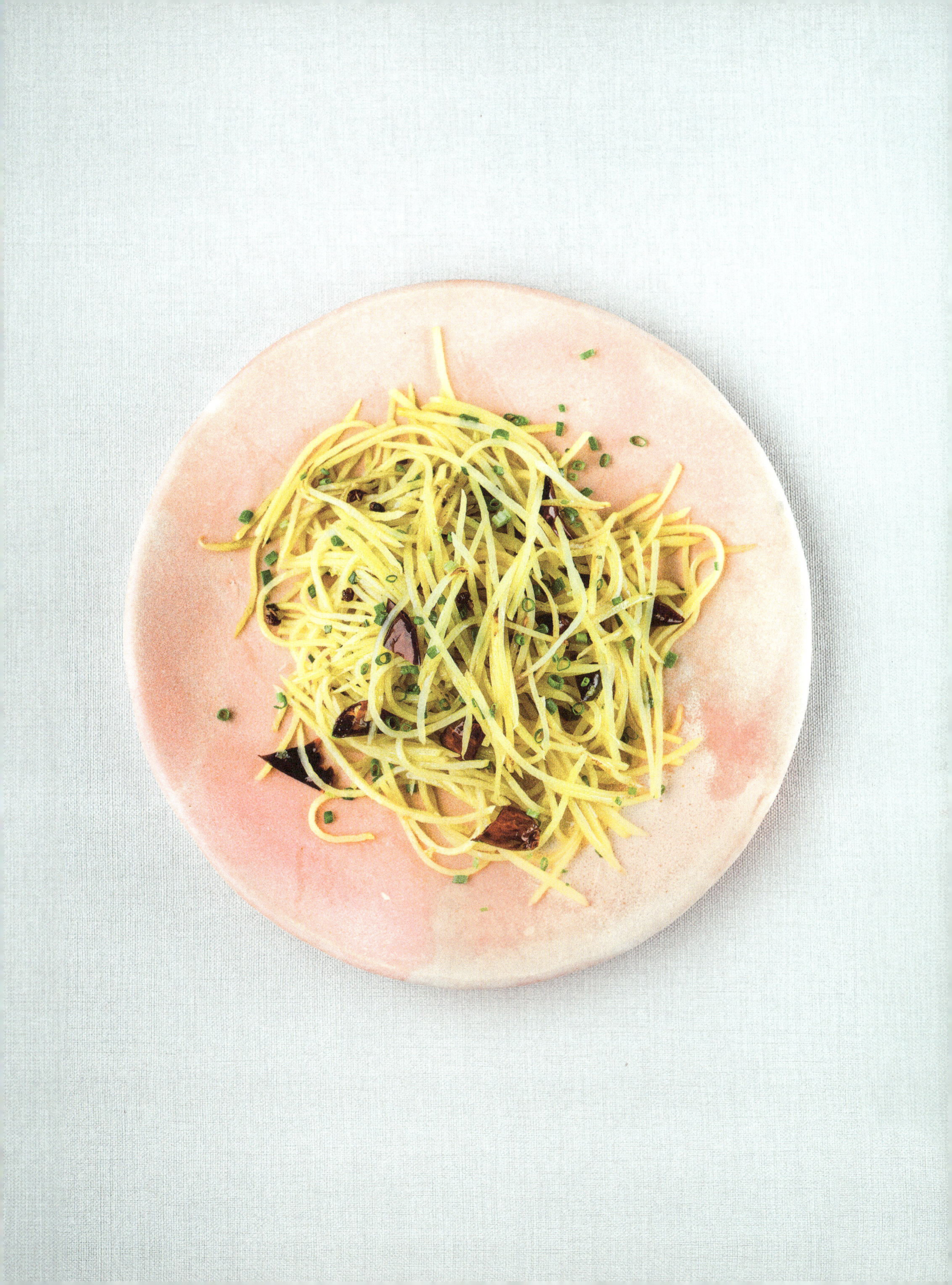

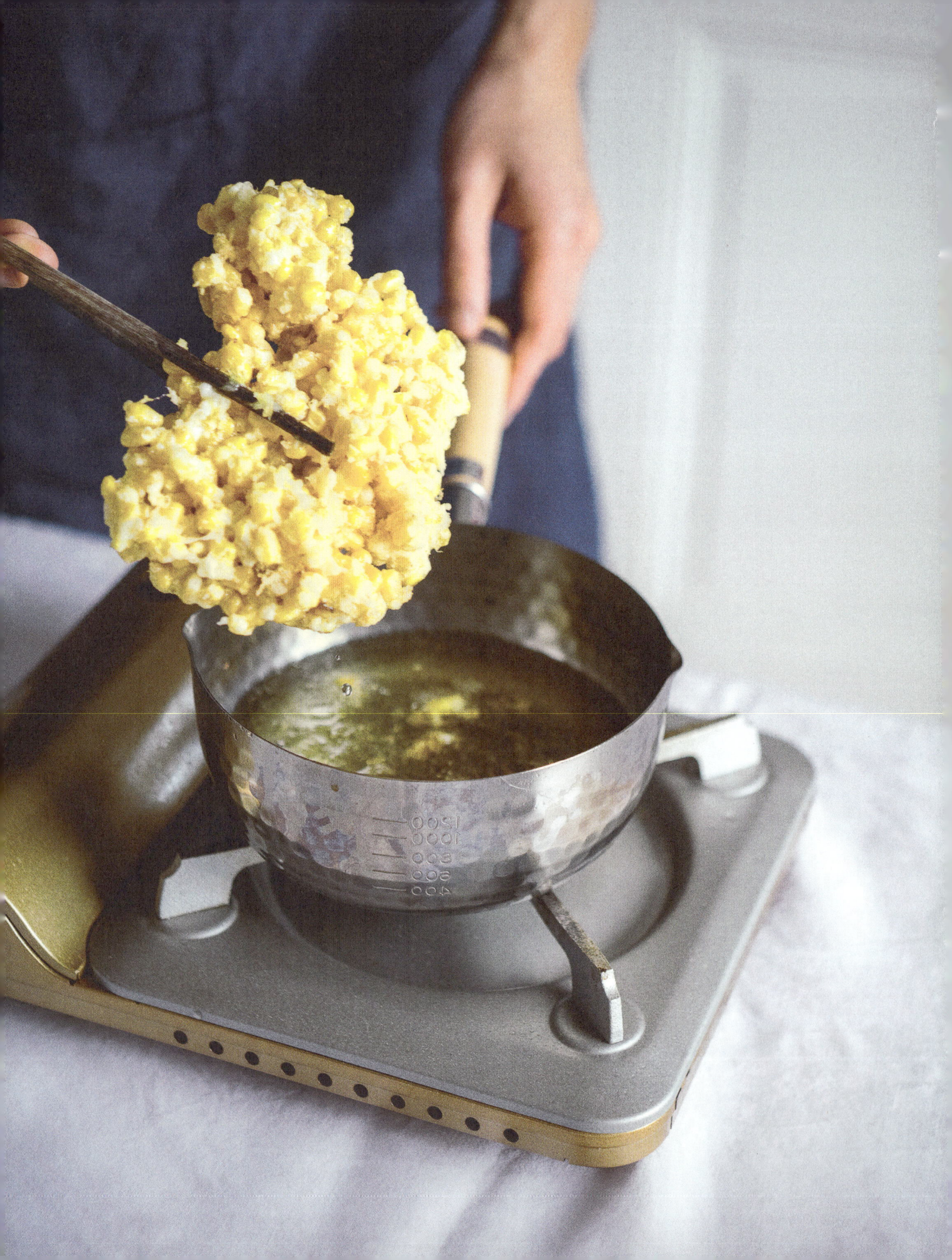

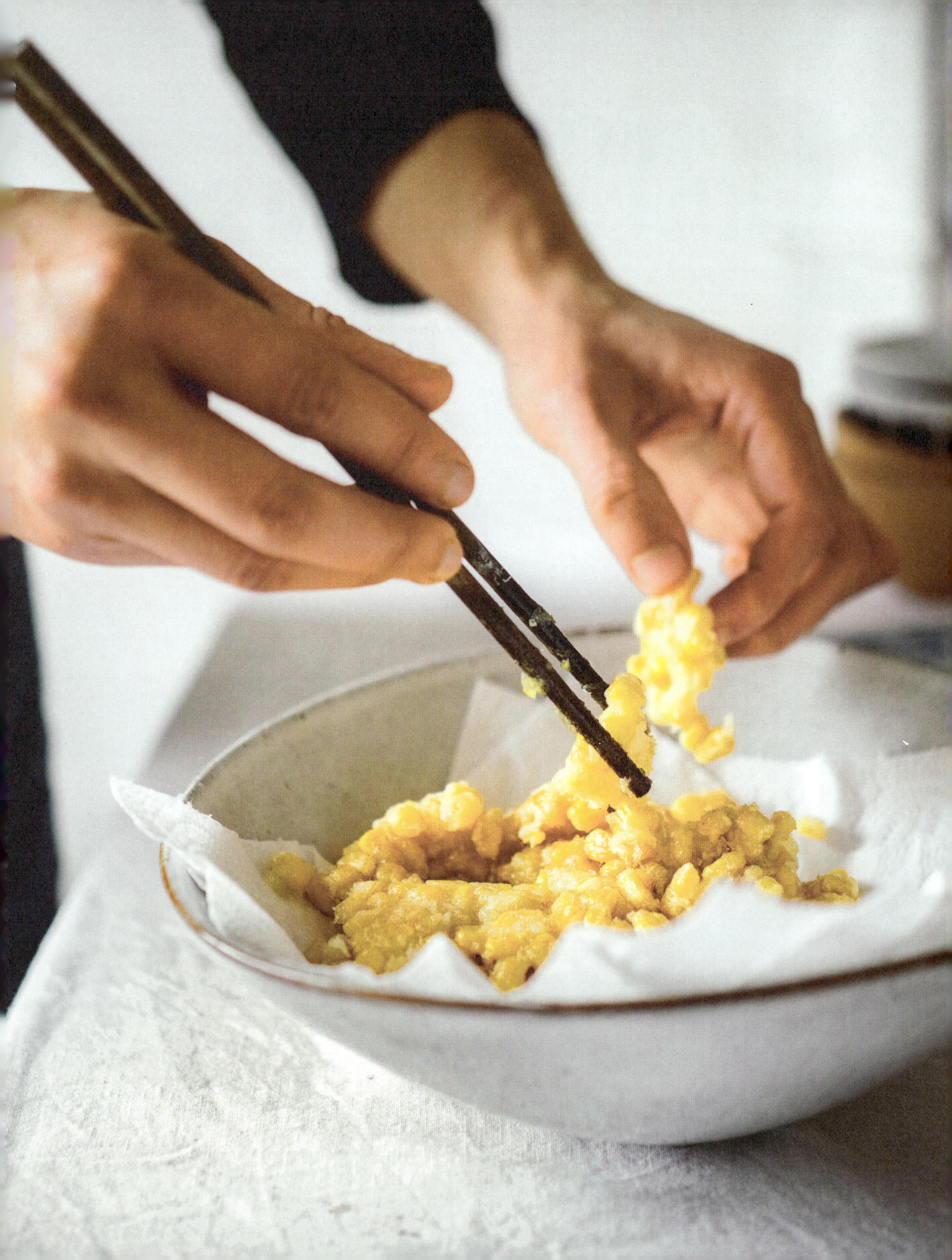

Fried Corn with Pepper and Salt

JIĀO YÁN YÙ MǏ

椒盐玉米

PREPARING 10 MINUTES

COOKING 10 MINUTES

THE FIRST TIME I TRIED THIS DISH AS AN APERITIF, A FRIEND TOLD ME IT WAS REALLY BETTER THAN POPCORN! THEY CAN'T BE COMPARED, BUT THE MIX OF SICHUAN PEPPERCORN AND SALT GOES WELL WITH THE NATURAL SWEET FLAVOUR OF CORN, WHICH IS NICE AND CRUNCHY THANKS TO DOUBLE FRYING. AND DON'T BE SCARED OFF BY THE NUMBER OF STEPS – IT'S ALL DONE VERY QUICKLY!

Serves 2 people

INGREDIENTS

For the corn

300g (10oz) canned sweetcorn (corn), drained
½ egg white
4 tbsp cornflour (cornstarch)
400ml (1¾ cups) neutral oil

For the aromatics

1 tsp chopped spring onion (scallion) white
2 garlic cloves, chopped
1 tsp chopped ginger
Dried chilli peppers (*optional*)

For the seasoning

½ tsp salt
½ tsp Sichuan peppercorn
½ tsp white pepper
½ tsp sugar

To serve

Chopped spring onion (scallion)

RECIPE STEPS

- Mix the seasoning ingredients together in a bowl and set aside.

- Mix the drained corn with the egg white. Sprinkle with the cornflour as you go, adding it in batches to avoid lumps.

- Pour the oil into a pot and heat to 180°C (350°F). Add half the corn kernels to the pot and fry for 1 minute, then remove them to a plate covered with kitchen paper and repeat the process with the remaining corn. (Frying is done in two batches to prevent the corn from clumping together.)

- Increase the temperature of the oil to 195°C (383°F) and fry the first batch of corn again, this time for 15 seconds. Repeat with the remaining corn and set aside.

FOR THE STIR-FRYING

- Heat a wok over a high heat and pour in ½ tablespoon of oil, just enough for the surface of the wok to be shiny. Add the aromatics, except the chilli peppers, and stir-fry for 10 seconds, then add the chilli peppers (if using) and stir-fry for a few seconds to release the flavours.

- Now add the corn and seasoning and continue cooking for 1 minute. Serve sprinkled with a little chopped spring onion.

GOOD TO KNOW
小提示

Thanks to the double frying, the corn will be particularly crispy.

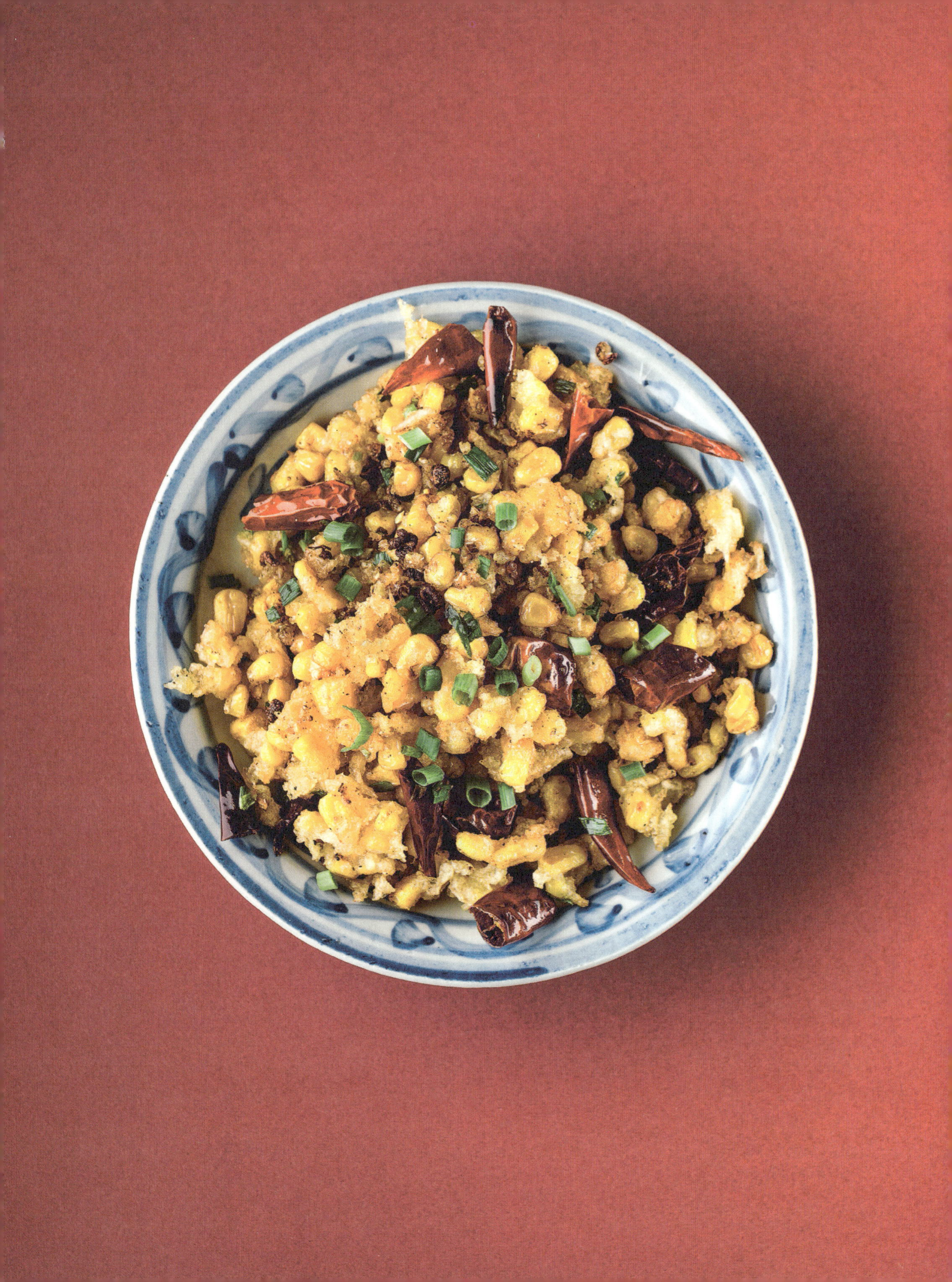

CHAPTER
04

Tofu
豆腐
DÒU FU

PP. 120-121: Tofu skin salad with red radishes ■ **PP. 122-123**: Silken tofu with century egg
PP. 126-127: Mapo tofu ■ **PP. 128-129**: Mr Jiang tofu ■ **PP. 130-131**: 5-spice tofu
PP. 132-133: Prawn-stuffed tofu ■ **PP. 134-135**: Silken steamed tofu with ham ■ **PP. 136-137**: Tofu "jerky"

From All Angles

Like a White Canvas

IN THE WEST, TOFU TENDS TO BE SEEN AS A MEAT SUBSTITUTE, WHOSE EXCLUSIVE INTEREST REMAINS ITS PROTEIN CONTRIBUTION IN A VEGETARIAN OR VEGAN DIET. YET IT IS ONE OF THE MOST VERSATILE PRODUCTS THERE IS. IT HAS AN INFINITE NUMBER OF SHAPES, TASTES AND TEXTURES.

MAKING TOFU: FROM THE BEAN TO THE FINISHED ARTICLE

Tofu is made from peeled soy beans that are ground and boiled to make soy milk.

A salted coagulant is added to curdle the milk. The mixture is then transferred to a fabric-covered mould and pressed to form a block. The tofu's texture will depend on the amount of water it contains. Silken tofu contains a lot of water, as it hardly gets pressed, while firm tofu contains much less.

• In Southern China, gypsum (or calcium sulphate), a natural mineral derived from rock sediments, is used, hence its Chinese name *shí gāo* (石膏), which means "stone plaster".

• In Northern China, magnesium chloride, better known as *nigari* or *lu shui* (卤水), a white powder extracted from seawater, is preferred. This northern tofu is supposed to be firmer.

• It is also possible to use an acidic agent such as gluconolactone, which will produce a very fine, tender tofu that is ideal to make the silken version (内脂豆腐, *nèi zhī dòu fu*).

CHOOSING THE RIGHT TEXTURE

SILKEN TOFU (嫩豆腐)

Silken tofu is delicate and has a texture akin to a flan or panna cotta. It can be eaten directly, with no preparation. I use it either in a quick salad recipe with a dash of soy sauce (p. 24) or I add it to a broth towards the end of the cooking process. The fresh version (豆花, *dòu huā*) is served warm for breakfast in much of Southern China, with various savoury or sweet seasonings.

MEDIUM OR SOFT TOFU (嫩豆腐)

This type of tofu is ideal if you are looking for a soft texture that remains easy to handle. I use it mainly in braised dishes like mapo tofu (p. 126) or I fry it in a pan with a drop of oil to obtain a grilled crust and a soft interior.

FIRM TOFU (卤水豆腐)

The basic white tofu and probably the most versatile. Its firm texture allows it to withstand any type of cooking, most notably wok cooking. I use it in my twice-cooked tofu jerky recipe (fried then braised, p. 136).

A FEW VARIANTS

5-SPICE TOFU (五香豆腐)

Firm or extra-firm tofu that is simmered in a broth made with soy sauce and spices. Once cooled, it is cut into blocks, sliced or julienned. Cooking gives it a caramel colour and a subtly salty and fragrant taste.

FRIED TOFU (油豆腐, 豆腐泡)

This is sold as cubes, triangles or sticks. The exterior is browned and slightly rubbery, while the interior is light and fluffy.

FERMENTED TOFU (豆腐乳)

Furu is a Chinese speciality that is quite rare in other countries. It is a soft tofu whose texture is akin to feta cheese, with a salty and umami taste.

TOFU SKIN (豆腐皮)

This is the thin layer that forms when cooking soy milk. Fresh tofu skin can be tricky to find in the West, but it is available in its dried form, in various shapes (sheets, tubes, knots...), which must be rehydrated before use.

GOOD TO KNOW
小提示

You could compare tofu to cheese, both in its production process and number of varieties. Tofu reflects regional diversity and the creativity of women and men spanning more than 2,000 years.

TOFU FOR ALL OCCASIONS

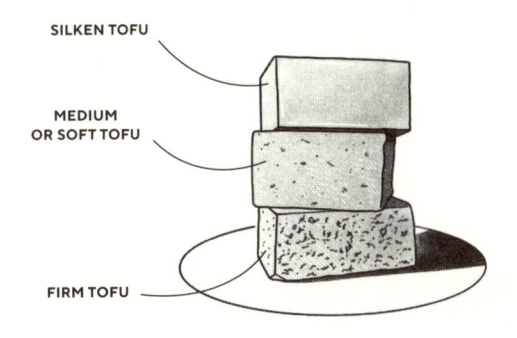

SILKEN TOFU

MEDIUM OR SOFT TOFU

FIRM TOFU

GOOD TO KNOW
小提示

Firm tofu can easily be frozen. Thawing it creates a spongy texture thanks to the expansion of the water as it solidifies, which is perfect for absorbing the liquid in a broth.

PLAIN TOFU
豆腐 | DÒU FU

FRIED TOFU
油豆腐 | YÓU DÒU FU

Perfect in soups, which highlight its spongy texture. It can also be stuffed (p. 132).

5-SPICE TOFU
五香豆腐 | WǓ XIĀNG DÒU FU

Ideal for making a quick stir-fried dish with minimal seasoning (p. 130).

TOFU SKIN
豆腐皮 | DÒU FU PÍ

A variant that works well in salads (p. 120).

FERMENTED TOFU
腐乳 | FǓ RǓ

Used as a garnish to accompany congee or as a condiment in a marinade or sauce.

Tofu Skin Salad with Red Radishes

LIÁNG BÀN FǓ ZHÚ

凉拌腐竹

PREPARING 100 MINUTES · COOKING 5 MINUTES

TOFU SKIN IS THE THIN LAYER THAT FORMS ON THE SURFACE OF SOY MILK DURING ITS PRODUCTION. IT IS USUALLY FOUND IN FROZEN OR DEHYDRATED FORM (THE FROZEN VERSION TASTES BETTER). IT HAS AN AMAZING TEXTURE NOT UNLIKE MEAT. IT HAS BEEN USED IN VEGETARIAN DISHES IN CHINA FOR HUNDREDS OF YEARS.

Serves 4 people

INGREDIENTS

For the tofu skin

- 80g (3oz) dried tofu skin (*see p. 118*)
- 1 litre (4⅓ cups) water
- 60g (2oz) red radishes, washed and thinly sliced with a mandoline or knife

For the sauce

- ½ tsp chopped garlic
- 1 tsp chopped spring onion (scallion)
- 2 tbsp neutral oil
- 1 tbsp soy sauce
- ½ tsp salt
- 1 tsp black rice vinegar
- 1 tsp Sichuan peppercorn oil
- 2 tsp chilli oil

To serve

Chopped coriander (cilantro)

FOR THE TOFU SKIN

- In a large bowl, soak the tofu skin in water for at least 1 hour to rehydrate. It is ready when no part of it feels hard to the touch.

- Bring the measured water to a simmer in a pot. Cook the tofu skin for 2 minutes over a medium heat, then drain on kitchen paper and set aside.

FOR THE SAUCE

- Mix the garlic and spring onion together in a bowl. Heat the neutral oil in a pan until it starts to lightly smoke, then immediately pour it into the bowl to release the flavours of the aromatics. Add the remaining sauce ingredients and mix well.

TO FINISH

- Add the tofu skin and radishes to the sauce bowl. Adjust the seasoning (spices, salt or vinegar) to taste. Marinate for at least 30 minutes in the fridge so that the tofu skin can absorb all the sauce.

- Sprinkle with a little coriander just before serving.

GOOD TO KNOW
小提示

The sauce can be modified to taste. Sichuan peppercorn oil can be replaced with sesame oil, and black rice vinegar with balsamic vinegar.

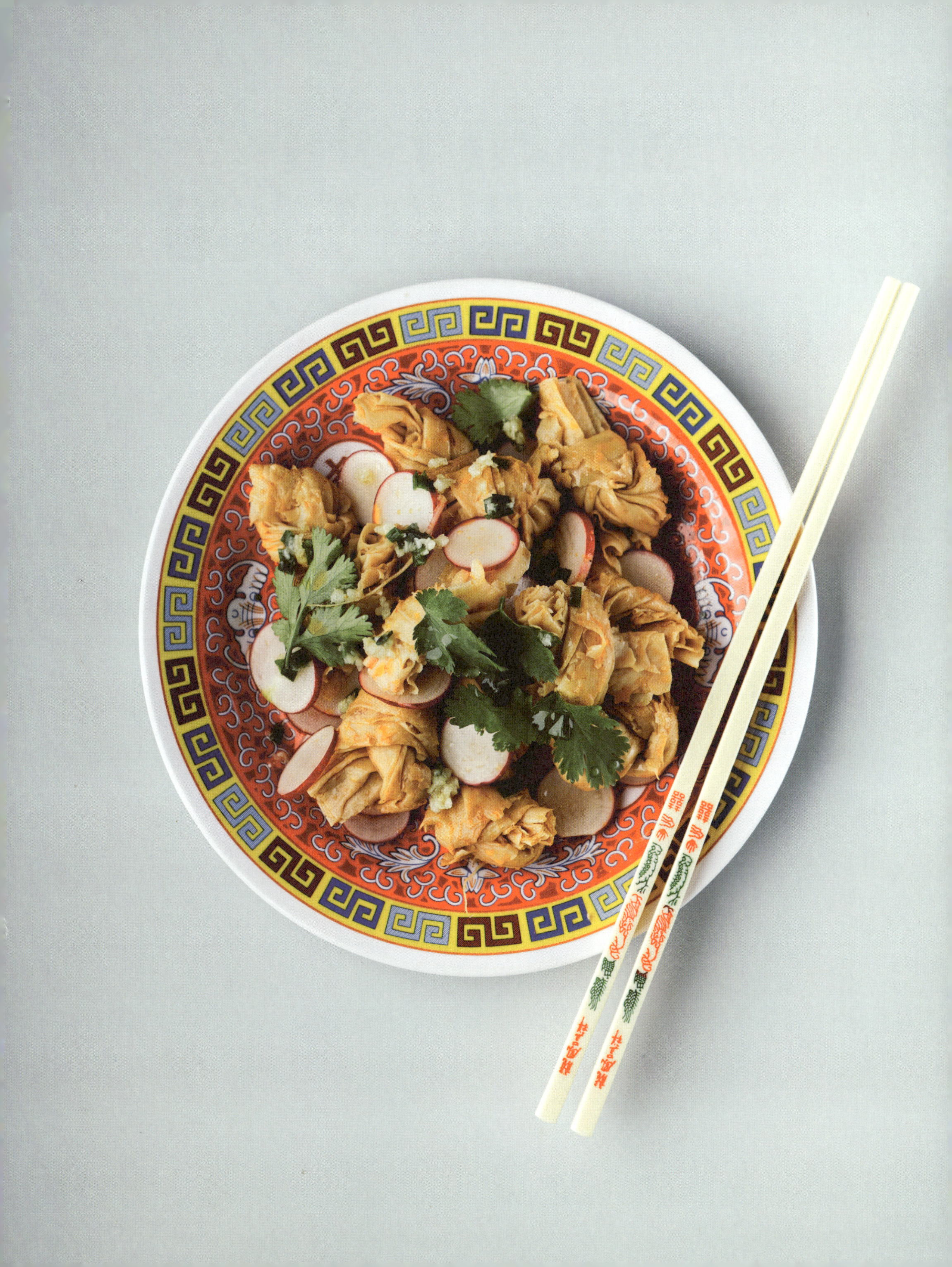

Silken Tofu with Century Egg

LIÁNG BÀN PÍ DÀN DÒU FU

凉拌皮蛋豆腐

PREPARING 10 MINUTES

COOKING 1 MINUTE

A CLASSIC RECIPE THAT IS TENDER, FRESH AND FULL OF UMAMI TO "COOK" THE SILKEN TOFU, WHICH IS USUALLY ENJOYED WITHOUT COOKING. FOR A STRONGER FLAVOUR, DO NOT HESITATE TO DOUSE IT WITH CHILLI OIL. ALSO, IF YOU HAVE NEVER TASTED CENTURY EGGS, THIS IS THE PERFECT DISH TO GIVE THEM A TRY!

Serves 2 people

INGREDIENTS

1 silken tofu block, about 500g (1lb 2oz)
1 century egg (see p. 140)
2 garlic cloves, chopped
1 tbsp chopped spring onion (scallion), plus a little extra to serve
2 tbsp neutral oil
2 tbsp soy sauce
2 tsp sesame oil
1 tsp dried mini shrimp (*xia pi*, optional)

RECIPE STEPS

- Remove the silken tofu from its packaging. To get perfect results, try to mimic the method for unmoulding a flan: make a small hole in each corner of the packaging to let the air escape, remove the lid, then flip the packaging over onto your serving plate and tap the top lightly. The tofu should slip out on its own.

- Cut the century egg into quarters with a knife, or here's a tip: use (unflavoured) dental floss to get cleaner results. Place the wedges on the tofu, then top with the garlic and spring onion.

- Heat the oil in a frying pan until it starts to smoke lightly, then pour this over the garlic and spring onion to release their flavours. Add the soy sauce, sesame oil and a few dried mini shrimp (see p. 32), if you like, to add some umami flavour. Finish with a scattering of spring onion.

GOOD TO KNOW
小提示

Century eggs remain a mystery to some, due to their unusual appearance and Western name. See p. 140 to learn more about this type of egg, which is obviously not a century old!

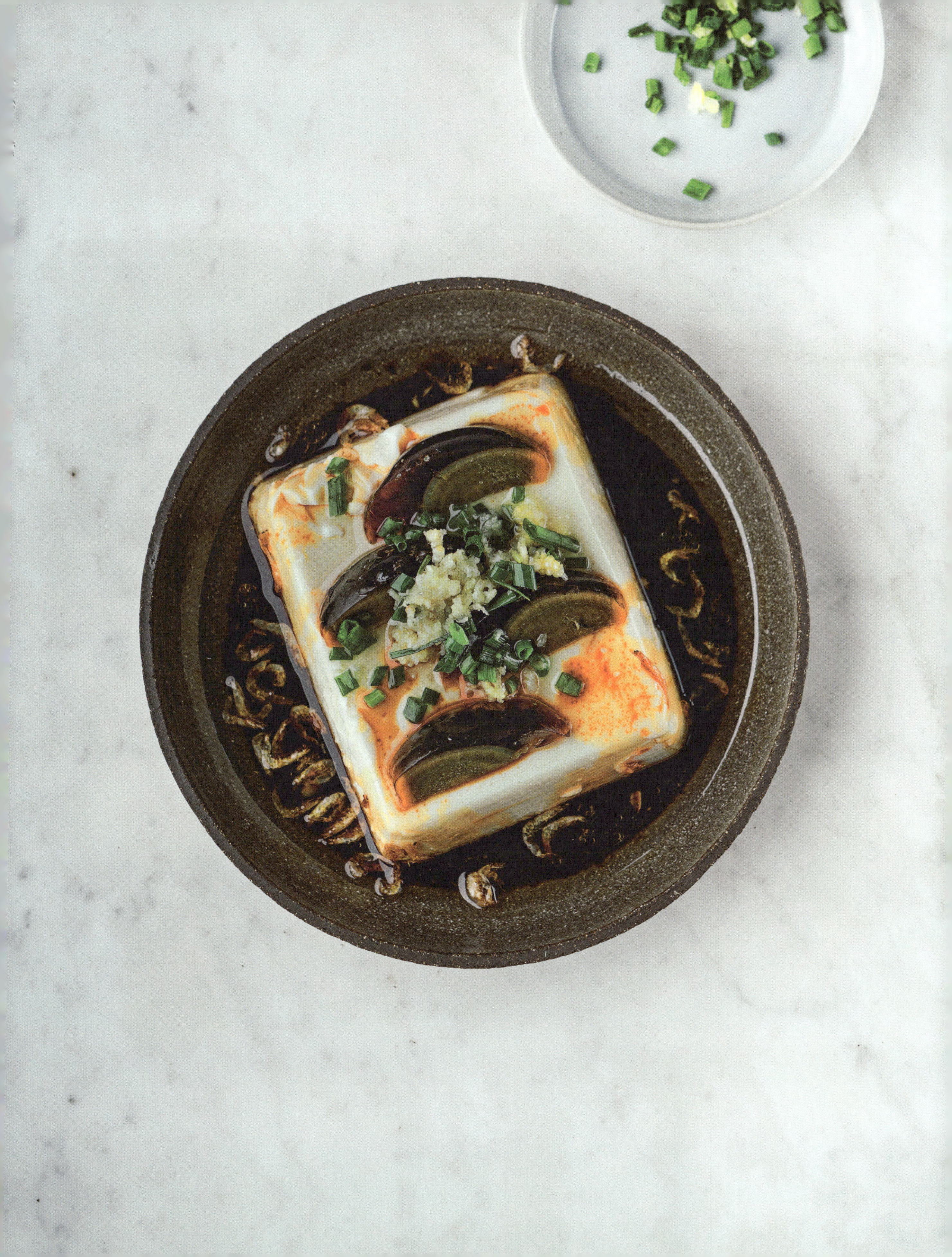

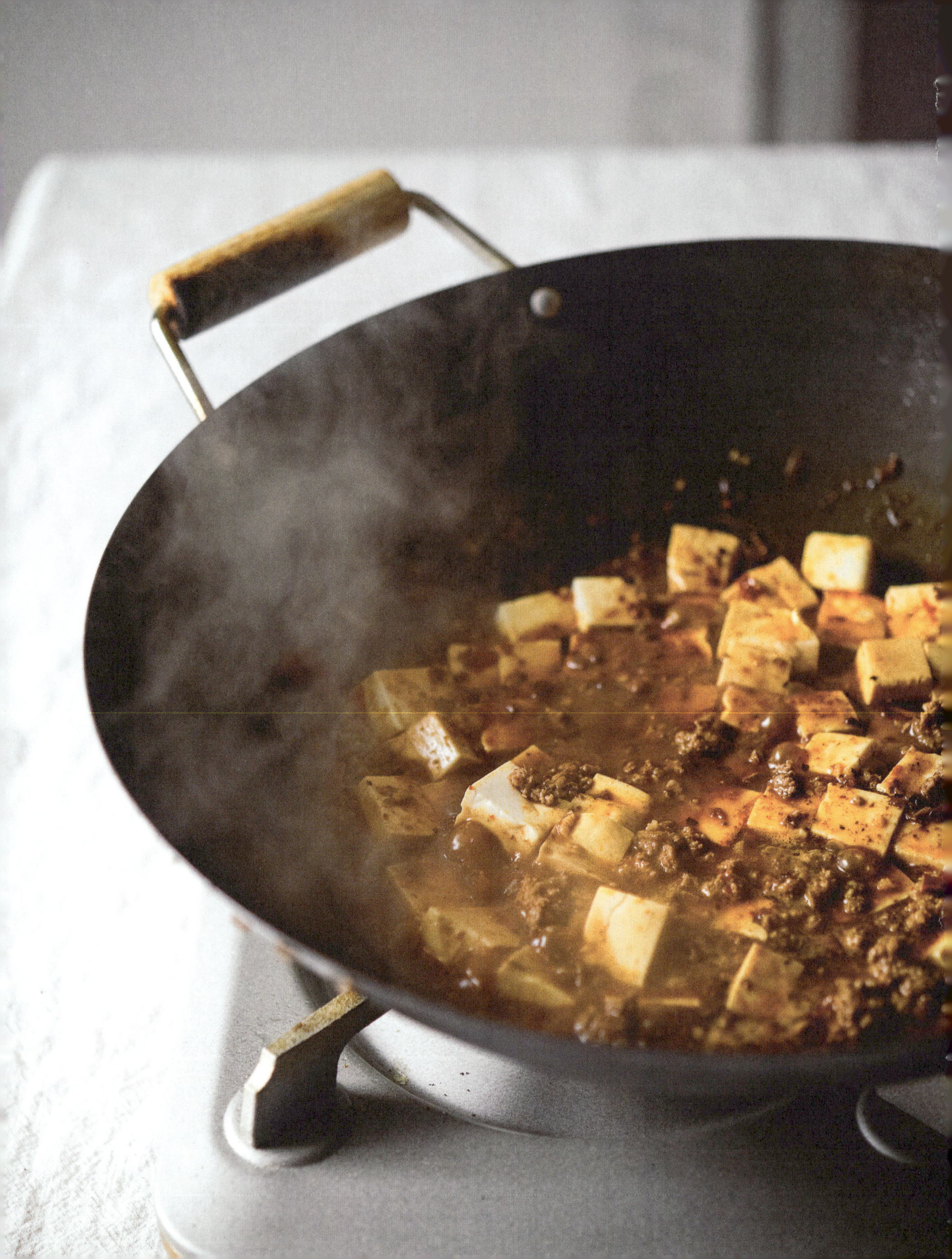

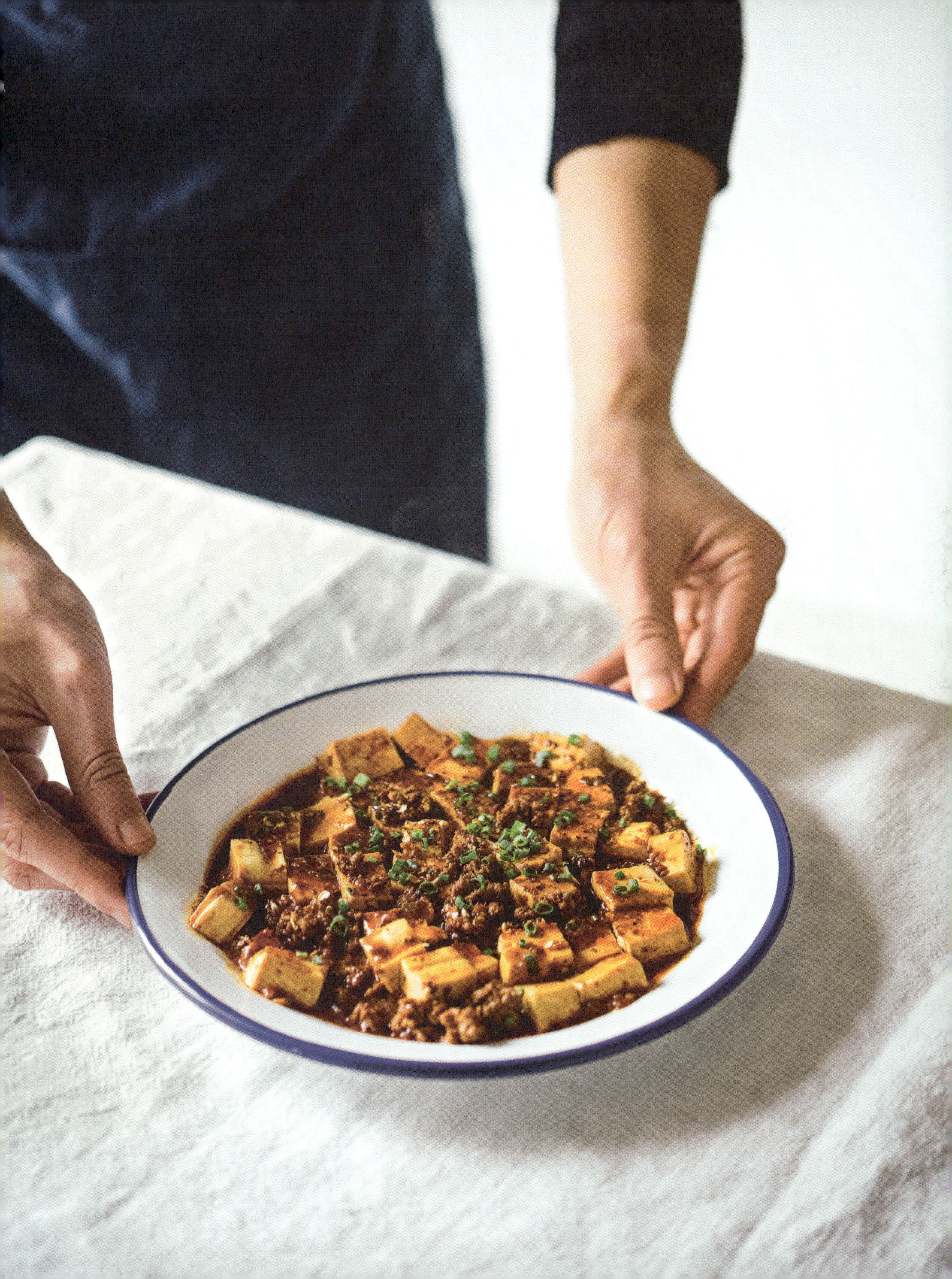

Mapo Tofu

MÁ PÓ DÒU FU

麻婆豆腐

PREPARING 5 MINUTES

COOKING 15 MINUTES

THERE ARE ALMOST AS MANY VERSIONS AS COOKS OF THIS SICHUAN DISH, WHICH IS ONE OF THE MOST FAMOUS RECIPES IN THE WORLD. MY VERSION IS INSPIRED BY THE ORIGINAL CHEN MAPO RECIPE, WHO IS SAID TO HAVE CREATED MAPO TOFU IN HIS SMALL RESTAURANT IN CHENGDU IN 1862.

Serves 4 people

INGREDIENTS

For the tofu

1 soft tofu block, about 500g (1lb 2oz), cut into 2cm (¾in) cubes
1 tbsp light soy sauce
1 tbsp neutral oil
80g (3oz) minced (ground) beef
½ tsp white pepper
Salt

For the sauce

2 tbsp neutral oil
1 tbsp chilli bean paste (*doubanjiang, see p. 36*)
2 garlic cloves, minced
1 tbsp fermented black soy bean sauce (*douchi, see p. 346*)
½ tbsp chilli powder
1 tsp soy sauce
150ml (⅔ cup) unsalted broth
2 tsp cornflour (cornstarch)
2 tbsp water

To serve

1 tbsp chopped spring onion (scallion)
1 tbsp Sichuan peppercorn

RECIPE STEPS

- Bring a large volume of water to the boil in a wok, add the tofu, 1 tablespoon of salt and the light soy sauce. Switch to a medium heat and blanch for 1 minute, then drain and set aside.

- Heat the wok over a medium heat and pour in the oil. When it starts to smoke, add the minced beef, ½ teaspoon of salt and the white pepper. Break the meat into small pieces with a spatula and fry for about 2 minutes until completely cooked, then remove from the wok and set aside.

FOR THE SAUCE

- Clean the wok and set it over a medium heat with the 2 tablespoons of oil. Pour in the chilli bean paste and fry it while stirring to release its flavour, about 10 seconds. Add the garlic, fermented soy bean sauce and chilli powder (see p. 36; I use the Chao Tian Jiao variety) and stir-fry for a few seconds without letting it burn.

- Gently add the tofu cubes to the wok, then the beef, soy sauce and broth (meat or vegetable-based, but unsalted; or use water if you don't have any broth). Bring to the boil, then switch to a low heat and let the tofu simmer in the sauce for 5 minutes.

- Mix the cornflour with the water, then add this mixture to the wok in three batches to gradually thicken the sauce until it coats the tofu.

- Transfer to a shallow dish and sprinkle with the chopped spring onion and Sichuan peppercorn to serve.

GOOD TO KNOW
小提示

I slightly decreased the amount of chilli pepper compared to the original recipe. Feel free to adjust the doubanjiang *and chilli powder quantity to taste. For a vegetarian version, replace the meat with shiitake.*

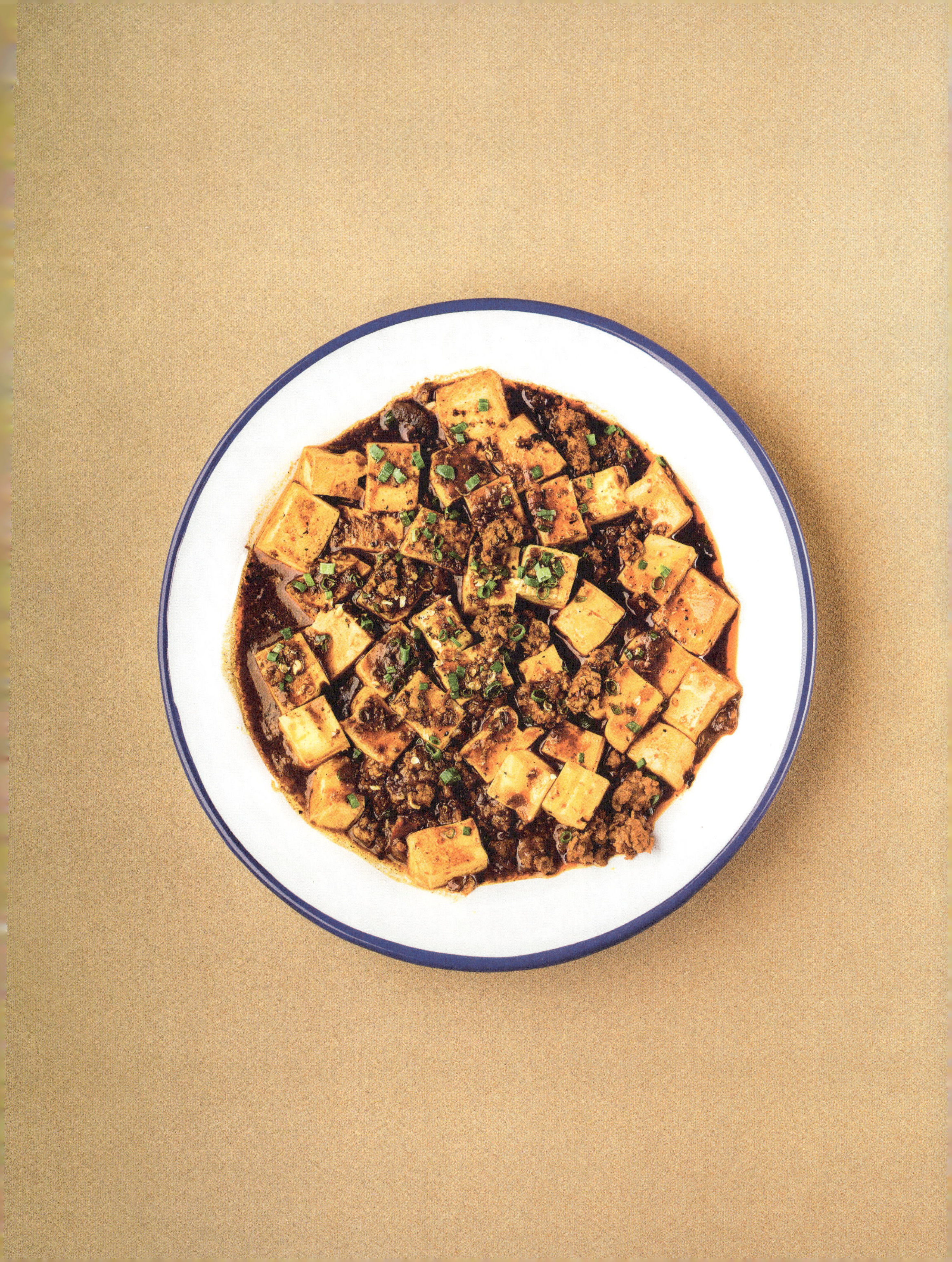

Mr Jiang Tofu

JIĂNG   SHÌ   LÁNG   DÒU   FU

蒋侍郎豆腐

PREPARING 20 MINUTES

COOKING 30 MINUTES

THIS RECIPE COMES FROM THE FAMOUS GASTRONOMY TREATISE *RECIPES FROM THE GARDEN OF CONTENTMENT* (随园食单), PUBLISHED IN 1792 BY POET YUAN MEI. AN EPICUREAN AND FINE OBSERVER OF THE CULINARY PRACTICES OF HIS TIME, HE HAD A PARTICULAR PASSION FOR TOFU AND THE SIMPLICITY OF GOOD PRODUCE.

Serves 4 people

INGREDIENTS

20 dried shrimp (*xia mi*)
2 tbsp lard or neutral oil
1 firm tofu block, about 500g (1lb 2oz), cut into 1cm (½in) squares
200g (7oz) fermented sticky rice (*jiu niang*, see p. 38)
100ml (6½ tbsp) water
2 tbsp light soy sauce
1 tsp cornflour (cornstarch)
Spring onion (scallion), cut into sticks, to serve

RECIPE STEPS

- Rehydrate the dried shrimp in a bowl of water. Meanwhile, add the lard (or oil) to a pan over a medium heat, then add the tofu. Brown it on one side for about 3 minutes, then repeat on the other side. (If you find that there is too much oil, you can wipe it off at the end of cooking with kitchen paper.)

- Drain the shrimp and add them to the pan.

- Put the fermented sticky rice in a sieve (strainer) over a bowl to collect the liquid, pressing well to collect each drop. Pour this liquid into the pan, then add the water.

- Simmer over a low heat for 30 minutes so that the tofu can soak up the flavours. There should still be some liquid left at the end of cooking.

- Mix together the soy sauce and cornflour and pour evenly over the tofu. Let the sauce thicken a little for about 30 seconds, then turn off the heat.

- Serve with a sprinkle of spring onion.

GOOD TO KNOW
小提示

Fermented sticky rice (see p. 38) and dried shrimp (see p. 32) can be found in any Chinese supermarket. To make lard yourself, see p. 344.

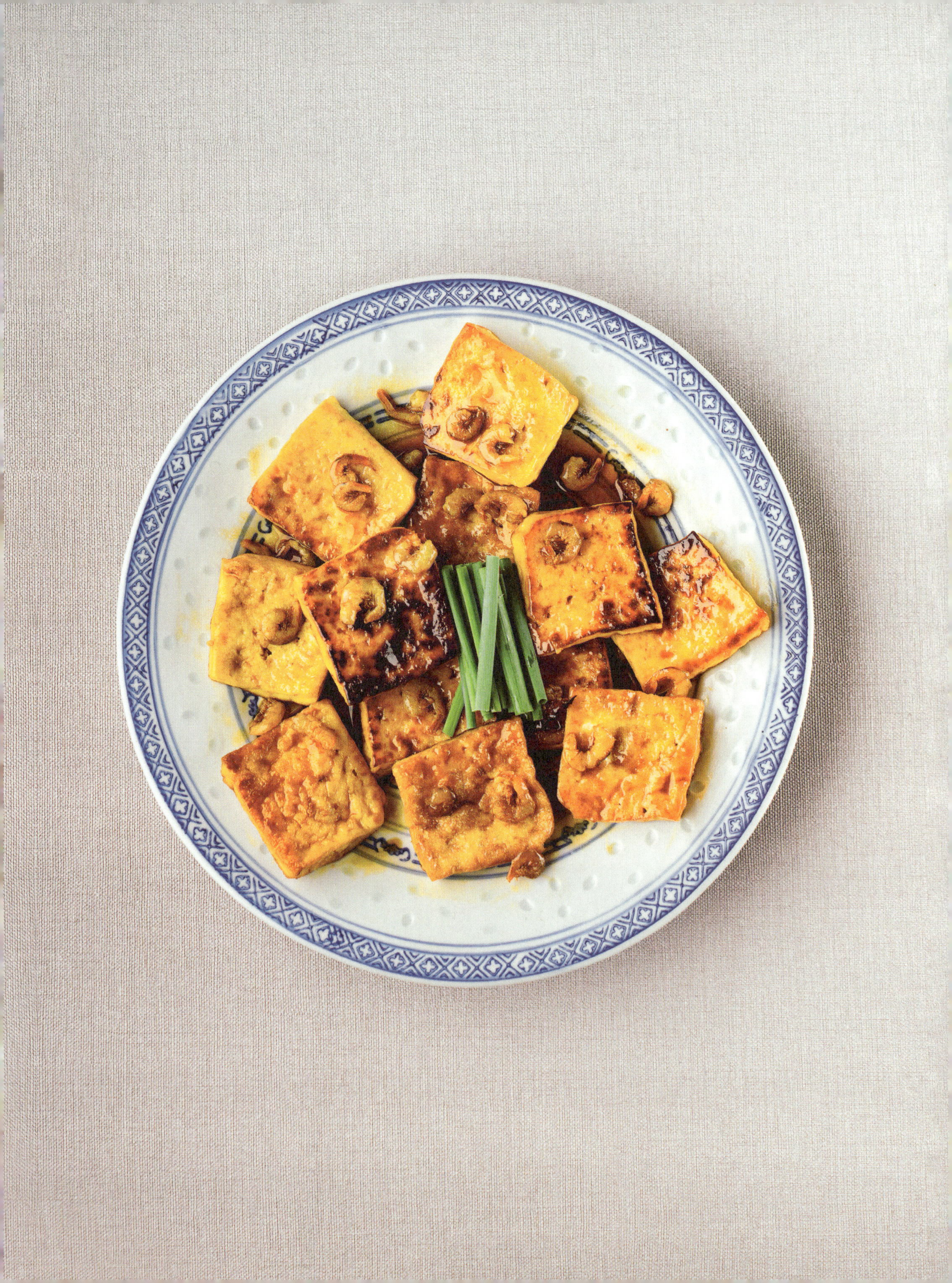

5-Spice Tofu

WǓ   XIĀNG   DÒU   FU

五香豆腐

PREPARING 5 MINUTES

COOKING 5 MINUTES

FRAGRANT TOFU, SOY SAUCE AND FRESH HERBS. AN INCREDIBLY SIMPLE AND QUICK DISH THAT IS ALWAYS UNANIMOUSLY LIKED AT THE TABLE.

Serves 4 people

INGREDIENTS

250g (9oz) 5-spice tofu in your preferred shape (*see p. 118*)
1 tbsp neutral oil
1 tsp sesame oil
2 tsp light soy sauce
1 handful of coriander (cilantro), chopped
1 tsp toasted white sesame seeds (*optional*)
White pepper and salt

RECIPE STEPS

- Rinse the tofu with cold water and drain well. Set aside.

- Heat a wok over a high heat. As soon as it starts smoking, pour in the neutral oil, then add the tofu. Fry for 1 minute over a medium heat.

- Pour in the sesame oil, then the soy sauce. Continue cooking for another 30 seconds, then add salt to taste. If you prefer a slightly more toasted tofu, extend the cooking time to 1–2 minutes.

- Turn off the heat and stir in the chopped coriander (leaves and stems). Add some white pepper and finally the toasted white sesame seeds. This dish can be enjoyed both hot and cold.

GOOD TO KNOW
小提示

5-spice tofu can be presented in different forms (see p. 118). For this recipe, I prefer to finely julienne it. If you don't like coriander (cilantro), replace it with a herb of your choice. I like to add Thai basil or tarragon to this dish.

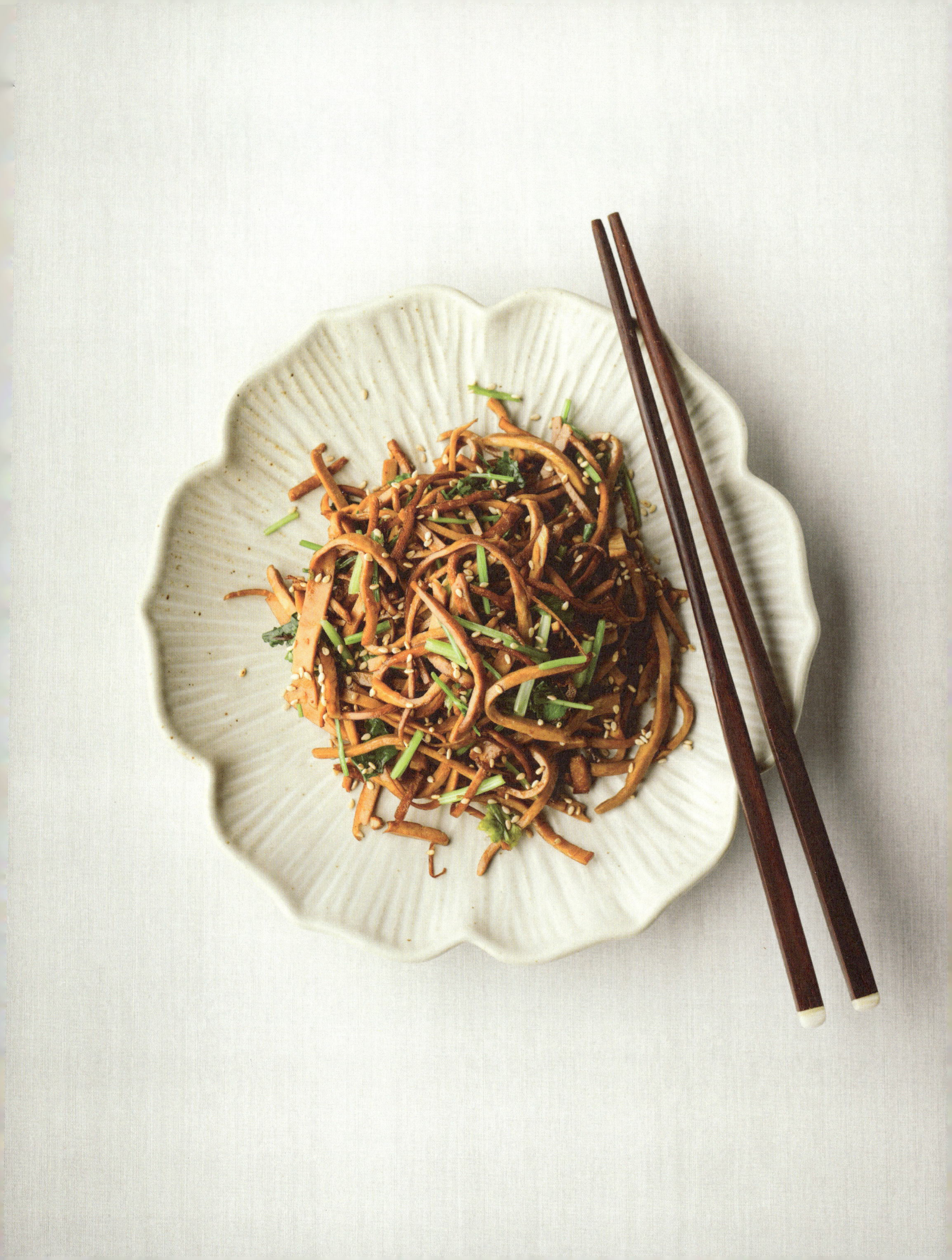

Prawn-Stuffed Tofu

XIĀ   HUÁ   NIÀNG   YÓU   DÒU   FU

虾滑酿油豆腐

PREPARING 20 MINUTES

COOKING 10 MINUTES

MY MOTHER WOULD STUFF THESE FRIED TOFU POCKETS WITH PORK AND SHIITAKE, AND WOULD THEN STEAM THEM. IT WAS DELICIOUS. THIS VERSION IS A PERSONAL REINTERPRETATION, WHICH COMBINES THE CRUNCHINESS OF WATER CHESTNUTS AND THE TENDERNESS OF PRAWNS.

🍴 Makes 8 tofu pockets

INGREDIENTS

For the tofu

30g (1oz) water chestnuts, cut into small cubes
120g (4¼oz) raw peeled prawns (shrimp), roughly chopped
2 tsp chopped shiso leaf, plus extra to serve
¼ tsp salt
¼ tsp Sichuan peppercorn
½ tsp sugar
½ tsp sesame oil
8 fried tofu pockets
½ tbsp neutral oil

For the sauce

½ tsp sugar
½ tsp soy sauce
1 tsp oyster sauce
½ tsp sesame oil
100ml (6½ tbsp) water
½ tbsp neutral oil
1 tsp fermented black soy bean sauce (douchi; optional)
1 tbsp cornflour (cornstarch) mixed with 3 tbsp water

FOR THE FRIED TOFU

- Prepare the stuffing: mix the water chestnuts and raw prawns in a bowl, add the chopped shiso, salt, Sichuan peppercorn, sugar and sesame oil.

- Using a small knife, cut a cross on one side of each of the fried tofu pieces, then push the flesh slightly inward with your finger to free up space for stuffing. Be careful not to puncture the pockets. Fill them with the stuffing, without letting the mixture overflow.

- Heat a non-stick pan over a medium heat and pour in the neutral oil. Once it becomes hot, add the stuffed tofu pockets, stuffing-side down, and let them brown for about 1 minute. If they stick a little, slide a spatula underneath to release them. Flip the pockets over and continue cooking for another minute, then remove from the pan and set aside.

FOR THE SAUCE

- Mix the sugar, soy sauce, oyster sauce and sesame oil with the 6½ tablespoons of water in a bowl.

- Heat the (wiped out) tofu pan over a medium heat and add the neutral oil. Once hot, pour in the fermented soy bean sauce (*douchi*) and stir-fry quickly to release the flavours, about 20 seconds. Add the soy sauce mixture, bring to the boil, then lower the heat. Add the stuffed tofu, cover and cook for 5 minutes, then turn off the heat.

TO SERVE

- Arrange the tofu pockets on a shallow plate. Reheat the sauce in the pan over a medium heat and stir in the cornflour and water mixture to create a thicker sauce. Pour the sauce into the dish and finish with a scattering of chopped shiso.

GOOD TO KNOW
小提示

Douchi sauce (see p. 346) is made from fermented black soy beans. If you don't have any, just increase the oyster sauce quantity. Frozen water chestnuts can be found in all Chinese supermarkets.

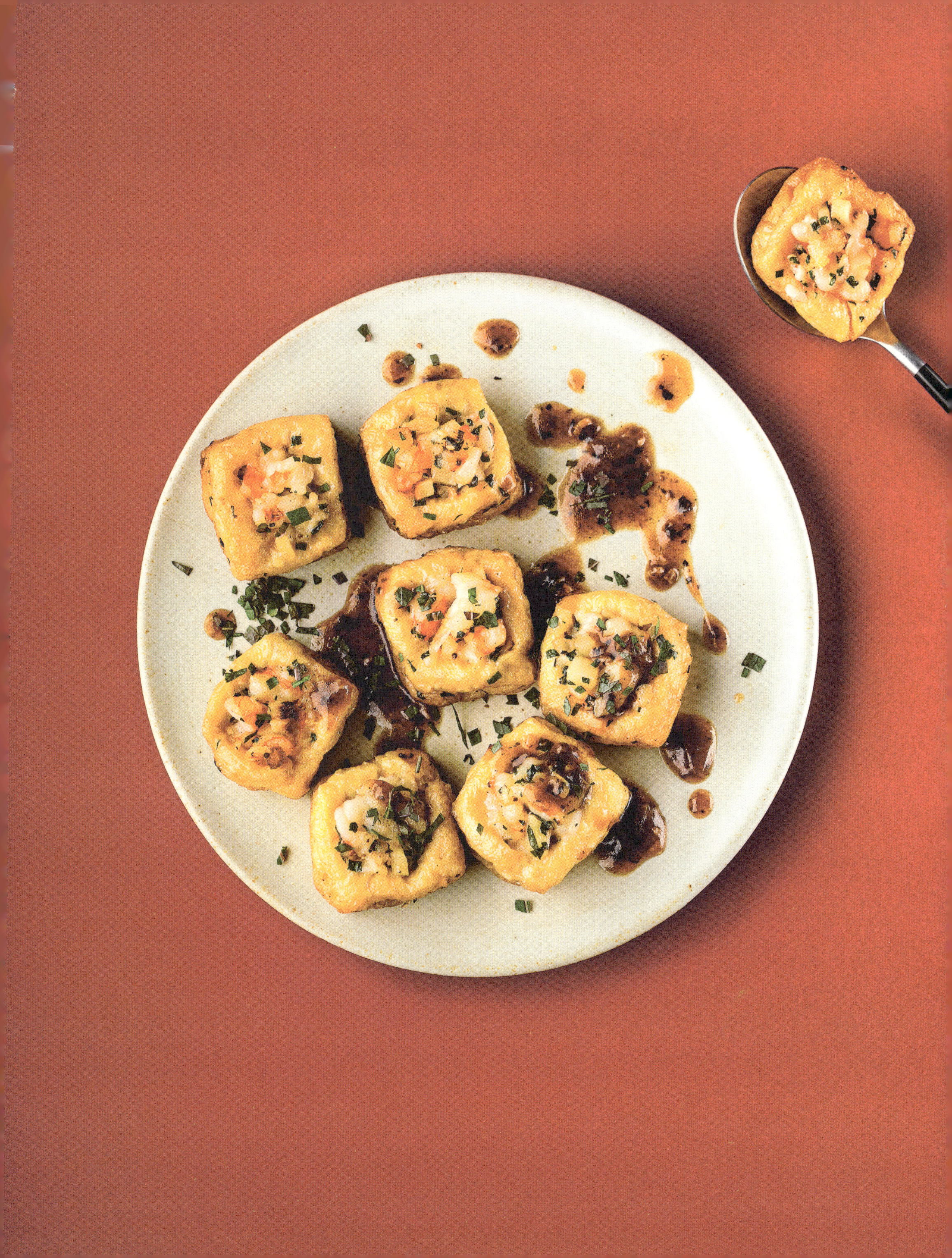

Silken Steamed Tofu with Ham

HUǑ　TUǏ　ZHĒNG　NÈN　DÒU　FU

火腿蒸嫩豆腐

PREPARING 10 MINUTES

COOKING 15 MINUTES

A DELICATELY SALTED DISH WITHOUT A DROP OF SOY SAUCE OR A GRAM OF SALT. A DISH WITH A VERY FINE BROTH WITHOUT ADDING LIQUID. THIS IS THE RESULT OF AN AMAZING ENCOUNTER BETWEEN SILKEN TOFU AND DRIED HAM.

🍴 Serves 2 people

INGREDIENTS

1 silken tofu block, about 400g (14oz)
40g (1½oz) jamón ibérico
1 tsp chopped spring onion (scallion)
2 garlic cloves, chopped
Dried chilli peppers (*optional*), cut into small pieces
1 tbsp neutral oil
2 tsp sesame oil

RECIPE STEPS

▪ Unmould the silken tofu directly onto a shallow plate (see p. 122 for the full technique). Cut it in 2 lengthways, then into slices 1.5cm (½in) thick. Insert a slice of ham between each pair of tofu pieces. They should be roughly the same size.

▪ Bring a pot of water to the boil. Place the plate in a steamer basket, then place that on top of the pot. Cover and cook for 15 minutes over a medium heat. The silken tofu will release liquid during cooking.

▪ Once the tofu has finished cooking, sprinkle it with the spring onion, garlic and dried chillies (if using).

▪ Heat the neutral oil in a pan. As soon as it starts smoking, turn off the heat and pour it over the aromatics to release their flavour. Finish with a drizzle of sesame oil.

▪ Enjoy with a spoon, combining a little tofu, ham and broth.

GOOD TO KNOW
小提示

The ham used in the original recipe is ham from Jinhua, a city famous for its pork in South-East China. The closest alternative is Iberian ham, both in taste and texture.

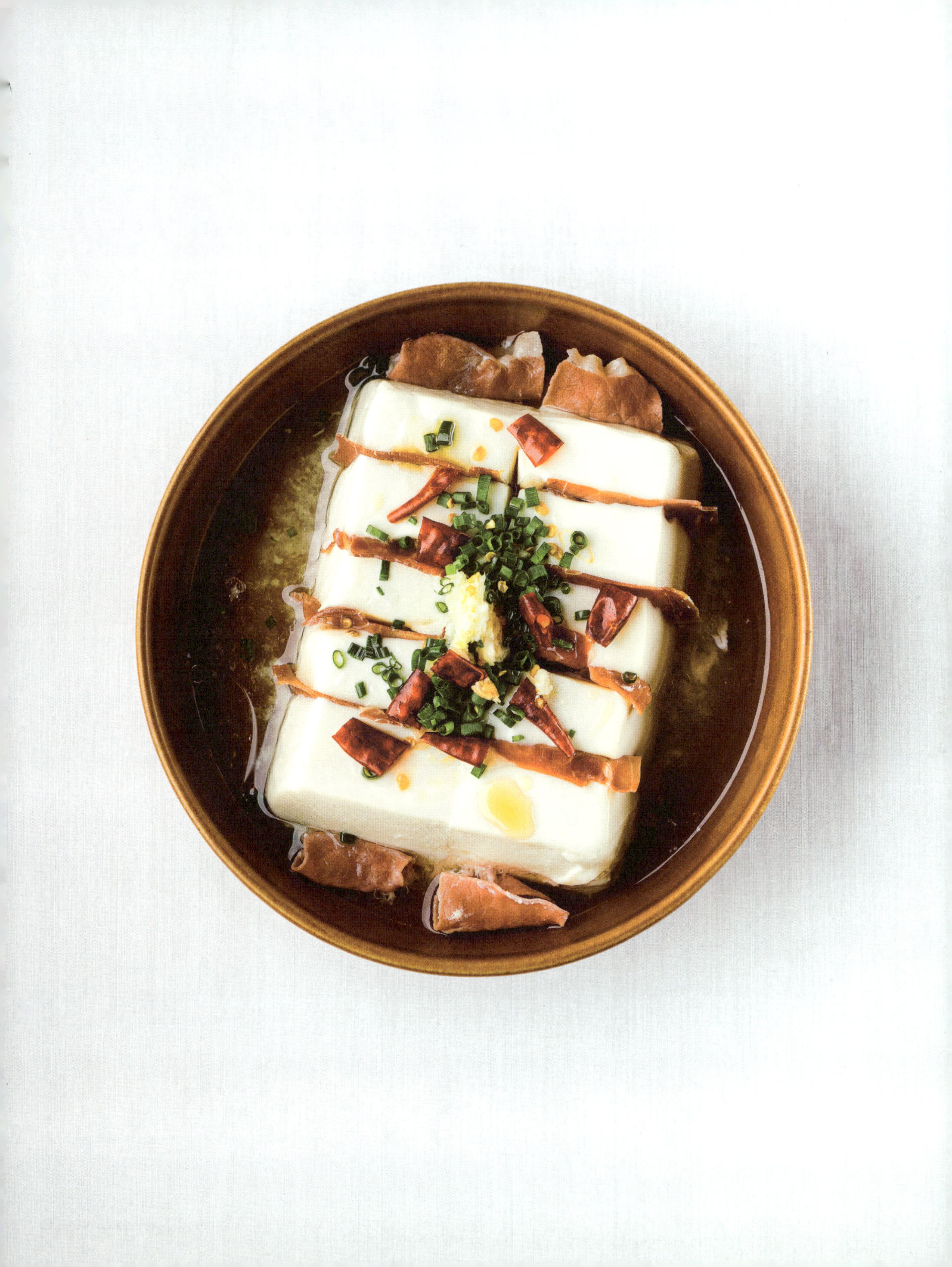

Tofu "Jerky"

LǓ ZHĪ DÒU FU GĀN
卤汁豆腐干

PREPARING 4 HOURS
COOKING 25 MINUTES

I RECENTLY STUMBLED UPON A VIDEO OF THIS TOFU SNACK THAT WAS BOUGHT FOR ME AT THE SUPERMARKET IN CHINA, WHEN I WAS YOUNG. IT REMINDED ME HOW MUCH I LIKED IT. IT WAS TOFU SOAKED IN A SPICE BROTH, THEN DRIED TO CONCENTRATE THE AROMAS. THE DOUBLE-COOKING METHOD ALSO CREATES A CHEWY TEXTURE, AS AMAZING AS IT IS PLEASANT.

Makes 20 slices

INGREDIENTS

500ml (2 cups) oil, for deep-frying
1 firm tofu block, about 400g (14oz), cut in half lengthways, then into slices 5mm (¼in) thick
20g (¾oz) rock sugar (or white sugar)
500ml (2 cups) warm water
1 star anise
1 chunk of cinnamon stick
½ tsp fennel seeds
1 piece of dried mandarin peel (*optional; see p. 30*)
2 tbsp honey
½ tsp toasted white sesame seeds
Pinch of ground cumin

RECIPE STEPS

- Heat the oil in a pan over a high heat. Once it reaches 180°C (350°F), add half the tofu slices, switch to a medium heat and fry for 5 minutes, keeping the temperature at around 160°C (320°F). The outside of the tofu should be hard and crispy. Place it on a plate lined with kitchen paper. Repeat the process with the remaining tofu.

- Remove the oil from the pan (you can filter and reuse it), leaving about ½ tablespoon in the pan. Heat over a medium heat, then add the rock sugar and let it caramelize. Keep an eye on the heat so the sugar does not burn. After about 8 minutes, you will have a caramel. Place the fried tofu pieces in the caramel, then add the warm water and spices (star anise, cinnamon, fennel seeds, and the dried mandarin peel if you have any). Bring to a simmer and cook over a medium heat for 15 minutes. Switch to a high heat at the very end of cooking to reduce the liquid.

- When the liquid is almost gone, switch to a low heat and pour in the honey. Continue cooking for about 5 minutes. Mix well.

DRYING AND TO SERVE

- Turn off the heat and let the tofu cool and dry in the fridge for 3–4 hours. The texture will become firmer and the flavours will intensify. Serve sprinkled with the toasted white sesame seeds and a pinch of cumin powder.

GOOD TO KNOW
小提示

This recipe pays tribute to the people of Suzhou, known for their sweet tooth. However, you can reduce the amount of honey and add some doubanjiang *(see p. 38) and a few chilli peppers for a saltier and spicier version.*

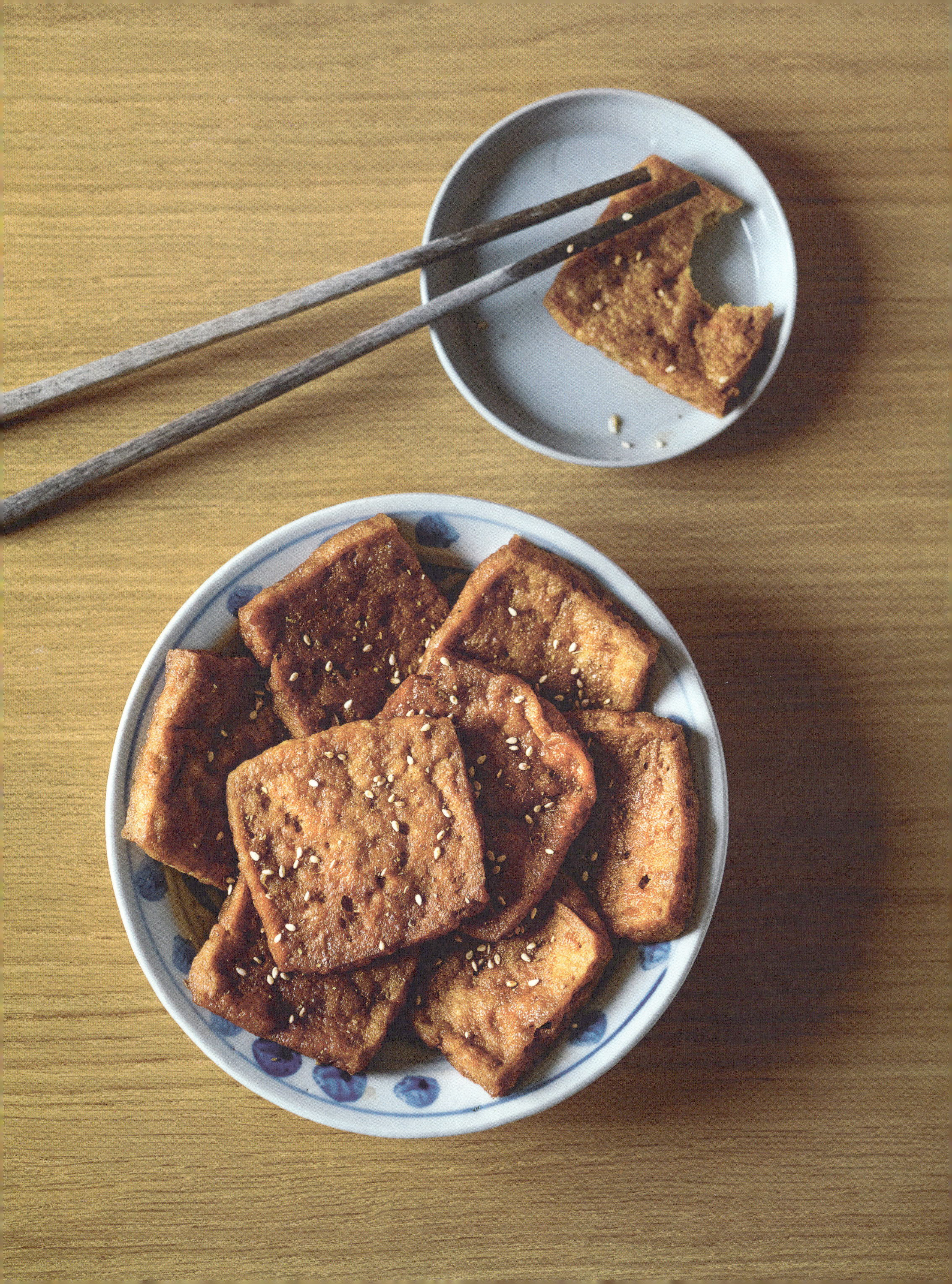

CHAPTER
05

Eggs

鸡蛋

JĪ DÀN

PP. 142-143: Steamed eggs ▪ **PP. 146-147:** Stir-fried tomatoes and eggs
PP. 148-149: Chinese spring onion omelette ▪ **PP. 150-151:** Black tea eggs
PP. 152-153: Dai-style fried egg salad ▪ **PP. 154-155:** Tiger skin eggs

From All Angles

An Infinite Number of Forms

SINCE CHICKENS WERE DOMESTICATED IN SOUTHEAST ASIA, MORE THAN 6,000 YEARS AGO, EGGS HAVE CONQUERED THE WORLD AND OUR PLATES. THANKS TO HUMAN CREATIVITY, THIS SIMPLE INGREDIENT, ONCE COOKED, IS SERVED IN AN INFINITE NUMBER OF SHAPES, TEXTURES AND TASTES, AND CHINESE CUISINE IS NO DIFFERENT.

EGGS IN ALL THEIR FORMS

Along with fish, eggs are probably the type of food I ate the most as a child. In a country with a wide variety of eating habits, eggs play a unifying role.

Fried eggs with tomatoes (see p. 164), for example, is a popular family dish from north to south, east to west, thanks to its versatility; you can eat eggs with rice, serve them as a garnish on noodles, or stuff them in dumplings. They are also common in soups (see p. 164): once beaten, they are gradually incorporated into the hot broth by swirling them with chopsticks. That creates small flakes that Chinese people poetically call "egg flowers" (蛋花, *dàn huā*).

Eggs can be steamed, too (see p. 142). Imagine a warm, comforting dish with a fluffy flan-like texture. The perfectly smooth surface trembles when tapped with the back of a spoon. A dash of soy sauce, like black paint on a pale yellow canvas, makes for a sublime finish.

NOT JUST CHICKEN

While fresh eggs eaten in China are mostly chicken eggs (and sometimes quail eggs), duck eggs are very popular once fermented or salted.

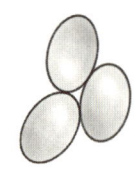

CHICKEN EGGS
鸡蛋 | JĪ DÀN

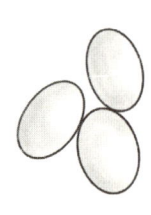

DUCK EGGS
鸭蛋 | YĀ DÀN

QUAIL EGGS
鹌鹑蛋 | ĀN CHÚN DÀN

A CENTURY, DID YOU SAY?

Let's talk about century eggs, whose name and dark colour can cause some confusion in the West.

They are called *pi dan* in Chinese (literally "egg skin"). The traditional method is to coat raw eggs with mud that is rich in lime, to which powdered rice husks (the outer shell of rice grains) and salt are added. Over time (40 to 50 days), this alkaline mixture transforms the egg's interior. The yolk becomes creamy and green, while the egg white acquires a gelatinous texture and a translucent amber colour. The taste can be compared to a hard-boiled egg, but slightly saltier and with a pronounced umami flavour.

A *pi dan* is also called a *song hua dan* ("pine egg") in China, because you can assess the quality of a century egg by looking for shapes that resemble pine branches on its surface.

MEMORY
回忆

I remember hard-boiled eggs marinated in black tea (see p. 150) that I bought from street vendors for half a yuan in the 1990s. They are a snack with an intense fragrance and delicate flavour.

Eggs   140   The Guide to Chinese Cooking

EGG DISHES

FRIED EGGS
荷包蛋 | HÉ BĀO DÀN

Perfect as a topping for a noodle soup or, more unusually, in a salad (p. 152).

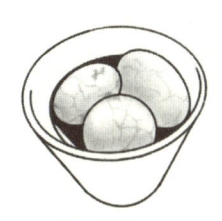

BLACK TEA EGGS
茶叶蛋 | CHÁ YÈ DÀN

A snack that can be found at small stalls or in local shops.

STEAMED EGGS
蛋羹 | DÀN GĒNG

An everyday dish that can be found throughout the country (p. 142).

EGG "FLOWER" SOUP
蛋花汤 | DÀN HUĀ TĀNG

This uses a technique that consists of gradually pouring beaten eggs into a hot broth (p. 164).

CENTURY EGGS
皮蛋 | PÍ DÀN

Usually eaten raw with congee or in a cold tofu dish (see p. 122).

HARD-BOILED QUAIL EGGS
水煮鹌鹑蛋 | SHUĬ ZHŬ ĀN CHÚN DÀN

Once cooked in water, these are added to a broth or just enjoyed on their own, soaked in soy sauce.

SALTED DUCK EGGS
咸鸭蛋 | XIÁN YĀ DÀN

These are highly popular and can be eaten with congee, and the yolk is often used in recipes, such as in sticky rice dishes or in a *liu sha bao* (see p. 286).

GOOD TO KNOW
小提示

To make salted duck eggs, the raw eggs are soaked in salted water (and possibly with added spices) for about a month. The chemical reaction that takes place will separate the fat contained in the yolk, which is particularly favoured for its dense, sandy texture and its rich and slightly salty taste.

Steamed Eggs

JĪ DÀN GĒNG

鸡蛋羹

PREPARING 3 MINUTES

COOKING 10 MINUTES

THESE EGGS, WHOSE TEXTURE IS A BIT LIKE A FLAN OR SILKEN TOFU, ARE A STAPLE OF POPULAR CHINESE CUISINE. IF YOU HAVE NEVER TASTED EGGS IN THIS FORM, YOU ARE IN FOR AN EXOTIC EXPERIENCE!

Serves 2 people

INGREDIENTS

3 medium eggs, about 180g (6oz)
270ml (scant 1¼ cups) water
¼ tsp salt
1 tsp sesame oil
1 tsp soy sauce
Chopped spring onion (scallion), to garnish

RECIPE STEPS

- Beat the eggs in a bowl and add the water and salt. Mix, then strain to remove the egg-white residue.

- Place the bowl in a steamer basket, cover with a plate (to prevent water vapour from falling back into the bowl and creating holes on the surface), and steam over a medium heat for 12 minutes. (If you use a pot filled with water, rather than a steamer, cooking will start once you bring the water to the boil.) Let the bowl stand in the steamer basket for another 5 minutes – the dish is cooked when the liquid has become barely solid and has the texture of silken tofu or flan. If your mixture is still very liquid, extend the cooking time by 3–5 minutes.

- Add the sesame oil, soy sauce and a sprinkling of chopped spring onion to serve.

GOOD TO KNOW
小提示

The ratio of egg to water is approximately 1:1.5, which is about 150ml (5oz) of water per 100g (3½oz) of egg. Adding salt is important, because it binds the egg proteins during the cooking process and increases your chances of reaching the desired texture. If you use broth instead of water, salt will not be needed.

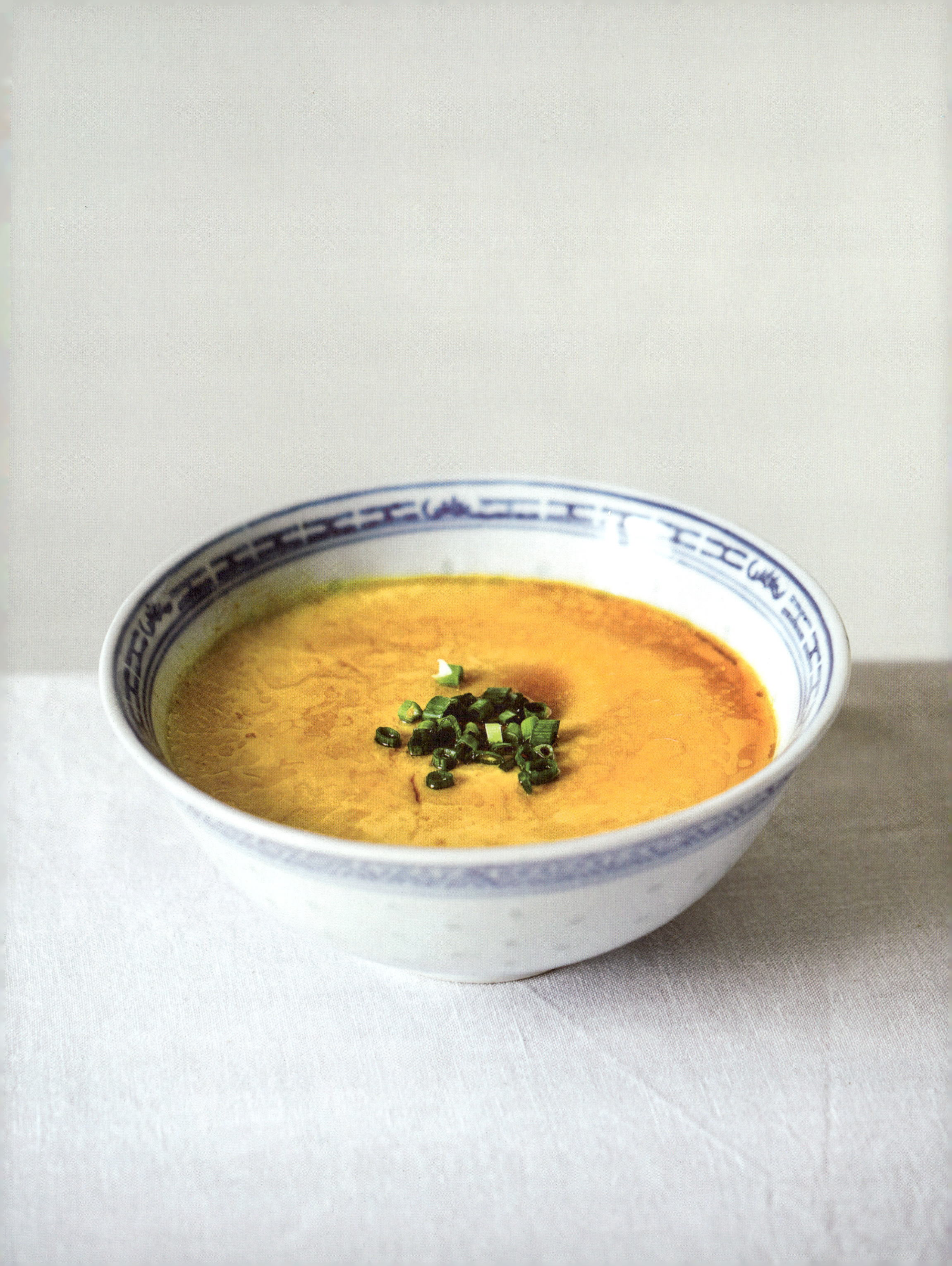

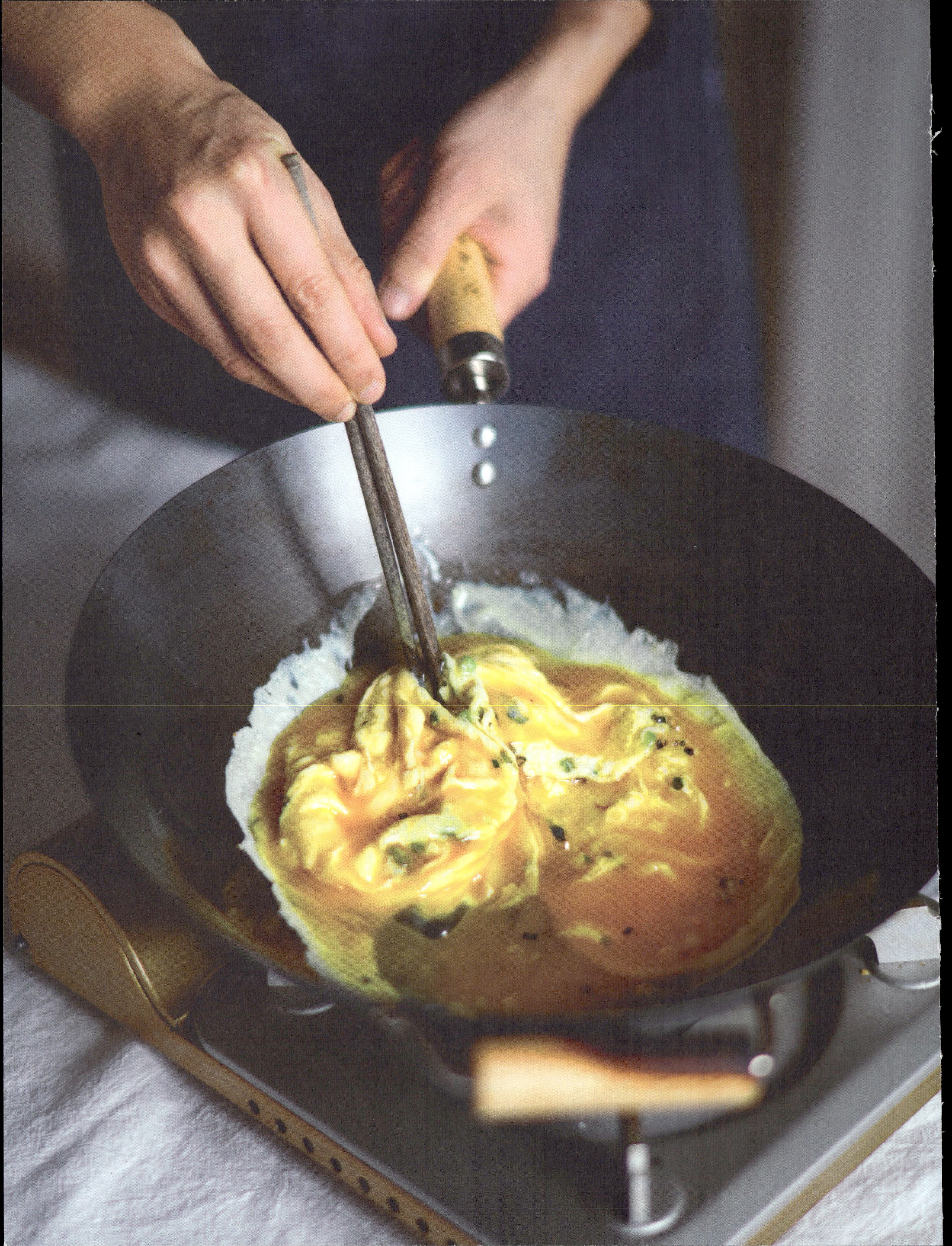

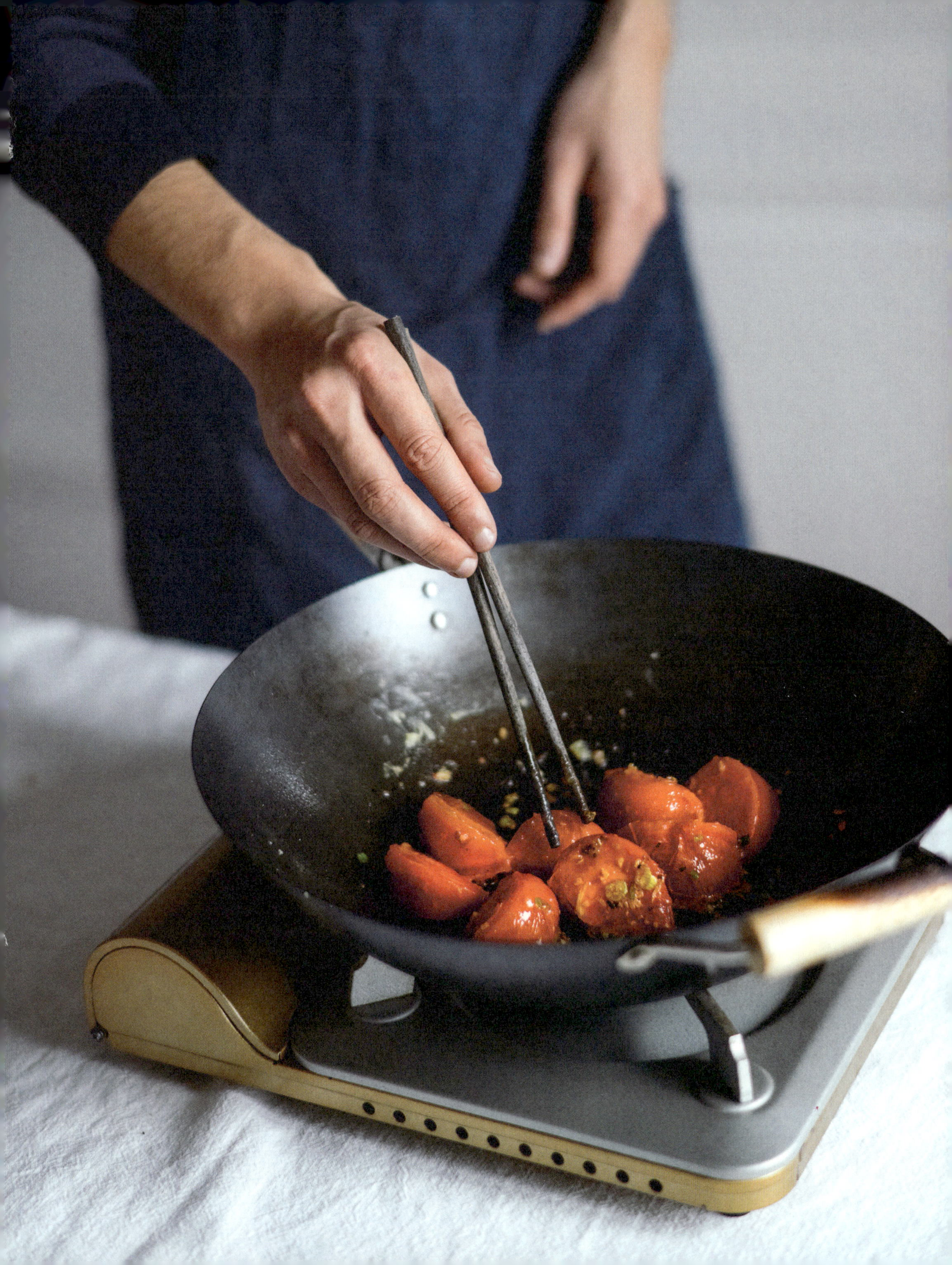

Stir-Fried Tomatoes and Eggs

FĀN QIÉ CHǍO JĪ DÀN

番茄炒鸡蛋

PREPARING 5 MINUTES

COOKING 12 MINUTES

THIS IS ARGUABLY THE MOST POPULAR EGG DISH IN CHINA. IT'S SIMPLE AND CHEAP, BUT SO COMFORTING. I HAVE TASTED MANY DIFFERENT VERSIONS, BUT MY FAVOURITE ONE WAS SERVED IN A SMALL RESTAURANT IN DALI, YUNNAN; THE EGGS ARE SLIGHTLY RUNNY, AND A HINT OF KETCHUP ENHANCES THE SWEETNESS OF THE TOMATOES.

🍽 Serves 2 people

INGREDIENTS

For the eggs

4 eggs
½ tsp salt
½ tsp sesame oil
1 tbsp Shaoxing wine
2 tbsp neutral oil
2 tsp chopped spring onion (scallion) white

For the tomatoes

300g (10oz) fresh or canned tomatoes
1 tsp cornflour (cornstarch)
2 tbsp water
1 tbsp ketchup
1 tbsp neutral oil
2 tsp chopped ginger
Salt or sugar, to taste

To serve

2 tsp chopped spring onion (scallion)

FOR THE EGGS

- Beat the eggs in a bowl and add the salt, sesame oil and Shaoxing wine.

- Heat a wok over a medium heat. Once it is hot, add the 2 tablespoons of oil and the spring onion white. Fry the onion for a few seconds to release the flavour. Add the eggs and do not touch them for the first 20 seconds. Then, gently tilt the wok to spread the liquid evenly. The aim is to obtain an omelette that is browned underneath but still runny on top, so do not overcook. After about 40 seconds, turn off the heat, slide the omelette from the wok and set aside.

FOR THE TOMATOES

- If using fresh tomatoes, cut them into quarters, removing the cores. You can also use canned, peeled whole tomatoes if you prefer. In a bowl, mix the cornflour with the 2 tablespoons of water and the ketchup.

- Reheat the wok over a medium heat. Once it is hot, add the tablespoon of oil, then the ginger. Fry for about 10 seconds to release the flavour. Add the tomatoes and cook for 4–5 minutes. They should soften slightly and release some juice. If you're using canned tomatoes, remember to pour in all the juice.

- Give the cornflour and ketchup mixture a stir and pour it over the tomatoes. Mix everything together and wait for the sauce to thicken. Season with a little salt and/or sugar to taste.

TO FINISH

- Add the omelette back into the pan and roughly break it into small pieces with a spatula. Turn off the heat and sprinkle with the spring onion to serve.

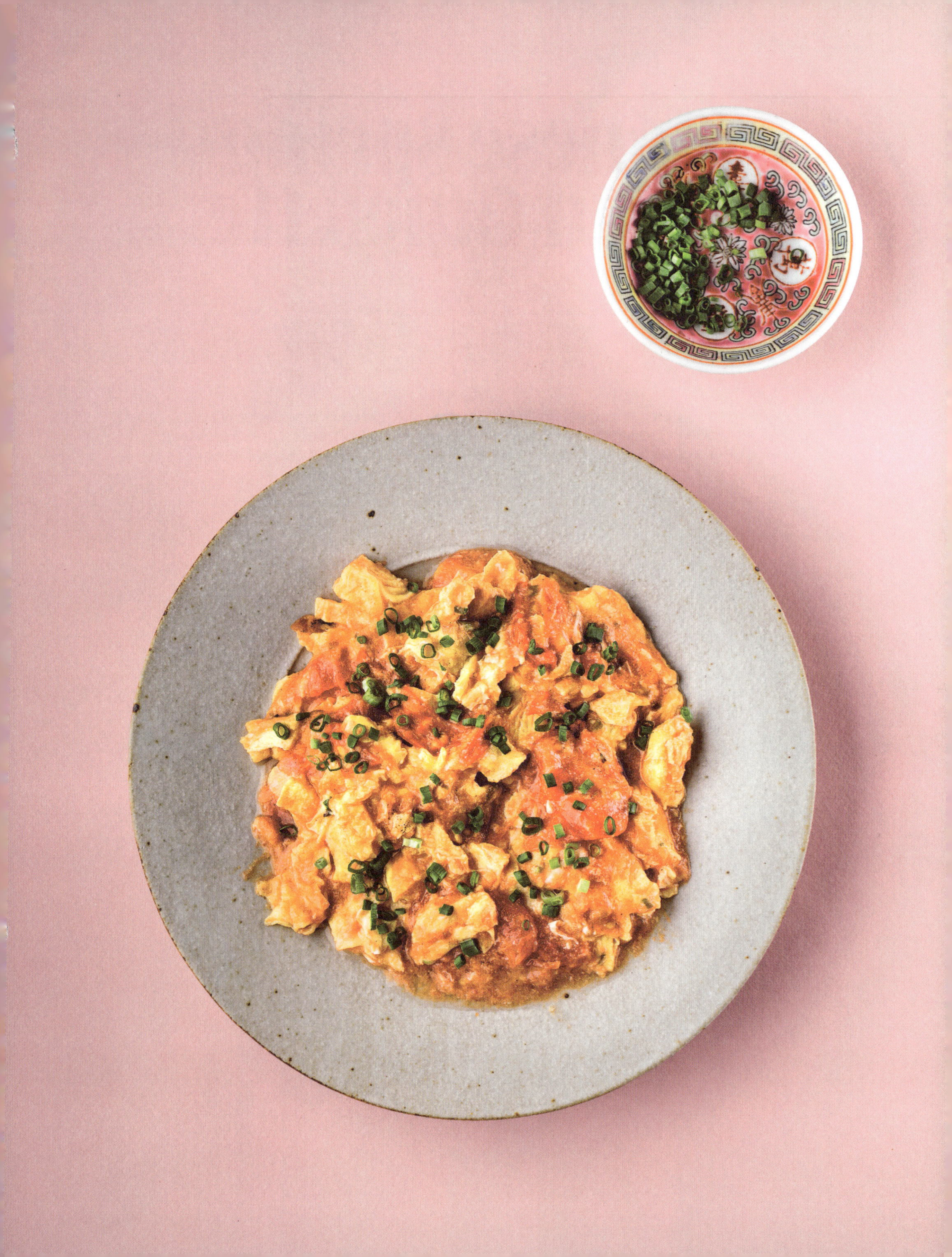

Chinese Spring Onion Omelette

JIǓ　CÀI　JĪ　DÀN　BǏNG

韭菜鸡蛋饼

Preparing 3 minutes

Cooking 12 minutes

FRIED EGGS WITH CHINESE SPRING ONION WERE OFTEN SERVED AT OUR FAMILY TABLE. THE INGREDIENTS ARE SIMPLE, BUT I LIKE THE EGGS' RICH TASTE WITH THE SUBTLE FLAVOUR OF THE CHINESE SPRING ONION, WHICH FOR ME IS BOTH A VEGETABLE AND A HERB.

Serves 4 people

INGREDIENTS

4 eggs
1 tsp fish sauce
1 tsp salt
2 tsp Shaoxing wine
1 tsp cornflour (cornstarch)
100g (3½oz) Chinese spring onions (chives), chopped
4 tsp neutral oil

RECIPE STEPS

- Beat the eggs in a bowl and add the fish sauce, salt, Shaoxing wine and cornflour. Stir in the chopped Chinese spring onions and mix well.

- Depending on your pan's size, you can make 1 to 4 omelettes. I use a small 16cm (6in) frying pan to make 4 mini omelettes. Heat the pan over a medium heat and add 1 teaspoon of the oil. Once it becomes hot, pour a quarter of the mixture and stir to distribute it well. When the surface is no longer runny, use your spatula to fold your omelette in two and let the underside brown for a few seconds, then flip it over to brown the other side.

- Repeat the process to make the other omelettes. You can serve them plain or with a sauce of your choice.

GOOD TO KNOW
小提示

This omelette goes well with a sweet and spicy sauce. For example, you can add a mango coulis to your Sichuan chilli oil (see p. 36).

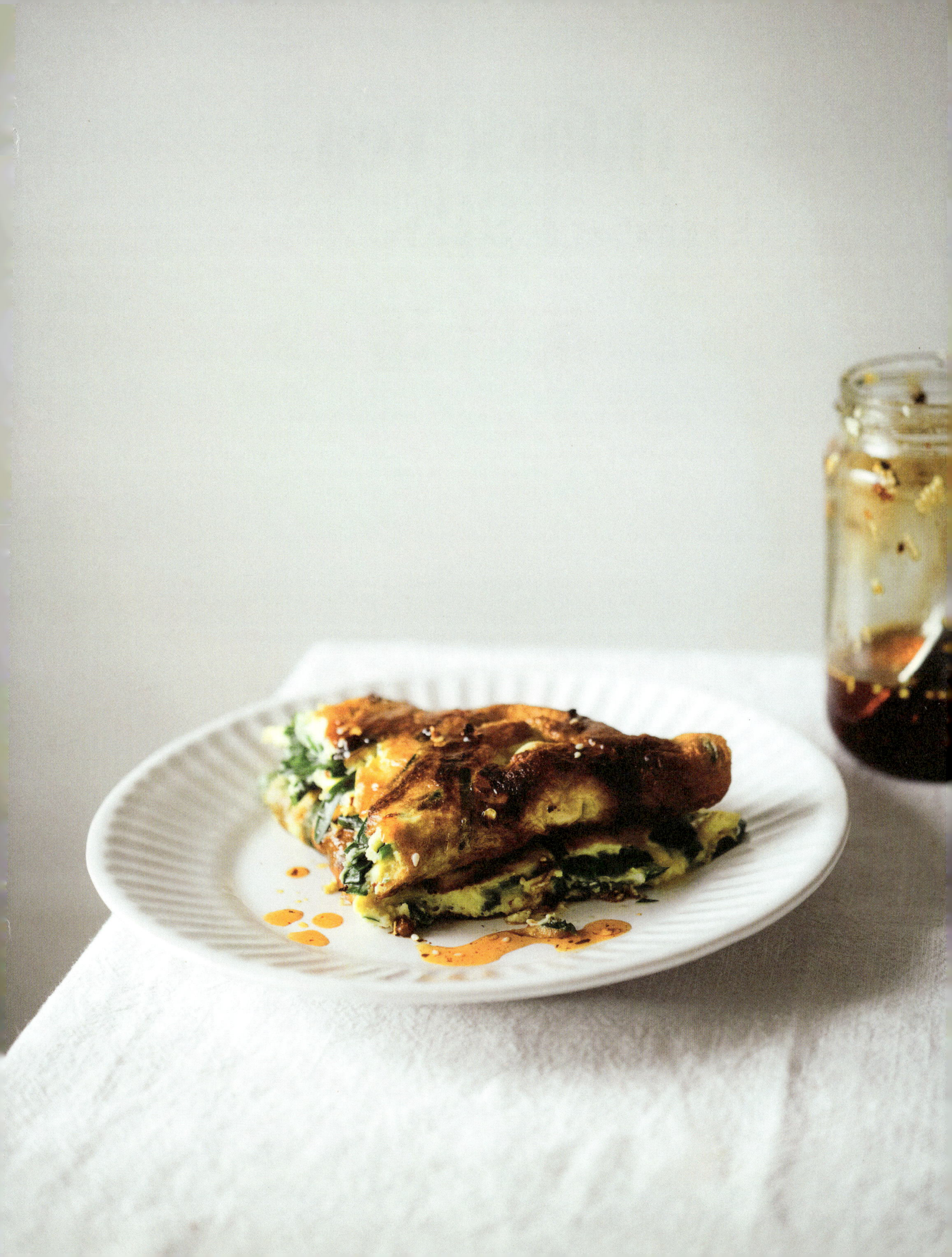

Black Tea Eggs

CHÁ YÈ DÀN

茶叶蛋

PREPARING 24 HOURS

COOKING 6 MINUTES

THESE EGGS, SOAKED IN A HOT AND VERY FRAGRANT MARINADE, ARE SNACKS THAT CAN BE FOUND EVERYWHERE IN CHINA. I OFTEN BOUGHT SEVERAL AFTER SCHOOL, IN THE '90S, AT HALF A YUAN PER PORTION. IN THIS RECIPE, I TRADED HARD-BOILED EGGS FOR SOFT, BUT FEEL FREE TO TEST THE ORIGINAL VERSION!

Makes 4 eggs

INGREDIENTS

For the eggs

4 eggs

For the marinade

1 tsp light soy sauce
1 tbsp dark soy sauce
1 star anise
½ tsp Sichuan peppercorn
½ cinnamon stick
½ tsp rock sugar (or white sugar)
½ tsp salt
1 tsp black tea
2 bay leaves *(optional)*

RECIPE STEPS

- For the marinade, pour 400ml (1¾ cups) of water into a pot, then add the soy sauces. Put the remaining ingredients in a muslin (cheesecloth) bag and add this to the pan. Bring to the boil, then turn off the heat and leave to infuse and cool completely. Discard the spice bag and transfer the marinade to a clean, dry container.

- Gently immerse the eggs in boiling water and cook for 6 minutes over a medium heat. Transfer them immediately to a bowl of iced water to stop the cooking process.

- Peel the cooled eggs and add them to the marinade. Let them marinate for at least 12 hours in the fridge, preferably for 24 hours. Eat within 3 days.

GOOD TO KNOW
小提示

In the original recipe, the eggs aren't peeled; instead you lightly tap the shells with the back of a spoon to make small cracks before marinating. It is more aesthetically pleasing, because the marinade will give it a marbled appearance, but the taste will be less pronounced.

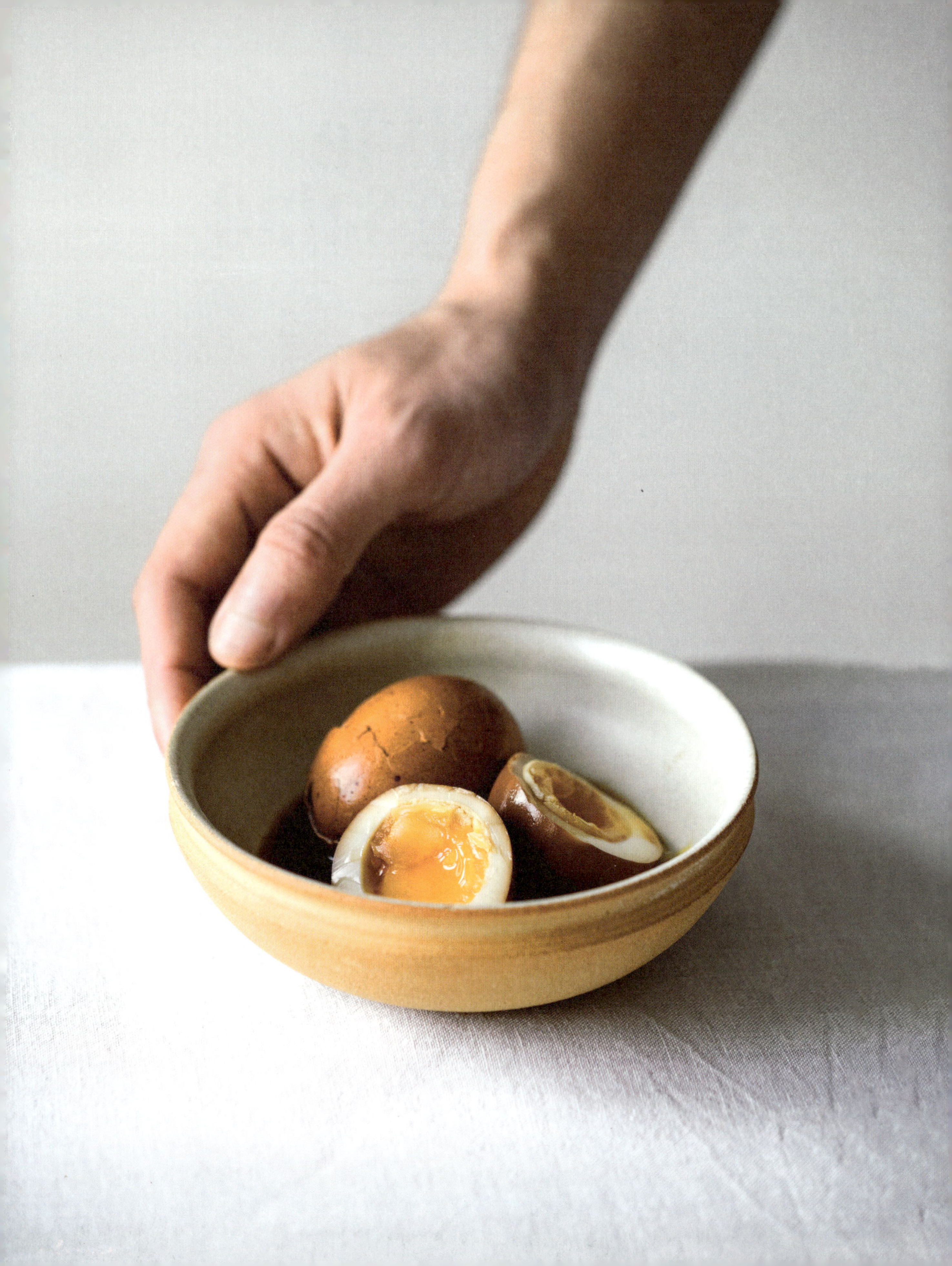

Dai-Style Fried Egg Salad

DǍI　WÈI　HÉ　BĀO　DÀN

傣味荷包蛋

Preparing 10 minutes

Cooking 5 minutes

CHINESE GASTRONOMY ALSO INCLUDES THE FOOD OF ITS 55 ETHNIC MINORITIES. FOR EXAMPLE, THE CUISINE OF THE DAI PEOPLE IN YUNNAN IS REMINISCENT OF THE FLAVOURS OF LAOS OR THAILAND. RAW INGREDIENTS ARE ACCOMPANIED BY AN ABUNDANCE OF FRESH HERBS, WITH A PREFERENCE FOR ACIDIC AND SPICY FLAVOURS. THE FOLLOWING RECIPE IS A GOOD INTRODUCTION.

Serves 2 people

INGREDIENTS

½ carrot, finely julienned
½ cucumber, finely julienned
½ red onion, chopped
2 bird's eye chillies, deseeded and finely chopped
½ tsp salt
2 tbsp lime juice
2 tbsp neutral oil
3 eggs
1 handful of long coriander (*ngo gai*), leaves picked
1 handful of mint leaves

RECIPE STEPS

- Put the carrot, cucumber, red onion and chillies in a bowl, then add the salt and lime juice and mix well.

- Heat a wok over a medium heat until it starts smoking. Add the oil, then the eggs immediately (you can do this in two batches if your wok is on the small side). Fry the eggs for 1–2 minutes. The idea is to make just-fried eggs with crispy edges.

- Add the eggs to the bowl, gently breaking them up into pieces. Finish with a few leaves of long coriander and mint.

GOOD TO KNOW
小提示

You can adapt the vegetable variety and quantity to taste, but the soul of this dish lies in the fried eggs, lime juice, fresh chilli pepper and both types of fresh herbs. Long coriander can be found in supermarkets that are well stocked with Southeast Asian products.

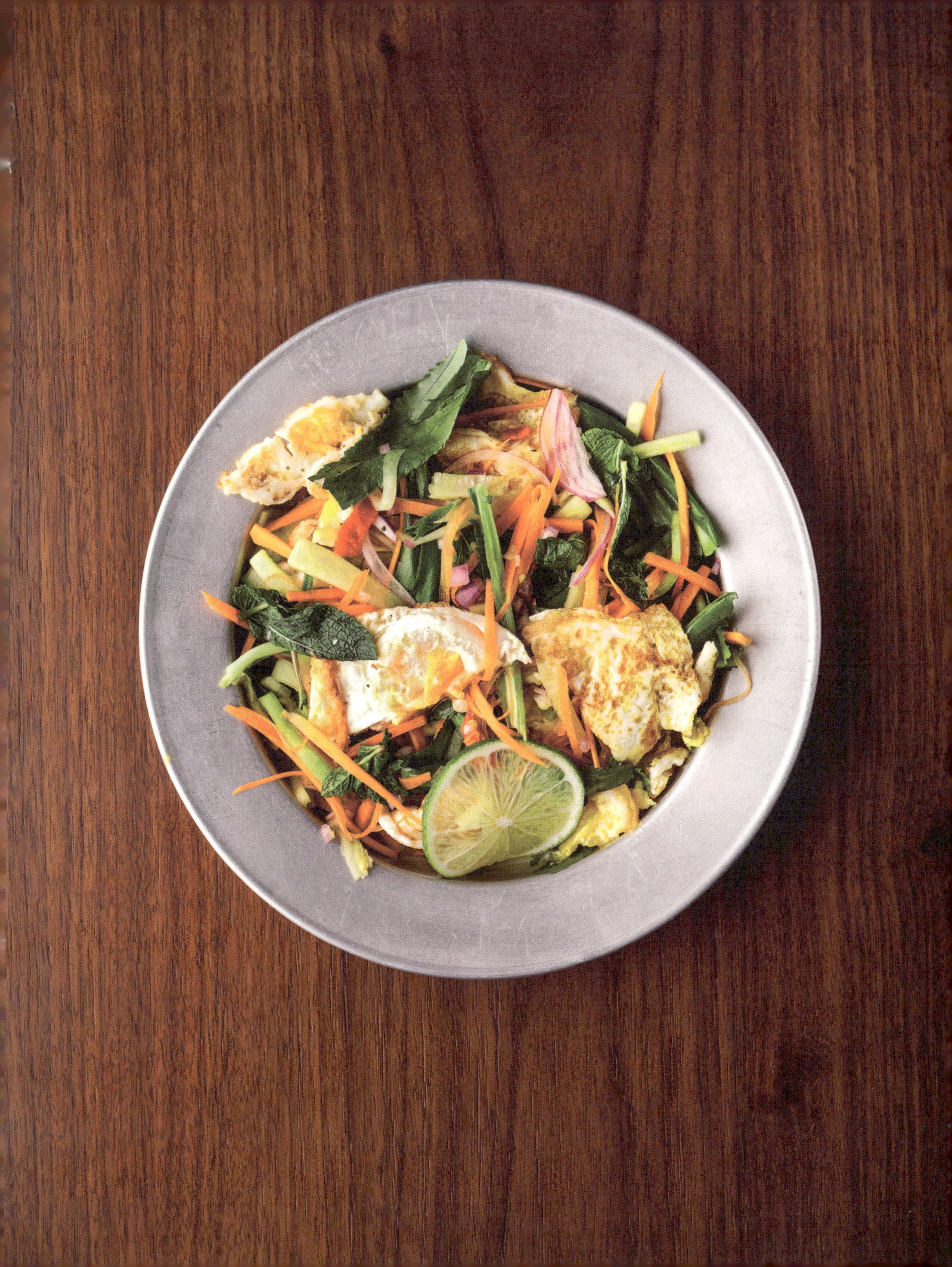

Tiger Skin Eggs

HǓ PÍ JĪ DÀN
虎皮鸡蛋

PREPARING 4 HOURS
COOKING 20 MINUTES

THIS EGG RECIPE FROM JIANGSU OWES ITS FAME NOT ONLY TO ITS UNUSUAL NAME, BUT ALSO TO ITS DOUBLE-COOKING METHOD AND LONG MARINATING TIME, WHICH CREATE A UNIQUE TASTE AND TEXTURE.

Makes 6 eggs

INGREDIENTS

For the eggs

6 eggs
300ml (1¼ cups) neutral oil

For the marinade

2 tbsp light soy sauce
1 tbsp dark soy sauce
1 tbsp sugar
1 tsp salt
400ml (1¾ cups) water

For the spices

1 star anise
½ tsp Sichuan peppercorn
2 dried chilli peppers
1 cinnamon stick

FOR THE EGGS

- First, hard boil the eggs. Bring 1 litre (4⅓ cups) of water to the boil in a pot. Gently add the eggs, then turn the heat down to a simmer and cook for 10 minutes.

- Prepare a large bowl of iced water and immerse the eggs immediately after cooking. Once cooled, peel them and let them dry.

- Heat the oil to 180°C (350°F) in a pan. Fry the eggs for about 2 minutes over a medium heat until the outsides are slightly browned. Remove the eggs and immerse them in cold water again for 10 minutes; this step is essential to let the skin "swell".

FOR THE MARINADE

- While cooking the eggs, pour all the marinade ingredients and all the spices into a pot. Bring to the boil, then turn off the heat and leave to infuse until the marinade is at room temperature. Remove the spices.

- Remove the eggs from the cold water and add them to the marinade. Leave them there for at least 4 hours, or preferably overnight in the fridge, which will allow them to soak up the flavours and take on a texture that is both al dente and elastic (which Chinese people call "qq").

- These eggs can be enjoyed cold, or warmed in a saucepan with their sauce.

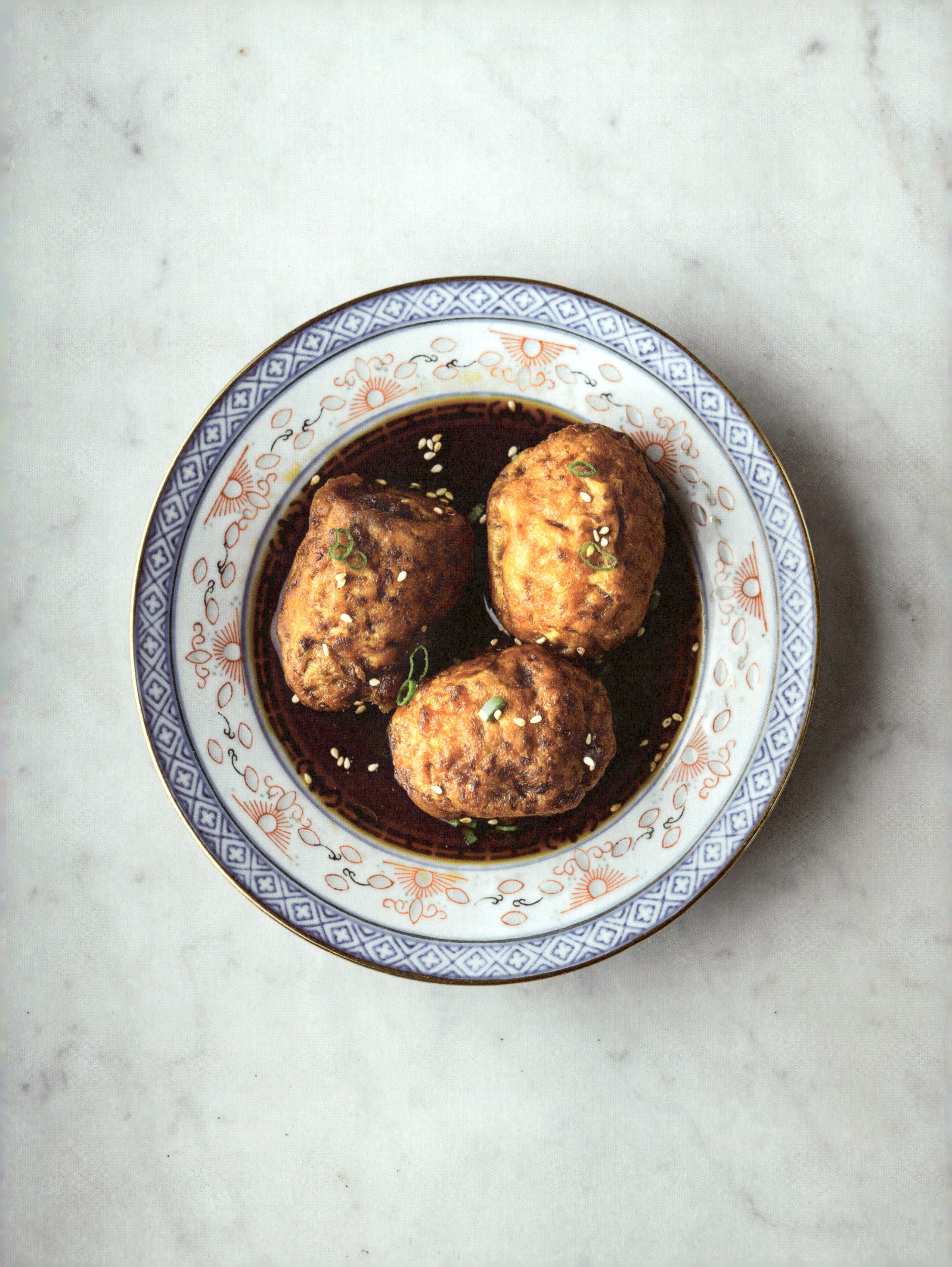

CHAPTER 06

Soups

汤
TĀNG

PP. 160-161: Base broths ■ **PP. 162-163:** "Milk" fish broth ■ **PP. 164-165:** Tomato and egg soup
PP. 166-167: Seaweed soup with dried shrimp ■ **PP. 168-169:** Wax gourd and corn soup ■ **PP. 170-171:** Hot and sour soup
PP. 172-173: Chicken soup with shiitake ■ **PP. 174-175:** Chicken meatball and vermicelli soup
PP. 176-177: Taro and trotter soup ■ **PP. 178-179:** Chinese-style borscht

From All Angles

Three Dishes and One Soup

MUCH MORE THAN A SIMPLE SOUP OR A VELOUTÉ SAUCE, A BROTH
IS AN ESSENTIAL ELEMENT IN A TRADITIONAL CHINESE MEAL.
A GOOD SOUP COMFORTS THE STOMACH, REHYDRATES
THE PALATE AND MAKES DISHES MORE DIGESTIBLE.

TO DRINK AND EAT

In China, starting the meal with a sip of hot soup is a common reflex.

To grasp its importance, you should know that traditionally, it is the only thing you drink during a meal. Water, tea or alcohol are not always included. When planning a Chinese meal, there are "dry" dishes and a "liquid" dish.

Soup (汤, *tāng*) most often refers to a light broth, served alone or with pieces of meat or vegetable. Like other dishes, the soup is placed in the middle of the table so that everyone can help themselves, ladling the soup into their own individual bowl. It is usually sipped from the bowl; chopsticks are used to eat the solid pieces.

DIFFERENT TYPES OF SOUP

Slow-simmered broth, quick tomato soup, or sweet soup to finish the meal… In China, the possibilities are endless.

The classic soup is generally made with meat (pork ribs, duck legs, whole chicken), tender cooked vegetables (taro, carrot, yam) and dried products to add some umami flavour (shiitake, for example). Everything is simmered over a low heat for at least 1 hour to extract a rich broth. Seasonings are kept to a minimum (salt, pepper), so as not to take over the natural taste of the broth.

It is also possible to make soups in a few minutes, such as tomato and egg soup (p. 164), or even just with boiling water poured over the ingredients (without any cooking), such as seaweed soup with dried shrimp (p. 166), which I make very regularly.

Finally, there is a category of sweet soups called *tong sui* (in Cantonese, as it is very popular in that region), which is usually served at the end of a meal or as a snack. You will find some inspiration in the chapter on sweets (pp. 350–371).

NOURISHING SOUPS

Given their highly digestible nature and gentle cooking methods to preserve nutrients, soups are often associated with health.

They are nourishing (养身汤, *yang shēn tāng*), and high-quality meat is usually associated with ingredients of Chinese medicine. Traditionally, it is common to give free-range chicken soup with goji berries and jujubes (see p. 35) to women who have given birth, to help their recovery during the famous "golden month".

There are no precise rules on how to eat soup. Personally, I like to start a meal with a few spoonfuls of soup before moving on to the rest. I have a similar ritual with noodle soups: I first eat a spoonful of broth, then taste the garnish, and finally the noodles.

MEMORY
回忆

I have kept a habit from my childhood: I really like to pour the soup of the day (we call it pao fan; *see the chapter on rice, p. 294) in my half-eaten rice bowl. The grains soaked in broth can still be enjoyed even if you are no longer hungry.*

CLASSIC CHINESE DINNER: THREE DISHES AND ONE SOUP

You start by tasting the broth, with a spoon or directly by drinking from the bowl. You then use chopsticks to eat the solid pieces.

DIFFERENT STEPS TO ENJOY A SOUP

01
Ladle the soup into your individual bowl.

02
Drink a few sips at the beginning of the meal.

03
Mix the soup with the rest of your rice.

Base Broths

GĀO TĀNG

高汤

PREPARING 5 MINUTES

COOKING 1-2 HOURS

A GOOD BROTH IS ESSENTIAL IN CHINESE CUISINE FOR NOODLE DISHES (WITH OR WITHOUT SOUP), IN CONGEE, IN QUICK SOUPS OR EVEN FOR COOKING RICE. CHICKEN AND PORK ARE GENERALLY USED AS A BASE. A 100% VEGETABLE BROTH IS RATHER RARE, BUT LEAVES MORE FREEDOM WHEN CHOOSING THE INGREDIENTS.

Makes 1 litre (4⅓ cups) of broth

INGREDIENTS

For the chicken & pork broth

- 1kg (2¼lb) chicken carcass and pork bones
- 1 tbsp Shaoxing wine
- 2 litres (8½ cups) hot water
- 1 piece of ginger, coarsely crushed
- A piece of spring onion (scallion)

For the vegetable broth

- 20g (¾oz) soy beans, rehydrated (*see method*)
- 8 dried shiitake mushrooms, rehydrated (*see method*)
- 1 onion, peeled and cut in half
- 1 corn cob, cut into 4–5cm (2in) pieces

FOR THE CHICKEN & PORK BROTH

- Put the chicken and pork in a large pot of cold water (with a ratio of 1:1 in my case, but there is no precise rule). Add the Shaoxing wine. Bring to the boil over a high heat, skimming off any foam, to remove impurities. Discard the water, return the pieces to the pot and add 2 litres (8½ cups) of fresh hot water, the coarsely crushed piece of ginger and the spring onion (see p. 28).

- Simmer for 2 hours over a low heat; remove the ginger and onion after 30 minutes. Do not add salt. At the end of the cooking time, strain the broth into a clean container – you will get approximately 1 litre (4⅓ cups) – then leave to cool.

- You can keep this broth for 3 days in the fridge. It can be frozen in individual portions; for example, I make 400ml (1¾-cup) portions.

FOR THE VEGETABLE BROTH

- The day before you want to make the broth, put the soy beans in cold water to rehydrate, then rehydrate the shiitake 1 hour beforehand, also in cold water. Drain.

- Pour 1.5 litres (6¼ cups) of water into a pot and add all the ingredients. Bring to the boil, then turn down the heat and simmer for 1 hour. At the end of the cooking time, strain the broth into a clean container and store it as for the chicken broth above.

GOOD TO KNOW
小提示

When making a vegetable broth, there are two things I find most important: umami flavour and a slightly sweet aftertaste. Shiitake and soy create some umami flavour, but you can also opt for kombu (mostly used in Japanese cuisine). Corn, widely used by my family in meat soups, adds some natural sweetness.

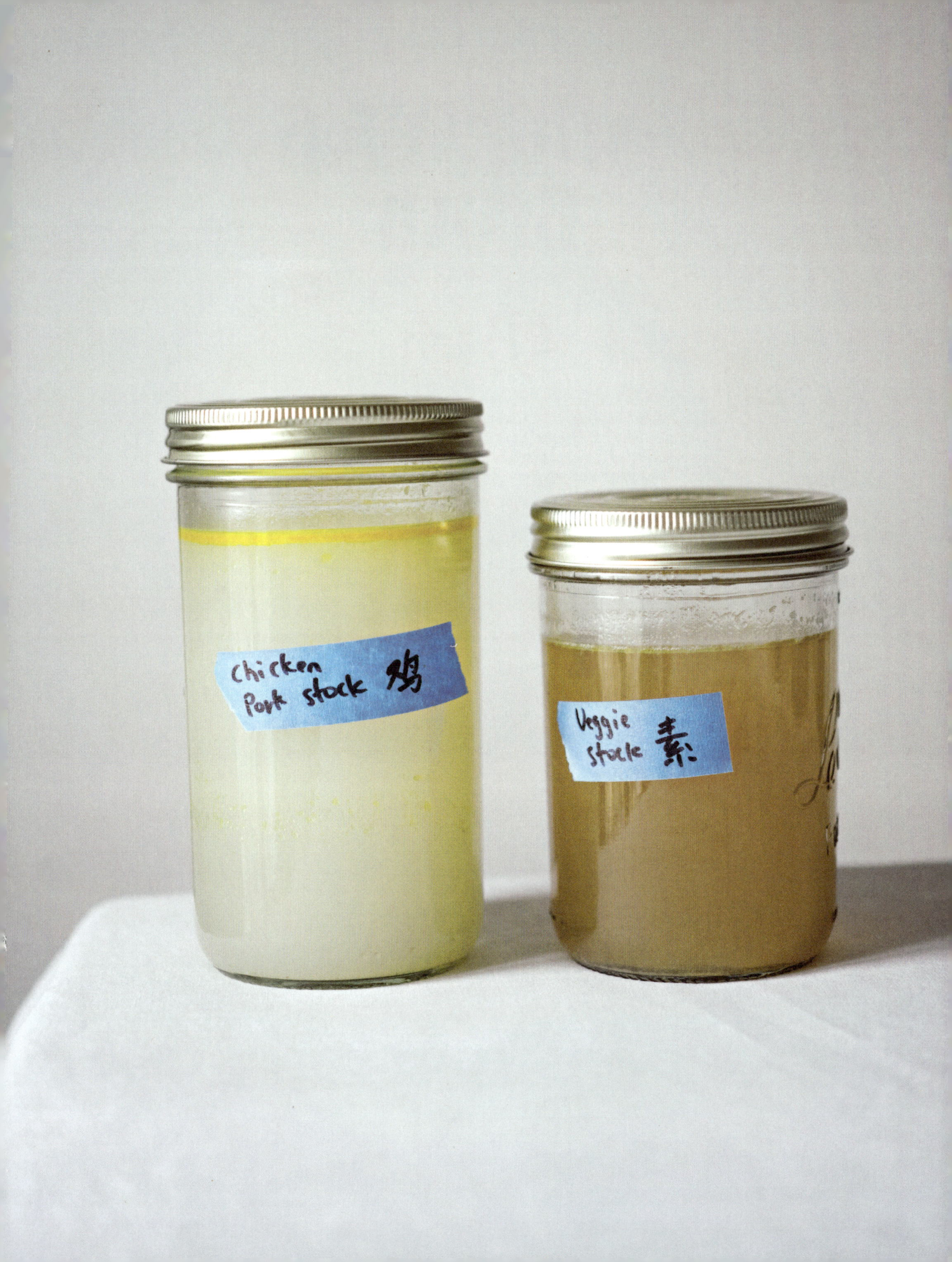
Chicken
Pork stock 鸡
Veggie
stock 素

"Milk" Fish Broth

NĂI TĀNG
奶汤

PREPARING 3 MINUTES

COOKING 20 MINUTES

THERE IS NO MILK IN THIS FISH BROTH. ITS MILKY COLOUR AND SLIGHTLY CREAMY TEXTURE ARE WHAT GAVE IT ITS NAME. THE SECRET OF THE RECIPE LIES IN TWO KEY STEPS: FRYING THE FISH IN A VERY HOT WOK AND COOKING IT IN BOILING WATER.

Serves 2 people

INGREDIENTS

About 300g (10oz) fish leftovers, preferably from a lean fish such as bass, bream or mullet
1 tbsp Shaoxing wine
3 ginger slices
1 tbsp neutral oil
A few whole spring onions (scallions), plus extra, chopped, to garnish
Salt and white pepper

RECIPE STEPS

- Put your fish leftovers (head and central bones) in a large bowl, add the Shaoxing wine and ginger slices, mix well, and marinate for 15 minutes. This step removes any unpleasant fishy smells. Remove the leftovers and drain on kitchen paper.

- Heat a wok over a medium heat until it starts smoking. Add the oil, then the fish carcasses and fry until the surface browns. Switch to a high heat, pour in 800ml (3½ cups) of boiling water and add the whole spring onions. It is important to keep the water boiling throughout the cooking process, about 8–10 minutes, to obtain a milky colour.

- At the end of the cooking time, strain the broth into your serving bowls. Season with salt and white pepper to taste and garnish with a little chopped spring onion. Drink the soup very hot, as the fish smell gets stronger when it cools down.

GOOD TO KNOW
小提示

Using fresh fish is paramount in Chinese cuisine, and even more so in this recipe. Do not use frozen fish – ideally, ask your fishmonger to fillet your fish and keep the leftovers to make this broth.

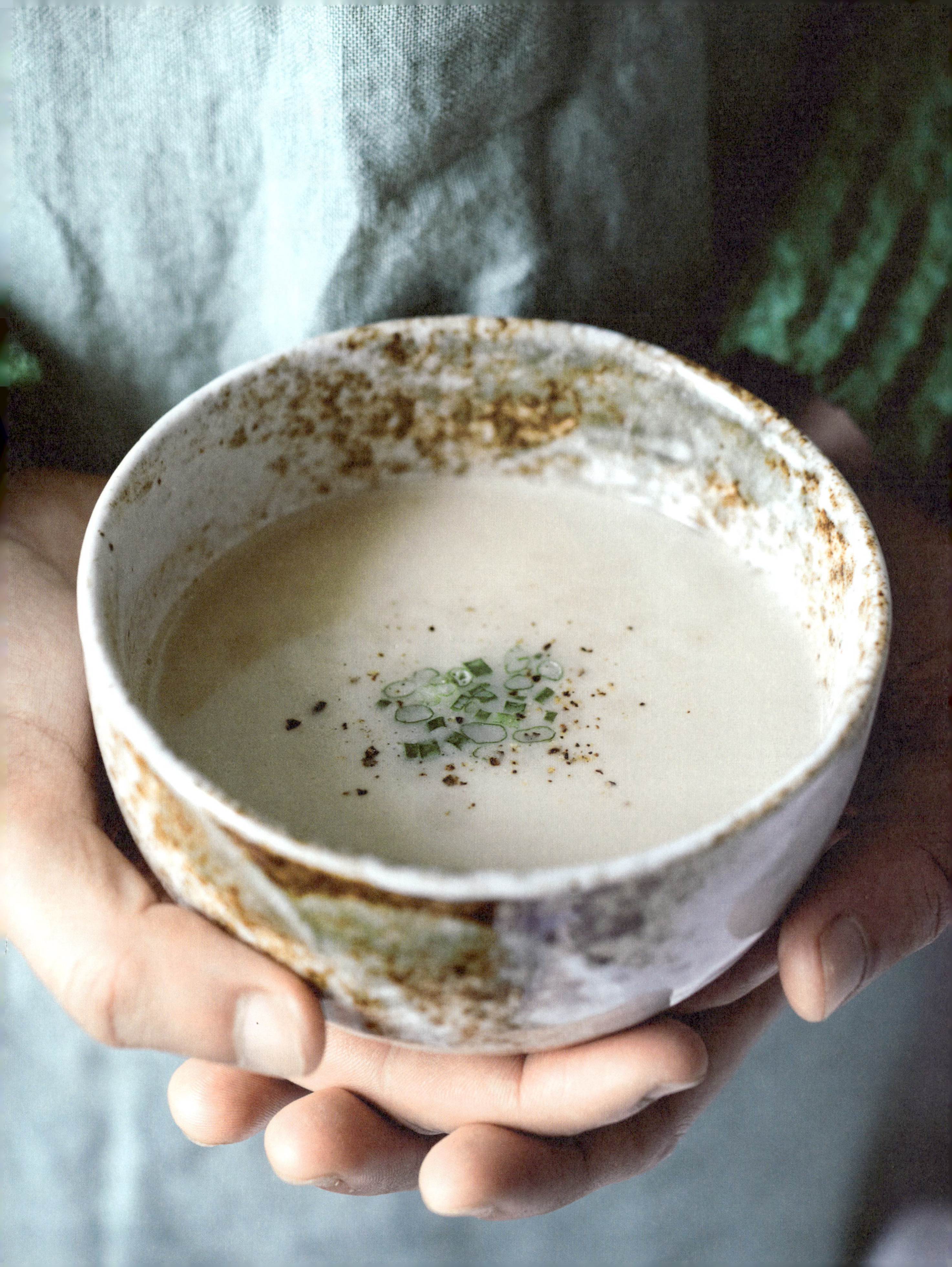

Tomato and Egg Soup

FĀN QIÉ DÀN HUĀ TĀNG

番茄蛋花汤

PREPARING 5 MINUTES

COOKING 8 MINUTES

THIS VERY SIMPLE SOUP IS PROBABLY ONE OF THE MOST POPULAR IN CHINESE HOUSEHOLDS. YOU CAN ACCOMPANY IT WITH RICE OR POUR IT DIRECTLY INTO YOUR RICE BOWL TO MAKE A *PAO FAN* (SEE P. 294).

🍴 Serves 4 people

INGREDIENTS

1 tsp chopped spring onion (scallion) white
2 tsp neutral oil
2 tomatoes, cut into quarters
2 tbsp cornflour (cornstarch)
3 tbsp water
3 medium eggs, beaten
1 tsp salt
¼ tsp white pepper
½ tsp sesame oil
Chopped spring onion (scallion) green, to serve

RECIPE STEPS

- Fry the spring onion with the oil in a hot wok for a few seconds. Add the tomatoes and fry for about 30 seconds, then pour in 800ml (3½ cups) of hot water and simmer the tomatoes for 2–3 minutes. I prefer tender tomatoes that haven't turned to mush.

- Mix the cornflour with the 3 tablespoons of water. Pour this gradually into the wok to thicken the soup (you can choose the amount, to taste). Next, gradually pour in the beaten eggs, using your chopsticks at the same time to swirl the water, which will distribute the eggs evenly.

- Season with the salt, white pepper and sesame oil, then turn off the heat and sprinkle with some chopped spring onion green to serve.

GOOD TO KNOW
小提示

Whether you use fresh seasonal tomatoes or whole canned tomatoes, their quality will largely determine the taste of this lightly seasoned soup.

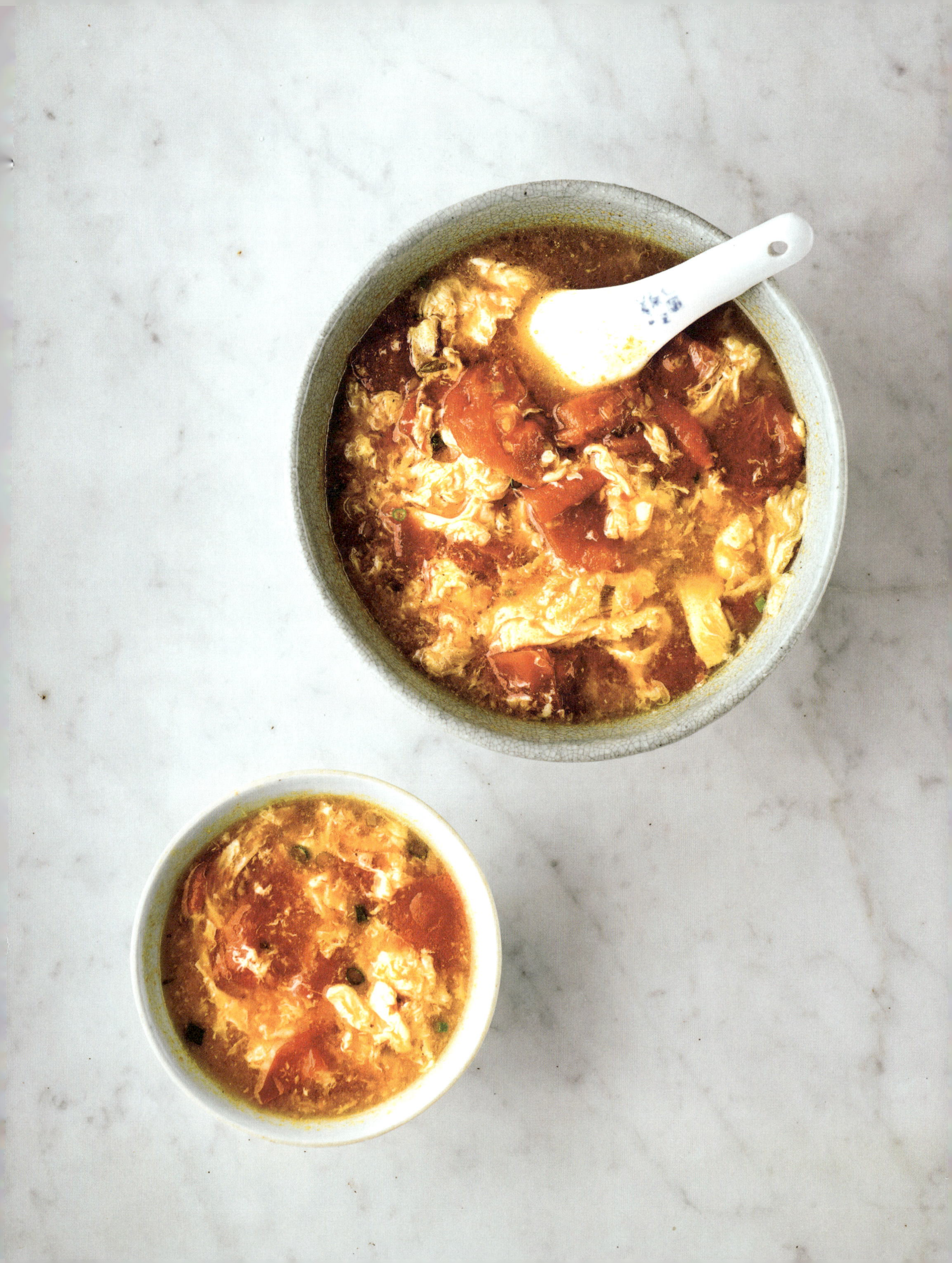

Seaweed Soup with Dried Shrimp

ZǏ　CÀI　XIĀ　PÍ　TĀNG

紫菜虾皮汤

PREPARING 3 MINUTES **COOKING 0 MINUTES**

THIS SIMPLE SOUP, RICH IN UMAMI, REMINDS ME OF MY FAMILY'S COASTAL ORIGINS. I PROBABLY DRANK DOZENS OF LITRES OF IT FROM A YOUNG AGE, AND I STILL HAVEN'T GOT TIRED OF IT. I DON'T USUALLY MEASURE THE QUANTITIES TOO MUCH FOR THIS RECIPE, SO FEEL FREE TO ADJUST THEM TO TASTE.

🍴 Serves 2 people

INGREDIENTS

1 handful of nori seaweed
  (*zi cai, see p. 32*), roughly torn
1 handful of dried mini shrimp
  (*xia pi, see p. 32*)
1 tsp black rice vinegar
½ tsp salt
¼ tsp white pepper
½ tsp sesame oil
Chopped spring onion (scallion)

RECIPE STEPS

- Place the seaweed in a large bowl, then add all the remaining ingredients, except the chopped spring onion.

- Pour in 500ml (generous 2 cups) boiling water, stir, and top with the spring onion.

GOOD TO KNOW
小提示

You can enrich the soup with a beaten egg, added just before pouring in the boiling water. Stir the soup at the same time to distribute the egg evenly.

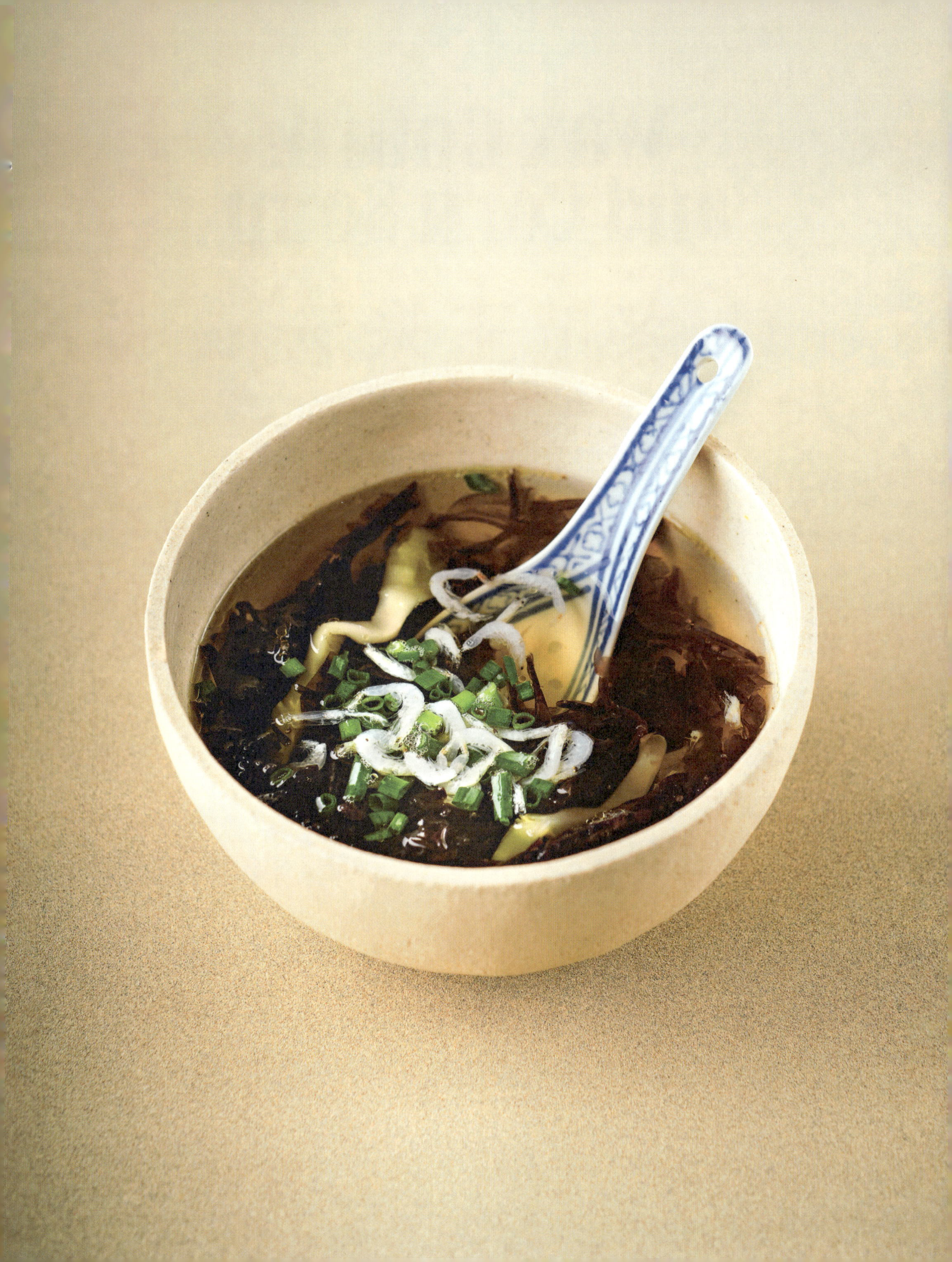

Wax Gourd and Corn Soup

DŌNG   GUĀ   YÙ   MĬ   TĀNG

冬瓜玉米汤

PREPARING 5 MINUTES

COOKING 30 MINUTES

WAX GOURD IS COMMONLY USED IN SOUPS IN CHINA. IN MY FAMILY, IT IS MOST OFTEN ASSOCIATED WITH PORK RIBS. HOWEVER, I SOMETIMES PREFER A LIGHTER BROTH THAT STILL MAINTAINS ITS UMAMI FLAVOUR.

Serves 4 people

INGREDIENTS

2 litres (8½ cups) poultry or vegetable broth (*see p. 160*) or water
600g (1lb 5oz) wax gourd, peeled and cut into 4–5cm (2in) pieces
1 corn cob, cut into 4cm (2in) pieces
½ tbsp salt
2 tbsp dried shrimp (*xia mi, see p. 32*)
1 tbsp goji berries
Chopped spring onion (scallion), to serve

RECIPE STEPS

- Bring the broth to the boil in a pot. (If you're using water, you can add 5 or 6 dried shiitake to add some flavour.) Add the gourd, corn, salt and dried shrimp (*xia mi*; these small and salty shrimp will add the umami flavour that the soup needs).

- Cook for 30 minutes at a constant simmer until the gourd is tender and soft.

- Five minutes before the end of the cooking time, add the goji berries. Serve hot, garnished with a sprinkling of chopped spring onion.

GOOD TO KNOW
小提示

Wax gourd (dong gua, literally "winter squash" in Mandarin) is a large gourd with firm, white flesh. Its taste isn't very pronounced, but it becomes slightly fibrous and tender after cooking, a texture that is appreciated in China. You can buy wax gourd from Asian supermarkets or specialist online retailers, but if you can't find it, feel free to try other squashes.

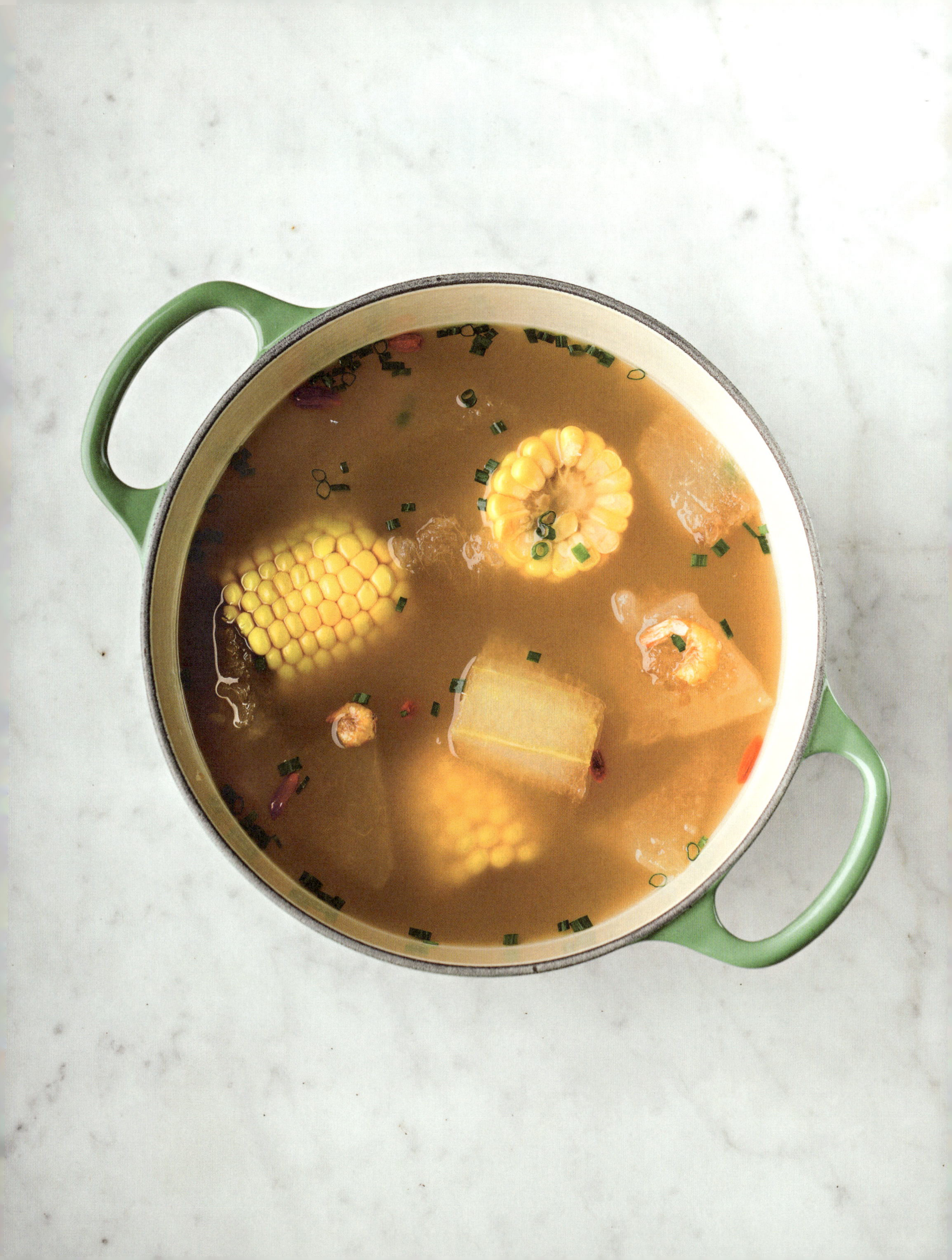

Hot and Sour Soup

SUĀN　LÀ　TĀNG

酸辣汤

PREPARING 75 MINUTES

COOKING 10 MINUTES

THIS SLIGHTLY THICK SOUP OWES ITS NAME TO ITS TWO MAIN SEASONINGS: BLACK RICE VINEGAR AND WHITE PEPPER.

Serves 4 people

INGREDIENTS

3 shiitake mushrooms
5g (⅛oz) dried black fungus
30g (1oz) bamboo shoots
1 tsp neutral oil
1 tsp salt
1 tsp white pepper
½ tsp dark soy sauce
50g (1¾oz) dried ham (preferably jamón ibérico) or shredded chicken, very thinly sliced
½ soft tofu block, about 200g (7oz) (*see p. 118*), cut into 2cm (¾in) cubes
2 tbsp cornflour (cornstarch)
2 tbsp water
2 eggs, beaten
1 tbsp black rice vinegar

To serve

1 tsp sesame oil
Chopped spring onion (scallion) and/or coriander (cilantro)

RECIPE STEPS

- Rehydrate the shiitake and black fungus for 1 hour in water (see p. 32 for more information on dried foods), then drain and finely julienne them. Cut the bamboo shoots into thin slices. If you are using fresh ones, blanch them for 30 seconds in boiling water after slicing them. Set aside.

- Heat the wok over a medium heat. Pour in the neutral oil and fry the shiitake for 30 seconds. Add 1 litre (4⅓ cups) of water and the salt, pepper and dark soy sauce. Bring to the boil, then lower the heat to a simmer. Add the black fungus, bamboo shoots and ham (or chicken) and cook for about 2 minutes.

- Add the tofu, then mix the cornflour and water in a bowl. Gradually pour into the soup, stirring constantly with a spoon or chopsticks. Once the soup has thickened, add the eggs little by little, distributing them evenly over the entire surface. Cook for a few seconds, stirring gently.

- Turn off the heat and add the black rice vinegar. I like this soup to taste like vinegar, as per the Chinese way, but you can adjust this to taste. Season with more salt and pepper if needed. Serve the soup in bowls topped with a dash of sesame oil and a sprinkling of spring onion and/or chopped coriander.

GOOD TO KNOW
小提示

This soup's ingredients are not set in stone, but in China, it is usually made with bamboo shoots, tofu, mushrooms, shredded meat (ham in this case to add as much umami flavour as possible) and duck blood.

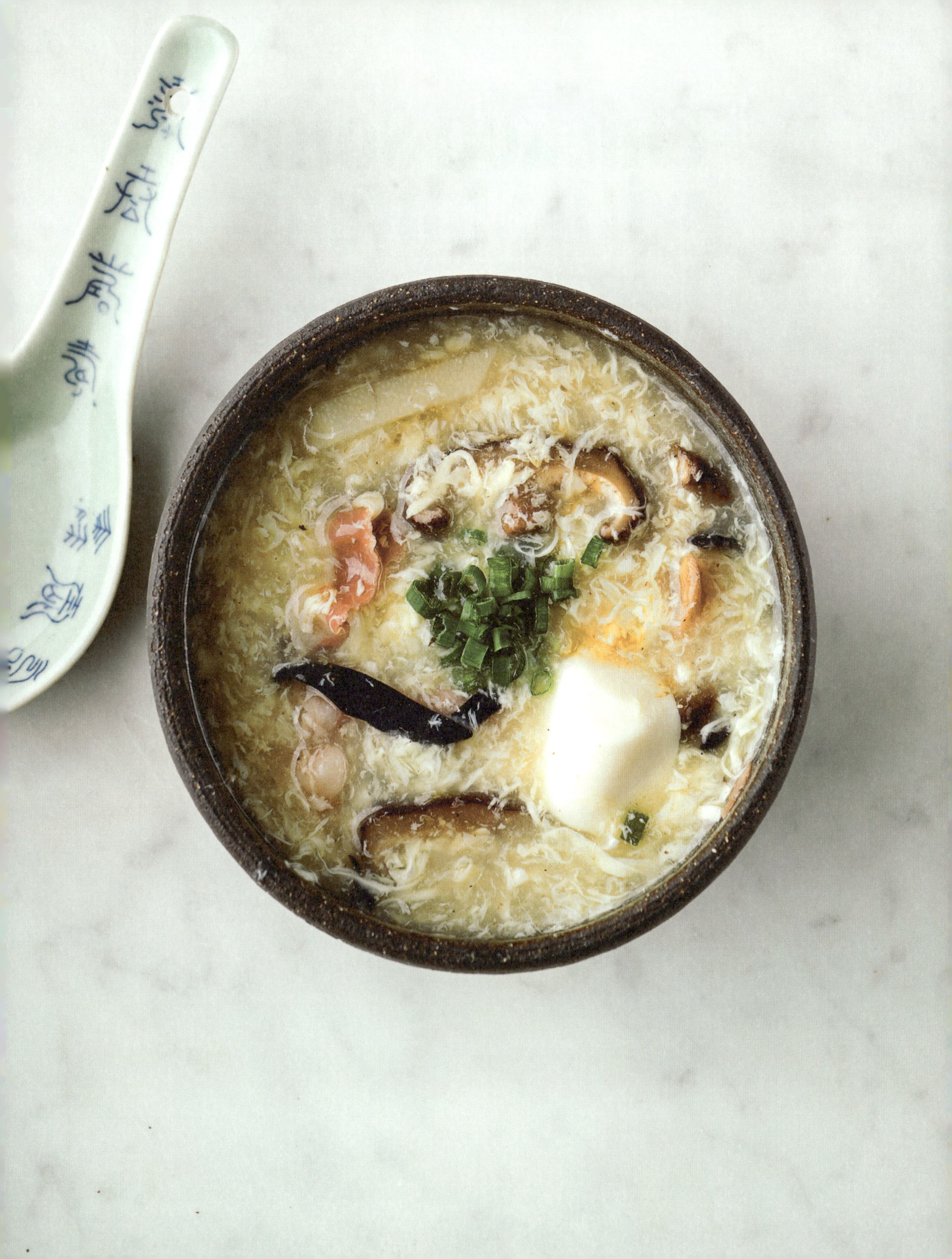

Chicken Soup with Shiitake

MÓ GŪ DÙN JĪ TĀNG

蘑菇炖鸡汤

PREPARING 15 MINUTES

COOKING 70 MINUTES

IN CHINA, CHICKEN SOUP IS ASSOCIATED WITH WELL-BEING. IT IS OFTEN SERVED TO SICK OR WEAKENED PEOPLE, SUCH AS NEW MOTHERS DURING THE GOLDEN MONTH. THE AIM IS TO PRESERVE THE CHICKEN'S UMAMI FLAVOUR, MEANING THAT STRONG SPICES SHOULD BE AVOIDED.

Serves 4 people

INGREDIENTS

600g (1lb 5oz) chicken (half a chicken, or only the legs), cut into 3–4cm (1½in) pieces
1 piece of ginger, about 3cm (1¼in), sliced
1 tbsp neutral oil
1 spring onion (scallion), white part cut into sticks, green part chopped
8 dried jujubes (*see p. 35*)
8 dried shiitake mushrooms, rehydrated
Vegetables of choice (*see note; optional*)
2 tsp goji berries
Salt

RECIPE STEPS

- Put the chicken pieces and ginger slices in a pot and fill with cold water. Bring to the boil over a high heat and skim off the foam, to remove any impurities. Take out the meat and set aside. Discard the water and ginger from the pot.

- In the same pot, heat the oil and add the spring onion white. Fry for about 10 seconds to release the flavour. Add the chicken pieces back in and lightly brown over a medium heat.

- Remove the spring onion white, pour in 2 litres (8½ cups) of boiling water and cook the chicken over a high heat for 5 minutes, skimming if necessary. Add the jujubes, shiitake and any vegetables if using, then switch to a low heat, cover and simmer for 1 hour.

- Five minutes before the end of the cooking time, stir in the goji berries. Finish with a little chopped spring onion green and add salt to taste. Serve hot with white rice.

GOOD TO KNOW
小提示

I like to use vegetables that add a touch of sweetness (carrot, corn) or that have a tender texture (turnip). If you are using a whole chicken, you can remove the parts that are too fatty to get a lighter broth, such as the rump or some areas of skin that is too thick.

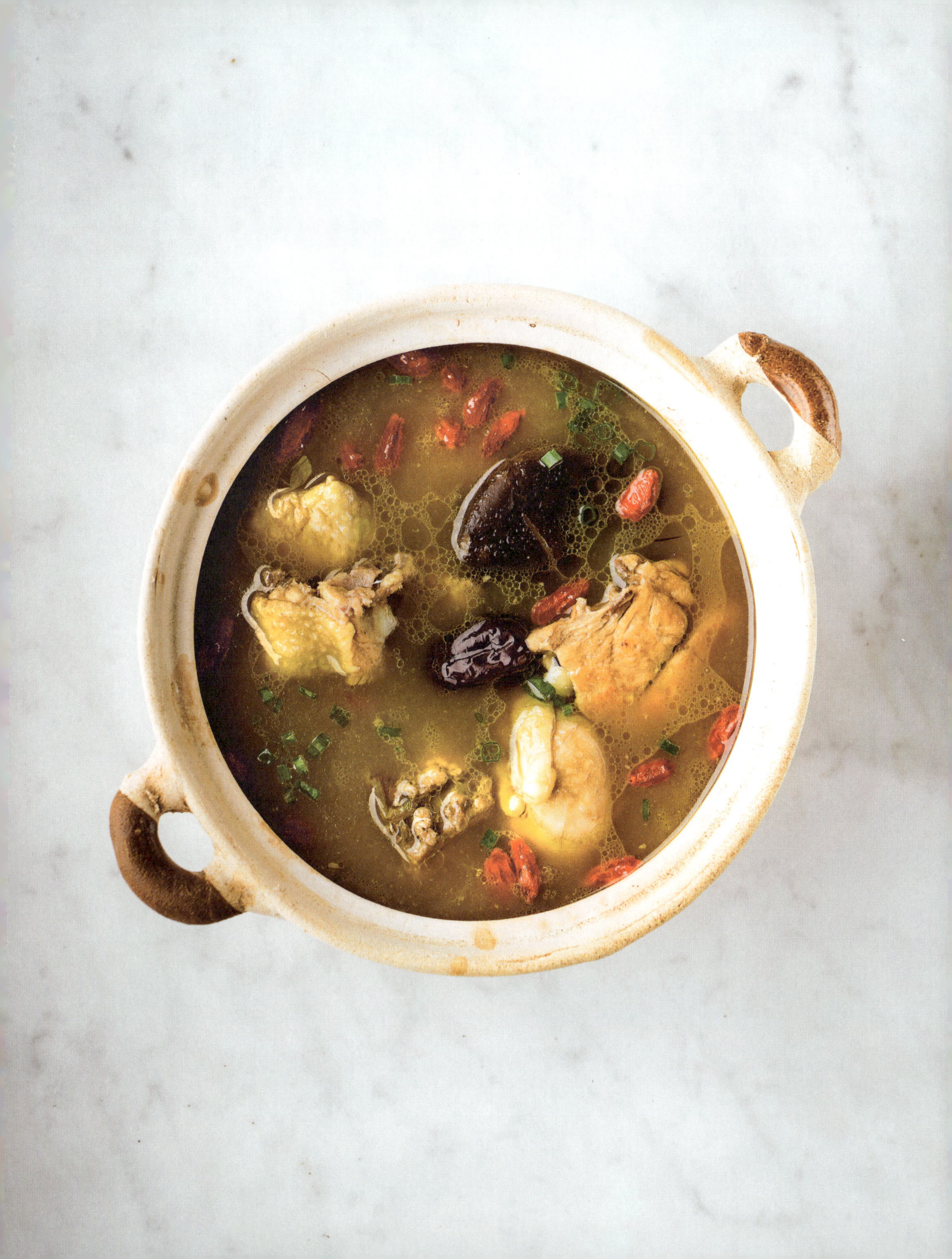

Chicken Meatball and Vermicelli Soup

JĪ WÁN ZI TĀNG

鸡丸子汤

PREPARING 15 MINUTES

COOKING 35 MINUTES

A GOOD CHINESE MEATBALL MUST ALWAYS HAVE A SPRINGY TEXTURE, MEANING THAT IT BOUNCES IN THE MOUTH, BUT WITHOUT THE EXCESS YOU FIND IN PROCESSED MEATBALLS. THE ONES IN THIS RECIPE SOAK UP THE SOUP DURING COOKING, WHICH IS WHY I DON'T SEASON THIS DISH TOO MUCH. I SEE IT AS THE ULTIMATE COMFORT FOOD!

Serves 2 people

INGREDIENTS

For the broth

1 litre (4⅓ cups) cold water
2 ginger slices
50g (1¾oz) mung bean vermicelli, soaked in warm water for 10 minutes, then drained
½ soft tofu block, cut into 3cm (1¼in) cubes
½ tsp salt
¼ tsp white pepper
Finely chopped spring onion (scallion), to serve

For the meatballs

1 chicken leg, about 200g (7oz), boned and finely chopped
1 tsp grated ginger
2 tsp chopped spring onion (scallion) white
2 tsp soy sauce
¼ tsp white pepper
¼ tsp 5-spice
½ tsp salt
1 tbsp water
2 tsp neutral oil
½ tsp cornflour (cornstarch)

FOR THE BROTH

- Pour the cold water into a pot, add the bones and skin from the chicken leg, then bring to the boil over a high heat, skimming off the foam, to remove any impurities. Switch to a low heat, add the ginger slices and simmer for 30 minutes (or until the liquid has reduced by a third).

FOR THE MEATBALLS

- Meanwhile, mix the chicken meat with the grated ginger, chopped spring onion white, soy sauce, white pepper, 5-spice and salt, then pour in the water, oil and cornflour. Use a whisk and a pair of chopsticks to mix, in quick circles going in the same direction, for about 1 minute, until it becomes sticky. This is the key step to making meatballs with the right texture. Shape the meatballs by hand.

TO FINISH

- Add the meatballs to the slightly simmering broth, then the vermicelli and tofu. The meatballs will take about 3–4 minutes to cook. Taste the broth, season with the salt and pepper (if needed) and sprinkle with spring onion to serve.

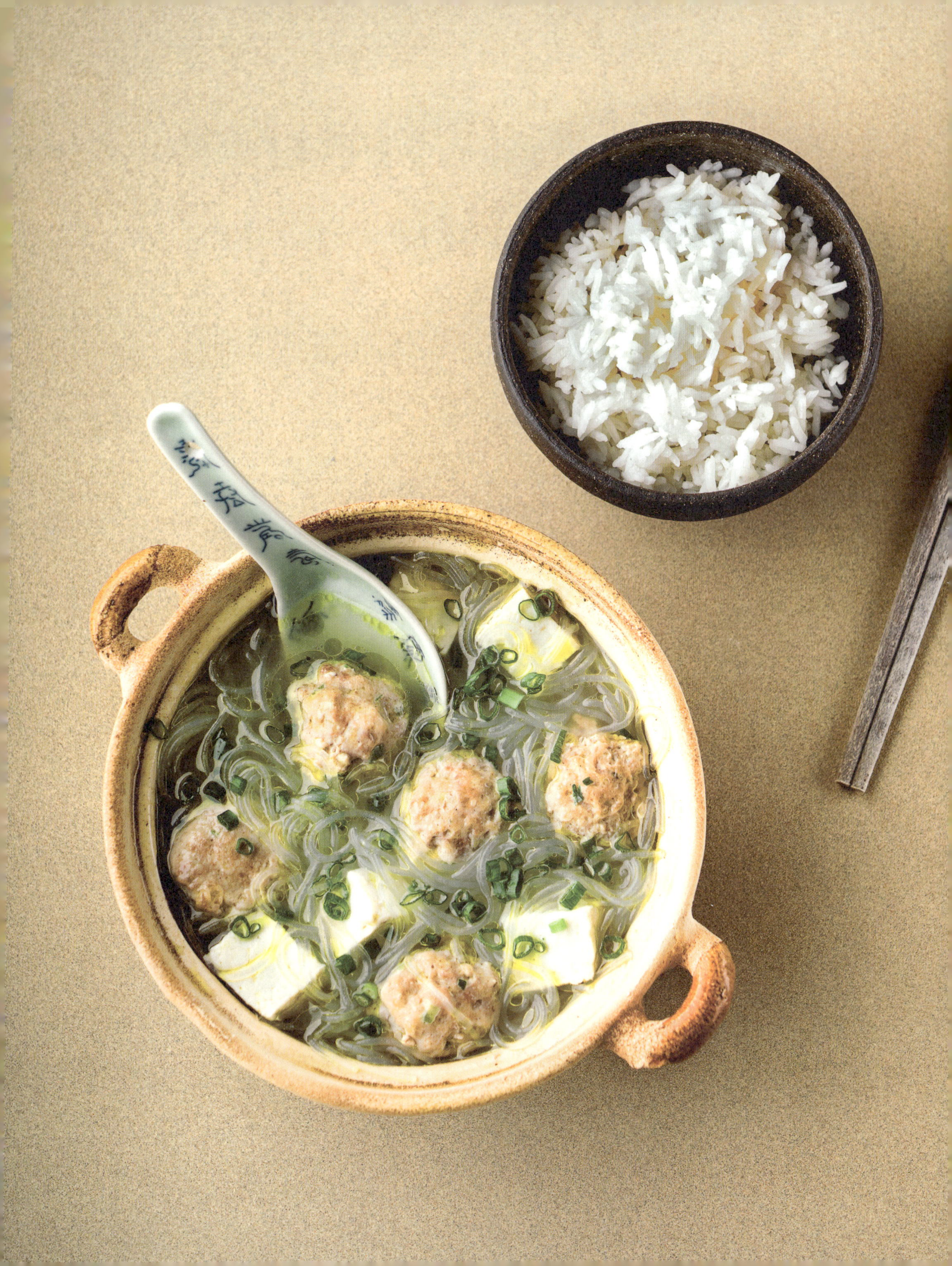

Taro and Trotter Soup

YÙ　NǍI　ZHŪ　TÍ　TĀNG
芋艿猪蹄汤

PREPARING 5 MINUTES

COOKING 2 HOURS

MY MOTHER REGULARLY MADE THIS SOUP AT HOME. I'M NOT A BIG FAN OF TROTTER, BUT IN THIS CASE, THE COMBINATION OF THE THREE INGREDIENTS WORKS WELL: A COLLAGEN-RICH BROTH, A VERY PLEASANT AND MILD SOY FLAVOUR, AND TENDER TARO.

Serves 6 people

INGREDIENTS

50g (1¾oz) soy beans, rehydrated (*see method*)
200g (7oz) pork ribs
200g (7oz) pig's trotters
20g (¾oz) ginger, sliced
2 tbsp Shaoxing wine
500g (1lb 2oz) taro, peeled and cut in half
200g (7oz) carrots, peeled and cut into 3-4cm (1½in) pieces
Finely chopped spring onion (scallion), to serve
Salt and white pepper

RECIPE STEPS

- The day before you want to make this soup, put the soy beans in cold water to rehydrate. Drain and set aside.

- Put the pork ribs and trotters in a pot of cold water and bring to the boil over a high heat, skimming off any foam, to remove any impurities. Drain and rinse.

- Put the meat back into the (clean) pot and add the soy beans, ginger, Shaoxing wine and 3 litres (3 quarts) of boiling water. Briefly bring to the boil, then turn the heat down, cover, and simmer over a low heat for 1½ hours.

- Add the taro and carrot pieces into the broth, stir, and continue cooking for another 30 minutes. The taro and carrots are ready when they become tender.

- Season at the end with salt and white pepper, and serve sprinkled with spring onion.

GOOD TO KNOW
小提示

If, like me, you mainly use meat to flavour broths without necessarily wanting to eat it, you can replace the pork ribs with pork bones.

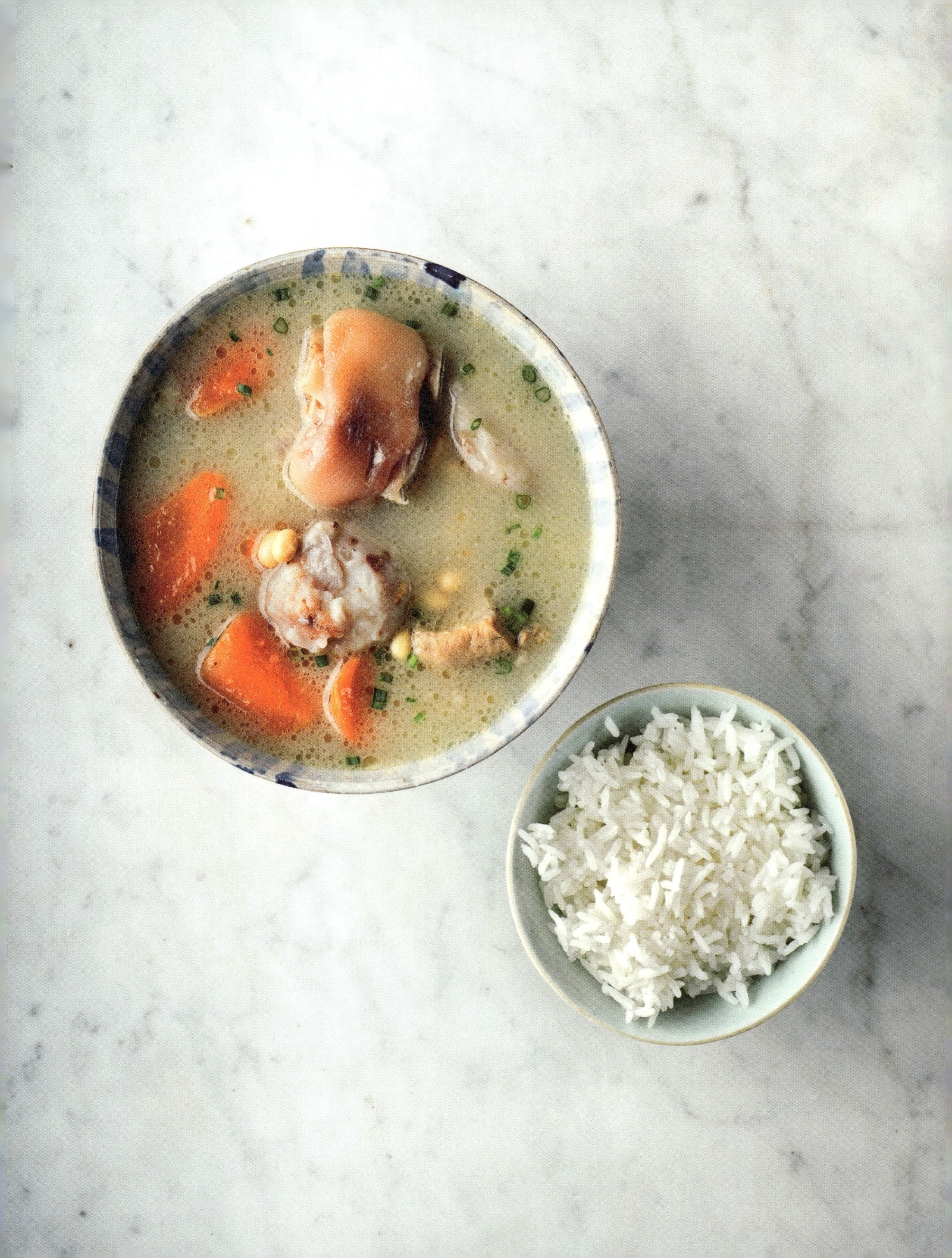

Chinese–Style Borscht

NIÚ　WĚI　LUÓ　SÒNG　TĀNG

牛尾罗宋汤

PREPARING 15 MINUTES

COOKING 2 HOURS

THIS SOUP IS A LEGACY OF THE "ROARING TWENTIES" IN SHANGHAI, WHICH WAS ALREADY A COSMOPOLITAN CITY 100 YEARS AGO. ITS RED COLOUR IS THE ONLY THING THAT REMAINS OF THE ORIGINAL VERSION IMPORTED BY BELARUSIAN REFUGEES. TOMATO HAS REPLACED BEETROOT AND OXTAIL IS OFTEN ADDED, MAKING IT A WINTER DISH THAT WARMS YOU UP.

🍴 Serves 4 people

INGREDIENTS

1kg (2¼lb) oxtail (beef tail), cut into chunks
2 tbsp plain (all-purpose) flour
2 tbsp neutral oil (or butter)
3 garlic cloves, minced
1 tsp Shaoxing wine
400g (14oz) canned tomatoes
½ tsp tomato paste
1 tsp salt
½ onion, chopped
300g (10oz) carrots, peeled and cut into large pieces
300g (10oz) potatoes, peeled and cut into large pieces
300g (10oz) white radish (*daikon*), peeled and cut into large pieces
Salt and black pepper
Chopped spring onion (scallion), to serve

RECIPE STEPS

• Rinse the oxtail pieces (it doesn't matter what size they are for cooking this recipe) with water in a large bowl, then drain. Coat the surface of the meat with a thin layer of flour on all sides. Heat a frying pan with 1 tablespoon of the oil over a medium heat, add the meat and brown on each side for about 5 minutes.

• Add the garlic and fry for a few seconds to release the flavour, then deglaze the pan with the Shaoxing wine. Transfer the ingredients to a pot and add the tomatoes, tomato paste and salt. Pour in enough hot water to cover the ingredients, then bring to the boil and simmer over a low heat for 1½ hours. (If you use a pressure cooker, reduce the cooking time by half.)

• Towards the end of the cooking time, heat a frying pan over a medium heat. Brown the chopped onion in the remaining tablespoon of oil for 1 minute, then add the carrots, potatoes and white radish and fry over a low heat for 5 minutes.

• Once the broth has simmered for 1½ hours, transfer the fried vegetables to the pot and simmer for another 30 minutes until all the ingredients are tender.

• Add salt to taste and serve with a sprinkling of freshly ground black pepper and chopped spring onion.

GOOD TO KNOW
小提示

This soup is quite rich, thanks to the oxtail. If I have any leftovers, I like to add noodles, topping up with a little soy sauce and black rice vinegar.

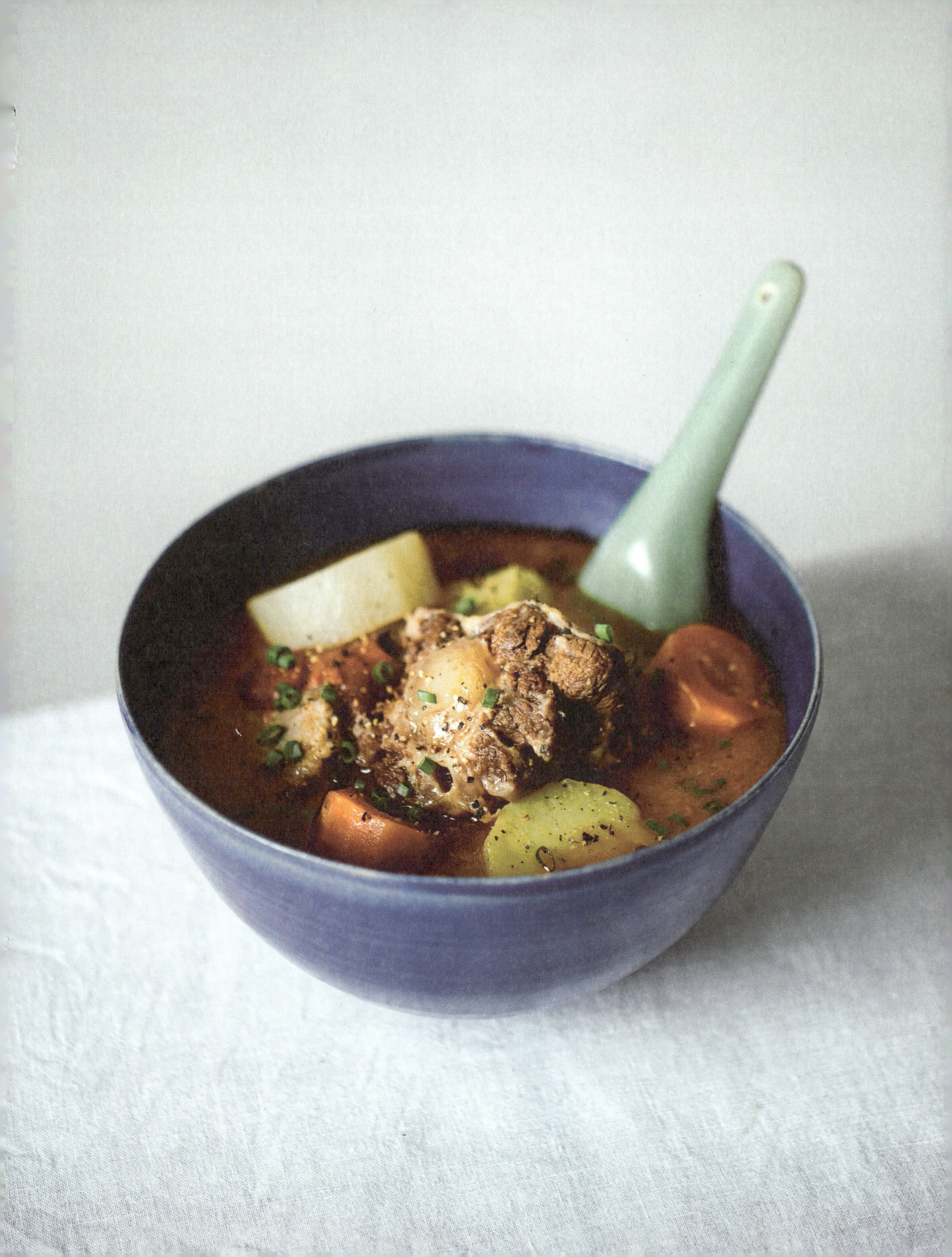

CHAPTER
07

Meat
肉
RÒU

PP. 186-187: Dongpo pork ■ PP. 188-189: Pork belly with rice flour
PP. 192-193: Steamed pork with dried mustard leaves ■ PP. 194-195: Crispy pork ■ PP. 196-197: Twice-cooked pork
PP. 198-199: Char siu ■ PP. 200-201: Sweet and sour pork ribs ■ PP. 202-203: Steamed pork ribs with douchi
PP. 204-205: Coca-Cola-flavoured chicken wings ■ PP. 206-207: Popcorn chicken ■ PP. 208-209: Beef with black pepper

From All Angles

When It Comes to Pork, Nothing Is Wasted

WHEN WE TALK ABOUT MEAT IN CHINA, PORK IS THE DEFAULT ANIMAL. ALL ITS PARTS (OR NEARLY) ARE CONSUMED, BECAUSE IN THE NOT SO DISTANT PAST, MEAT WAS A RARE PRODUCT THAT WAS RESERVED FOR SPECIAL OCCASIONS.

A HISTORY OF PORK

Pork has become the most popular meat in the country since the beginning of the Ming dynasty, nearly 700 years ago.

Mutton and beef were prized by the ruling class, whether under the Mongols or Manchu, the last two Chinese dynasties. But pigs had the advantage of being omnivorous, easy to raise in dense areas of the kingdom, and had less agricultural or military use than other livestock. That is why pork became the meat of the people.

CHOICE CUTS

Chinese people have created an incredibly high number of pork recipes. Pork belly is the most popular cut, given that its 7:3 ratio of 70% lean meat and 30% fat is ideal for wok cooking.

Pork ribs, spare ribs and trotters, rich in collagen, are also very popular.

Pork kidneys, finely cut and meticulously cut on the diagonal, are fried with vegetables in a wok.

Pork blood is valued for its texture, which is similar to silken tofu and often served in small pieces in a broth.

As for the intestines, they are cleaned out and cut up before simmering for hours in a broth that is used to make a soup of rice vermicelli (猪脏粉, *zhū zàng fěn*), a Wenzhou speciality and a dish from my childhood that I still enjoy.

OTHER MEATS

• Poultry (chicken, duck) is very popular. Cantonese people are particularly fond of it and have become masters in preparing it. You will find a few of these recipes in this book (Coca-Cola-flavoured chicken wings, p. 204; popcorn chicken, p. 206).

• Beef, which is more expensive, comes in third place, although it has become more common with the improvement of living standards.

• In the North and especially the North-West, mutton and lamb are historically associated with the (formerly) nomadic people of Inner Mongolia or the Muslim Chinese people of the Xinjiang or Qinghai regions. Lamb skewers or grilled rack of lamb have become popular dishes all over China.

• In Xizang (Tibet), yak meat is ubiquitous.

• The most surprising, perhaps, is Sichuan's love of rabbit meat. The meat is fried with chilli peppers and Sichuan peppercorn, while the head, once braised with spices, is a popular snack. You are now prepared for such a dish if you ever set foot in Chengdu…

MEMORY
回忆

Despite the explosion (or catching up) of meat consumption, Chinese cuisine has kept an inherently frugal approach to meat. Always pre-cut (and therefore portioned) before cooking, meat is shared with the whole table, alongside other dishes of vegetables, tofu and soup.

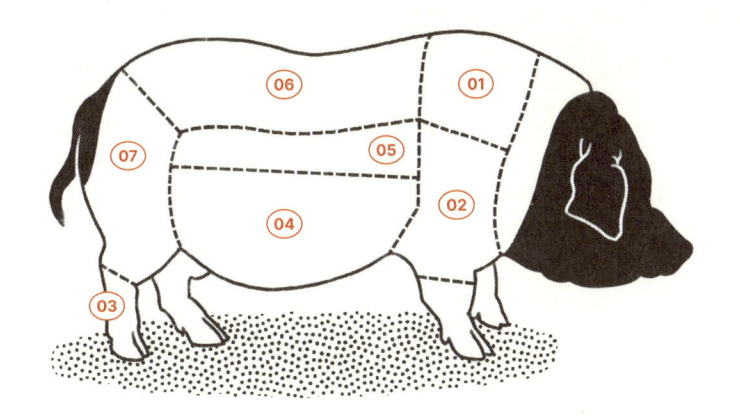

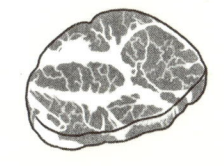

01
SPARE RIB
梅花肉 | MÉI HUĀ RÒU

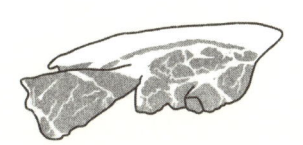

02
KNUCKLE OF HAM
前腿肉 | QIÁN TUǏ RÒU

03
TROTTER
猪蹄 | ZHŪ TÍ

04
BELLY
五花肉 | WǓ HUĀ RÒU

05
FILLET
里脊肉 | LǏ JĪ RÒU

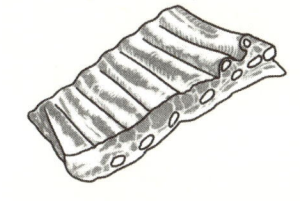

06
RIB
猪排骨 | ZHŪ PÁI GǓ

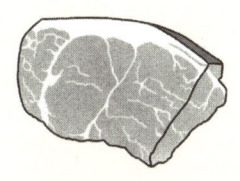

07
HAM
后腿肉 | HÒU TUǏ RÒU

TECHNIQUE 5

Preparing the Meat

MEAT PREPARATION FOLLOWS 3 MAIN PRINCIPLES:
1) CUTTING; AS THERE IS NO KNIFE AT THE TABLE, EVERYTHING MUST BE CUT BEFOREHAND IN THE KITCHEN.
2) BLANCHING, TO NEUTRALIZE UNPLEASANT SMELLS, TO WHICH CHINESE PEOPLE ARE VERY SENSITIVE.
3) TENDERIZING, TO ACHIEVE A VELVETY TEXTURE, WHICH IS AN OBSESSION IN CHINESE CUISINE.

CUTTING

刀工

DĀO GŌNG

Here are the 3 most common types of cuts for stir-fried dishes.
A little tip: you can freeze the meat for 30 minutes to make it firmer and easier to cut.

SLICES
片 / PIÀN

Find the grain of the meat (see the "good to know" section) and cut into thin slices of 2–3mm (⅛in) against the grain. Keep the knife at an angle of 45° to make wider slices.

STICKS
丝 / SĪ

Cut into thicker slices of about 5mm (¼in), then into sticks. To go faster, you can spread the meat slices like cards on your countertop.

CUBES
丁 / DĪNG

Cut the meat first into 1cm (½in) wide strips along the grain, then cut into small cubes.

RESTAURANT SECRETS

In restaurants, it is common to fry marinated meat in an oil bath at 150°C (300°F) for about 10 seconds before browning it.

This technique, called *guo you* ("dunk in oil"), helps the meat to maintain its shape and "lock" in the texture and juice. It is best to add the meat pieces gradually, to prevent them from clumping together in the oil.

At home, to avoid using too much oil, the *guo shui* technique ("dunk in water") is preferred, which involves blanching marinated meat in simmering water.

To avoid "washing off" your marinade during this pre-cooking stage, add a little oil to the meat to create a protective layer (oil and water do not mix) and do not blanch the meat for more than 30 seconds. Drain before frying it.

GOOD TO KNOW
小提示

The grain of the meat refers to the direction of muscle fibres, which are more or less visible depending on the type of meat (chicken < pork < beef) and the cut (fillet < thigh).

It is recommended to "cut against the grain" if the fibres are highly visible, which means cutting perpendicular to the grain to shorten the fibres. This will make chewing easier and therefore give the meat a softer mouthfeel.

BLANCHING

焯水

CHĀO SHUǏ

The notion of neutralizing "strong smells" (腥味, xing wei) in Chinese cuisine involves treating the meat before cooking it, especially for braised or simmered dishes, most often with ginger and Shaoxing wine.

01
Cut the meat to the size required for the recipe. Immerse it in a pot with enough cold water to cover the meat. Add a few ginger slices (no need to peel it in this case) and 1–2 tablespoons of Shaoxing wine.

02
Set over a high heat, without covering, and remove any foam (which is made of coagulated proteins) from the surface as you go, using a strainer or skimmer.

03
Turn off the heat once the water boils. Drain the pieces of meat and let them cool before using them for the rest of the recipe.

TENDERIZING

变嫩

BIÀN NÈN

"Velveting" is the English term for a three-step process commonly used in Chinese cuisine for stir-fried dishes. The goal is to keep the meat juicy with a texture that "slides in the mouth", like velvet.

01
Marinate the meat according to the recipe (in Shaoxing wine, soy sauce, minced garlic...) and massage well to make it absorb the seasoning.

02
Add a little cornflour (cornstarch) and massage again for a few seconds. The starch makes a protective layer that will help retain the meat juices during cooking. Marinate for 15 minutes to 1 hour, depending on the meat's thickness and texture.

03
Then, pour over 1 tablespoon of neutral oil per 500g (1lb 2oz) of meat and mix. This prevents the pieces from clumping and sticking together when cooking.

Dongpo Pork

DŌNG　　PŌ　　RÒU

东坡肉

PREPARING 15 MINUTES

COOKING 2 HOURS

THIS RECIPE OWES ITS NAME TO THE FAMOUS POET SU DONGPO, WHO IS SAID TO HAVE INVENTED IT IN 1089 WHEN HE LIVED IN HANGZHOU. THE PORK STANDS OUT IN THIS RECIPE WITH ITS SHINING RED COLOUR, ITS MELTING FAT, ALL WITHOUT USING A SINGLE DROP OF OIL. IT IS ONE OF THE BEST-KNOWN MEAT DISHES IN CHINA, AND REPRESENTS THE COOKING TECHNIQUE CALLED *HONG SHAO* (*SEE P.50*).

Serves 4 people

INGREDIENTS

600g (1lb 5oz) pork belly, with the skin
10 spring onions
8 ginger slices
150ml (⅔ cup) good-quality Shaoxing wine, such as Huadiao (*see p. 24*)
60g (2oz) rock sugar (*see p. 27*)
4 tbsp light soy sauce
1 tbsp dark soy sauce
2 bay leaves

RECIPE STEPS

• Blanch the pork in boiling water (see p. 185) and let it cool in an ice bath so that it firms up. Drain. Using a sharp knife, cut the meat into 4cm (1½in) squares. It doesn't matter if some pieces are a bit larger.

• Line the bottom of a pot with the spring onions (folded in 2) and the ginger slices. This prevents the meat from sticking to the bottom of the pot, and adds flavour.

• Place the meat in the pot, skin side down (you can tie each piece of pork so that it keeps its shape as well as possible during cooking, but this isn't essential). Add the Shaoxing wine, rock sugar, soy sauces and bay leaves and enough water to cover the meat. Bring to the boil, then cover and simmer for 2 hours over a low heat.

• At the end of the cooking time, switch to a medium heat for a few minutes so that the liquid starts to reduce and to finish colouring the meat. Remove the pieces of meat and continue reducing the sauce until thick, but do not reduce it too much, or it will turn into a viscous caramel (if this happens, just add a drop of hot water to loosen).

• Put the pork on a plate, pour over the sauce and serve with white rice. This dish will taste even better heated up the following day.

GOOD TO KNOW
小提示

If you use a pressure cooker, like most Chinese households, reduce the cooking time by half.

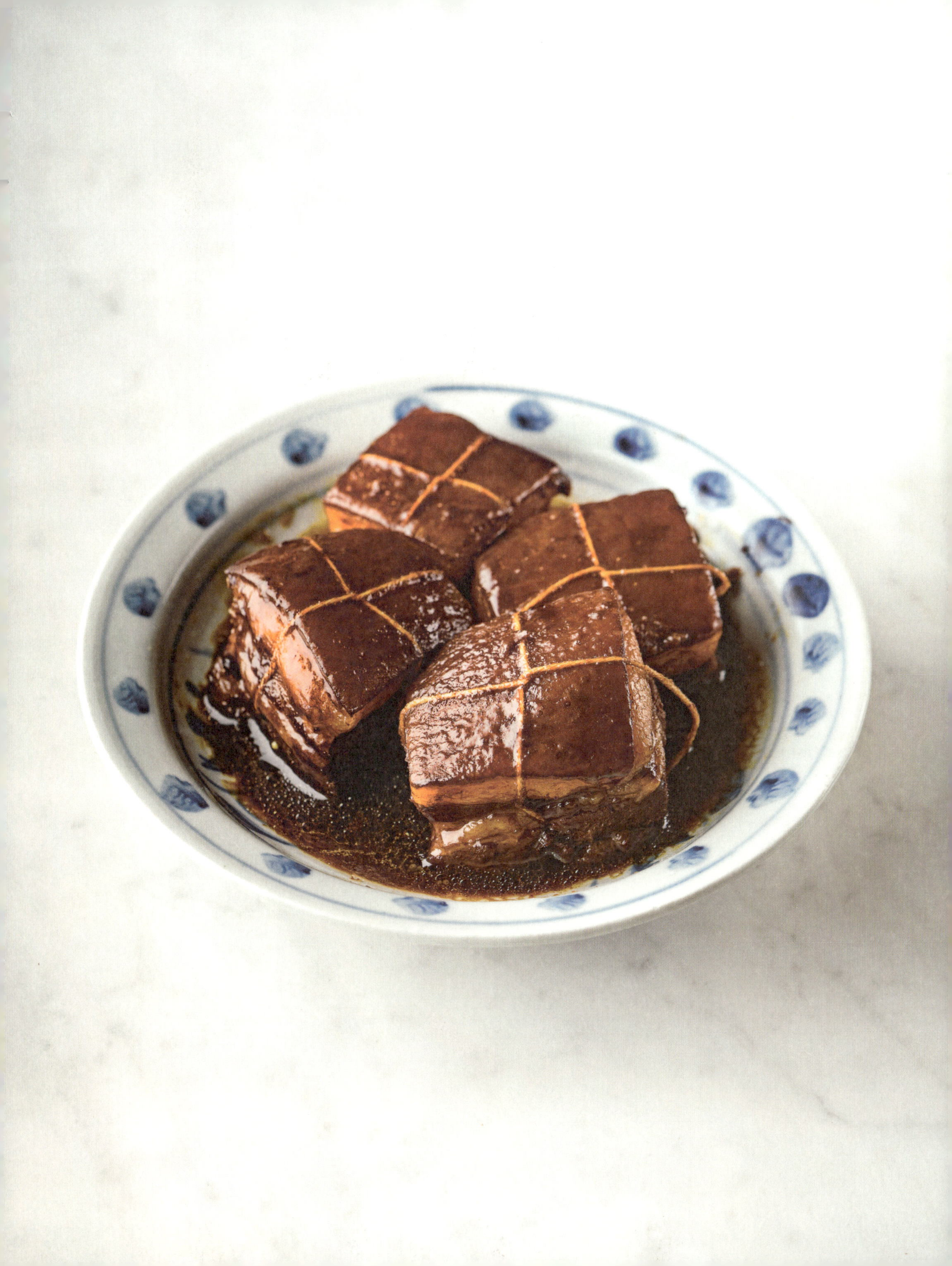

Pork Belly with Rice Flour

FĚN ZHĒNG RÒU

粉蒸肉

PREPARING 45 MINUTES

COOKING 90 MINUTES

THIS *KOU ROU* (MEAT THAT IS STEAMED FOR SEVERAL HOURS) DISH, OF SICHUAN ORIGIN, IS A RECENT DISCOVERY FOR ME. POTATOES OR SWEET POTATOES CAN BE ADDED DURING COOKING. I ALSO LIKE TO WRAP THE MEAT WITH A SHISO LEAF; IT MAKES FOR AN INCREDIBLE COMBO.

Serves 4 people

INGREDIENTS

For the pork belly

400g (14oz) pork belly, with the skin
1 tbsp light soy sauce
1 tsp dark soy sauce
1 tsp salt
1 tsp sugar
½ tsp Sichuan peppercorn
1 tsp chopped ginger
½ tsp 5-spice
1 tsp chilli bean paste (*doubanjiang*)
1 egg white
Chopped spring onion (scallion)
A few shiso leaves (*optional*)

For the rice powder

20g (¾oz/2 tbsp) jasmine rice
20g (¾oz/2 tbsp) sticky rice
¼ tsp star anise
¼ tsp fennel seeds
½ cinnamon stick, broken
½ tsp Sichuan peppercorn

FOR THE RICE POWDER

- Wash both rices and toast over a low heat in a wok or frying pan for 6–7 minutes until lightly browned. Transfer to a blender, then add the star anise, fennel seeds, cinnamon and Sichuan peppercorn and blend until you obtain a powder similar to fine breadcrumbs.

FOR THE PORK

- Cut the belly into roughly 1cm (½in) slices. Transfer to a large container and pour over the soy sauces, salt, sugar, Sichuan pepper, ginger, 5-spice and chilli bean paste. Massage the marinade into the meat. Add the egg white and mix, then coat each piece of meat in the rice powder. Leave to marinate for 30 minutes.

- Place the pieces of meat in a bowl, skin side down. Bring your steamer to the boil. Place the bowl in your steamer basket and cook for 1½ hours over a medium heat. Remember to add water to the steamer from time to time to prevent it from drying out.

- To serve, place a plate on top of the bowl and flip the bowl over, holding the plate firmly in place. Sprinkle the pork with chopped spring onion and enjoy with a bowl of rice or some shiso leaves. The dish will be even better when warmed up the next day!

GOOD TO KNOW
小提示

To ensure that the meat does not lose its shape during cooking, choose a piece of belly that is large enough, at least 6cm (2½in), and do not cut it too thinly; aim for at least 1cm (½in).

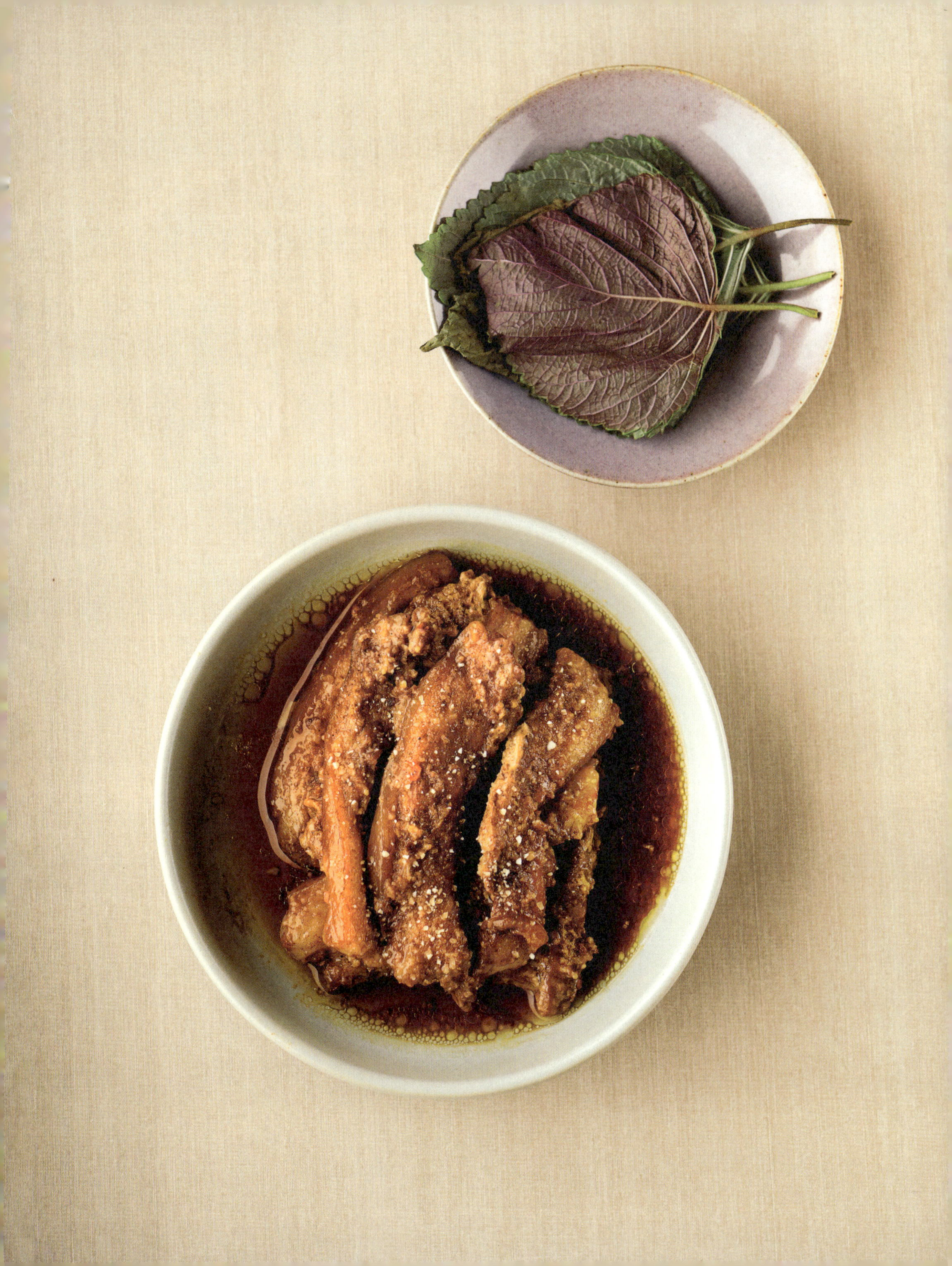

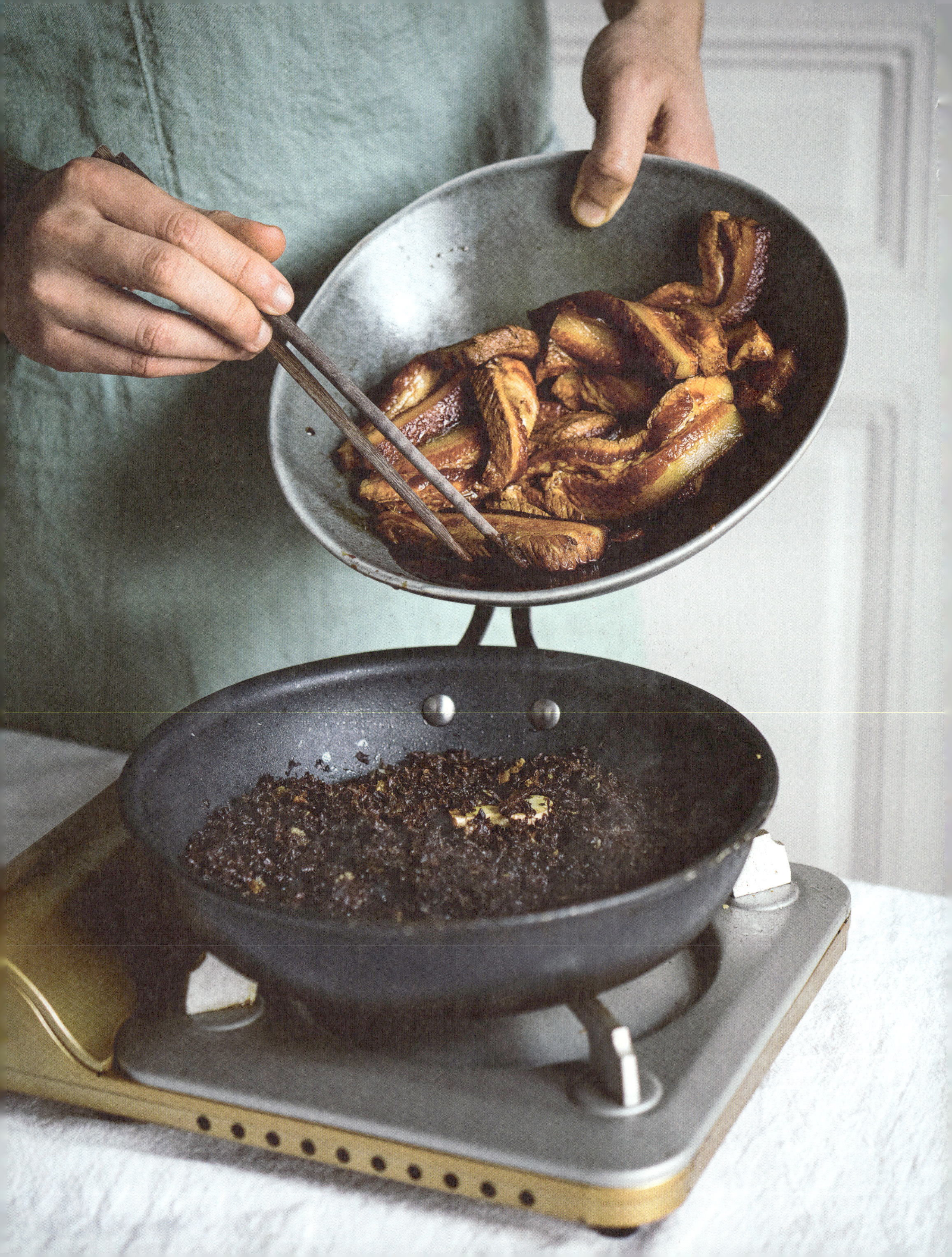

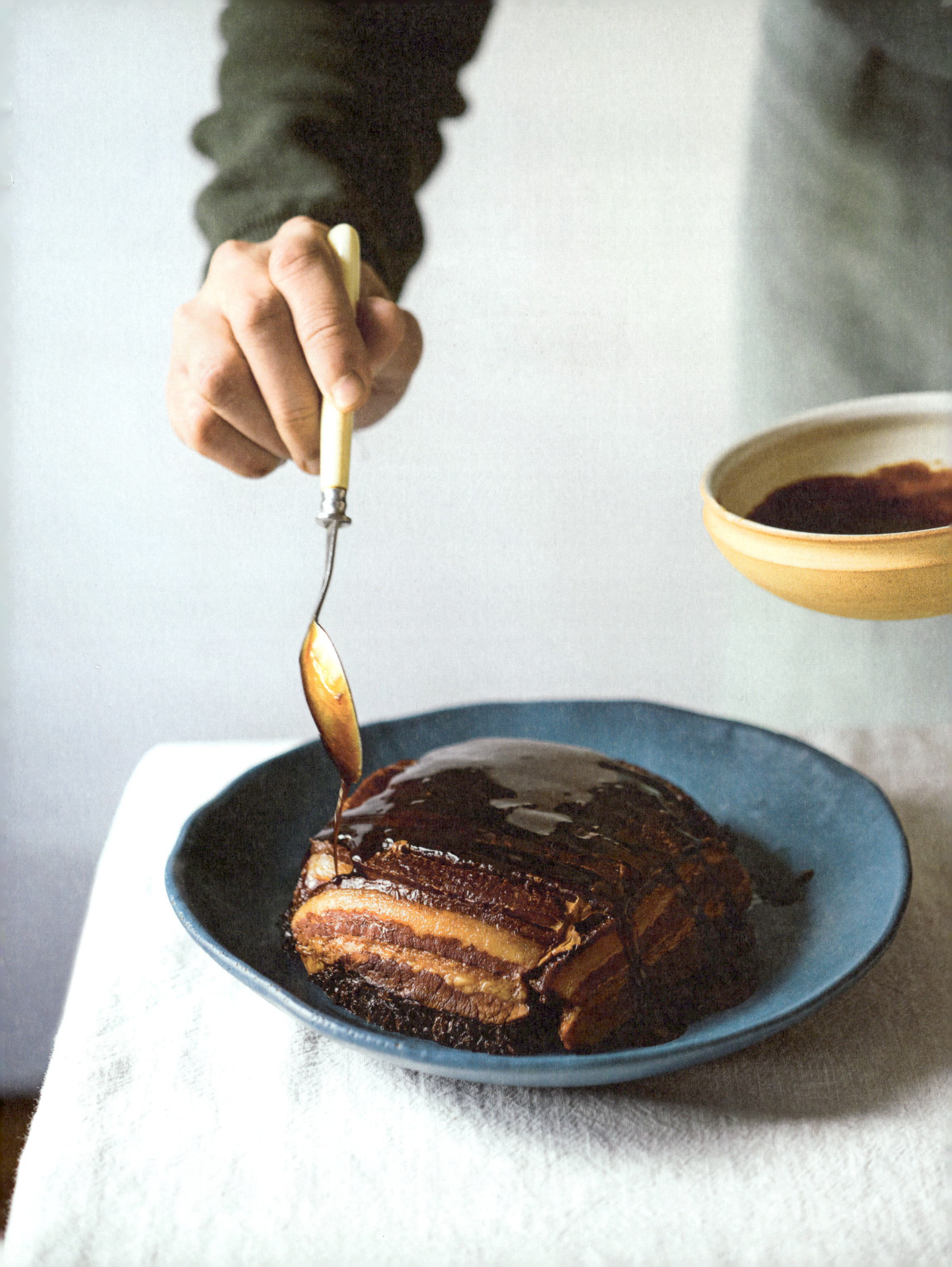

Steamed Pork with Dried Mustard Leaves

MÉI CÀI KÒU RÒU

梅菜扣肉

PREPARING 15 MINUTES

COOKING 100 MINUTES

IN CHINESE, THE TERM *XIA FAN CAI* (LITERALLY "THE DISHES THAT BRING DOWN RICE") REFERS TO ALL DISHES THAT MAKE IT POSSIBLE TO EASILY DOWN TWO BOWLS OF RICE. THE TERM INCLUDES THIS RECIPE. IT'S THE FIRST ONE I THOUGHT OF WHEN WRITING THIS BOOK. THE PORK BELLY'S FAT AND THE SCENT OF DRIED MUSTARD LEAVES BLEND PERFECTLY.

Serves 4 people

INGREDIENTS

For the pork belly

50g (1¾oz) dried mustard leaves (*mei cai*, see p. 38)
500g (1lb 2oz) pork belly, with the skin
3 ginger slices
1 tbsp dark soy sauce
4 tbsp neutral oil
3 garlic cloves, chopped
2 star anise
Finely chopped spring onion (scallion), to serve

For the sauce

3 tbsp light soy sauce
1 tbsp dark soy sauce
1 tsp sesame oil
1 tsp sugar
1 tbsp Shaoxing wine
¼ tsp white pepper

FIRST STEPS

- Rehydrate the dried mustard leaves in cold water for 1 hour. Put the pork belly with the 3 slices of ginger in cold water, bring to the boil, then drain (see p. 185). Prick the skin all over with a fork, to later help the marinade to penetrate more easily. Rub the pork all over with the dark soy sauce and leave to dry on a rack for about 30 minutes.

SECOND STEPS

- Pour 3 tablespoons of the oil in a frying pan over a low heat. Once hot, place the pork belly skin side down, then cover immediately and keep the lid closed, otherwise the power of the splashes may send it flying! Cook for 5 minutes until the skin is browned and hardened. Turn off the heat and wait a few minutes before opening. Cut the meat into 1cm (½in) slices.

- Prepare the sauce: mix all the ingredients in a bowl, then add the pork slices and let them marinate for a few minutes.

- Drain the mustard leaves. Pour the remaining 1 tablespoon of oil into a hot frying pan and fry the mustard leaves wth the garlic, star anise and 1 tablespoon of the marinade for about 3 minutes over a low heat to release the flavours.

FINAL STEPS

- In a bowl just big enough to fit the meat, place the pork skin side down, packing the slices tightly together. Place the fried mustard leaves on top, if possible up to the brim, then rest the 2 star anise on top of the leaves. Place in your steamer, cover and cook for 1½ hours over a medium heat.

- When cooking is finished, pour the juices into a frying pan and reduce over a low heat.

- To serve, place a plate on top of the bowl containing the pork and flip the bowl over, holding the plate firmly in place. Pour some of the reduced juices over the pork and sprinkle with finely chopped spring onion. The dish can be enjoyed right away with rice (a lot of rice!), but it will taste even better the next day.

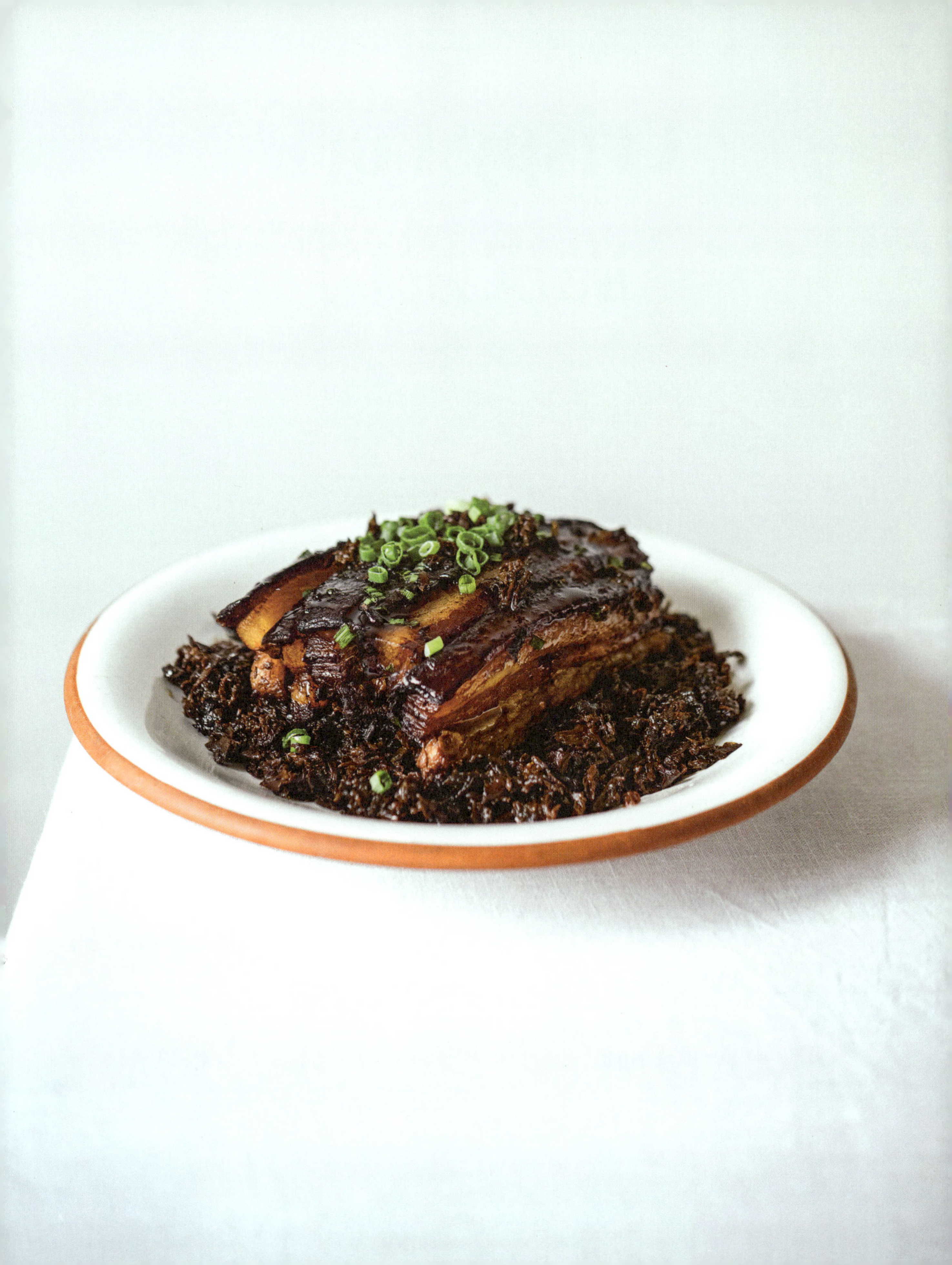

Crispy Pork

CUÌ PÍ SHĀO RÒU

脆皮烧肉

PREPARING 12 HOURS

COOKING 50 MINUTES

THIS MIGHT BE ONE OF THE MOST FAMOUS CANTONESE DISHES ABROAD. IT IS DIFFICULT INDEED TO RESIST THE COMBINATION OF THE CRISPY SKIN AND THE TENDERNESS OF HIGHLY FRAGRANT MEAT IN A SINGLE BITE.

Serves 4 people

INGREDIENTS

For the pork belly

600g (1lb 5oz) pork belly, with the skin
A few ginger slices
1 tsp white vinegar

For the spices

2 tsp salt
2 tsp sugar
1 tsp 5-spice
½ tsp white pepper
1 tsp garlic powder *(optional)*

TO PREPARE THE PORK

- Place the pork, skin side down, and the ginger slices in a pot and pour in enough cold water to cover the meat. Bring to the boil, then switch to a low heat and cook for 5 minutes. Drain well.

- Prick the skin all over with a fork (which should go in easily after cooking) to make small, shallow holes over the entire surface. This step is essential to give the skin the puffed-up appearance that is so characteristic of the dish.

- Using a knife, make cuts on the meat side, as deep as two thirds of its thickness, and 2cm (¾in) apart.

- Mix all the spices together and massage them into the meat, especially in the notches, without putting any on the skin. If you do, wipe them off with kitchen paper. Cover the skin with the vinegar, which will make it crisp up during cooking. Place the meat on a rack and chill overnight to let it dry.

TO COOK

- Take the meat out of the fridge. The skin should be hard. Make a kind of mould with aluminium foil around the meat (like a box), just letting the skin stick out the top. Place on a rack and bake for 20 minutes at 190°C (170°C fan/375°F/Gas 5). Put a sheet lined with aluminium foil under the rack, as the meat can release juice during cooking. Raise the temperature to 210°C (190°C fan/415°F/Gas 6–7) and cook for another 20 minutes. The skin will "burst" and form a hard and crispy crust.

- Take the meat out of the oven – collect the juices (which can be reused) – and let it stand for a few minutes. With a good knife, cut the pork at the notches (the skin is quite hard), then into smaller pieces. Serve with a good bowl of rice.

GOOD TO KNOW
小提示

Although ovens may vary, do not cook for more than 1 hour, to prevent the meat from becoming too dry. Similarly, monitor the temperature so as not to burn the skin. It will be ready when it becomes browned and "puffed".

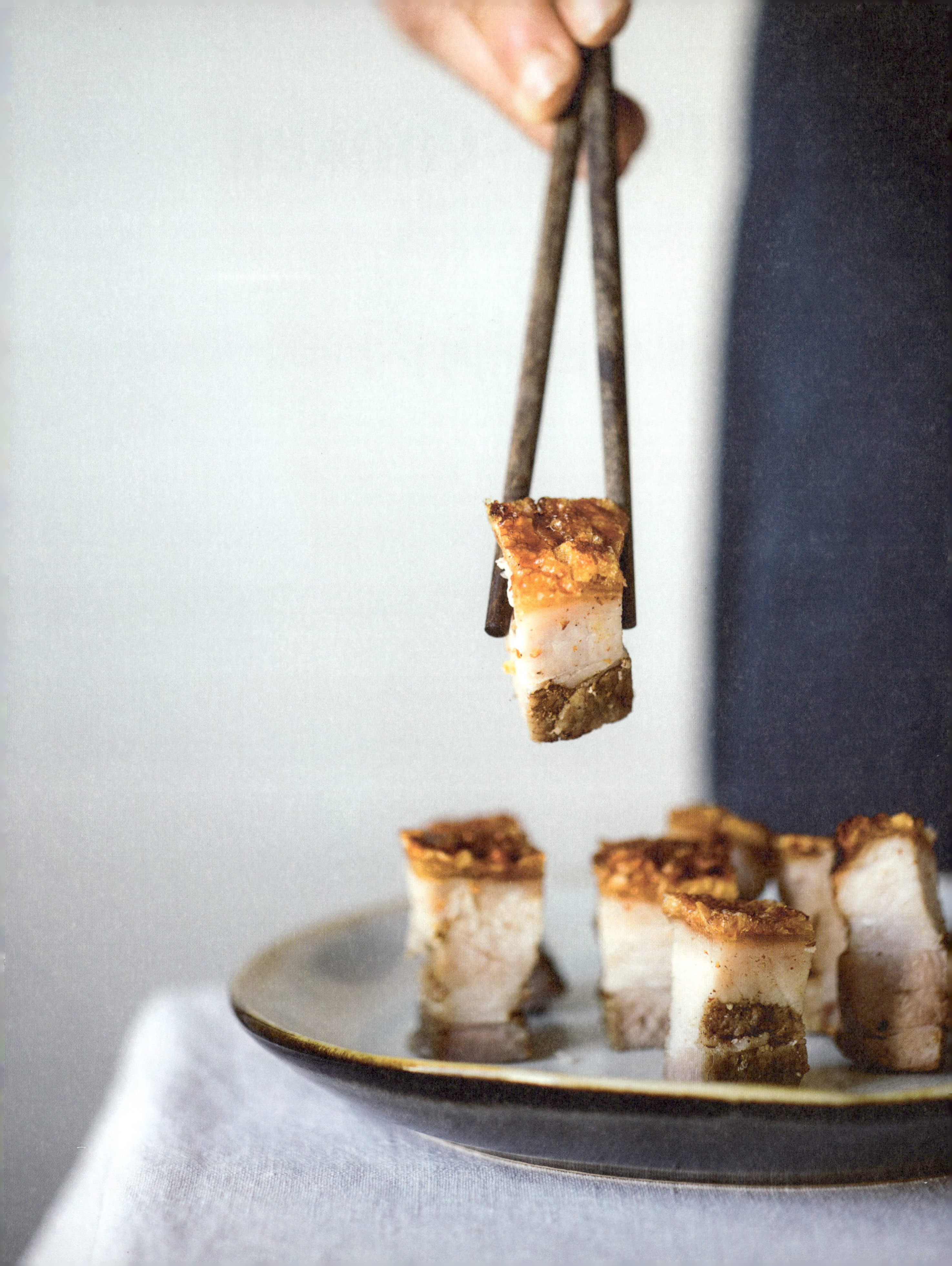

Twice-Cooked Pork

HUÍ GUŌ RÒU

回锅肉

Preparing 5 minutes · *Cooking 25 minutes*

THIS SICHUAN FAMILY DISH OWES ITS NAME TO THE DOUBLE COOKING OF THE PORK, WHICH IS FIRST BLANCHED, THEN STIR-FRIED IN A WOK. THE DELICATE TEXTURE OF THE SLIGHTLY FATTY MEAT IS THIS RECIPE'S APPEAL. THE FAT MELTS OFF WITH THE WOK'S HEAT AND BLENDS PERFECTLY WITH THE SUBTLE TASTE OF LEEKS AND *DOUBANJIANG*, THE REGION'S SIGNATURE CONDIMENT.

Serves 2 people

INGREDIENTS

- 250g (9oz) pork belly, with the skin
- 10g (¼oz) ginger, minced
- 2 tbsp neutral oil
- 20g (¾oz) chilli bean paste (*doubanjiang*, see p. 36)
- 10g (¼oz) sweet soy bean paste (*tian mian jiang*, see p. 38)
- 10g (¼oz) fermented black soy beans (*douchi*, see p. 346), rinsed, drained and coarsely crushed
- 1 tsp Sichuan peppercorn
- ½ tsp sugar
- 100g (3½oz) leeks (preferably baby leeks), chopped

RECIPE STEPS

- Place the pork belly and minced ginger in a pot filled with cold water. Bring to the boil over a high heat, then switch to a low heat and cook for 15–20 minutes, depending on the meat's thickness. Check by piercing the meat with a fork – it is cooked if you no longer see any red.

- Remove the meat from the pot and plunge it into iced water to firm it up, then cut it into very thin slices – roughly 2mm (⅛in) – with a sharp knife.

- Heat a wok over a high heat and pour in the oil. Fry the pork belly quickly for about 1 minute. The meat will curl up on itself and shrink, losing fat. Switch to a medium heat, add the chilli bean paste (*doubanjiang*) and sweet soy bean paste (*tian mian jiang*) and fry for 10 seconds to release their flavours, then add the crushed fermented soy beans (*douchi*), Sichuan peppercorn, sugar and chopped leeks. Stir-fry for about 1 minute and serve.

GOOD TO KNOW
小提示

In Sichuan, young garlic shoots (green garlic), harvested before the bulb forms, are used instead of leeks. It looks like a thin leek and has a subtle and sweet taste. As it is not easily found, leek is a good substitute.

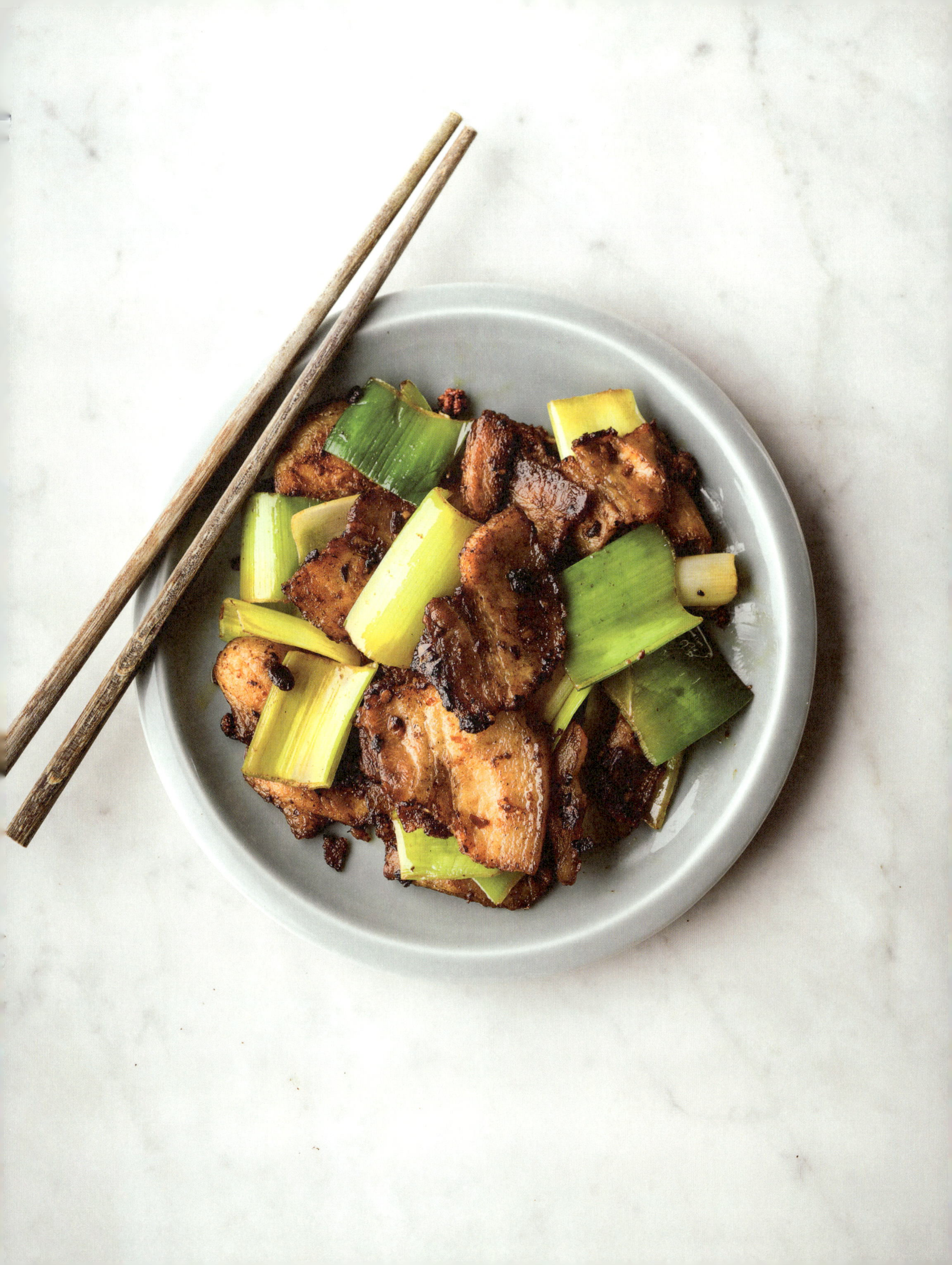

Char Siu

MÌ ZHĪ CHĀ SHĀO RÒU

蜜汁叉烧肉

PREPARING 6 HOURS

COOKING 40 MINUTES

STAR OF CANTONESE ROTISSERIE, CHAR SIU IS A LACQUERED PORK DISH EASILY RECOGNIZABLE BY ITS DARK RED COLOUR AND SWEET AND SAVOURY TASTE. IT IS FOUND AS A GARNISH IN ALL DISHES IN THAT REGION: STIR-FRIED RICE, BAO, NOODLES... IT GOES WITH EVERYTHING!

Serves 4 people

INGREDIENTS

For the spare ribs

600g (1lb 5oz) spare rib
2 tsp honey

For the marinade

3 garlic cloves, roughly chopped
3 ginger slices
1 tbsp red yeast rice
1 piece of red fermented tofu, about 15g (½oz) (see p. 38)
½ tsp 5-spice
1 tbsp Shaoxing wine
3 tbsp soy sauce
1 tbsp oyster sauce
1 tbsp sugar
2 tbsp honey
1 tbsp hoisin sauce

RECIPE STEPS

• Cut the spare rib in half, about 5cm (2in) thick. Mix all the marinade ingredients in a bowl, then pour into a plastic ziploc bag (or Tupperware). Add the meat and massage to coat it well with marinade. Close the bag by expelling the air and marinate the meat in the fridge for at least 6 hours, preferably overnight.

• Remove the meat 30 minutes before cooking and place it on a rack. Mix the 2 teaspoons of honey with 2 teaspoons of the marinade and cover the entire surface of the meat.

• Bake for 20 minutes at 180°C (160°C fan/350°F/Gas 4), placing a baking sheet lined with aluminium foil underneath. After 20 minutes, remove the meat and baste it in the sauce again. Turn it over and put it in the oven for another 20 minutes.

• Remove the meat from the oven and let it rest for a few minutes. Cut into thin strips and serve with rice.

GOOD TO KNOW
小提示

Red yeast rice and fermented tofu (furu) *are the two ingredients that give colour to this dish. If you have to choose only one, opt for the fermented tofu, which also adds flavour.*

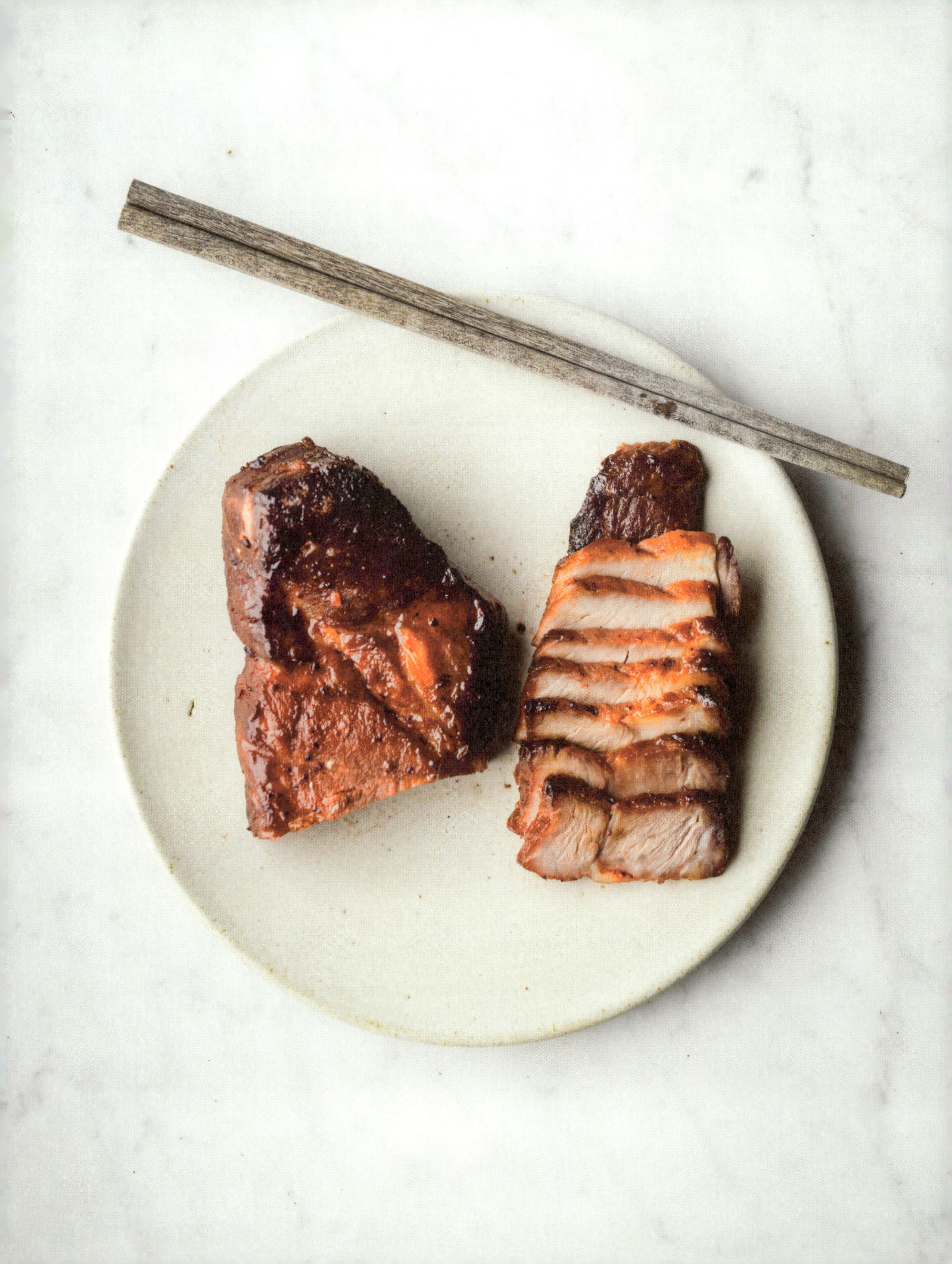

Sweet and Sour Pork Ribs

TÁNG   CÙ   PÁI   GŬ

糖醋排骨

PREPARING 15 MINUTES

COOKING 35 MINUTES

HERE IS THE FAMOUS CARAMEL PORK'S AUTHENTIC RECIPE, WHICH IS MADE WITH PORK RIBS IN CHINA. THIS IS AN ABSOLUTE CLASSIC, SURPRISINGLY SIMPLE AND ALMOST IMPOSSIBLE TO GET WRONG.

Serves 4 people

INGREDIENTS

500g (1lb 2oz) pork ribs
1 tbsp soy sauce
2 tbsp Shaoxing wine
3 tbsp black rice vinegar
2 salted dried plums (*huamei, see p. 32; optional*)
1 tbsp neutral oil
30g (1oz) rock sugar (or regular sugar)
4 thin ginger slices
½ tsp toasted white sesame seeds

RECIPE STEPS

- Cut the pork ribs along the bones. Then cut each rib in 2 to make smaller pieces. (Use a Chinese cleaver – see p. 44 – or ask your butcher to do it for you.) Pour a large volume of cold water into a pot, immerse the pork ribs and bring to the boil, skimming off any foam. This step both pre-cooks the meat and removes any impurities. Remove the meat and drain.

- Mix the soy sauce, Shaoxing wine, vinegar and 300ml (1¼ cups) of water in a bowl. Add the dried plums, if using, and set aside.

- Now make the caramel that will create the dish's characteristic colour. Pour the oil into a frying pan over a low heat, then add the pieces of rock sugar (or regular sugar). Keep over a low heat, stirring if necessary, until the sugar is melted and takes on a caramel colour (see p. 50 for guidance).

- Add the pork ribs to the pan and brown them on all sides, then add the ginger slices. Pour over the sauce.

- Cover the pan and leave on a low heat for 30 minutes. Then, remove the lid and increase the heat to reduce the sauce. Taste and adjust with a little more vinegar if necessary (it counterbalances the fat and sugar). Serve sprinkled with the toasted white sesame seeds.

GOOD TO KNOW
小提示

Salted dried plums (huamei) *are both sweet and acidic, which matches the dish's flavour profile while adding a subtle fruity touch. You can find them in Chinese supermarkets. They can also be replaced by dried mandarin peel* (chen pi, *see p. 32*).

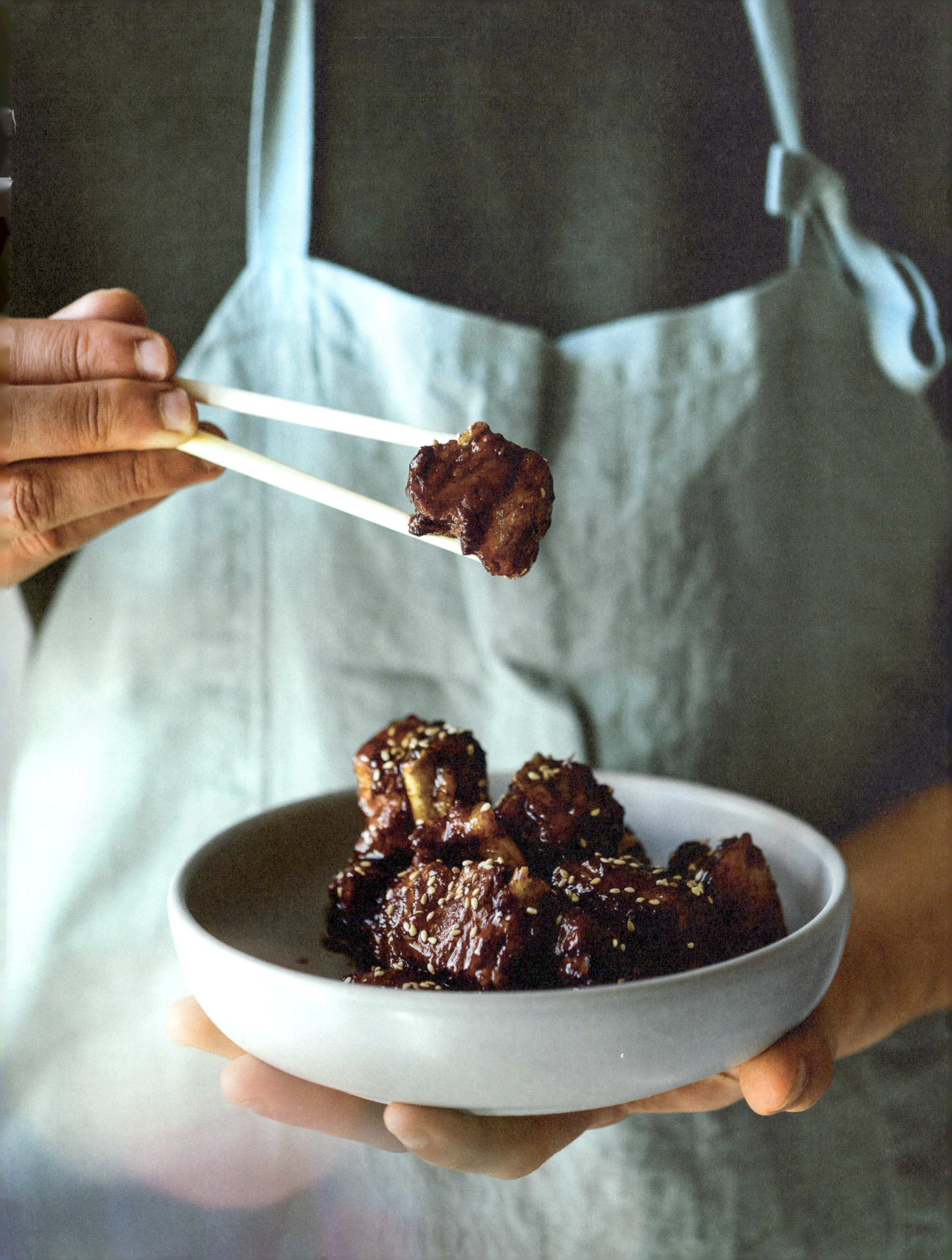

Steamed Pork Ribs with Douchi

DÒU CHǏ ZHĒNG PÁI GǓ

豆豉蒸排骨

PREPARING 40 MINUTES

COOKING 20 MINUTES

THESE PORK RIBS ARE TRADITIONALLY SERVED IN A STEAMER BASKET DURING A DIM SUM MEAL. THE FERMENTED BLACK SOY BEANS, WITH THEIR SALTY AND UMAMI FLAVOUR, ARE THE BASIS OF THE MARINADE.

Serves 2 people

INGREDIENTS

For the pork ribs

250g (9oz) pork ribs
1 tbsp white rice vinegar
½ tsp salt
1 tbsp cornflour (cornstarch)
½ tsp sesame oil
Chopped red chilli (*optional*)
Chopped spring onion (scallion)

For the marinade

1 tbsp fermented black soy beans (*douchi, see p. 346*), rinsed, drained and coarsely chopped
1 tbsp neutral oil
½ tbsp chopped garlic
½ tbsp chopped ginger
½ tbsp chopped red onion
½ tsp chopped dried mandarin peels (*optional, see p. 32*)
½ tbsp Shaoxing wine
½ tbsp soy sauce
½ tsp sugar
¼ tsp white pepper
½ tsp oyster sauce

TO PREPARE THE PORK RIBS

▪ Cut the pork ribs into bite-sized chunks, about 3cm (1in). Use a Chinese cleaver for this (see p. 44) or ask your butcher to do it for you. Soak the ribs in a bowl of water with the vinegar for 30 minutes. This step blanches and tenderizes the meat. Rinse, then drain on kitchen paper.

▪ Meanwhile, prepare the marinade. Fry the fermented soy beans (*douchi*) in a wok over a low heat for about 1 minute, without oil, to release the flavours. Remove from the wok and set aside.

▪ Pour the oil into the wok and add the garlic, ginger and red onion, and the dried mandarin peels if using. Fry over a medium heat for 20 seconds, then add the fermented soy beans back in and cook for 30 seconds more. Pour in the Shaoxing wine and soy sauce, then, after another 20 seconds, stir in the sugar, white pepper and oyster sauce. Set aside.

▪ Transfer the pork ribs to a bowl and sprinkle with the salt. Massage the meat, then cover with the cornflour to form a thin layer, which is very important to help the meat "retain" the marinade during cooking. Pour over the marinade and massage again, then leave to stand for at least 30 minutes.

TO COOK

▪ Arrange the ribs on a plate, in a single layer (or use 2 plates and 2 steamer baskets if necessary) and steam them over a high heat for 12 minutes. Serve drizzled with the sesame oil and sprinkled with some chopped fresh chilli and spring onion.

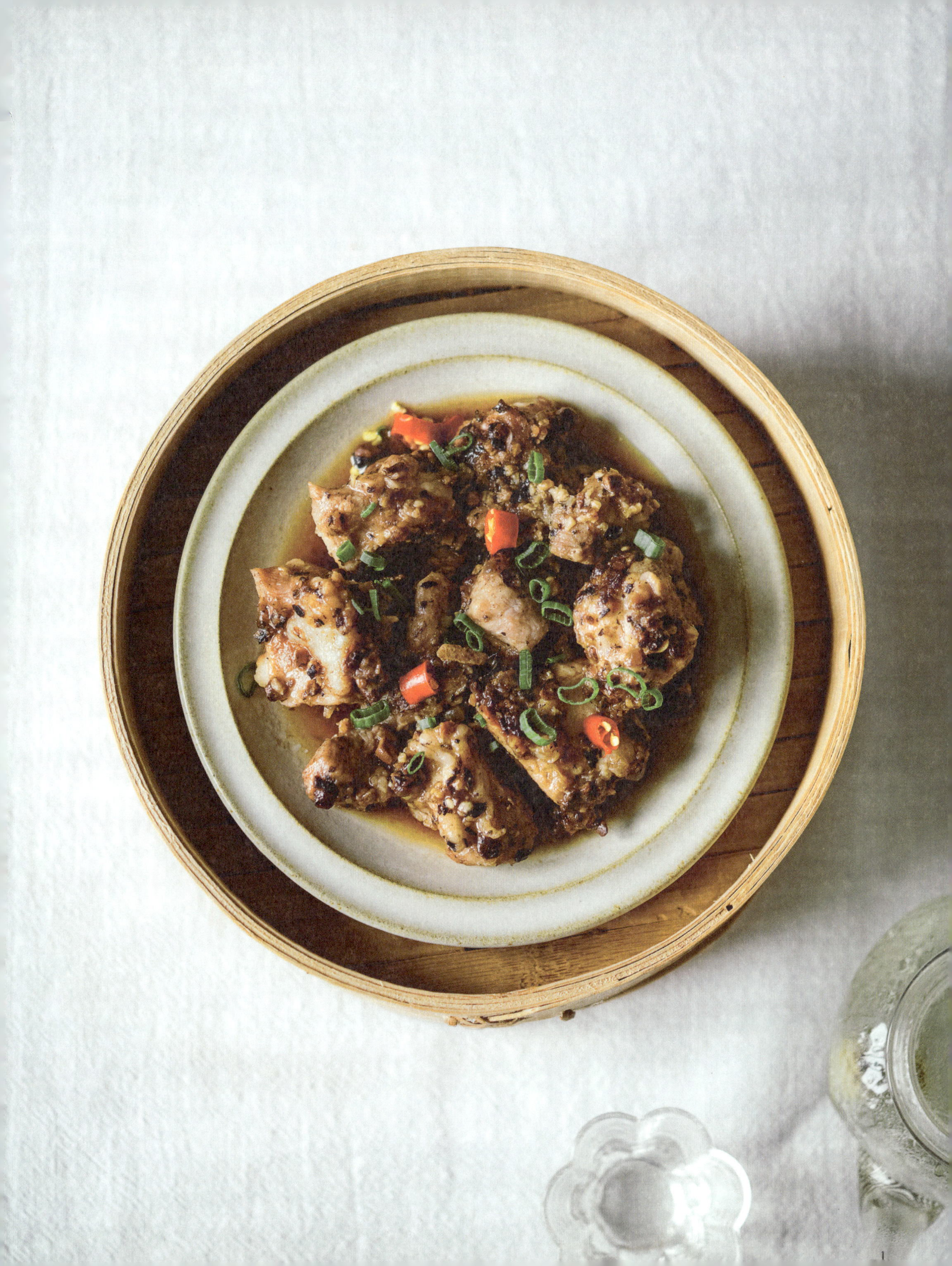

Coca-Cola-Flavoured Chicken Wings

KĚ LÈ JĪ CHÌ

可乐鸡翅

PREPARING 5 MINUTES *COOKING 20 MINUTES*

YES, YOU READ THE NAME OF THIS DISH CORRECTLY. AND I DIDN'T INVENT THIS RECIPE! COKE WILL ADD SOME SWEETNESS AND CREATE A CARAMEL COLOUR, EXACTLY LIKE THE BRAISING TECHNIQUE CALLED *HONG SHAO* (SEE P. 50), BUT IN A SIMPLIFIED VERSION. CHILDREN LOVE IT (JUST LIKE I DID) – I WONDER WHY...

🍴 Serves 2 people

INGREDIENTS

12 chicken wings
1 tbsp neutral oil
10g (¼oz) ginger, finely julienned
½ tbsp light soy sauce
½ tbsp dark soy sauce
1 tbsp Shaoxing wine
330ml (1½ cups) Coca-Cola
A pinch of salt
Toasted white sesame seeds
Lime juice (*optional*)

RECIPE STEPS

- Make 2 cuts on each of the chicken wings, on the skin side.

- In a frying pan, heat the oil over a medium heat, then add the ginger and fry it for about 15 seconds to release the flavours.

- Add the chicken wings, skin side down first, and brown on both sides for about 3–4 minutes. Pour in the soy sauces, Shaoxing wine and Coca-Cola (the equivalent of a can), then add the pinch of salt. Bring to the boil, lower the heat and simmer for 15 minutes, covered.

- Briefly increase the heat to reduce the juices until you get a thick sauce. Serve with a sprinkling of toasted white sesame seeds and a drizzle of lime juice, if you like.

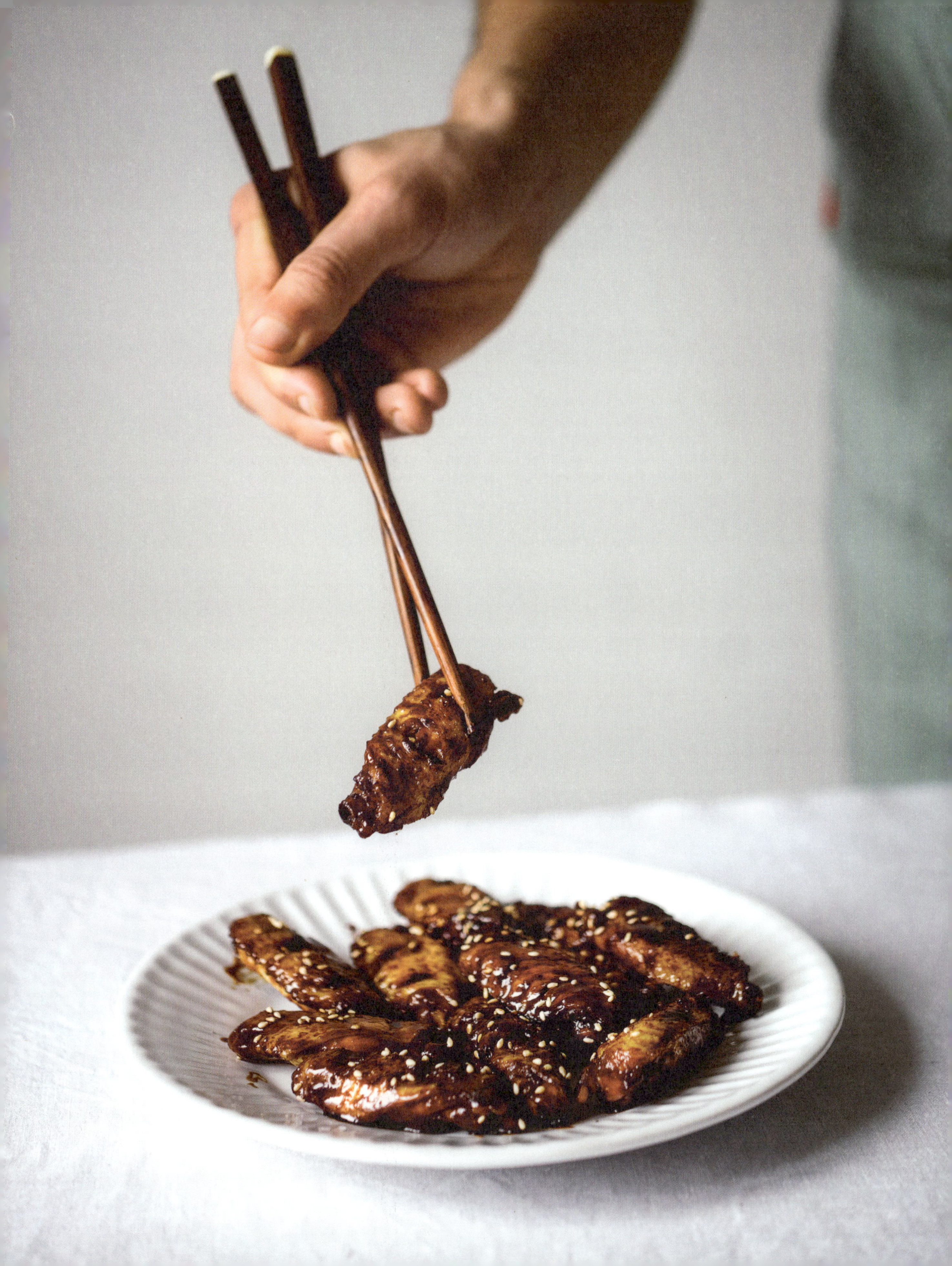

Popcorn Chicken

TÁI　WĀN　YÁN　SŪ　JĪ
台湾盐酥鸡

PREPARING 75 MINUTES

COOKING 8 MINUTES

PEOPLE IN TAIWAN LOVE FRIED CHICKEN, LIKE ALMOST EVERYWHERE IN THE WORLD. THE LOCAL RECIPE IS VERY POPULAR IN NIGHT MARKETS. THE SECRET LIES IN THE MARINADE: FERMENTED TOFU (SEE P. 118) AND 5-SPICE, TWO OF THE ISLAND'S KEY INGREDIENTS.

Serves 2 people

INGREDIENTS

2 boneless, skinless chicken legs, about 450g (1lb), cut into bite-size pieces (about 3cm/1¼in)
3 tbsp sweet potato starch (*see note below*)
500ml (generous 2 cups) neutral oil
A few Thai basil leaves
Salt and white pepper, to taste

For the marinade

1 piece (about 15g/½oz) of red or white fermented tofu, (*see p. 38*)
2 tsp soy sauce
1 tsp Shaoxing wine
2 tsp grated garlic
½ tsp 5-spice
1 egg white

FOR THE MARINADE

- To make the marinade, place the fermented tofu in a large bowl and mash it with a fork. Pour in the soy sauce and Shaoxing wine and mix until smooth. Add the garlic and 5-spice, then add the chicken pieces and mix again. Add the egg white, massage into the chicken, and mix everything for a final time. Cover and marinate in the fridge, preferably overnight but for at least 1 hour.

TO COOK

- Remove the bowl from the fridge and mix in the sweet potato starch. In a pot, heat the oil over a medium heat to 180°C (350°F). Add the chicken pieces (the temperature of the oil will drop to 140°C/275°F) and fry for 2 minutes. Remove the chicken pieces from the pot onto a plate covered with kitchen paper and set aside.

- Using a spider, remove any residue left in the oil, then reheat the oil to 200°C (400°F) over a medium heat. Fry the chicken pieces a second time for about 30 seconds, to make them crispy. Remove them from the oil as before and then add your basil leaves. Fry them for about 10 seconds, at around 170°C (325°F), until crisp. Be careful, as the water contained in the leaves might make the oil spit slightly.

- Arrange everything on a plate and season with salt and white pepper to serve.

GOOD TO KNOW
小提示

Sweet potato starch is usually favoured for its larger grains, to make the typical rough texture of Taiwanese fried chicken. It can be found in Chinese supermarkets. Otherwise, you can replace it with cornflour (cornstarch); the appearance will be smoother but will not impact the taste.

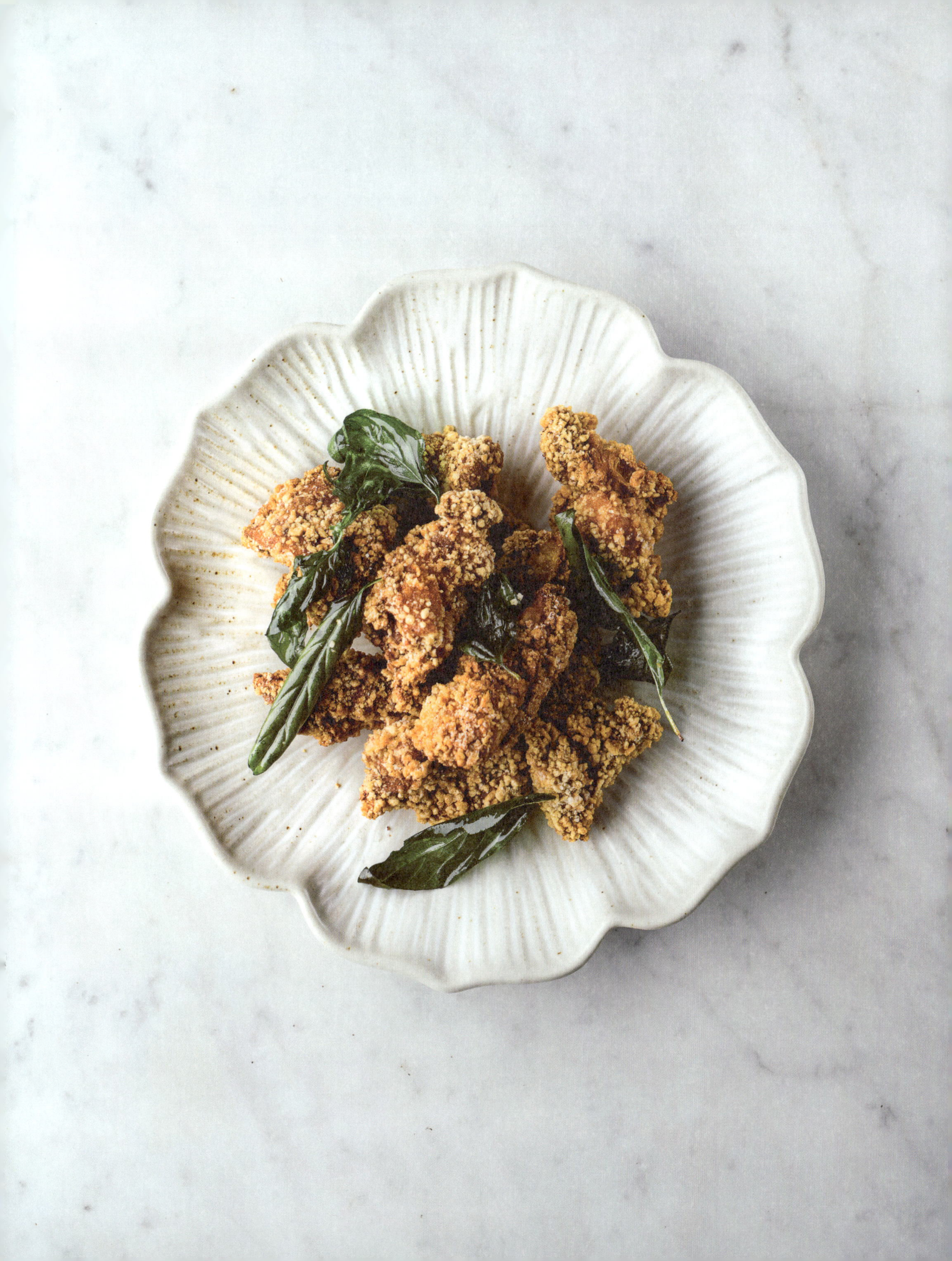

Beef with Black Pepper

HĒI JIĀO NIÚ LIǓ

黑椒牛柳

PREPARING 15 MINUTES

COOKING 5 MINUTES

CANTONESE CUISINE IS RENOWNED FOR ITS ABILITY TO ALWAYS INNOVATE, TO DRAW ON EXTERNAL TECHNIQUES AND INGREDIENTS TO ELEVATE ITS DISHES. THIS RECIPE SEEMS SO CLOSE AND YET SO FAR FROM A TRADITIONAL PEPPER STEAK. WHILE IT BORROWS SOME "WESTERN" INGREDIENTS SUCH AS KETCHUP OR BLACK PEPPER, THE MARINADE AND COOKING TECHNIQUES ARE TYPICALLY CANTONESE.

Serves 2–3 people

INGREDIENTS

250g (9oz) beef fillet
2 tbsp neutral oil
½ onion, about 100g (3½oz), chopped
1 tsp chopped garlic
A few dried chilli peppers
2 spring onions (scallions), cut into 6cm (2½in) pieces

For the marinade

1 tsp soy sauce
1 tsp sugar
1 tbsp Shaoxing wine
1 egg white
1 tbsp cornflour (cornstarch)
1 tbsp neutral oil

For the sauce

1 tsp soy sauce
1 tsp ketchup
½ tsp black rice vinegar
½ tsp ground black pepper
¼ tsp sesame oil
1 tbsp water

RECIPE STEPS

- Mix all the sauce ingredients together in a small bowl.

- Tap the beef fillet all over with the back of a knife to tenderize it, then cut it finely against the grain into slices 5mm (¼in) thick. Transfer the meat to a bowl and add the soy sauce, sugar, Shaoxing wine and egg white. Massage it so that it absorbs all the liquid (the bottom of the bowl must be empty). Add the cornflour and massage again to distribute it, then add the oil to prevent the pieces from sticking together.

- Heat the wok over a medium heat and pour in the 2 tablespoons of oil. Once hot, add the beef and stir-fry quickly for 1 minute. You should no longer see any pink. Transfer to a bowl, leaving as much oil as possible in the wok.

- Heat the wok again over a medium heat. Add the onion, and fry for about 1 minute to soften it, then add the garlic, dried chillies and spring onions, and continue cooking for 20 seconds to release the flavours. Add the meat back in, stir-fry for 15–20 seconds, then pour the sauce down the sides of the wok and mix well. Do not exceed 1 minute of cooking time after adding the beef, so it remains tender.

- Arrange on a plate and finish with a generous helping of black pepper, to taste.

GOOD TO KNOW
小提示

See p. 185 for more information on the marinating technique known as velveting, which gives the meat a tender texture and velvety mouthfeel.

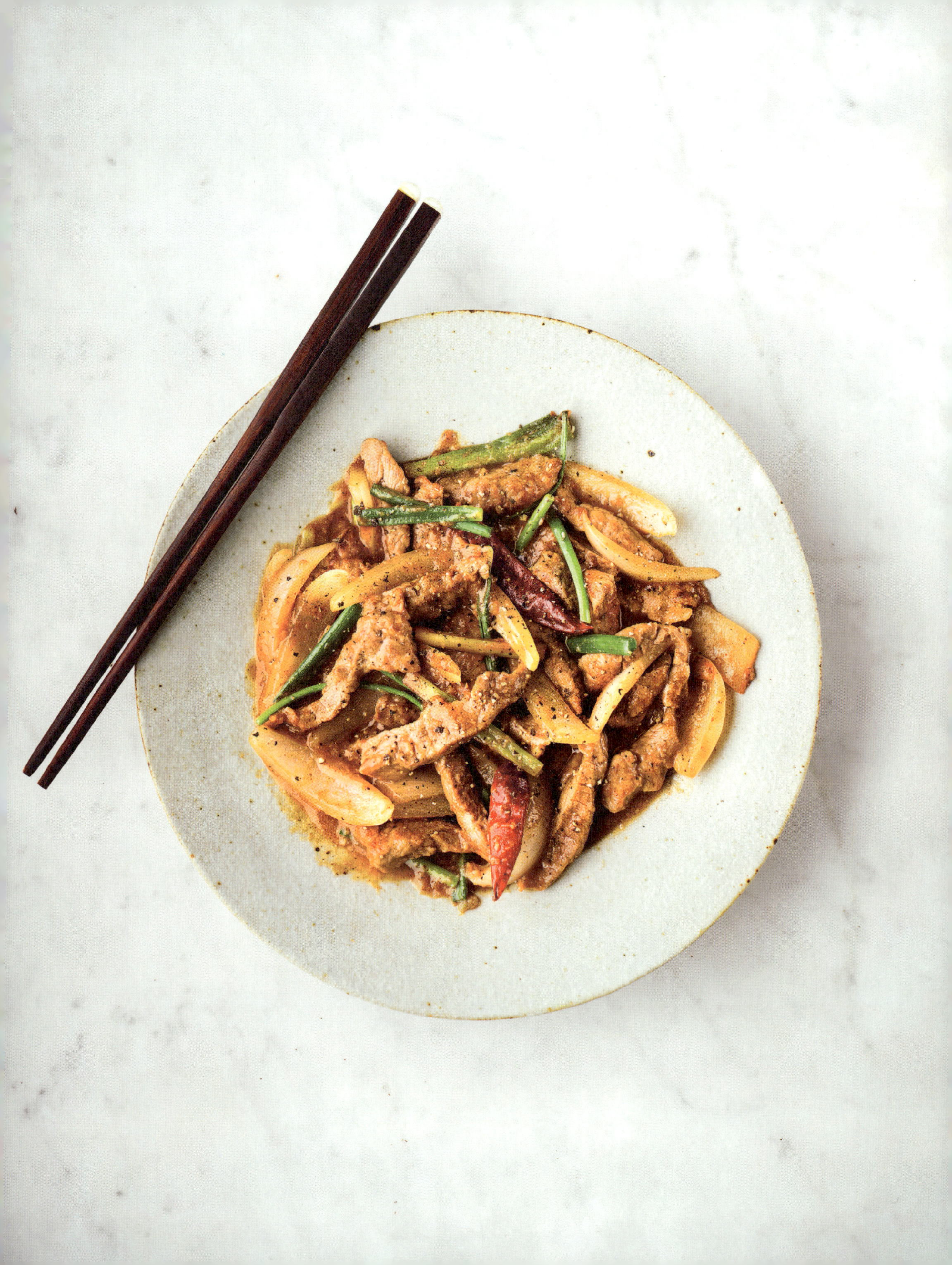

CHAPTER
08

Fish

鱼

YÚ

PP. 214-215: Steamed sea bream ▪ **PP. 216-217**: Suan cai minced fish
PP. 218-219: Chilli fish pot ▪ **PP. 220-221**: Fried cockles with garlic and chilli
PP. 222-223: Steamed scallops with rice vermicelli ▪ **PP. 224-225**: Stir-fried squid with celery
PP. 226-227: Oyster pancake ▪ **PP. 228-229**: Prawns with Sichuan peppercorn and salt

From All Angles

The Precious Sea

GIVEN CHINA'S 14,500KM (9,000 MILES) OF COASTLINE, TWO OF THE LARGEST RIVERS IN THE WORLD (THE YANGTZE AND THE YELLOW RIVER) AND COUNTLESS LAKES, WATER HAS ALWAYS PROVIDED CHINESE COOKS WITH A WEALTH OF PRODUCE.

EXTREME FRESHNESS AND UMAMI

Daily catches or dried products, extremly fresh or with a long shelf life, seafood is ubiquitous and incredibly versatile.

In China, a fresh fish is a fish that is still alive. In speciality restaurants, huge aquariums stand at the entrance (which is almost an experience in itself!), and customers choose what will end up on their plate as well as the cooking method, all in less than 30 minutes.

On the other hand, I do not know of any other country with such a pronounced taste for dried products: shrimp, seaweed, cuttlefish, scallops, fish of all kinds… There is an unimaginable variety. Drying concentrates the flavours and transforms all these ingredients into natural flavour enhancers. For me, this is one of the main secrets of Chinese cuisine. The famous XO sauce, invented in Hong Kong, is supposed to enhance the taste of any dish and is made of dried products (ham, shrimp and scallops with spices).

FROM RAW TO COOKED

Unlike their Japanese neighbours, Chinese people rarely eat raw fish.

That practice, which was common until the beginning of the Qing dynasty (17th century), is now limited to a few local specialities, such as *yusheng* (a kind of sashimi served with chopped vegetables) in Chaozhou, in the Guangdong province, or raw crab marinated in Shaoxing wine, in Wenzhou. Even oysters are roasted with garlic sauce or made into pancakes (see p. 226).

Chinese people are very sensitive to the natural taste of seafood products (原味, *yuan wei*). Steaming is very popular, as it preserves the delicate flesh of most fish (see p. 214). Thanks to the wok, prawns/shrimp (see p. 228) or some shellfish (see p. 220) can be quickly stir-fried. If the dishes are more liquid-based, fish is added to the broth at the end, to simply blanch it (see p. 216).

Regardless of the method, it is common to use Shaoxing wine, ginger or onion (in the marinade or during cooking) to remove any unpleasant fishy smells (腥味, *xīng wèi*).

SYMBOL OF PROSPERITY

During Chinese New Year, serving a beautiful whole fish is traditional.

Words are important in China, and fish is pronounced "鱼, *yu*", a homonym for "余, *yu*", which means abundance. In general, the dishes considered to be the most luxurious are almost all linked to the sea: abalone, shark fin soup or sea cucumber. It's hard to imagine a great meal without a few iodized flavours.

MEMORY
回忆

I grew up in Wenzhou, a coastal city in southeastern China, famous for its seafood. From belt fish (also known as large-head hairtail) to local velvet crabs (small, perennial crabs), to slipper lobsters, to jellyfish, to "blood" cockles, to algae of all kinds, the ocean was invited to the table almost every day.

THE YELLOW SEA | 黄海 | HUÁNG HǍI

ABALONE
鲍鱼 | BÀO YÚ

SEA CUCUMBER
海参 | HǍI CĀN

SEA URCHIN
海胆 | HǍI DǍN

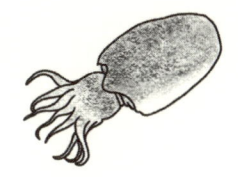

CUTTLEFISH
墨鱼 | MÒ YÚ

THE EAST CHINA SEA | 东海 | DŌNG HǍI

LARGE YELLOW CROAKER
黄鱼 | HUÁNG YÚ

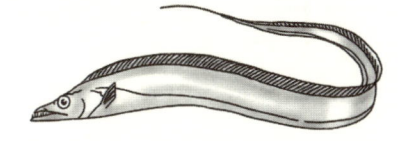

SCABBARD FISH
带鱼 | DÀI YÚ

BLOOD COCKLES
血蚶 | XUÈ HĀN

BLUE CRAB
梭子蟹 | SUŌ ZI XIÈ

SILVER POMFRET
鲳鱼 | CHĀNG YÚ

MANTIS SHRIMP
皮皮虾 | PÍ PÍ XIĀ

THE SOUTH CHINA SEA | 南海 | NÁN HǍI

HUMPBACK GROUPER
老鼠斑 | LǍO SHǓ BĀN

LEOPARD CORAL GROUPER
东星斑 | DŌNG XĪNG BĀN

FRESHWATER | 淡水 | DÀN SHUǏ

GRASS CARP
草鱼 | CǍO YÚ

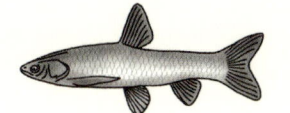

BLACK CARP
青鱼 | QĪNG YÚ

COMMON CARP
鲤鱼 | LǏ YÚ

RED SWAMP CRAYFISH
小龙虾 | XIǍO LÓNG XIĀ

Steamed Sea Bream

QĪNG ZHĒNG YÚ

清蒸鱼

PREPARING 15 MINUTES — COOKING 10 MINUTES

STEAMED FISH IS BOTH A DAILY AND A FESTIVE DISH IN THE COASTAL REGIONS OF CHINA. THE BASIC RECIPE IS REALLY SIMPLE, AND CAN BE APPLIED TO ANY WHITE FISH (SEA BREAM, TURBOT, BASS…). THE KEY HERE IS FRESHNESS, SO NO FROZEN FOOD!

Serves 4 people

INGREDIENTS

For the sea bream

1 sea bream
1 tsp salt
Ginger: some thinly sliced; some finely julienned
Spring onions (scallions): some cut into sticks; some finely julienned
2 tbsp neutral oil

For the sauce

3 tbsp soy sauce
1 tsp sugar
2 tbsp poultry broth (or water)

FOR THE FISH

- Scale, gut and clean the fish, including the gills (ask your fishmonger to do this if necessary). Massage the outside of the fish with the salt for about 10 seconds, which reduces unpleasant smells. Rinse both inside and out with clean water. Drain.

- Spread your ginger slices and spring onion sticks over a large plate, then place the fish on top, again to help reduce unpleasant smells, but also to flavour the flesh.

- Place a steamer rack (see p. 44) in your wok and add water to the base of the wok. Bring to the boil over a high heat, then add the bream on top of the rack. Cover with a lid and cook for 8 minutes, then turn the heat off and let it stand for 3 minutes. You can check the cooking by sticking a fork in the thickest part of the fish. If the flesh is opaque (not translucent) and comes off easily, then it is ready.

- Meanwhile, mix the sauce ingredients in a small bowl. If you don't have broth, you can use water.

TO SERVE

- Transfer the bream to a plate (discard the cooking water) and pour in the sauce. Place your julienned ginger and spring onion on top of the fish. Heat the oil in a wok until it starts to smoke and pour it immediately over the ginger and spring onion to release their flavour.

GOOD TO KNOW
小提示

In China, fish is usually served whole, which requires a very large steamer. A wok's diameter is perfect for this, but if you don't have one, you can cut the fish in half, to fit your steamer basket, then "gather" it back together when serving. The recipe also works with a fillet or fish steak; just reduce the cooking time depending on the size.

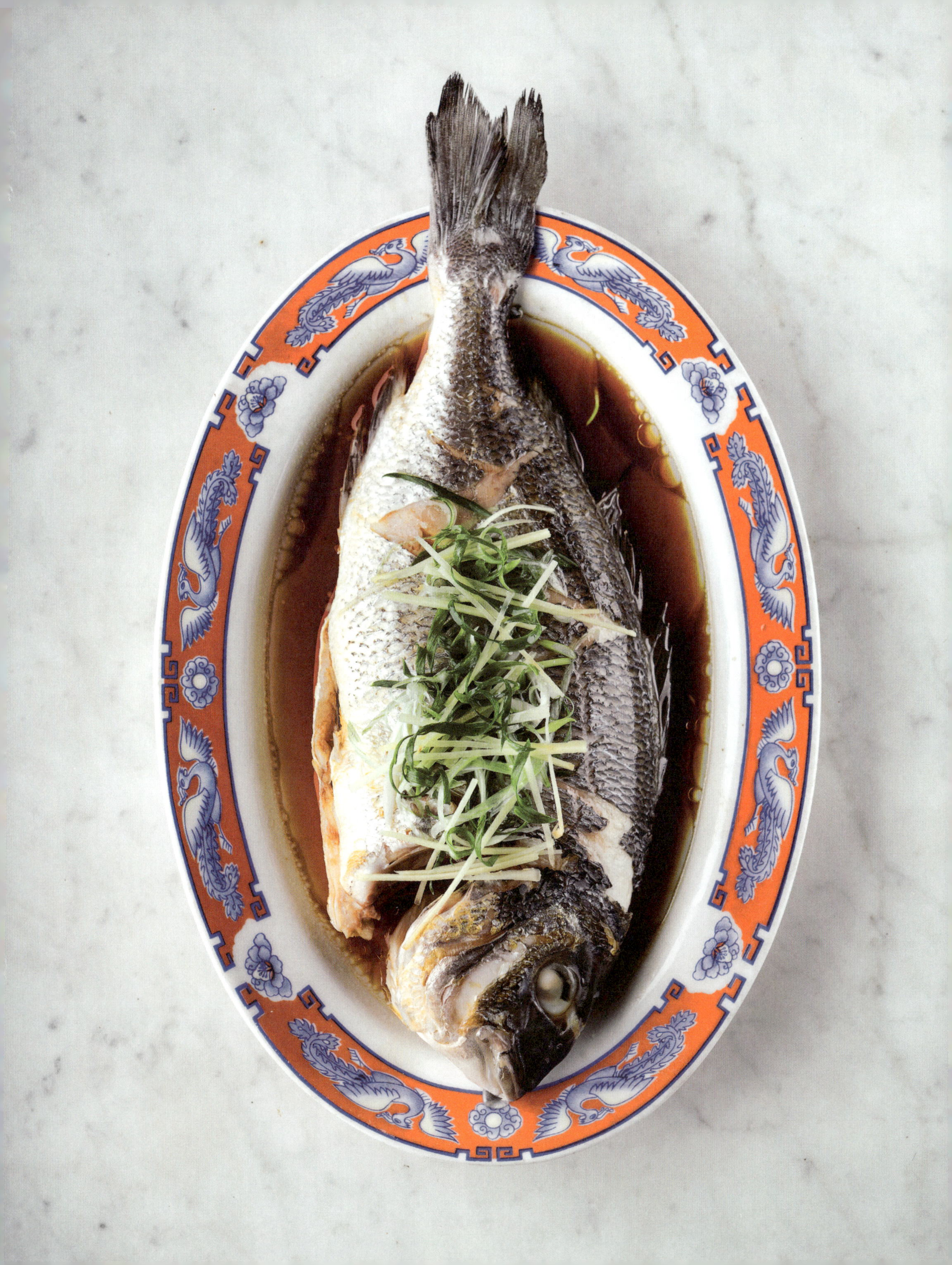

Suan Cai Minced Fish

SUĀN CÀI PIÀN YÚ

酸菜片鱼

PREPARING 15 MINUTES

COOKING 10 MINUTES

SUAN CAI (SEE P. 38) IS A KIND OF CHINESE SAUERKRAUT, BUT WITH A CRISPER TEXTURE AND A MORE ACIDIC TASTE, THAT IS OFTEN FOUND ALONGSIDE RICE OR NOODLE DISHES. HOWEVER, IT ALSO GOES PERFECTLY WITH FISH DISHES. THE FOLLOWING RECIPE (USING PERCH) IS ONE OF MY FAVOURITES.

Serves 4 people

INGREDIENTS

500g (1lb 2oz) skinless white fish fillet, cut into 3–4mm (⅛in) slices
½ tsp salt + ½ tbsp
1 tsp Shaoxing wine
1 egg white
1 tbsp cornflour (cornstarch)
2 tsp neutral oil
3 ginger slices

For the vegetables

1 tbsp neutral oil
2 spring onions (scallions), chopped, white and green parts separated
100g (3½oz) *suan cai*, chopped
¼ pointed cabbage, about 200g (7oz), tough heart discarded and leaves chopped
½ tsp salt
½ tsp soy sauce

For the sauce

2 tbsp oil
4 garlic cloves, chopped
100ml (6½ tbsp) water
1 tsp soy sauce
½ tsp sugar
¼ tsp white pepper

TO PREPARE THE FISH

- Put the fish slices in a bowl and add the ½ teaspoon of salt and the Shaoxing wine. Massage with your hand until you feel a slightly sticky texture. Pour in the egg white, mix well, then stir in the cornflour and mix again. Add the oil and mix for a final time – you're looking for a "slippery" texture to the fish. Rest in the fridge while you prepare the vegetables.

FOR THE VEGETABLES

- Heat the wok over a medium heat until it starts smoking. Pour in the oil, then immediately add the spring onion white and cook for 10 seconds. Stir in the *suan cai*, fry for about 20 seconds, then add the cabbage and salt. Continue cooking for about 3 minutes until the leaves become soft. Pour in the soy sauce, mix and turn off the heat. Remove from the wok and place on a serving plate.

TO COOK THE FISH

- Bring 2 litres (8½ cups) of water to the boil in the (clean) wok over a medium heat. Add the ½ tablespoon of salt, the ginger slices and the fish. Leave the fish to simmer for 2–3 minutes, without touching it, then carefully remove it from the wok with a spider or skimmer. Place on top of the vegetables.

FOR THE SAUCE

- Heat the wok again over a medium heat, pour in the 2 tablespoons of oil, then add the chopped garlic and fry until lightly browned (it should not burn, but lower the heat if necessary). Add the water, then the soy sauce, sugar and white pepper and cook to reduce the sauce slightly.

- Pour the sauce over the fish and sprinkle with your chopped spring onion green.

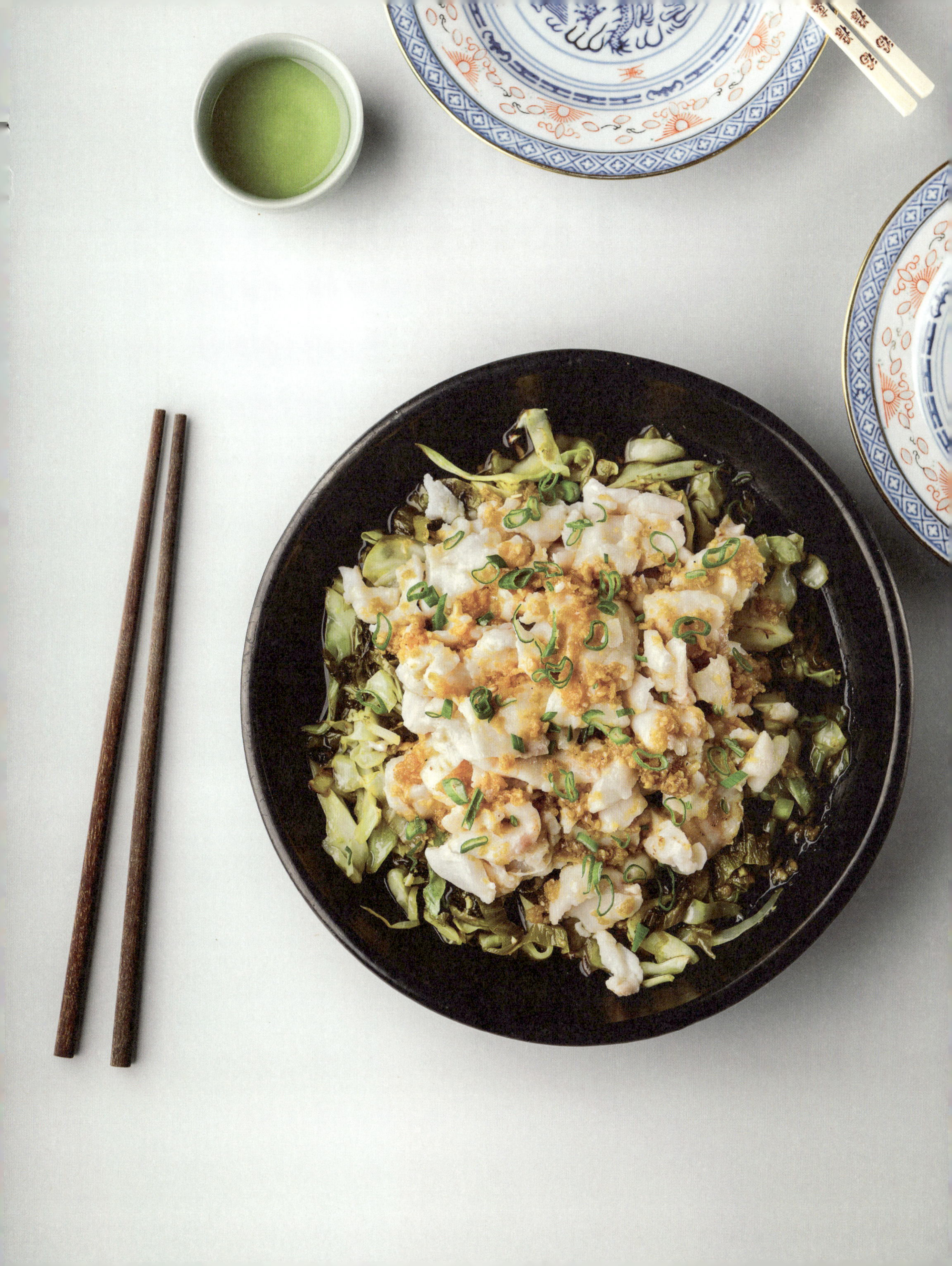

Chilli Fish Pot

SHUǏ　ZHǓ　YÚ

水煮鱼

PREPARING 15 MINUTES　　*COOKING 10 MINUTES*

THIS IS ONE OF SICHUAN'S ICONIC DISHES, WHOSE FLAVOUR IS QUITE ADDICTIVE AND STANDS OUT TO EVERYONE WHO TASTES IT. DO NOT BE INTIMIDATED BY ITS SCARLET COLOUR – IT ISN'T AS SPICY AS YOU IMAGINE! YOU CAN MAKE IT WITH ANY WHITE FISH: SEA BREAM, MULLET, BASS…

Serves 2 people

INGREDIENTS

For the fish

- 1 skinless bass fillet, about 200g (7oz), cut into very thin sashimi-size slices (retain the head and spine for the broth)
- ½ tsp salt
- ¼ tsp white pepper
- 1 tsp Shaoxing wine
- ½ egg white
- 2 tsp cornflour (cornstarch)
- 1 tsp neutral oil

For the broth

- 5 tbsp neutral oil
- 10 dried chilli peppers
- 2 tsp Sichuan peppercorn
- A few Chinese cabbage leaves, each cut into 3 pieces
- 1 tbsp chilli bean paste (*doubanjiang*)
- 3 ginger slices
- 2 garlic cloves, minced
- ½ tsp salt
- 1 tsp sugar
- Chopped coriander (cilantro)

TO PREPARE THE FISH

- Put the fish in a bowl with the salt, white pepper, Shaoxing wine and egg white. Gently massage the fish to let the flavours penetrate. Mix in the cornflour, in two batches to avoid clumping, then pour in the teaspoon of neutral oil to prevent the pieces from sticking – you're looking for a "slippery" texture to the fish.

TO COOK

- For the broth, heat a wok over a low heat and pour in 1 tablespoon of the neutral oil. Fry the dried chilli peppers and Sichuan peppercorn for about 2 minutes, then remove from the wok and crush them roughly in a mortar or with a knife. Set aside.

- Blanch the Chinese cabbage leaves in boiling water for 30 seconds, then drain and place in a large bowl.

- Place the (clean) wok over a medium heat and add another tablespoon of the oil. Once hot, fry the chilli bean paste (*doubanjiang*) for 15 seconds, then add the fish head and bones and brown them. Pour in 1 litre (4⅓ cups) of boiling water, then add the ginger and garlic. Bring to the boil, then season with the salt and sugar. Add the bass slices and cook for about 40 seconds. Turn off the heat and adjust the seasoning if necessary.

- Pour the broth into the large bowl, over the cabbage. You can remove the fish head and bones at this point if you wish (in China, everything is kept in). Add the crushed chilli and Sichuan peppercorn mix, then heat the remaining 3 tablespoons of oil until smoking and pour over the spices to release their flavours. Finish by sprinkling with a little chopped coriander.

GOOD TO KNOW
小提示

In this case, the broth is not meant to be drunk; it is there to add flavour to the dish. You can enrich this recipe with other vegetables or firm tofu. You can also adjust the amount of dried chilli peppers to your taste.

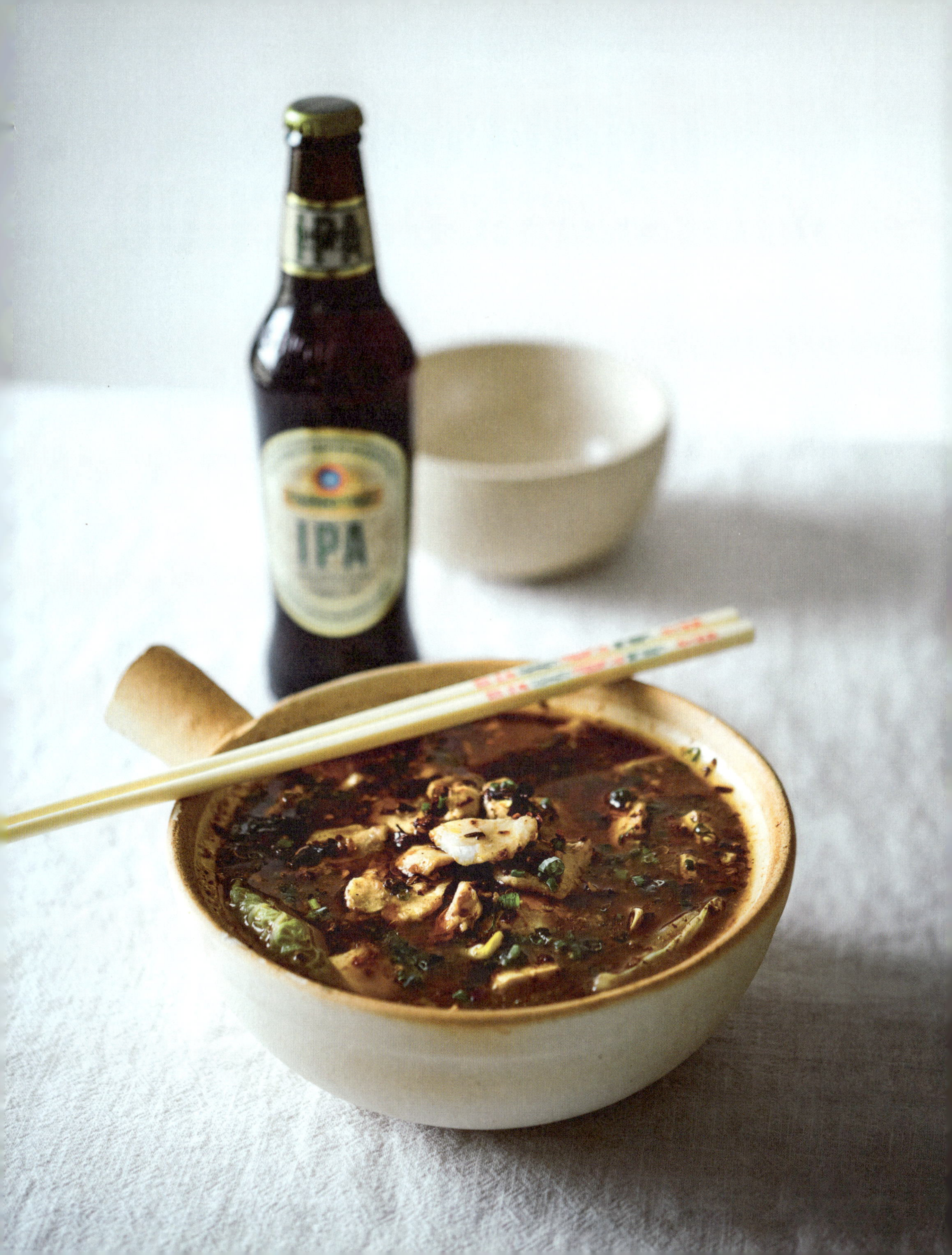
IPA
IPA

Fried Cockles with Garlic and Chilli

CHǍO HUĀ GÉ

炒花蛤

PREPARING 2 HOURS

COOKING 3 MINUTES

WENZHOU IS KNOWN FOR ITS SEAFOOD, ESPECIALLY SHELLFISH. THE FOLLOWING RECIPE FOLLOWS A SPECIFIC LOGIC: AROMATICS TO ADD FLAVOUR, LIMITED SEASONING TO LET THE IODIZED TASTE STAND OUT, AND A QUICK BURST OF HEAT FROM THE WOK TO INTENSIFY THE FLAVOURS.

Serves 2 people

INGREDIENTS

300g (10oz) cockles
1 tbsp neutral oil
2 garlic cloves, chopped
2 tsp chopped shallot
A few dried chilli peppers
1 tsp soy sauce
½ tsp sugar
Coriander (cilantro), or Thai basil, to serve

RECIPE STEPS

- Disgorge the cockles (see p. 83) in salted water 2 hours before cooking.

- Heat a pan over a medium heat and pour in the oil. Once hot, fry the garlic, shallot and chilli peppers for 10 seconds to release the flavours. Add the drained cockles and stir-fry for 2–3 minutes until they are all open (discard any that don't open). Pour in the soy sauce and sugar, and sprinkle with a few coriander leaves to serve. (Or try Thai basil – although less traditional, it also works very well.)

GOOD TO KNOW
小提示

You can use clams or tellin instead of cockles. I like to make this dish slightly spicy, without letting the chilli take over the flavour of the cockles. Instead of dried chillies, you can opt to add a drizzle of chilli oil (see p. 36) when serving.

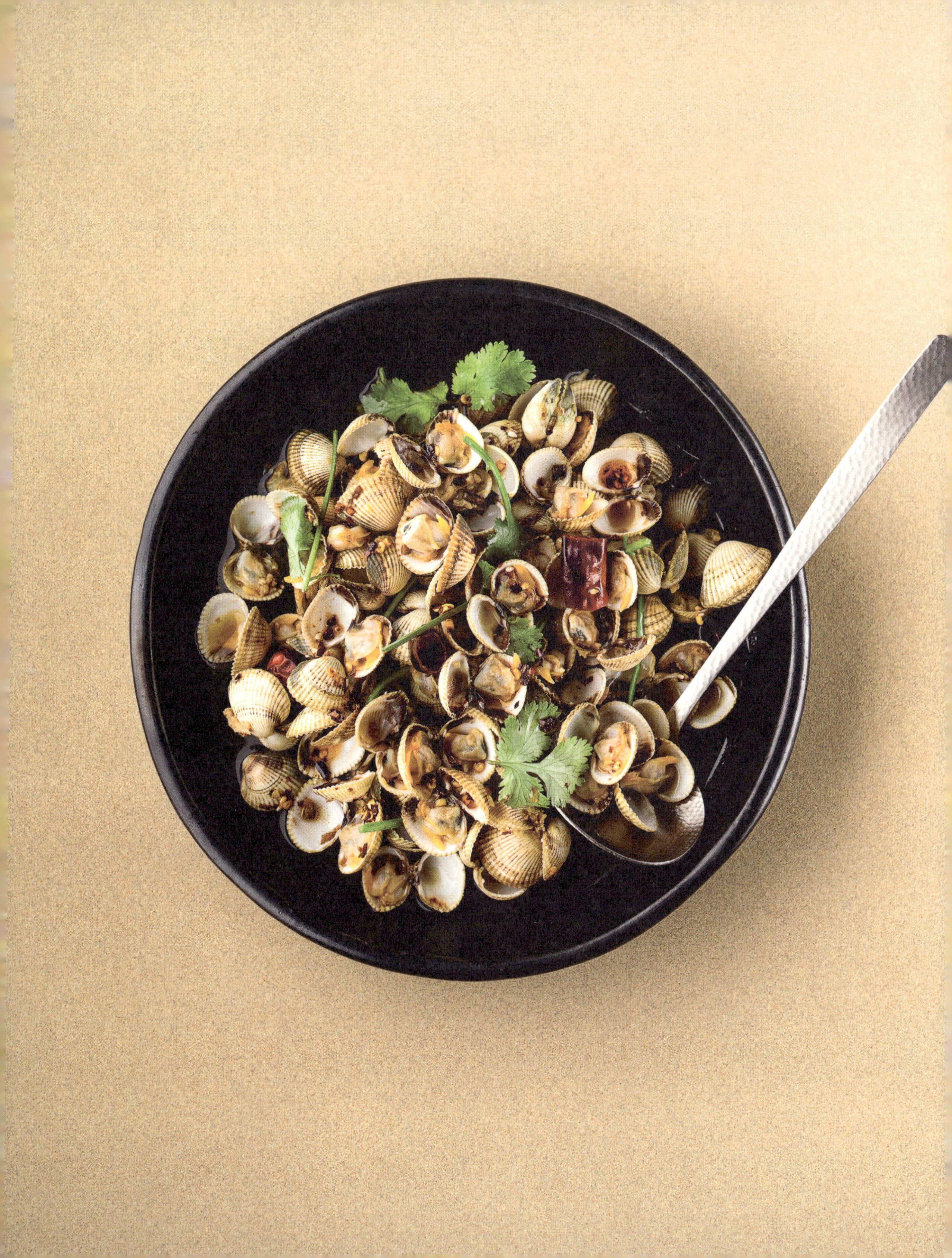

Steamed Scallops with Rice Vermicelli

FĚN   SĪ   ZHĒNG   SHÀN   BÈI

粉丝蒸扇贝

Preparing 25 minutes

Cooking 4 minutes

IN CHINA, SHELLFISH ARE RARELY EATEN RAW. WHILE OYSTERS, ABALONE OR RAZOR CLAMS ARE HIGHLY POPULAR IN NIGHT MARKETS, GRILLED AND SERVED WITH A GOOD BEER, STEAM COOKING IS ALSO A GOOD ALTERNATIVE TO PRESERVE THE TENDERNESS OF THE FLESH. THE FOLLOWING RECIPE IS OFTEN SERVED IN MY FAMILY ON FESTIVE DAYS, SUCH AS CHINESE NEW YEAR.

Makes 8 scallops

INGREDIENTS

8 scallops (retain the shells)
1 tbsp Shaoxing wine
¼ tsp white pepper
60g (2oz) mung bean vermicelli (see p. 232)
Chopped spring onion (scallion), or herb of your choice, to serve

For the sauce

3 tbsp neutral oil
1 garlic bulb, cloves separated and chopped
3 tsp light soy sauce
1 tsp oyster sauce
1 tsp sugar
3 tbsp water

RECIPE STEPS

- Marinate the scallops with the Shaoxing wine and white pepper for 15 minutes.

- Meanwhile, rehydrate the vermicelli in warm water for 10 minutes while you prepare the sauce.

- In a hot frying pan, over a low heat, add the neutral oil and then half the garlic. Brown for a few minutes, without letting it burn. Place the remaining garlic in a bowl, pour in the hot oil and the browned garlic, and mix. Add the rest of the sauce ingredients and mix again.

- Drain the vermicelli. Place a handful in each scallop shell, then add ½ teaspoon of the sauce and a marinated scallop. Bring your steamer water to the boil, put the shells into the steamer, cover and cook over a medium heat for about 4 minutes. Do not overcook the scallops – it is better to undercook them slightly rather than the opposite.

- Place on a serving plate, drizzle a little of the sauce into each shell and sprinkle with some chopped spring onion (or herb of your choice).

GOOD TO KNOW
小提示

You can replace the oyster sauce with douchi sauce (see p. 346) if you have some to hand – it's my favourite version!

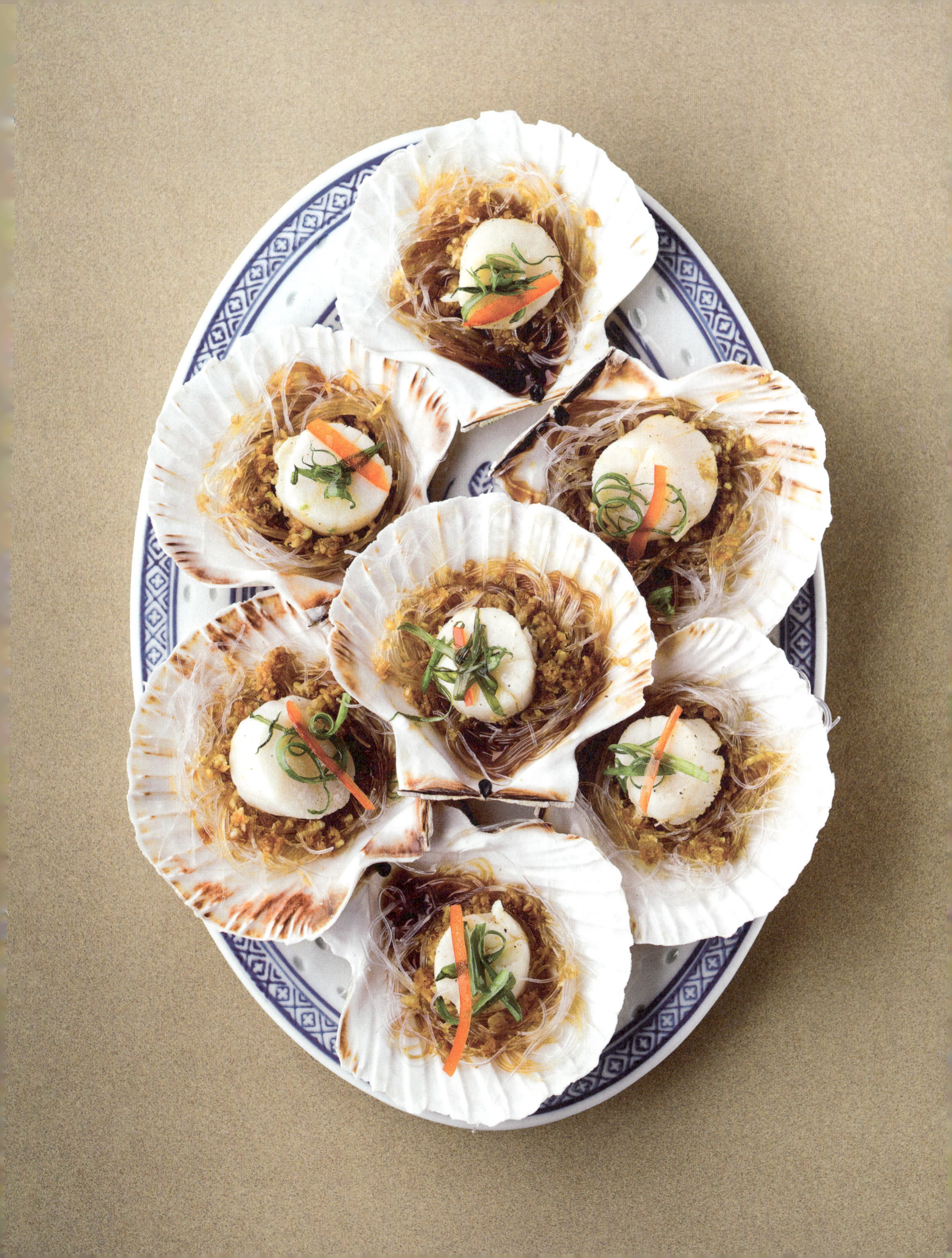

Stir-Fried Squid with Celery

QÍN　CÀI　CHǍO　YÓU　YÚ

芹菜炒鱿鱼

PREPARING 10 MINUTES

COOKING 5 MINUTES

SQUID (OR CALAMARI) IS OFTEN SEEN ON CHINESE TABLES; SMALL NOTCHES ARE MADE ON ITS SURFACE TO CREATE THE IMPRESSION OF DRAGON SCALES AFTER COOKING.

🍴 Serves 2 people

INGREDIENTS

1 whole squid, about 300g (10oz)
2 celery sticks, cut into 6cm (2½in) lengths
1 tbsp neutral oil
2 tsp red onion, chopped
¼ red bell pepper, julienned
1 tsp oyster sauce
1 tsp dark soy sauce
White pepper, to taste

RECIPE STEPS

- Remove the non-edible parts of the squid (mouth, innards), or ask your fishmonger to prepare it for you. Separate the body from the tentacles (which are also edible, so save them for another recipe). Open the body and spread it on a board. Make some diagonal cuts with a sharp knife, approximately 2mm (⅛in) apart, in one direction and then in the opposite direction. Cut the flesh into small rectangles, about 6 x 4cm (2½ x 1½in).

- Blanch the squid pieces for 15 seconds in boiling water. They will curl up and form small tubes. Set aside. In the same water, blanch the chopped celery sticks (they should be the same length as the squid, for aesthetic purposes) for about 30 seconds. Drain and set aside.

- In a hot wok placed over a high heat, add the oil, then the red onion and bell pepper. Stir-fry for 30 seconds, then add the celery and continue cooking for about 1 minute (the vegetables should be cooked but remain crisp). Add the squid, oyster sauce, soy sauce and a little white pepper, stir-fry for 30 seconds, then serve.

GOOD TO KNOW
小提示

I used Chinese celery in this version, which is thinner than classic celery. Feel free to cut your regular-size sticks in half lengthways if they are too thick, to speed up cooking.

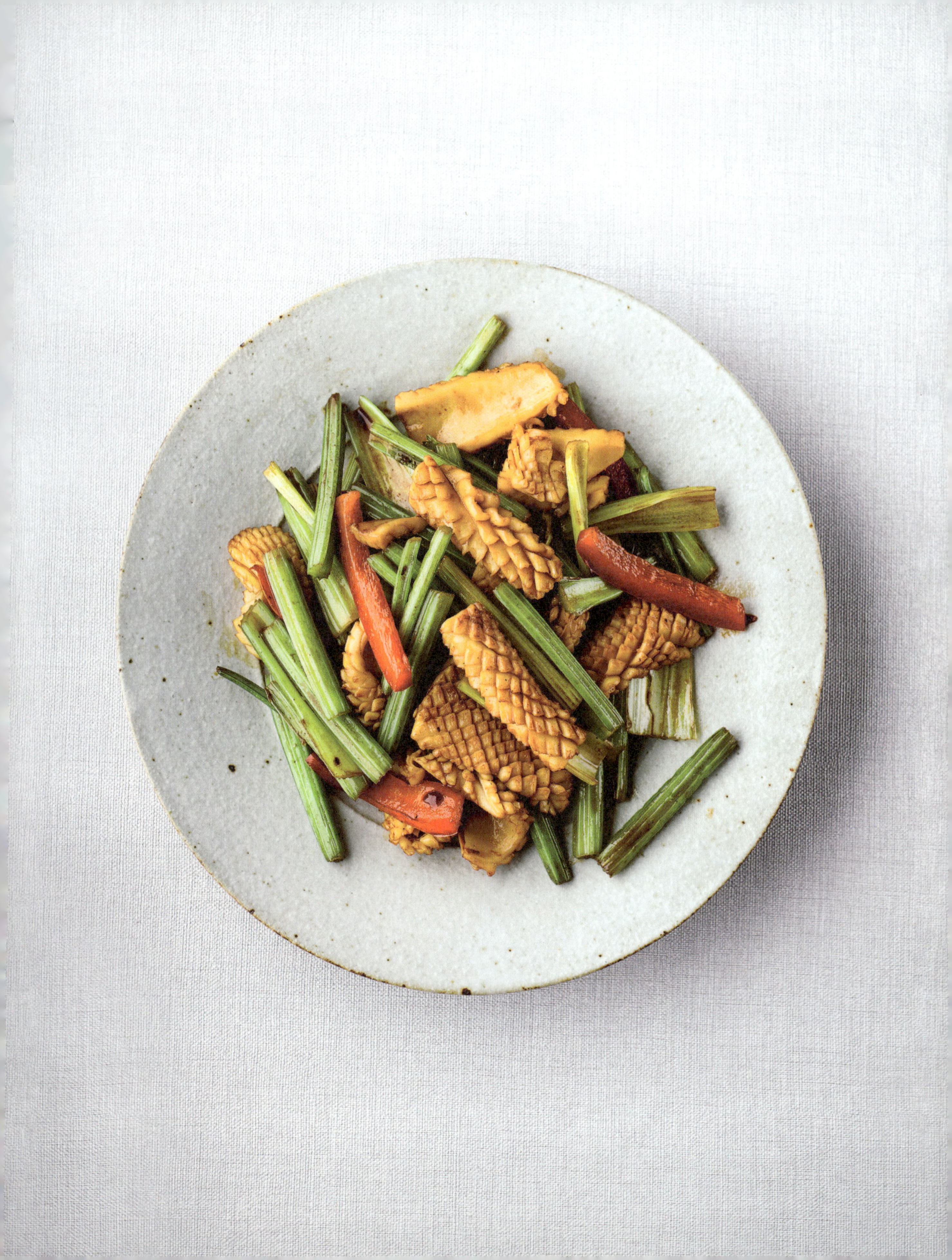

Oyster Pancake

HÁO LÀO
蚝烙

PREPARING 15 MINUTES *COOKING 5 MINUTES*

IN CHINA, OYSTERS ARE EATEN BOTH RAW AND COOKED. FOR EXAMPLE, GRILLING IS A VERY POPULAR COOKING METHOD. BUT I HAVE A SOFT SPOT FOR THIS CHAOZHOU (CANTON) SPECIALITY, WHICH HIGHLIGHTS THE UMAMI AND THE FLAVOUR OF THE OYSTERS.

🍴 Makes 1 large pancake

INGREDIENTS

100g (3½oz) oyster meat, from about 12 oysters (*see method*)
70ml (4½ tbsp) oyster water (*see method*)
30g (1oz/about ¼ cup) sweet potato starch
1 tsp fish sauce
½ tsp white pepper
1 tbsp chopped spring onion (scallion)
1 tbsp neutral oil or lard
1 egg, beaten
Chopped coriander (cilantro), to serve

RECIPE STEPS

- Open the oysters, pick out the meat and reserve the water, straining to remove any shell debris.

- In a bowl, mix the oyster meat and water (it is already very salty, so there is no need to add salt in the recipe), the sweet potato starch, fish sauce, white pepper and spring onion. Feel free to add a little more water as you go. The mixture should be quite thick. If it is too liquid, it will be difficult to get a crispy coating.

- Heat the oil or lard in a wok or frying pan over a medium heat. Add the oyster mixture and let it brown for about 2 minutes, then pour in the beaten egg and cook until it just starts to set. Flip the pancake over and brown on the other side for about 2 minutes.

- Arrange on a plate and sprinkle with chopped coriander. Locals like to add fish sauce to this dish, but personally, I prefer a slightly fruity chilli sauce.

GOOD TO KNOW
小提示

100g (3½oz) of oyster meat corresponds to about a dozen oysters. If possible, use sweet potato starch with large grains for extra crunchiness. You can find it under the name "di gua fen" (粗地瓜粉) *in most Chinese supermarkets.*

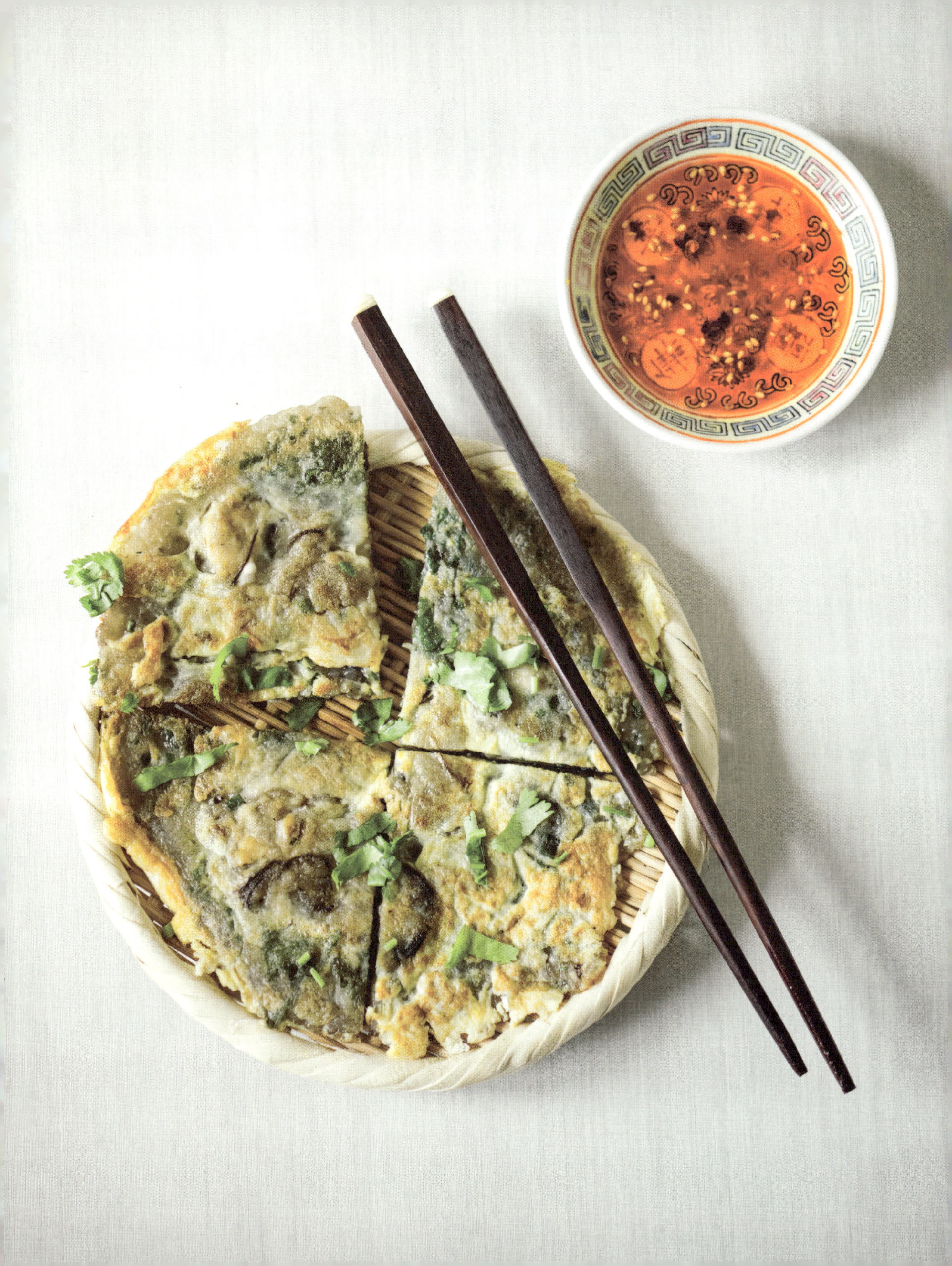

Prawns with Sichuan Peppercorn and Salt

JIĀO   YÁN   JIĀ

椒盐虾

PREPARING 12 MINUTES

COOKING 8 MINUTES

THIS RECIPE IS A SPECIALITY OF MY AUNT IN FRANCE, WHO TREATS US EACH TIME WITH THESE WOK-FRIED PRAWNS. THE SICHUAN PEPPERCORN AND SALT COMBO SEEMS SIMPLE, BUT IS WONDERFULLY EFFECTIVE. THE AROMATIC INGREDIENTS ADD BOTH FLAVOUR AND COLOUR. NO CHANGES NEEDED!

🍴 Makes 10 prawns

INGREDIENTS

10 jumbo prawns (shrimp), unpeeled
2 tbsp cornflour (cornstarch)
300ml (1¼ cups) sunflower or rapeseed (canola) oil
1 small piece of ginger, about 10g (¼oz), peeled and chopped
2 garlic cloves, chopped
2 spring onions (scallions), white parts only, chopped
¼ red bell pepper, chopped
2 shallots, chopped
½ tsp salt
½ tsp Sichuan peppercorn
Finely chopped spring onion (scallion) green, to serve

RECIPE STEPS

▪ Lay a prawn flat on a board and, with a sharp knife, make a shallow slit down the back to remove the digestive tract without removing the shell. Repeat with all the prawns, but leave the heads on, which will add flavour.

▪ Roll the prawns into the cornflour to coat them, and shake them to remove any excess. Heat a wok or pot over a high heat and pour in the oil. When the temperature reaches 180°C (350°F), add the prawns and fry them for about 45 seconds. They should be golden brown, with a crispy crust. To avoid using too much oil, frying can be done in two batches. Drain on kitchen paper.

▪ Heat a wok over a medium heat. When it starts to smoke, pour in 1 tablespoon of the frying oil, followed by the ginger, garlic, spring onions, pepper and shallots. Fry for approximately 30 seconds. When the mixture is nice and flavoured, switch to a high heat and add the prawns. Season with the salt and Sichuan peppercorn and stir-fry for about 30 seconds to mix everything. Sprinkle with chopped spring onion green to serve.

GOOD TO KNOW
小提示

Salt and Sichuan peppercorn can be toasted before mixing and grinding to create stronger flavours. It is a very common mix found in many dishes in China.

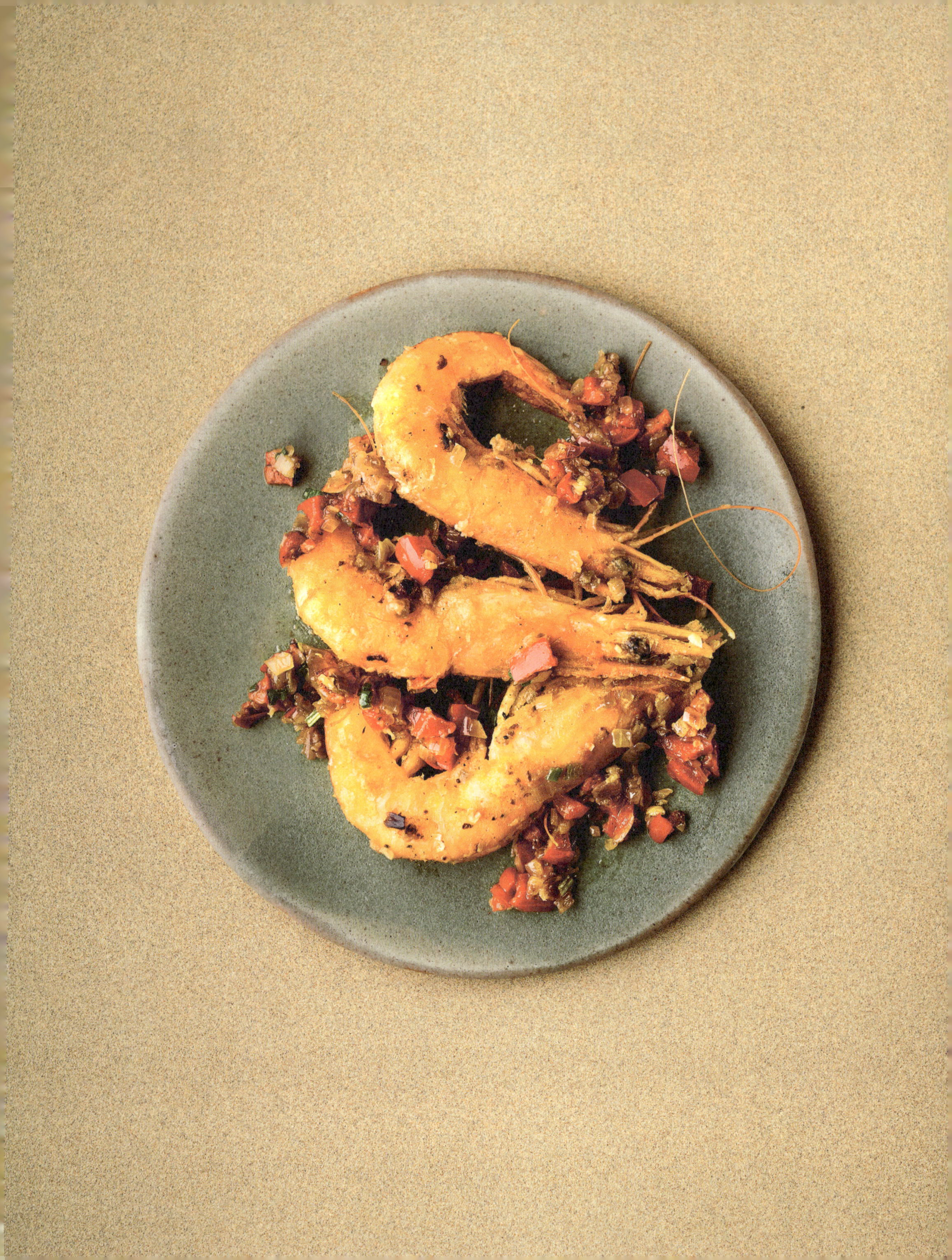

CHAPTER 09

Noodles

面条

MIÀN TIÁO

PP. 236-237: Kansui noodles ▪ **PP. 238-239**: Egg and tomato noodles
PP. 240-241: Cold noodles with sesame sauce ▪ **PP. 242-243**: Zha jiang noodles ▪ **PP. 244-245**: Dan dan noodles
PP. 246-247: 4 noodle sauces ▪ **PP. 248-249**: Yangchun noodles ▪ **PP. 250-251**: Braised beef noodle soup
PP. 252-253: Stir-fried chow fun with beef ▪ **PP. 254-255**: Stir-fried rice vermicelli

From All Angles

The Land of Noodles

CHINA IS A COUNTRY THAT CAN NEVER GET ENOUGH NOODLES! THE FIRST WRITTEN RECORDS OF NOODLES DATE BACK TO THE HAN DYNASTY, MORE THAN 2,000 YEARS AGO (BUT THEY WERE PROBABLY MADE LONG BEFORE THEN). THERE ARE MORE THAN 1,200 VARIETIES IN THE COUNTRY, AND JUST AS MANY RECIPES.

AN EVERYDAY DISH

Noodle restaurants (面馆, *mian guan*) can be found in any corner of the country. It is one of the best options to eat (well) quickly, at low prices and at any time of the day.

From a distance, you can see the smoke coming out of the huge pot of boiling water in which fresh noodles are cooking. Next to it, there are a dozen bowls containing different seasonings, pickles and fresh herbs. Meat simmers for a long time in advance, while vegetables are blanched at the same time as the noodles are made.

In China, it is rare to make noodles yourself, as they can be easily purchased. While many young people like to go for instant noodles from the supermarket, it is possible to prepare a quick meal with fresh or dried noodles and a home-made sauce (see p. 246), all in less than 15 minutes.

MIAN OR *FEN*?

In China, different types of noodles are distinguished by their raw ingredients and their manufacturing method.

Noodles made from wheat flour are generally called "面, *mian*" (or mein in Cantonese), while "粉, *fen*" noodles are made from starch, most often rice starch or mung bean, which is usually translated as "vermicelli". The production has remained largely artisanal, even today, which is why a wide range of techniques can be found throughout the regions.

- There are flat and long noodles in the north (手擀面, *shou gan mian*), which are cut directly with a knife.

- Further west, in Lanzhou, we will find the famous stretched noodles (拉面, *la mian*), the ancestors of the Japanese ramen.

- Knife-grated noodles (刀削面, *dao xiao mian*) are a speciality of the Shanxi province. The chef holds the pasta block in their hand, then grates it and throws the noodles in boiling water.

- In Wenzhou, thin wheat noodles (素面, *su mian*) are dried in the sun like huge curtains of white threads, which makes for an impressive sight.

WITH OR WITHOUT SOUP

In the same way that there are many techniques for shaping noodles, there are different ways to eat them, depending on the region.

In Wenzhou, noodles, whether rice or wheat, are generally served with broth, which is why the expression "noodle soup" seems to be a pleonasm. But this is not necessarily the case elsewhere.

Dan dan noodles (see p. 244) can be served with or without soup. You will find the same thing if you are ever in Chongqing and choose to taste what locals affectionately call "little noodles" (小面, *xiao mian*), an iconic breakfast of the city.

In this chapter, you will find both fried noodles and noodles cooked in water, served in a broth or with a sauce.

GOOD TO KNOW
小提示

You can buy a wide variety of noodles, fresh or dried, in Chinese supermarkets, if you don't have the courage to make them yourself (see p. 234). And feel free to freeze fresh noodles to use them at any time.

DIFFERENT METHODS FOR SHAPING NOODLES

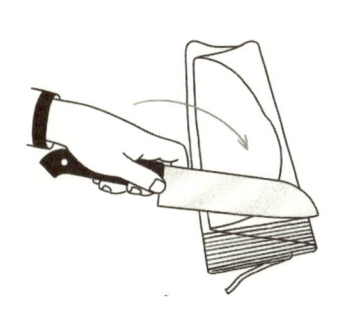

HAND-ROLLED NOODLES
手擀面 | SHǑU GǍN MIÀN

HAND-STRETCHED NOODLES
拉面 | LĀ MIÀN

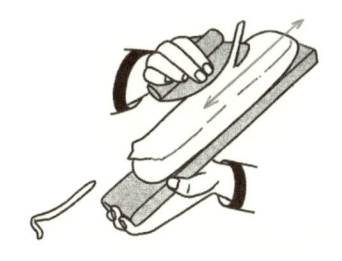

HAND-GRATED NOODLES
刀削面 | DĀO XIĀO MIÀN

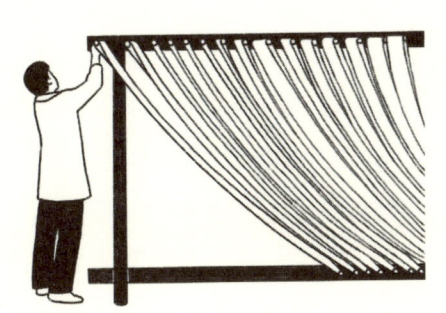

SU MIAN
素面 | SÙ MIÀN

BIANG BIANG NOODLES

面

BIÁNG BIÁNG MIÀN

Making hand-stretched noodles (*la mian*) requires a specific technique, so much so that there are many schools specializing in this training in Lanzhou, their city of origin. *Biang biang* noodles from Shaanxi are a more accessible alternative. They are easily recognizable by their shape, long and wide, and their al dente texture in the mouth.

SERVES 4: 400g (14oz/3 cups) T55 (bread/all-purpose) flour ▪ 4g (1 tsp) salt ▪ 200ml (scant 1 cup) water ▪ 2 tbsp vegetable oil

01
Mix the flour and salt. Add the water as you go, while mixing with chopsticks or with your hands.

02
Knead by hand for 3 minutes until a ball is formed. At this point, it should feel somewhat hard and not very smooth.

03
Cover the dough and let it stand for 30 minutes.

04
The dough should now be easier to work with. Knead it for another 1 minute until it forms **a smooth ball.**

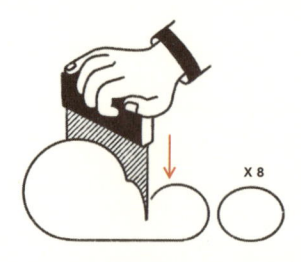

05
Divide it into 8 sections.

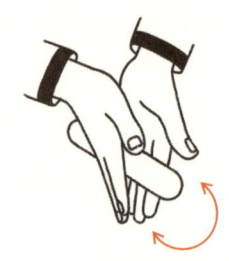

06
Form each piece into **a small sausage** about 10cm (4in) long by rolling it in your hand.

07
Place the dough on a plate and **generously cover it with oil** so that the entire surface is well covered.

08
Cover with film (plastic wrap) and let stand at room temperature (20°C/68°F) for 2 hours.

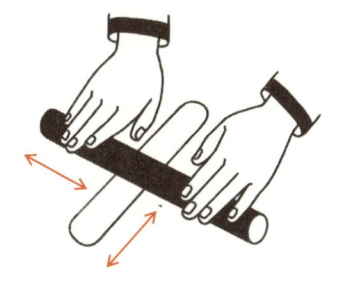

09
Using a rolling pin, **roll each "sausage"** lengthways, roughly 15cm (6in) long, then widthways, roughly 8cm (3in) wide. The edges should be slightly thinner than the centre.

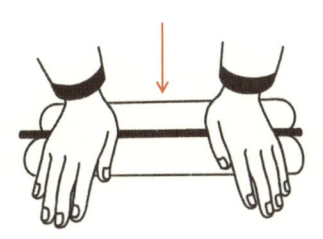

10
Working with one piece of dough at a time, make **a crease in the middle** with a chopstick to allow the noodle to split into two later.

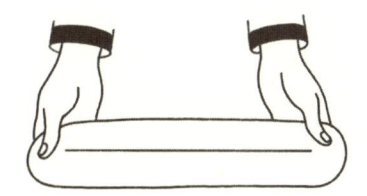

11
Wedge the dough between **your thumb and the other three fingers (index finger, middle finger, ring finger), with the palm of your hand pointing upwards**, which allows you to exert less pressure on the dough and reduce the risk of breakage.

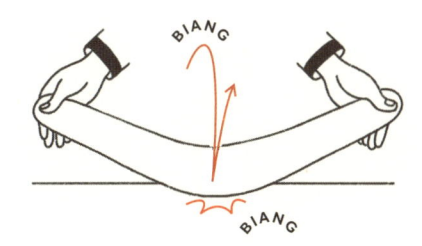

12
Stretch gently, then, when you feel resistance, **bounce the dough** on your countertop (hence the sound "biang biang") to continue stretching it to the desired thickness.

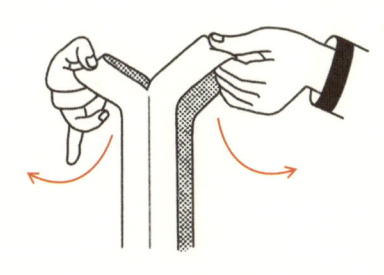

13
Separate the noodle at the fold and break just one of the two ends to obtain a very long noodle, known as the famous belt noodle.

14
Cook your noodle in boiling water for 1 to 2 minutes depending on the thickness, aiming for an al dente texture.

GOOD TO KNOW
小提示

This bizarre name, biang biang, is an onomatopoeia that supposedly refers to the sound of noodles bouncing on the countertop (it might take some imagination). Its Chinese character is particularly complex (between 42 and 57 strokes depending on the version), so it is common to write it directly in phonetics, even in China.

Kansui Noodles

JIĂN　SHUǏ　MIÀN

碱水面

PREPARING 90 MINUTES

COOKING 2 MINUTES

KANSUI IN JAPANESE (OR *JIAN SHUI* IN MANDARIN) TRANSLATES TO "ALKALINE WATER". COMPOSED OF POTASSIUM BICARBONATE AND WATER, IT IS AN ESSENTIAL INGREDIENT TO MAKE THESE SLIGHTLY YELLOW NOODLES, WITH AN *AL DENTE*, ELASTIC TEXTURE, WHICH ARE HIGHLY POPULAR IN CHINA. AS THE DOUGH IS QUITE HARD (42% HYDRATION), A PASTA MACHINE IS STRONGLY RECOMMENDED.

Serves 4

INGREDIENTS

500g (3¾ cups) plain (all-purpose) flour
5g (1 tsp) salt
1 tsp *kansui* (see note)
210ml (scant 1 cup) water
Cornflour (cornstarch), for dusting

RECIPE STEPS

- Mix the flour and salt. Mix the *kansui* and water, then gradually add to the flour, while continuously mixing. This allows the flour to better absorb the liquid. You should obtain a fairly dry and firm dough. Knead the dough by hand until it forms a fairly rough ball. Cover with a cloth (or film/plastic wrap) and let it stand for 1 hour.

- Knead the dough again for 2–3 minutes – it should be a little easier to work with. Form into a ball and divide it into 4 pieces. Choose a piece and cover the others in the meantime. Flatten the dough piece to form a rectangle 4mm (⅛in) thick and run it through your pasta maker at the widest level (level 0). Fold both sides over the centre, then run it through your pasta maker again to make straight edges. Set your pasta maker to level 1 and run your dough strip through it. Then adjust to level 2, and so on until level 4 or 5, depending on the desired thickness, ideally 1.5–2mm (1/12in).

- Sprinkle the surface of the dough with a little cornflour, then use the fine-cut ("spaghetti") setting on your pasta maker (the al dente texture of this dough is less suitable for making large noodles). Repeat the process with the other three dough pieces.

GOOD TO KNOW
小提示

Kansui is available in small bottles in Chinese supermarkets, but it is easy to make it yourself. Spread 100g (3½oz) of bicarbonate of soda (baking soda) in an oven dish lined with foil and bake for 1 hour at 100°C (80°C fan/215°F/Gas ¼). You should then have 70g (2½oz) of powder (do not handle it with your hands). Store in a jar, then simply mix 1 portion of the powder with 4 portions of water to obtain the kansui.

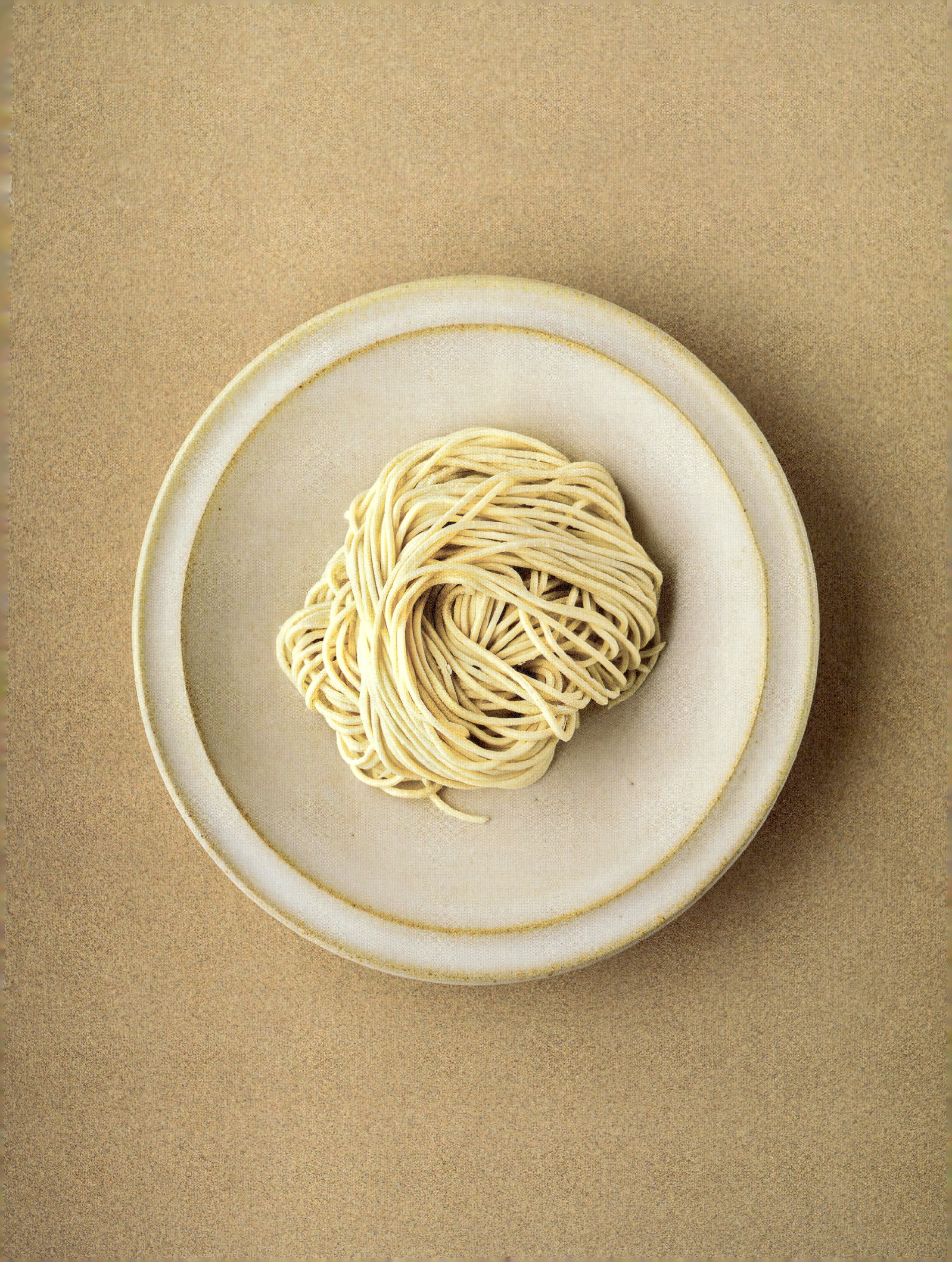

Egg and Tomato Noodles

JĪ　DÀN　FĀN　QIÉ　MIÀN

鸡蛋番茄面

Preparing 10 minutes　　*Cooking 10 minutes*

THE EGG-AND-TOMATO COMBO IS A VERY SIMPLE FILLING THAT YOU NEVER GET TIRED OF. IT IS POSSIBLE TO USE THE BASE RECIPE (SEE P. 146) OR TO FOLLOW THE SIMPLIFIED VERSION HERE TO GO WITH *BIANG BIANG* NOODLES (SEE P. 234). THE SAUCE CONSISTS OF THE THREE ESSENTIAL INGREDIENTS OF SHAANXI, THE PROVINCE WHERE THESE NOODLES ARE FROM: VINEGAR, GARLIC AND CHILLI PEPPER.

Serves 2 people

INGREDIENTS

300g (10oz) *biang biang* noodles

For the sauce

1 tsp tomato paste
1 tsp cornflour (cornstarch)
½ tsp sugar
2 tbsp water
2 tbsp neutral oil
3 eggs, beaten, and mixed with ½ tsp salt
1 tbsp finely chopped spring onion (scallion) white
200g (7oz) tomatoes, quartered

To finish (per bowl)

½ tsp soy sauce
½ tsp black rice vinegar
1 garlic clove, chopped
1 tsp chilli powder
1 tbsp finely chopped spring onion (scallion) green
1 tbsp neutral oil

FOR THE SAUCE

- In a bowl, combine the tomato paste, cornflour, sugar and water and set aside.

- Heat a wok over a medium heat until it starts to smoke. Add 1 tablespoon of the oil, then the eggs. Allow them to swell with the heat for about 40 seconds, making sure they remain a little runny. Remove from the wok and set aside.

- Heat the same wok over a medium heat and add the second tablespoon of oil followed by the spring onion white; fry for about 10 seconds to release the flavour. Add the fresh tomatoes and cook for 2–3 minutes – they should soften up to release some juice. Give the tomato paste and cornflour mixture a stir and pour into the wok, then mix and wait for the sauce to thicken. Add the eggs back in, roughly breaking them up, and let them cook for about 30 seconds, then remove the wok from the heat.

TO SERVE

- Cook the noodles in boiling water for 1–2 minutes (see p. 235) and drain. For each person: mix the soy sauce and vinegar in a large bowl and half your noodles, then pour in half of the tomato and egg sauce. Add the chopped garlic, chilli powder and spring onion green, then heat the tablespoon of oil until it starts to smoke and immediately pour it over the aromatics to release their flavours.

- Mix well and enjoy hot.

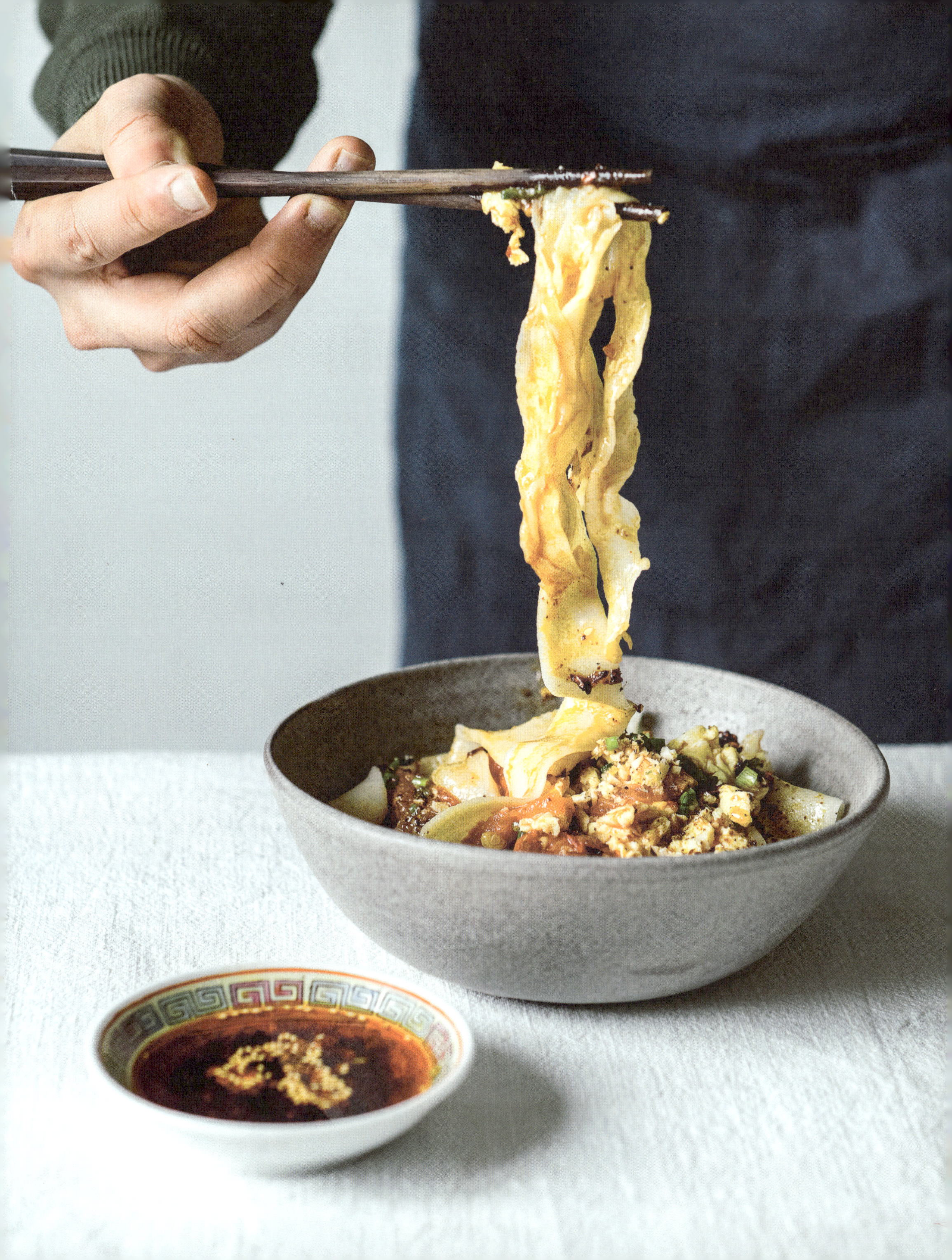

Cold Noodles with Sesame Sauce

MÁ   JIÀNG   LIÁNG   MIÀN

麻酱凉面

PREPARING 8 MINUTES

COOKING 3 MINUTES

THIS NOODLE RECIPE IS UNANIMOUSLY LIKED, ESPECIALLY IN HOT WEATHER. ALMOST EVERYTHING RELIES ON THE SAUCE. YOU WILL FIND MANY VARIATIONS DEPENDING ON WHETHER YOU ARE IN BEIJING OR SICHUAN. MY RECIPE A BIT OF A HYBRID OF THE DIFFERENT REGIONS.

🍴 Serves 2 people

INGREDIENTS

For the noodles

300g (10oz) noodles, of the la mian type *(see p. 232)*
A few cherry tomatoes
1 tsp grated white radish, *(optional)*
Finely chopped or shredded spring onion (scallion)
¼ tsp toasted sesame seeds

For the sesame sauce

3 tbsp Chinese sesame paste *(see p. 40)*
1 tbsp soy sauce
2 tsp black rice vinegar
2 tsp sesame oil
1 tsp sugar
½ tsp salt
2 garlic cloves, grated
2 pinches of Sichuan peppercorn
2 tbsp water

RECIPE STEPS

- Mix the sauce ingredients in a large bowl. You can adjust the amount of water depending on the consistency you want; however, do not dilute too much.

- Cook the noodles according to the packet instructions, then tip them into a colander and run them under cold water for a few seconds (which gives them a firmer texture). Drain and transfer to the bowl with the sauce. Mix well.

- Serve topped with cherry tomatoes, white radish (if using), spring onion and toasted sesame seeds.

GOOD TO KNOW
小提示

You can use other vegetables if you like – ideally crunchy and juicy ones such as cucumbers, red radishes or mung bean sprouts.

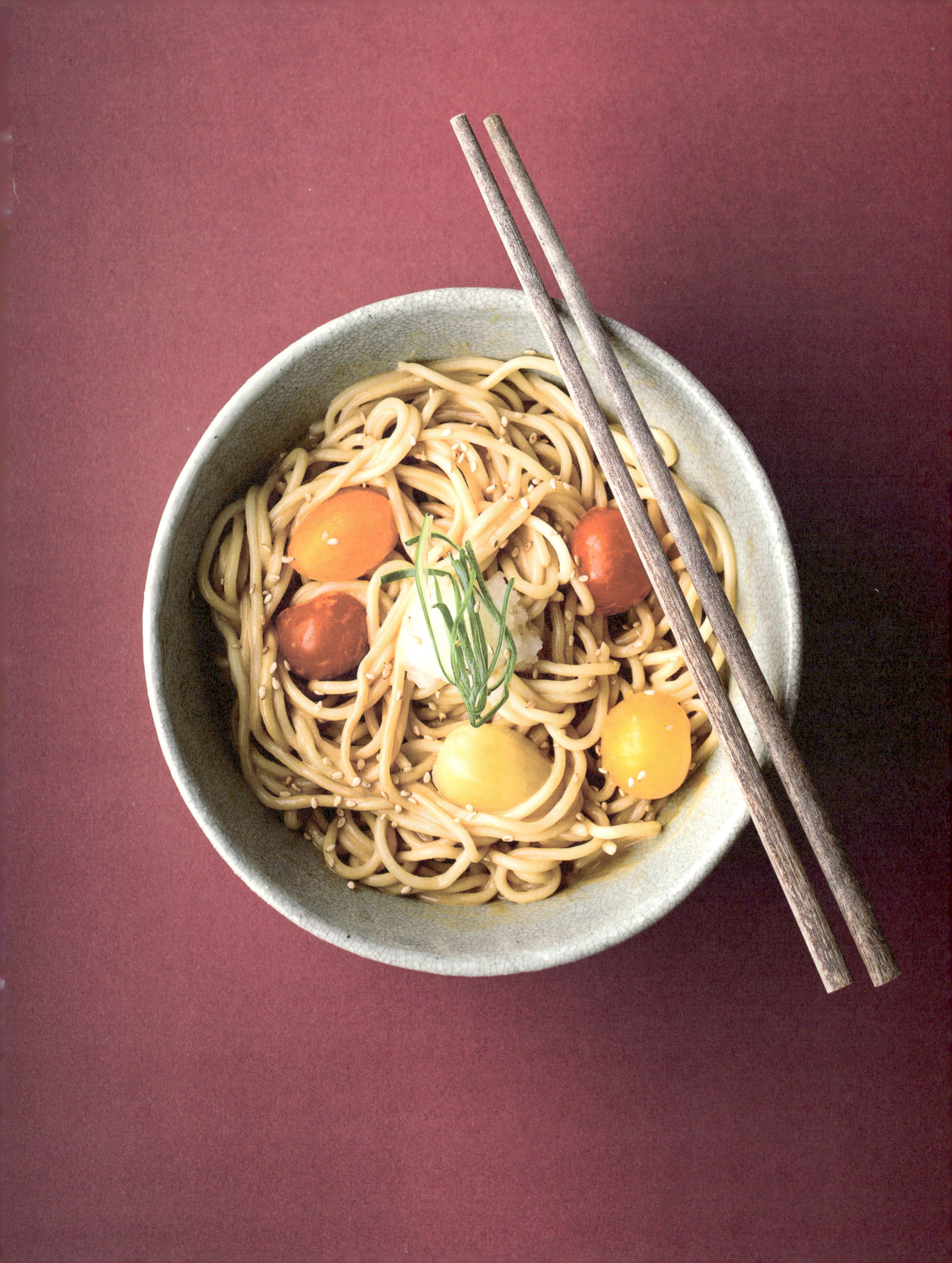

Zha Jiang Noodles

LǍO　BĚI　JĪNG　ZHÁ　JIÀNG　MIÀN

老北京炸酱面

Preparing: 10 minutes　　*Cooking: 30 minutes*

THESE NOODLES ARE AN ICON OF OLD BEIJING CUISINE. *ZHA JIANG* LITERALLY MEANS "STIR-FRIED SAUCE". HOWEVER, IT IS MORE OF A SIMMERED SAUCE WITH DIFFERENT FERMENTED SOY PASTES. THIS DISH IS SO POPULAR THAT IT WAS ADOPTED IN KOREA UNDER THE NAME *JAJANGMYEON*, WHERE IT BECAME JUST AS FAMOUS AS THE ORIGINAL.

Serves 4 people

INGREDIENTS

- 250g (9oz) pork belly
- 2 tbsp neutral oil
- 60g (2oz) fermented sweet soy bean paste (*tian mian jiang*, see p. 38)
- 80g (3oz) fermented salted soy bean paste (*huang dou jiang*, see p.10)
- 3 tbsp Shaoxing wine
- 50g (1¾oz) red onion, chopped
- 1 tsp finely chopped ginger
- 1 tsp finely chopped garlic
- 1 star anise
- 15g (½oz) rock sugar (or regular sugar)
- Fresh noodles of choice, about 150g (5½oz) per person
- Cucumber, carrot, red radishes, bean sprouts (*optional*), to serve

FOR THE PORK

- First prepare the pork belly. Separate the fat from the lean meat and cut into small cubes: 5mm (¼in) for the lean meat and 1cm (½in) for the fat (which will reduce a lot during cooking). Fry the fat in a pan over a low heat, with the oil. When the pieces are slightly browned and have reduced by half, remove them with a spider or skimmer, leaving the oil in the pan.

FOR THE SAUCE

- Meanwhile, in a large bowl, mix the fermented sweet soy bean paste, the fermented salted soy bean paste and the Shaoxing wine. (Alternatively, you can use only *tian mian jiang*, but if you do, use 180g (6¼oz) because it is less salty.)

- In the same pan you used for the pork fat, fry the red onion over a low heat for 5 minutes until lightly browned. Discard the onion and keep the fragrant oil. Stir-fry the ginger and garlic for a few seconds in that oil, then add the soy paste mixture, the star anise, the sugar and the pork (both lean meat and browned fat), and simmer for 20 minutes without covering. Your *zha jiang sauce* is done.

TO SERVE

- Cook your chosen noodles in a large volume of boiling water (in two batches if necessary). Drain and divide between 4 bowls. Add 2 tablespoons of the sauce to each bowl (not too much at first, as it is quite salty!) and then add your choice of toppings, usually finely julienned crisp vegetables such as cucumber, carrots and bean sprouts. Mix it all together and enjoy!

GOOD TO KNOW
小提示

This noodle dish is eaten hot in winter and cold in summer. Preferably use la mian *noodles (see p. 232). In Beijing,* zha jiang *sauce is also used on rice, on pancakes with vegetables or on a plain bao.*

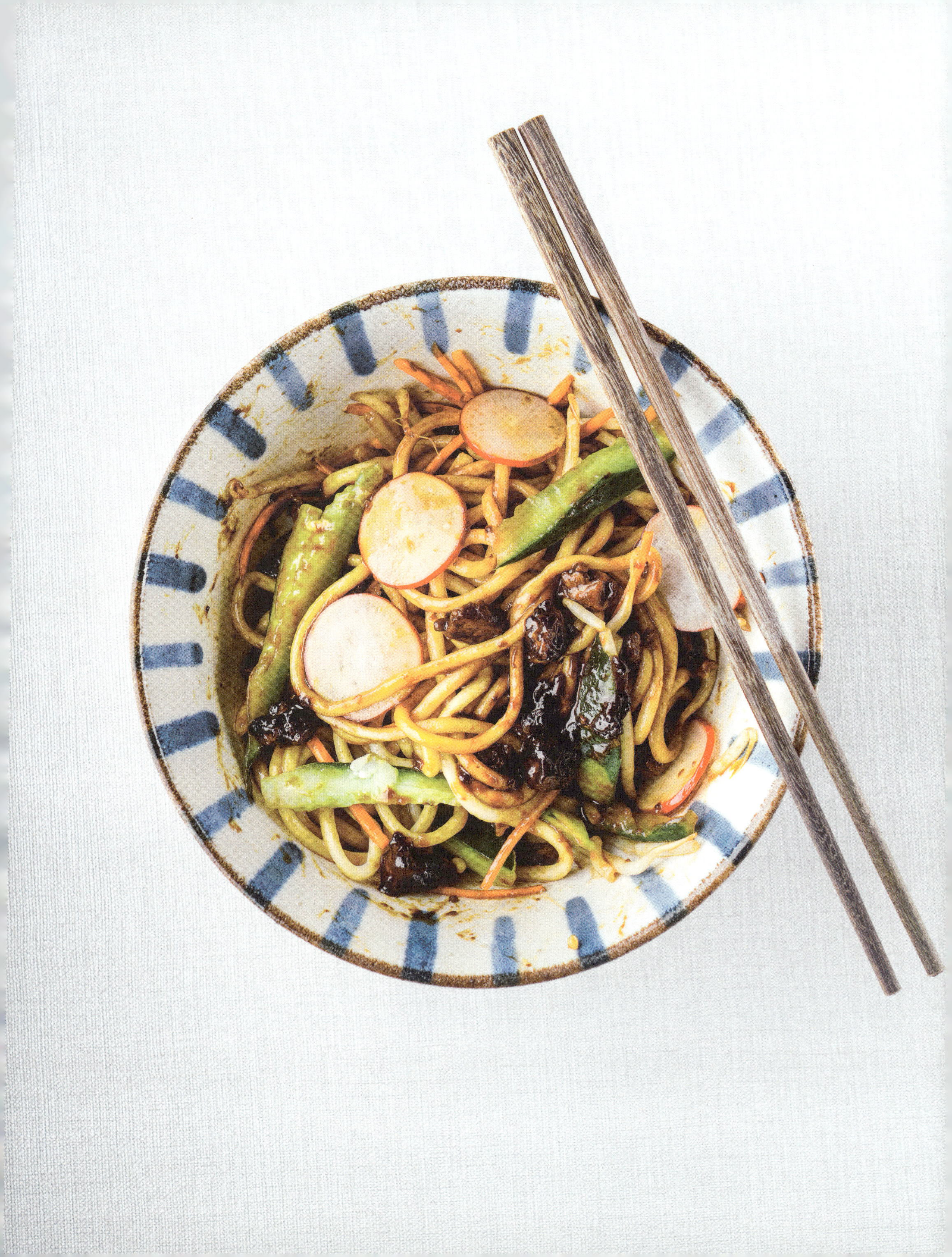

Dan Dan Noodles

DÀN　DÀN　MIÀN
担担面

PREPARING 5 MINUTES

COOKING 10 MINUTES

IF YOU COULD ONLY HAVE ONE NOODLE RECIPE, IT SHOULD BE THIS ONE! THE SAUCE IS A PERFECT HARMONY OF TASTE, ALL AT ONCE SALTY, VINEGARY, SPICY AND WITH A GOOD DOSE OF UMAMI. NO WONDER THAT IN RECENT YEARS, THIS DISH HAS BECOME THE FACE OF SICHUAN CUISINE IN THE REST OF THE WORLD.

Serves 2 people

INGREDIENTS

For the noodles

- 1 tbsp neutral oil
- 100g (3½oz) minced (ground) beef
- 1 tbsp Shaoxing wine
- 1 tsp dark soy sauce
- ½ tbsp fermented mustard leaves (*ya cai, see p. 38; optional*)
- 300g (10oz) fresh noodles
- Toasted peanuts, crushed
- Finely chopped spring onion (scallion)
- 2 garlic cloves, grated
- Sichuan peppercorn, to taste

For the sauce

- 3 tbsp sesame paste
- 1 tbsp chilli oil (*see p. 342*)
- 1½ tbsp light soy sauce
- 1 tbsp sesame oil
- 1 tbsp black rice vinegar
- 1 garlic clove, chopped
- 6 tbsp noodle cooking water

FOR THE SAUCE

- In a large bowl, mix all the sauce ingredients together (except the noodle cooking water, which you will add at the end to dilute the sauce).

FOR THE BEEF

- Heat a wok over a medium heat until it starts smoking. Add the oil, then the minced beef (in the traditional recipe, minced pork is used). Fry the meat quickly until lightly browned, for about 2–3 minutes. Deglaze with the Shaoxing wine, then stir in the dark soy sauce, and the fermented mustard leaves (*ya cai*) if using. Stir-fry for 1 minute, then turn off the heat and set aside.

TO SERVE

- Cook the noodles until al dente in a large volume of boiling water, according to the instructions on the packet.

- Add the 6 tablespoons of noodle cooking water to the sauce and mix, then divide the sauce between 2 serving bowls. Drain the noodles and add half to each bowl. Mix again, add the beef, then top with a few toasted crushed peanuts, some chopped spring onion and the grated garlic. Personally, I like to add some freshly ground Sichuan peppercorn and a drizzle of home-made chilli oil to finish.

GOOD TO KNOW
小提示

Dàn dan noodles can also be enjoyed as a soup. Simply add more cooking water to the sauce or, better yet, replace the noodle cooking water with a good home-made broth (see p. 160) at the time of serving.

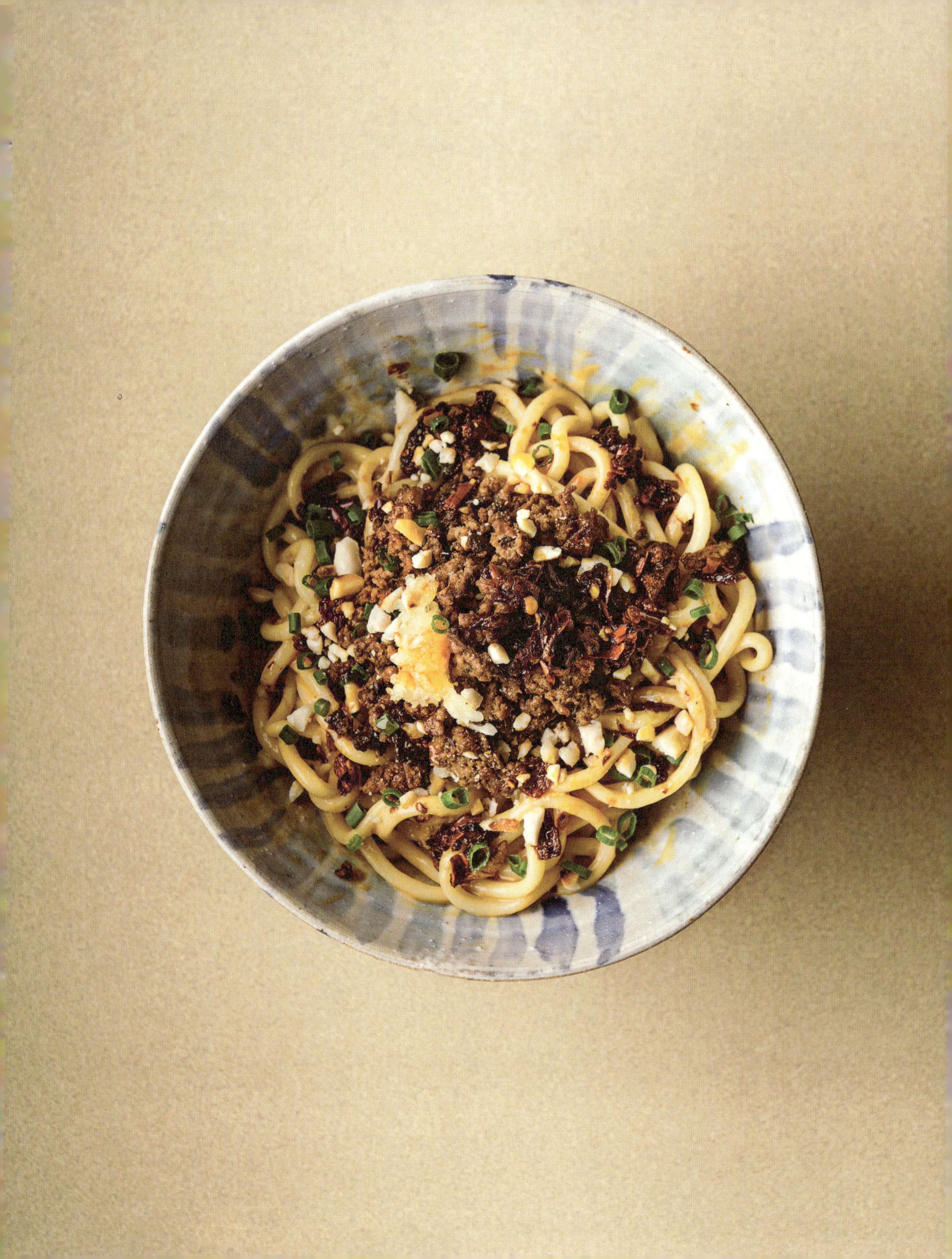

4 Noodle Sauces

SWEET & SPICY
甜水面酱
TIÁN SHUĬ MIÀN JIÀNG

This sauce is inspired by a Sichuan dish called "sweet water noodles", which refers to a special sweet soy sauce (recipe p. 348) that is very flavourful.

MAKES 1 BOWL:

1 tbsp sweet soy sauce
1 tbsp sesame paste
1 tsp chilli oil (see p. 36)
½ tsp finely chopped garlic
¼ tsp Sichuan peppercorn (optional)
A few toasted peanuts, coarsely crushed

Combine the sweet soy sauce, sesame paste and chilli oil in a small bowl. Arrange your cooked noodles of choice in a large bowl, pour in the sauce, then add the garlic, Sichuan peppercorn and a few coarsely crushed toasted peanuts. Mix and enjoy.

SALTY & FLAVOURFUL
葱油面酱
CŌNG YÓU MIÀN JIÀNG

This ultra-simple sauce is based on a key ingredient: spring onion oil (see p. 340), widely used in Shanghai to season the locals' favourite noodles.

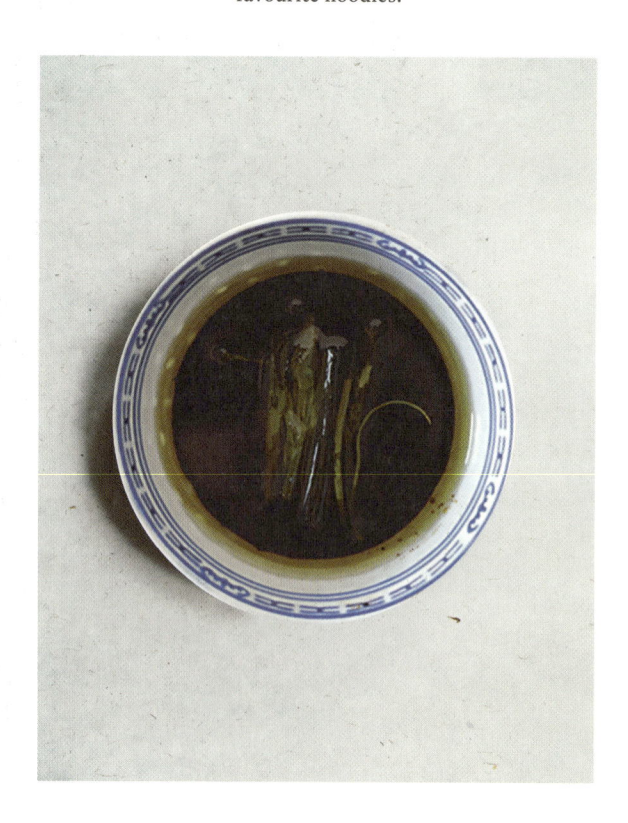

MAKES 1 BOWL:

2 tbsp spring onion (scallion) oil
1 tbsp light soy sauce
½ tsp sugar
1 tsp lard (optional)

Heat all the ingredients in a pan over a low heat until fragrant and the sugar dissolves. Transfer the sauce to a bowl, add your cooked noodles of choice. Mix and enjoy. (If you just made your spring onion oil – see p. 340 – you can sprinkle with some of the fried spring onions when serving.)

THERE ARE ENDLESS VARIETIES OF NOODLE RECIPES IN CHINA,
BUT THE SECRET TO THEIR SUCCESS OFTEN LIES IN A GOOD SAUCE.
HERE ARE FOUR YOU CAN USE WITH ANY TYPE OF NOODLES
YOU HAVE ON HAND TO MAKE AN EXPRESS DISH.

BIANG BIANG
油泼辣子
YÓU PŌ LÀ ZI

This is the classic base sauce for biang biang noodles (see p. 234), which tastes like vinegar, as well as salty and spicy. Purists will use the old vinegar of Shanxi, which is stronger and more full-bodied!

MAKES 1 BOWL:

- 1 tbsp black rice vinegar
- 1 tsp light soy sauce
- 1 tsp finely chopped garlic
- 2 tsp finely chopped spring onion (scallion)
- 2 tsp chilli powder (see p. 36)
- 2 tbsp neutral oil
- Sichuan peppercorn
- Salt

Place your cooked noodles of choice in a large bowl, add the vinegar and soy sauce, then sprinkle the garlic, spring onion and chilli powder (I use the *er jing tiao* variety in this example) on top. Heat the oil until it starts smoking and then pour it over the aromatics to release their flavours (you should hear a "pssshh" sound). Finish with a pinch of ground Sichuan peppercorn and salt.

IODIZED & CREAMY
蚝油酱
HÁO YÓU JIÀNG

Let's head to Guangdong to make a salty and iodized sauce. Nori powder, which is easier to find, replaces the traditional dried shrimp eggs (虾籽, *xiā zǐ*).

MAKES 1 BOWL:

- 1 tbsp oyster sauce
- 1 tsp spring onion (scallion) oil (p. 340)
- ½ tsp sesame oil
- 1 tsp lard (*optional*)
- 1 tsp toasted nori powder

Mix all the ingredients, except the nori powder, in a large bowl. Add your cooked noodles of choice, mix again, then sprinkle over the nori.

Yangchun Noodles

YÁNG　CHŪN　MIÀN

阳春面

PREPARING 3 MINUTES

COOKING 5 MINUTES

DO NOT BE FOOLED BY ITS SIMPLE APPEARANCE AND THE SCANT AMOUNT OF GARNISH. SIMPLY MENTIONING THIS NOODLE DISH TO SOMEONE FROM SHANGHAI WILL PROBABLY MAKE THEM VERY NOSTALGIC. THE COMBINATION OF JUST A FEW INGREDIENTS IN A HOT BROTH IS ENOUGH TO BRING COMFORT.

Makes 2 bowls

INGREDIENTS

For the noodles

700ml (2¾ cups) pork bone broth (*see p. 306*)
300g (10oz) thin noodles

Per noodle bowl

1 tbsp lard (*see p. 344*)
½ tbsp soy sauce
⅛ tsp sugar
⅛ tsp white pepper
Finely chopped spring onion (scallion)

RECIPE STEPS

- Bring the broth to the boil in a pot. (It can be replaced with chicken broth, if you prefer; see p. 160.) At the same time, cook the noodles in another pot, following the instructions on the packet. As soon as they are cooked, run them under cold water for a few seconds to give them a more al dente texture.

- To each bowl, add the lard, soy sauce and sugar, then pour in half the broth, which should be very hot. Mix to dilute the lard. Add half the noodles immediately and finish with the white pepper and chopped spring onion to serve.

GOOD TO KNOW
小提示

Lard is the soul of this dish, but if you don't have any on hand, it is possible to replace it with sesame oil (1 tablespoon is enough), or better yet, spring onion (scallion) oil. It will, of course, taste different.

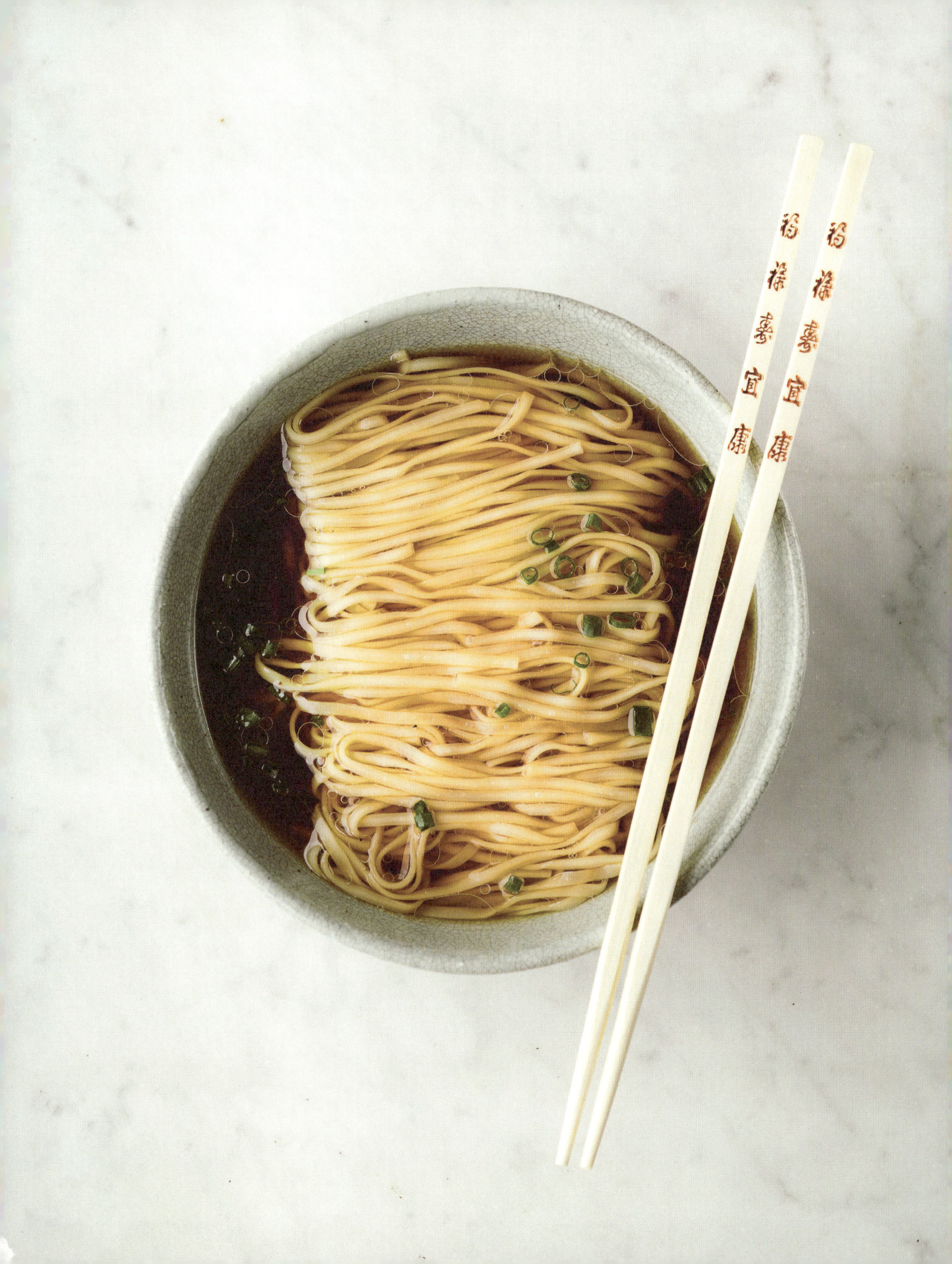
福祿壽宜康
福祿壽宜康

Braised Beef Noodle Soup

HÓNG   SHĀO   NIÚ   ROÙ   MIÀN

红烧牛肉面

PREPARING 10 MINUTES *COOKING 2½ HOURS*

IN A COUNTRY KNOWN FOR ITS PIGS, THIS BEEF NOODLE DISH WINS ALL THE POPULARITY CONTESTS! THERE IS THE LANZHOU VERSION, WITH A CLEAR AND FRAGRANT BROTH AND HAND-STRETCHED NOODLES, BUT ALSO THE SICHUAN VERSION, SPICIER DUE TO THE ADDITION OF *DOUBANJIANG* (*SEE P. 38*). IN TAIWAN, IT TOOK ON A LITTLE FRUITY FLAVOUR, AND THAT'S THE RECIPE YOU WILL FIND HERE.

🍴 Makes 6 bowls

INGREDIENTS

For the broth

2 tbsp neutral oil
10g (¼oz) chopped ginger
1 bunch of spring onions (scallions), cut into 5cm (2in) lengths
1 garlic bulb, halved widthways
1 tbsp chilli bean paste (*doubanjiang*)
3 tbsp Shaoxing wine
1 tbsp dark soy sauce
100ml (6½ tbsp) light soy sauce
30g (1oz/2½ tbsp) sugar
1kg (2¼lb) beef shank, cut into 7–8cm (3in) pieces
4 litres (4 quarts) water
1 tomato, cut into quarters
½ apple (*optional*)
2 star anise
2 bay leaves
1 cinnamon stick
1 tsp fennel seeds
1 tsp Sichuan peppercorn

For each bowl

1 tsp soy sauce
1 tsp black rice vinegar
½ tsp sesame oil
⅛ tsp white pepper
150g (10oz) fresh noodles
A handful of pak choi (bok choy)
Chopped coriander (cilantro)

FOR THE BROTH

- Heat the oil over a medium heat in a large pot. Add the chopped ginger (unpeeled), the spring onions, and the garlic bulb, which should be placed cut side down. Add the chilli bean paste (*doubanjiang*) and fry for 1–2 minutes.

- Deglaze the pan with the Shaoxing wine, add the two soy sauces and then the sugar. Place the pieces of beef shank into the pot and fry for 1–2 minutes, then add the water, tomato and apple (if using).

- Put the whole spices (star anise, bay, cinnamon, fennel and Sichuan peppercorn) in a muslin (cheesecloth) bag and place the bag in the broth. Cook over a high heat until just coming to the boil, then switch to a low heat and simmer, covered, for 2–2½ hours. The meat should be tender but remain slightly firm – leave it to rest and cool slightly in the broth so that it absorbs the flavours. Remove the beef pieces and cut them into slices of about 3–4mm (⅛in). Filter the broth and discard the spice bag.

TO SERVE

- In each serving bowl, combine the soy sauce, vinegar, sesame oil and white pepper. Cook the noodles in a large volume of boiling water, according to the packet instructions, then drain (keep the cooking water) and place in the bowl. Pour in a generous ladleful of hot broth (about 300ml/1¼ cups) and top with a few leaves of pak choi (blanched for a few seconds in the noodle water), the slices of beef and a little fresh coriander.

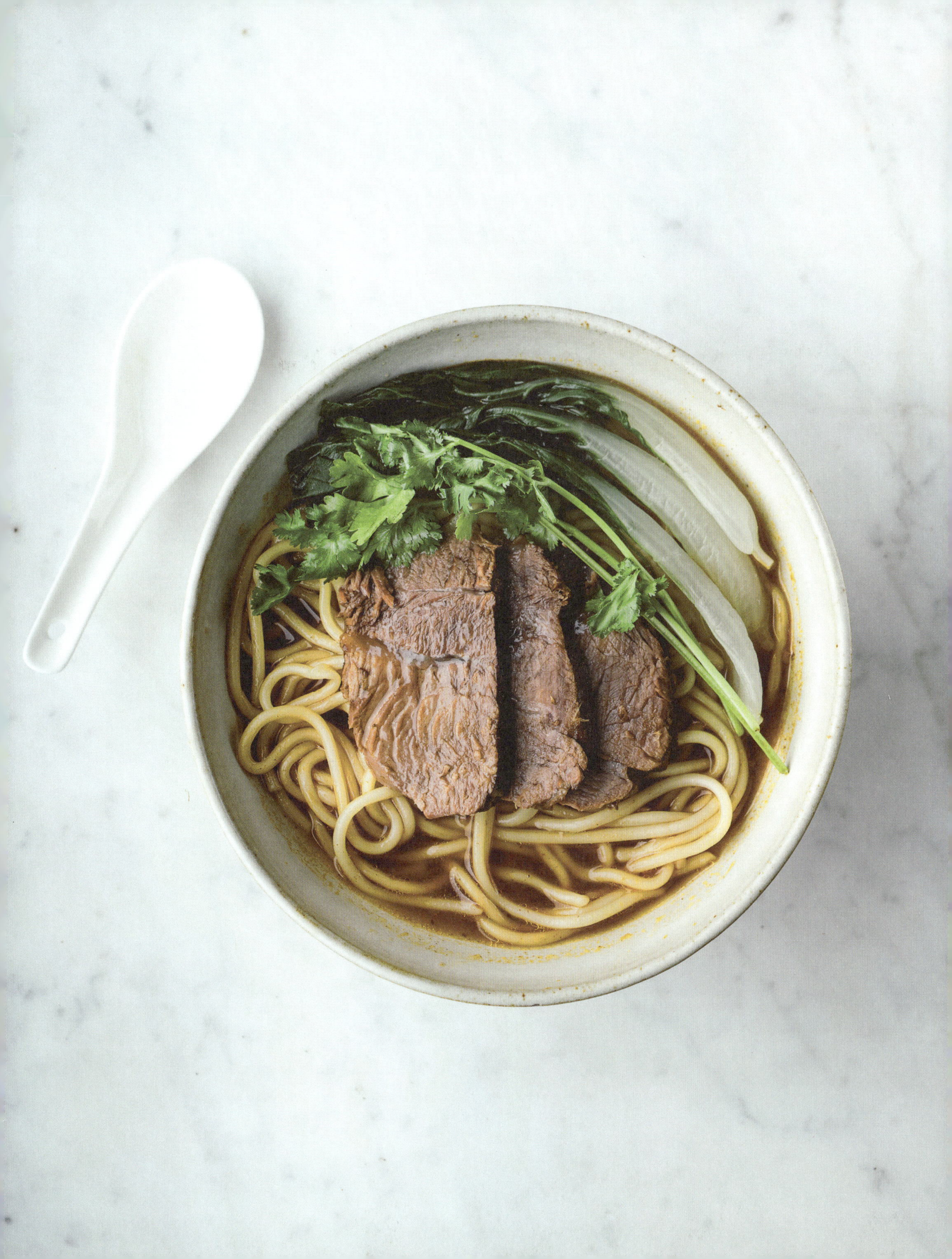

Stir-Fried Chow Fun with Beef

GĀN CHǍO NIÚ HÉ

干炒牛河

PREPARING 15 MINUTES

COOKING 5 MINUTES

HE FEN IS A VERY POPULAR RICE PASTA IN CANTONESE CUISINE. THE WOK STIR-FRIED VERSION (*CHOW FUN* IN CANTONESE), WITH THIN SLICES OF BEEF, IS ONE OF ITS MOST ICONIC DISHES. FOR ME, IT WORKS AS A GAUGE TO JUDGE A CANTONESE RESTAURANT'S MASTERY OF *WOK HEI*, THE FAMOUS SMOKY TASTE THAT THE WOK GIVES WHEN AT THE RIGHT TEMPERATURE.

Serves 2 people

INGREDIENTS

For the chow fun

- 100g (3½oz) beef fillet, cut against the grain into 3mm (⅛in) slices
- 300g (10oz) rice noodles (*see note*)
- 2 tbsp neutral oil
- 10g (¼oz) ginger, about 5cm (2in) long, very finely julienned
- 50g (1¾oz) spring onions (scallions), white and green parts separated and each cut into 5cm (2in) lengths
- 50g (1¾oz) Chinese spring onions (chives), cut into 5cm (2in) lengths
- 80g (3oz) mung bean sprouts
- 1 tsp light soy sauce
- 1 tsp dark soy sauce
- Salt, to taste (*optional*)

For the marinade

- ½ tsp soy sauce
- ¼ tsp sugar
- ¼ tsp cornflour (cornstarch)
- ½ tsp neutral oil

RECIPE STEPS

- First make the marinade. Put the beef into a bowl and add the soy sauce and sugar for the marinade, then mix with your fingers or a chopstick. Stir in the cornflour, mix again, then add the oil and set aside.

- Meanwhile, open the packet of rice noodles and gently separate any noodles that have stuck together.

- Heat 1 tablespoon of the oil in your wok over a high heat. Once hot, add the beef and fry for 40 seconds, until the meat is sufficiently cooked (no pink). Remove from the wok and set aside.

- Heat the remaining 1 tablespoon of oil in the wok over a medium heat. Once hot, add the ginger and fry for a few seconds to release the aromas. Stir in the spring onion white, the Chinese spring onion and the mung bean sprouts. Switch to a high heat and stir-fry for about 1 minute. The mung bean sprouts should no longer feel raw, but they should remain crisp. Add the rice noodles, beef, spring onion green and light and dark soy sauces and stir-fry in the wok, keeping everything moving to prevent the noodles from sticking – they cook very fast, about 2 minutes.

- Taste (before turning off the heat) to adjust the seasoning with a pinch of salt if necessary.

GOOD TO KNOW
小提示

Rice noodles/pasta can be found in the chilled section of some Chinese supermarkets. Do not hesitate to show them the Chinese name, he fen (河粉).

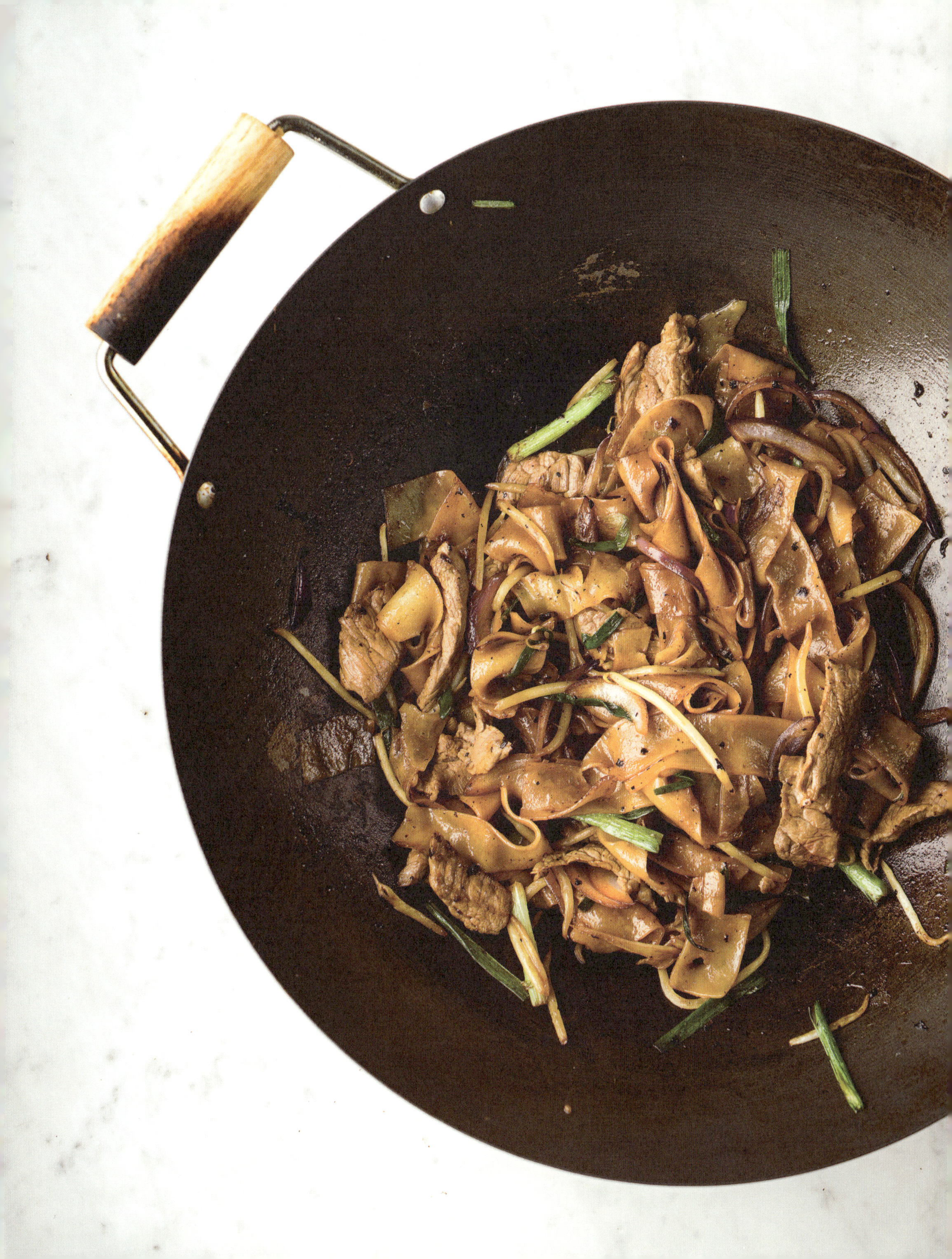

Stir–Fried Rice Vermicelli

CHǍO   FĚN   GĀN

炒粉干

PREPARING 20 MINUTES

COOKING 10 MINUTES

THIS WENZHOU DISH IS VERY COMMON IN *YE XIAO* RESTAURANTS, ESPECIALLY ON SUMMER EVENINGS. THE VERY THIN VERMICELLI ARE STIR-FRIED IN A WOK OVER A HIGH HEAT TO OBTAIN THE *WOK HEI*, THE SUBTLE SMOKY TASTE CAUSED BY THE MAILLARD REACTION. TO PREPARE IT LIKE THE LOCALS, PLAN TO ACCOMPANY IT WITH A GOOD COLD BEER.

Serves 2 people

INGREDIENTS

2½ tbsp neutral oil
2 eggs, beaten
½ onion, chopped
3 shiitake mushrooms, soaked in warm water for 30 minutes, then drained and chopped
25g (about 1oz) carrot, finely julienned with a knife or mandoline
150g (5½oz) pointed cabbage, chopped
100g (3½oz) rice vermicelli (see p. 232), soaked in water for 20 minutes, then drained
80g (3oz) mung bean sprouts
1 tbsp soy sauce
1 tsp salt
½ tbsp oyster sauce

FOR THE EGGS

- Heat your wok over a medium heat, add ½ tablespoon of the neutral oil, then pour in the eggs. Make an omelette and break it into small pieces with a spatula, then remove from the wok and set aside.

FOR THE STIR-FRY

- Set the wok over a high heat, with the remaining 2 tablespoons of oil. Stir-fry the onion for 20 seconds, then add the shiitake, carrot and pointed cabbage and stir-fry for about 1 minute, until the cabbage softens slightly. Stir in the vermicelli, mung bean sprouts, soy sauce and salt and continue cooking for about 3–4 minutes. It is important to maintain a high heat and to stir constantly, so that all the moisture contained in the vermicelli evaporates without having the food stick to the wok. If the vermicelli get tangled, use tongs or a chopstick to untangle them.

- Add the omelette pieces and stir-fry for another 30 seconds, then pour in the oyster sauce and add a little more salt if necessary. Give everything a final stir and serve.

GOOD TO KNOW
小提示

The choice of fillings and garnishes are quite unrestricted here. In Wenzhou, dried pork belly marinated in soy sauce (jiang you rou, **酱油肉**) *is often added, which you can sometimes find in Chinese supermarkets. You will need to cut the pork into small pieces and steam it for 10 minutes before using.*

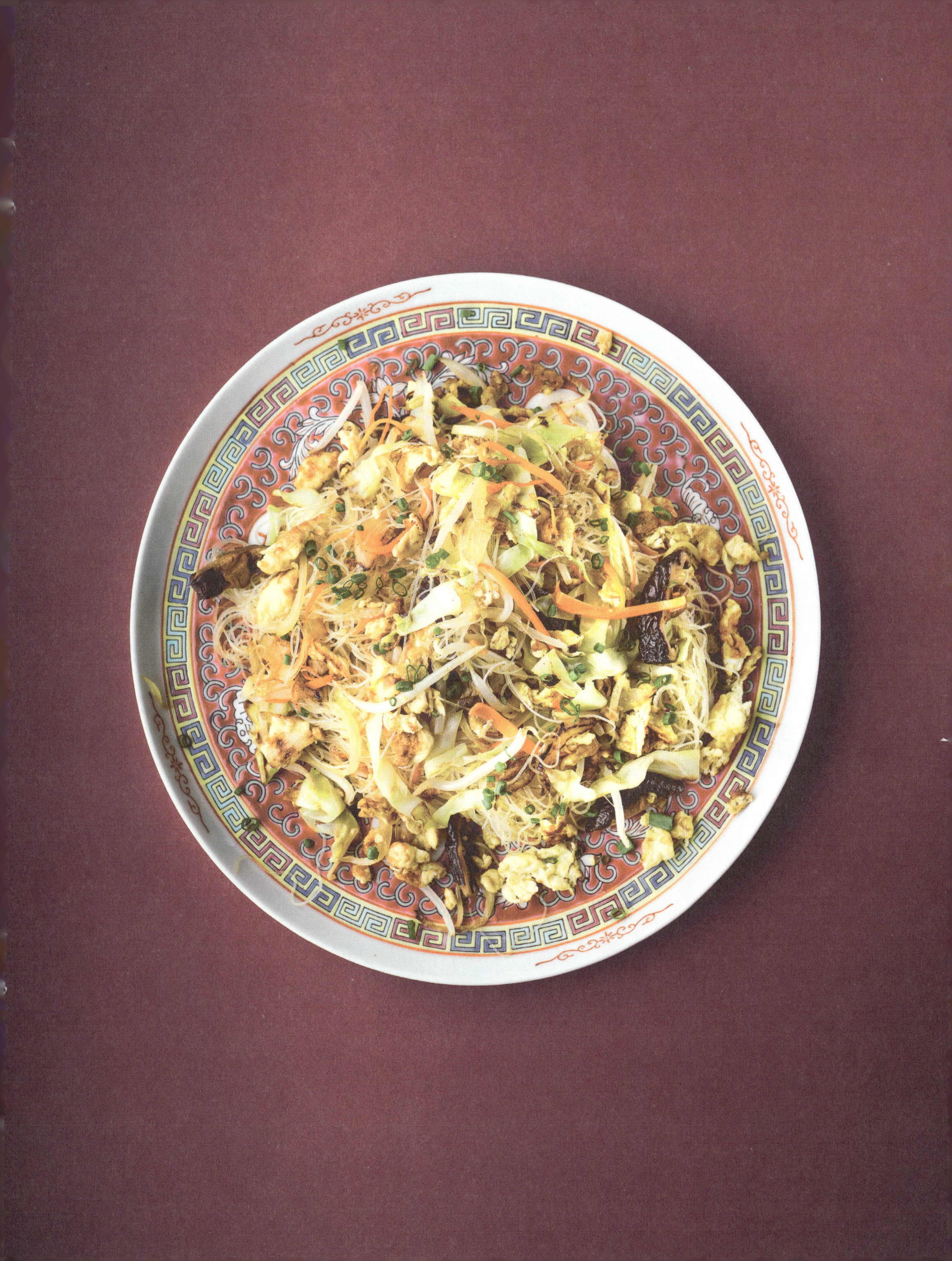

CHAPTER 10

Dumplings
饺子
JIǍO ZI

PP. 260-261: Dumpling dough   **PP. 262-263**: 4 types of vegetarian stuffing   **PP. 264-265**: Folding the dumplings
PP. 266-267: Cooking dumplings   **PP. 268-269**: Zhong dumplings   **PP. 272-273**: Wonton soup

From All Angles

A Taste of the New Year

THERE IS NO DIRECT TRANSLATION FOR THE MANDARIN WORD "DUMPLING".
WHAT WE ALWAYS CALL "CHINESE DUMPLING" CAN DESCRIBE VERY DIFFERENT DISHES,
DEPENDING ON THE TYPE OF FLOUR, THE SHAPE OF THE DOUGH, THE TYPE OF STUFFING,
THE FOLDING METHOD, THE DUMPLING'S SIZE, THE COOKING METHOD…

JIAO ZI, THE NORTHERN DUMPLINGS

Jiao zi could be described as the default dumplings, and are therefore the most well known. They are shaped like half-moons and eaten all over the country.

In the North, they are both an everyday food and an essential dish during the Chinese New Year (p. 374). It has become a kind of ritual for the whole family to get together to make *jiao zi* for the most important meal of the year.

When cooked with water, their most typical cooking method, they are called *shui jiao* (*shui* means water). A cup of black rice vinegar is never far away. Pan-fried dumplings, which you might know better under the Japanese term "gyoza", are also very popular. They are called *jian jiao* (煎饺) or *guo tie* (锅贴) in China.

MORE DELICATE PRESENTATIONS IN THE SOUTH

In the south of the country, dumplings are smaller and have more intricate shapes, but they are rarely eaten as a main dish.

Wontons are a good example (混沌), made with very thin dough, with a texture that slides in the mouth (thanks to the addition of egg in the flour) and a smaller amount of stuffing. As is often the case in China, each region has its own version of the same dish. For example, wonton is called *chao shou* (抄手) in Sichuan, where it is served with sweet soy sauce and chilli oil (see p. 36). It becomes *yun tun* (云吞) in Guangdong, presented as a soup. This is my favourite version.

DIM SUM DUMPLINGS

We can list a very large number of different dumplings in Cantonese dim sum.

The most famous ones are probably the prawn-stuffed dumplings called *xia jiao* (but better known by their Cantonese name *har gow*), which have a translucent stuffing thanks to the wheat starch used to make them.

There is also *shao mai* (or *siu mai* in Cantonese), which are shaped like a purse, with a yellow dough due to the addition of an alkaline agent in the flour, like ramen noodles.

The recipes in this chapter focus mainly on *jiao zi*, but the techniques (especially for the stuffing) apply to all types of dumplings.

GOOD TO KNOW
小提示

Gyoza became popular in Japan after World War II, when they were brought back by Japanese soldiers who returned from the conquered territory of North-East China. In Japanese kanji script, gyoza is written exactly the same way as jiao zi: 饺子. It's come full circle.

THE MAIN DUMPLINGS FROM NORTH TO SOUTH

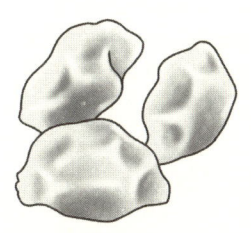

JIAO ZI
饺子 | JIĂO ZI

The basic northern dumplings, usually cooked in water and served with rice vinegar.

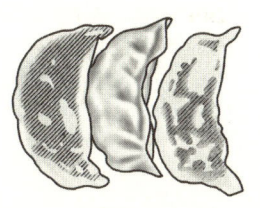

GUO TIE
锅贴 | GUŌ TIĒ

Roasted dumplings, longer in shape and with a slightly finer dough than *jiao zi*.

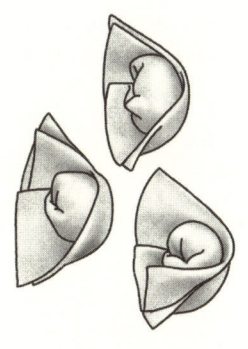

WONTON
馄饨 | HÚN TUN

Small dumplings in the form of a Chinese ingot with a very thin skin, usually served as a soup in the South.

SHAO MAI
烧麦 | SHĀO MÀI

Purse-shaped steamed dumplings. The stuffing changes radically depending on the region.

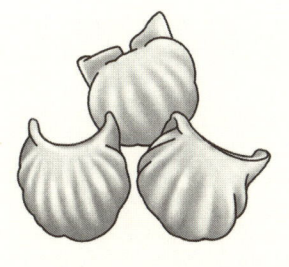

XIA JIAO
虾饺 | XIĀ JIĂO

Iconic dumplings of Cantonese dim sum (south) with translucent dough and prawn (shrimp) stuffing.

DUMPLING DOUGH

饺子皮

JIAO ZI PÍ

Dumpling dough is a small, thin disc made from wheat flour. A successful dough should be sufficiently flexible and elastic, without sticking to the countertop.

PREPARATION: 20 mins, **REST:** 1 hour 15 mins, **MAKES** 30 dumplings
250g (generous 1¾ cups) T55 (bread/all-purpose) flour ■ 2g (½ tsp) salt ■ 120ml (½ cup) water

01
Mix the flour and salt, then add the water gradually. Knead the dough for 1 minute until it no longer sticks to your fingers.

02
The dough should be slightly dry. Let it rest for 15 minutes, covered with film (plastic wrap).

03
Knead again for 1–2 minutes until you form a ball with a smooth surface. Cover again and let it rest for 1 hour.

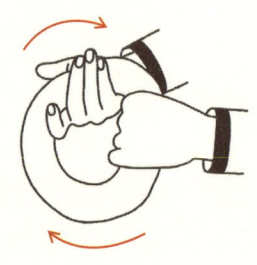

04
Lightly cover the countertop with flour. Make a hole in the middle of the ball, then form a "ring" circle of about 4cm (1½in) in diameter.

05
Cut the circle to get 2 rolls, then divide into 12g (½oz) pieces.

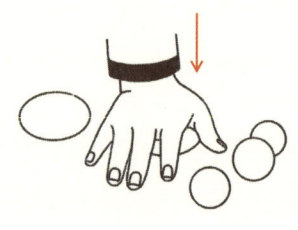

06
Lightly roll each dough piece on the countertop to form a ball, then flatten it with your palm.

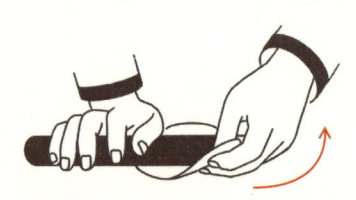

07
Using a dumpling rolling pin (p. 45), flatten each disc while turning it with the other hand until you obtain a circle shape 9cm (3½in) in diameter.

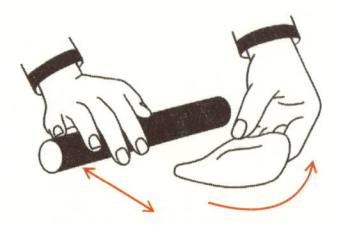

08
With this technique, the edge of the discs should be thinner than the centre; if not, the dough might be too thick when you come to making folds.

GOOD TO KNOW
小提示

If you are new to this, try to work in batches of 6–10 discs and use them immediately to prevent them from drying out. If possible, try to make them with two people, one to make the discs and the other to add the stuffing and to fold.

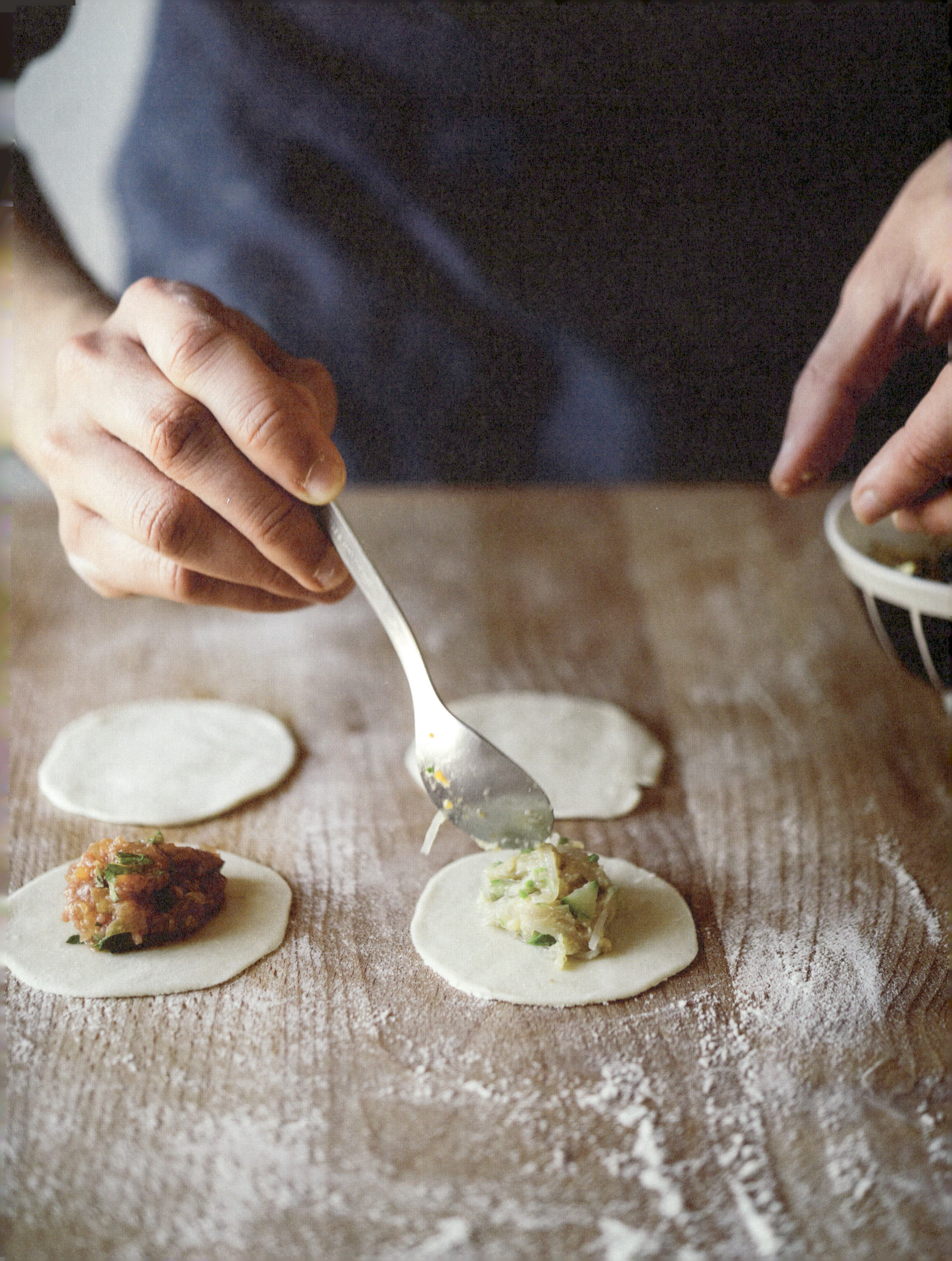

4 Types of Vegetarian Stuffing

AUBERGINE & ASPARAGUS
茄子芦笋
QIÉ ZI LÚ SǓN

TOMATOES & EGGS
番茄鸡蛋
FĀN QIÉ JĪ DÀN

SPRING

MAKES 30 DUMPLINGS:

20g (¾oz) mung bean vermicelli
100g (3½oz) asparagus
250g (9oz) aubergine (eggplant)
1 tbsp vegetarian oyster sauce
1 tbsp sesame oil
½ tsp salt
1 pinch of pepper

01 Rehydrate the vermicelli in boiling water to soften them up. Drain and coarsely chop. **02** Peel the asparagus, cut off the base, and blanch the spears in boiling salted water for 3–4 minutes. Check the doneness with a knife; it should penetrate easily with some slight resistance. Cut into small cubes. **03** Cut the aubergine into 4–5cm (1½–2in) pieces and steam until the flesh is tender, for about 10 minutes. **04** Mix the vermicelli with the asparagus and aubergine and season with the vegetarian oyster sauce, sesame oil, salt and pepper, then mix again.

SUMMER

MAKES 30 DUMPLINGS:

300g (10oz) tomatoes
1 tsp salt + ⅓ tsp
2 eggs (about 120g/4¼oz)
½ tsp Shaoxing wine
1 tsp sesame oil
1 tbsp vegetable oil
½ tsp sugar
1 pinch of pepper
A sprinkle of chopped herbs of your choice

01 Blanch the tomatoes for about 40 seconds in boiling water and remove the skin. Cut into small cubes, then add the 1 teaspoon of salt. Leave to disgorge (see p. 83) for 30 minutes and drain; do not keep the juice. **02** Beat the eggs in a bowl and add the Shaoxing wine, sesame oil and remaining ⅓ teaspoon of salt. Add the oil to a pan over a medium heat and scramble the eggs. **03** Add the diced tomatoes to the pan, then the sugar, pepper and chopped fresh herbs of your choice. Mix.

THE RATIO IS APPROXIMATELY 12G (SCANT ½OZ) OF DOUGH PER 14G (½OZ) OF STUFFING. COMPARED TO MEAT-BASED STUFFING, VEGETARIAN STUFFING HAS A HIGHER TENDENCY TO CRUMBLE. YOU CAN USE A STICKY VEGETABLE AS A BINDER BASE (AUBERGINE/EGGPLANT, PUMPKIN), OR AN AROMATIC OIL (SESAME, WALNUT). VEGETABLES THAT CONTAIN TOO MUCH WATER SHOULD ALSO BE DISGORGED (SEE P. 83) BEFORE BEING ADDED TO THE STUFFING; OTHERWISE, IT MIGHT DILUTE THE FLAVOUR.

SHIITAKE & TOFU
香菇豆腐
XIĀNG GŪ DÒU FU

AUTUMN

MAKES 30 DUMPLINGS:

60g (2oz) dried shiitake mushrooms
120g (4¼oz) fresh shiitake mushrooms
200g (7oz) 5-spice tofu (*see p. 118*)
1 tbsp vegetable oil, plus extra for frying
2 tsp soy sauce
½ tbsp chopped spring onion (scallion) white
1 pinch of ground Sichuan peppercorn
1 pinch of pepper

01 Rehydrate the dried shiitake. **02** Chop the shiitake (both the fresh and rehydrated) into thin strips. Coarsely chop the 5-spice tofu. **03** Fry the mushrooms and tofu in a frying pan in a little oil for 2–3 minutes, then season with the soy sauce. **04** In a bowl, add the chopped spring onion white, then heat the tablespoon of oil until very hot and pour this over the onions to release the flavours. **05** Mix this with the mushrooms and tofu, then season with the Sichuan peppercorn and pepper.

PUMPKIN & EGGS
南瓜鸡蛋
NÁN GUĀ JĪ DÀN

WINTER

MAKES 30 DUMPLINGS:

5g (⅛oz) dried black fungus
250g (9oz) pumpkin
2 eggs (about 120g/4¼oz)
1 tbsp vegetable oil
½ tsp salt
1 pinch of pepper
1 tsp finely chopped onion

01 Rehydrate the black fungus in boiling water for 1 minute, then drain and coarsely chop (it will gain a lot of volume). **02** Peel the pumpkin, cut it into small pieces and steam for 15 minutes until completely soft. **03** Beat the eggs, then heat the oil over a medium heat and scramble the eggs, seasoning them with the salt and pepper and finally adding the onion. **04** Mix the black fungus and pumpkin with the scrambled eggs.

FOLDING THE DUMPLINGS

包饺子

BĀO JIAO ZI

Here are three folding methods: the simplest (the one we teach children), the most common (the one we use at home), and the fastest, used in restaurants to mass-produce dumplings. I'm also adding a basic method for wontons, whose dough is square-shaped. Don't panic if you don't succeed the first time. The most important thing is to know how to "close" your dumpling to stop the stuffing from coming out during cooking.

THE SIMPLEST

01
Fold your dough disc to form a half-moon, pinching slightly in the middle to make it stick.

02
Pinch the borders to close the dumpling.

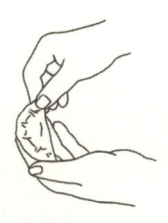

03
These dumplings do not stand upright, so they are reserved instead for cooking with water, like zhong dumplings (see p. 268).

THE MOST COMMON

01
Fold your dough disc to form a half-moon, pinching slightly in the middle to make it stick.

02
Pinch the end of one side to create a first fold.

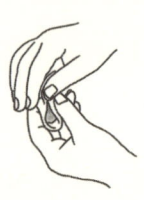

03
Fold again to create a second fold.

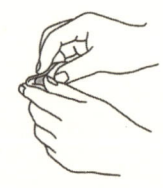

04
Repeat on the other side (that makes four moves) to close the dumpling.

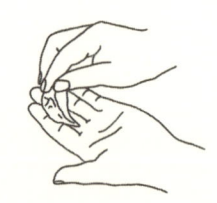

05
These dumplings stand upright, so they are perfect for making *guo tie* (see p. 259).

GOOD TO KNOW
小提示

There are no precise rules on the ratio of dough to stuffing. Some prefer a thin dough and a lot of stuffing, others will appreciate slightly smaller dumplings with less stuffing. I use a ratio of 12g (scant ½oz) of dough to 18g (¾oz) of stuffing, but if you're new to making them, reduce the amount of stuffing a little to make it easier to fold.

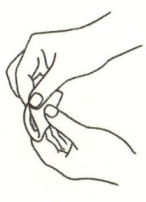

THE FASTEST

01
Pinch the end of one side to create a first fold.

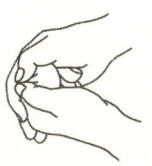

02
Wedge the dumpling between your thumbs and the rest of your hand.

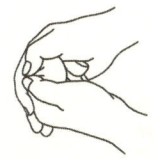

03
Press lightly towards the centre to "pack" the stuffing.

SPECIAL FOLDING FOR WONTONS

01
Fold the dough square in half to form a mini rectangle.

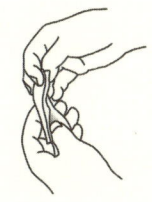

02
Hold both corners of the rectangle.

03
Fold down the excess dough while slightly pushing the stuffing down.

04
Bring the two corners in and press to stick them together, to form a small Chinese gold ingot shape (called *yuan bao*).

COOKING DUMPLINGS

煮饺子

ZHU JIAO ZI

The diversity of dumplings in China explains their various cooking methods. Those that are cooked with water are the most popular and are a staple in the north of the country. Steam cooking is associated with southern cuisine, especially in Cantonese dim sum. As for pan-fried dumplings, they are served as a side dish.

WATER

01
In a pot, bring a large volume of water to the boil over a medium heat. Add a pinch of salt, then the dumplings, in batches to avoid overcrowding the pan and prevent them from sticking to each other.

02
Without touching the dumplings, stir the water to create a "whirlpool", so that the dumplings don't stick to the bottom.

03
Cook for about 6–8 minutes in simmering water (depending on the stuffing) until the dumplings float to the surface. Drain and serve with a sauce or in a soup (p. 272).

PAN

01
Pour a thin layer of oil into a non-stick pan.

02
Place the dumplings in the pan, turn on the heat and lightly brown the bottom over a medium heat for 1–2 minutes.

03
Add water up to about one third of the dumplings' height.

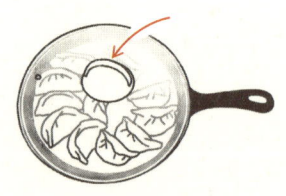

04
Cover and cook for about 6–7 minutes (longer if they have a meat stuffing) or until the water has evaporated completely.

05
Remove the lid and continue cooking for about 1 minute to grill the underside of the dumplings. Enjoy with your chosen sauce.

THE SAUCE
酱汁

Black rice vinegar (or acidity in general) is an indispensable part of the sauce that goes with dumplings. I add a pinch of salt, a bit of chopped garlic and some chilli oil. I regularly use soy sauce or oyster sauce (to add some salt), coriander (cilantro), spring onion (scallion) or ginger, fragrant oils (sesame oil, Sichuan peppercorn oil) or a hint of sugar to balance everything out.

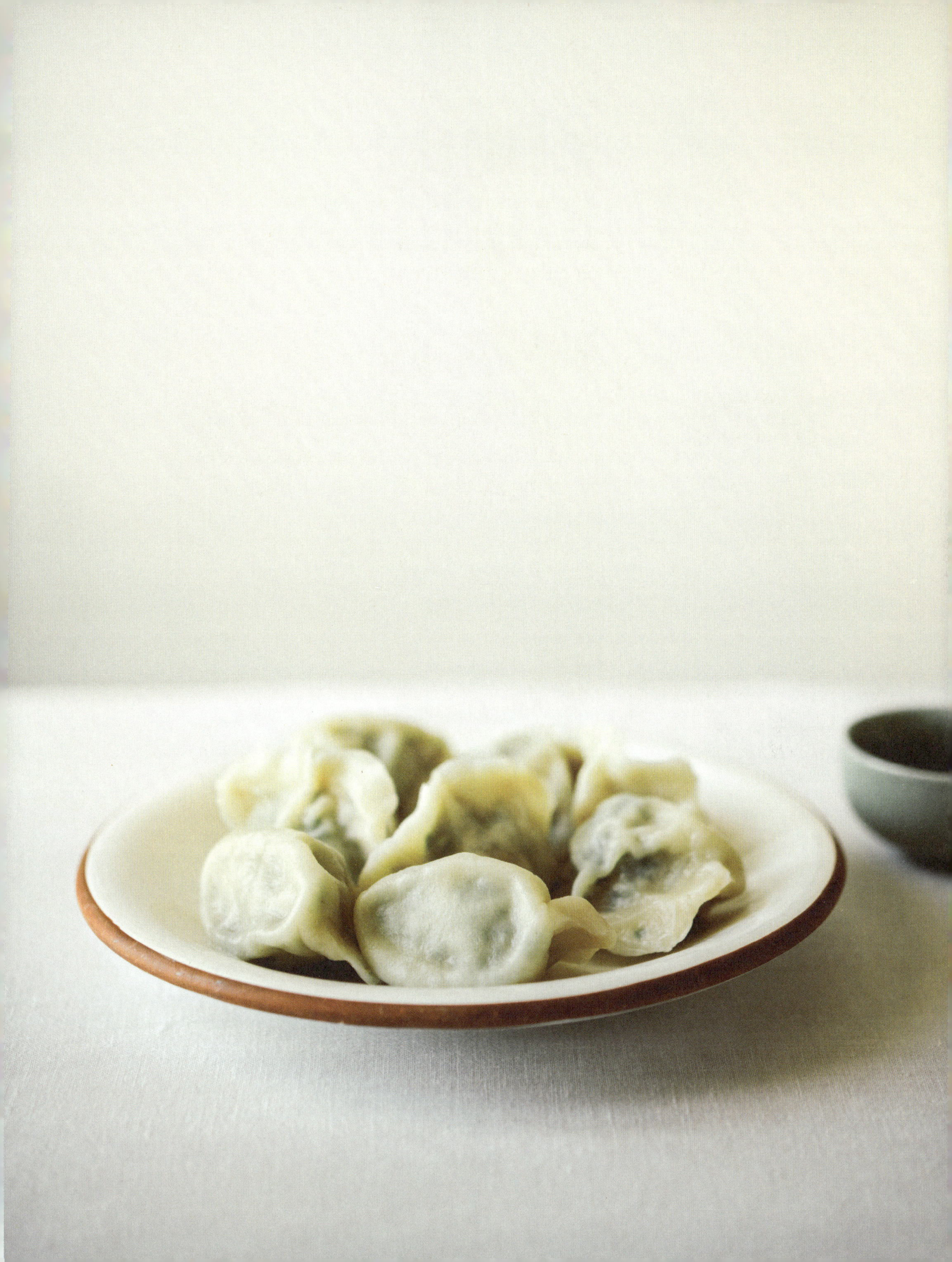

Zhong Dumplings

ZHŌNG SHUǏ JIĂO

钟水饺

PREPARING 105 MINUTES

COOKING 2 MINUTES

THESE PORK-STUFFED DUMPLINGS ARE BEST KNOWN FOR THEIR HIGHLY FLAVOURFUL SAUCE: A MIXTURE OF CHILLI OIL AND SWEET SOY SAUCE, WHICH IS RARE IN CHINA. THIS CHENGDU SPECIALITY IS EATEN AS A SNACK (AS A STARTER) RATHER THAN AS A MAIN COURSE.

Makes 24 dumplings

INGREDIENTS

For the dough

180g (6¼oz/1¼ cups) T55 (bread/all-purpose) flour
2g (½ tsp) salt
1 egg white (about 35g/1¼oz)
50ml (3 tbsp) water

For the stuffing

½ tsp Sichuan peppercorn
3 ginger slices, about 2mm (⅛in) thick
30ml (2 tbsp) boiling water
200g (7oz) minced (ground) pork (preferably 15–20% fat)
½ tsp Shaoxing wine
½ tsp sesame oil
½ tsp salt
¼ tsp sugar
⅛ tsp white pepper

For the sauce (per bowl)

1 tbsp chilli oil (*see p. 36*)
½ tbsp sweet soy sauce (*p. 348*)
1 tsp grated garlic

FOR THE DOUGH

- Follow the steps for making dumpling dough (see p. 260), mixing the flour, salt and egg white in a bowl and gradually adding the water. (Zhong dumplings are generally smaller than standard dumplings, at approximately 10g/¼oz and 7cm/3in in diameter, compared to 12g/½oz and 9cm/3½in.)

FOR THE STUFFING

- In a bowl, infuse the Sichuan peppercorn and ginger slices in the boiling water for 10 minutes. Drain and allow to cool.

- In another bowl, mix the pork with the remaining stuffing ingredients, then add the infusion and quickly mix in one direction for 1 minute to obtain a sticky texture. Chill while you prepare the dough.

FOLDING AND COOKING

- Form discs of dough. When folding, remember to cover the rest of the dough with a cloth or film (plastic wrap) to prevent it from drying out. Place 10g (¼oz) of your stuffing in the centre of a disc and fold the edges, pinching in the middle to form a half-moon (see the simple method, p. 264). Repeat the process with the rest of the dough to make all your dumplings.

- Cook in boiling salted water, in batches of 8–12 depending on the size of your pan, for 2 minutes. Your dumplings should start to float.

- Drain and put them in a bowl. Add the chilli oil, sweet soy sauce and freshly grated garlic. Mix and enjoy.

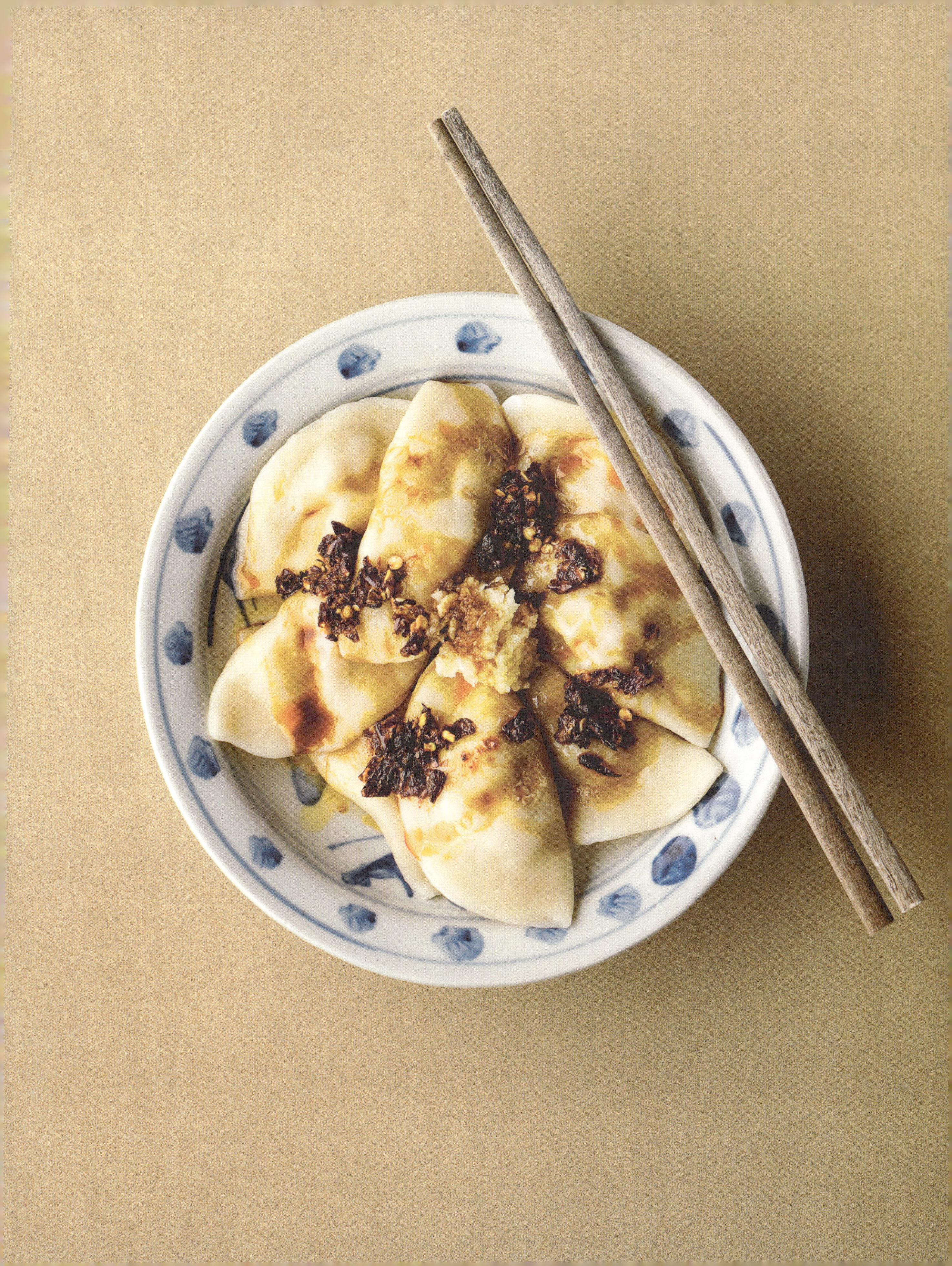

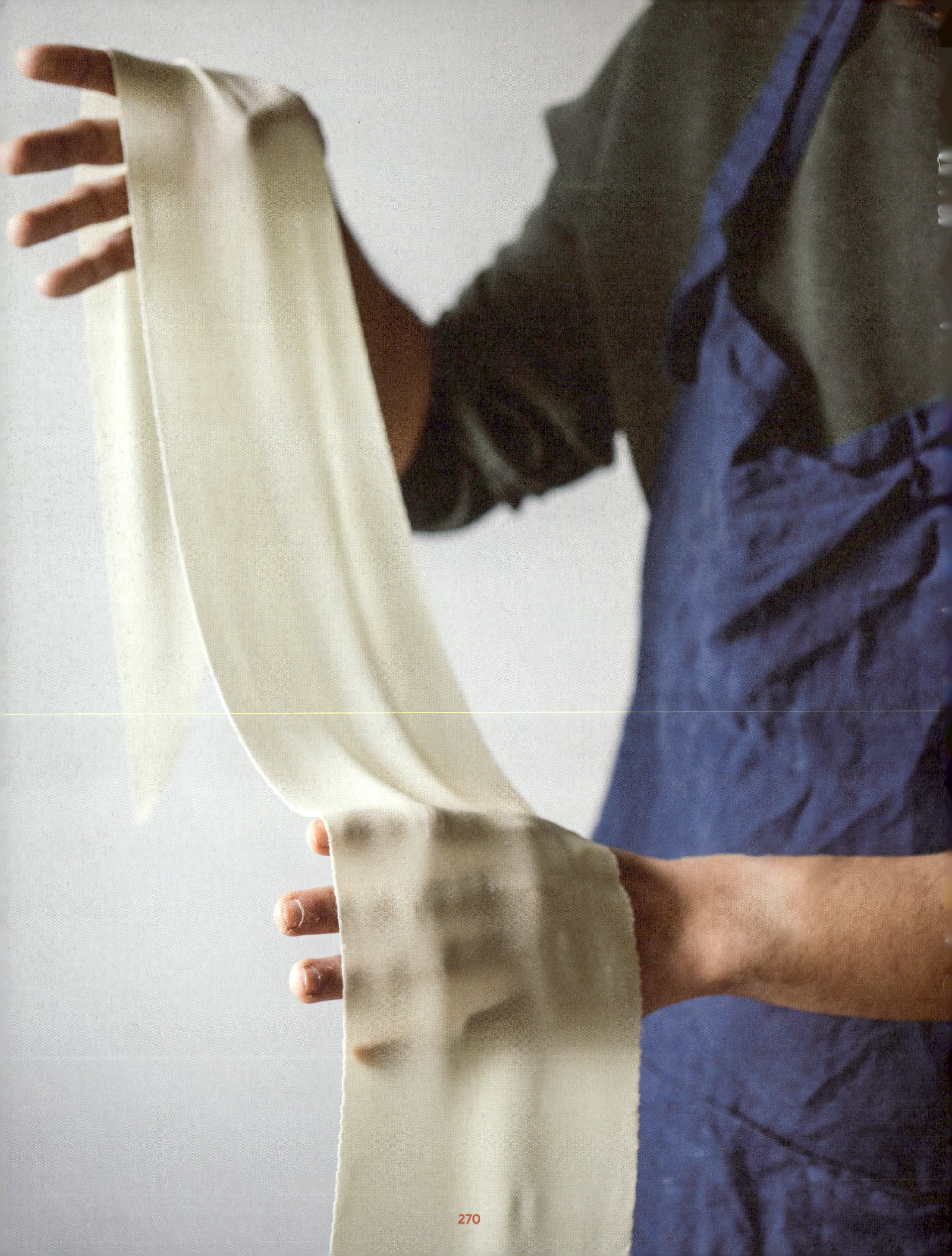

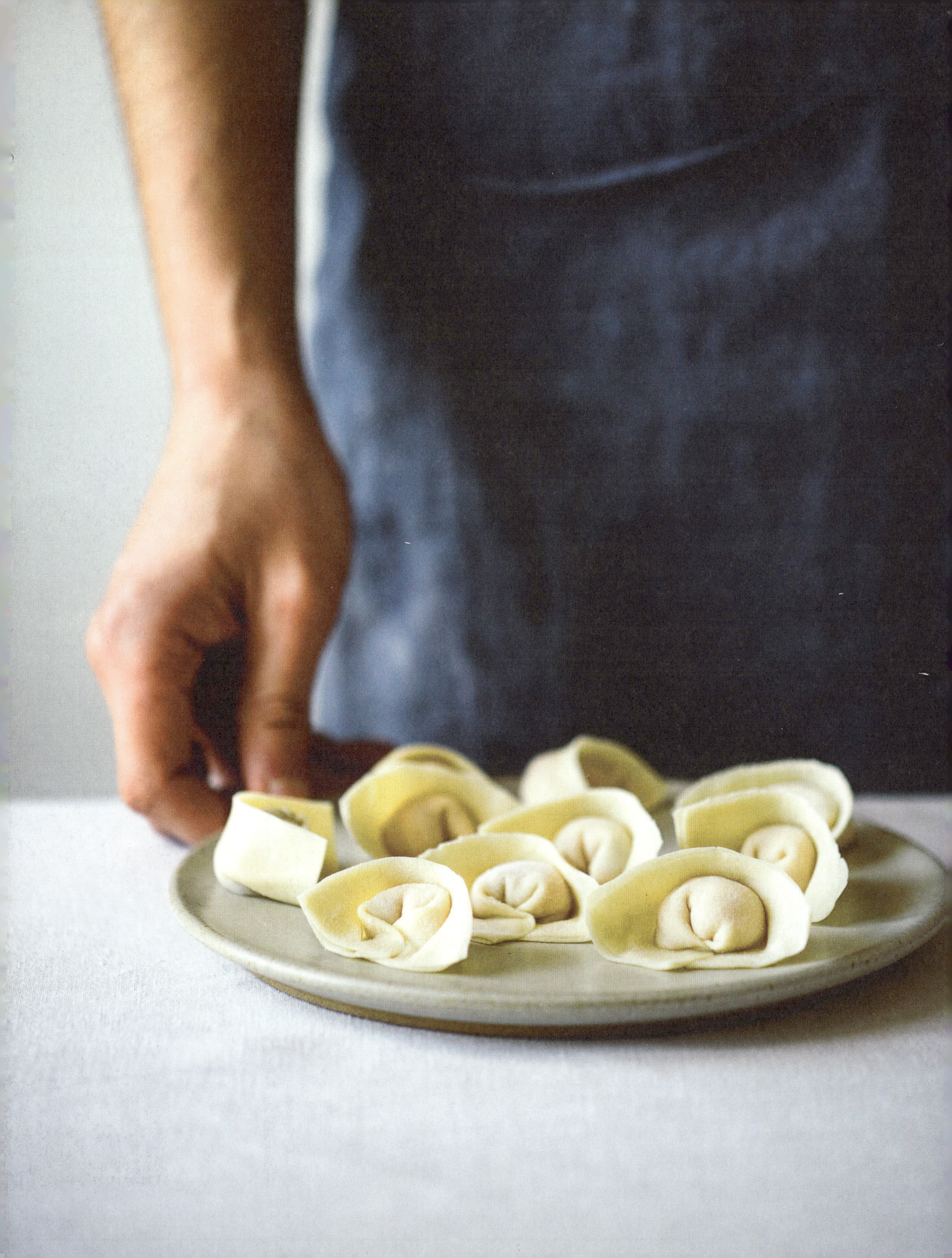

Wonton Soup

HÚN TUN TĀNG

馄饨汤

PREPARING 2 HOURS — *COOKING 2 MINUTES*

WONTONS ARE SMALL DUMPLINGS WITH VERY THIN DOUGH, TRADITIONALLY SERVED WITH A PORK FILLING, AND ARE POPULAR IN EASTERN AND SOUTHERN CHINA. IN WENZHOU, MY HOMETOWN, THEY ARE EATEN AS A SOUP FOR BREAKFAST. IF YOU MAKE THE DOUGH YOURSELF, I STRONGLY ADVISE BEGINNERS TO USE A PASTA MAKER TO ACHIEVE THE NECESSARY THINNESS.

🍽 Makes 30 wontons

INGREDIENTS

For the dough

120g (4¼oz/scant 1 cup) T55 (bread/all-purpose) flour
2g (½ tsp) salt
1 egg white (about 35g/1¼oz)
20ml (1 tbsp) water
A little cornflour (cornstarch)

For the stuffing

200g (7oz) minced (ground) pork (30% fat)
1 tsp sesame oil
½ tsp Shaoxing wine
½ tsp salt
¼ tsp white pepper
¼ tsp finely grated ginger
1 egg yolk

For the broth (per bowl)

¼ tsp salt
½ tsp sesame oil
1 tsp vinegar
300ml (1¼ cups) boiling water, or hot unsalted broth (see p. 160)
Finely chopped spring onion (scallion), to serve

FOR THE DOUGH

- Mix the flour, salt and egg white in a bowl and gradually add the water. Mix and knead to obtain a fairly dry and rough dough. Cover with film (plastic wrap) and let it rest for 15 minutes. Knead again to form a slightly smoother ball. Cover and let it rest for another hour.

- Divide the dough into 4 and run it through the pasta maker on the last setting (level 9 on my machine) to obtain a translucent dough. Sprinkle your dough strip with a thin layer of cornflour, to prevent it from sticking, and cut into 7cm (3in) squares of about 6g (⅕oz). If you don't use the dough squares right away, cover them (with a cloth or film) to prevent them from drying out.

FOR THE STUFFING

- In a bowl, mix the pork with the other stuffing ingredients. Use your hand to mix, turning quickly in one direction until you obtain a sticky texture after about 1 minute. Store in the fridge.

FOLDING AND STUFFING

- Follow the technique on p. 265. I use about 6g (⅕oz) of dough for 8g (¼oz) of stuffing.

COOKING AND SERVING

- Put the salt, sesame oil and vinegar into each of your serving bowls. You can add other classic toppings, such as dried mini shrimp (*xia pi*, p. 32), nori seaweed (*zi cai*, p. 32), fermented mustard (*zha cai*, p. 38) or omelette cut into thin strips. All these ingredients add salt and umami.

- Cook the wontons for about 1½ minutes in boiling water until they float to the surface, then drain. Place the wontons in your serving bowls and pour over the boiling water (you can reuse the wonton cooking water) or hot unsalted broth. Sprinkle each bowl with finely chopped spring onion and serve.

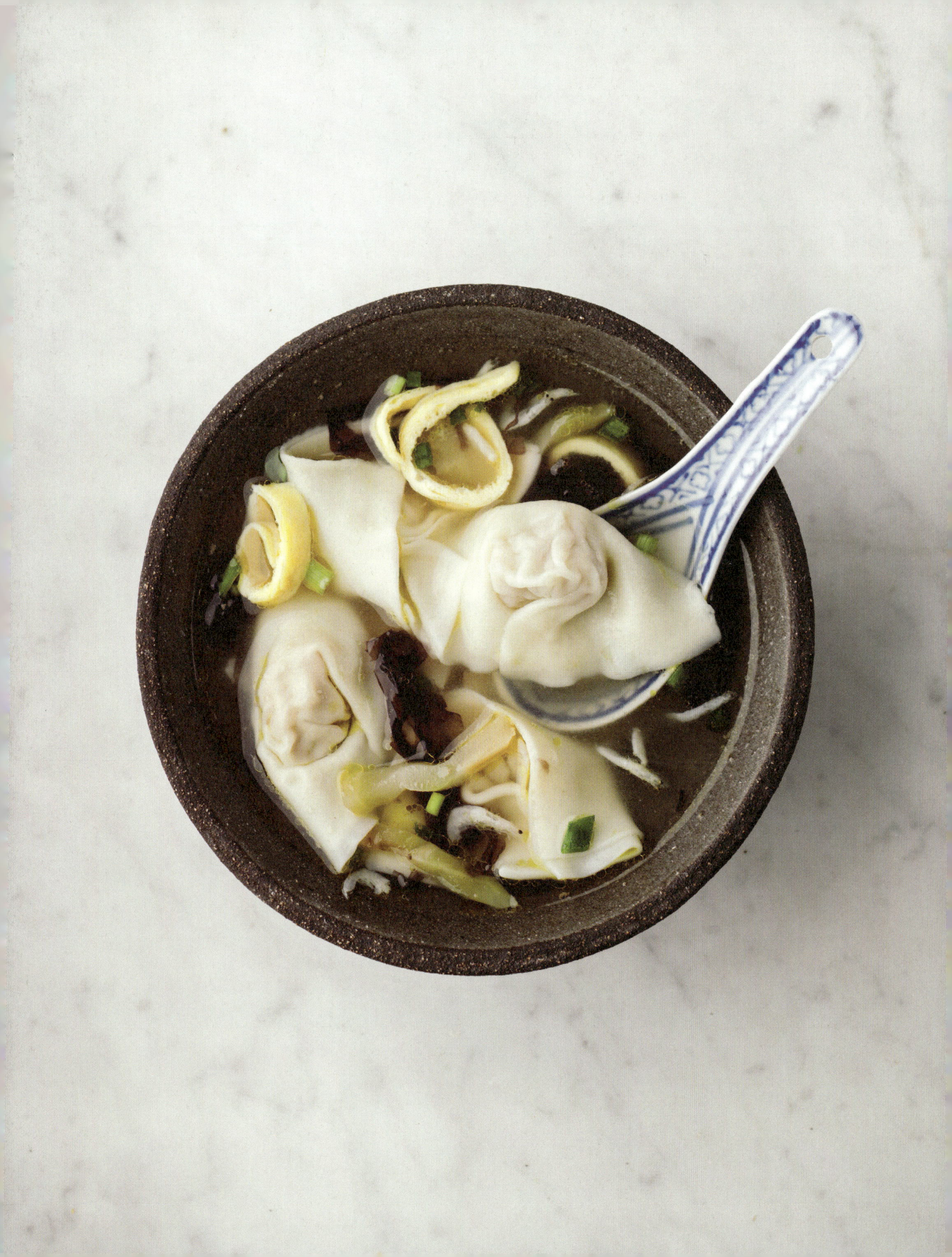

CHAPTER
11

Bao Zi
包子
BĀO ZI

PP. 278–279: Bao zi ■ **PP. 280–281:** Jian bao ■ **PP. 282–283:** Folding bao
PP. 284–285: Gua bao ■ **PP. 286–287:** Liu sha bao

From All Angles

The Soul of Breakfast

BAO ARE THOSE WHITE, FLUFFY, STEAMED BUNS THAT CAN BE FOUND ALL OVER CHINA. SALTY OR SWEET, STUFFED OR PLAIN, BIG AS A BURGER OR SMALL AS A MACARON, THERE IS SOMETHING FOR EVERYONE.

MORNING DELIGHTS

For Chinese people, bao (or *bao zi*) are above all associated with breakfast. At dawn, in the street, you can see huge bamboo baskets stacked in front of small stalls. A thick steam continuously rises out of them. Quickly, people flock to pick up their *bao zi*.

It is a dish that is eaten on the go, accompanied by fresh soy milk. Basic *bao zi* are often stuffed with ground pork (*rou bao*), but there is usually a vegetarian version (*cai bao*) made out of a mixture of Chinese cabbage, leafy green vegetables, tofu or shiitake.

TO EACH THEIR BAO

MANTOU AND HUA JUAN

This term refers to a bao without filling, popular in the north of the country. In the South, *mantou* is served as a starch to go along with dishes, like rice. It is most commonly rectangular, with slightly rounded edges. There is also *hua juan* (literally "flowery roll"), a plain bao that is shaped like braided rolls. The spring onion (scallion) added to the dough gives it a pleasant flavour.

XIAO LONG BAO

These bao, which are popular in the Jiangnan region (see p. 10), are distinguished by their small size, very thin dough and regular folds. The basic filling consists of ground pork and pork jelly that melts at the cooking stage, hence the broth that flows out after the first bite. I have a soft spot for the ones stuffed with crab paste, when they are accompanied by Zhenjiang vinegar and finely julienned ginger. They can be enjoyed throughout the day, especially in early autumn.

SHENG JIAN BAO

These typical Shanghai bao, which are among the locals' favourite breakfasts, are cooked like grilled dumplings. They are first fried in a frying pan, folds down, to obtain a crispy crust, before adding water to finish with steam cooking and thus reach the characteristic softness of bao. Just before serving, they are sprinkled with sesame seeds and chopped spring onions (scallions). They are often served with a light pork bone broth offered by the restaurant (see the simplified recipe without pork gelatine on p. 280).

CHAR SIU BAO

This is one of the best-known bao, associated with Cantonese dim sum (see p. 258). As its name suggests, it is stuffed with *char siu*, sweet and savoury lacquered pork (see p. 198), and easily recognizable by its cracks after cooking which give a glimpse of the filling.

SWEET BAO

There is a wide variety of sweet bao, usually served as a snack. Traditional fillings typically include black sesame, azuki bean paste (*dou sha* in Chinese), a mixture of duck egg yolk and butter (*nai huang*) and lotus seeds. There are also sweet and savoury versions, such as the famous "bao with flowing sand" (see p. 286).

GOOD TO KNOW
小提示

The name xiao long refers to the small steamer baskets in which xiao long bao are served.

DIFFERENT TYPES OF BAO

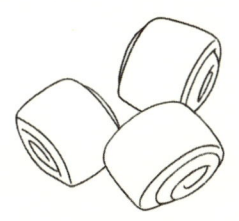

MANTOU
馒头 | MÁN TOU

A plain bao that is usually served as a side dish to go with other savoury dishes.

HUA JUAN
花卷 | HUĀ JUĂN

A plain bao with a braided shape and covered with spring onion (scallion).

XIAO LONG BAO
小笼包 | XIĂO LÓNG BĀO

Small bao with very thin dough, containing broth and usually a pork filling.

SHENG JIAN BAO
生煎包 | SHĒNG JIĀN BĀO

A Shanghai speciality, this is a small bao that is grilled, then steamed.

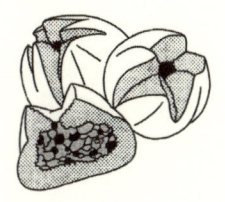

CHAR SIU BAO
叉烧包 | CHĀ SHĀO BĀO

A bao stuffed with Cantonese lacquered pork, usually served as part of a dim sum meal.

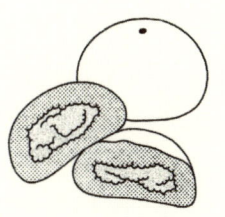

NAI HUANG BAO
奶黄包 | NĂI HUÁNG BĀO

A sweet bao made with salted duck egg yolk, butter, milk and custard powder.

BAO ZI

包子

BĀO ZI

Bao zi are soft, white rolls that can be found at breakfast almost everywhere in China. They usually have a pork-based filling, but depending on the region, there are infinite versions (meat + green vegetables, herbs, tofu, fermented cabbage…). The dumpling stuffing techniques can also be applied to bao (see pp. 262–265).

MAKES 8 BAO: FOR THE DOUGH: 330g (2½ cups) T55 (bread/all-purpose) flour ▪ ½ tsp sugar ▪ ½ tsp dry yeast ▪ 180ml (¾ cup) water
FOR THE FILLING: 100g (3½oz) raw prawns (shrimp) ▪ 120g (4¼oz) chopped pork belly ▪ 1 tsp light soy sauce
¼ tsp dark soy sauce ▪ 1 tsp sesame oil ▪ 1 tsp oyster sauce ▪ ¼ tsp white pepper
1 tbsp chopped spring onion (scallion) ▪ 1 tsp grated ginger ▪ 2 tsp Shaoxing wine

01
Prepare the dough: mix the flour, sugar and yeast in a large bowl. Add the water as you go, then knead for about 3 minutes until you obtain a ball that does not stick to your fingers. At this point, it should not be completely smooth.

02
Cover the dough with film (plastic wrap) and let it rest for about 1½ hours at room temperature (21°C/70°F). It will double in volume.

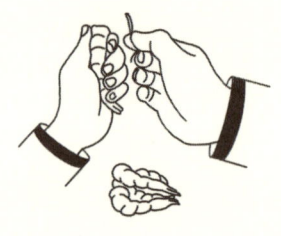

03
Prepare the filling: peel the prawns and cut them into small cubes, retaining their texture. In a bowl, mix the prawns with the other ingredients, then stir quickly with a fork until sticky. Store in the fridge.

04
When **the dough has doubled in volume**, knead it to knock out any trapped air, then form it into a roll.

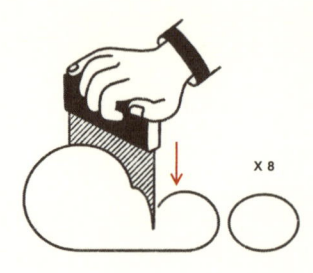

05
Divide the dough into 8 pieces of about 60g (2oz) each.

06
Working with one piece at a time, covering the others with film to prevent them from drying out, fold in **the edges of each dough piece towards the centre**, then roll it quickly on the countertop, exerting light pressure with your palm to form a ball.

07
Flatten with your palm and **roll with the rolling pin into a disc 12cm (5in)** in diameter. The edges should be thinner than the centre.

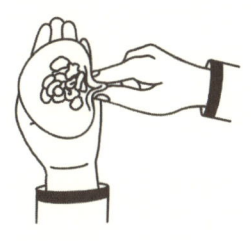

08
Place 35g (1¼oz) **of your chosen stuffing in the middle.**

09
Form a first fold by pinching with the index and ring fingers of your right hand (for right-handed people). Use the index finger to make a **second fold.** The index finger must always come back to the initial point to keep the folds in place.

10
Repeat until **the last fold is made at the initial point** to close the bao zi. The most important thing here is not the aesthetics, especially if you are just starting out, but to close the bao well to prevent any juice from the filling from leaking during cooking.

11
If there is a little excess dough on top, you can remove it (see the folding steps in detail on p. 282).

12
Line your steamer basket with slightly perforated baking paper (to let the steam circulate). Arrange the bao zi, leaving at least 1cm (½in) between each one.

15 MIN

3 MIN

13
Add 500ml (generous 2 cups) of boiling water to a pot of the same diameter as your steamer and place the basket on top. Leave the bao **to rise for another 15 minutes, without covering.** The bao zi will gain slightly in volume.

14
Cover the basket and set the pan over a medium heat. Once the water reaches boiling point (you should see steam rising out of the basket), leave the bao to steam for **15 minutes**.

15
Turn off the heat and leave the bao for another **3 minutes**, covered, then enjoy.

Jian Bao

JIĀN BĀO

煎包

PREPARING 90 MINUTES · COOKING 12 MINUTES

JIAN BAO, SMALL BAO GRILLED IN A PAN, ARE VERY POPULAR IN SUZHOU AND SHANGHAI (WHERE THEY ARE CALLED *SHENGJIAN MANTOU*, 生煎馒头, IN SHANGHAINESE). THEY ARE USUALLY SOLD IN FOURS. I ATE UP HUNDREDS OF THEM DURING MY UNIVERSITY EXCHANGE YEAR IN SHANGHAI. HERE IS A SIMPLIFIED VERSION, WITHOUT PORK GELATINE BUT WITH A JUICY FILLING.

Makes 20 bao

INGREDIENTS

For the dough

200g (7oz/1½ cups) T55 (bread/all-purpose) flour
1g (3 pinches) dry yeast
½ tsp sugar
115ml (7 tbsp) water
Neutral oil, for frying

For the stuffing

3 ginger slices
1 piece of spring onion (scallion) white
½ tsp Sichuan peppercorn
40ml (2½ tbsp) boiling water
200g (7oz) minced (ground) pork
½ tsp salt
1 tsp soy sauce
1 tsp sugar
½ tbsp Shaoxing wine
½ tbsp sesame oil
¼ tsp white pepper

To serve

Toasted black sesame seeds
Finely chopped spring onion (scallion) green
Black rice vinegar

FOR THE DOUGH

- Mix the flour, yeast and sugar, then add the water gradually. Knead until you form a slightly smooth ball that does not stick to your fingers. Let it rise for 30 minutes at room temperature (20°C/68°F), covered, to prevent it from drying out.

- Once the dough has risen by about 50%, transfer it to the fridge to slow its rise down.

FOR THE STUFFING

- Infuse the ginger, spring onion white and Sichuan peppercorn in boiling water for 5 minutes. Strain and allow the water to cool. Mix the pork with the remaining ingredients, then add the infused water. Mix with your hand, always turning in the same direction, until you obtain a sticky texture. Store in the fridge.

FOLDING THE BAO

- Divide the dough into 15g (½oz) portions, then follow the folding technique for a conventional *bao zi* (p. 279), using 15g (½oz) of filling per bao. Note that the dough keeps rising while you fold the bao. If you are starting out (and are not very fast), cook the first batch of bao as soon as they are ready.

COOKING THE BAO

- Heat a frying pan over a medium heat and pour in 1 tablespoon of neutral oil. Place the first 10 bao in the pan, folds-side down. Leave a space of at least 1cm (½in) between the bao, as they will swell while cooking.

- Grill for 1–2 minutes over a medium heat so that the bottom is nicely browned. Next, add boiling water (up to one third of the baos' height), then switch to a low heat, cover and cook for about 8–10 minutes. The bao are ready when the water has completely evaporated and you hear crackling in the pan (these *jian bao* don't puff up as much as the classic *bao zi*). Repeat for the second batch. Sprinkle with a few toasted black sesame seeds and finely chopped spring onion green, and enjoy with black rice vinegar for dipping, to cut through the fats.

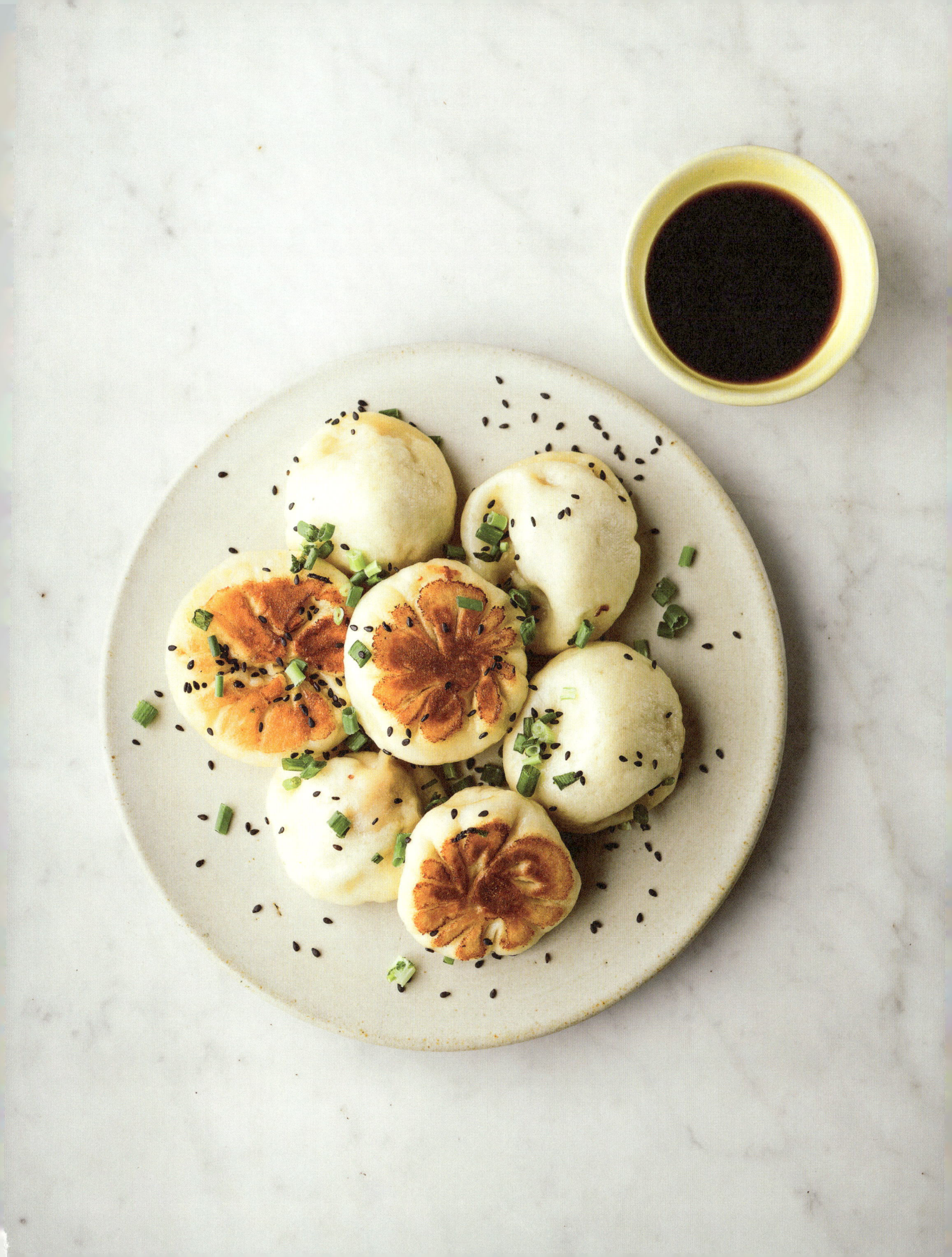

FOLDING BAO

包包子

BĀO BĀO ZI

Visually, it is easy to distinguish a savoury bao from a sweet one. The former has about ten folds, while the latter is perfectly smooth. This is usually explained by the need to perfectly seal the bao if it has a sweet filling, which is often more liquid; the conventional folding method increases the risks of leakage.

SAVOURY BAO

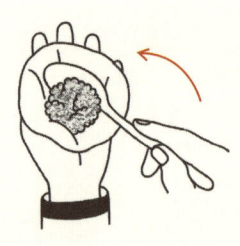

01
Place your filling on your disc of dough. If you are starting out, do not add too much filling, to facilitate folding.

02
Form a first fold by pinching the edge of the dough with **the index finger (inside) and ring finger (outside) of your right hand.**

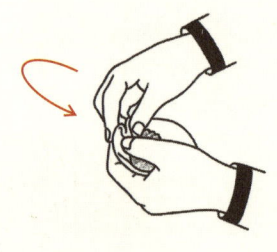

03
Use the index finger to make a second fold. The **thumb should always stay at the initial point to keep the folds in place.**

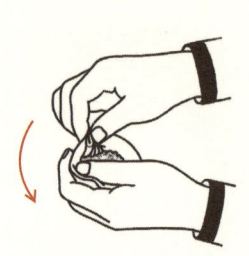

04
Use the thumb of your left hand to **hold the filling** to prevent it from overflowing.

05
Repeat until **the last fold is made at the initial point to close the bao.**

06
If there is excess dough, **you can remove it.**

GOOD TO KNOW
小提示

*These instructions are for a right-handed person.
When cooking, sweet bao are placed folds-down (smooth-side up),
while savoury bao are placed folds-up.*

SWEET BAO

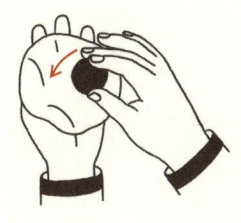

01
Place your filling on your disc of dough.

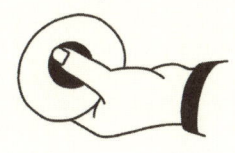

02
Press on the filling
with your left thumb.

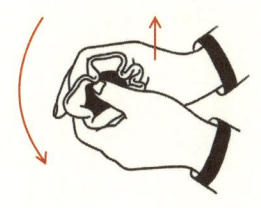

03
At the same time, **lift the dough
around the filling with your right hand**,
while turning the bao, until the filling
is completely covered.

04
Pinch to close the bao.

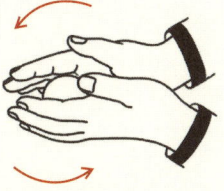

05
Place the bao **folds-down on the countertop
and slightly roll the bao to obtain
a round shape** (if you haven't already
obtained that shape).

Gua Bao

GUÀ BĀO

刈包

PREPARING 105 MINUTES

COOKING 120 MINUTES

ORIGINALLY FROM THE FUJIAN PROVINCE, GUA BAO HAS BECOME ONE OF THE FACES OF TAIWANESE STREET FOOD IN RECENT YEARS. PORK WEDGED IN SOFT BREAD – THAT'S ALL IT NEEDED TO RECEIVE THE NICKNAME OF "TAIWANESE BURGER".

Makes 8 gua bao

INGREDIENTS

For the buns

250g (9oz/1¾ cup plus 2 tbsp) plain (all-purpose) flour
1 tsp sugar
½ tsp dry yeast
135ml (generous ½ cup) water
1 tsp neutral oil, for brushing

For the pork belly

500g (1lb 2oz) pork belly (with the rind), cut into 10cm (4in) pieces
1 tbsp neutral oil
2 tbsp light soy sauce
1 tbsp dark soy sauce
25g (scant 1oz) rock sugar
1 tbsp Shaoxing wine
3 garlic cloves, peeled
2 star anise
1 cinnamon stick
3 bay leaves

For the toppings

½ cucumber, finely sliced with a mandoline
1 carrot, finely julienned
½ red onion (preferably pickled), finely chopped
1 tbsp crushed peanuts

FOR THE BUNS

- Follow the steps for the *bao zi* on p. 278 to make and prove the dough. Divide the dough into 8 pieces of about 48g (1¾oz) each. Roll the pieces into balls, flatten them and spread with the rolling pin to form ovals about 10cm (4in) long. Lightly brush them with the oil to prevent them from sticking before folding them in half.

- Line a steamer basket with baking paper. Place the bao in the basket, cover and let them rise for another 15 minutes. Bring some water to the boil in a pot. Place the steamer basket on top and leave the buns to steam over a medium heat for 10 minutes, then turn the heat off and leave to stand for 5 minutes.

FOR THE PORK BELLY

- While your dough is proving, cook the pork. Put the pieces of pork belly into a pot filled with enough cold water to cover the meat. Bring to the boil over a high heat, skimming off any foam to remove impurities, then rinse the pork and drain.

- Heat the tablespoon of oil in a pot over a medium heat and fry the pork so that each side is slightly browned. Add the remaining ingredients and enough water to cover the meat. Bring to the boil, then switch to a low heat and simmer for 2 hours, covered, until the meat and rind become tender.

- Remove the pork from the pot and cut into 2cm (¾in) slices. Strain the aromatics from the liquid, then reduce the broth over a medium heat until thickened.

TO SERVE

- Add a couple of slices of pork to each gua bao, then top with your cucumber, carrot and red onion. Finish with a drizzle of the reduced juices and a handful of crushed peanuts.

GOOD TO KNOW
小提示

If you don't have time to make the dough, you can find the buns in the frozen section of Asian supermarkets. You can replace the meat used here with Dongpo pork (see p. 186) or breaded pork.

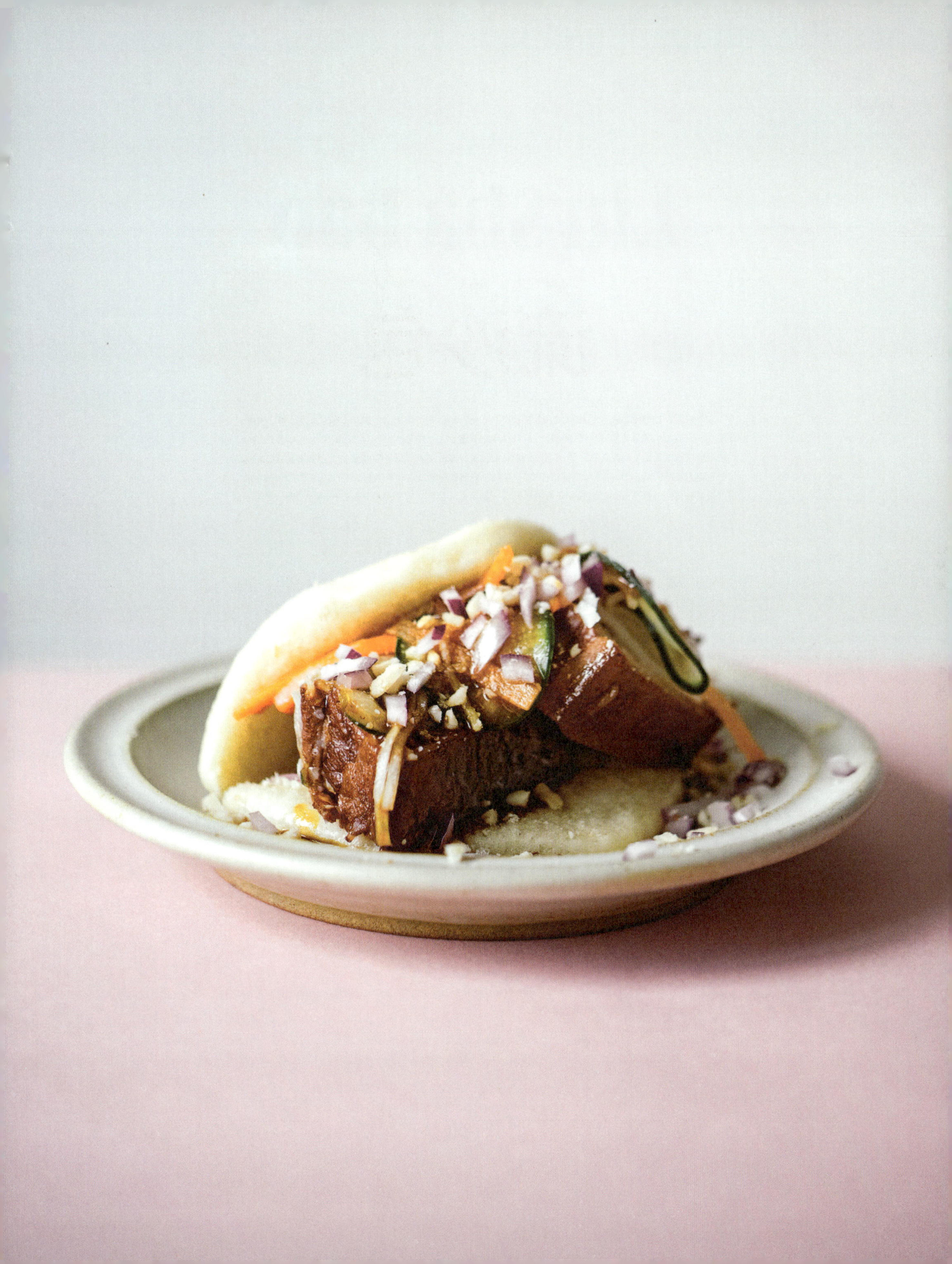

Liu Sha Bao

LIÚ　SHĀ　BĀO

流沙包

PREPARING 150 MINUTES

COOKING 10 MINUTES

THESE TYPICAL CANTONESE BAO ARE PART OF DIM SUM MEALS (P. 258). THE LITERAL TRANSLATION OF THEIR NAME, "BAO WITH FLOWING SAND", REFERS TO THE USE OF SALTED DUCK-EGG YOLK, WHICH CREATES A GRAINY TEXTURE, GOLDEN COLOUR AND SALTY TASTE. WHEN YOU OPEN UP THESE SOFT BAO, THE LIQUID IN THE CENTRE ALWAYS HAS AN EFFECT ON THE PERSON EATING IT.

Makes 8 bao

INGREDIENTS

For the dough

200g (7oz/1½ cups) T45 flour (00 flour)
30g (1oz/2½ tbsp) sugar
3g (scant 1 tsp) dry yeast
5g (⅛oz/1 tsp) baking powder
½ egg white
80ml (5 tbsp) milk

For the filling

4 salted duck-egg yolks, about 48g (1¾oz)
1 tbsp cornflour (cornstarch)
1 tbsp custard powder (or pastry cream powder)
2 gelatine sheets, about 4g (⅛oz)
2 tbsp hot water
60g (2oz/¼ cup) butter
70g (2½oz/⅓ cup) sugar

FOR THE FILLING

- Steam the duck egg yolks (see p. 140) for 10 minutes over a medium heat. Allow to cool, then chop them very finely and mix (or blend) them with the cornflour and the custard powder.

- In a small pot over a low heat, mix the gelatine with the hot (but not boiling) water to dissolve it. Stir in the butter and sugar until melted and then pour this liquid into the egg and cornflour mixture, stirring until you have a homogenous, soft-textured mixture. Roll the filling in film (plastic wrap) and put it in the freezer for 1 hour, to make it easier to work with.

FOR THE DOUGH

- Mix the flour, sugar, yeast and baking powder in a bowl. Add the egg white, then gradually add the milk. Knead until you obtain a non-sticky dough. Let it rest for 1½ hours at room temperature (20°C/68°F). The dough should double in volume.

- Knock back the dough, then form a roll and divide it into eight 40g (1½oz) pieces. Flatten the pieces with your palm and spread them with a rolling pin to form discs 10cm (4in) in diameter. This is similar to the dumpling dough technique (see p. 260).

TO ASSEMBLE

- Take the filling out of the freezer and divide it into 20g (¾oz) balls (keep the filling chilled as you go, so it does not soften too much). Place a portion of filling on a disc and close the bao by following the sweet bao folding technique (p. 283). Repeat with the rest of the dough discs and filling.

- Line two steamer baskets with baking paper, then divide the bao between them. Cover and let rise at room temperature for 45 minutes (or 15 minutes over steam, with the heat turned off).

- Steam the bao over a medium heat for 7 minutes, then turn off the heat and wait 3 minutes before opening. Enjoy your bao warm.

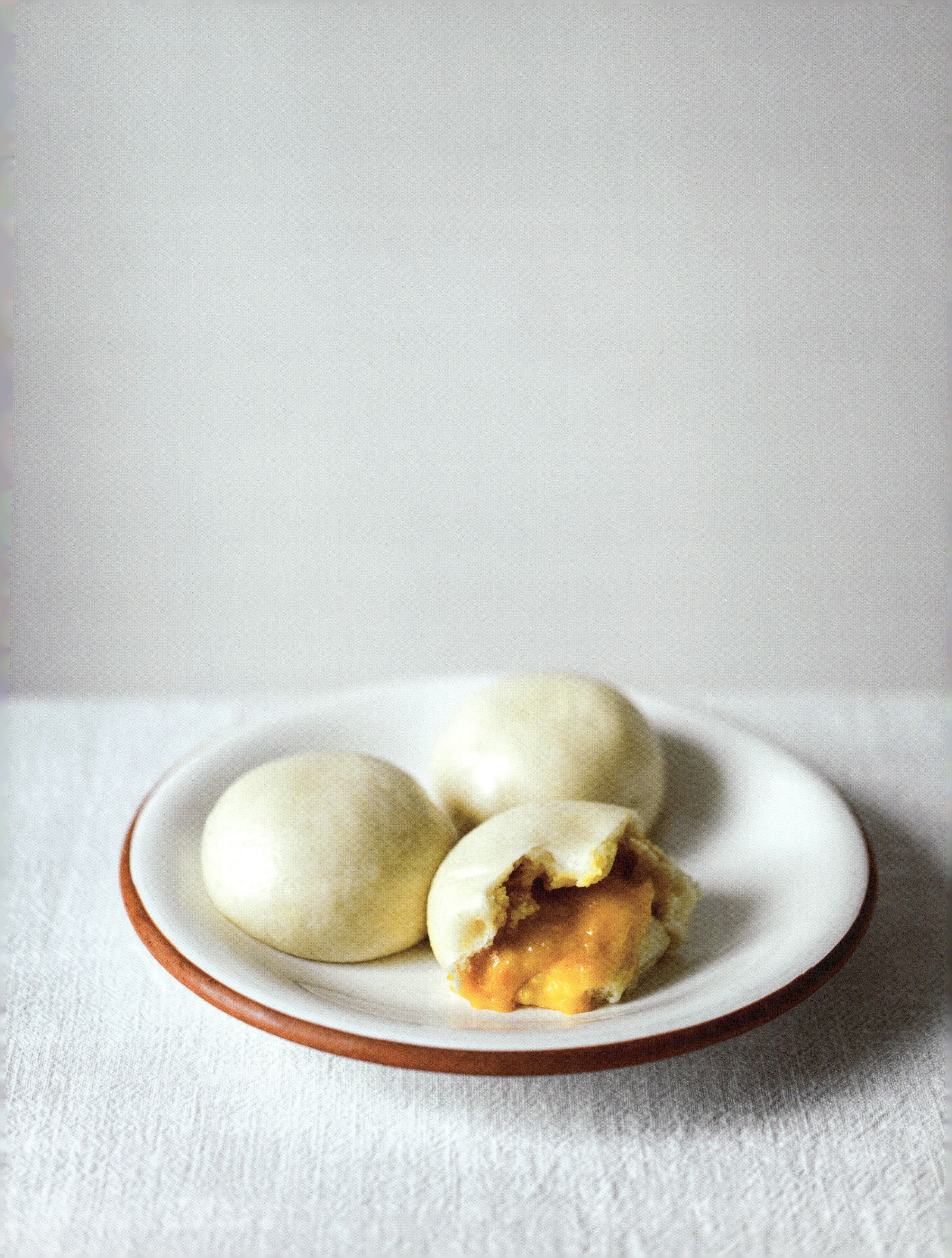

CHAPTER
12

Rice
米饭
MI FÀN

PP. 292-293: White rice ▪ **PP. 294-295:** Seafood pao fan ▪ **PP. 296-297:** Egg fried rice
PP. 298-299: Clay pot rice ▪ **PP. 300-301:** Lu rou fan ▪ **PP. 302-303:** Beef congee
PP. 304-305: Pumpkin millet congee ▪ **PP. 306-307:** Sticky rice with pork broth and shiitake
PP. 308-309: Lo mai gai ▪ **PP. 310-311:** Cheung fun ▪ **PP. 312-313:** Wok stir-fried nian gao

From All Angles

There's More than Just White Rice

RICE IS CHINA'S STAPLE FOOD, ESPECIALLY IN THE SOUTH OF THE COUNTRY, BUT IT IS NOT LIMITED TO WHITE RICE. HERE IS A LITTLE OVERVIEW OF EVERYTHING YOU CAN DO WITH THIS PLANT.

EVERYDAY RICE

In China, dishes accompany rice, not the other way around. The word *xia fan* (下饭), "bring down the rice", is often used to describe a dish that goes well with rice.

There are two main categories of white rice in China:

- Indica rice (灿米, *càn mǐ*), a medium-grain and relatively firm rice traditionally grown in the South. It is the one I grew up with, and includes Thai rice (also called jasmine rice), which is probably the most well-known variety.

- Japonica rice (粳米, *jīng mǐ*), rounder, short-grained, with a soft and sticky texture. It is generally associated with the North-East (but also with Japan, as its name suggests), notably with the city of Wuchang, which produces one of the most famous rice grains in the country.

Many dishes can be made from white rice. Leftover rice cooked the day before is perfect for making *chao fan* (fried rice, see p. 296). You can also add a hot broth to make *pao fan* (p. 294), or cook the rice in a clay pot to prepare *bao zai fan* with a beautiful golden rice crust (p. 298).

CONGEE, THE REMEDY FOR GLOOMY DAYS

Congee (*zhou* in Mandarin) is a rice porridge popular for breakfast in Southern China.

The rice is boiled in a large volume of boiling water until the grains burst, which creates a more or less liquid texture. Easy to digest, congee is traditionally a dish associated with sick days.

Basic congee (白粥, *bái zhōu*) has no taste, except for the subtle flavour of rice. It's a blank page that leaves you the freedom to compose. Cantonese people are by far the experts in that area, making plain or seasoned congee in both sweet and savoury forms (p. 302), some thick, others thinner and more liquid. There is even a congee fondue, much like Chinese fondue, where the broth is replaced by a very liquid congee base.

RICE IN ALL ITS FORMS

In China, rice is eaten at any time of the day, and cooked in many ways.

Wenzhou's sticky rice (p. 306) will forever trigger nostalgic memories for me. *Nian gao*, a kind of soft and slightly sticky rice cake, are delicious in a stir-fried dish (p. 312).

Rice noodles are a southern speciality called *mi mian* (米面) or *he fen* (河粉), depending on the region. The fresh versions are wide and flat, and they can be found in the chilled section of some Chinese supermarkets. They are used either in a noodle soup or in a stir-fried dish (see p. 252). Rice vermicelli, much thinner, is always sold in its dried form. They are delicious in a stir-fried dish (see p. 254).

And finally, sticky rice flour is widely used in China for sweet dishes; you can find out more about that in the last chapter of this book.

GOOD TO KNOW
小提示

Since its domestication more than 10,000 years ago on the banks of the Yangtze River, rice has been inseparable from Chinese culture. It contributed to the development of civilization, shaped landscapes via rice fields, and inspired countless poets and painters. Rice can be used to make wine, vinegar and even paper.

WHITE RICE AND RICE-BASED FOODS

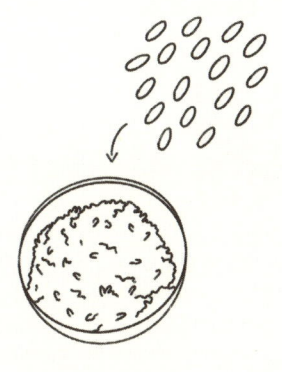

JAPONICA RICE
粳米 | JĪNG MǏ

Japonica rice is a short-grain rice with a soft and sticky texture, usually associated with North-East China.

INDICA RICE
灿米 | CÀN MǏ

Indica rice is a medium-grain rice, relatively firm and traditionally grown in the South.

RICE NOODLES
米面 | MǏ MIÀN

THIN VERMICELLI
粉丝 | FĚN SĪ

LARGE VERMICELLI
粉干 | FĚN GĀN

RICE CAKE
年糕 | NIÁN GĀO

RICE FLOUR
粘米粉 | ZHĀN MǏ FĚN

White Rice

BÁI MǏ FÀN

白米饭

Preparing 3 minutes

Cooking 25 minutes

PERSONALLY, FOR A LONG TIME, MAKING RICE MEANT POURING WATER INTO A MACHINE (PRESSURE COOKER, SEE P. 44) AND PRESSING A BUTTON. I HAD TO COOK MY FIRST RICE IN A POT DURING MY STUDIES, WHEN I WAS 20. SINCE THEN, I HAVE FOLLOWED THE SAME RECIPE EVERY TIME I DON'T HAVE A RICE COOKER ON HAND.

Serves 4 people

INGREDIENTS

200g (7oz/1 cup) jasmine rice
400ml (14oz/1¾ cups) water

RECIPE STEPS

- Put the rice in your cooking pot and rinse with tap water. Use your hand to stir the grains gently, then drain. Repeat the process a second time. This step is not mandatory, as it depends on the type of rice, but it removes a good amount of the starch, which leaves a whitish layer at the end of cooking (the starch has no impact on taste but it doesn't look very nice).

- Pour the measured water into the pot at a 2:1 ratio with the rice, or about 2cm (¾in) above the rice, and bring to the boil over a medium heat. Allow the water to evaporate until level with the surface of the rice, which takes about 8 minutes. You should see small "craters" appear in the top of the rice, through which steam escapes.

- At that point, lower the heat to as low as possible, cover and cook for 12 minutes. Turn off the heat and leave the lid on for another 5 minutes. The rice is now ready. In Chinese cuisine, good rice should not be too dry or too wet – the grains should be soft and slightly sticky while still staying separate from each other.

GOOD TO KNOW
小提示

The most common mistake here is to let the water completely evaporate before covering (and this happens very quickly). If you do, the rice will be too dry. Remember to cover and switch to a low heat as soon as you see the water at the surface of the rice.

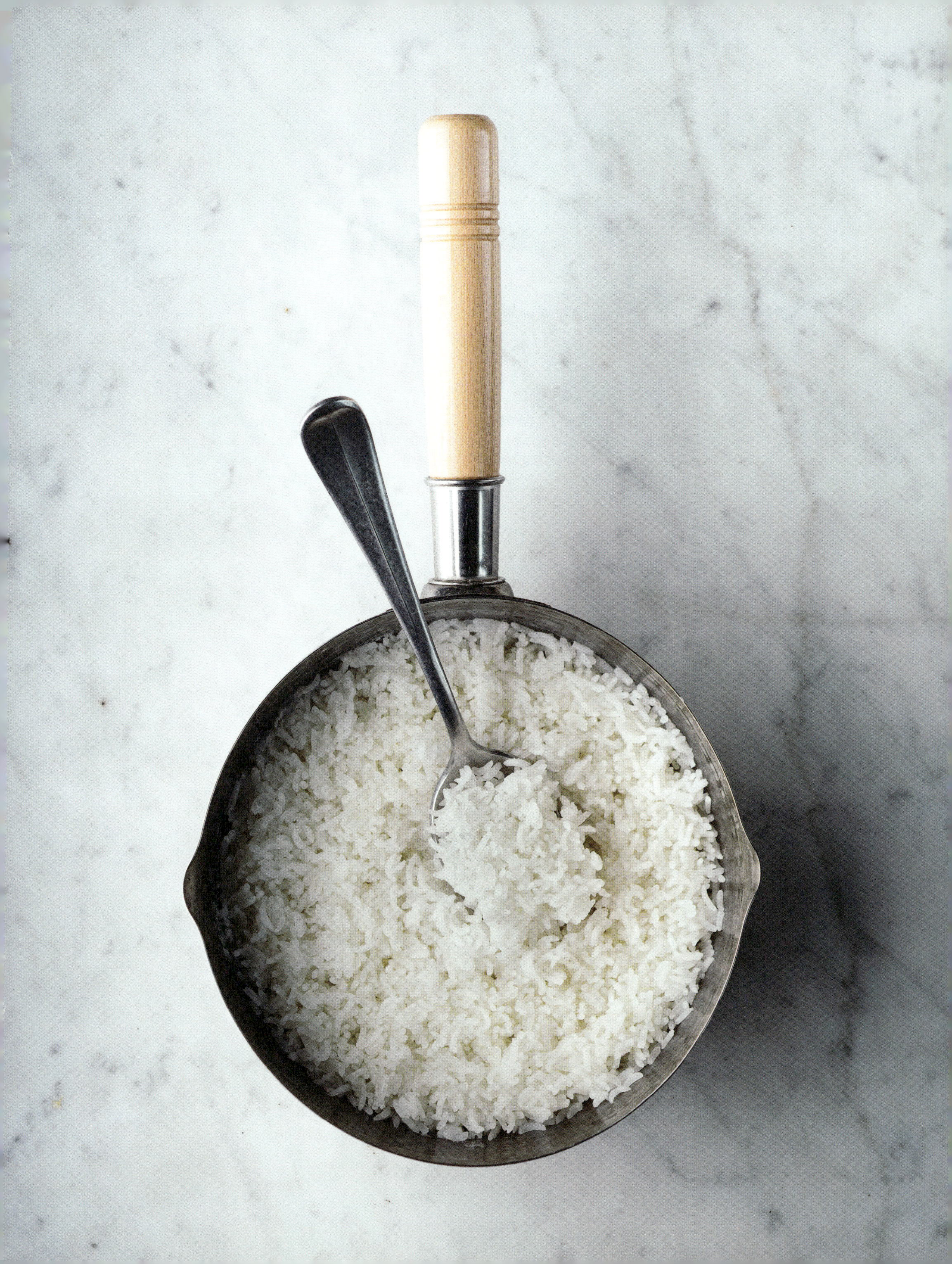

Seafood Pao Fan

HĂI　XIĀN　PÀO　FÀN

海鲜泡饭

PREPARING 15 MINUTES

COOKING 25 MINUTES

PAO FAN LITERALLY MEANS "SOAKED RICE". IT'S USUALLY REFERRING TO ADDING COOKED RICE TO A SOUP THAT WAS ALREADY MADE. I'VE ALWAYS LIKED IT THAT WAY, BUT WE CAN ALSO USE THIS IDEA TO CREATE A DISH. THIS VERSION IS A TRIBUTE TO MY HOMETOWN, WENZHOU, KNOWN FOR ITS ABUNDANCE OF SEAFOOD.

Serves 4 people

INGREDIENTS

½ tbsp neutral oil
¼ onion, chopped
50g (1¾oz) fresh shiitake mushrooms, chopped
800g (1¾lb) cooked rice
150g (5½oz) squid, cleaned and sliced into thin strips
8 mussels, cleaned
8 scallops
2 prepared sea urchins (*optional*)
Finely chopped spring onion (scallion), to serve

For the prawn broth

1 tbsp neutral oil
3 ginger slices
8 fresh jumbo prawns (shrimp), peeled, deveined and heads removed but shells and heads retained (keep a few prawns with their heads on, if you like to serve them that way)
1 tbsp Shaoxing wine
1 tbsp tomato paste
2 litres (8½ cups) water (or home-made broth, *see p. 160*)
1 tsp salt
½ tbsp fish sauce

FOR THE PRAWN BROTH

- Heat a wok over a medium heat and pour in the tablespoon of oil. Fry the ginger for a few seconds, then add the prawn heads and shells and let them brown. Remove the ginger and deglaze the wok with the Shaoxing wine. Pour in the tomato paste and water (or home-made broth), then bring to the boil and cook, covered, over a low heat for 20 minutes. Strain the broth back into the wok and add the salt and fish sauce.

FOR THE SEAFOOD AND RICE

- Meanwhile, heat the ½ tablespoon of oil in a frying pan over a medium heat. Fry the onion and shiitake for about 2 minutes, then transfer them to the prawn broth.

- Add the cooked rice to the broth, followed by the seafood: squid, mussels, prawn flesh and scallops (I usually brown them for 2 minutes in a pan with a bit of butter beforehand, but it's optional). Cook for about 3 minutes over a medium heat.

- Present in individual bowls and dress with some sea urchin roe (if using) and finely chopped spring onion. You can serve this dish with a squeeze of lemon juice or a drizzle of chilli oil (see p. 36), if you like.

GOOD TO KNOW
小提示

I adapted the recipe with seafood that can easily be found outside China. You should ideally choose seasonal and local produce, if you can.

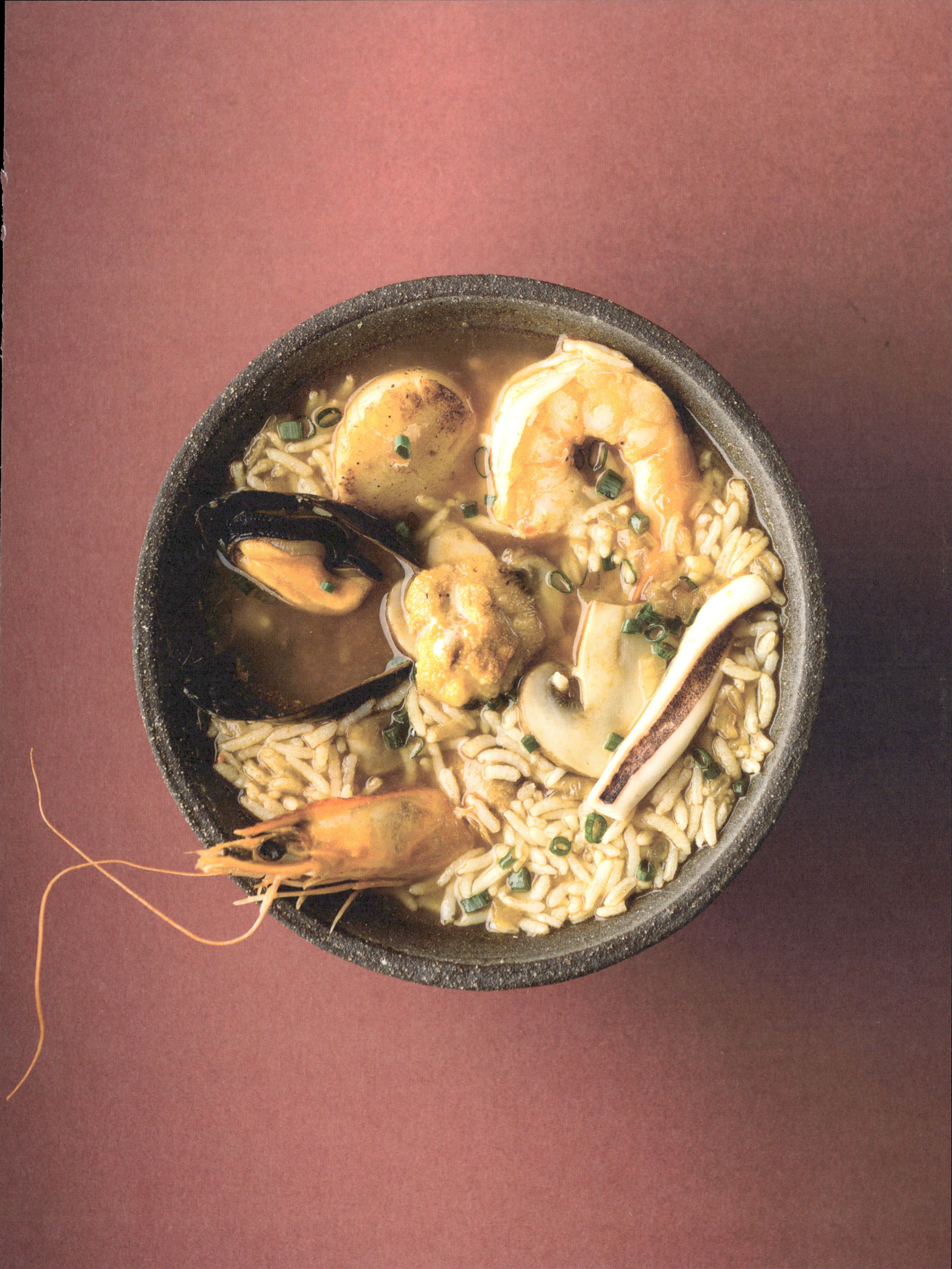

EGG FRIED RICE

蛋炒饭

DÀN CHǍO FÀN

This is a basic fried rice that I often make at home. The dried shiitake and dried mini shrimp add umami, while the corn creates some crunchiness and a slight sweetness.

SERVES 2 PEOPLE: 10g (¼oz) dried shiitake mushrooms ▪ 3 eggs ▪ 300g (10oz) cooked rice ▪ 3 tbsp neutral oil
1 tbsp chopped spring onion (scallion) white ▪ 50g (1¾oz) corn, fresh or canned, well drained ▪ 1 tbsp soy sauce
1 tbsp chopped spring onion (scallion) green ▪ 2 tsp dried mini shrimp (*xia pi*) ▪ Salt and white pepper (*optional*)

01
Set up: Rehydrate the shiitake, then drain and cut into strips. Separate the egg whites from the yolks.

02
Mix the rice (cooked then cooled and dried) with the egg yolks. Massage for a few seconds to mix well and separate the rice grains if they form clusters. Set aside.

03
Heat your wok over a medium heat. Once hot, add 1 tablespoon of the oil, then the **spring onion white, shiitake and corn. Fry for 1 minute until the mushrooms are cooked,** then remove from the wok and set aside.

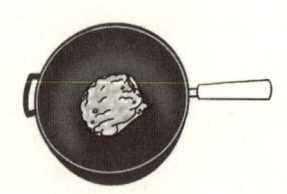

04
Heat the wok over a high heat. As soon as it starts to smoke, add the remaining 2 tablespoons of oil, then the egg white, and **stir quickly with a spatula for about 30 seconds to form small threads of egg white.**

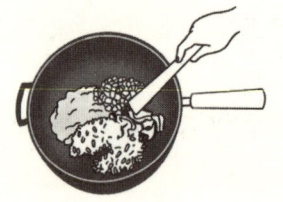

05
Add the rice and mix quickly to prevent it from sticking to the wok. **Keeping a high heat is very important here.**

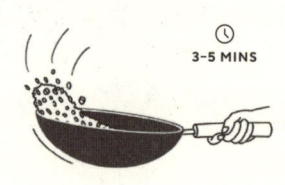

06
Stir-fry the rice, stirring constantly for 3–5 minutes to let all the moisture evaporate until **all the grains are separated and dry.**

07
Add the spring onion white, corn and shiitake mixture, and stir-fry for 30 seconds. Then pour the soy sauce onto the side of the wok and stir-fry for another 30 seconds.

08
Adjust the seasoning with a little salt and white pepper if necessary. **Add the chopped spring onion green and the dried shrimp,** mix for a few seconds, and the dish is ready.

GOOD TO KNOW
小提示

Three golden rules, regardless of the type of rice you fry:
1) use cooked then cooled and dried rice;
2) keep the wok very hot throughout;
3) do not overload the wok.

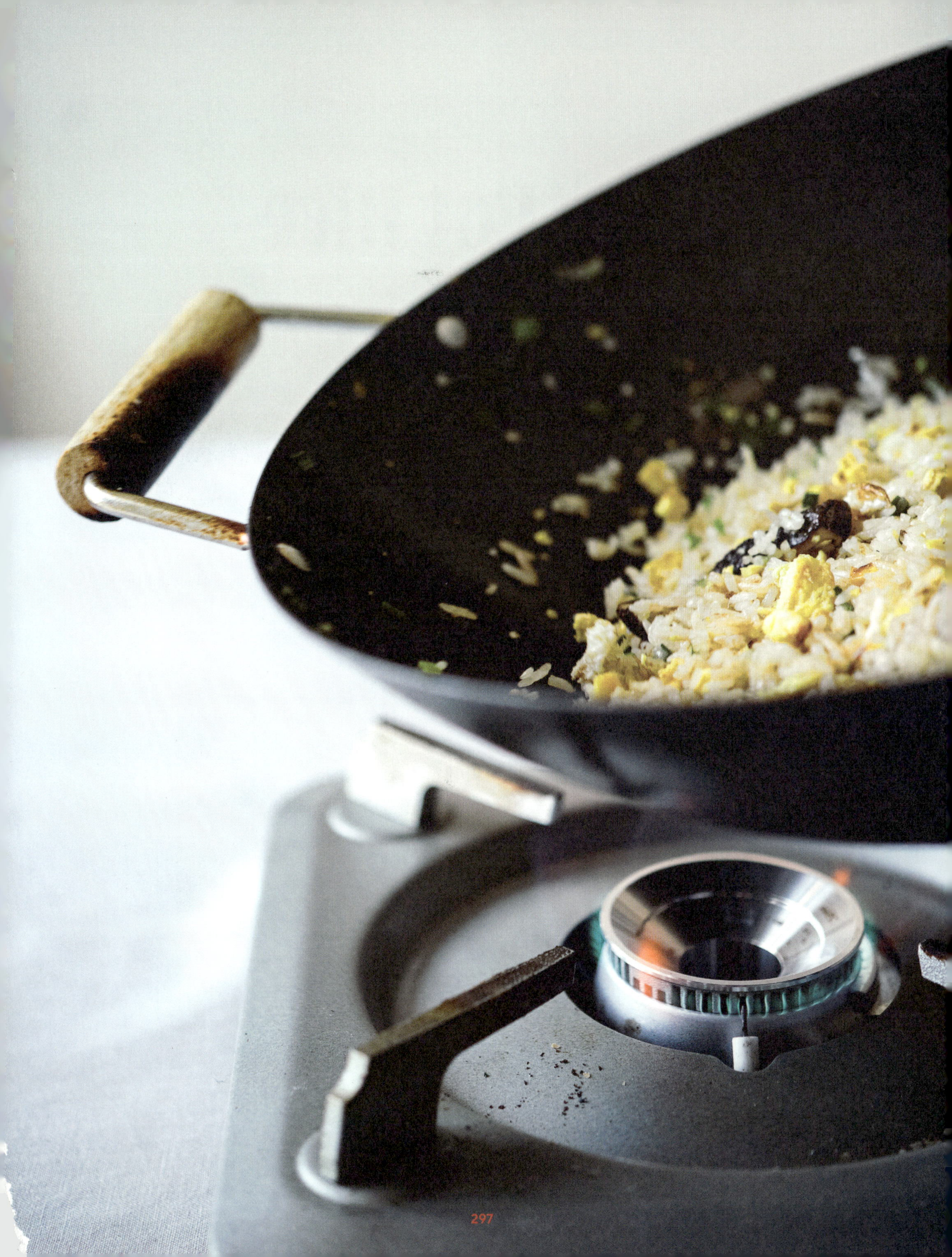

Clay Pot Rice

HUÁ JĪ BĀO ZĬ FÀN

滑鸡煲仔饭

PREPARING 45 MINUTES — *COOKING 20 MINUTES*

THE CLAY POT (*SHA GUO* IN MANDARIN, *SEE P. 44*) IS USED IN CHINESE CUISINE FOR ITS HEAT DIFFUSION CAPACITIES AND ITS ABILITY TO KEEP FOOD WARM ONCE IT'S OFF A HEAT SOURCE. CLAY POT RICE, FOUND THROUGHOUT THE CANTON AREA, IS ITS BEST REPRESENTATION.

🍽 Serves 2 people

INGREDIENTS

For the rice

2 dried shiitake mushrooms
150g (5½oz) boneless chicken legs, cut into small pieces
200g (7oz/1 cup) rice
340ml (1½ cups) boiling water
100g (3½oz) Cantonese sausage (*lap cheong*, optional), cut into strips
2 mini pak choi (bok choy) leaves, washed
1 tsp neutral oil
Coriander (cilantro) and spring onion (scallion), finely chopped

For the marinade

1 tsp soy sauce
1 tsp Shaoxing wine
1 tsp oyster sauce
⅛ tsp white pepper
1 tsp cornflour (cornstarch)
1 tbsp neutral oil

For the sauce

1 tbsp neutral oil
2 tbsp light soy sauce
1 tsp dark soy sauce
1 tbsp oyster sauce
2 tsp sugar
80ml (5 tbsp) water

FOR THE CHICKEN

- Rehydrate the shiitake (see p. 32) in warm water for 30 minutes. Put the chicken pieces in a bowl, add the shiitake and all the marinade ingredients (except the oil) and mix well. Finish by adding the 1 tablespoon of oil and leave the chicken to marinate for at least 30 minutes.

FOR THE RICE

- Rinse the rice and drain. Lightly oil the bottom of the clay pot (*sha guo*) using kitchen paper, then add the rice. Pour in the boiling water and heat the *sha guo* over a medium heat, then cover. The water will boil, then evaporate after 6–7 minutes (you have to listen for it). Remove the lid – there should be no water left on the surface. Add the marinated chicken, shiitake, sausage strips (if using) and mini pak choi leaves.

- Cover again and cook over a low heat. After 5–6 minutes, you will hear some light crackling sounds, meaning the water has completely evaporated. Pour the 1 teaspoon of oil directly on the edges of the lid. It will seep into the *sha guo* and help to create a grilled rice crust. Cook for another 4–5 minutes, then turn off the heat and check the rice. Extend the cooking time for a few minutes if necessary.

FOR THE SAUCE

- Mix all the sauce ingredients together in a bowl and pour half over the rice – you should always make a little more to adjust to taste. Sprinkle with coriander and spring onion and serve with any extra sauce on the side.

GOOD TO KNOW
小提示

Clay pot rice is more of a cooking technique rather than a precise recipe. You will find a dozen different toppings in any clay pot restaurant in Guangzhou or Hong Kong. It's up to you to add the meat and vegetables you prefer.

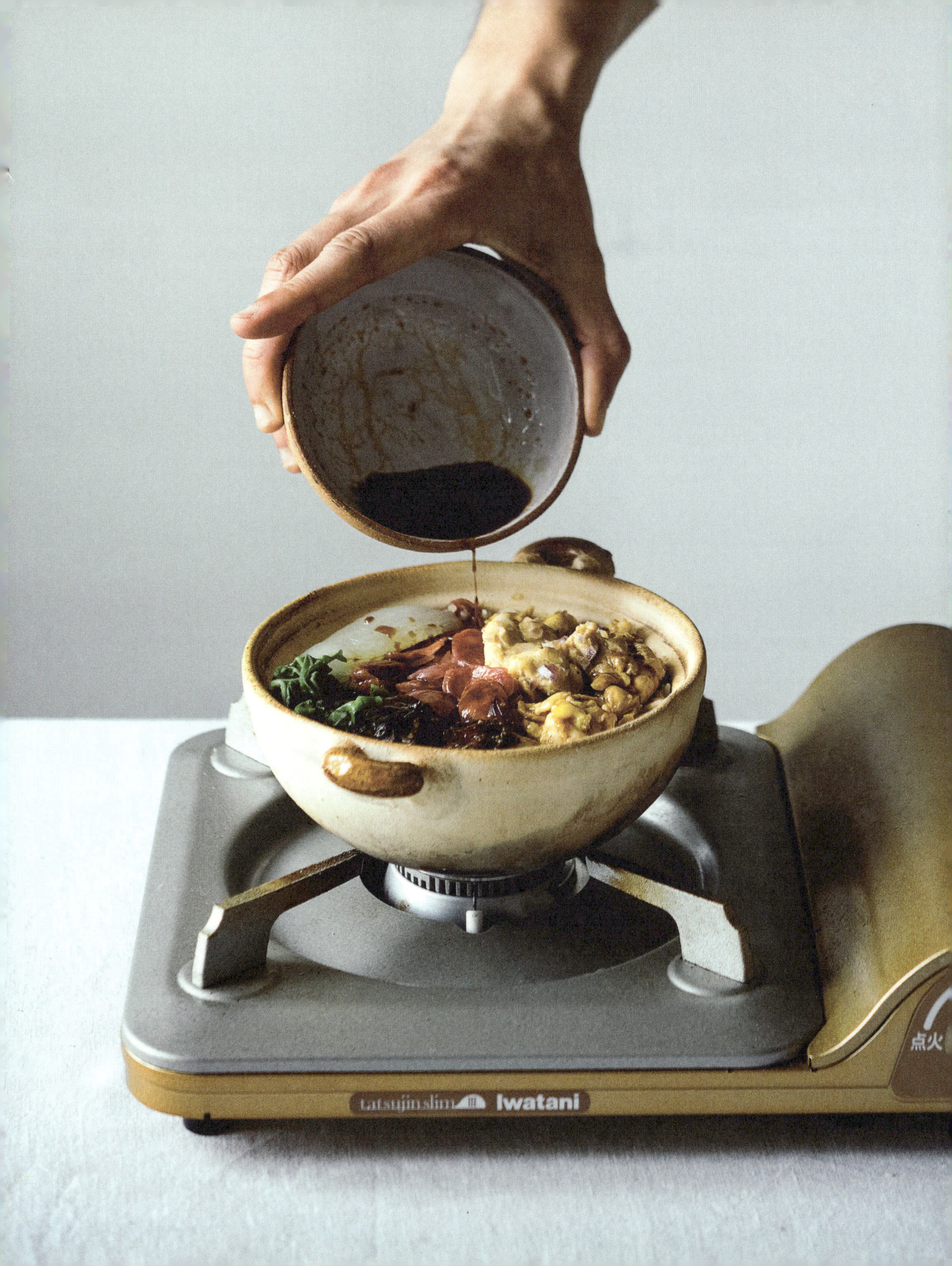
tatsujin slim
Iwatani
点火

Lu Rou Fan

LǓ RÒU FÀN

卤肉饭

PREPARING 5 MINUTES   *COOKING 60 MINUTES*

SERVED IN ALL HOUSEHOLDS BUT ALSO IN STREET STALLS IN TAIWAN, THIS EVERYDAY DISH BELONGS TO THE CATEGORY CALLED *XIA FAN CAI* (LITERALLY "DISH THAT BRINGS DOWN RICE"), AS THE SIMMERED AND FLAVOURFUL PORK WOULD MAKE YOU EASILY GOBBLE UP TWO BOWLS OF RICE!

Serves 4 people

INGREDIENTS

4 eggs
600g (1lb 5oz) pork belly, ideally 30% fat, cut into thin slices or sticks about 2mm (⅛in) wide
1 tbsp neutral oil *(optional)*
100g (3½oz) shallots, chopped
3 spring onions, white and green parts separated and finely chopped
8 garlic cloves, chopped
1 tbsp sugar
½ tsp 5-spice
¼ tsp white pepper
2 tbsp soy sauce

RECIPE STEPS

- Cook the eggs for 10 minutes in boiling water, then immerse them in cold water to stop the cooking process. Peel and set aside.

- Heat a pot over a medium heat and add the pork (if your meat is too lean, you can add 1 tablespoon of oil). Stir regularly, until the meat is slightly browned and releases a good amount of fat, about 8–10 minutes.

- Add the shallots and continue cooking for about 1 minute to release the flavours. Then add the spring onion white and fry for 30 seconds before adding the garlic. After 30 seconds, sprinkle in the sugar and cook for about 3 minutes, which will help brown the meat.

- Add the 5-spice, white pepper, soy sauce and hard-boiled eggs. Mix and pour in enough water to completely cover the ingredients.

- Bring to the boil, then switch to a low–medium heat, cover and simmer for 40 minutes. The meat should be very tender. If there is still a lot of liquid at the end of cooking, reduce over a high heat. Enjoy with white rice and sprinkled with the spring onion greens, if you like.

GOOD TO KNOW
小提示

You usually find leafy green vegetables (spinach, pak choi/bok choy) along with the eggs to accompany the meat. Simply blanch any greens quickly in boiling water and drain.

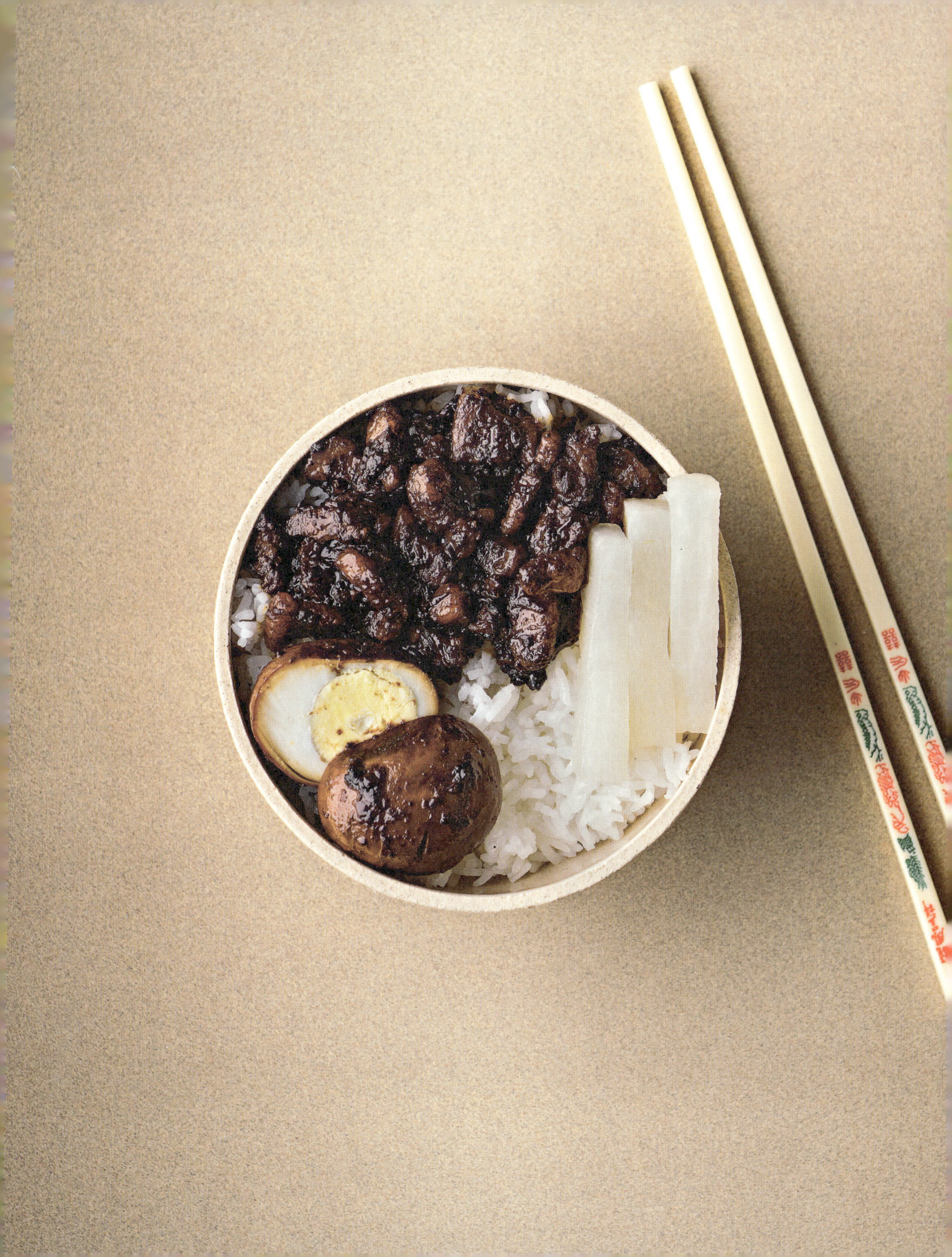

Beef Congee

SHĒNG GǓN NIÚ RÒU ZHŌU

生滚牛肉粥

PREPARING 40 MINUTES

COOKING 40 MINUTES

CONGEE, OR *ZHOU* IN MANDARIN, IS A KIND OF RICE PORRIDGE COOKED WITH A LARGE VOLUME OF WATER. IT PLAYS A MAJOR PART IN THE DAILY DIET OF THE SOUTH OF THE COUNTRY. SERVED PLAIN, IT REPLACES RICE TO ACCOMPANY DISHES, BUT IT CAN ALSO BE SERVED ALONE, AS IS THE CASE HERE.

Serves 4 people

INGREDIENTS

For the congee

- 200g (7oz) beef fillet, cut into 2–3mm (⅛in) slices aganist the grain (*see p. 184*)
- 2 tsp cornflour (cornstarch)
- 2 tsp neutral oil
- 1.2 litres (5 cups) water
- 60g (2oz/generous ¼ cup) rice, rinsed and drained
- 2 tsp salt
- A handful of shredded iceberg lettuce
- 4 eggs
- Finely chopped spring onion (scallion), to serve

For the marinade

- 1 tbsp soy sauce
- 1 tbsp oyster sauce
- 1 tbsp Shaoxing wine
- 1 piece of dried mandarin peel (*see p. 32, optional*)
- ¼ tsp white pepper
- 1 tsp grated ginger

FOR THE MARINADE

- Put the beef into a bowl and pour in all the marinade ingredients (if you don't have any dried mandarin peels, use ½ teaspoon of sugar). Massage the meat with this mixture, then add the cornflour and mix again. Pour in the 2 teaspoons of oil and mix for a final time to prevent the pieces from sticking together. Marinate in the fridge for 30 minutes.

FOR THE CONGEE

- Bring the water to the boil in a casserole, then switch to a medium heat and add the rinsed and drained rice. Cook for about 40 minutes, without covering (the water should not stop boiling). The rice is cooked when the grains have "exploded" and have amalgamated with the water. If you prefer a less liquid texture, reduce to the desired consistency.

- Turn off the heat and add the salt and the marinated beef, then throw in the shredded lettuce and mix.

TO SERVE

- Ladle the congee into your serving bowls and break a raw egg in the middle of each. The congee's heat will cook it. Sprinkle with chopped spring onion to finish.

GOOD TO KNOW
小提示

Jasmine or sushi rice (Japonica) is generally used for congee. The rice to water ratio varies from 1:10 to 1:20. I personally prefer a very liquid congee, so I opted here for the ratio of 1:20.

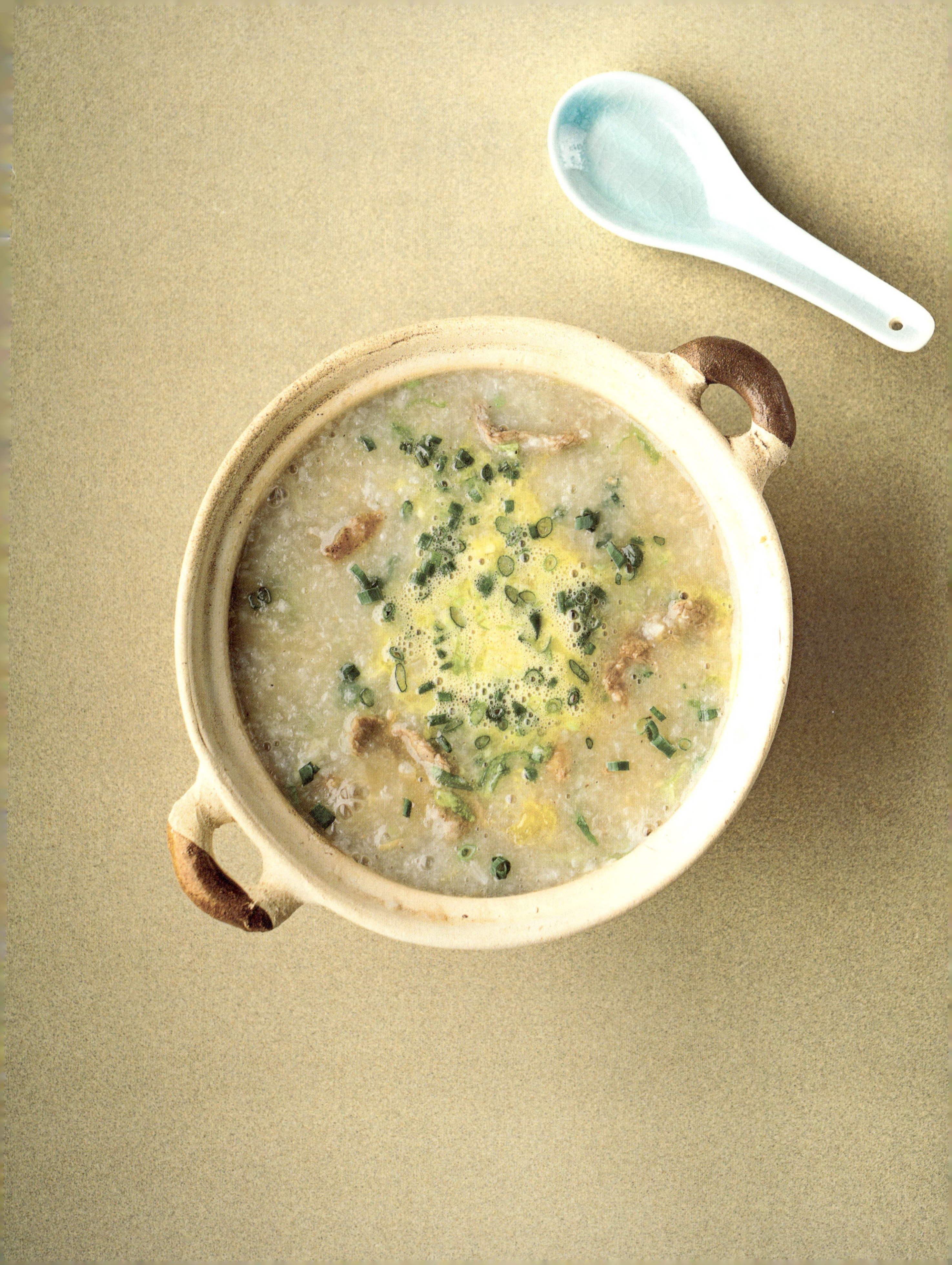

Pumpkin Millet Congee

NÁN GUĀ XIĂO MĬ ZHŌU

南瓜小米粥

Preparing 10 minutes

Cooking 30 minutes

MILLET CONGEE, A POPULAR CEREAL IN NORTHERN CHINA, IS AN EXCELLENT ALTERNATIVE TO THE CLASSIC RICE-BASED VERSION. THE PUMPKIN WILL MAKE THE CONGEE SLIGHTLY SWEET AND VERY COLOURFUL, PERFECT FOR A DIGESTIBLE AND NUTRIENT-RICH BREAKFAST.

Serves 4 people

INGREDIENTS

2 litres (8½ cups) water
120g (4¼oz/generous ½ cup) millet grains, rinsed and drained
30g (1oz/2 tbsp) sticky rice, rinsed and drained
200g (7oz) pumpkin flesh, cut into small cubes
A few jujubes (*see p. 35; optional*)
15g (½oz/2 tbsp) goji berries
30g (1oz/2½ tbsp) sugar

RECIPE STEPS

- Bring the water to the boil in a pot. Add the millet, sticky rice, pumpkin pieces and jujubes, then cover and cook for 30 minutes over a medium heat (the water should not stop boiling). Leave a small opening between the pot and lid, to prevent the congee from overflowing. Stir occasionally.

- After 30 minutes, turn off the heat and add the goji berries and sugar. Mix well. I prefer to use brown sugar (called "red sugar" in Chinese), but white sugar is also suitable.

- Serve in small bowls. You can enjoy the congee on its own, or serve it instead of rice as part of a classic meal.

GOOD TO KNOW
小提示

Pumpkin can be replaced with winter squash, and sticky rice with jasmine rice. And as with all congees, you can adjust the amount of water according to your preference.

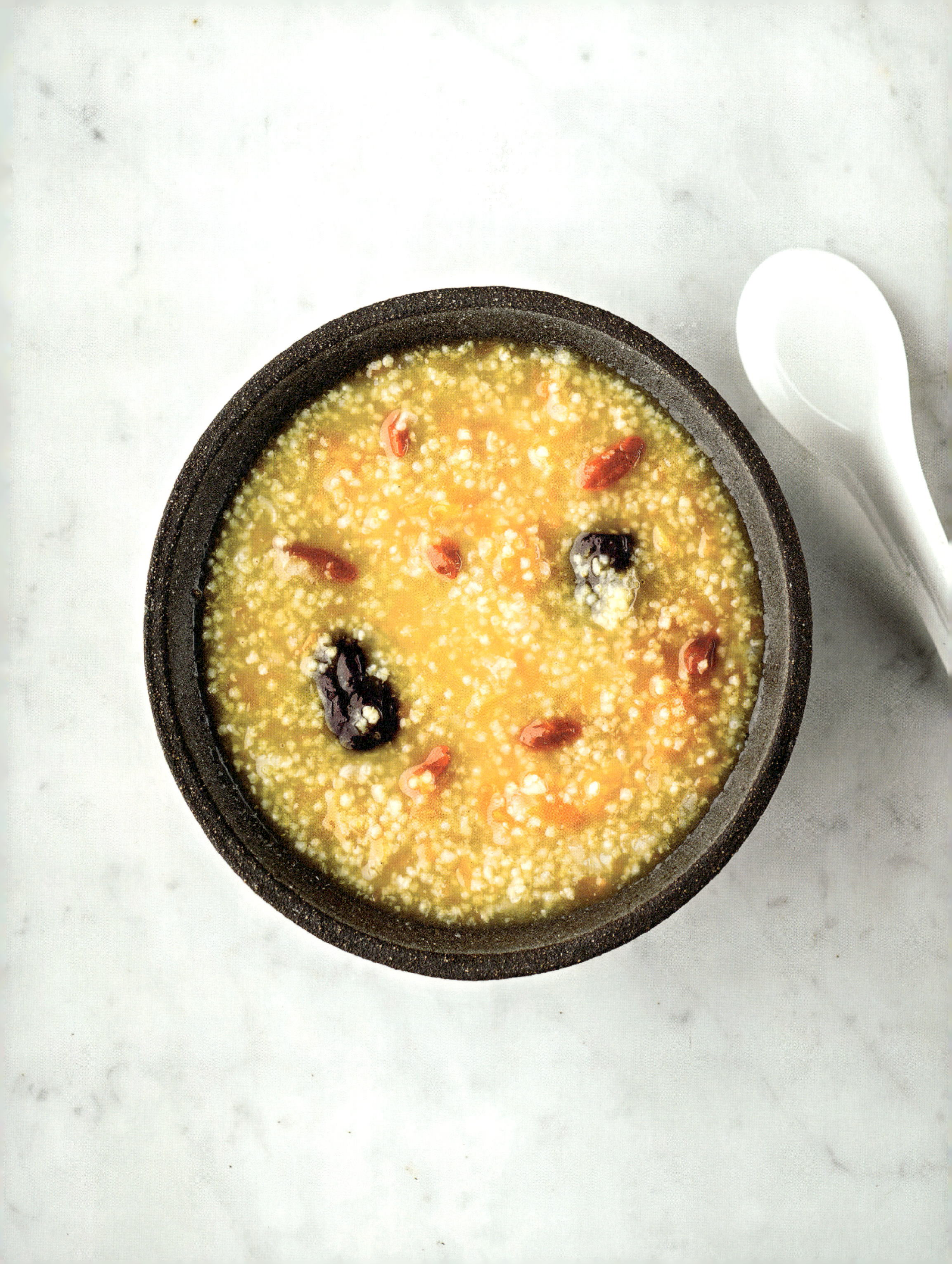

Sticky Rice with Pork Broth and Shiitake

NUÒ MǏ FÀN

糯米饭

PREPARING 130 MINUTES

COOKING 30 MINUTES

MY LOVE OF THIS DISH RUNS DEEP AND STIRS A LOT OF CHILDHOOD MEMORIES. IT'S MY NUMBER ONE BREAKFAST WHEN I RETURN TO WENZHOU AND IT ALWAYS MAKES ME NOSTALGIC. THE BROTH'S SMELL, THE STALL'S LIVELINESS, THE SOY MILK'S SWEETNESS THAT ALWAYS GOES WITH THIS DISH... IT'S LIKE I'M BACK THERE ALREADY.

🍴 Serves 2 people

INGREDIENTS

For the rice

200g (7oz/1 cup) sticky rice
Finely chopped spring onion (scallion), to serve

For the broth

5 dried shiitake mushrooms
1 tbsp oil
1 tsp chopped ginger
1 tsp chopped garlic
1 tsp chopped spring onion (scallion) white
150g (5½oz) pork, chopped (with 20% fat if possible)
1 tbsp Shaoxing wine
1 tbsp light soy sauce
½ tsp salt
½ tsp sugar
Shiitake soaking water

For the toppings (optional)

Dried shrimp (*xia mi*)
Dried pork (*rou song*)
Fried doughnut (*you tiao*)
Fermented mustard (*zha cai*)

FOR THE STICKY RICE

- Soak the sticky rice in water for at least 2 hours (overnight if possible). Drain, then steam the rice. The traditional method is to line the bottom of a bamboo steamer basket with a muslin-like (cheesecloth) fabric, to place the rice on it and to cook for 30 minutes over a medium heat. But you can use your usual steaming method. The rice should be a little dry but soft, and the grains should be well separated.

FOR THE BROTH

- Rehydrate the shiitake (see p. 32), perhaps while the sticky rice cooks, then drain (keeping the soaking water) and chop finely. Heat the oil in a wok over a medium heat and fry the ginger, garlic and spring onion white for about 20 seconds to release the flavours. Add the shiitake and the chopped pork, and fry for 2–3 minutes. Once the pork is cooked, pour in the Shaoxing wine, then the light soy sauce, salt and sugar. Add the mushroom soaking water (top up with fresh water if necessary) until the ingredients are covered. Simmer on a low heat for 15 minutes.

TO SERVE

- Divide the rice between 2 bowls, pour in the broth (I prefer it when it's really liquid) and sprinkle with spring onion and any toppings of choice. Enjoy immediately.

GOOD TO KNOW
小提示

I've included the classic toppings as an option here, because if you can't find any of them, it should not prevent you from making the recipe. In my opinion, the broth is the heart of this dish. For more information on these ingredients, see p. 32 (dried shrimp), p. 326 (fried doughnut) and p. 38 (fermented mustard).

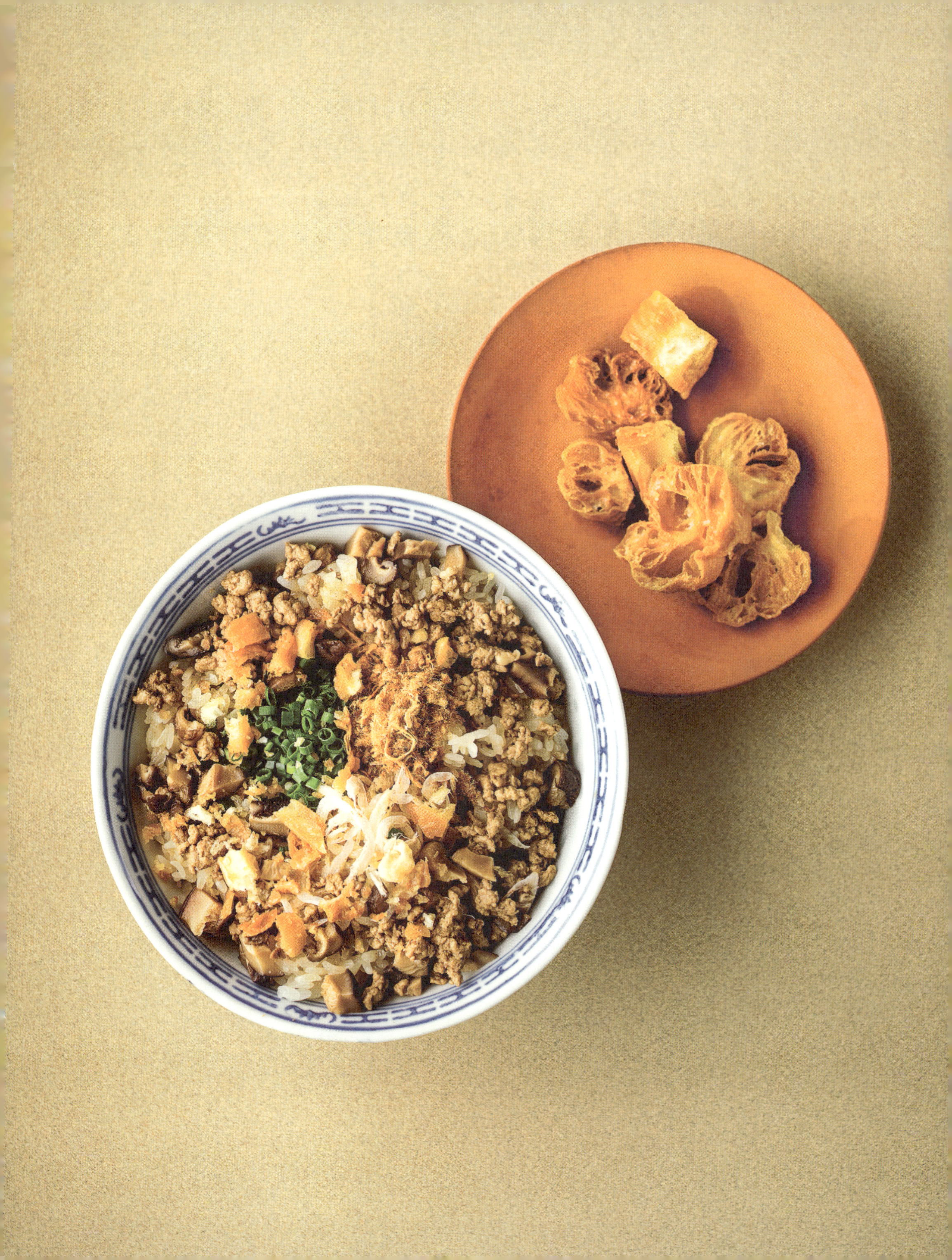

Lo Mai Gai

NUÒ MǏ JĪ

糯米鸡

PREPARING 90 MINUTES + SOAKING TIME

COOKING 60 MINUTES

LO MAI GAI (LITERALLY "CHICKEN STICKY RICE" IN CANTONESE) IS A DISH THAT IS OFTEN FOUND IN DIM SUM MEALS (SEE P. 258). SOFT STICKY RICE IS STUFFED WITH CHICKEN (AMONG OTHER THINGS) AND WRAPPED IN A LOTUS LEAF, WHICH ADDS A SUBTLE FLAVOUR DURING THE STEAMING PROCESS.

Makes 6 *lo mai gai*

INGREDIENTS

For the lo mai gai

400g (14oz/2 cups) sticky rice
6 dried shiitake mushrooms, about 15g (½oz)
10g (¼oz) dried shrimp (*xia mi, see p. 32*)
6 dried lotus leaves (*see p. 35*)
1 tbsp neutral oil

For the marinated chicken

100g (3½oz) boneless chicken leg
½ tsp grated ginger
2 tsp oyster sauce
2 tsp Shaoxing wine
¼ tsp white pepper
1 tsp sesame oil

For the sauce

1 tbsp chopped shallot
1 tsp dark soy sauce
1 tbsp light soy sauce
½ tsp sugar
½ tbsp oyster sauce
½ tsp salt
50ml (3 tbsp) mushroom or shrimp soaking water

FOR THE RECIPE PREP

- Soak the sticky rice for at least 4 hours (but preferably overnight), then drain.

- Rehydrate the shiitake and dried shrimp (see p. 32), and keep the soaking water. Rinse the lotus leaves to remove any impurities, and use a large container (such as a large oven tray) to rehydrate them in cold water for at least 1 hour before use. The leaves should be soft enough to fold without breaking.

- Meanwhile, cut the chicken leg into small pieces, about 3cm (1¼in) wide and 1cm (½in) thick, and mix with the other marinade ingredients. Marinate for 30 minutes.

TO COOK THE RICE

- Line a large steamer basket with a muslin cloth (cheesecloth) and place the soaked and drained rice in a layer about 2cm (¾in) thick. Cover and cook over a medium heat for 30 minutes. If you have a small basket, divide into two baskets for even cooking. When the rice is cooked, transfer to a large bowl and set aside.

FOR THE SAUCE

- Prepare the sauce by mixing all the ingredients together in a bowl, then pour half of this sauce into the sticky rice. Mix to let the rice absorb it. Heat a wok over a high heat and pour in the tablespoon of neutral oil, then turn the heat down to medium and add the marinated chicken, shiitake and dried shrimp. Fry for 1 minute, then add the remaining sauce and continue cooking for 1–2 minutes. Set aside.

TO ASSEMBLE AND STEAM

- Lay a lotus leaf flat. Place a layer of rice in the middle, then a layer of stuffing (chicken, shiitake and dried shrimp), then add another layer of rice (the stuffing must be completely covered). Fold the leaf as you would a gift to close, while pressing the inside so that the rice holds while cooking. Repeat for the remaining leaves and filling and steam over a medium heat for 25 minutes. Enjoy straight away.

- To warm up the *lo mai gai*, simply steam again for 8 minutes.

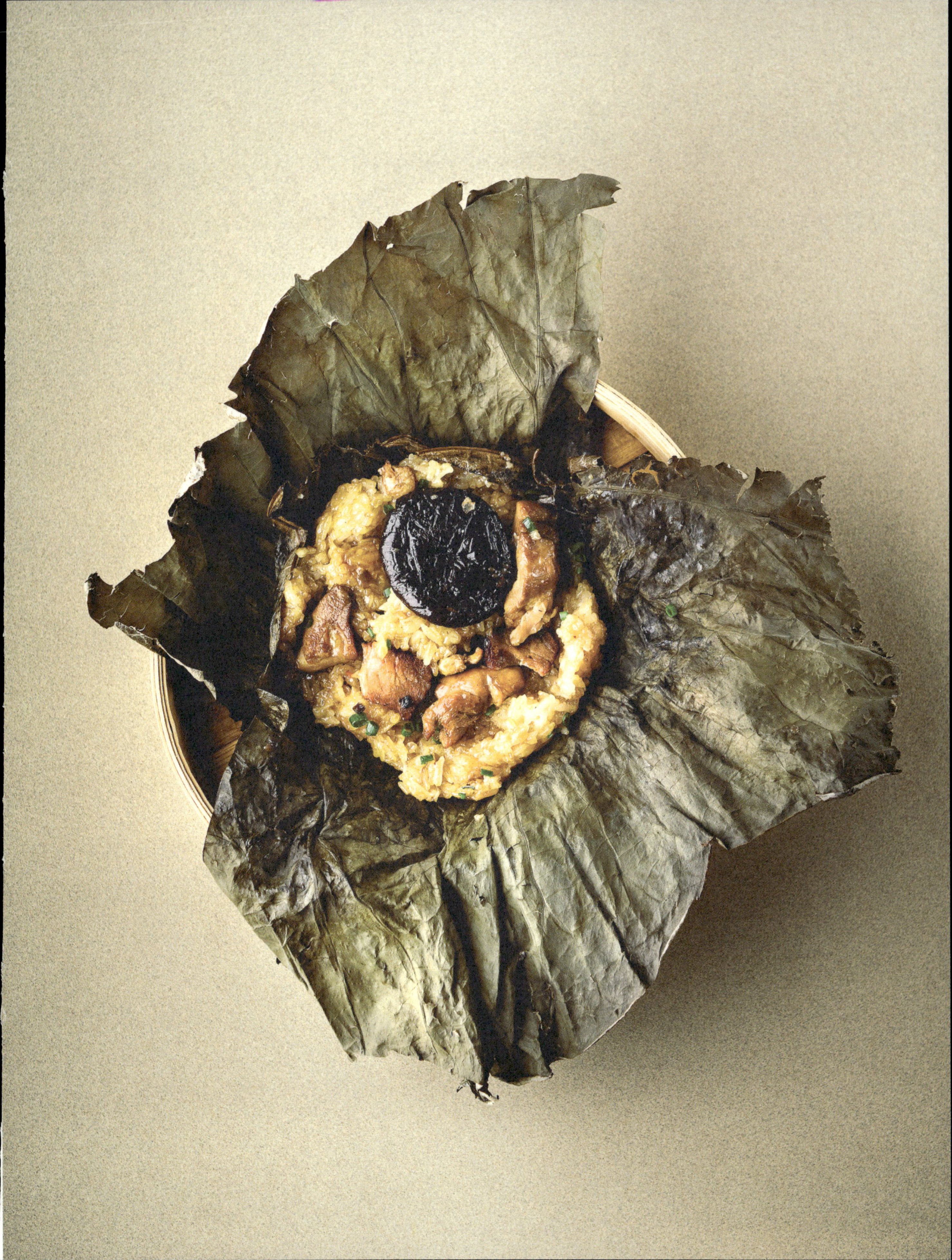

Cheung Fun

CHÁNG   FĚN

肠 粉

PREPARING 5 MINUTES   COOKING 20 MINUTES

THESE RICE FLOUR-BASED PANCAKES ARE ONE OF CANTON'S TRADITIONAL BREAKFASTS. THEY ARE STEAMED, WHICH MAKES THEM TRANSLUCENT AND ELASTIC. THEY CAN BE EATEN PLAIN WITH A SAUCE OR STUFFED (WITH PRAWNS/SHRIMP, MEAT, HERBS...). RESTAURANTS MAKE THEM USING SPECIFIC EQUIPMENT. HENCE, THIS IS A HOME-MADE VERSION, WHICH IS A LITTLE THICKER BUT ALSO MUCH EASIER TO MAKE.

Makes 10 pancakes

INGREDIENTS

For the cheung fun

70g (2½oz/½ cup) rice flour
40g (1½oz/⅓ cup) wheat starch
15g (½oz/2 tbsp) cornflour (cornstarch)
¼ tsp salt
250ml (9oz/1 cup) water
½ tbsp neutral oil

For the sauce

2 tbsp spring onion oil (see p. 340)
2 tbsp light soy sauce
2 tsp oyster sauce
1 tsp sugar
5 tbsp water

For the stuffing (optional)

Finely chopped cooked prawns (shrimp) or meat
Chopped fresh herbs
Chopped spring onion (scallion)

RECIPE STEPS

- Mix all the sauce ingredients in a bowl and set aside.

- Combine the rice flour, wheat starch and cornflour in a bowl, then add the salt and water and mix until you obtain a homogenous texture.

- Pour 2cm (¾in) of water into a wok or frying pan, which should ideally measure at least 24cm (9½in) in diameter, then place a steamer rack (see p. 44) in the middle with a rimmed flat plate on top. Make sure that the height of the rack plus the plate does not prevent a lid from closing.

- Bring the water to the boil, then switch to a medium heat. To make each *cheung fun*, repeat the following process: cover the plate in the wok with a thin layer of oil. Stir the flour and water mixture again (the starch and flour tend to collect at the bottom of the bowl) and pour a thin layer onto the plate, just enough to cover it.

- Place a lid on the wok and steam over a high heat for 1-2 minutes. Little bubbles appearing between the plate and your *cheung fun* indicate that it's ready. Remove the plate and let the pancake cool a little before peeling it off with a silicone spatula.

FOR THE STUFFING

- At that point, you can add your choice of filling: traditionally, it should be finely chopped cooked prawns or meat, with fresh herbs (such as coriander/cilantro) and spring onion.

- Roll your *cheung fun* to enclose the stuffing and repeat the process until you have used up all your ingredients. Serve with the sauce.

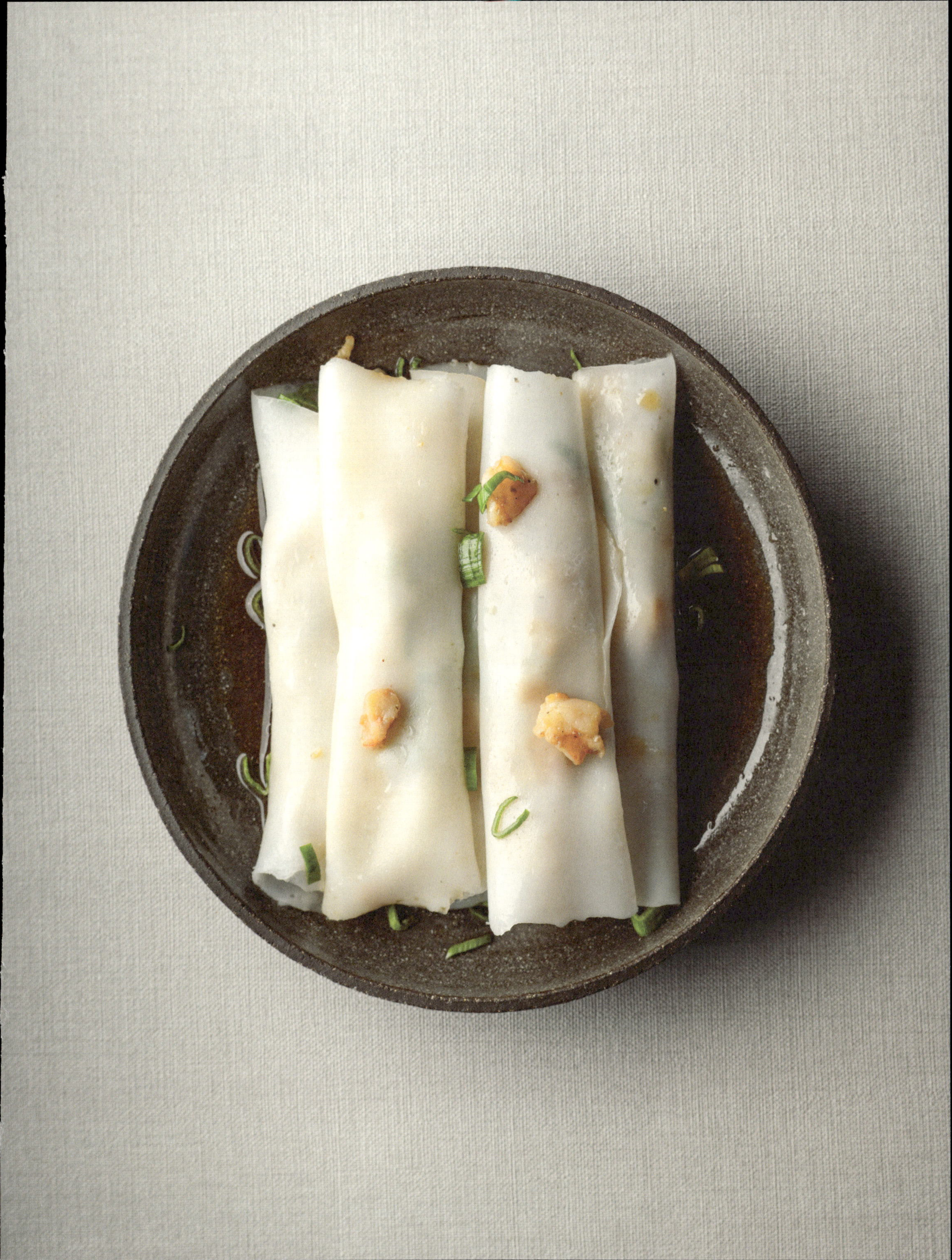

Wok Stir-Fried Nian Gao

CHǍO   NIÁN   GĀO

炒年糕

PREPARING 10 MINUTES + SOAKING TIME

COOKING 8 MINUTES

NIAN GAO ARE CAKES MADE OUT OF STICKY RICE. IN MY REGION (ZHEJIANG), *NIAN GAO* ARE SHAPED LIKE SMALL OVAL SLICES THAT ARE OFTEN FOUND IN SOUPS OR STIR-FRIED DISHES.

Serves 2 people

INGREDIENTS

3 dried shiitake mushrooms
1 tbsp neutral oil
2 garlic cloves, chopped
150g (5½oz) chicken breast, cut into small pieces
100g (3½oz) pak choi (bok choy) leaves
100g (3½oz) spinach leaves, tough stems removed
250g (9oz) *nian gao* (see note), rinsed and separated
¼ tsp sesame oil

For the sauce

1 tbsp light soy sauce
¼ tsp dark soy sauce
1 tbsp oyster sauce
Black rice vinegar
1 tsp sugar
100ml (6½ tbsp) mushroom soaking water

RECIPE STEPS

- Rehydrate the shiitake for 30 minutes in warm water (or you can also use fresh mushrooms), then cut them into strips. Keep the soaking water for the sauce.

- Mix the sauce ingredients together in a bowl and set aside.

- Heat the neutral oil in a wok over a medium heat and fry the garlic for a few seconds, then add the chicken. Let the meat brown – it should not be completely cooked through at this stage. Add the mushrooms, pak choi and spinach. Pour in the sauce, then add the *nian gao* on top. Cover to let the steam soften the *nian gao* for about 2–3 minutes. They tend to stick to the bottom of the wok, even in a non-stick pan, which is why you need to leave the meat and vegetables underneath.

- When the *nian gao* are soft, mix everything together with a spatula. If you use vegetables that cook quickly instead of those listed here (mung bean sprouts, for example), add them at this point and fry for 1 minute. Make sure all the ingredients are cooked properly, including the chicken.

- Turn off the heat and drizzle with the sesame oil to serve.

GOOD TO KNOW
小提示

The traditional Wenzhou recipe I grew up with used pork belly instead of chicken, marinated in soy sauce, then sun-dried (jiang you rou, 酱油肉). *Nian gao are sold vacuum-packed in the chilled section of most Chinese supermarkets. After washing them, you need to separate any cakes that are stuck together.*

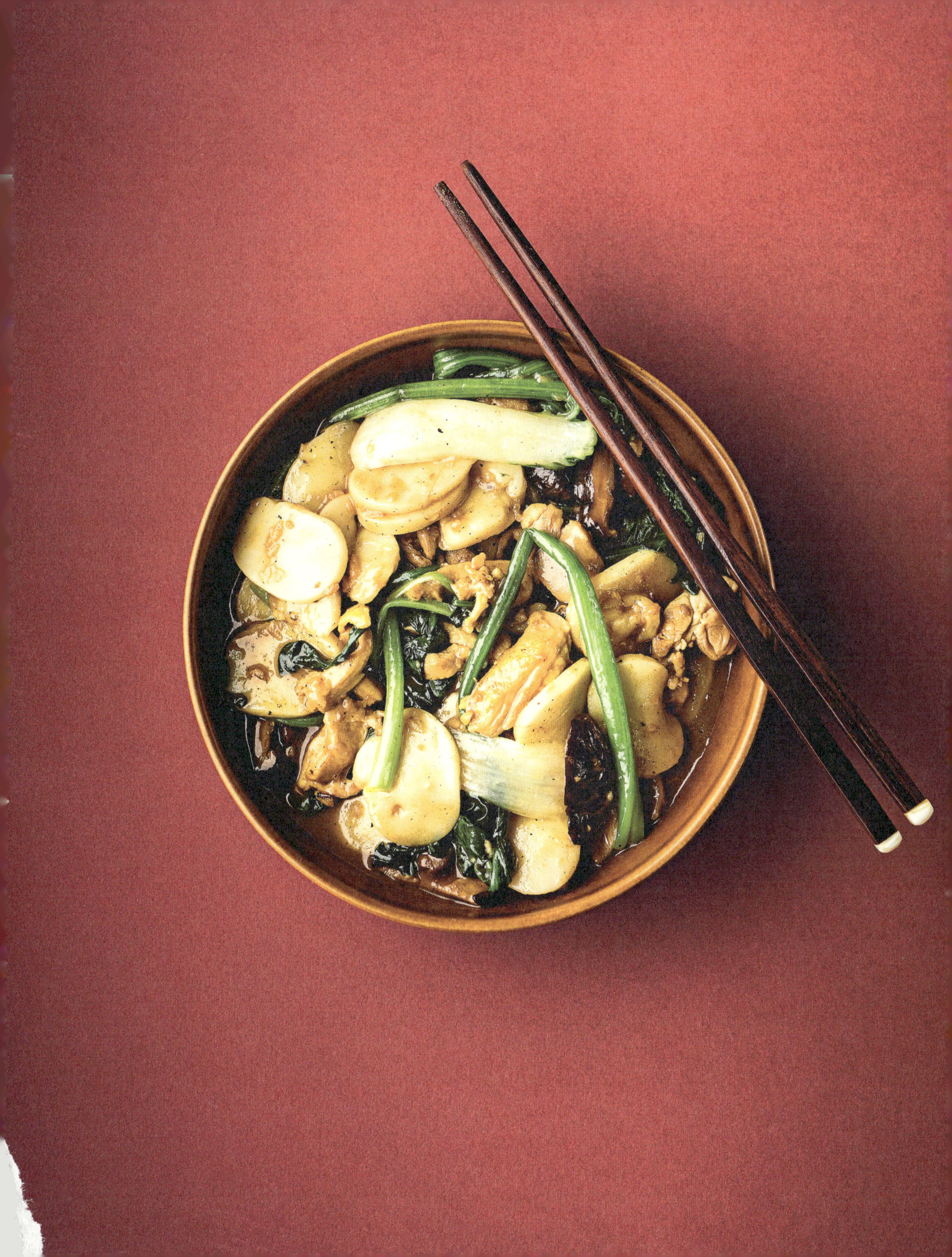

CHAPTER
13

Snacks
小吃
XIĂO CHĪ

PP. 318-319: Spring onion pancakes ■ **PP. 320-321:** Mustard leaf pancakes
PP. 322-323: Jian bing ■ **PP. 324-325:** Soy milk ■ **PP. 326-327:** You tiao ■ **PP. 330-331:** Liang fen
PP. 332-333: White radish cake ■ **PP. 334-335:** Strange-tasting peanuts

From All Angles

At Any Time of the Day

THERE IS A SET OF CHINESE DISHES CALLED *XIAO CHI*.
XIAO MEANS "SMALL" AND *CHI* MEANS "EAT". THEY CAN BE DESCRIBED
AS MORE OR LESS HEARTY SNACKS EATEN OUTSIDE OF LUNCH OR DINNER,
BUT IN REALITY THEY ARE FAR MORE THAN SIMPLE SNACKS.

THE SOUL OF STREET FOOD

Much like a hot dog in New York or a sweet crêpe in Paris, *xiao chi* are found first and foremost on the street. The difference is that in China, you can eat it throughout the day.

It starts at breakfast, which is mostly eaten outside, where a huge number of small restaurants are busy offering bao, cakes, noodle soups and dumplings of all kinds (see p. 257). Then, in most Chinese cities, there are areas dedicated to takeaway meals (*xiao chi jie*). Historically, they are located next to temples, the ultimate stop-off point. This is very much the case in Shanghai, Nanjing, Suzhou and Changsha, for example, where *xiao chi jie* have become major tourist attractions in themselves.

At nightfall, night markets take over, especially in the south of the country, where the temperature is mild for a large part of the year. The warm evenings mean you can stroll from one stall to another, grazing as you go, or sit in one of the *dai pai dong*, small open-air restaurants that are a Hong Kong staple.

REGIONAL ORIGIN, NATIONAL POPULARITY

The strong internal migration in China, occurring since the 1980s, has popularized *xiao chi* throughout the country, but their name remains inseparable from their region and city of origin.

Whether it's lamb skewers from Xinjiang, "stinky" tofu from Hunan, *jian bing* (a type of pancake, see p. 322) from Tianjin, or *rou jia mo* (a mini sandwich with simmered meat) from Xi'an, *xiao chi* have local origins and ingredients. In Taiwan, *xiao chi* are deeply rooted in the local culture, as evidenced by some 300 night markets spread across the island. The dishes are often Chinese in origin, but they evolved over time with local, Japanese or even Western influences, before being reintroduced on the mainland.

SOME POPULAR CHINESE STREET FOOD SNACKS

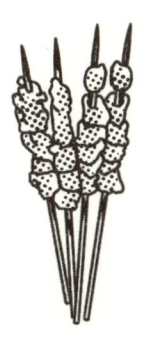

LAMB SKEWER
羊肉串 | YÁNG RÒU CHUÀN

A Uyghur cumin-flavoured speciality.

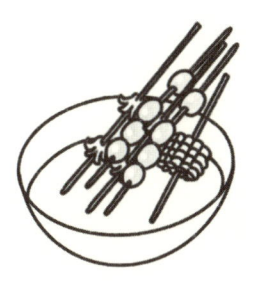

MA LA TANG
麻辣烫 | MÁ LÀ TÀNG

Skewers of all kinds in a hot and spicy broth.

HAWTHORN SKEWER
冰糖葫芦 | BĪNG TÁNG HÚ LU

A Peking speciality consisting of caramel-coated hawthorn berries.

BUBBLE TEA
珍珠奶茶 | ZHĒN ZHŪ NǍI CHÁ

A Taiwanese drink made of milk, tea and tapioca pearls.

RICE NOODLE ROLL
肠粉 | CHÁNG FĚN

A rice-flour pancake stuffed with meat or prawns (shrimp).

"STINKY" TOFU
臭豆腐 | CHÒU DÒU FU

Fermented tofu that is fried and usually served with a chilli sauce.

ROU JIAO MO
肉夹馍 | RÒU JIĀ MÓ

A small bread-roll sandwich stuffed with simmered meat.

CHONGQING NOODLES
重庆小面 | CHÓNG QÌNG XIĂO MIÀN

A true symbol of Chongqing, these noodles can be enjoyed with or without soup.

SPRING ONION PANCAKES

葱油饼

CŌNG YÓU BǏNG

These small pancakes are based on two simple ingredients: fat (traditionally lard) and spring onion (scallion). The result is a pancake with different layers, crispy on the outside and soft on the inside. The scent of spring onion intensifies during cooking, as it does with spring onion oil (see p. 340).

MAKES 6 PANCAKES: 150g (5½oz) chopped spring onions (scallions) ▪ Oil for cooking the pancakes
FOR THE DOUGH: 350g (2½ cups) T55 (bread/all-purpose) flour ▪ 2g (¾ tsp) dry yeast ▪ 1 tbsp neutral oil
250ml (2 cups) hot water (70°C/158°F) ▪ Spring onion oil (see p. 340; optional)
FOR THE OIL PASTE (YOU SU): 50g (1¾oz) lard (or neutral oil) ▪ 40g (¼ cup) flour ▪ 6g (generous 1 tsp) salt

01
For the dough, mix together the **flour, yeast, oil and water.**

02 (3 MINS)
Knead the dough until you form a ball that should not stick to your fingers. Sprinkle with some spring onion oil, if you like, which will strengthen the spring onion's flavour.

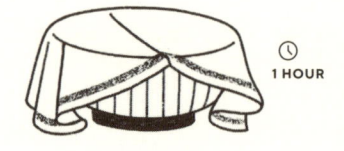

03 (1 HOUR)
Let the dough **stand for 1 hour, covered with a cloth** to prevent it from drying out.

04
Meanwhile, mix the oil paste ingredients together in a bowl and set aside.

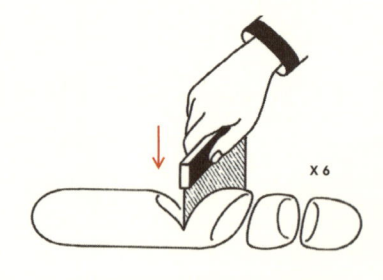

05
Knead the dough again to create a smooth ball. **Shape into a long "sausage"** and divide it into 6 pieces.

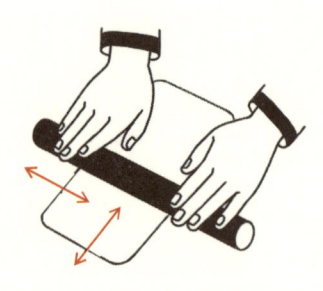

06
Roll out a piece of dough with a rolling pin to a thin rectangle of about 30 x 8cm (12 x 3in) and 3mm (⅛in) thick.

GOOD TO KNOW
小提示

You can freeze the pancakes and reheat them in a pan (without thawing them beforehand and without adding fat). These pancakes are great on their own (savoury and flavourful) but can also be garnished with meat, pickles and salad to make a complete meal.

07
Add a layer of oil paste to the dough with a brush. Cover generously with some chopped spring onion (about 25g/1oz).

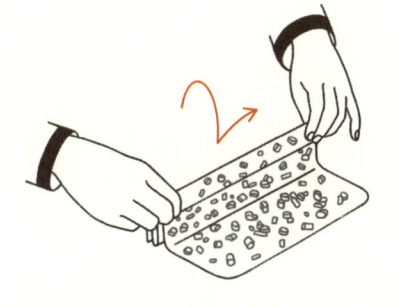

08
Fold the dough widthways little by little to create a long roll.

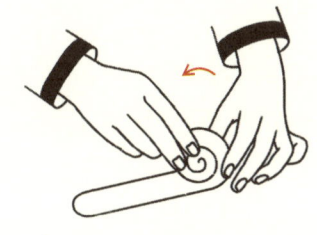

09
Then, **roll up into a "snail"** to form a circle.

10
Flatten the pancake by squeezing it with your palm, then repeat the process with the other 5 dough pieces. Let the pancakes rest for 15 minutes, covered with a cloth or film (plastic wrap), which will allow for easier rolling.

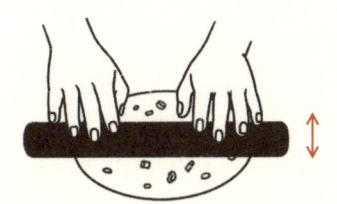

11
Spread the pancakes out with a rolling pin. They should be about **12cm (5in)** in diameter, or more if you prefer a thinner pancake. It doesn't matter if some spring onion pokes out of the dough.

12
Heat a thin layer of oil in a pan over a medium heat. **Brown the pancakes for 1–2 minutes on each side.**

Mustard Leaf Pancakes

WĒN ZHŌU MÀI BǏNG

温州麦饼

PREPARING 90 MINUTES
COOKING 20 MINUTES

I GREW UP WITH THESE PANCAKES FILLED WITH *MEI CAI* (FERMENTED MUSTARD LEAVES) AND PORK; THEY ARE A WENZHOU SPECIALITY. THERE ARE DIFFERENT VERSIONS, WHICH ARE MORE OR LESS THICK, FROM SOFT TO CRISPY. AT HOME, WE EAT THEM ALONG WITH A WHITE CONGEE, BUT THEY ARE DELICIOUS WITHOUT ACCOMPANIMENT AND CAN BE ENJOYED AS A TREAT.

Makes 6 pancakes

INGREDIENTS

For the dough

500g (1lb 2oz/3¾ cups) plain (all-purpose) flour
½ tsp salt
275ml (9½oz/scant 1¼ cups) hot water
Neutral oil, for frying

For the filling

200g (7oz) dried mustard leaves (*mei cai*, see p. 38)
200g (7oz) pork belly (ideally 50% fat), finely sliced
20g (¾oz) dried mini shrimp (*xia pi*, see p. 32)
30g (1oz) spring onions (scallions), chopped
1 tsp salt
½ tsp sugar
1 tsp lard (*optional; see p. 344 for home-made*)

FOR THE DOUGH AND FILLING

- Rehydrate the dried mustard leaves (*mei cai*) in warm water for 30 minutes.

- Meanwhile, mix the flour and salt in a bowl, then gradually add the hot water – which should be about 75°C (167°F), made up of three quarters boiling water and one quarter room-temperature water – while mixing with a chopstick. (Hot water helps to create a soft dough that is easier to spread; this kind of dough is called *tang mian*, 烫面.) Knead for 1 minute until the ball no longer sticks to your fingers. It does not need to be smooth. Cover with a cloth or film (plastic wrap) while you prepare the filling.

- Rinse the rehydrated *mei cai* twice with water, then drain. Heat a dry pan over a medium heat and fry the leaves, without adding any fat. Stir regularly to prevent them from burning – they are ready once they are dry.

- Mix the pork belly with the *mei cai*, dried shrimp, spring onions, salt, sugar and lard, if you have some.

TO SHAPE

- Divide the dough into 6 pieces of about 125g (4½oz), then shape into discs of about 8cm (3in) in diameter. Add 75g (2½oz) of the filling to each disc, then fold the dough by turning it with your hand to encase the filling. Gently roll out each pancake with your rolling pin, starting from the middle and spreading out to the edges to distribute the filling evenly, until it is about 2mm (⅛in) thick. It does not matter if a little of the filling leaks out.

TO COOK

- Heat a pan over a medium heat and pour in ½ teaspoon of oil. Use a brush to spread it well. Cook each pancake for about 2–3 minutes on each side (adding more oil as necessary); they should be properly browned. Cut into quarters and enjoy hot.

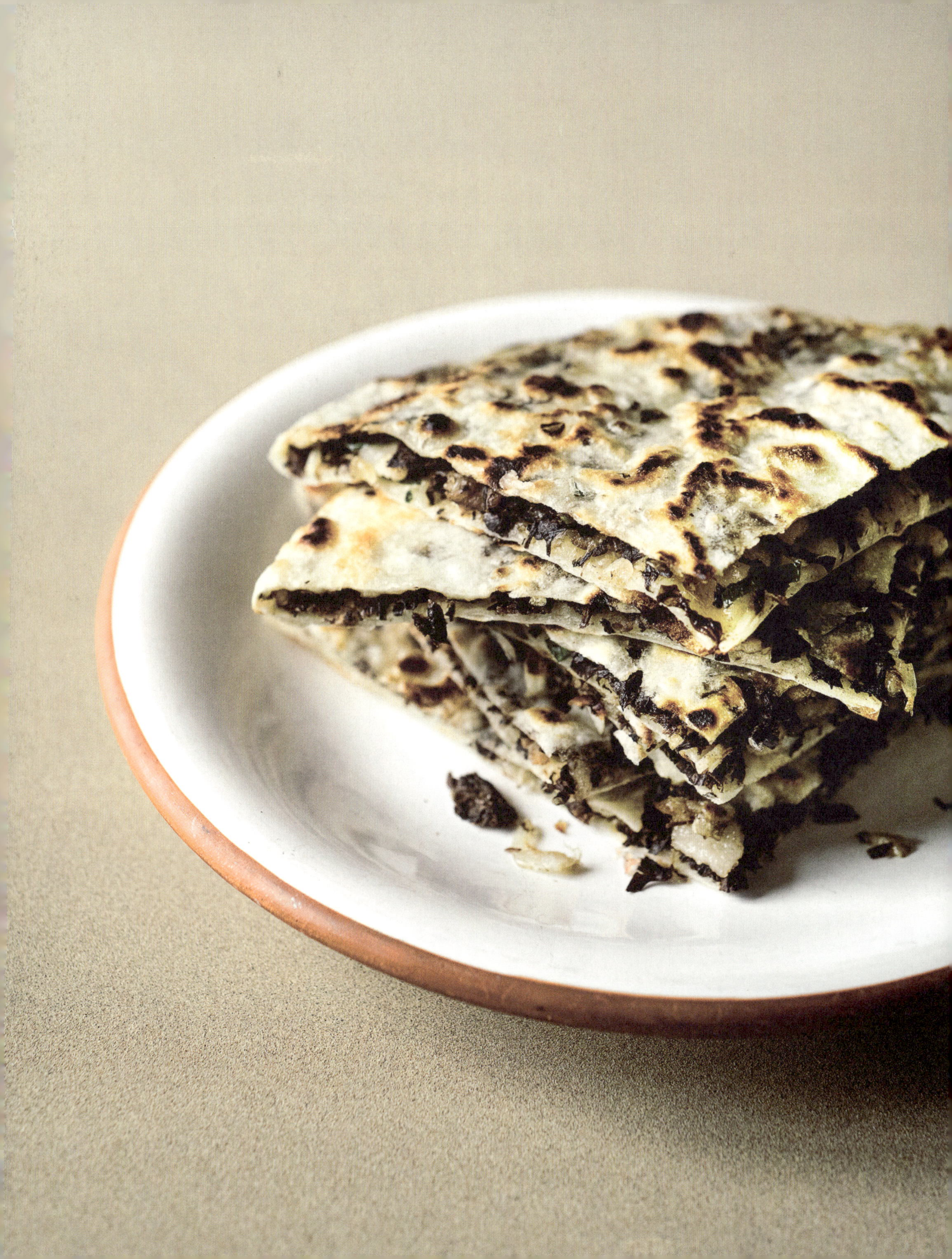

Jian Bing

JIĀN BǏNG GUǑ ZI
煎饼果子

Preparing 10 minutes
Cooking 30 minutes

JIAN BING (LITERALLY "PAN-FRIED PANCAKES") ARE TRADITIONALLY SERVED FOR BREAKFAST IN NORTHERN CHINA (TIANJIN, BEIJING, SHANDONG). ITS BASIC VERSION IS VEGETARIAN AND CONSISTS OF THREE ESSENTIAL ELEMENTS (NOT INCLUDING TOPPINGS): A FLUFFY PANCAKE, TWO FERMENTED SOY SAUCES AND A CRISPY LAYER IN THE MIDDLE, MADE OUT OF FRIED DOUGH OR FRIED DOUGHNUT (SEE P. 326).

Makes 4 pancakes

INGREDIENTS

For the pancake batter

65g (2¼oz/½ cup) T55 flour (bread/all-purpose flour)
65g (2¼oz/½ cup) mung bean flour
205ml (7oz/scant 1 cup) water

For the sauce

2 tbsp sweet soy bean paste (*tian mian jiang, see p. 38*)
1 tbsp chilli bean paste (*doubanjiang, see p. 38*)
2 tsp sugar
1 block of fermented tofu, about 15g (½oz); *optional*
2 tbsp water

For the topping

200ml (scant 1 cup) neutral oil
8 wonton wrappers
4 eggs
Chopped coriander (cilantro)
Finely chopped spring onions (scallions)
A handful of toasted black sesame seeds

RECIPE STEPS

- Heat the oil in a wok to 160°C (320°F). Make a few cuts on the wonton wrappers (to prevent them from losing their shape while cooking), then immerse them in the oil and fry until browned, for about 1 minute. Set aside. (Once the oil is cold, you can filter and reuse it.)

- Next, prepare the pancake batter: mix all the ingredients together in a bowl until you have a thick batter.

- Prepare the sauce: mix the sweet soy bean paste, chilli bean paste, sugar and fermented tofu in a bowl, then add the water at the end to dilute the mixture. The fermented tofu (see p. 118) will add a salty and umami flavour.

TO COOK THE PANCAKES

- Heat a non-stick pan (or better still, a crêpe maker if you have one) over a medium heat. Lightly oil the surface and pour in a ladleful of your batter – about 60g (2oz) for a 28cm (11in) frying pan – and spread it evenly to make a thin layer (this will be easier if you have a spreader).

- When the batter is no longer runny, break an egg on top of the pancake and spread it over the entire surface. Cook for about 30 seconds, until the egg is barely liquid, then add a handful of chopped coriander and spring onions, and some toasted black sesame seeds. Flip the pancake and cover it with 1 teaspoon of the sauce (or more, to taste). Finally, add two of the fried wonton wrappers, breaking them up if necessary to arrange them more easily.

- Fold in the two sides, then fold the pancake in half and repeat with the remaining batter, toppings and sauce. Enjoy hot.

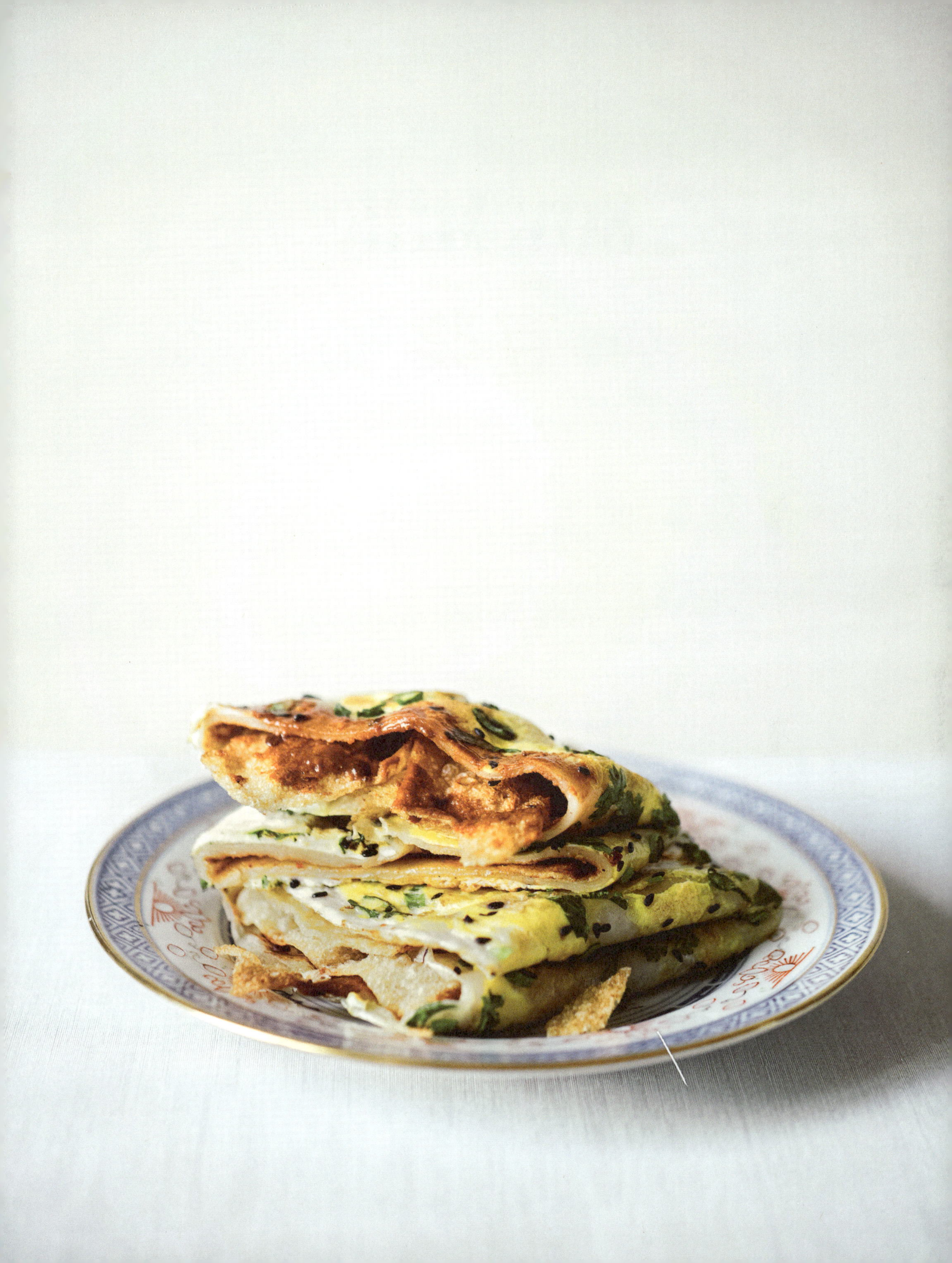

Soy Milk

DÒU　JIĀNG

豆浆

PREPARING 12 HOURS · COOKING 25 MINUTES

FRESH SOY MILK (OR "SOY PORRIDGE" IF YOU TRANSLATE IT LITERALLY) IS AN ICONIC BREAKFAST DRINK.

Makes 2 glasses

INGREDIENTS

170g (6oz) yellow soy beans
720ml (25oz/3 cups) water

RECIPE STEPS

- Soak the soy beans in water for at least 12 hours. The beans will gain in volume, and their film will become easier to remove by rubbing them in your hands. Once you've rubbed off the film, rinse with fresh water and drain. (If you bought already-peeled soy beans, simply soak and drain them.)

- Mix the soy beans with the measured water for about 1 minute until smooth, then strain through a very fine sieve, or use a muslin cloth (cheesecloth). Press and squeeze to collect as much liquid as possible. The residue, called *dou zha* and better known as *okara* in Japan, can be used as a base for making protein pancakes.

- Bring the soy milk to the boil in a pot. Lower the heat so that the liquid remains simmering and cook for about 20 minutes. Remove any foam from the surface.

GOOD TO KNOW
小提示

Soy milk is always drunk hot at breakfast, served in a bowl. To make a sweet version, simply add sugar or honey. The savoury version, found in the south of the country, is much denser. You usually add a hint of soy sauce, some nori seaweed (zi cai, see p. 32), pieces of fried doughnut (you tiao, see p. 326), dried mini shrimp (xia pi, see p. 32), and a bit of spring onion (scallion).

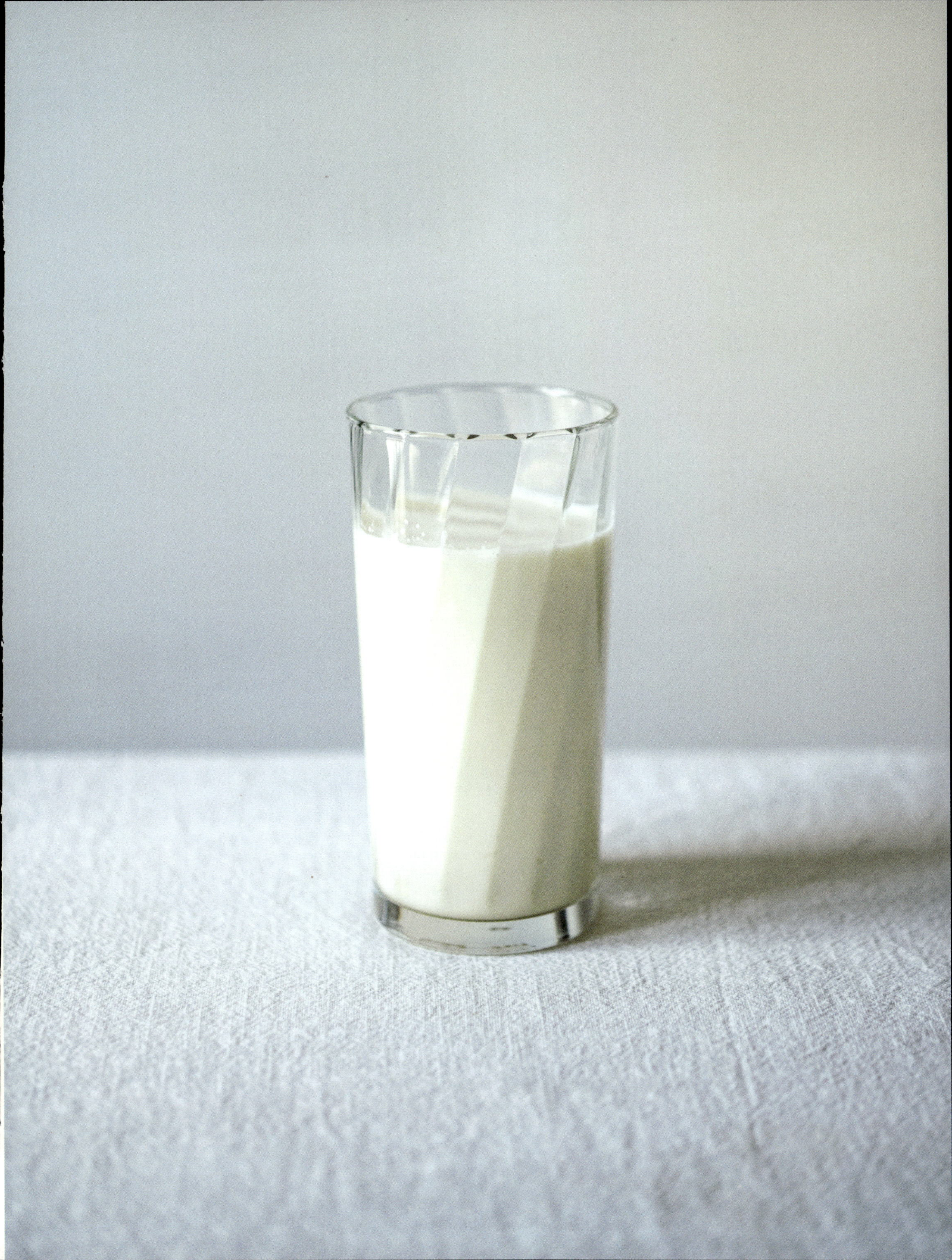

You Tiao

YÓU   TIÁO

油条

PREPARING 75 MINUTES   *COOKING 25 MINUTES*

THIS LONG FRIED DOUGHNUT IS THE SOUL OF BREAKFAST AND IS FOUND ALMOST EVERYWHERE IN CHINA. THERE ARE INFINITE WAYS TO EAT IT: ON ITS OWN WITH SOY MILK (P. 324), DUNKED IN CONGEE (P. 304), AS A FILLING IN A PANCAKE (P. 322) OR IN STICKY RICE (P. 306), JUST TO NAME A FEW EXAMPLES.

🍴 Makes 8 *you tiao*

INGREDIENTS

250g (9oz/about 1¾ cups) T55 (bread/all-purpose) flour, plus extra for dusting
½ tsp salt
½ tsp baking powder
½ tsp bicarbonate of soda (baking soda)
1 egg
130ml (4½oz/½ cup) water
500ml (generous 2 cups) neutral oil, for frying

RECIPE STEPS

▪ In a bowl, mix together the flour, salt, baking powder and bicarbonate of soda. Add the egg, then gradually add the water. Mix until all the flour is incorporated. The dough should not be too dry or too sticky, and there is no need to knead it. Add a teaspoon of oil over the entire surface, then cover and let it stand at room temperature for 1 hour.

▪ Sprinkle a little flour on the countertop, then fold the dough (which should be quite elastic and flexible) like an envelope to form a thick rectangle. Spread the dough with a rolling pin until you obtain a rectangle 1cm (½in) thick, about 10cm (4in) wide and 40cm (16in) long.

▪ Heat the frying oil in a wok to 180°C (350°F). Meanwhile, cut the dough widthways into strips 3cm (1in) wide. Place one strip on top of another, then make a deep fold lengthways to stick them together.

▪ Slightly stretch the dough, pressing firmly on both sides to make the layers stick (as they can tend to separate while cooking). Place in the hot oil and wait until the doughnut rises to the surface and slightly hardens (5–10 seconds). Flip it quickly with tongs or a chopstick to inflate the doughnut.

▪ Once the *you tiao* reaches its maximum size (after about 20–30 seconds), continue cooking for about 2 minutes until browned. Drain on kitchen paper and serve.

GOOD TO KNOW
小提示

You can freeze any leftover you tiao. *To heat them up, bake them at 200°C (180°C fan/400°F/Gas 6) until the inside is warm.*

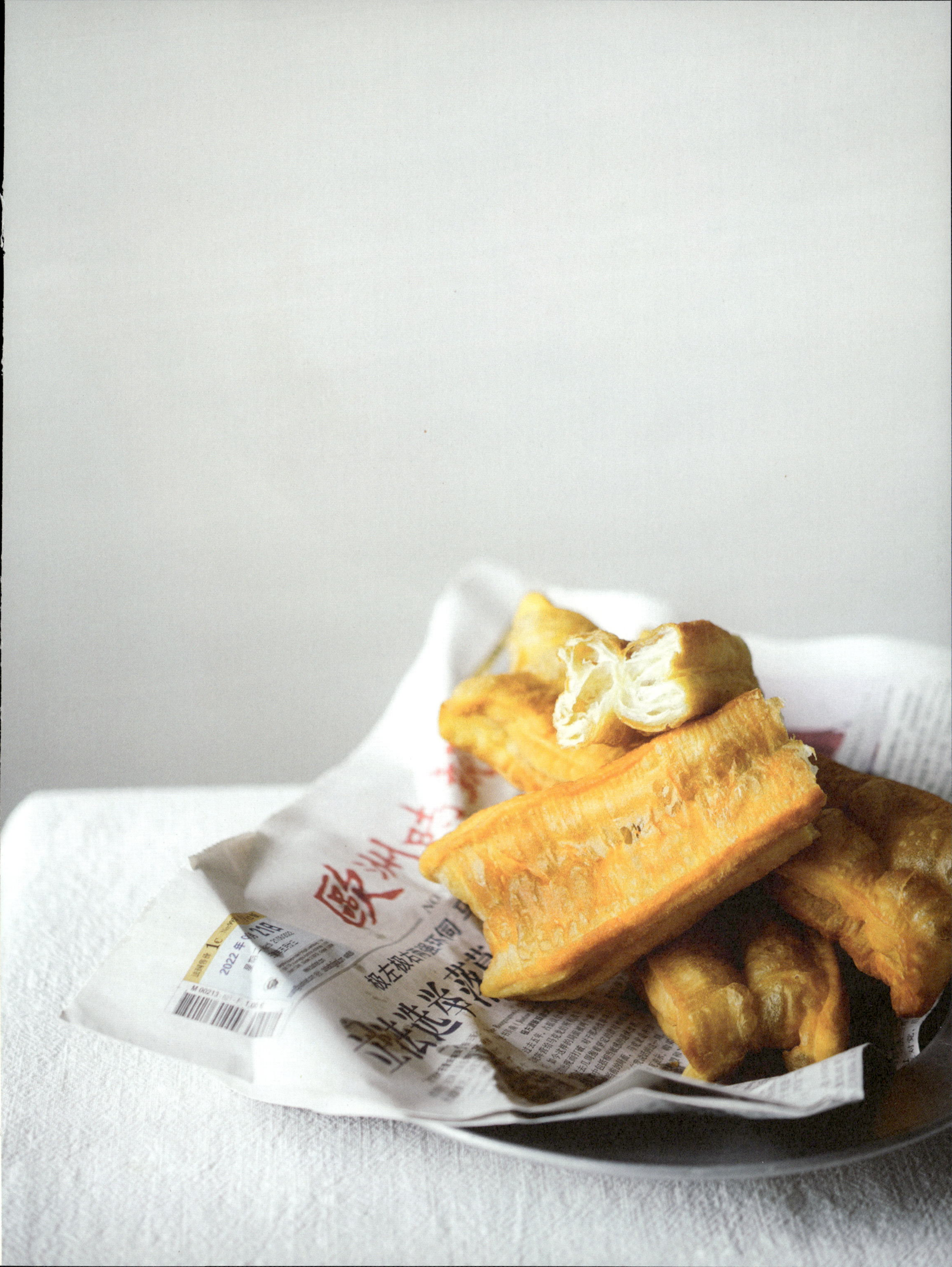
2022 年

328

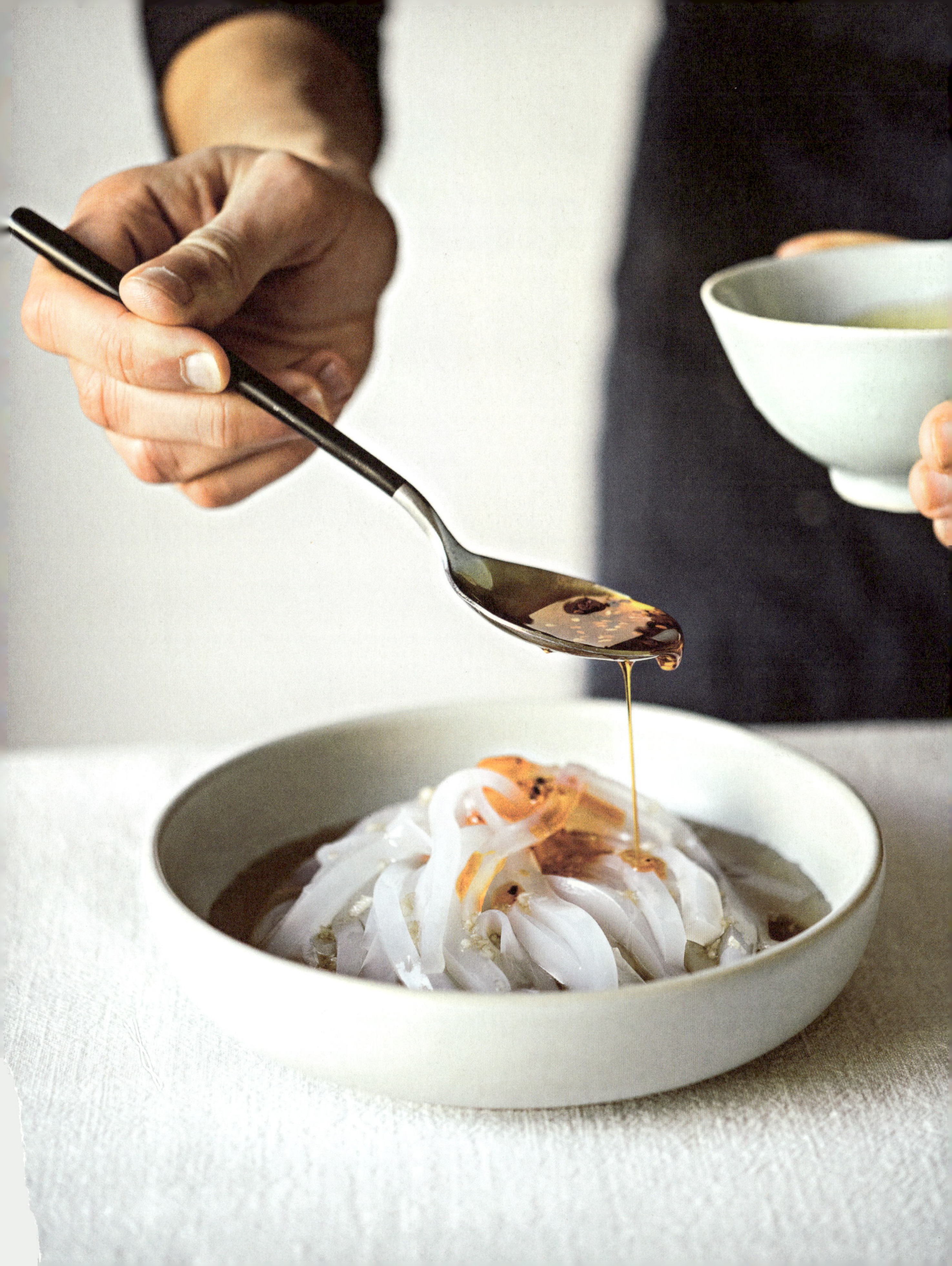

Liang Fen

LIÁNG FĚN

凉粉

PREPARING 4 HOURS

COOKING 10 MINUTES

MUNG BEAN JELLY IS A SUMMER SNACK FOUND IN MANY NORTHERN REGIONS. ITS TRANSLUCENT APPEARANCE AND SILKY TEXTURE ALWAYS AMAZE THOSE WHO TRY IT FOR THE FIRST TIME. THIS DISH IS SERVED FRESH, USUALLY WITH A TASTY AND SPICY SAUCE.

Serves 4 people

INGREDIENTS

For the *liang fen*

80g (3oz/scant ⅔ cup) mung bean flour
750ml (26oz/3 cups) water
½ tsp sodium carbonate (*optional; see note*)

For the sauce (per serving)

2 tbsp black rice vinegar
200ml (scant 1 cup) water
2 garlic cloves, chopped
1 tsp salt
1 tsp sesame oil
½ tsp sugar
Finely chopped spring onion (scallion)
Chilli oil, to taste (*see p. 36, or p. 342 for home-made*)

FOR THE LIANG FEN

- Mix the mung bean flour with 200ml (7oz/scant 1 cup) of the water. Heat the remaining 550ml (19oz/generous 2 cups) of water in a pot without bringing it to the boil, then add the sodium carbonate.

- Add the flour mixture into the pot over a low heat, keeping the temperature at around 50°C (122°F) – you should just see small bubbles at the bottom of the pot. The mixture will thicken (this is the gelatinization process). Mix regularly with a spatula for about 8–10 minutes until you obtain a white jelly without any small white chunks, which should be translucent and thick.

- Remove the jelly from the pot, transfer it to a container and allow to cool. The mixture will solidify, which makes it easy to unmould.

- Meanwhile, mix together the vinegar, water, garlic, salt, sesame oil and sugar for the sauce and set aside.

TO SERVE

- Cut the cooled jelly block into sticks, place into your serving bowls and mix with the sauce. Sprinkle with spring onion and add a drizzle of chilli oil, to taste, if you like. Store any leftovers in the fridge and eat within 48 hours.

GOOD TO KNOW
小提示

Sodium carbonate is an alkaline agent that increases the elasticity of the liang fen and limits the risk of it breaking. It can be made at home: spread a thin layer of bicarbonate of soda (baking soda) on a baking tray and bake for about 1 hour at 100°C (210°F).

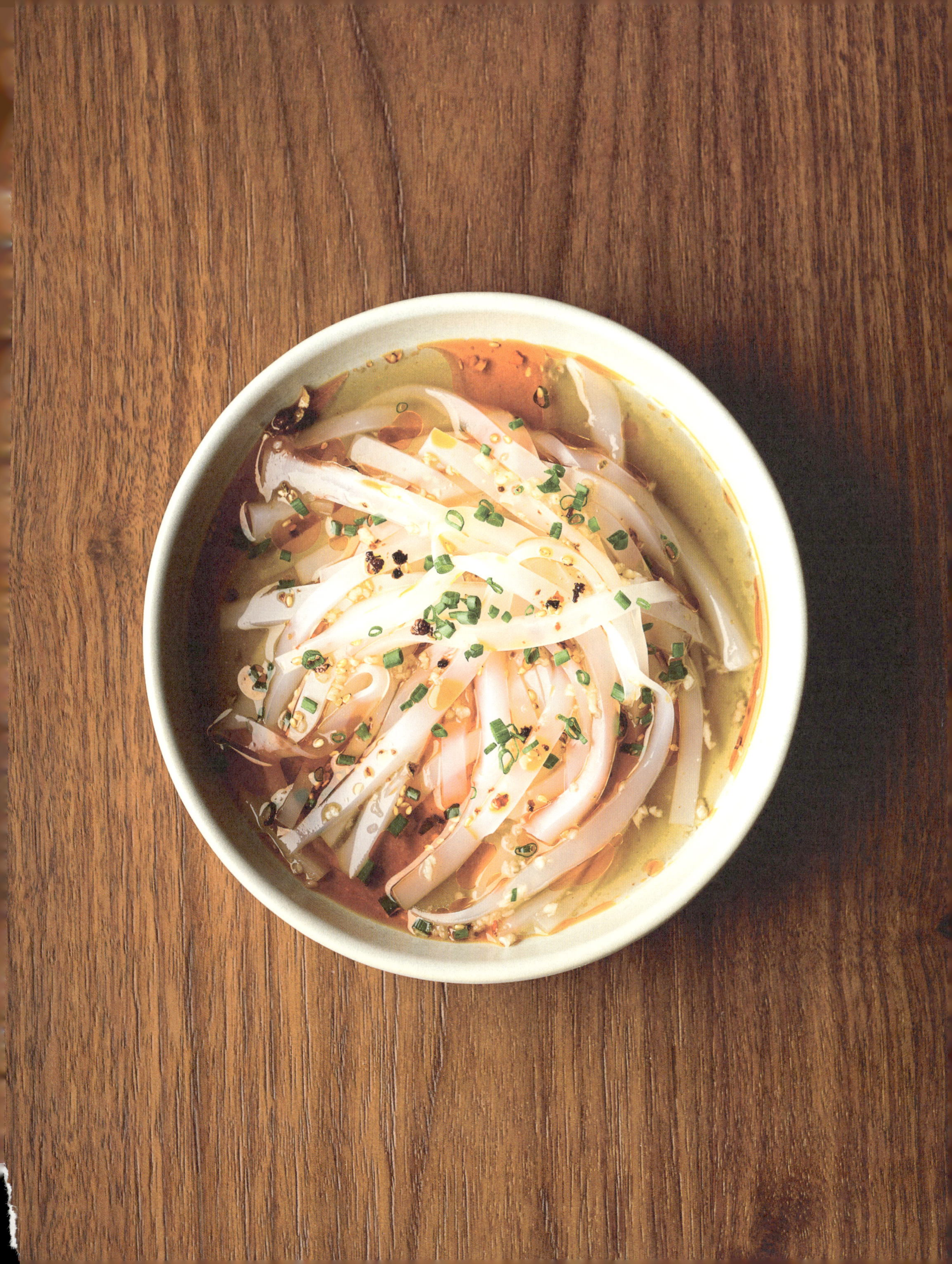

White Radish Cake

LUÓ BO GĀO

萝卜糕

PREPARING 75 MINUTES

COOKING 75 MINUTES

THIS SALTY "CAKE" MADE FROM WHITE RADISH IS ONE OF THE TRADITIONAL DISHES EATEN DURING CHINESE NEW YEAR IN GUANGDONG. MANY DRIED INGREDIENTS ARE ADDED TO CREATE A HIT OF UMAMI FLAVOUR IN VARIOUS LUXURIOUS FORMS: SHIITAKE, SCALLOPS, SHRIMP, HAM…

Serves 10 people

INGREDIENTS

700g (1lb 9oz) white radish, peeled and finely julienned with a mandoline
½ tbsp salt
2 dried shiitake mushrooms
20g (¾oz) dried shrimp
 (*xia mi*, see p. 32)
Neutral oil for frying and greasing
1 tbsp chopped red onion
80g (3oz) *char siu*, chopped
 (*see p. 198, optional*)
200g (7oz/1½ cups) rice flour
½ tsp soy sauce
½ tsp oyster sauce
¼ tsp white pepper
½ tsp sugar

FOR THE BATTER

- Disgorge the radish strips with the ½ tablespoon of salt for 15 minutes (see p. 83). Drain and discard the liquid, but you don't have to rinse the radish. Meanwhile, rehydrate the dried shiitake for 2 hours and the shrimp for 30 minutes, then chop into 5mm (¼in) cubes. Keep the soaking water.

- Heat ½ tablespoon of neutral oil in a frying pan over a medium heat. Fry the red onion, dried shrimp and *char siu* for about 1 minute to release their flavours. Add the shiitake and white radish and cook for 10 minutes over a low–medium heat to release the water contained in the radish.

- Mix 250ml (1 cup) of the shiitake and shrimp soaking water with the rice flour in a bowl, and pour this into the frying pan. Season with the soy sauce, oyster sauce, white pepper and sugar. Mix for about 2 minutes until you have a fairly dense batter.

TO STEAM THE "CAKE"

- Oil the bottom of a heatproof container (to fit your steamer basket) and line it with a sheet of baking paper. Transfer the batter mixture to the container and steam for about 1 hour. The exact cooking time will depend on the height of your "cake" (it is 6cm/2½in high in this example).

TO SERVE

- Allow the cake to cool, then unmould it and cut into small rectangular pieces, about 1cm (½in) thick. Heat 1 teaspoon of oil in a pan over a medium heat and brown the cake pieces for about 2 minutes on each side. This step is not mandatory, but it adds some crunchiness, which contrasts with the soft interior. Enjoy hot.

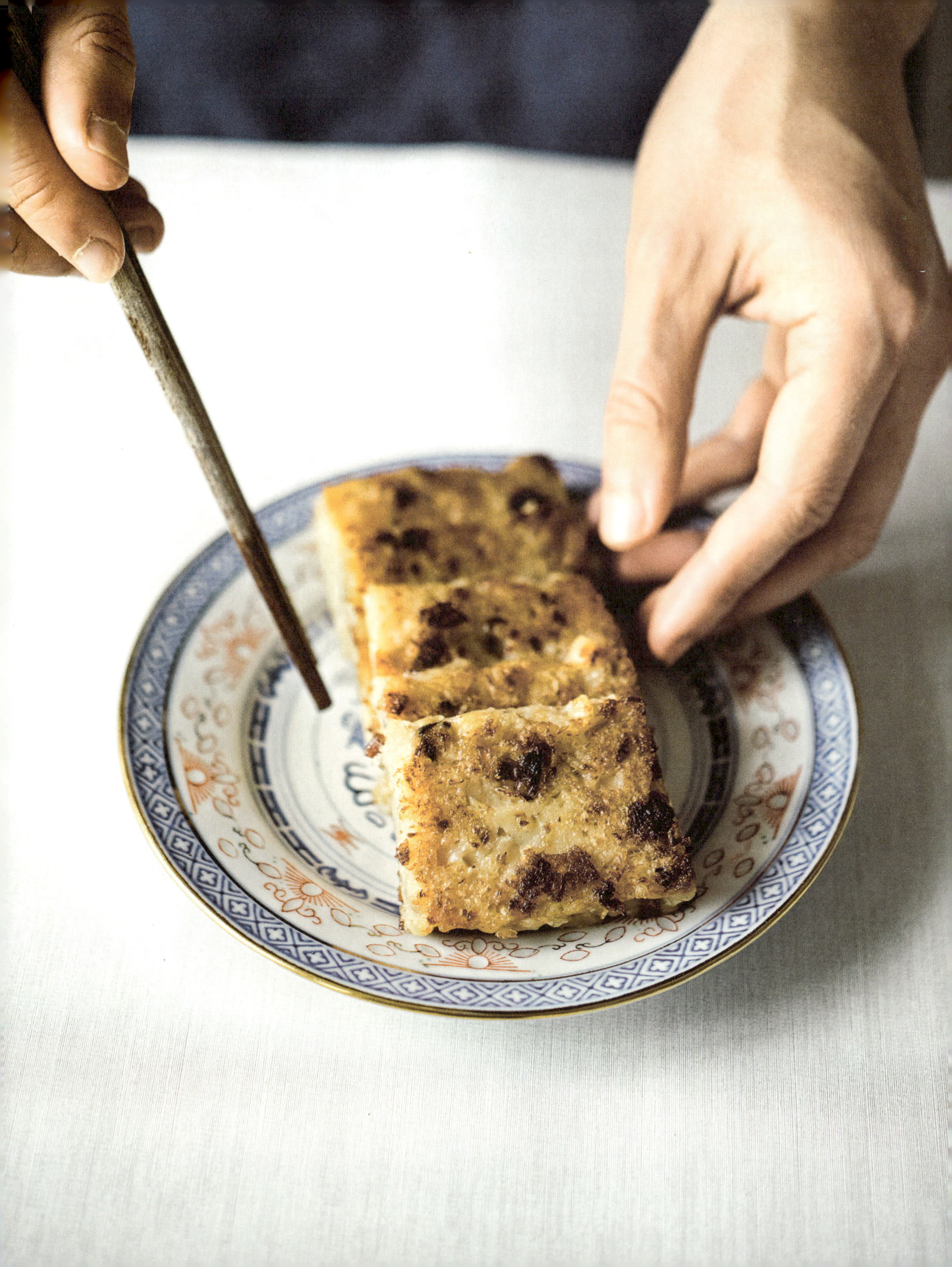

Strange–Tasting Peanuts

GUÀI   WÈI   HUĀ   SHĒNG

怪味花生

Preparing 5 minutes · *Cooking 15 minutes*

PEANUTS ARE THE DEFAULT SNACK IN CHINA. THEY ARE NIBBLES TO ENJOY ON THE TRAIN, AT THE TABLE TO ACCOMPANY A BEER OR WITH TEA. THIS CRISPY VERSION WITH A SWEET, SALTY, SPICY AND SMOKY TASTE (HENCE THE NAME "STRANGE", BECAUSE THE FLAVOUR IS COMPLEX) IS ONE OF MY FAVOURITES.

🍴 Serves 4 people

INGREDIENTS

For the peanuts

300g (10oz/2¼ cups) peanuts
1 egg yolk
30g (1oz/about ¼ cup) cornflour (cornstarch)
500ml (17oz/2 cups) oil

For the caramel

2 tbsp water
30g (1oz/2½ tbsp) sugar

For the spice mix

½ tsp chilli powder
½ tsp salt
½ tsp ground cumin
¼ tsp curry powder
¼ tsp ground cinnamon
½ tsp white sesame seeds

FOR THE PEANUTS

- In a bowl, mix the peanuts with the egg yolk, which should become slightly sticky. If you wash the nuts beforehand, remember to drain and dry them thoroughly before adding the egg.

- Stir in the cornflour in two batches, and shake well each time to distribute evenly. Put the peanuts in a fine sieve and gently shake to remove any excess flour; a thin layer is sufficient.

- Heat the oil in a wok over a medium heat to 160°C (320°F). Add the peanuts and fry for about 5 minutes. Do not touch them at first to allow a crust to form. Drain on plenty of kitchen paper and set aside. (You can filter the oil and reuse it.)

- Meanwhile, mix together all the ingredients for the spice mix and set aside.

FOR THE CARAMEL

- Pour the water and sugar into the (clean) wok to make a blond caramel. Start over a medium heat to let the water evaporate; large bubbles will appear, then smaller ones. The texture will become syrupy and the colour will begin to change. Switch to a low heat and monitor the colour. As soon as the caramel turns dark blond (just before it reaches the typical colour of a brown caramel), turn off the heat and add the peanuts and the spice mix. Shake to let the spiced caramel coat each peanut.

- Transfer to a plate and leave to cool, which will allow the peanuts to become even crisper.

GOOD TO KNOW
小提示

You can change the spice ratio or add others to taste. My preferred trio is chilli, salt and cumin. I adapt the rest according to what I have on hand.

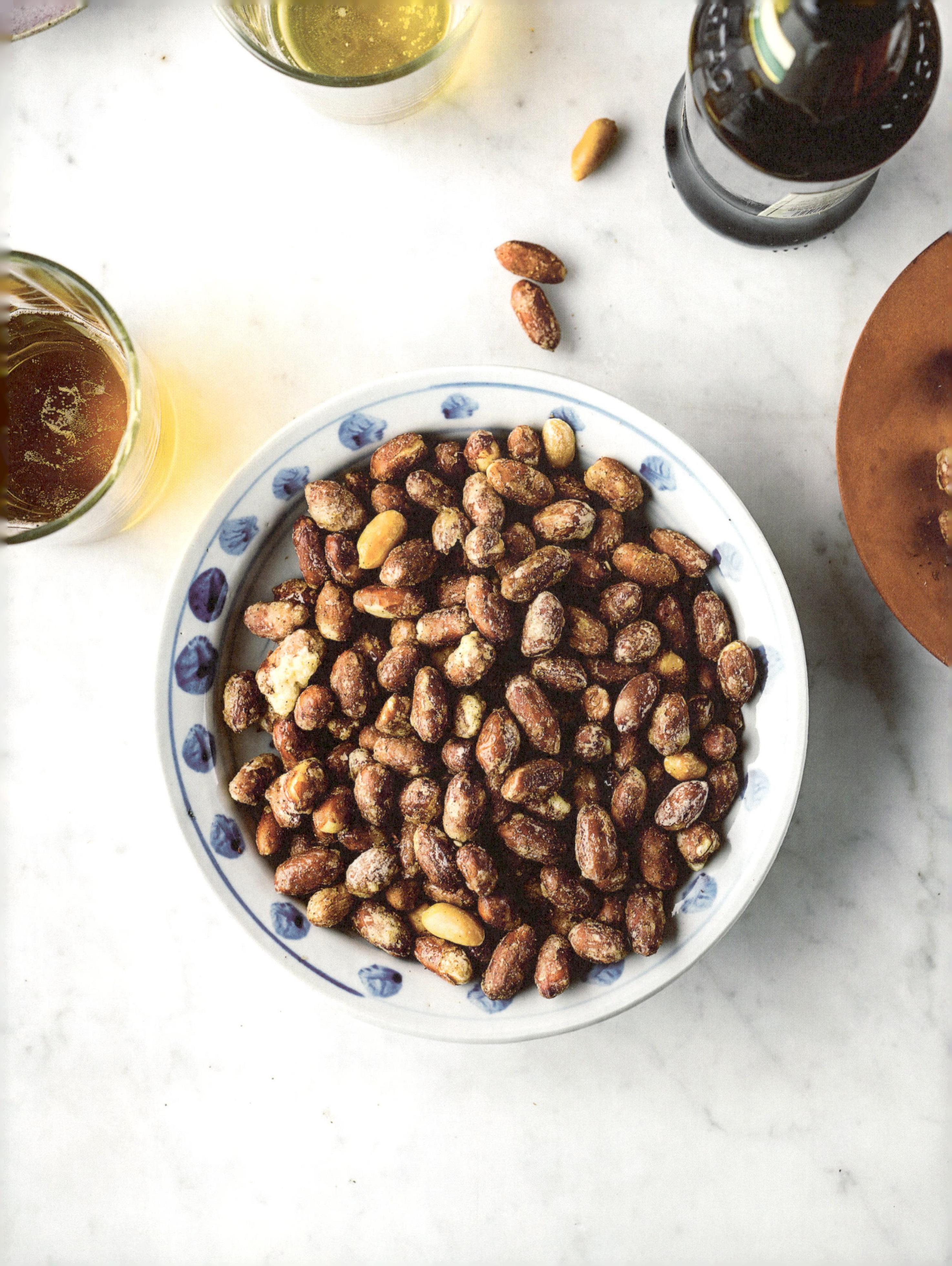

CHAPTER 14

Condiments

酱料

JIÀNG LIÀO

PP. 340–341: Spring onion oil ▪ **PP. 342–343:** Sichuan chilli oil ▪ **PP. 344–345:** Lard
PP. 346–347: Fermented black soy bean sauce ▪ **PP. 348–349:** Flavoured sweet soy sauce

From All Angles

It All Starts with a Good Sauce

JIANG IS ONE OF THE MOST COMMONLY USED WORDS IN CHINESE CUISINE. IT ORIGINALLY REFERRED TO CONDIMENTS MADE OUT OF FERMENTED SOY, WHICH INCLUDES SOY SAUCE. HOWEVER, THE WORD HAS COME TO BE A CATCH-ALL TERM FOR ALL TYPES OF SAUCES.

FAT, THE FOUNDATION OF A GOOD SAUCE

Chilli oil is ubiquitous in Chinese cuisine (see p. 36). In spite of this somewhat generic name (as each region has its own variant), the type we usually mean is Sichuan chilli oil.

It combines three things Chinese people like in a dish: the colour (色, *sè*), the fragrance (香, *xiāng*) and the taste (味, *wèi*). The oil is bright red and very aromatic, thanks to the infusion of a mixture of spices. The chilli pepper does not dominate the other flavours; the taste is quite complex. The original recipe combines three types of chilli pepper, each contributing to one of the desired characteristics.

Much like lard (see p. 344) and spring onion oil (see p. 340), chilli oil is used as a base to create a wide variety of sauces. You can mix it with black rice vinegar to make a typical dumpling sauce. You can also add sesame paste, which is already half the work needed to make dan dan noodle sauce. Other examples of its use can be found in the noodle sauce recipe section (see p. 246).

JIANG, AN IMPROVED VERSION

While it is technically possible to make soy sauce and other fermented soy pastes (see p. 346) at home, it isn't always worth it, as the process is long and tedious.

However, transforming these raw products to adapt them to taste is within everyone's reach.

Sweet soy sauce is a good example. Highly popular in some countries, it is pretty much unknown in China, where the term "salted soy sauce" would sound redundant. There is a sweet version in Sichuan (see p. 348), but it is relatively unknown in the rest of the country.

All the recipes in this chapter can be easily stored (in a closed jar, in the fridge), ready to use whenever a dish calls for something extra. For example, *douchi* sauce (p. 346) is one of my favourite condiments for stir-fried dishes, because it can add a salty, sweet and umami flavour all on its own.

GOOD TO KNOW
小提示

Jiang is everywhere. It is the sauce you add to noodles, the one in which you dip Chinese fondue ingredients, or the one that adds some umami flavour to a stir-fried dish.

ICONIC BRANDS

HENG SHUN
恒顺

Flagship product: Rice vinegar
Founded in 1840

Combine this with soy sauce and you will get the default dipping sauce in China.

JUAN CHENG
鹃城牌

Flagship product: Chilli bean paste (*doubanjiang*)
Founded in 1981

The soul of Sichuan cuisine and found in the famous *mapo tofu* recipe (see p. 126).

LAO GAN MA
老干妈

Flagship product: Chilli oil
Founded in 1996

The Spicy Chilli Crisp range is the most universal condiment in China (for rice, noodles, dumpling sauces, etc.).

WANG ZHI HE
王致和

Flagship product: Fermented tofu (*fu ru*)
Founded in 1669

This can be eaten as it is (with rice) or incorporated as an ingredient in a marinade.

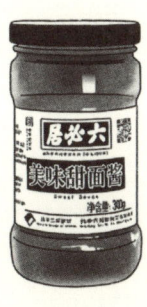

LIU BI JU
六必居

Flagship product: Fermented sweet bean paste (*tian mian jiang*)
Founded in 1530

The iconic sweet and savoury taste of the sauce goes perfectly with Peking duck.

LEE KUM KEE
李锦记

Flagship product: Oyster sauce
Founded in 1880

A must for stir-fried dishes in Cantonese cuisine and the secret ingredient for a delicious fried rice.

Spring Onion Oil

CŌNG YÓU
葱油

PREPARING 5 MINUTES · COOKING 25 MINUTES

SPRING ONION-INFUSED OIL IS VERY POPULAR IN SHANGHAI AND JIANGSU CUISINE. ITS INCREDIBLE FLAVOUR ENHANCES ANY DISH INSTANTLY. I USE IT TO MAKE NOODLE SAUCE (SEE P. 246), IN PANCAKES (SEE P. 318) OR AS A BASE FOR A CHILLI OIL (SEE P. 36).

Makes 300ml (1¼ cups)

INGREDIENTS

100g (3½oz) spring onions (scallions)
300ml (1¼ cups) neutral oil
50g (1¾oz) shallots, peeled and halved lengthways

RECIPE STEPS

- Wash the spring onions, then drain and dry with kitchen paper. Cut them into roughly 8cm (3in) long sticks, separating the white parts (including the root; nothing is thrown away) from the green.

- Heat a wok (or pan) over a medium heat and pour in the oil. When the temperature reaches 140°C (285°F), switch to a low heat and add the shallots and spring onion whites. Cook until lightly browned for about 10–15 minutes. Remember to monitor the temperature – do not let the onions burn, or your oil will taste bitter. If you don't have a thermometer, you can check the temperature with a piece of spring onion: if the onion floats with small bubbles around it, the temperature is about right.

- Once lightly browned, remove the shallot and spring onion white, and add the spring onion greens. Let them infuse in the oil for about 10 minutes, again until lightly browned.

TO STORE

- Filter the oil and store it in a sealed jar. It can be kept in the fridge for at least one month. It is possible to reuse the shallots and fried spring onions as a garnish; for example in noodles, fried rice or even a salad.

GOOD TO KNOW
小提示

You can use only spring onions if you wish to stay true to the original recipe. The oil to spring onion ratio is 2:1, so 100ml (3½oz) oil per 50g (1¾oz) spring onion.

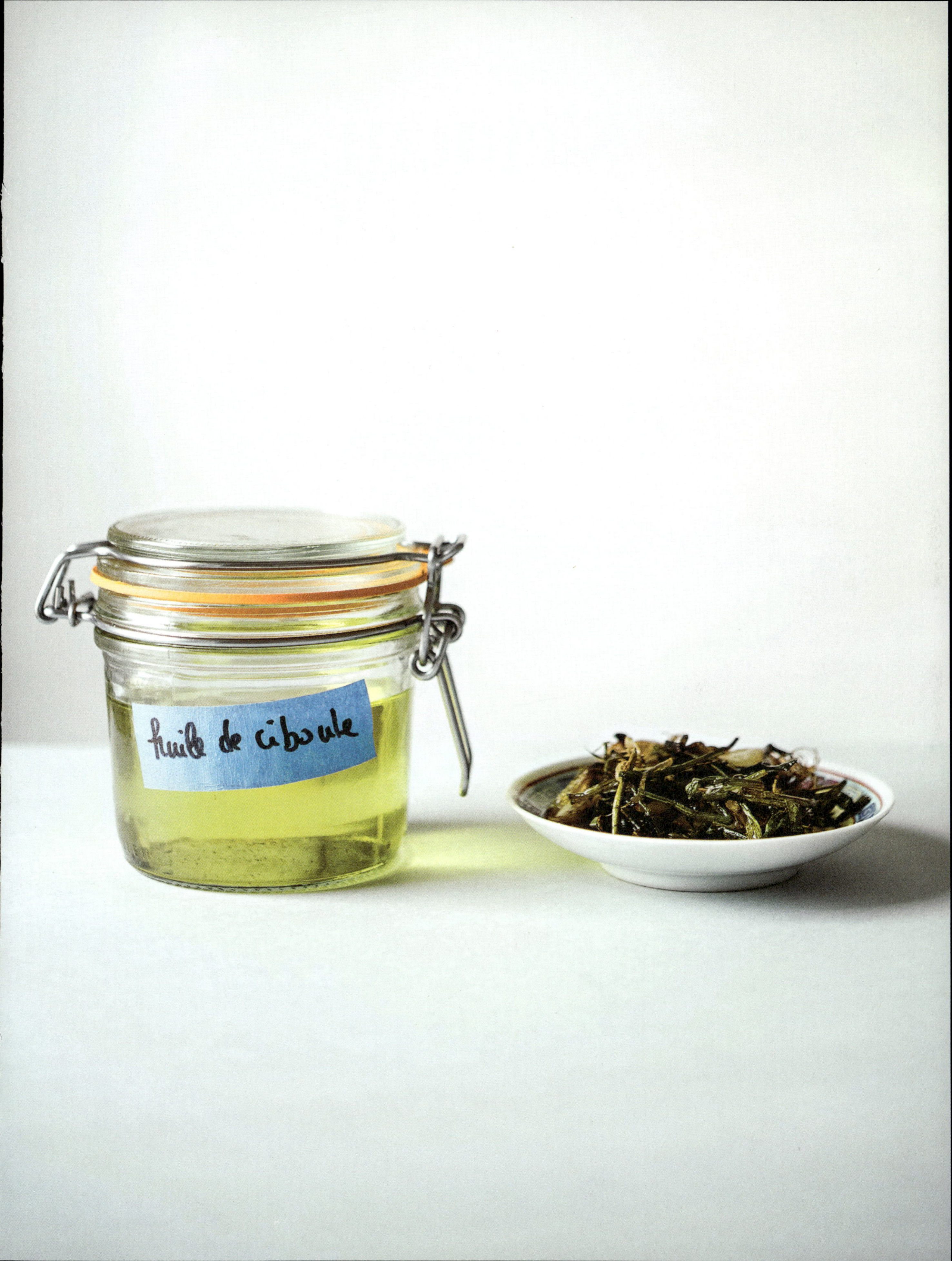
huile de ciboule

Sichuan Chilli Oil

SÌ CHUĀN LÀ YÓU

四川辣油

PREPARING 12 HOURS

COOKING 15 MINUTES

THIS OIL IS THE SOUL OF SICHUAN CUISINE. IT IS COMPLEX AND PARTICULARLY FLAVOURFUL, MUCH LIKE THE DIVERSITY OF SICHUAN CUISINE, WHICH ISN'T SIMPLY JUST SPICY.

Makes 400ml (1¾ cups)

INGREDIENTS

450ml (scant 2 cups) neutral oil
50g (1¾oz) spring onion (scallion) white, cut into short sticks
2 bay leaves
½ cinnamon stick
1 tbsp Sichuan peppercorn
1 star anise
40g (1½oz/⅓ cup) chilli powder (*see note*)
1 tbsp white sesame seeds

RECIPE STEPS

- Heat the oil in a small pot to 120°C (248°F). Add the spring onion white, bay leaves, cinnamon, Sichuan peppercorn and star anise. Infuse for about 15 minutes, until the spring onion sticks are browned (but don't let them burn). Remove the aromatics using a strainer or slotted spoon, then heat the oil to 160°C (320°F).

- In a heat-resistant bowl, mix the chilli powder (adjust the quantity to taste, but perhaps decrease it the first time) and the sesame seeds. Pour over the hot oil in 2 or 3 batches, to prevent it from overflowing. The heat should be high enough to make the chilli pepper "fizzle" without burning it. Mix well and let it cool.

STORING AND USAGE

- Transfer to a clean, dry jar and let it infuse for at least 12 hours before use. The oil should be stored at room temperature, but cooling it will extend its shelf life (at least 3 months, possibly much longer).

- A basic sauce usually consists of chilli oil, rice vinegar, soy sauce (or salt), some grated garlic and a bit of freshly ground Sichuan peppercorn.

GOOD TO KNOW
小提示

The choice of chilli pepper will impact the oil's taste and colour. Er jing tiao is the variant that is traditionally used in Sichuan, but it is difficult to find in other countries. Try asking your local Sichuan restaurant for some, as they often import them from China. Alternatively, you can replace it with Korean chilli powder (gochugaru), which will, however, be less fragrant.

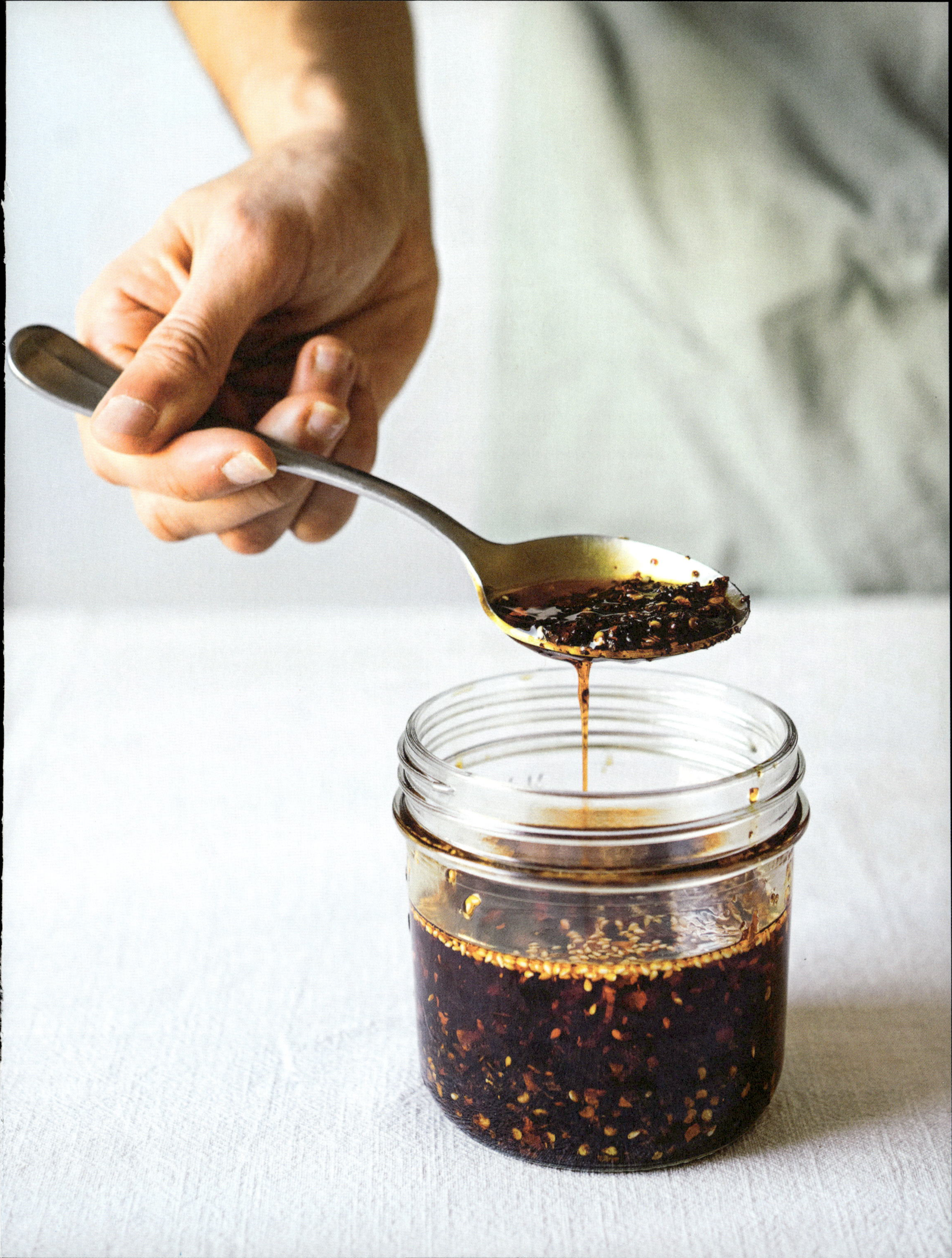

Lard

ZHŪ YÓU
猪油

PREPARING 6 HOURS • COOKING 75 MINUTES

PORK FAT WAS THE BASIC FAT IN CHINA FOR A LONG TIME, BOTH FOR STIR-FRIED DISHES AND FOR TRADITIONAL PASTRIES. NOWADAYS, VEGETABLE OILS ARE PREFERRED, AS THEY ARE CHEAPER AND EASIER TO PRESERVE. BUT ITS FLAVOUR REMAINS HIGHLY POPULAR IN MANY DISHES, SUCH AS, FOR EXAMPLE, A SIMPLE STIR-FRIED RICE WITH SOY SAUCE.

Makes 400g (14oz)

INGREDIENTS

500g (1lb 2oz) pork fat (see note)
100ml (6½ tbsp) water
A few ginger slices (optional)

RECIPE STEPS

• Cut the pork fat into 2–3cm (1in) cubes. Transfer them to a pot, add the water and bring to the boil over a medium heat. Water helps to distribute the heat better and prevents the pieces at the bottom from cooking too quickly at first.

• When the water has almost completely evaporated, switch to a low heat. At this point, the fat will start to turn into a yellow oil. It is important to maintain a low heat and stir occasionally to prevent the fat from burning, which will affect the colour and taste of the finished product. You can add a few ginger slices to neutralize any unpleasant smells.

• Scoop up some of the oil every 15 minutes with a ladle and pour into a bowl, which will allow the remaining fat to render into oil more easily. This will take between 40 minutes and 1 hour, until the fat browns and reduces by about two thirds of its volume.

• Let the oil cool, then transfer to a clean, dry jar. Keep the lard in the fridge for at least 1 month; it will turn white as it solidifies. You can extend its shelf life by adding a bit of salt while it is still liquid, or by transferring it to the freezer in ice-cube trays.

GOOD TO KNOW
小提示

Rindless pork loin fat is the most suitable type to make lard. You can also use belly fat, which is easier to find (remember to remove all the meat and rind), or leaf lard (the fat surrounding the pig's kidneys), which makes a more delicate lard, better suited to baking.

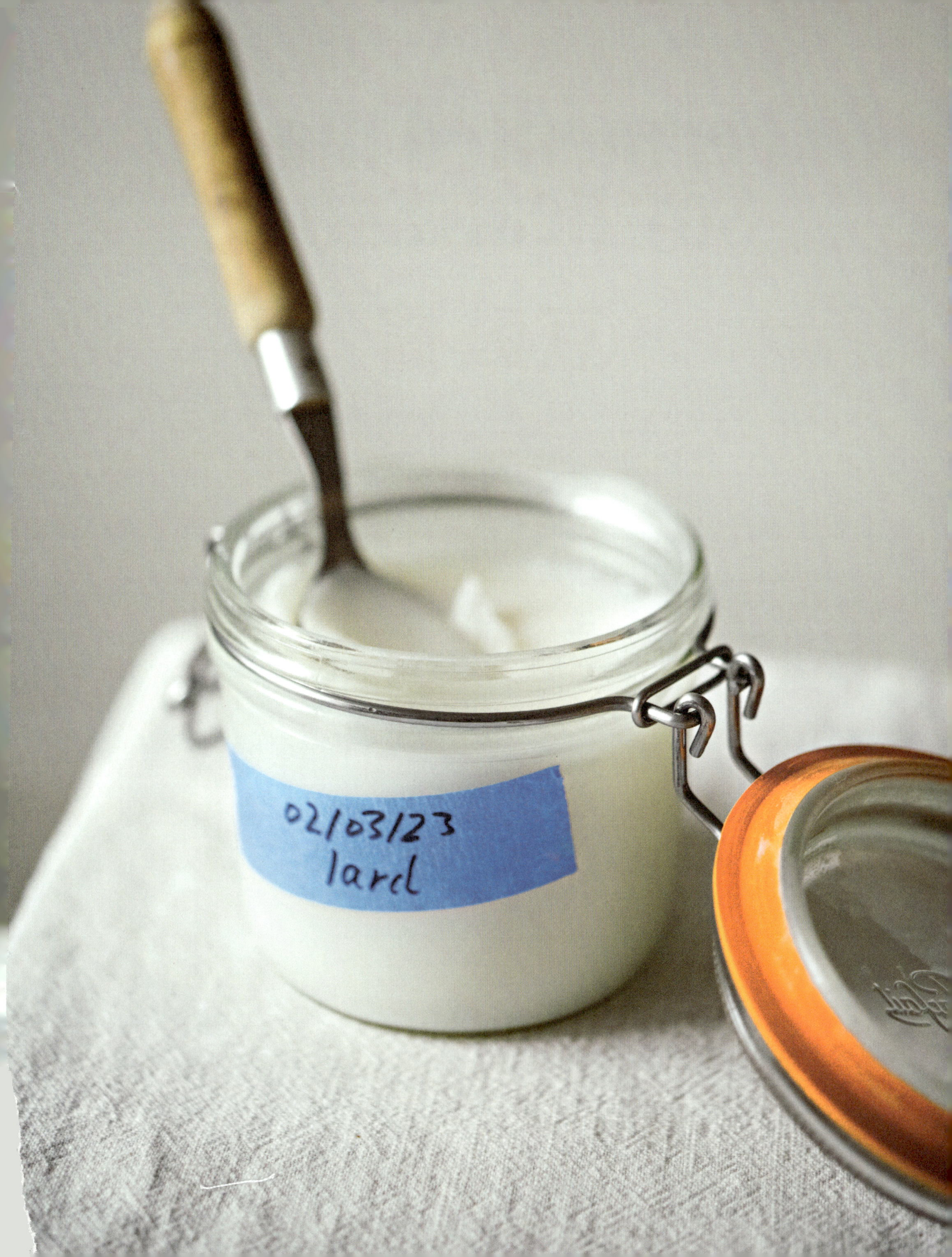
02/03/23
lard

Fermented Black Soy Bean Sauce

DÒU CHǏ JIÀNG

豆豉酱

Preparing 5 minutes · Cooking 20 minutes

I WOULD SAY THAT THIS SAUCE, MADE OUT OF FERMENTED BLACK SOY BEANS (*DOUCHI*, SEE P. 38), GARLIC AND SOY SAUCE, HAS THE POWER TO ENHANCE ANY DISH'S FLAVOUR. IT IS USED IN SOUTHERN CHINA AND ESPECIALLY IN GUANGDONG, MOST NOTABLY IN STIR-FRIED AND STEAMED DISHES.

Makes 300g (10oz)

INGREDIENTS

200g (7oz/1½ cups) fermented black soy beans (*douchi*)
3 tbsp neutral oil
1 spring onion (scallion) white (or 1 onion), minced
2 tbsp soy sauce
1 tbsp sugar
2 tbsp Shaoxing wine
2 tbsp chopped garlic
1 tsp chopped ginger

RECIPE STEPS

- Rinse the fermented black soy (*douchi*), drain, then coarsely chop with a knife, retaining some texture.

- Heat the oil in a pan over a medium heat. Add the spring onion white and the *douchi* and fry for about 2 minutes until the *douchi* absorbs the oil.

- Add the soy sauce, sugar and Shaoxing wine, and switch to a low heat. Simmer for 10 minutes, stirring regularly, to prevent the mixture from burning. Finally, add the garlic and ginger and continue cooking for 5 minutes. The *douchi* will release some of the oil that it has absorbed during this process.

- Transfer the sauce to a bowl and let it cool completely. You can keep it for at least 2 months in the fridge, in a closed jar.

GOOD TO KNOW
小提示

You can try this sauce (½–1 tablespoon) in most stir-fried dishes (vegetables, rice), but also in steamed dishes or even on your grilled meats. You could also add some finely chopped fresh chillies into the mix at the end, if you like.

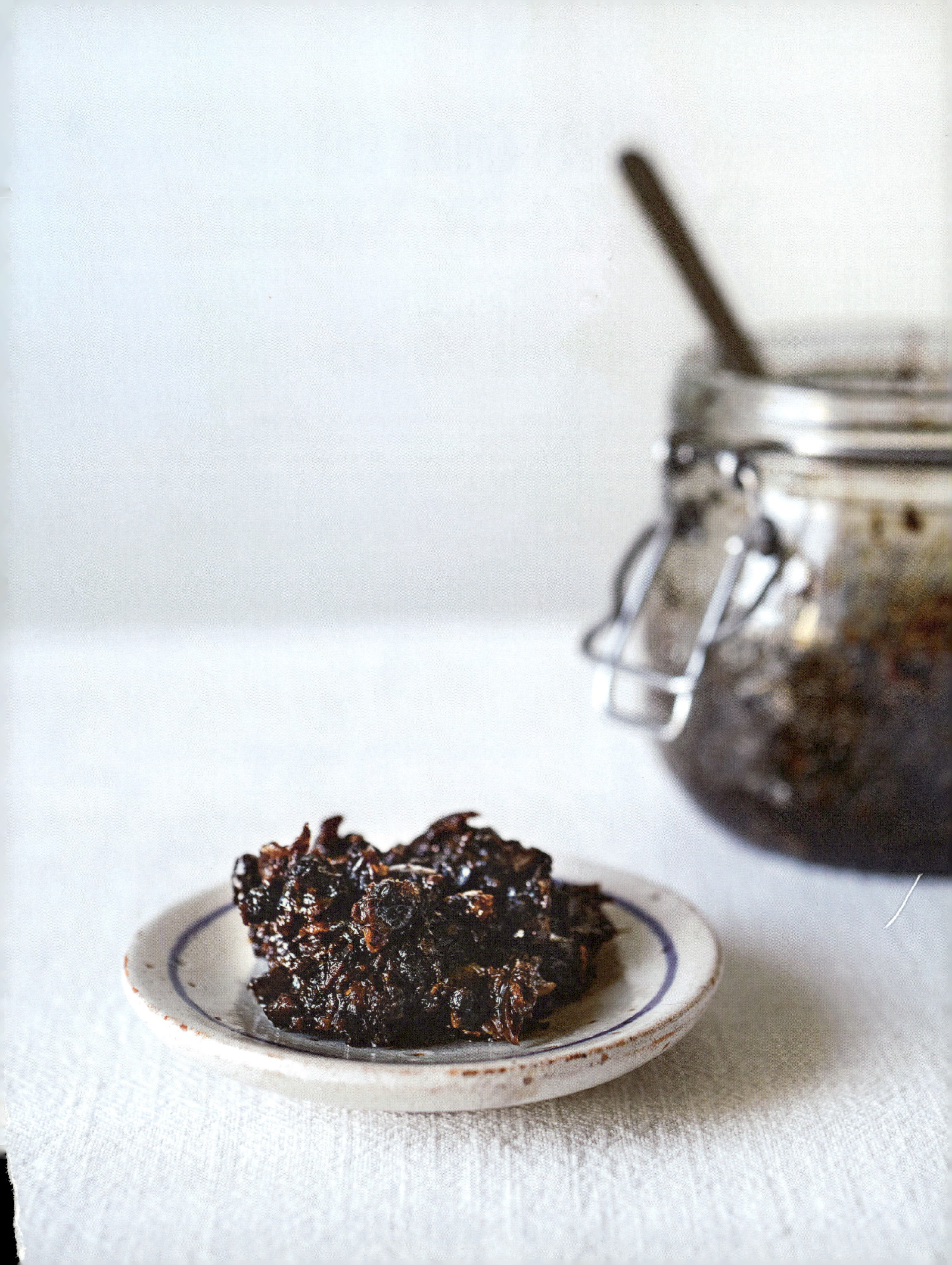

Flavoured Sweet Soy Sauce

FÙ ZHÌ JIÀNG YÓU

复制酱油

PREPARING 5 MINUTES

COOKING 30 MINUTES

THIS SOY SAUCE IS ONE OF SICHUAN CUISINE'S FLAGSHIP CONDIMENTS. IT IS A SIMPLE MATTER OF SIMMERING A GOOD SOY SAUCE OVER A LOW HEAT WITH SUGAR AND SPICES, WHICH ADDS AROMATIC COMPLEXITY. THERE ARE INFINITE VARIATIONS IN SICHUAN. FEEL FREE TO EXPERIMENT WITH OPTIONAL INGREDIENTS IF YOU HAVE SOME ON HAND.

Makes about 300ml (1¼ cups)

INGREDIENTS

450ml (scant 2 cups) soy sauce
150g (5½oz/¾ cup) brown sugar
80g (3oz) rock sugar (or use regular white sugar)
1 star anise
2 bay leaves
½ cinnamon stick
½ tsp fennel seeds
2 shiitake mushrooms (*optional*)
1 brown cardamom pod (*optional*)
1 slice of Chinese liquorice (*optional*)
2 cloves (*optional*)

RECIPE STEPS

▪ Pour the soy sauce and sugars into a small pot, then place all the spices and aromatics into a muslin (cheesecloth) bag and add the bag to the pot. Bring to the boil, then switch to a low heat and simmer for 30 minutes. The sauce should reduce by a third and have a slightly thick texture; it should cling to the back of a spoon.

▪ Allow to cool completely and remove the spice bag. Transfer the sauce to a clean jar, to be stored away from light and heat. If you don't use it often, place the sauce in the fridge, where it will keep for at least a year.

GOOD TO KNOW
小提示

Combine this sweet soy sauce with chilli oil (see p. 342) to make one of Sichuan's most irresistible sauces, found in dishes like zhong dumplings (see p. 268).

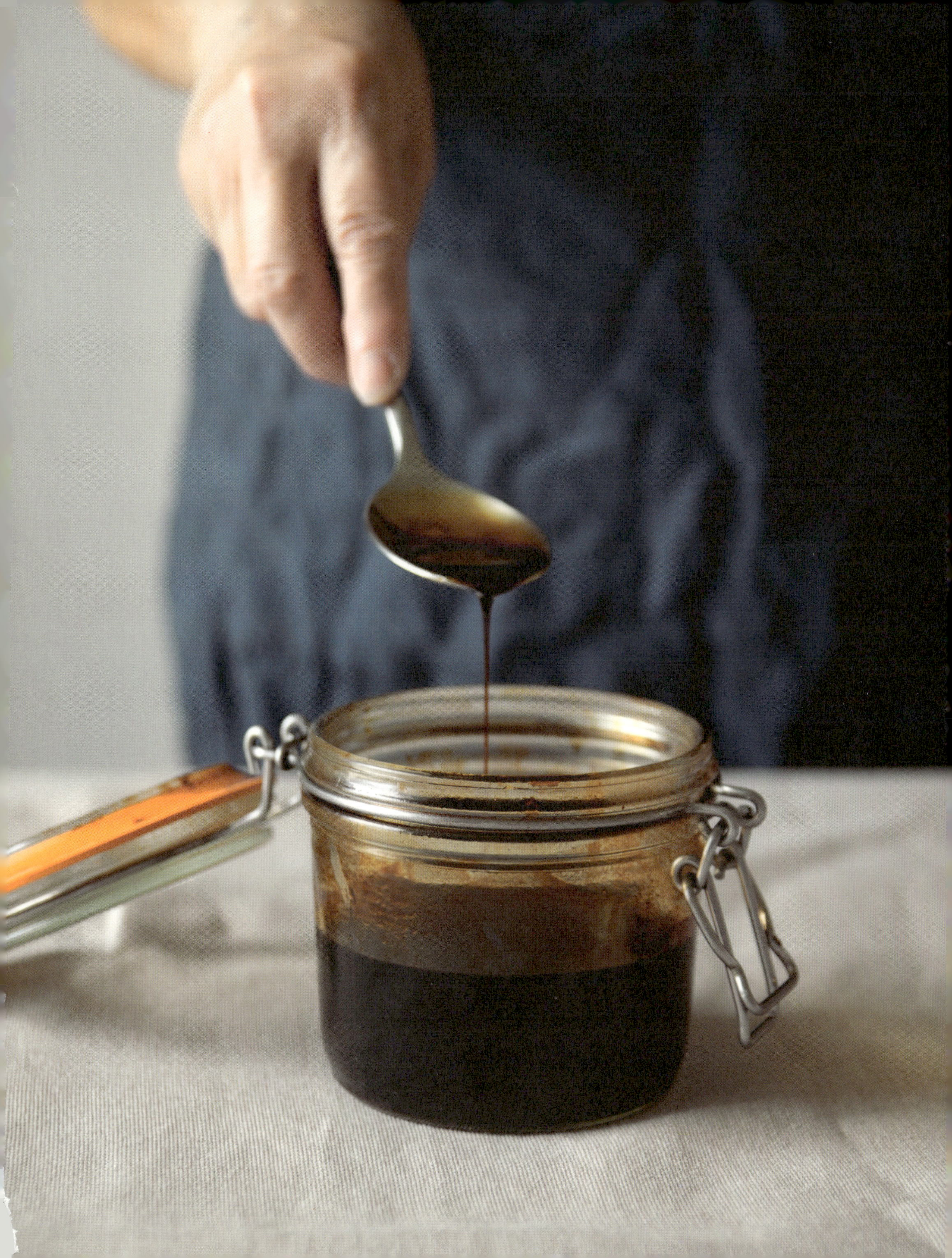

CHAPTER 15

Sweets
甜品
TIÁN PIN

PP. 354–355: Pumpkin sticky rice cakes ▪ **PP. 356–357**: Pear and white mushroom soup
PP. 358–359: Sticky rice with brown sugar ▪ **PP. 360–361**: Red mung bean soup ▪ **PP. 362–363**: Pineapple cakes
PP. 364–365: "Pineapple" brioche ▪ **PP. 366–367**: Tang yuan with black sesame ▪ **PP. 368–369**: Honey candied kumquats
PP. 370–371: Pomelo mango sago

From All Angles

More than a Simple Dessert

IN CHINA, THE CONCEPT OF DESSERT DOES NOT REALLY EXIST.
A MEAL USUALLY ENDS WITH SOME SEASONAL FRUITS. BUT THAT DOESN'T MEAN
THAT SWEETS DON'T HAVE A PLACE IN CHINESE CUISINE – FAR FROM IT.

A HISTORY OF TEA

In China, sweets are historically associated with the centuries-old tea culture. In tea houses (茶楼, *chá lóu*), a proper sweet dish is served with the drink to help to balance the bitterness.

They serve small pastries which are pleasant to look at, and which, of course, match the type of tea, just like pairing food with the proper wine.

The famous *dim sum* meals, which feature small sweet or savoury dishes served in steamer baskets, were first created to accompany tea towards the end of the 19th century in Guangdong (see p. 10).

HYBRID PASTRIES

While many countries are known for their sweet pastries, China has a preference for savoury dishes. Most Western pastries are too sweet or too "heavy" for the Chinese palate.

A lighter, fresher sweet touch is much preferred, especially at the end of a meal, where the dessert is often a fruit plate by default. However, there is a classic sweet, often presented as a puff pastry (酥, *su*) with a fairly substantial texture, which is made with lard instead of butter.

The popularity of Western pastries, which first came to territories such as Hong Kong, Macau and Shanghai, led to some interesting hybrid recipes, such as the "pineapple" brioche (p. 364), pineapple cake (p. 362) or *pastéis de nata*, a legacy of the Portuguese colonization of Macau that was later popularized by KFC.

STICKY RICE AND "SWEET SOUPS"

Let's start by mentioning all the dishes made with sticky rice flour, very popular when you're looking for a soft and sticky texture: *tang yuan* (see p. 366), sticky rice balls filled with black sesame, served as a soup during the lantern festival, or *ludagun*, the famous Peking snack made with sticky rice paste filled with red mung bean paste. Its strange name (literally "the rolling donkey") refers to the dark beige roasted soy powder that covers the whole exterior.

In a more liquid form, we can mention "sweet soups" (糖水, *táng shuǐ*), particularly popular in Guangdong. Served hot or cold depending on the season, they are drunk as much as they are eaten. The ingredients vary greatly (fruits, mung beans, medicinal herbs...) and often have a therapeutic effect. Red mung bean soup, for example (see p. 360), is supposed to calm your "inner fire" on hot days.

GOOD TO KNOW
小提示

The recipes in this chapter are just a sample of the different forms of sweet food you will find in China. Some will be served as a dessert, others as a snack.

SWEETS + TEA

PASTRIES
点心 | DIǎN XĪN

THE DEFAULT "DESSERT"

FRUIT PLATE
水果盘 | SHUǏ GUǑ PÁN

SWEETS AS A SNACK

LU DA GUN
驴打滚 | LÚ DǍ GǓN

PASTÉIS DE NATA
蛋挞 | DÀN TÀ

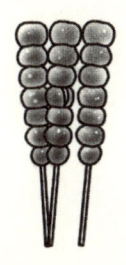

HAWTHORN SKEWER
冰糖葫芦 | BĪNG TÁNG HÚ LU

SWEET SOUP
糖水 | TÁNG SHUǏ

Pumpkin Sticky Rice Cakes

NÁN GUĀ BǏNG

南瓜饼

PREPARING 15 MINUTES

COOKING 20 MINUTES

I ASSOCIATE THESE SLIGHTLY CRISPY CAKES WITH A VERY SOFT INTERIOR WITH THE END OF A LARGE MEAL, JUST BEFORE THE FRUITS ARE SERVED. STICKY RICE FLOUR GIVES IT ITS TYPICAL ELASTIC TEXTURE, AND THE PUMPKIN ADDS A NATURALLY SWEET FLAVOUR.

🍴 Makes 8 cakes

INGREDIENTS

200g (7oz) pumpkin flesh, cut into small pieces
150g (5½oz/scant 1¼ cups) sticky rice flour, plus extra if needed
50g (1¾oz/¼ cup) sugar
4 tbsp breadcrumbs
200ml (7oz/scant 1 cup) neutral oil, for frying

FOR THE PUMPKIN

- Steam the pumpkin for 15 minutes, until the flesh is tender, then mash with a fork to make a purée.

FOR THE DOUGH

- In a bowl, mix the sticky rice flour and sugar, then add the pumpkin purée and knead to mix well until you have a slightly sticky ball of dough. If it's too sticky, add a little more rice flour (start with 1 teaspoon) until you reach the desired texture.

- Turn the dough out onto the countertop and roll it into a ball, then divide it into 8 pieces of about 40g (1½oz) each. Form these into little balls, then lightly flatten them with the palm of your hand. Dunk them one by one in the breadcrumbs to coat.

TO COOK

- Heat a wok or frying pan over a medium heat and add the oil. When the temperature of the oil reaches 170°C/325°F (you can test this with a few breadcrumbs – if small bubbles form around them immediately, and the crumbs don't burn, the oil is ready), add the cakes – the oil should come halfway up the sides of the cakes. Fry for about 2 minutes on each side, until golden.

- Transfer the cakes to a plate lined with kitchen paper and let them cool for a few minutes before enjoying them while they are still hot.

GOOD TO KNOW
小提示

You can replace the pumpkin with winter squash, if you prefer, and you can also add extra fillings and flavours of your choice, such as black sesame or azuki bean paste.

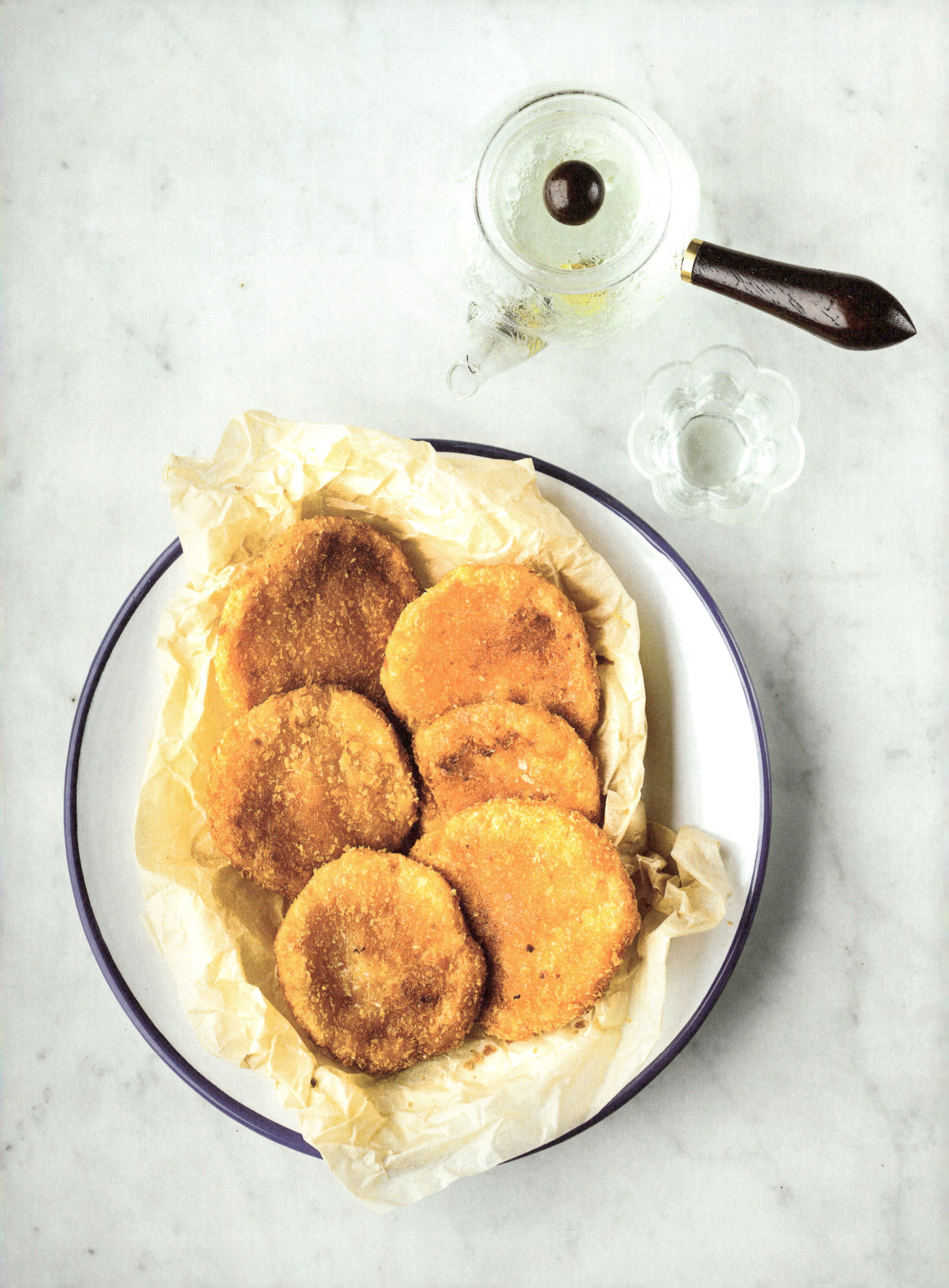

Pear and White Mushroom Soup

XIĂO　DIÀO　LÍ　TĀNG

小吊梨汤

PREPARING 35 MINUTES

COOKING 40 MINUTES

THIS PEAR SOUP IS VERY POPULAR IN WINTER IN NORTHERN CHINA (ESPECIALLY IN BEIJING). ACCORDING TO TRADITIONAL CHINESE MEDICINE, IT RELIEVES DRY THROATS AND MOISTENS THE LUNGS. IT ALSO SERVES AS AN INTRODUCTION TO THE WORLD OF *TANG SHUI* (糖水), WHICH ARE SWEET SOUPS SERVED ON THEIR OWN OR AT THE END OF A MEAL.

Serves 4 people

INGREDIENTS

20g (¾oz) white mushrooms (*see note*)
800ml (3½ cups) water
1 nashi pear, about 250g (9oz), washed, peeled and cut into 4cm (1½in) pieces
30g (1oz) rock sugar
3 salted dried plums (*huamei, optional*)
A handful of goji berries (*optional*)

RECIPE STEPS

▪ Rehydrate the white mushrooms for about 30 minutes, then drain and shred them by hand into small pieces of about 2–3cm (1in). Bring the fresh water to the boil in a pot, then switch to a low heat, add the white mushrooms and simmer for 30 minutes until they soften.

▪ Add the pieces of pear to the pot along with the sugar, and the dried plums if using. (You can also add the nashi peels and core for extra flavour, but if you do, place them in a muslin/cheesecloth bag in order to remove them easily.) Continue cooking for another 10 minutes.

▪ Remove the bag (if using) and add the goji berries. This soup can be eaten hot or cold.

GOOD TO KNOW
小提示

The white mushroom (Tremella fuciformis, or yin er in Chinese, literally "silver ears") turns slightly yellow as it dries. This form is what can be found in Chinese supermarkets. Despite its neutral taste, it is popular in China for its gelatinous texture and medicinal properties.

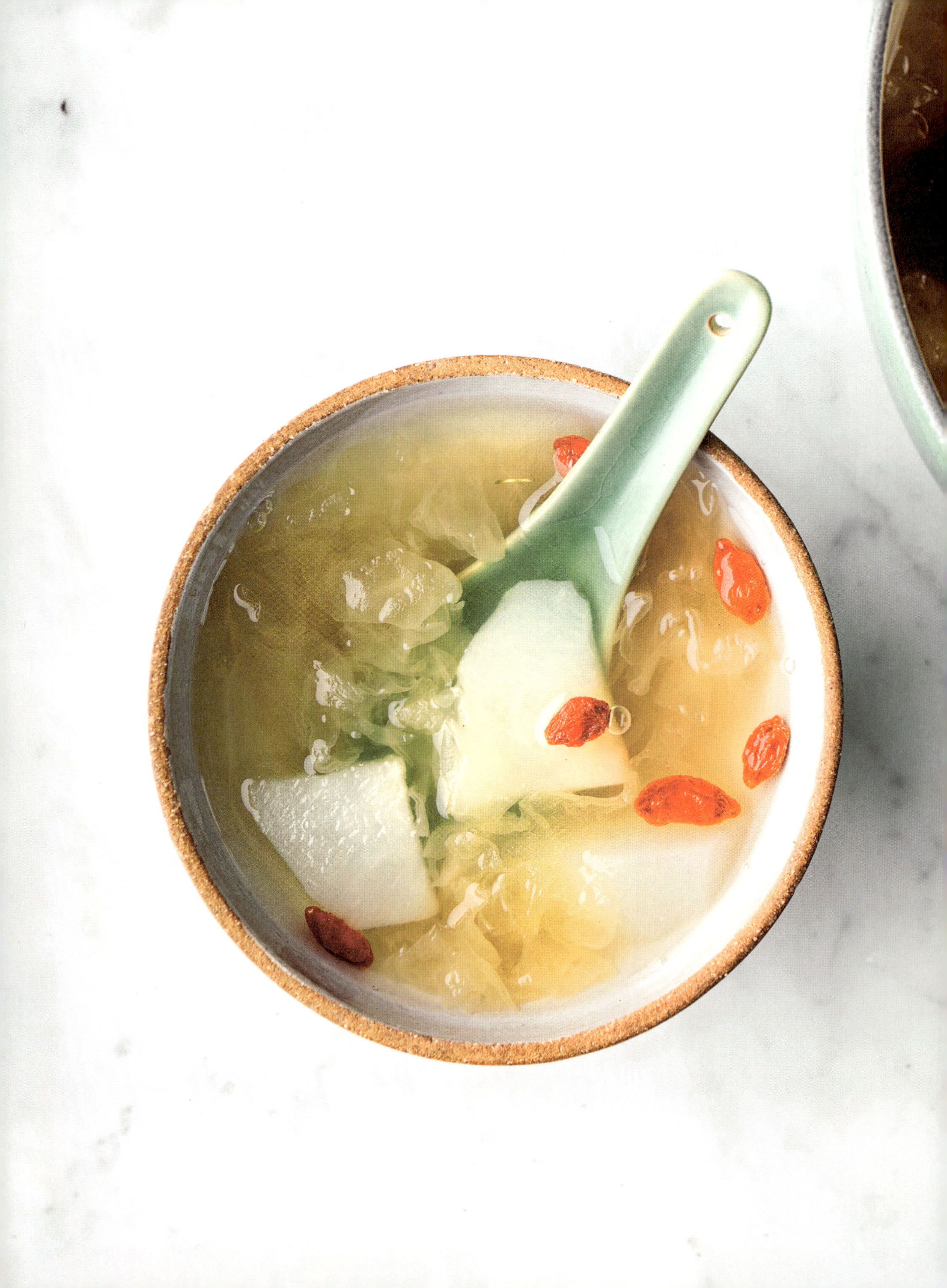

Sticky Rice with Brown Sugar

HÓNG　TÁNG　CÍ　BĀ

红糖糍粑

PREPARING 10 MINUTES

COOKING 35 MINUTES

CIBA (PRONOUNCED "TSI BA") IS A STICKY RICE SNACK FOUND IN ALMOST ALL REGIONS OF SOUTHERN AND SOUTH-EASTERN CHINA. THE VERSION SHOWN HERE IS POPULAR IN CHONGQING, WHERE IT IS AN ESSENTIAL PART OF CHINESE FONDUES, ANOTHER SPECIALITY OF THE REGION.

🍴 Makes about 20 *ciba*

INGREDIENTS

For the sticky rice

1 tbsp neutral oil
250ml (1 cup) water
130g (4½oz/1 cup) sticky rice flour
30g (1oz/¼ cup) cornflour (cornstarch)
30g (1oz/¼ cup) roasted soy powder

For the sugar syrup

50g (¼ cup) brown sugar
100ml (6½ tbsp) water

RECIPE STEPS

- In a bowl, mix the oil with the water, then add the sticky rice flour and cornflour. Mix until you obtain a fairly liquid paste, then transfer to a dish and steam for 30 minutes over a medium heat.

- After steaming, the warm dough becomes sticky and very malleable. Mix it with a spatula for 1 minute, which will make the dough a little more elastic.

- Divide the dough with a pair of scissors or a knife to make small balls roughly 20g (¾oz) each. Put the roasted soy powder on a plate and roll the balls around on the plate to coat them evenly in the powder. Your *ciba* are done.

- For the sugar syrup, pour the brown sugar and water into a small pan and cook over a low heat until you have a syrup (more or less liquid, to taste). Transfer to a small bowl.

- Enjoy the *ciba* drizzled with a little syrup.

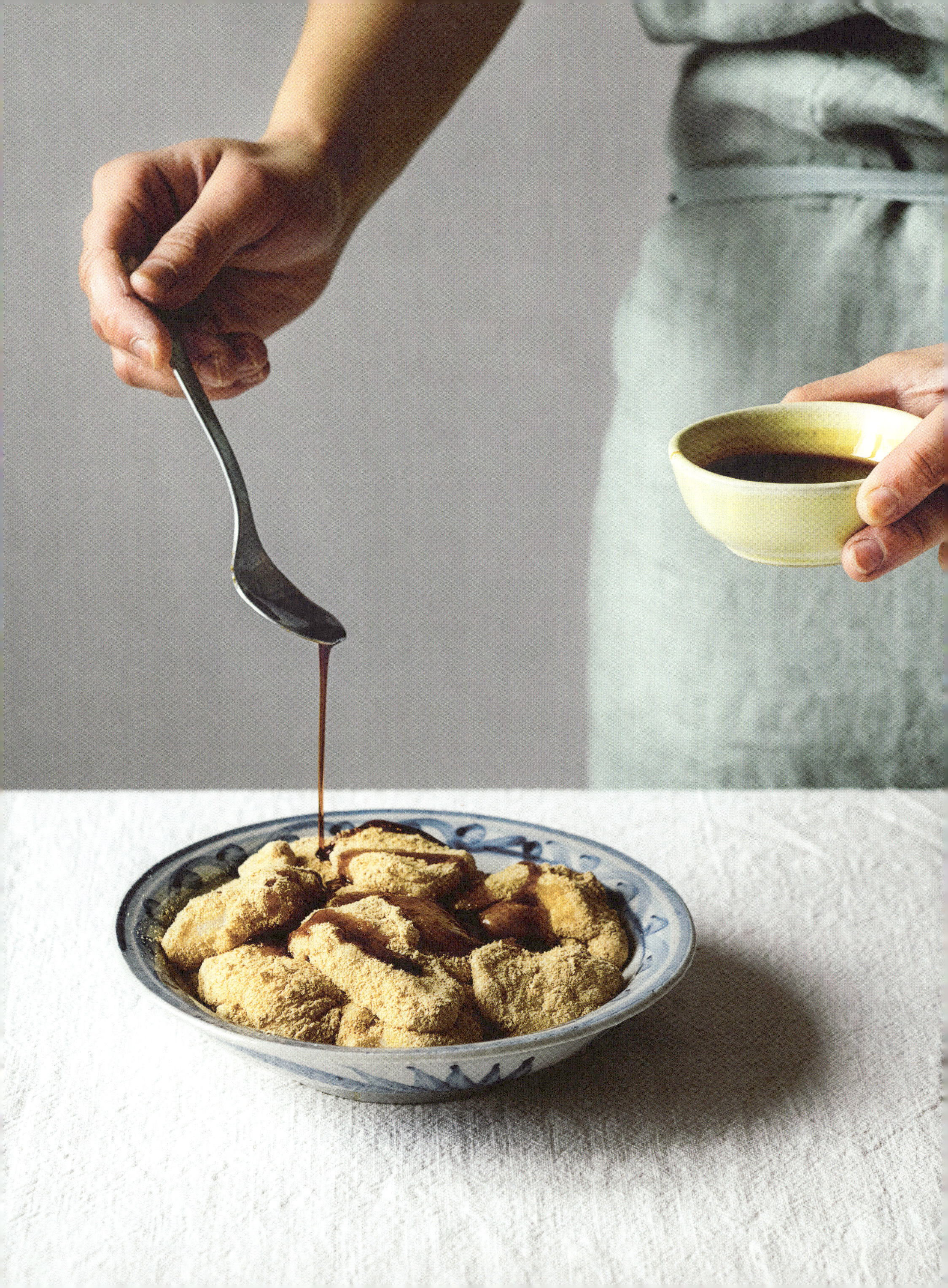

Red Mung Bean Soup

HÓNG   DÒU   BĪNG

红豆冰

PREPARING 12 HOURS

COOKING 50 MINUTES

IN CHINESE CUISINE, RED MUNG BEANS (ALSO CALLED AZUKI BEANS) ARE OFTEN USED IN SWEET DISHES. THIS SUMMER SOUP REMINDS ME OF MY CHILDHOOD YEARS IN WENZHOU, ALBEIT A SLIGHTLY DIFFERENT VERSION; WE WOULD USE GREEN MUNG BEANS, AND NO COCONUT MILK.

Serves 6 people

INGREDIENTS

200g (7oz/generous 1 cup) red mung (azuki) beans
2 litres (8½ cups) water
Sugar, to taste
400ml (1¾ cups) coconut milk, to serve

RECIPE STEPS

- Wash the red mung beans, then transfer them to a freezer-proof container and fill with cold water to cover. Freeze overnight (this will reduce the cooking time).

- Bring the 2 litres (8½ cups) water to the boil in a pot and add the frozen mung beans. Cover and cook for 50–60 minutes over a medium heat until the mung beans soften and the grains "pop" slightly (in Chinese, we say that the grains have "flowered"). If they haven't popped, cook for a bit longer.

- Once the beans are ready, add sugar to taste, mix and leave to cool.

- To serve, add a portion of mung beans to the bottom of a glass, top up with some of the liquid, then add plenty of ice, and finally a dash of coconut milk – a good few tablespoons per person.

GOOD TO KNOW
小提示

Red mung beans are naturally sweet, which explains why they are often found in East Asian desserts. If you have a pressure cooker, you can reduce the cooking time by half.

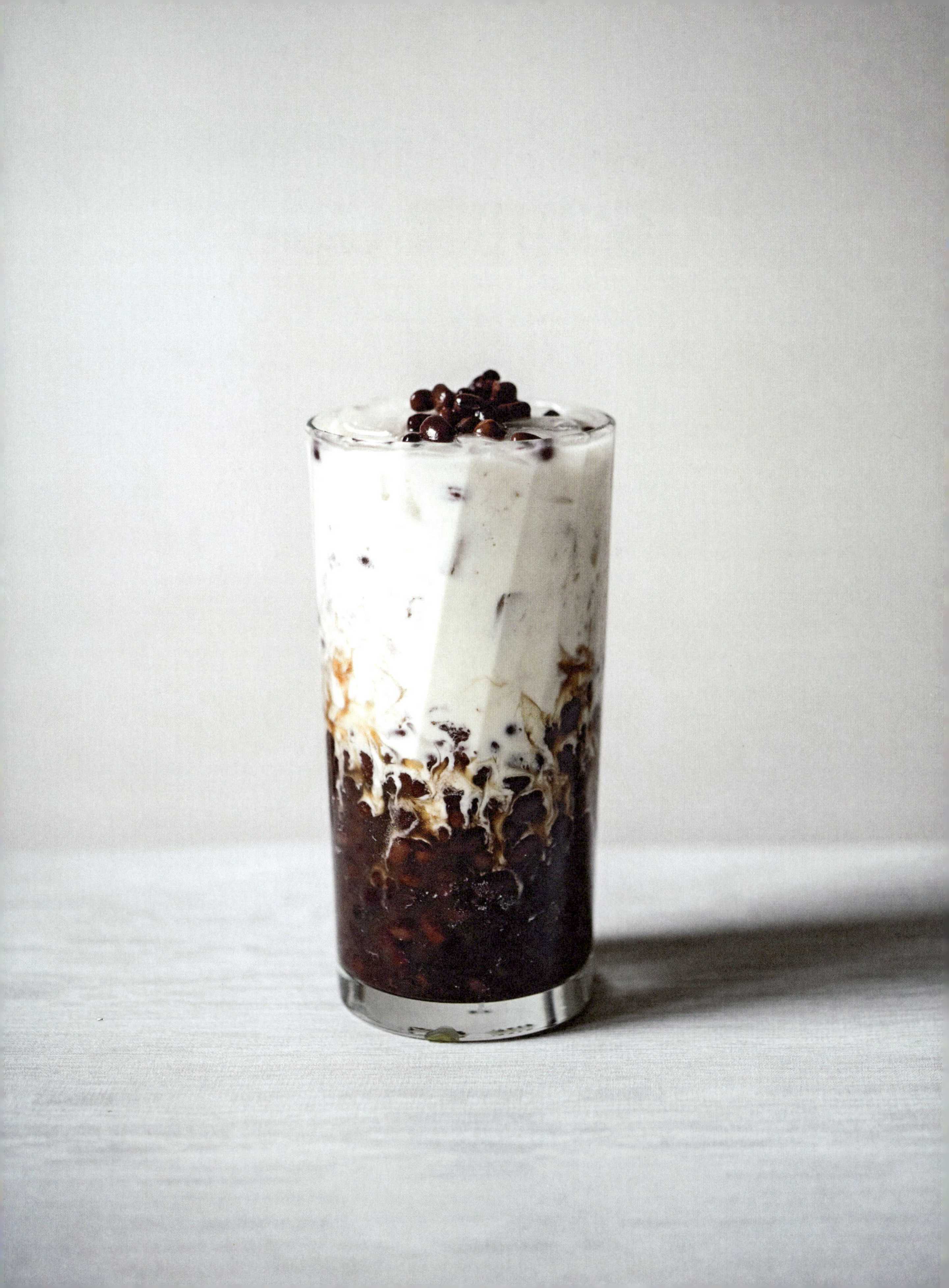

Pineapple Cakes

FÈNG LÍ SŪ

凤梨酥

PREPARING 40 MINUTES + RESTING TIME

COOKING 35 MINUTES

THESE BISCUITS, WITH THEIR SHORTBREAD TEXTURE AND PINEAPPLE CORE, ARE ICONIC IN TAIWANESE CUISINE. THE ISLAND IS FAMOUS FOR THIS FRUIT, WHICH WAS INTRODUCED IN THE 18TH CENTURY. IT IS KNOWN LOCALLY AS *FENG LI*, UNLIKE IN THE REST OF THE SINOPHONE WORLD, WHERE IT IS CALLED *BO LUO*.

Makes about 18 cakes

INGREDIENTS

For the dough

125g (4½oz/scant 1 cup) T45 flour (00 flour)
25g (1oz/scant ¼ cup) milk powder
125g (4½oz/1 stick plus 1 tbsp) butter, slightly softened
1 egg yolk
20g (¾oz/2¼ tbsp) icing (powdered) sugar

For the filling

750g (1lb 10oz) fresh pineapple (or use canned), finely chopped
80g (3oz/6½ tbsp) sugar
40g (1½oz) maltose (or 20g/¾oz honey)

FOR THE DOUGH

- Sift the flour and milk powder together into bowl to obtain a very fine powder.

- In a large bowl, beat the butter with an electric mixer for 2–3 minutes until smooth. Pour in the egg yolk and icing sugar and continue beating to mix well. Set the mixer to minimum speed and gradually add the flour and milk powder, mixing until the flour is no longer visible. Wrap the dough in film (plastic wrap) and leave to rest in the fridge for 30 minutes.

FOR THE FILLING

- Put the pineapple into a frying pan, add the sugar and heat over a medium heat, stirring regularly so that the water in the pineapple evaporates. Once the mixture becomes slightly sticky, stir in the maltose (or honey, which is sweeter), then switch to a low heat and continue cooking until the filling is slightly caramelized, like pineapple jam, but not too brown. Remove from the heat and leave to cool, then divide into portions of about 15g (½oz) and place in the fridge for 30 minutes.

TO ASSEMBLE

- Shape the chilled filling portions into small balls and place half of them on a plate (keep the other half in the fridge to prevent them from softening too much). Remove the dough from the fridge – it should be soft but not sticky – and form it into a roll, then divide it into portions of about 18g (¾oz).

- Roll a dough portion in your hands to make a ball and make a hole in the centre big enough to accommodate a portion of filling. Add a filling ball to the hole, close up and re-roll (see the sweet bao technique, p. 282), then press lightly to form a flattened cylinder. Repeat the process for the remaining dough and filling.

- Place the cakes on an oven tray lined with baking paper and bake for about 12 minutes at 180°C (160°C fan/350°F/Gas 4) until lightly browned. Leave to cool before serving.

- The cakes will keep for several days in an airtight container lined with kitchen paper.

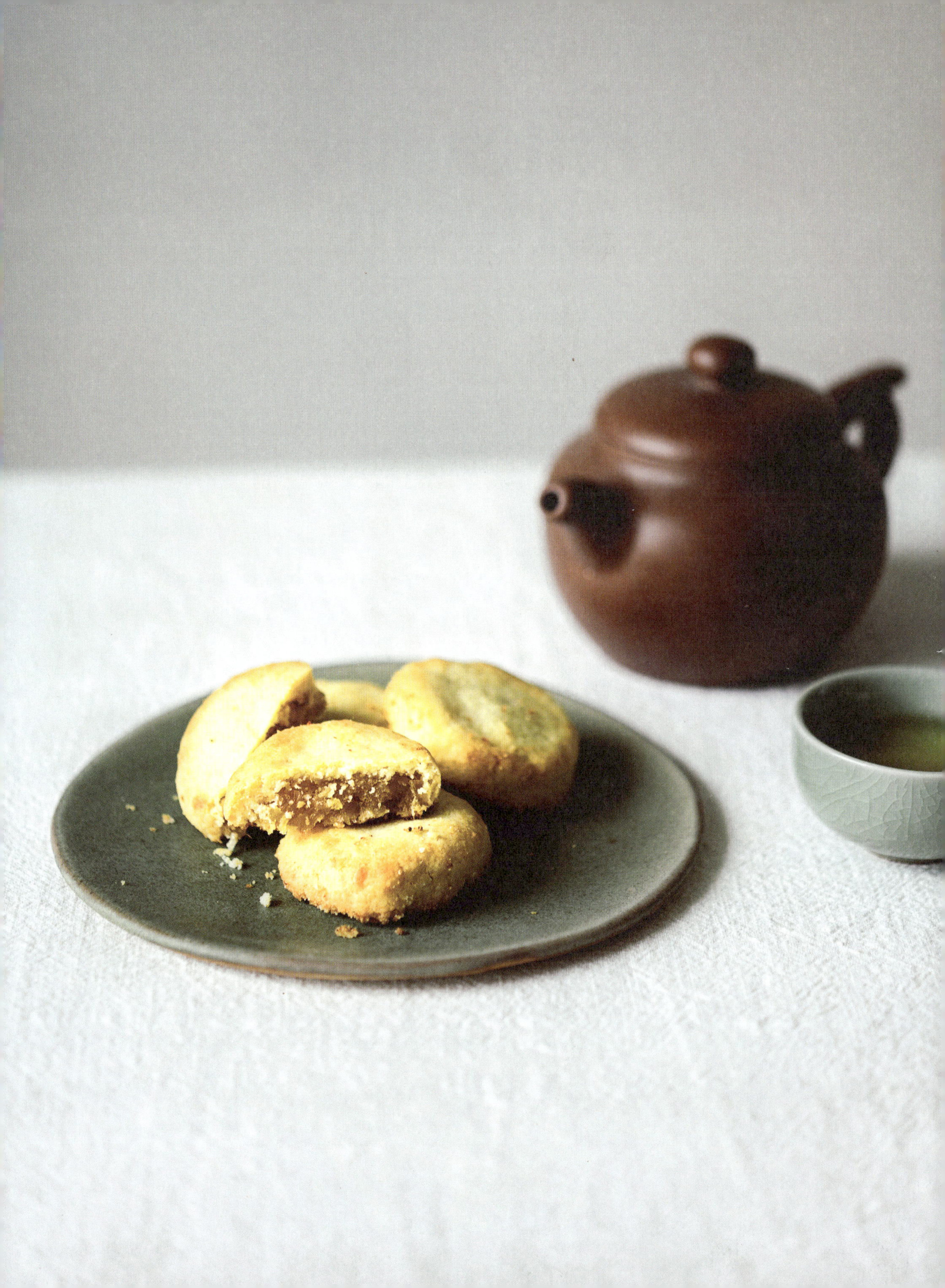

"Pineapple" Brioche

BŌ LUÓ BĀO

菠萝包

PREPARING 40 MINUTES + RESTING TIME

COOKING 15 MINUTES

THESE SOFT AND SWEET BRIOCHES ARE CLASSICS IN *CHA CHAAN TENG*, HONG KONG CAFES WHERE YOU CAN FIND WESTERN DISHES ADAPTED TO LOCAL FLAVOURS. THE CRUST IS MEANT TO BE REMINISCENT OF PINEAPPLE BARK (WITH A LITTLE IMAGINATION). HOWEVER, IF YOU LOOK FOR THIS FRUIT IN THE INGREDIENTS… THERE IS NONE!

Makes 8 brioches

INGREDIENTS

For the *tangzhong*

30g (1oz/scant ¼ cup) T65 (strong/bread) flour
120ml (4oz/½ cup) water

For the dough

310g (11oz/scant 2¼ cups) T65 (strong/bread) flour
5g (⅛oz/1 tsp) salt
35ml (2½ tbsp) milk
50ml (3 tbsp) full-fat (heavy) cream
1 egg, about 50g (1¾oz)
8g (¼oz) instant yeast
45g (1½oz/scant ¼ cup) sugar
30g (1oz/2 tbsp) soft butter

For the topping

2 egg yolks
1 tsp vanilla extract
70g (2½oz/5 tbsp) soft butter
50g (1¾oz/¼ cup) sugar
110g (3¾oz/generous ¾ cup) plain (all-purpose) flour
3g (scant 1 tsp) bicarbonate of soda (baking soda)

FOR THE *TANGZHONG*

- Mix the flour and water in a small pot. Heat over a low heat and stir regularly. The mixture will thicken to the texture of béchamel sauce (when it reaches about 65°C/150°F, if you have a thermometer). Turn off the heat and set aside.

FOR THE DOUGH

- Pour the flour, salt, milk, cream, egg, yeast, sugar and *tangzhong* into the bowl of your electric mixer. Give it a good stir with a spatula, then mix on medium speed for about 2 minutes until you have a dough. Add the softened butter and continue mixing for about 8 minutes. The dough should be smooth and elastic.

- Let the dough rest for 1½ hours at room temperature in a lightly oiled bowl, covered with film (plastic wrap). It will double in volume.

- Divide the dough into 8 pieces of about 65g (2¼oz), then roll up each piece: fold the edges towards the centre and roll quickly on the countertop, maintaining a gentle pressure with your palm – this will help create smooth balls. Let the balls rest for another 30 minutes, on a tray covered with film. They will double in volume.

FOR THE TOPPING

- In a bowl, mix 1 of the egg yolks with the vanilla extract, softened butter and sugar, then add the flour and bicarbonate of soda and mix with a spatula until you have a smooth, soft dough.

TO ASSEMBLE

- Divide the topping dough into 8 pieces of about 30g (1oz). Roll each piece into a ball on the countertop and then flatten and roll it into a thin layer (between 2 sheets of film to prevent it from sticking). Place this layer gently on top of the rested dough balls and brush each bun with the remaining egg yolk.

- Place the buns on an oven tray lined with baking paper and bake for about 15 minutes at 195°C (175°C fan/200°F/Gas 6) until lightly browned. Eat warm or cold.

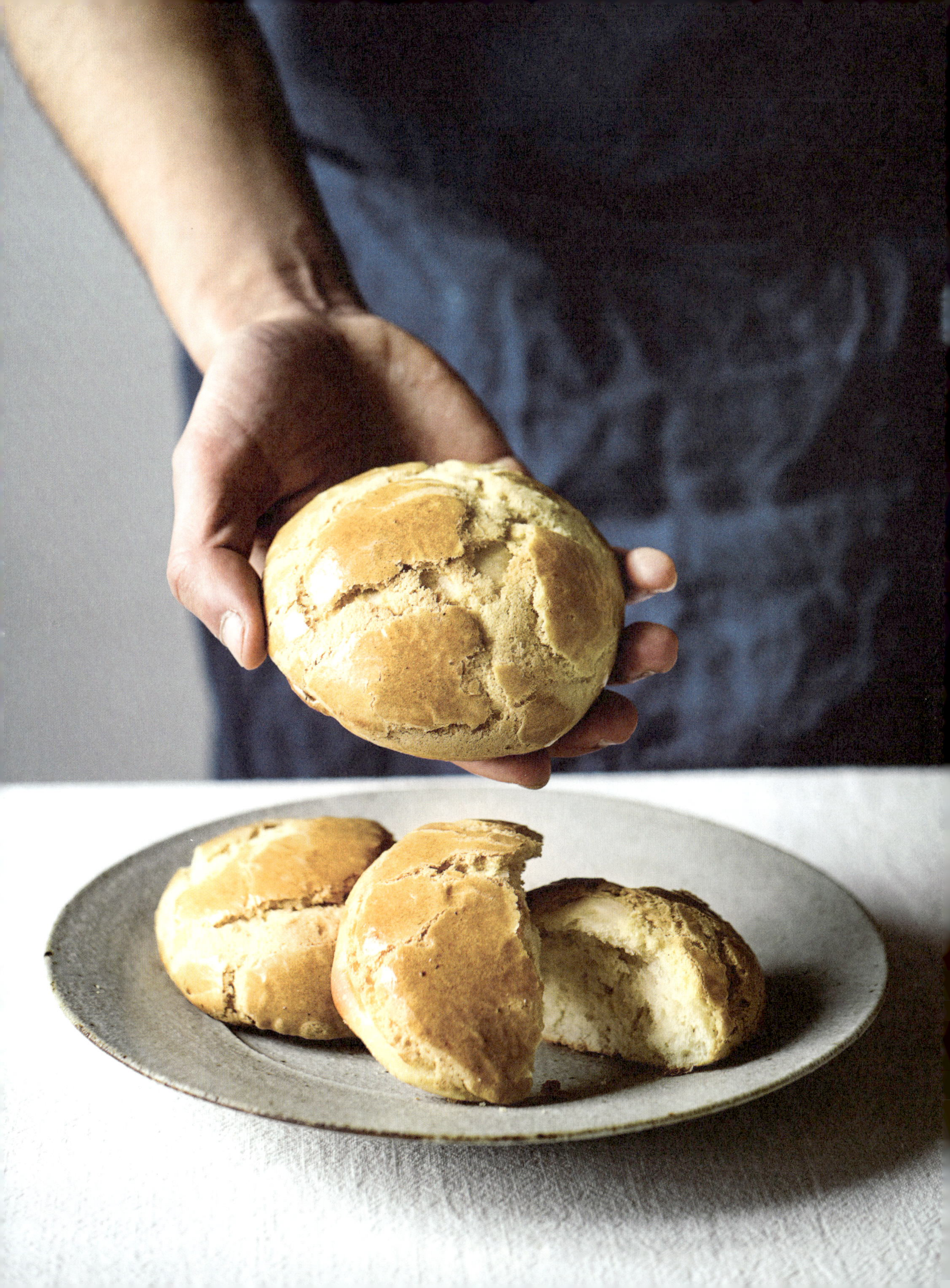

Tang Yuan with Black Sesame

ZHĪ　MÁ　TĀNG　YUÁN
芝麻汤圆

PREPARING 90 MINUTES 　　*COOKING 5 MINUTES*

THESE SOFT, STICKY LITTLE BALLS WITH A FLOWING BLACK SESAME HEART ARE TRADITIONALLY ENJOYED AT THE LANTERN FESTIVAL. NOWADAYS, THEY ARE RARELY HOME-MADE. HOWEVER, MUCH LIKE DUMPLINGS, THE PREPARATION PROCESS IS ALSO A TIME FOR FAMILY BONDING.

Makes about 20 *tang yuan*

INGREDIENTS

For the filling

110g (3¾oz/1 cup) plain black sesame seeds
60g (2oz/¼ cup) melted lard (or unsalted butter)
40g (1½oz/3¼ tbsp) sugar
20ml (1 tbsp) water

For the dough

200g (7oz/1½ cups) sticky rice flour
95ml (6½ tbsp) boiling water
60ml (4 tbsp) room temperature water

For the soup (for each bowl)

100ml (6½ tbsp) *tang yuan* cooking water (*see method*)
1 tbsp fermented sticky rice (*jiu niang, see p. 38; optional*)
1 pinch of dried osmanthus flowers

FOR THE FILLING

- Wash the sesame seeds, then toast them in a dry frying pan over a low heat. Toast for 8–10 minutes, stirring with a spatula to prevent them from burning, until they become slightly swollen and easy to crumble.

- Grind the sesame seeds into a powder, then mix with the melted lard, sugar and water. Spread it out in a thin layer over a tray and leave it in the freezer for about 1 hour – this makes the mixture easier to work with.

- Using your hands, roll the chilled filling into about 20 balls, roughly 10g (¼oz) each, and place them on a tray lined with film (plastic wrap) to prevent them from sticking. Freeze them while you make the dough.

FOR THE DOUGH

- In a bowl, mix the sticky rice flour and boiling water, then add the room-temperature water and mix until the dough no longer sticks to the edges of the bowl. Form it into a ball and cover it with film to prevent it from drying out.

TO SHAPE THE *TANG YUAN*

- Take a 15g (½oz) portion of the dough (cover the rest with film while you work) and roll it in your hands to make a ball, then make a hole in the centre with your thumb big enough to accommodate a portion of filling. Add a chilled black sesame ball to the hole, then close up and re-roll (see the sweet bao technique, p. 282). To keep the outside spotless, have a towel on hand to wipe your sesame-stained fingers as you go. Place the *tang yuan* on a plate lined with film and repeat for the remaining dough and filling.

- Bring a pot of water to the boil and cook the *tang yuan* over a medium heat for about 2 minutes. To prevent them from clumping together, swirl the water with a chopstick just after adding the *tang yuan* and do not overload the pan. They are ready when they start floating to the surface and have gained half their size in volume.

- To each small serving bowl, add the 100ml (6½ tbsp) of cooking water and the fermented rice. Add the *tang yuan*, then sprinkle with the dried osmanthus flowers.

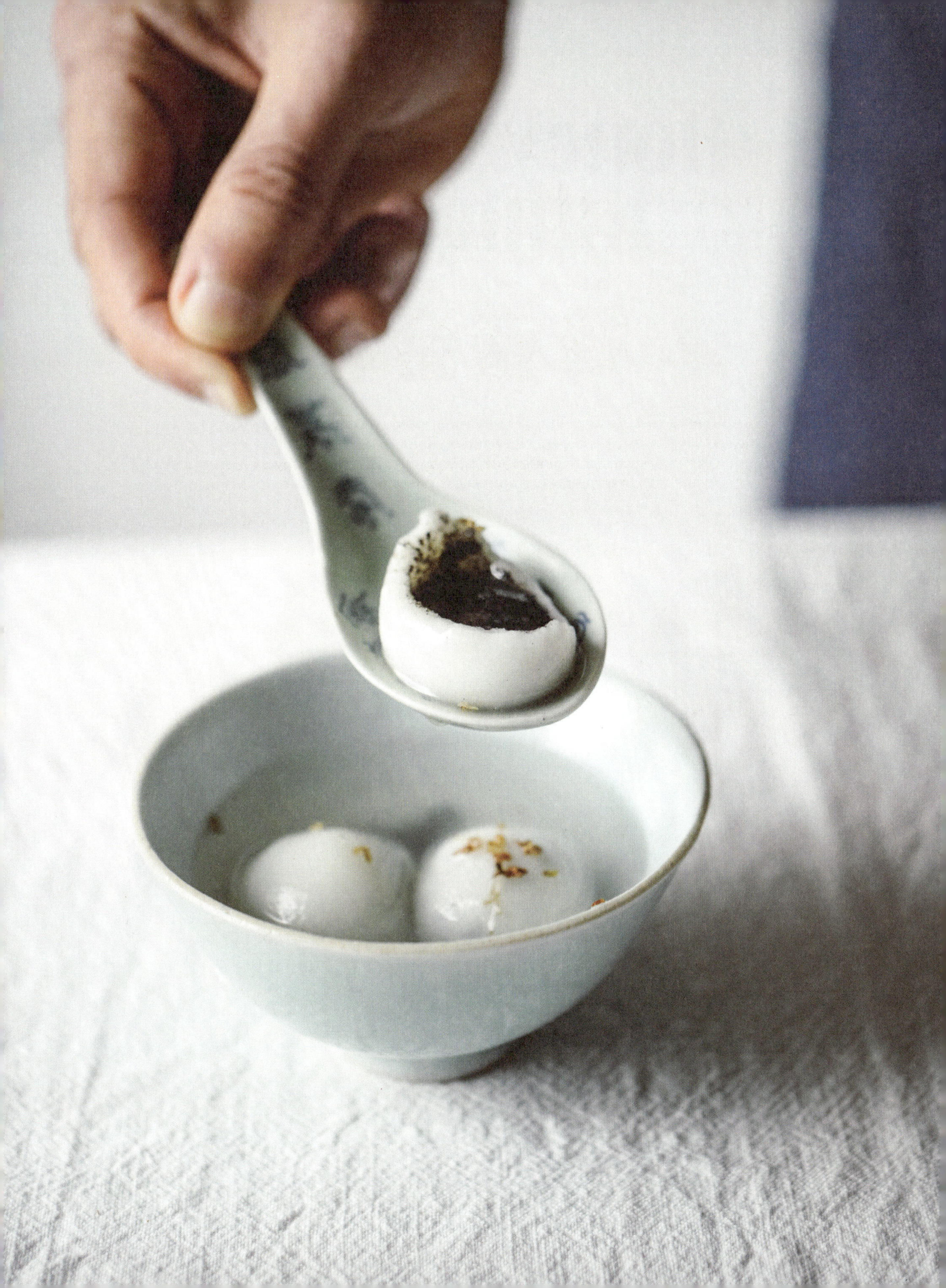

Honey Candied Kumquats

FĒNG MÌ JĪN JIÉ

蜂蜜金桔

PREPARING 5 MINUTES

COOKING 30 MINUTES

KUMQUAT IS A SMALL, SWEET AND ACIDIC CITRUS FRUIT WITH A SLIGHT BITTERNESS THAT TASTES VERY PLEASANT. IT IS COMMONLY USED IN CHINA TO SOOTHE COUGHS, MOST NOTABLY COMBINED WITH HONEY. ONCE CANDIED, THE KUMQUATS CAN BE ENJOYED AS A SWEET (CANDY), OR INFUSED IN HOT WATER, WHICH FEELS GREAT TO HAVE IN THE MORNING.

Makes 1 jar

INGREDIENTS

150g (5½oz) rock sugar (or white sugar)
300g (10oz) kumquats, washed
300ml (1¼ cups) water
75g (2½oz/5 tbsp) honey

RECIPE STEPS

- Heat the rock sugar and water in a pot over a low heat until the sugar has completely dissolved.

- Add the kumquats to the pot and let them cook for about 30 minutes until you have a thick caramel and almost translucent fruits.

- Leave to cool a little (not completely, or the caramel will solidify) and then transfer the mixture to a clean jar. Cover with the honey, which will not only add flavour, but will also help to preserve the fruit.

- The kumquats will keep for at least 1 month in the fridge.

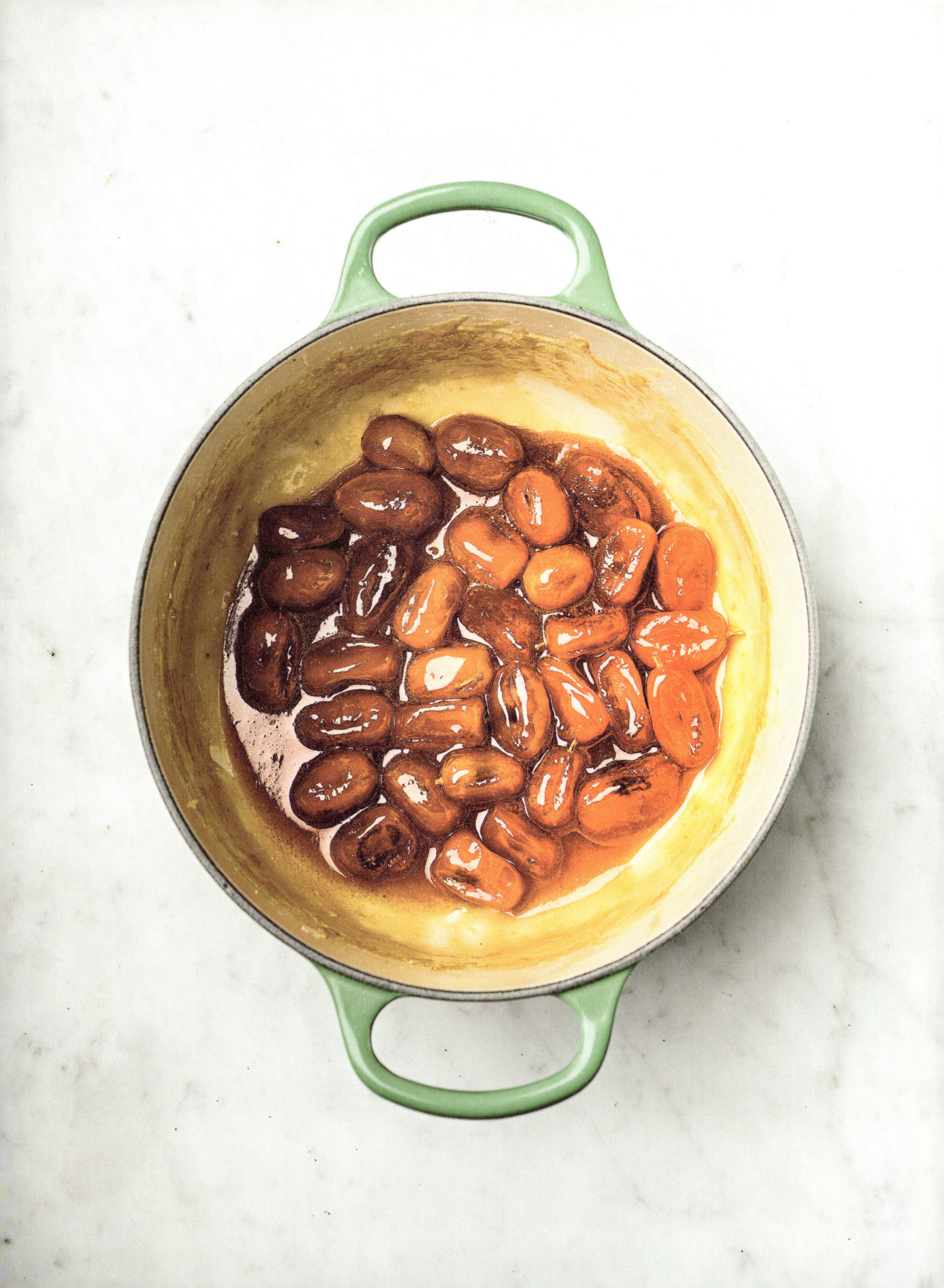

Pomelo Mango Sago

YÁNG ZHĪ GĀN LÙ

杨枝甘露

PREPARING 5 MINUTES

COOKING 20 MINUTES

THIS REFRESHING DESSERT WAS INVENTED IN THE '80S AT THE LEI GARDEN RESTAURANT IN HONG KONG. ITS CHINESE NAME, WHICH CAN BE TRANSLATED AS "WILLOW BRANCH DEW", REFERS TO GUANYIN, THE GODDESS OF COMPASSION IN CHINESE BUDDHISM, WHO HOLDS A WILLOW BRANCH IN HER HAND THAT IS SUPPOSED TO QUENCH THE PEOPLE'S THIRST.

Makes 2 glasses

INGREDIENTS

For the solid part

40g (1½oz) tapioca pearls
80g (3oz) grapefruit flesh, torn into small pieces
80g (3oz) mango flesh, cut into 2cm (¾in) cubes

For the liquid part

150ml (⅔ cup) coconut milk
80ml (5 tbsp) milk (or plant-based milk of your choice), unsweetened
1 tbsp sugar
100g (3½oz) mango flesh

FOR THE SOLID PART

- Bring 1 litre (4⅓ cups) of water to the boil in a pot over a high heat. Add the tapioca pearls, then switch to a low heat and cook for 12 minutes until you see only a small white dot in the centre. Turn off the heat and leave the pearls in the water for another 8 minutes. They will become completely translucent. Remove, rinse with cold water and drain.

FOR THE LIQUID PART

- While the tapioca pearls are cooking, heat the coconut milk and cow or vegetable milk in a pot, then add the sugar, which should dissolve. Let it cool before setting aside in the fridge.

- Take 50ml (3 tbsp) of this mixture and combine with the 100g (3½oz) of mango flesh. The texture should be slightly thick. Set aside in the fridge.

TO SERVE

- In each serving glass, place a layer of grapefruit, a layer of mango cubes and a layer of tapioca pearls. Pour over the sweet coconut milk mixture, then top with the mango mixture. Finish up with a few pieces of grapefruit, and enjoy straight away.

GOOD TO KNOW
小提示

Try to pick a ripe and sweet mango to avoid the fibrous texture of an unripe fruit.

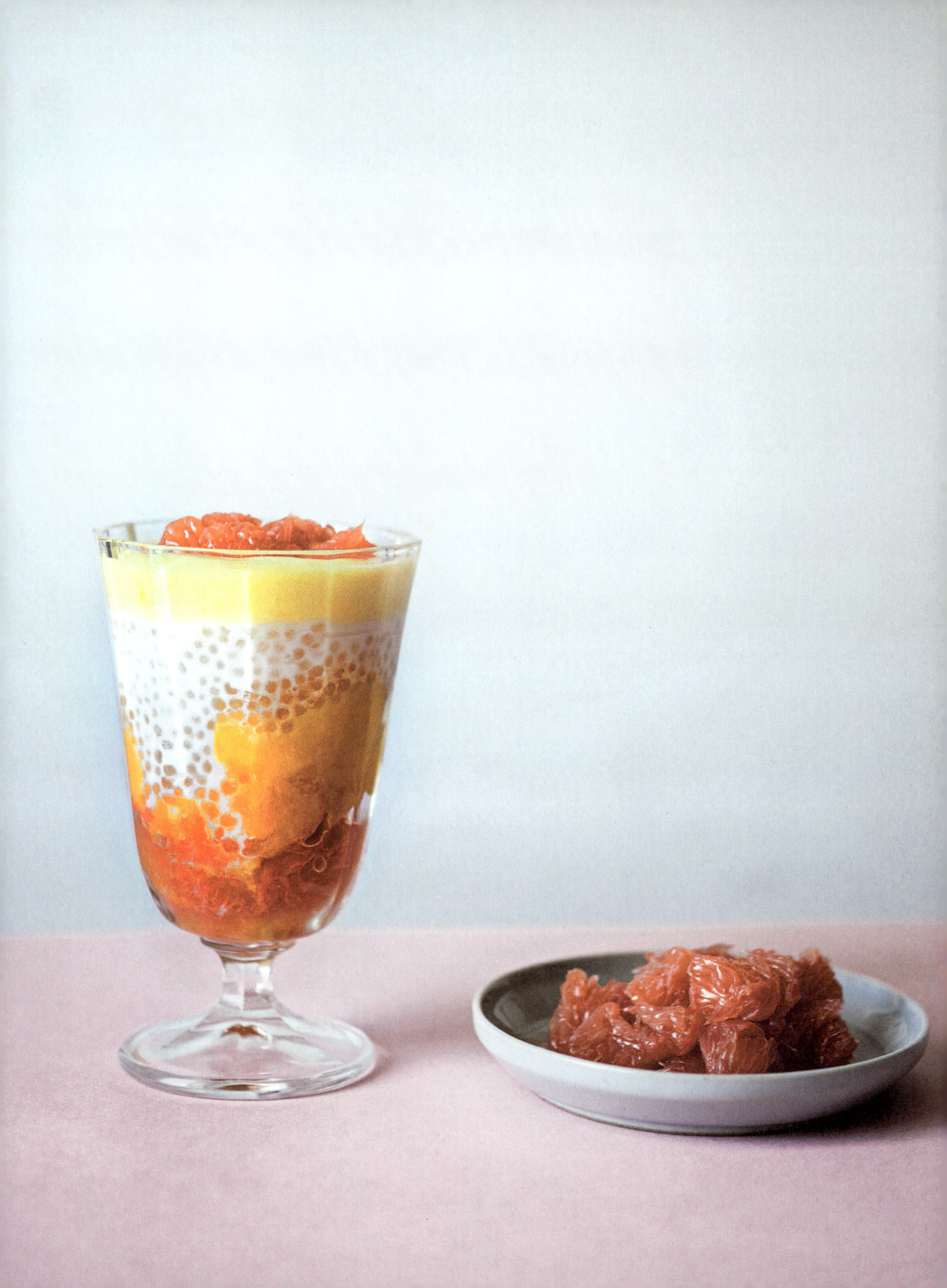

Appendices

附录

FÙ LÙ

BONUS 1

Festive Dishes

THE FOUR TRADITIONAL FESTIVALS ARE ONE OF THE PILLARS OF CHINESE CULTURE, AND ARE CELEBRATED BEYOND THE BORDERS OF THE COUNTRY, IN ASIA AND ALSO EVERYWHERE THE CHINESE DIASPORA IS PRESENT.

01 CHINESE NEW YEAR

新年 / XĪN NIÁN

Date: The first day of the lunar calendar.

What is celebrated: The Chinese New Year, which historically celebrates the arrival of spring (hence its other name, "spring festival", 春节), lasts several days. It is the most important celebration of the year. The meal, which takes place the night before (年夜饭, *nián yè fàn*), is a family reunion comparable to Christmas in Europe or Thanksgiving in North America.

Associated dishes: The meal menu is quite flexible nowadays, and may vary by region. But there are a few dishes with special significance that are usually present on the table.

- **DUMPLINGS**: Making dumplings together with the family is a mandatory step in northern China. Their shape is reminiscent of gold ingots (元宝, *yuan bao*) used in imperial China, and they symbolize good fortune.

- **NIAN GAO**: In the south of the country, sticky rice cakes are preferred (see p. 354). The character "糕, *gao*" (cake), is a homonym of "高, *gao*" (rise), meaning that eating *nian gao* amounts to "rising from year to year".

- **FISH**: Just like seafood, fish is very popular during large meals. Furthermore, the term "鱼, *yu*" (fish), is also a homonym of "余, *yu*" (surplus), used in the expression *nian nian you yu*, which translates to "having surplus [wealth and food] every year".

02 QINGMING FESTIVAL

清明节 / QĪNG MÍNG JIÉ

Date: The first day of the fifth solar period of the Chinese calendar, which corresponds to April 4th, 5th or 6th, depending on the year.

What is celebrated: It is a commemoration of the dead. You could compare it to All Saints' Day in the West. During this festival, you pay a visit to your ancestors, which involves sweeping the graves (扫墓), praying and making offerings.

Associated dish: *Qing tuan* (literally "green ball") is the dish served during the Qingming Festival. Traditionally native to Jiangnan (see p. 10), the dumplings are found everywhere in China today, but they remain mostly popular in that region, such as Shanghai or Hangzhou. The balls consist of a paste made of sticky rice flour mixed with Chinese wormwood juice and a sweet or savoury filling. They are steamed, then usually drizzled with sesame oil.

GOOD TO KNOW
小提示

Chinese New Year is a time for giving gifts, especially food, to relatives and loved ones. From ginseng to dried products, tea or fruit baskets, each type of food has an intrinsic value and a special meaning.

⓪③ DRAGON BOAT FESTIVAL
端午节 / DUĀN WŬ JIÉ

Date: The fifth day of the fifth month in the lunar calendar – *duan wu* literally means "beginning of the fifth".

What is celebrated: It is a day of tribute to the poet Qu Yuan, who died that day more than 2,000 years ago. He was a Chu State minister and committed suicide by throwing himself into the Miluo River (Hunan province), in despair as his kingdom was about to be defeated by the enemy. The Dragon Boat Race was born as a way for villagers to commemorate this patriotic figure.

Associated dish: *Zong zi* is the iconic dish to enjoy on this day. It is made of stuffed sticky rice wrapped in bamboo leaves and steamed.

The stuffing varies by region, but there is always a pork version (肉粽), sometimes associated with salted duck-egg yolk. In my region, the sweet stuffing is most often made with candied jujube.

⓪④ MID-AUTUMN FESTIVAL
中秋节 / ZHŌNG QIŪ JIÉ

Date: The fifteenth day of the eighth month in the lunar calendar, which corresponds to mid-September to early October in the Gregorian calendar.

What is celebrated: In the Chinese culture, it is the best day to admire the full moon with your family, hence its other name, "moon festival". Legend has it that Houyi, an outstanding archer who saved Earth from disaster by eliminating nine of the ten suns, was rewarded with an elixir of immortality. His secret was unfortunately discovered, and one of his malicious apprentices wanted to take it. His wife, Chang'e, had no other choice but to swallow this elixir.

She became an immortal goddess forced to stay on the moon, forever separated from Houyi. This festival, which commemorates Chang'e, is a time of reunion.

Associated dish: Moon cake is a classic dish that is offered and enjoyed at this time. The traditional version consists of a thick, sweet and fluffy paste wrapped around a sweet filling (lotus seed paste, azuki bean paste) or savoury filling (ham, salted duck-egg yolk), which is then baked in the oven. Its round shape is meant to be reminiscent of the moon, and Chinese characters on the dough generally indicate the ingredients of the filling.

BONUS 2

Tea Time

IN CHINA, TEA IS NOT JUST A DRINK BUT A WAY OF LIFE.
HERE IS A SHORT OVERVIEW ON HOW IT IS ENJOYED
IN VARIOUS REGIONS.

01 SICHUAN: RELAXING IN TEA HOUSES

Nowhere else in China are there as many tea houses (茶馆, *chá guǎn*) as in Sichuan. It is estimated that there are 10,000 in Chengdu alone, the province's capital. Indoors or outdoors in a park, you will see locals gathered around bamboo tables everywhere, quietly sipping their tea.

For Sichuanese people, tea houses are much more than just a food and drink outlet; they are an essential part of local life. You go there to play mahjong, have your ears cleaned and spend the whole afternoon chatting with friends.

Up until the 1960s, you could go to a tea house to get some hot water in huge flasks, as it was cheaper than heating up a fire at home.

- **What is served?**

Mainly green tea served in *gaiwan*, large cups with a lid. A teapot with a long spout is traditionally used to pour boiling water, which cools to 80°C/175°F as it reaches the cup, the ideal temperature for steeping green tea.

02 GUANGDONG: THE *YUM CHA* TRADITION

For Cantonese people, tea (*yum cha*) is usually accompanied by an assortment of side dishes, whether steamed or fried, served in bamboo baskets (*dim sum*), traditionally brought round on a small cart (although that is increasingly rare). In restaurants, in the early morning, you can see elderly people reading their newspapers; then, a little later, families with children, and tourists, come and go throughout the day. The tea is often overshadowed by the food, but this has not always been the case.

Towards the end of the 19th century, these establishments were simple tea stalls – as this thirst-quenching drink is particularly well suited to the subtropical climate of the region – and they were intended to be resting places for workers. Food was later offered to retain customers. The food started out by being quite rustic (bao, pancakes), and gradually developed to attract a wealthier clientele. That is how the first tea houses appeared in Guangzhou. They are the ancestors of the restaurants we know today.

- **What is served?**

In China, tea is known to "cut the fat" and help with digestion. It is a must in *dim sum* restaurants and is served at the beginning of the meal. The price is low and is calculated per head. Most people opt for one of the following teas: jasmine, chrysanthemum, oolong (like *tieguanyin*), black and pu'er.

GOOD TO KNOW
小提示

Much like wine, certain types of tea are paired with certain dishes, not only based on the taste, but also according to the supposed virtues of each tea family. Green tea, which is mostly "yin", is preferred in summer, while black tea, classified as "yang", is preferred in winter.

---

03 TIBET: BUTTER TEA

Butter tea (*po cha* in Tibetan) is usually the first thing you are served when you are welcomed by a Tibetan family. This drink, enriched with yak butter, brings warmth, fats and vitamins to a harsh region where fruits and vegetables are desperately lacking.

The history of tea in Tibet is associated with the mythical Tea Horse Road (茶马古道, *chá ma gu dào*), a network of mule paths that connected this immense territory to Sichuan. Traders sold black tea produced in Ya'an, (雅安) in Sichuan in exchange for horses (among other products), which were in high demand for the Chinese imperial army.

▪ What is served?

Butter tea can be surprising at first because of its salty taste and very rich texture. The drink should almost be thought of as a soup rather than a tea.

The traditional version is to boil black tea "crumbs" – a fermented tea pressed into a brick. The infusion is transferred to a long wooden cylinder, a kind of Tibetan churn called *chandong* (nowadays, this is done with a blender), then salt, milk and a good dose of yak butter is added. Everything is mixed together, and the drink is ready.

BONUS 3

Food Is the Best Medicine

THIS SENTENCE APPLIES WHOLEHEARTEDLY TO CHINESE CUISINE. THE NOTION OF HEALTH THROUGH COOKING, IN LINE WITH TRADITIONAL CHINESE MEDICINE, IS INDEED STILL VERY PRESENT IN CHINA. FROM COOKING METHODS TO INGREDIENT COMBINATIONS, TO THE SEASONALITY OF PRODUCTS, FOOD PREVENTS AILMENTS AS MUCH AS IT CURES THEM.

01 DISTANT ORIGINS

In the founding text of Chinese medicine, *The Yellow Emperor's Classic of Internal Medicine* (黄帝内经, *Huang Di Nei Jing*), written more than 2,000 years ago (475–221 BCE), there was already mention of the link between food and health. In Chapter 81, Section 22, the authors recommend a diet comprising 5 cereals (rice, soy, sesame, wheat and millet), 5 fruits (date, plum, chestnut, apricot and peach), 5 meats (mutton, beef, pork, chicken, dog) and 5 vegetables (squash, Chinese spring onion, mung bean sprout, shallot and onion).

The number 5 is more of a symbol (like the 5 elements of the Chinese representation of the universe: metal, wood, water, fire, earth) than an exact number. The underlying idea is to have a varied and as balanced a diet as possible.

This book, which is among the oldest of traditional Chinese medicine, was probably one of the first nutritional-health texts written in the history of humanity.

02 THE BALANCE BETWEEN "HOT" AND "COLD"

Long before the discovery of modern nutrition (with the concepts of calories, carbohydrates and vitamins), Chinese medicine introduced the idea of classifying foods according to their impact on the human body.

On the one hand, there are so-called "hot" foods (热, *re*), which are usually cooked at high temperatures (fried, grilled/broiled), high in calories (oil-producing) and strongly flavoured (chilli pepper, spices). On the other hand, "cold" foods (寒, *han*) encompass the majority of green vegetables and low-calorie ingredients (tofu, seaweed, crustaceans). In the middle, there are "neutral" foods, mainly made of starches, fish or lean meat. Note that the terms "hot" and "cold" do not describe the temperature of the food itself.

An excess of "hot" food would inevitably cause what is called a "fire surge" (上火, *shang huo*), a concept known to all Chinese people. This phenomenon would result, for example, in an inflammation of the gums, a sore throat or the appearance of mouth ulcers. These symptoms should thus be combated with "cold" foods. As you may have realized, the fundamental principle of Chinese nutrition is based on the search for balance between "hot" and "cold" foods. It is therefore common to see them combined in the same dish. For example, you will eat stir-fried vegetables (cold) with garlic or chilli peppers (hot), or mutton (hot) simmered with white radish (cold).

COLD 寒 | HÁN
Bamboo shoots, tomatoes, seaweed, crab, soy sauce

COOL 冷 | LĚNG
Wheat, leafy green vegetables, soy milk, cheese, green tea

NEUTRAL 平 | PÍNG
Rice, potatoes, shiitake mushrooms, milk, white fish, pork

WARM 温 | WĒN
Onion, coriander (cilantro), cherries, pumpkin, coffee, mutton, salmon, alcohol

HOT 热 | RÈ
Black peppercorns, cinnamon, ginger, chilli pepper, mustard seeds

"A saint must know how to heal before the disease appears."

圣人不治已病治未病

The Yellow Emperor's Classic of Internal Medicine

03 WHEN FOOD BECOMES MEDICINE

Since pharmacopoeia plays an important role in Chinese medicine, the boundary between medicine and food has always been quite porous. There are concoctions made purely for medical purposes, prepared from a dozen dried ingredients (leaves, roots, seeds, mushrooms…), prescribed in quantities adapted to each patient. They are usually dark in colour and taste very bitter. I always drank them reluctantly when I was a child.

Other culinary ingredients with medicinal connotations have long made their way into the kitchen. This is the case with ginseng or goji berries, which are seen as "nourishing" (补, *bu*) in Chinese medicine, meaning that they participate in strengthening certain organs or "vital energy" (气, *qi*). They are most often found in soups (as in the recipe on p. 172), as this cooking method better preserves nutrients.

And finally, there are a large number of ingredients that are used in Chinese medicine as much as in everyday cooking. These include ginger, star anise, Chinese liquorice or Chinese yam (whose Chinese name literally means "mountain medicine").

04 AN OUTDATED OR ENTIRELY MODERN CONCEPT?

The West usually views traditional Chinese medicine as a pseudo-science, so the concept of "hot" and "cold" foods can simply appear as a folk remedy to the uninitiated. The reality is more complex, and since I am not a doctor, I prefer to focus on the underlying, more universal notions.

Seasonality is an essential element in Chinese cuisine. The importance of an ingredient's medicinal properties has led to a natural interest in raw and fresh foods and, particularly, seasonality. Frozen or canned products aren't very widespread in China, despite the increasingly urban lifestyle. Nothing beats a live fish or seasonal fruit or vegetable.

An individualized diet is another precept derived from Chinese medicine (the same symptom does not always require the same treatment, depending on the individual). Apart from ingredients' intrinsic properties, what we should eat also depends on our own physiology and on external factors, such as the climate and the season. Unlike the West, China has no notion of superfoods; everything is more a question of balance.

INDEX 1

Recipes

Bamboo shoots with chilli oil 70	Kansui noodles 236
Base broths 160	Lard 344
Beef congee 302	Liang fen 330
Beef with black pepper 208	Liu sha bao 286
Black tea eggs 150	Lo mai gai 308
Braised beef noodle soup 250	Lu rou fan 300
Char siu 198	Mapo tofu 126
Cheung fun 310	"Milk" fish broth 162
Chicken meatball and vermicelli soup 174	Mouth-watering chicken 72
Chicken soup with shiitake 172	Mr Jiang tofu 128
Chilli fish pot 218	Mustard leaf pancakes 320
Chinese spring onion omelette 148	Oyster pancake 226
Chinese-style borscht 178	Pear and white mushroom soup 356
Clay pot rice 298	"Pineapple" brioche 364
Coca-Cola-flavoured chicken wings 204	Pineapple cakes 362
Cold noodles with sesame sauce 240	Pomelo mango sago 370
Crispy pork 194	Popcorn chicken 206
Dai-style fried egg salad 152	Pork belly with rice flour 188
Dan dan noodles 244	Prawn-stuffed tofu 132
Dongpo pork 186	Prawns with Sichuan peppercorn and salt 228
Egg and tomato noodles 238	Pumpkin millet congee 304
Fermented black soy bean sauce 346	Pumpkin sticky rice cakes 354
5-spice braised beef top rump 76	Red mung bean soup 360
5-spice tofu 130	Roasted asparagus in butter-soy sauce 98
Flavoured sweet soy sauce 348	Romaine lettuce with oyster sauce 92
Four happiness kaofu 64	Seafood pao fan 294
Fried cockles with garlic and chilli 220	Seaweed salad with cucumber 60
Fried corn with pepper and salt 114	Seaweed soup with dried shrimp 166
Fried mangetout with lap cheong 100	Shredded chicken with sesame oil 74
Gua bao 284	Sichuan chilli oil 342
Hand-torn cabbage 86	Sichuan fried green beans 102
Honey candied kumquats 368	Silken steamed tofu with ham 134
Hot and sour soup 170	Silken tofu with century egg 122
Jian bao 280	Smashed cucumber salad 58
Jian bing 322	Soy milk 324
Julienned potato salad 110	Spinach with sesame sauce 66

Spring onion oil	340
Steamed aubergine salad	56
Steamed eggs	142
Steamed pork ribs with douchi	202
Steamed pork with dried mustard leaves	192
Steamed scallops with rice vermicelli	222
Steamed sea bream	214
Steamed white radish balls	108
Sticky rice with brown sugar	358
Sticky rice with pork broth and shiitake	306
Stir-fried celery with cashew nuts	96
Stir-fried Chinese spring onions with soy bean sprouts	84
Stir-fried chow fun with beef	252
Stir-fried garlic scapes and pork	94
Stir-fried rice vermicelli	254
Stir-fried squid with celery	224
Stir-fried tomatoes and eggs	146
Strange-tasting peanuts	334
Suan cai minced fish	216
Sweet and sour pork ribs	200
Tang yuan with black sesame	366
Taro and trotter soup	176
Three treasures of the Earth	106
Tiger skin eggs	154
Tofu "jerky"	136
Tofu skin salad with red radishes	120
Tomato and egg soup	164
Twice-cooked pork	196
Wax gourd and corn soup	168
White radish cake	332
White radish pickles	68
White rice	292
Wok cauliflower	88
Wok stir-fried nian gao	312
Wonton soup	272
Yangchun noodles	248
You tiao	326
Yu xiang aubergine	104
Zha jiang noodles	242
Zhong dumplings	268

Ingredients

A
Asparagus 98, 262
Aubergine (eggplant) 56, 104, 106, 262

B
Bacon 88
Bamboo shoots 70, 170
Bay leaf 76, 150, 186, 250, 284, 342, 348
Beef 244
    Beef fillet 208, 252, 302
    Beef shank 250
    Beef top rump 76
    Oxtail 178
Bell pepper
    Green pepper 106
    Red pepper 96, 224, 228
Bicarbonate of soda (baking soda) 326, 364
Black sesame 280, 322, 366
Black tea 15, 150
Breadcrumb coating 354
Broccoli 80
Broth 32, 96, 104, 126, 160, 162, 168, 250, 294
    Chicken broth 160, 214
    Pork broth 134, 248, 276, 284, 306
    Vegetable broth 136, 174, 218, 272
Brown cardamom 30, 74, 348
Butternut squash 304, 354

C
Cabbage
    Cauliflower 88
    Chinese cabbage 80, 218, 276
    Choudou cabbage 86
    Pointed cabbage 86, 216, 254
Carrot 108, 152, 176, 178, 242, 254, 284
Cashew nuts 96
Celery 96
Char siu 332
Chicken
    Chicken breast 312
    Chicken carcass 160
    Chicken leg 72, 74, 172, 174, 206, 308
    Chicken wings 204
Chilli bean paste (doubanjiang) 38, 104, 126, 188, 196, 218, 250, 322
Chilli peppers
    Bird's eye chilli 36
    Er jing tiao chilli pepper 36, 247
    Xiao mi la chilli 36, 102
Chinese celery 81, 224
Chinese liquorice 348
Chinese mustard
    Dried mustard leaves (mei cai) 38, 192, 244, 320
    Fermented mustard (zha cai) 38, 306
Chinese spring onion (chive) 84, 148, 252
Cinnamon 30, 64, 76, 136, 150, 154, 188, 250, 284, 334, 342, 348
Clams 220
Cloves 30, 76, 348
Coca-Cola 204
Cockles 220
Coriander (cilantro) 72, 74, 120, 130, 170, 218, 220, 226, 250, 298, 322
Corn 114, 160, 168, 296
Cucumber 58, 60, 152, 242, 284
Cumin 30, 136, 334
Curry powder 334
Custard powder 286

D
Douchi sauce 108, 126, 132, 196, 202, 346
Dried lily flowers 35, 64
Dried mandarin peel 136, 202, 302
Dried osmanthus flowers 366
Duck blood 170

E
Egg 142, 146, 148, 150, 152, 154, 238, 254, 300, 302, 322
    Century egg 122
    Egg white 94, 114, 188, 206, 208, 216, 218, 268, 272, 286
    Egg yolk 272, 334, 362, 364
    Salted duck egg 286

F
Fennel seeds 30, 76, 136, 188, 250, 348
Fish
    Bass 162, 218
    Mullet 162, 218
    Sea bream 162, 214, 218
    White fish 216
Fish sauce 148, 226, 294
5-spice 30, 76, 174, 188, 194, 198, 206, 300
Fried doughnut (you tiao) 306, 326
Full-fat fresh cream 364

G
Garlic 28
Gelatin 286
Ginger 28, 56, 72, 74, 76, 94, 146, 160, 174, 176, 186, 192, 250, 294
Goji berries 34, 35, 168, 172, 304, 356
Grapefruit 370
Green beans 102
Green garlic 196

H
Ham 134, 170
Hoisin sauce 198
Honey 136, 198, 362, 368

I
Iceberg lettuce 302

J
Jujube 172, 304

K
Kansui 236
Kaofu 64
Ketchup 108, 146, 208
Kumquat 368

L
Lard 40, 41, 128, 226, 247, 248, 318, 344, 366
Leek 196
Lemon 68, 152, 204, 294
Long coriander (ngo gai) 152
Lotus leaf 35, 308

M
Maltose 362
Mango 148, 370
Milk 286, 362, 364
    Plant milk 306, 324, 326, 360, 370
Millet 304
Mint 152

Mirin 70
Mung bean sprouts 84, 242, 252, 254
Mushrooms
    Black fungus 32, 33, 64, 170, 263
    Shiitake 32, 64, 108, 160, 170, 172, 254, 263, 294, 296, 298, 306, 308, 312, 332, 348
    White mushroom 356
Mussels 294

N

Nashi pear 356
Nian gao 312
Noodles 236, 242, 244, 248, 250, 252
    Biang biang noodles 234, 238
    La mian noodles 232, 240

O

Oil
    Chilli oil 36, 70, 72, 120, 122, 244, 246, 268, 294, 330, 342
    Sesame oil 40
    Spring onion oil 246, 247, 310, 340
Onion 160, 178, 208, 242, 254, 284
Oyster sauce 27, 92, 132, 247, 308, 310
Oysters 226

P

Pak choi (bok choy) 250, 298, 312
Peanut butter 40
Peanuts 64, 74, 244, 246, 284, 334
Pineapple 362, 364
Pork 268, 272, 306
    Cantonese sausage (lap cheong) 100, 298
    Pork belly 88, 102, 186, 188, 192, 194, 196, 242, 278, 284, 300, 320
    Pork bone 160, 248
    Pork ribs 176, 200, 202
    Pork shoulder 198
    Pork tenderloin 94
    Trotter 176
Potato 110, 178, 188
    Agria potato 106
    Bintje potato 106
Prawns (shrimp) 132, 228, 278, 294
    Dried shrimp (xia mi/xia pi) 32, 122, 128, 166, 168, 296, 308, 320, 332
Pumpkin 304, 354

R

Red bean paste 276
Red radish 120, 242
Rice
    Fermented rice (jiu nig) 39, 128, 366
    Jasmine rice 188, 302, 304
    Rice vermicelli 254
    Sticky rice 188, 304, 306, 308, 354, 358
    White rice 74, 172, 186, 292, 300
Roasted soy powder 358
Romaine lettuce 92

S

Salted dried plum (huamei) 200, 356
Salted soy bean paste (huang dou jiang) 242
Scallops 222, 294
Sea urchin 213
Seaweed 60
    Nori seaweed (zi cai) 33, 166
Sesame paste 40, 66, 244, 246
Sesame sauce 66, 240
Shallots 76, 220, 228, 300, 340
Shaoxing wine 24, 74, 76, 94, 146, 148, 162, 176, 186, 200, 222, 242, 250
Shiso 132, 188
Sichuan peppercorn 27, 40, 41, 150
Soy beans 38, 160, 176, 324
Soy sauce 24, 198, 206, 214, 346, 348
    Dark soy sauce 24, 76
    Light soy sauce 24, 64, 76, 98, 128, 192, 222, 284, 310
Spinach 66, 312
Spring onion (scallion) 28, 186, 250, 252, 318, 320, 340
    Spring onion green 104, 110, 252, 296
    Spring onion white 74, 96, 104, 106, 110, 114, 146, 164, 172, 174, 216, 228, 238, 252, 263, 280, 296, 300, 306, 342, 346
Squid 224, 294
Star anise 30, 64, 74, 76, 136, 150, 154, 188, 192, 242, 250, 284, 342, 348
Sugar
    Brown sugar 348, 358
    Icing (powdered) sugar 362
    Rock sugar 27, 76, 136, 150, 186, 200, 242, 348, 356, 368
Sweet chilli sauce 148
Sweet soy bean paste (tian mian jiang) 38, 76, 196, 242, 322

T

Tapioca 370
Taro 176
Tarragon 130
Tellin 220
Thai basil 206, 220
Tofu
    Fermented tofu 118, 198, 206, 322
    Firm tofu 118, 128, 136
    5-spice tofu 118, 130, 263
    Fried tofu 118, 132
    Silken tofu 118, 122, 134
    Soft tofu 118, 126, 170, 174
Tofu skin 118, 120
Tomato paste 178, 238, 294
Turmeric 72, 74
Turnip 172

V

Vanilla 364
Vinegar
    Black rice vinegar 24, 56, 330
    Rice vinegar 24, 68
    White rice vinegar 70
    White vinegar 56

W

Water chestnut 132
Wax gourd 168
White radish 68, 108, 178, 332
White sesame 56, 72, 136, 204, 342
Winter squash 263, 304, 354
Wonton wrappers 322

Y

Yeast
    Baking powder 286, 326
    Dry yeast 278, 280, 284, 286, 318
    Instant yeast 364
    Red yeast rice 198

From its inception to its publication, it took a year and a half to complete this book.

Nothing would have been possible without the fine team of Éditions du Chêne. Thank you Emmanuel for your trust and kindness. Thank you Faris for your constant patience and support. Thank you Sabine for your keen eye.

Without the involvement of photographers, illustrators and graphic designers, this book would only be a long chunk of text. Thank you Franck for your beautiful photos, which brought the recipes to life. Thank you Marie, Fabien, Léa and Clément for your drawings that have been able to transcribe my thoughts. And a big thank you to Benoit and his team, without whom we would not have such a beautiful object in our hands.

Thank you Lynda and Lucy for your invaluable help during the long shooting days. Churning out ten dishes a day in my tiny kitchen was not a sure bet.

Thank you Yoann for being my cheerleader from the beginning.

Thank you to my parents, who have always left me free to venture out and who have been so enthusiastic about seeing the book, despite their usual modest demeanour. I always think back to my grandmother, Mingliu, in front of a mustard leaf pancake (p. 320). She made me some so many times during my childhood and taught me the comfort of simple and frugal cooking.

And finally, this book is a tribute to those who opened my eyes to Chinese cuisine. My thoughts go out to all these small restaurants, often family-run, which are the true protectors of local cuisine everywhere I go in China. To all the writers (like Wang Zengqi), who know how to handle words much better than I do, thank you for transporting me to the China of yesteryear, which is nothing more than a memory now. To all the creators and chefs who accompanied me for hundreds of hours, watching the most incredible and improbable dishes and techniques.

I still have so much to learn; this is just the beginning.

DK LONDON
Editorial Director Cara Armstrong
Project Editor Izzy Holton
Senior Designer Tania Gomes
Senior Production Editor Tony Phipps
Senior Production Controller Stephanie McConnell
Jackets and Sales Material Coordinator Emily Cannings
DTP and Design Coordinator Heather Blagden
Art Director Maxine Pedliham

Editorial Sarah Epton

Editorial coordination and layout: EliLoCom
Translation and proofreading: Jeanne de Rougemont / EliLoCom, www.elilocom.fr

Le Guide de la Cuisine Chinoise © Hachette Livre (Editions du Chêne), 2023
All photography by Franck Juery.
All illustrations by Parpaing Studio, except:
Léa Hybre: p. 9, 46–47, 48–49, 50–51, 53, 79, 117;
Clément Chassagnard: p. 22–23, 82–83, 184–185.

First published in Great Britain in 2025 by
Dorling Kindersley Limited
20 Vauxhall Bridge Road
London SW1V 2SA

The authorised representative in the EEA is
Dorling Kindersley Verlag GmbH. Arnulfstr. 124,
80636 Munich, Germany

Copyright © 2025 Dorling Kindersley Limited
A Penguin Random House Company
10 9 8 7 6 5 4 3 2 1
001-344824-Jan/2025

All rights reserved. No part of this publication may be reproduced, stored in or introduced into a retrieval system, or transmitted, in any form, or by any means (electronic, mechanical, photocopying, recording, or otherwise), without the prior written permission of the copyright owner. A CIP catalogue record for this book is available from the British Library.

ISBN: 978-0-2417-1564-2

Printed and bound in Malaysia

www.dk.com